THE ROUTLEDGE FILM
MUSIC SOURCEBOOK

The Routledge Film Music Sourcebook is an annotated, thematically organized collection of approximately eighty source readings pertaining to film music dating from its beginnings to the present, from the United States and other select countries around the globe. The documents represent a wide variety of music-related issues that were heatedly debated during cinema's early decades and which, by and large, remain of concern today.

Each document is prefaced by a brief introduction that gives details on both the author and the particular issue at hand. Also, each group of documents is prefaced by a longer introduction that puts the collective information and opinions that follow into a historical context. The organizational scheme is at the same time chronological and thematic in a pattern that alternates between aesthetic and practical considerations.

James Wierzbicki teaches Musicology at the University of Sydney.

Nathan Platte teaches Musicology at the University of Iowa.

Colin Roust teaches Music History at Roosevelt University's Chicago College of the Performing Arts.

THE ROUTLEDGE FILM MUSIC SOURCEBOOK

EDITED BY

JAMES WIERZBICKI, NATHAN PLATTE, AND COLIN ROUST

Routledge
Taylor & Francis Group

NEW YORK AND LONDON

First published 2012
by Routledge
711 Third Avenue, New York, NY 10017

Simultaneously published in the UK
by Routledge
2 Park Square, Milton Park, Abingdon, Oxon OX14 4RN

Routledge is an imprint of the Taylor & Francis Group, an informa business

Library of Congress Cataloging-in-Publication Data
  The Routledge film music sourcebook / edited by James Wierzbicki,
  Nathan Platte, and Colin Roust. — 1st ed.
  p. cm.
  1. Motion picture music—History and criticism I. Wierzbicki,
  James. II. Platte, Nathan. III. Roust, Colin. IV. Routledge (Firm)
  ML2075.R68 2011
  781.5'4209—dc22   2011007417

ISBN: 978–0–415–88873–8 (hbk)
ISBN: 978–0–415–88874–5 (pbk)

Typeset in Sabon
by Florence Production Ltd, Stoodleigh, Devon
Printed and bound in the United States of America on acid-free paper by
Edwards Brothers, Inc.

IN MEMORY OF JOHN BARRY
(NOVEMBER 3, 1933–JANUARY 30, 2011)

CONTENTS

PREFACE

Even a hundred years ago, film music had its critics. "Civilization is not a crab," grumbled Louis Reeves Harrison in 1911, "but theatrical managers walk sideways if not backwards when they allow their musicians to play the wrong accompaniment."[1] Without good film music, Harrison suggested wryly, civilization itself suffered.

Harrison's argument still resonates among a growing body of film-music fans, students, and scholars. More than ever, music remains a critical component of film's cultural, artistic, and economic viability. New commentators continue to bring insights to the possibilities and problems that arise in film music's production, implementation, and promotion. Along with music-minded writers for other trade journals that documented the cusp between nickelodeon cinema and silent film's heyday, Harrison simply got the ball rolling. Once set in motion, the basic argument over film music—what it is, what it could be, what it *should* be—has never abated. Searching for intelligent commentaries on the nature and purpose of film music, the researcher willing to roll up his sleeves and dig deep into archives worldwide will find hundreds—no, thousands—of documents.

For the film-music scholar such a bounty of literature is perhaps exhilarating, yet the plenitude presents problems. With more than a century's worth of material available, it can be difficult for students, teachers, and enthusiasts to know where to begin or how to digest discussions about unfamiliar films and practitioners. Even more discouraging is the dispersion of sources, a problem that has long plagued even specialists in the field. A few years after Roy Prendergast in 1977 bemoaned the apparent fact that there is no "body of intelligent and perceptive writing on the subject" of film music, he was corrected by Martin Marks. "There is in fact an extensive literature on the subject," Marks wrote, but "it is far from easy to come by, and this is one reason for its own neglect. Books on film music pass speedily out of print, while articles lie scattered and buried in ephemeral or out-of-reach journals."[2] This remains an issue today. The Internet has improved access by means of newspaper databases and online archives, but many of these resources are available only to subscribing universities, and databases will not necessarily guide readers to or through the most salient articles. And, of course, much of the literature has not been digitized. *The Routledge Film Music Sourcebook* offers one response to the challenge by presenting a rich spectrum of readings that explore film music from a variety of perspectives.

How and Why *This* Volume?

What began as a casual conversation over breakfast as we three co-authors fortified ourselves for participation in the 2008 version of New York University's "Music and the Moving Image" conference, ended as a lively discussion as to how we could present old source material in a new and different way. Wouldn't it be interesting, we thought, if we could offer modern-day readers not just the intellectual gist of the arguments but also the full range of the intense and often biased passions that fueled them? And so began our original plan, for a carefully annotated anthology of English-language source readings.

It was to cover—for reasons that seemed logical enough from a historical point of view—the beginnings of film music's 'mainstream' flow until its diversification in the years following World War II.

But why stop with World War II? And why limit the project to documents originally published in English? These were questions asked not just by the acquisitions editor of our publisher but also by the anonymous reviewers who took a serious look at our original proposal. Encouraged by these very sensible suggestions, we set about considerably broadening our scope for inclusion in what ended up as *The Routledge Film Music Sourcebook*.

Organization

The eight sections of the *Sourcebook* are arranged chronologically and reflect the collection's historical breadth. Our goal was to cull the literature for selected, representative documents of their day. They begin during the "silent" era, with feisty columns from the weekly trade presses, heady speculations on the future of what seemed to be a brand new art form, and practical advice from musicians who thrived during the silent film's heyday. They end in the most recent decades, with commentaries that alternately ruminate upon film music's now substantial history and project its future trajectories.

The other sections correspond with important flash points in cinema's history. In one, we explore early sound film, which forced commentators to renegotiate music's role vis-à-vis the filmic image. The next section is rooted in the era of the classical-style film, when Hollywood studios sought to standardize scoring methods as a means of increasing productivity and—perhaps accidentally—raising musical quality. The anthology then deals with innovations that ultimately fractured classical-style norms and heralded a postwar boom of writings on film music; articles by Lawrence Morton and Hans Keller, for example, signal the rise of the "serious" film music critic, who advocated for the art form's betterment through purely musical aesthetics. Sea changes in the cinema of the 1960s and 1970s—for better or worse, depending on one's perspective—occupy the writers featured in the fifth section, while the sixth section focuses on two often overlooked facets of the film music economy: the sometimes strained relationships between film studios and the unionized musicians they have employed, and the increasing importance of the often very lucrative soundtrack album. The final sections foreground technological and production innovations that over the last twenty years have revolutionized the way in which film music is composed, recorded, and perceived.

Within this historical framework, each section of the anthology is divided into subsections that are organized by theme. These subsections have been designed with the classroom in mind. Readings are grouped in order to highlight both correspondences and conflicts among writers that in turn might serve as material for discussion among students.

Criteria for Selection

International representation was a key concern in the selection of articles. Many of the selections were first published in the United States, but they are balanced by readings from China, England, France, Germany, Italy, and Russia. By devoting substantial space to film music beyond Hollywood, this anthology not only exposes readers to a broad range of insights and methods but also acknowledges an important shift in the field of film-music studies, that is, toward greater engagement with international cinemas and their respective literatures. While some names, such as Dmitry Shostakovich and Hans Erdmann, might be familiar to many readers, others, such as Gianandrea Gavazzeni and Nikolai Kryukov, likely are not. Together they represent important voices from national cinemas whose contributions to this anthology are crucial, and we are proud to note that their comments are offered here in their first English translations.

Along with presenting many international voices, the anthology draws together authors from diverse professional backgrounds. In the pages that follow, film composers, music directors, concert hall conductors, labor reporters, film critics, music critics, conservatory professors, and even publicists share their variously overlapping and disparate perspectives. While these writers focus primarily on the narrative feature film, their arguments and observations span an impressive gamut, from the delicious abstractions of John Cage to the meticulous pragmatism of Erno Rapee, from the political concerns of Wang Yunjei to the commercial reportage of Catherine Applefeld Olson. Brought together in a single volume, these writers demonstrate that there are as many different ways of discussing film music as there are approaches to composing it.

Using This Volume

Our editorial method is designed to make these documents easily readable by a general audience and to make them readily available for students and scholars. Organized both chronologically and thematically, each group of readings is prefaced by an introduction that places its component items in a broad context, and each document in turn is prefaced by a much briefer introduction that gives specific information about its author and highlights its important insights.

For notes, our policy has been "as few as possible, as many as necessary." Indeed, most of the annotations simply identify persons, or explain terms, that doubtless were familiar to the documents' original readers but may or may not be familiar to readers today. Rather than provide information on individual film titles as they occur in the anthology, we have opted for a comprehensive filmography—arranged alphabetically by title, and including nation of origin, date, director, studio, and composer—at the back of the book. It is our sincere hope that redundancies resulting from our editorial approach will be not just forgiven but appreciated. As mentioned above, the anthology's design was prompted by considerations of its potential use in the classroom. While some readers may well choose to proceed cover to cover through all this material, it seems more likely that the volume's contents will merely be sampled, in bits and pieces thoughtfully assigned by film-music instructors who have their own unique pedagogic agendas. Mindful of this, and mindful of the ways in which most collections of source readings are put to use, we have no expectations that readers of one section will have read all that came before.

Our treatment of documents, we trust, is appropriate to the diverse material at hand. Items originally published in Chinese, French, German, Italian, and Russian have been translated precisely yet cast into idiomatic modern English; particularly flavorful terms or phrases from languages other than English have been not only translated but also included, verbatim, either in bracketed insertions or in notes. Items originally published in English for the most part retain their sometimes quirky grammar and spellings, but punctuation and the treatment of numbers have been adjusted to reflect the modern American style. Without comment, we have adjusted titles of songs and films so that the former are in double quotation marks and the latter are in italics; where a name is misspelled, as is often the case with Dimitri Tiomkin's given name or with Michel Legrand's surname, it is silently corrected; we let accents/diacritical marks appear or not, as in the originals, and we let stand diverse spellings of transliterated Russian names and such words as "filmmaker," "theater," "disc," and "aesthetic." Beyond that, our policy in regard to the material presented here has been one of "hands off." When we have something to say, we say it upfront in our introductions; otherwise, we comfortably and confidently let our authors speak for themselves.

To the Student

One of the key items in *The Routledge Film Music Sourcebook* is the set of responses by thirty-five French musicians to a simple question that was asked in 1919 by the Paris-based journal *Le Film*: Do you think that there is a new path that music is to follow by associating with cinematography? The diversity of responses range from enthusiastic assertions of film music's artistic promise to outright denial of the genre's ability ever to transcend its commercial origins. As some of those respondents to the questionnaire likely often said about something or other, "Plus ça change, plus c'est la même chose"— the more things change, the more they stay the same.[3]

Prodded by developments not just technological but also economic and societal, film music of course has changed much over the past century. Yet through all the changes there have persisted questions that seem as important to audiences as to filmmakers and composers. Just how much music should there be in the accompaniment to a narrative film? How often, and for what reasons, should the general "mood" of the music shift? How carefully synchronized with filmic images should musical gestures be? What is the effect when the music plays not "with" the film's action but, somehow, "against" it? What is the effect of no music at all? How much attention should a film's accompanying music call to itself? Is it a good thing or a bad thing if the audience actually notices the music? What happens if a film score includes pre-existing music that a large portion of the audience recognizes? Is there a place in the film score for popular music, or for classical music? Does truly 'good' music—music that, quite on its own, stands up to repeated listening—have a place at all in the cinema?

We suspect you will find not only that these questions have endured over the years but also that their definitive answers have yet to be found. To those interested in film music's history and film music's future, this anthology offers proof that the fundamental issues have, in fact, been under discussion for quite a long time. And doubtless these same issues will continue to challenge us for a long time to come. As they say, "plus ça change . . ."

ACKNOWLEDGMENTS

A project of this scope has been, and still is, daunting. We are indebted to numerous individuals who helped to ease the process of compiling readings for *The Routledge Film Music Sourcebook*. We spread our net wide, and thus we are hugely indebted to all our global colleagues who pointed us in the direction of materials that we might at least consider for this ever-expanding anthology of film-music source readings. In particular, we owe thanks to Knut Holtsträter in Germany, Antonio Ferrara in Italy, Séverine Abhervé in France, and Joys Cheung in Hong Kong, without whose suggestions this collection would be much less rich.

We likewise owe thanks to the various institutions—the University of Michigan, Oberlin College, Bowling Green State University, Roosevelt University's Chicago College of the Performing Arts, the University of Iowa, the University of Sydney—that actually paid us salaries while we struggled to put together this massive volume. We owe thanks, too, to all the staff at Routledge—Constance Ditzel, Denny Tek, Mike Andrews, Janice Baiton, and Sarah Stone—who helped to bring this book into being.

Most importantly, we owe thanks to the persons closest to us, those individuals who day upon day have tolerated our often grumpy moods and in various ways reminded us that, yes, this whole project might actually be worth doing. We thus most especially acknowledge (in alphabetical order) Amy, Anna, Benjamin, Diane, Elle, Eva, and Helene, without whose constant support this book never would have been completed.

Part 1

"SILENT" FILM

1

EARLY APPROACHES TO FILM ACCOMPANIMENT

Standard historical accounts of film music assert that musical accompaniment of moving pictures originated during the earliest days of moving picture exhibition in the mid-1890s.[1] It is perhaps reassuring to know that music was indeed "there" with these early films, but the quality, type, source, and function of this music was by no means consistent from place to place or year to year. There were no norms to which to adhere, and practices, not to mention expectations, varied. Some moving pictures were accompanied by pianists, small orchestras, or phonographs. At other times the accompaniment was not musical. Lecturers provided commentary for certain films, and the performance of live sound effects was another non-musical option. Sometimes there was no accompaniment at all. Even in the years following 1905, as nickelodeon theaters sprang up across the downtowns of America, often occupying multiple storefronts in a single block, musical tastes and standards continued to vary widely, defined only by individual exhibitors and the musicians they hired.

Rick Altman, who has meticulously documented these uneven years of experimentation and novelty in *Silent Film Sound*, argues that exhibitors experienced a "crisis of the late aughts" when the rapid proliferation of nickelodeons (often clustered together in one part of town) created unprecedented levels of competition.[2] If there were not enough films for each nickelodeon in town to show different titles, what would differentiate the product of one theater from another? Sound, and more particularly music, was one crucial facet over which the exhibitor exercised profound influence. Recently launched trade publications such as *Film Index*, *Moving Picture World*, and *Moving Picture News* began covering musical topics in sporadic articles in the late aughts, and by the end of 1910 both *Film Index* and *Moving Picture World* had initiated weekly columns devoted exclusively to improving the standards of musical accompaniment in moving picture theaters. In 1912, *Movie Picture News* joined the fray with its own column. Taken together, these columns represent the earliest sustained, published dialogue on the relationship between music and film.

In very general terms, the authors justified the importance of their columns by two simple precepts: 1) musical accompaniment had a *profound* impact upon the moving picture experience and should be valued by exhibitors and musicians accordingly; 2) improved musical accompaniment would not only boost receipts at individual theaters but would also culturally advance the entire moving picture industry. Beyond these initial points, the discursive topography became increasingly uneven. On whose shoulders did this improvement lie? Was it the responsibility of the musicians or of the exhibitors and film producers? How would these changes impact silent cinema's placement within the spectrum of other musical arts? In other words, from what was film music being improved and to what heights need it aspire? Should it be operatic (or, heaven forbid, Wagnerian), or did it just need to be better than cheap vaudeville? For whom were these improvements intended? Were they to provide uplift to the working-class spectator or merely to attract the already refined ears of a more discerning and "moneyed clientele"?[3]

Clearly, the *rationales* for improving musical accompaniment in the moving picture houses were just as important to the trade press columnists as the *means* by which these improvements would be accomplished. Over the next two years, *Film Index*'s Clyde Martin, *Moving Picture World*'s Clarence E. Sinn, and Louis Reeves Harrison (who did not write a regular column yet produced memorable articles for *Moving Picture World*) wrestled with the issues from different vantage points, sometimes appealing directly to the exhibitor and at other times writing for music directors and performers.[4] Although the authors unanimously agreed that musical accompaniment should be consistent with the dramatic tone of the picture, they often disagreed (either with each other or with their correspondents) on the qualitative role that music should assume in the moving picture theater.

Louis Reeves Harrison likened the cinema-music relationship to opera, suggesting that music's profound cultural capital could enhance the film industry's reputation more effectively than any other element of exhibition:

> By way of a start in intellectual exercise, give some consideration to the fact that grand opera is not much more than a grand pantomime with the story told so clearly by action that the sense of it can be caught by the eye while the ear is charmed. . . . [T]he emotion conveyed is not exactly that set forth in the music, that method of expression is too vague and comprehensive, but it stimulates emotions aroused by the situation, by the series of events, by gestural and facial expression, just as in moving pictures. In both cases, words are not absolutely essential, but the right sort of music is essential to complete enjoyment of the drama. The music of the opera is not sacrificed to the drama, but is supported by it. The pictured drama is not sacrificed to the music, but is so powerfully influenced by it as to become wonderfully effective or absolutely repelling according to the accompanying tone of the picture.[5]

In contrast, Clarence Sinn acknowledged that film accompaniment, like orchestral accompaniment in the live theater, must support the drama of the film, but not overwhelm or dominate, as in opera. Acknowledging that films themselves were still in a state of early development, Sinn saw little purpose in lavishing them with music that would be significantly more complicated than their narratives:

> It is not impossible that a day may come when the best of dramatists will write the film stories, and the best of composers supply the music thereto. Should that time ever come, we might reasonably expect to see (or hear) the thematic method worked out to its logical development. Music for the pictures is still in the formative period, and we are all working, each in his own way, to give it some definite shape.[6]

Similarly, Clyde Martin emphasized that music for pictures was altogether different from concert music. Although he acknowledged that better quality films deserved more elaborate and thoughtful musical accompaniments, Martin noted that most films did not require this degree of investment, and he recommended that players focus their energies on improvisations:

It does not take a renowned soloist to play the pictures, it takes what is commonly known as a fakir [*sic*]. My advice to a musician with ambitions to become a picture player, is, throw away your music, improvise, and study expression.[7]

There is a special urgency in the music columns of the early 1910s; musical practices were changing rapidly and any anticipated outcome was uncertain at best. Consequently, the literature has a trajectory, with multiple authors contributing to solve a common problem. As 1913 approached, the feeling of musical crisis began to fade, with even the vituperative Harrison noting optimistically in December 1912 that "the musical photodrama has not yet arrived, but it seems to be on its way."[8] This tone differs strikingly from Harrison's condemnation, in January 1911, of the musical tendencies of Lily Limpwrist, Freddy Fuzzlehead, and Percy Peashaker.[9]

Due in large part to the effectiveness of the trade press columns, musical expectations for accompanying films entered a period of relative stability and were grounded by certain fundamental standards. These included artful transitions between musical selections and the continuous playing of music throughout the picture, the subordination of musical decisions and selections to the film's narrative, and the use of music to enhance the film's overall tone (as opposed to music that might emphasize unimportant details or undermine the film's seriousness).[10] Obviously, musical accompaniment from theater to theater still depended upon an exhibitor's financial and musical resources, but the expectation of what music *should* do in relation to a moving picture was no longer an open question. If a musician departed from the norm, that was his or her prerogative, but there was now a norm from which to depart. Today, these trade press columns remain remarkably relevant, as the debated issues of music-and-film technique, audiences' perception of music, and the use of music to elevate film's cultural status continue to resonate in current studies that frequently overlook these initial conversations.[11]

1.1 MUSIC FOR THE PICTURE

Clarence E. Sinn

Just as Louis Reeves Harrison's vituperative attacks on musical accompaniment were being published in Moving Picture World *in late 1910 and early 1911, a very different voice joined the conversation in the very same journal. Clarence E. Sinn, who had served as music director at Chicago's Orpheum Theater and also worked for the Criterion Theatre, wrote his column for musicians rather than exhibitors and adopted a more moderate and sympathetic tone, often referring to his correspondents as "Brother ___."*

Whereas Harrison decried film musicians' shortcomings, Sinn proposed attainable solutions: "Much has been said in criticism of the music accompanying moving pictures, but so far I have noticed few practical suggestions have been offered which would put the novice on the right road."[12] Sinn's initial column, which is reproduced here along with the editor's introduction, outlines many of the themes and techniques that Sinn would elaborate upon in later columns, such as emphasizing "the general character of the picture," building a substantial music library for varied dramatic situations, and avoiding musical jokes that "get a laugh where none was intended." In later columns, Sinn upheld his epithet of "cue music man" by offering musical suggestions for specific productions and printing cue sheets submitted by readers. Sinn accomplishes this task to an extent here with a brief discussion of musical selections for Auld Robin Gray (1910), although later columns would feature more detailed outlines.

In contrast to Harrison, who repeatedly encouraged film musicians to aspire to the standards of opera, Sinn was less comfortable with operatic analogies, preferring instead to compare musical accompaniment for films with the more direct techniques of pantomime and stage melodrama: "The moving picture drama (or photoplay) is simply a play in pantomime, and the accompanying music is essentially the same as that of a play given on the stage."[13] This point is worth emphasizing as Sinn has often been depicted as a veritable Wagnerite; this notion is misleading because it overlooks Sinn's often-expressed ambivalence toward applying Wagnerian methods to moving pictures.[14]

In addition to writing a regular music column for Moving Picture World, Sinn also published music anthologies for theater pianists and orchestras.

Foreword

It is gratifying to see how the broadminded exhibitors, those who aim to show the pictures to the best advantage, are fast taking to the idea that good and appropriate music does not only enhance the beauty of the picture but gives it life. From every town we hear that such and such a theater has discharged the music killer, the man or woman at a low salary who believed that any old ragtime music was good enough for motion pictures, to engage more experienced musicians. It is surprising to note how many theaters are improving the sound effects while many of them are adding a violinist; in fact, many other instrument players. The demand for good music is such that it is now as much of a rivalry between exhibitors to brag of their good orchestra as it is of bragging of the quality of their pictures. In other words, the managers are now taking as much interest in the music as in the projection of the pictures, and the great demand for extra musical accessories, like the Deagan electric bells,[15] xylophones, chimes, automatic orchestras, pipe-organs, etc., shows that, in the very near future, moving picture theaters will be real concert halls and that the public will go to the shows not only for the sake of seeing pictures but to hear good music.

A full orchestra costs less than two cheap vaudeville acts and is more profitable to the exhibitor. Good music captivates and pleases, while cheap vaudeville acts give a very unfavorable reputation to a moving picture theater.

Realizing, therefore, the importance of the music, we make no apology for introducing this new department to [Moving Picture] World readers. We believe that Mr. Sinn will find a hearty response to his suggestions and invite every exhibitor and orchestra leader to write him for particular information or offer suggestions, addressing same to Music Department, Moving Picture World, Drawer 727, Chicago, Ill.

J.M.B.[16]

Much has been said in criticism of the music accompanying moving pictures, but so far as I have noticed few practical suggestions have been offered which would put the novice on the right road to "working up" his pictures musically. I am daily in receipt of inquiries whose general purport is: "What shall I play—where shall I play it—and why?" It is the purpose of these articles to try and give a few hints along these lines which the writer hopes may stimulate interest among his fellow-workers in this great field, and invite questions which will be answered so far as lies in his power.

The moving picture is almost infinite in its variety of subjects, but for the present we may divide them roughly into three classes: scenic, industrial, and dramatic—the last including all pictures in which the characters enact a story. The moving picture drama (or photoplay) is simply a play in pantomime, and the accompanying music is essentially the same as that of a play given on the stage. There is this distinction, however. In the drama proper, music is only introduced at intervals to heighten the effect of certain scenes, while in pantomime it is continuous, or nearly so. The reason is apparent. The drama depends upon both speech and action to convey its story: the eye and ear of the auditor are in sympathy; we see the action and hear the words. This sympathy of eye and ear must exist else there is no sustained interest—no intelligent appreciation of the story. To hold this double interest the stage manager employs as accessories, lights, scenery, music—always keeping in view this sympathy between the eye and ear.

Pantomime depends solely upon the action to convey its story, and appeals to the eye alone. Now the ear demands gratification as well as the eye, and, to this end, music is employed, but whenever possible it should be consistent with the story and not merely a concert program on the side.

Certain forms of music are accepted as suitable accompaniments for certain situations; as soft and plaintive for pathetic scenes, stormy and turbulent for the violent ones, etc. All the emotions have some sort of musical analogy and if these are correctly applied the dramatic effect is heightened and the interest of the auditor is intensified. If, on the other hand, the music be incongruous, the attention is diverted and the interest is lessened. Bear in mind that the picture is the show—that it [is] what the audience is paying for— and any accessory (musical or otherwise) should carry out and amplify the impression intended by the producer.

A picture was shown some time ago containing a scene wherein Pharaoh's daughter discovers the infant Moses in the bulrushes. The pianist played "Oh, You Kid."[17] He got a laugh which is probably what he wanted, but at what a sacrifice. The whole picture was dignified and serious, and the music should have sustained that character throughout.

It is the general character of the picture which you must observe. Taken altogether, what is the predominant feature? Is it pathetic, mysterious, tragical or comical? Work up to this general effect whatever it is. The producer takes great pains to convey certain impressions and preserve a certain atmosphere, and it is his due that these unities be preserved so the audience may receive his story in the same spirit in which it is told. To begin with, you should have a good library, which in these days of cheap music is not difficult. A few marches and waltzes, though these are indispensible, are not sufficient. Long andantes such as "Traumerei," "Flower Song," "Angel's Serenade" and the like are useful.[18] The intermezzo, valse lento, and gavottes make convenient "fill-ins" where the scene is neutral yet the general character of the picture is subdued or pathetic. Religious music, national airs (of different countries), Oriental music and dances are frequently called for. Popular songs are useful, especially in sentimental pictures and comedies. The titles of these, if well known, frequently carry out the suggestion of the picture, but care should be taken that the music is also in keeping with the scene. Don't try to get a laugh when none was intended, as it only cheapens your work and hurts the picture. Your library should also include some melodramatic music, such as mysterious, agitato, "Hurrys" for combats, storms, fire scenes, etc. These are in constant demand.

Overtures, medleys, popular selections, etc., have their place also, but as a general rule it is not wise to use them in dramatic pictures, as the chances are a lively movement will come at a time when you should be playing a slow one, and vice versa. I suspect this is at the bottom of a great many criticisms that have appeared lately. Some of the scenic and most of the industrial pictures as a rule do not require special music—there's a good place for your concert music. Once in a long time you will get a picture that runs in a dead level—no high lights or deep shadows—very difficult to shade musically as nothing in particular happens. An overture or selection is probably as good as anything else, but be careful.

Some intensely dramatic pictures are tuned to one pitch, yet are full of suggestions as to the musical setting. "Auld Robin Gray" is a recent and easy example. We open the picture with the song "Auld Robin Gray"[19] once through, the same as if we were taking up the curtain on the stage. As it would be monotonous to repeat the song over and over throughout the picture, we relieve it occasionally; "My Highland Laddie"[20] in the first scene, Tosti's "Good-bye"[21] at the parting scene—always filling in with the titular song. I heard the "Wedding March" played for the wedding scene; while this might be criticized, it accented the scene and did not detract from the general effect. After that "Auld Robin Gray" until the end with all the expression possible.

In the next article we will take up this matter of incidental music in more detail. (To be continued.)

From *Moving Picture World* 7, no. 22 (November 26, 1910), 1227.

1.2 PLAYING THE PICTURES

Clyde Martin

On the spectrum between the outspoken, boisterous Louis Reeves Harrison and the more careful Clarence E. Sinn, Clyde Martin of Film Index *occupies a middle ground in tone and outlook. Like Harrison, Martin cited both poor musicians and poor exhibitors for the problems in the moving picture theater. In one column, Martin blamed the appalling drum effects on managers who have only "given [the drummer] a job in the picture house to keep him off the streets at night."[22] Like Sinn, Martin also understood that moving picture musicians were often victims of circumstance:*

> I find that the musicians in the west are making every effort to play the pictures and some of them are making a pretty good stab at it, but nine out of every ten are handicapped by a noisy house, the buzzing of fans, the rattle of the machine, and the conversation of the ushers with their friends in the back rows and still the manager wonders why his piano player does not make good.[23]

In general, Martin encouraged musicians to accept the status of their modest occupation and not bring illusions of musical grandeur to the theater: "It does not take a renowned soloist to play the pictures, it takes what is commonly known as a fakir."[24] Unlike Sinn, who encouraged close adherence to prescriptive instructions known as cue sheets, Martin envisioned a more flexible and improvisatory approach that would allow the accompanist to follow the on-screen action without the tight constraints of a printed score. While Martin explained that such accompanying skills required practice, advance preparation, and refinement, his cavalier choice of words caused trouble. Mr. A. Picker of Ironwood, Michigan, was the first to protest, arguing that "a faker is not a musician." Martin responded testily, but ultimately conceded the point on April Fool's Day of 1911:

> *March 18th, without home or friends, occurred the death of 'faking.' This little fellow seemed to have no excuse for living, he had lived just long enough to become a burden. 'Faking' made his home with Mr. Martin and during the last days of his life proved to be such a misunderstood person, that death came as a relief to all who knew him. 'Faking' is survived by his twin-brother 'Improvise.' May he rest in peace.[25]*

In the column included in this collection, Martin's advice takes the form of a litany of practical, and rather specific, suggestions. Not limiting himself to musical concerns, Martin illustrates how the careful selection of sound and percussion effects can enhance a moving picture's spectacular qualities. Martin also devotes considerable space to expounding on one of the chief musical concerns of the era: the absolute necessity for continuous *musical accompaniment.*

Since I have been conducting my articles in *The Index* I have received many letters from musicians asking suggestions for appropriate music for certain releases that have been booked in their theatres for some future date. It is very gratifying indeed to know that the musicians in the better class of theatres are looking after the details of the picture music and bettering their own conditions, as well as the conditions of the theatres.

I will be glad to receive suggestions at any time from picture musicians, and [if] at any time I can be of service and give advice on appropriate music for any certain release I will do so, either by letter or through the columns of The Index.

Last week I received an inquiry from a Western exhibitor asking for a list of the most important traps and effects to be used by the drummer and behind the screen. From the tone of the letter I was led to believe the exhibitor was located in a small town with a limited number of amusement seekers to draw from, but was willing to take a chance at educating more picture fans by improving his show as much as his income would allow. I believe there are many more of the smaller exhibitors that are willing to spend a little money on effects, and for their special benefit I publish the list I believe to be complete for the small town show.

On the drummer's rack I would advise, as the most essential effects:

Sand Blocks	Triangles
Castanets	Tambourine
Crash Cymbal	Telephone

Wood Block   Electric Door Bell
Tom Tom

The balance of the effects should be handled from behind the screen and you should make it a point to have a competent person in charge of the concealed effects, as the least mistake on the part of your effect man may ruin a scene or possibly a whole picture. The most important line of effects to be used behind the screen consists of

Baby Cry	Midway Musette
Rooster Crow	Dog Bark
Hen Cackle	Chimes
Mocking Bird Whistle	Gongs
Steamboat Whistle	Cow Bawl
Sleigh Bells	Revolver
Tugboat Whistle	Wind Machine
Locomotive Whistle	Auto Horn
Horse Hoof Imitation	Thunder Sheet
Train Imitation	

It is seldom that you will find use for some of these effects, but it is well to have them on hand. Take, for instance, such a picture as "The Legacy," that clever production by the Vitagraph Company; just think what a help your tug and steamboat whistles would be to the scene where the old couple is shown on the ferry, crossing over to the New York side.[26] The reason I mention this picture in particular, the first matinee this picture was run in our theatre the effect man was on the job, but the only thing he had was one tug and one steamboat whistle, and the Hudson River was a very tame affair that afternoon. But after the matinee I searched the town over and scared up fifteen or twenty good whistles. That night every one around the theatre with a good pair of lungs was on the job, and when the ferry scene came on, well, we nearly made the Hudson backwater to Albany. And the best part of it was the scene got a big hand and the picture caused so much comment the management kept the picture on and featured it for four days, matinee and night. This is what convinces me that the audience wants effects.

By the way, did you use a phonograph on the effect list when you run [sic] the Edison release of October 11?[27] There was another chance for an inexpensive effect to make the hit of the show. Give them something different whenever you get the chance, and you will soon have them talking about your show, and when you get them talking you can get their loose change.

Another impressive effect that can be worked by the drummer is a roll on the crash cymbal. Don't run a good thing in the ground, but wait until you get such a picture as the Pathe release of Saturday, October 8, "An Indian's Gratitude," and in the scene where the Indian turns and falls over the 250-foot cliff you can make your audience stand up if you will give a roll on the crash cymbal.[28] Don't work this on every little fall; wait for a novelty like this Pathe picture and then you will take the audience by surprise.

The use of a thunder sheet is very seldom called for, unless you use it in such a picture as the Vitagraph release of November 19, "Francesca Da Rimini."[29] Through the last scenes of the picture, during the approaching storm, try and work the effect of distant thunder, and then, when the cripple raises his dagger to kill, work up the scene with loud thunder from behind the screen, a roll on the crash cymbal is the drummer's end of the work; then, when the bolt of lightning strikes the lovers dead, muffle the vibration of the cymbal and thunder sheet so that the second they fall to the floor the house is quiet, and let the piano music fade away with the light on the picture. By handling the climax in this way it will be in keeping with the conception the producer has portrayed.

A musician should never stop playing through the showing of a picture. This is a great mistake that you will frequently find in the big houses as well as the small ones. This is one reason why I say there is no orchestra that can play the picture properly, for the simple reason the music of an orchestra is limited, and they are obliged to stop at times in the middle of a picture and wait their chance to go ahead.

This point was illustrated to me while on a short trip to Chicago. I happened to stroll into one of the largest picture houses in that city and, I believe, there was a Biograph on the screen.[30] When I entered I was surprised not to hear music. By the time I was seated I had come to the conclusion the orchestra was either eating their lunch in the pit or had sent a representative to the box office with a request for more money. I had still another surprise coming, for, at the finish of the picture every one in the orchestra sat up, took notice, and, as the last ten feet of the film passed through [the] machine they struck a chord and went into the introduction of the illustrated song. I went from there to a five-cent picture house just around the corner and found the same picture on the program that I had just seen at the larger house. The music at the five-cent house consisted of piano and drums, and when this same picture was thrown on the screen you would have been surprised to hear what the piano player made out of the picture. It is the same old story every place you go; an orchestra either plays long andantes and waltzes, or they sit and watch the picture.

Another thing that should be remembered by the musicians: Don't cut your chaser short. If it is the last show for the evening play until nearly every one is out of the house. By doing this you send them away in good spirits. If you are running illustrated songs or a spotlight song in connection with the pictures, and you have a song that has made a hit with the crowd it is a very good idea to play the chorus over for a chaser. I figure if I can play a chaser that will have the audience humming as they leave the theatre I have won a good point. In my next article I will show how it is possible to advertise a picture in such a way as to help the musicians in their work.

From *Film Index*, no. 24 (December 10, 1910), 5.

1.3 JACKASS MUSIC

Louis Reeves Harrison

Louis Reeves Harrison (1857–1921) was a writer of multiple talents who worked as a journalist, author, and scriptwriter.[31] From 1908 to 1920 he expressed his strong opinion on a variety of topics in Moving Picture World. *From reviews of individual films to detailed discussions of cinematic melodrama, Harrison did much to shape the tenor of discourse in the trade press:*

I confess that I like [melodrama] when it is not underdone, but then I am somewhere half-way between the holy mountain of high criticism and the abyss of low taste. I can enjoy grand opera or Coney Island according to circumstances . . . the main question at any place of entertainment is, "Do we like it or do we feel as though we were not getting our money's worth?"[32]

Harrison's self-appointed duty in many of his columns was to culturally navigate the film industry through the ambiguous and potentially treacherous middle ground between high-brow and low-brow, between "legitimate" entertainment and cheap amusements, between grand opera and Coney Island. "I am ranged on the side of motion-pictures," he wrote. "I believe they are capable of tremendous development, and everything I say is intended to promote their advancement."[33]

It was not long before Harrison turned his critical eye to musical accompaniment. His spirited diatribe, "Jackass Music" (enlivened with droll sketches by H. F. Hoffman[34]) has achieved the level of a trade press "classic" and has been cited and discussed frequently.[35] *Speaking more to exhibitors than musicians, Harrison used the tried-and-true technique of merciless ridicule as a means of encouraging reform. Positing exhibitors as social pillars of the community, Harrison opened his article with a smart dash of metaphorical backhand: "Civilization is not a crab, but theatrical managers walk sideways if not backwards when they allow their musicians to play the wrong accompaniment."*[36] *In particular, Harrison believed music was key to elevating both the industry's cultural status and the middle-class appeal: "Inappropriate music may 'do' for an unintelligent part of the audience, but what is the use of driving away the intelligent portion? . . . Better music means better patronage and more of it."*[37]

While "Jackass Music" remains justly famous, the article is only a part of a series of editorials by Harrison published between November 1910 and April 1911 that harped upon the shortcomings of moving picture musical accompaniment.[38]

Civilization is not a crab, but theatrical managers walk sideways if not backwards when they allow their musicians to play the wrong accompaniment to the right composition whether of song or picture. O, what a noise when the lights are turned low and Lily Limpwrist takes her place at the usual instrument of torture! With a self-conscious smirk she gives a poke to her back switch, dabs her side teasers with both patties, rolls up her sleeves and tears off "That Yiddisher Rag." She bestows a calm smile on the box-of-candy young man in the first row, but the presentation on the screen fails to divert her "I-seen-you" glances any more than if it was the point of a joke.

The chorus-girl who attempts to pose as a prima-donna, with little more equipment that a tuft of bleached hair, a pair of high-heeled slippers and a cigarette voice can be tolerated, we often endure the howling and screeching of a Tommy trying to sing "Come into the Garden Maud," but when Lily Limpwrist assails our unprotected organs of hearing with her loony repertoire it seems a shame to throw away ten cents on such a performance, to say nothing of the time wasted. We sit patiently through the act of an imported star, who commends to our attention the interesting intelligence "Me Rag, moy Beoss usedter droive em cryzy at the Croiterion," we submit to the inanities of the chin-whiskered, pillow-paunched Dutch comedian, who says: "Vot it is, is it? Ask me," and we even tolerate the Irish comedian, shaved yesterday, who looks like an undertaker out-of-a-job when he wails in a hold-over voice: "Where thuh dear-ol Sha-hamrock gurrows," but there is a limit.

LILLY
LIMPWRIST

Lily is all right at home, when her mother importunes her to "play something and don't wait to be teased," or still better as a summer-eve girl on a Coney-Island boat, but no man will ever marry a girl who plays dance while the pictured man is in a death struggle: she would probably be *at* one when the real one was in trouble. The girl of sympathy will play music in accord with the pictured story, the girl of ambition will try to improve the quality of her work, the girl of sense will try to improve the quality of the performance, draw patronage instead of driving it away, benefit the management, and show to others who are looking for pianists that she is not a fat-wit but a woman of ideas and good taste.

The performance of Lily Limpwrist is a poetic dream compared to the diabolical dipso-mania of Freddy Fuzzlehead and Percy Peashaker when they cut loose between the "vodeveal" acts. Gee! *Non compos mentis* and *le diable au corps*[39] for theirs and a free pass to Matteawan for what they have done to kill the box-office receipts at moving-picture shows. Percy is really a wonder. When there is water in the picture it goes to Percy's cerebrum. If there is a lake shown on the screen, no matter if it is a mile away, calm or stormy, he shakes his box of peas so that we may know that it is principally made of water. Realism becomes intense when a vessel appears and Percy blows a whistle "Oo-Oo" to enforce the fact that it is a steamer and not a full-rigged ship. "Bow-wow" indicates that we are looking at a dog and not a door-mat. "Honk-honk" gives one a thrilling remembrance of crossing Broadway after the theatre with fifty cow-boy taxis in full pursuit, and he is a master of such startling effects as clapping two blocks of wood together when an old nag candidate for the glue factory trots along a country road. But Percy's star act, the one that gets a laugh, is his imitation of a baby crying no matter whether the one on the screen is nursing or merely dying. Percy is a comparatively new type of the egomaniac, but whether we must humor him or put him in a padded cell must be left to the alienists.

PATHOS

If you were to ask a large proportion of the audience what should be done to Freddy Fuzzlehead they would vote to shoot him, but I am in favor of slow torture, making the punishment fit the crime, put him in a room where there is another of his kind playing with the piano and let him die a lingering death. Ten thousand dollars a day is spent to amuse people with moving pictures good, bad and indifferent, but all are bad or indifferent when Fuzzlehead does his long-eared stunt. Ten millions of people pay their nickels and dimes to see the moving pictures, and these shock-headed kleptopianoacs steal their pleasure away in order to practice the accompaniment for the song-and-dance comedians, those who come on the stage and say "I will now sing you a little ballad entitled 'Show you are a clod-hopper by keeping time with your feet.'" The same comedian who gets no applause from the long-suffering audience and asks if they are hand-cuffed, or says to the piano man, *sotto voce*, "Did y'ever s-see sucha lotta dubs?" The hallroom lobster on the stage is "great" to Fuzzlehead, the boob action exactly suits the boob at the piano, the moving pictures are rot, he could do better himself if he had time, but he would say the same thing if he was shown the treasures of the Louvre or the Palace of Luxembourg. Ten thousand dollars a day is spent to *produce* the moving pictures, and it would be impossible to say how much more to keep going the ten thousand motion-picture theatres throughout the country. These pictures are not all masterpieces, many of them are very crude, but the whole art is in a primitive state, is constantly improving, and the exhibitions are kept alive by their production. People go every day to see the pictures, once in a while for the variety entertainment, and it is not only asinine but unbusiness-like to lower the grade of musical accompaniment when the lights are turned down. Inappropriate music may "do" for an unintelligent part of the audience, but what is the use of driving away the intelligent portion? All other parts of the theatrical working force move in harmony, like the wheels of a clock, but these fatheads against the stage apron are like the clock alarm that goes off when you don't need it and never when you do. Attention of managers to the comfort of patrons would help matters some, and little higher salaries would help a great deal to get suitable music. Better music means better patronage and more of it, and superior patronage means a demand for superior photoplays. Suitable music is an essential. If the drummer can not be taught to subordinate his morbid craving for attention to the general effect, cut him out altogether and pay more for a pianist who can improvise softly during scenes of pathos or utilize operatic selections for the dramatic effects.

Bangity-bang-bang. Bing-bang-bang.

Desperate Desmond has got Claude Eclaire in a tight place, but no matter, the "rag" is on; "hit it up."

Bangity-bang-bang! Bing-bang-bang!

There is a tender-hearted mother dying in the little play, the world around her is subdued and silent, her face is pale, her frame attenuated, her respiration is heavy with sighs of sorrow and unsatisfied desire to have her children properly cared for. Tears are falling like her life illusions, she is overcome with her double burden of pain and sorrow, her eyes, inflamed by the fever of unattained hopes, turn beseechingly to the infinite power above, a last faint sigh, the eyes close forever:

Bangity-bang-bang! Bing-bang-bang![40]

From *Moving Picture World* 8, no. 3 (January 21, 1911), 124–25.
Illustrations by H. F. Hoffman.[41]

2

DREAMS OF THE FUTURE

The years surrounding World War I were arguably the most optimistic, the most feverishly excited, the film industry has ever experienced. On the eve of the conflict not just embryonic Hollywood but also its equivalents throughout Europe more or less simultaneously hit upon the idea of "feature films" that differed markedly from their one-reel predecessors not just in terms of their running time but also in terms of their displayed spectacle and the complexity of their narrative content. Many of the silent-film features of course amounted to little more than commercial entertainments, albeit with glorious production values and cast members well on their way to becoming movie "stars." At the same time, a significant number of the early features aspired to both the scope and the depth of the best that traditional story-telling genres—novels and plays, opera and ballet—had to offer.

As early as 1911 multi-reel epics were being produced in Italy; within a year or two large-scale films were being made as well in France and the United States, and often they were released in the company of originally composed orchestral scores.[1] Although such films found congenial homes in existing opera houses and vaudeville theaters, to meet audience demand exhibitors in cities around the world rushed to build "movie palaces" whose seating capacities fairly dwarfed those of most earlier cinema-specific venues.[2] Whether or not they were distributed with originally composed scores, the feature films that played in the movie palaces were inevitably accompanied by orchestras or by a newly invented instrument called the theater organ.[3]

Outbreak of hostilities in the summer of 1914 disrupted film production almost everywhere in Europe, but it had no effect whatsoever on film production in Hollywood. Hollywood's dominant influence on cinema worldwide throughout the twentieth century is often attributed to the sheer number of films—huge, in comparison with the output of any other nation—that Hollywood over the years has been able to generate. But surely Hollywood's ascendance is due at least in part to the simple fact that in the middle of the twentieth century's second decade, when the Old World was being torn apart by war, filmmaking in the New World rolled peacefully along. During the war, Hollywood flourished; after the war, the European film industries strived first to recover and then to catch up.

The writers gathered in this section offer a mix of American wartime and French postwar perspectives on the relationship between music and the still relatively new phenomenon of the feature film. Readers will note the strongly worded negative opinions from certain of the French commentators, who declare in no uncertain terms that cinema is nothing more than "photographed pantomime" and is simply "depressing for the masses."[4] But readers will also note that the majority of these comments project not cynicism but optimism. Indeed, one of the most remarkable threads that links these many opinions is the one that suggests that the combination of music and moving pictures *could be* a genuine "art" form.

Likely to the chagrin of the French composer Claude Terrasse and the American critic Carl Van Vechten, film in the immediate wake of World War I did not move boldly in the direction of "cinematographic opera" or the Wagnerian *Gesamtkunstwerk* (the "complete art work," with virtually all its elements determined by a single author). One suspects, though, that Terrasse, Van Vechten, and others who between 1916 and 1919 had been perhaps naively hopeful took at least a modicum of comfort in knowing that film music in general by the early 1920s had indeed settled into a standard—and apparently quite viable—functional mode.

2.1 MUSIC FOR THE MOVIES

Carl Van Vechten

Carl Van Vechten (1880–1964) was a polymath aesthete who during the early decades of the twentieth century contributed importantly, as both critic and practitioner, to many areas of American culture. Born in Cedar Rapids, Iowa, he earned a liberal arts degree at the University of Chicago in 1903 and then relocated to New York. He established himself first as a writer on music, serving as a reviewer for the New York Times *and then, in 1910–11, as program annotator for the* New York Philharmonic; *an unabashed champion of musical modernism, he wrote enthusiastically about such "cutting edge" composers as Leo Ornstein, Erik Satie, Arnold Schoenberg, Igor Stravinsky, and other "cutting edge" composers, and his essays were readily published in such books as the precociously titled* Music After the Great War *(1915),[5]* Music and Bad Manners *(1916),* Interpreters and Interpretations *(1917), and* The Merry-Go-Round *(1918). In the 1920s Van Vechten concentrated on literature, vociferously singing the praises of African-American writers representative of the so-called Harlem Renaissance and at the same time producing novels of his own.[6] In the 1930s he turned to photography, creating not only praiseworthy landscapes and still lifes but also iconic portraits of the period's leading figures in literature, music, theater, and dance.*

In this chapter from Music and Bad Manners, *Van Vechten contributes to the idea—perhaps a myth, really—that the earliest exhibitors of motion pictures looked to musical accompaniment as a palliative to audience anxieties triggered by the "appalling" silence of flickering on-screen images. By 1916, however, film accompaniment had evolved far beyond its tentative initial stages and settled into a common practice that laid the foundation, at least in essence, for film music today. Van Vechten likely remembered his youthful exposure to catch-as-catch-can accompaniments for brief vaudeville and nickelodeon film shows in Cedar Rapids and Chicago. But the movies he saw in New York c.1915–16 would have been enormously more sophisticated not just in terms of their narrative content but also in terms of their dramatically relevant musical support. The films he addresses here are clearly of the "modern" sort, not the one- or two-reel entertainments previously offered by a cartel of East Coast producers but, rather, the two- or three-hour, star-studded dramas regularly delivered by ambitious independent producers based for the most part in Southern California. The venues in which he experienced these films would have been not humble nickelodeons that accommodated a hundred or so patrons but, rather, brand new "movie palaces" seating more than a thousand. And the film music he heard, a far cry from accompaniments provided by lone pianists or two- or three-man ensembles, would have been delivered either by a large orchestra or the recently invented theater organ.*

Van Vechten was foresighted in his observation that "the moving picture demands a new kind of music," not mere "sentimental accompaniment" but music whose formal principles were in line with those of the emerging cinema fare. Indeed, his description of this new film music—offered in his final paragraph—seems apt for a great many European and American film scores from the 1990s.

Despite the fact that it would seem that the moving picture drama has opened up new worlds to the modern music, no important composer, so far as I am aware, has as yet turned his attention to the writing of music for the films. If the cinema drama is in its infancy, as some would have us believe, then we may be sure that the time is not far distant when moving picture scores will take their places on the musicians' book-shelves alongside those of operas, symphonies, masses, and string quartets. In the meantime, entirely ignorant of the truth (or oblivious to it, or merely helpless, as the case may be) that writing music for moving pictures is a new art, which demands a new point of view, the directors of the picture theatres are struggling with the situation as best they may. Under the circumstances it is remarkable, on the whole, how swiftly and how well the demand for music with the silent drama has been met. Certainly the music is usually on a level with (or of a better quality than) the type of entertainment offered. But the directors have not definitely tackled the problem; they still continue to try to force old wine into new bottles, arranging and re-arranging melody and harmony which was contrived for quite other occasions and purposes. Even when scores have been written for pictures the result has not shown any imaginative advance over the arranged score. It is strange, but it has occurred to no one that the moving picture demands a *new* kind of music.

The composers, I should imagine, are only waiting to be asked to write it. Certainly none of them has even shown any hesitancy about composing incidental music for the spoken drama. Mendelssohn wrote strains for *A Midsummer Night's Dream* which seemed pledged to immortality until Granville Barker ignored them;[7] the Wedding March is still in favour in Kankakee and Keokuk. Beethoven illustrated Goethe's *Egmont*; Sir Arthur Sullivan penned a score for *The Tempest*; Schubert was inspired to put down some of his most ravishing notes for a stupid play called *Rosamunde*; Grieg's *Peer Gynt* music is more often performed than the play.[8] More recent instances of incidental music for dramas are Saint-Saëns's score for Brieux's *La Foi*, Mascagni's for *The Eternal City*, and Richard Strauss's for *Le Bourgeois Gentilhomme*.[9] Is it necessary to continue the list? I have only, after all, put down a few of the obvious examples (passing by the thousands upon thousands of scores devised by lesser composers for lesser plays) that would spring at once to any musician's mind. Of course it has usually been the poetic drama (do we ever hear Shakespeare or Rostand without it?) which has seemed to call for incidental music but it has accompanied (with more or less disastrous consequences, to be sure) the unfolding of many a "drawing-room" play: especially during the eighties.

When the first moving picture was exposed on the screen it seems to have occurred to its projector at once that some kind of music must accompany its unreeling. The silence evidently appalled him. A moving picture is not unlike a ballet in that it depends entirely upon action (it differs from a ballet in that the action is not necessarily rhythmic)—and

19

whoever heard of a ballet performed without music? Sound certainly has its value in creating an atmosphere and in emphasizing the "thrill" of the moving picture, especially when the sound is selected and co-ordinated. It may also divert the attention. On the whole, more photographed plays follow the general lines of *Lady Windermere's Fan* or *Peg o' My Heart* than of poetic dramas such as *Cymbeline* or *La Samaritaine*.[10] The problem here, however, is not the same as in the spoken drama. For in motion pictures a poetic play sheds its poetry and becomes, like its neighbour, a skeleton of action. There is no conceivable distinction in the "movies" (beyond one created by preference, or taste, or the quality of the performance and the photography) between Dante's *Inferno* and a picture in which the beloved Charles Chaplin looms large. The directors of the moving picture companies have tried to meet this problem; that they have not wholly succeeded so far is not entirely their fault.

It is no easy matter, for example, in a theatre in which the films are changed daily (this is the general rule even in the larger houses), for the musicians (or musician) to arrange a satisfactory accompaniment for 5,000 feet of action which includes everything from an earthquake in Cuba to a dinner in Park Lane, and it is scarcely possible, even if the distributors be so inclined (as they frequently are nowadays) to furnish a music score which will answer the purposes of the different sized bands, ranging from a full orchestra to an upright piano, *solo*. As for the pictures without pre-arranged scores, the orchestra leaders and pianists must do the best they can with them.

In some houses there is an attitude of total disrespect paid towards the picture by the *chef d'orchestre*. He arranges his musical programme as if he were giving a concert, not at all with a view to effectively accompanying the picture. In a theatre on Second Avenue in New York, for example, I have heard an orchestra play the whole of Beethoven's First Symphony as an accompaniment to Irene Fenwick's performance of *The Woman Next Door*. As the symphony came to an end before the picture it was supplemented by a Waldteufel waltz, *Les Patineurs*. The result, in this instance, was not altogether incongruous or even particularly displeasing, and it occurred to me that if one had to listen to music while the third act of *Hedda Gabler* were being enacted one would prefer to hear something like Boccherini's celebrated minuet or a light Mozart dance rather than anything ostensibly contrived to fit the situation. In the latter instance the result would be sure to be unbearable bathos.

On the other hand there are certain players for pictures who remind one by their methods of the anxiety of Richard Strauss to describe every peacock and bean mentioned in any of his opera-books. If a garden is exposed on the screen one hears *The Flowers That Bloom in the Spring*; a love scene is the signal for *Un Peu d'Amour*; a cross or any religious episode suggests *The Rosary* to these ingenuous musicians; Japan brings a touch of *Madame Butterfly*; a proposal of marriage, *O Promise Me*; and a farewell, Tosti's *Goodbye!* This expedient of appealing through the intellect to the emotions, it may be admitted, has the stamp of approval of no less a composer than Richard Wagner.

Lacking the authority of real moving picture music (which a new composer must rise to invent) the safest way (not necessarily the *best* way) is the middle course—one method for this, another for that. One of the difficulties is to arrange a music score for a theatre with a large orchestra, where the leader must plan his score—or have it planned for him—for an entire picture before his orchestra can play a note. Music cues must be definite; twenty bars of *Alexander's Ragtime Band*, seventeen of *The Ride of the Valkyries*, ten of *Vissi d'Arte*, etc. An ingenious young man has discovered a way by which music and action may be exactly synchronized. I feel the impulse to quote extensively from the somewhat vivid report of this achievement, published in one of the motion picture weekly journals: "Here was a man-sized job—how to measure the action of the picture to the musical score, so that they would both come out equal to every part of the picture, and would be so exact that any orchestra might take the score and follow the movement of the play with absolute correctness. It was a question primarily of mathematics, but even so it was some time before a system of computation was devised before the undertaking was gotten down to a certainty. As an illustration, on the opening night of one of the most notable photoplay productions now before the public, the orchestra, notwithstanding a three weeks' rehearsal, found at the conclusion of the picture that it was a page and half behind the play's action in the musical setting." Then we learn that Frank Stadler of New York "provided the remedy for this condition of affairs." It is impossible to resist the temptation to quote further from this extremely racy account. "He remembered that Beethoven had overcome the difficulty of proper timing for his sonatas by a mechanical arrangement known as the metronome, invented by a friend of his. This is an arrangement with a little bell attached which may be set for the movement of the music and used as an exact guide to the right measure, the bell giving warning at the expiration of each period so that the leader knows whether he is in time or not." Mr. Stadler then began the measurement of a film with a metronome, a stenographer, and a watch. He found that the film ran ten feet to every eight seconds and he set the metronome for eight second periods accordingly. "The stenographer made a note of the action of the picture each time the bell rang, with the result that when the entire picture had been run Mr. Stadler had a complete record of the production. All that was necessary then was to select from the classics and the popular melodies the music which would give a suitable atmosphere and a harmonious accompaniment to the theme of the play, so synchronizing the music with the eight second periods that every bar of it fitted the spirit of the many score of scenes of the production."

The single-man orchestra, the player of the upright piano, need not make so many preparatory gestures. He may with impunity, if he be of an inventive turn of mind, or if his memory be good, improvise his score as the picture unreels itself for the first time before what may very well be his astonished vision; and, after that, he may vary his accompaniment, as the shows of the day progress, improving it here or there, or not, as the case may be, keeping generally as near to his original performance as possible. Of course he puts a good deal of reliance on rum-ti-tum shivery passages (known to orchestra leaders as *"agits"*—an abbreviation of *agitato*; a page or two of them is distributed to every member of a moving picture band) to accompany moments of excitement. This music you will remember if you have ever attended a performance of a Lincoln J. Carter melodrama in which a train was wrecked, or a hero rescued from the teeth of a saw, or a heroine pursued by bloodhounds.[11] (Those were the good old days!) Recently I heard a pianist in a moving picture house on Fourteenth Street in New York eke out a half-hour with similar poundings on two or three well-used chords (well used even in the time of Haydn). The scenes represented the whole of a two-act opera, and the ambitious pianist was trying to give the audience the effect of singers (principals and chorus) and orchestra, with his three chords. (Shades of Arnold Schoenberg!)

A certain periodical devoted to the interests of the moving picture trade conducts a department as first aid to the musical conductors and pianists who figure at these shows. In a recent number the editor of this department gives it as his solemn opinion that musicians who read fiction are the best equipped for picture playing. Then, with an almost tragic parenthesis, he continues, "Reading fiction is the last diversion that the average musician will follow. He feels that all the necessary romance is to be found in his music." Facts are dead, says this editor in substance, but fiction is living and should make you weep. When you cry, all that remains for you to do is to think of a tune which will synchronize with the cause of your tears; this will serve you later when a similar scene occurs in a film drama.

There is one tune which any capable moving picture pianist has found will synchronize with any Keystone picture (for the benefit of the uninitiated I may state that in the Keystone farces some one gets kicked or knocked down or spat upon several times in almost every scene).[12] I do not know what the tune is, but wherever Keystone pictures are shown, in Cedar Rapids, Iowa; Grand Rapids, Michigan; Chicago, and even New York, I have heard it. When a character falls into the water (and at least ten of them invariably do) the pianist may vary the tune by sitting on the piano or by upsetting a chair. In one theatre I have known him to cause glass to be shattered behind the screen at a moment when the picture exposed a similar scene. How Marinetti would like that![13]

However, the day of this sort of thing is rapidly approaching its close, I venture to say. Some of the firms are already issuing arranged music scores for their productions (one may note in passing the score which accompanied Geraldine Farrar's screen performance of *Carmen*, largely selected from the music of Bizet's opera, and Victor Herbert's original score for *The Fall of a Nation*, a score which does not take full advantage of the new technique of the cinema drama). It will not be long before an enterprising director engages an enterprising musician to compose music for a picture. For the same reason that d'Annunzio, very early in the career of the moving picture, wrote a scenario for a film, I should not be surprised to learn that Richard Strauss was under contract to construct an accompaniment for a screened drama.[14] It will be very loud music and it will require an orchestra of 143 men to interpret it and probably the composer himself will conduct the first performance, and, later, excerpts will be given by the Boston Symphony Orchestra and the critics will say, in spite of Philip Hale's diverting programme notes, that this music should never be played except in conjunction with the picture for which it was written. Mascagni is another composer who should find an excellent field for his talent in writing tone-poems for pictures, although he would contrive nothing more daring than a well-arranged series of illustrative melodies.[15]

But put Igor Stravinsky, or some other modern genius, to work on this problem and see what happens![16] The musicians of the future should revel in the opportunity the moving picture gives them to create a new form. This form differs from that of the incidental music for a play in that the flow of tone may be continuous and because one never needs to soften the accompaniment so that the voices may be heard; it differs from the music for a ballet in that the scene shifts constantly, and consequently the time-signatures and the mood and the key must be as constantly shifting. The swift flash from scene to scene, the "cut-back," the necessary rapidity of the action, all are adapted to inspire the futurist composer to brilliant effort; a tinkle of this and a smash of that, without "working-out" or development; illustration, comment, piquant or serious, that's what the new film music should be. The ultimate moving picture score will be something more than sentimental accompaniment.

From *Music and Bad Manners* (New York: Alfred A. Knopf, 1916), 43–54.

2.2 THE SURVEYS OF *LE FILM*: MUSIC AND THE CINEMA

(Les Enquêtes du *Film*: La musique et le cinema)

Le Film *began as a weekly trade journal in 1914 under the editorship of Henri Diamant-Berger. Following the Easter 1919 issue, Lyonel Robert became the new editor and changed the journal's direction, making it a popular monthly magazine sold principally at news stands in Paris. During the summer of 1919* Le Film *conducted a survey focused on the relationship between music and film. Robert's letter of June 30 was reproduced at the beginning of the article. Thirty-three responses were published in the August 15 issue, with two late-arriving contributions in the September 15 issue. Each response is prefaced by an introductory comment from Robert, presented both here and in the original in italics.*

The musicians who responded represent a broad spectrum of French musical life, including composers, critics, conductors, instrumentalists, teachers, and publishers. They ranged from musical conservatives, such as Vincent d'Indy and Maurice Moszkowski, to members of the avant-garde, such as Georges Auric and Claude Terrasse. Their opinions likewise ranged widely, from utter dismissals of film music as a genre to unbounded hopes that film music offered completely new hopes for modern composers.

Of the thirty-three respondents, thirteen eventually had at least one film score among their credits. In film music, Auric easily proved to be the most prolific, between 1930 and 1969 composing music for 120 feature films, more than a dozen short films, and a half-dozen television series. But Fernand Le Borne also occupies a prominent place in French film music history; early in the twentieth century he was the musical director for Pathé's Films d'Art and in this capacity not only scored several films but also hired Camille Saint-Saëns to compose the music for L'Assassinat du Duc de Guise *(1908). Henri Rabaud's short film career began in grand style, with the highly publicized gala premiere of* Le Miracle des Loups *(1924) at the Paris Opéra's Palais Garnier. That film was produced by a new art film company, the Société des Films Historiques, and it brought Rabaud into contact with novelist Henry Dupuis-Mazuel, director Raymond Bernard, and actor Charles Dullin. These four celebrated artists would also work together on the Société's second film,* Le Joueur d'Echecs *(1927).*

Continuing our series of surveys, we address ourselves this time to musicians in the following terms:

> Without doubt, you have heard—or heard about—the score that Camille Erlanger[17] wrote for the cinematic 'libretto' *La Suprême Epopée* (Salle Marivaux, April 1919). When death surprised your late colleague, he was working on music for a new film. In addition, Mascagni should be finishing a special score for a great film in the making entitled *Iris*.*[18]
>
> At the moment when French cinematography, reborn after five years of war, strives to become an art—or at the very least to bring to its productions an increasingly serious and artistic character—we would like to hear your view

on the following question: Do you think that there is a new path for music to follow by associating with cinematography? Should this music conform to the conventions of incidental music as it is already used in theaters—or could it take advantage of the differences between current theatrical and cinematographic conceptions in order to expand its technique and search for new modes of expression?

To judge by the eagerness of responses and by the very importance of those who responded—as well as by the real interest of many responses—it seems that our question was asked at the right moment, and that the problem it raises is one many would like to see resolved. But who will make the first steps toward this new formula—publishers, exhibitors, screenplay writers, or musicians? If *Le Film* provoked a useful response and if it can contribute to the realization of a solution, it will be very happy to render this service to art, artists, and cinematography.

—Lyonel Robert

A discordant note is necessary. It is difficult for us to see an esteemed master like Vincent d'Indy[19] *profess such contempt for cinema, but it is his right after all:*

Since, in my opinion, cinema has nothing to do with art and since its effects have always seemed to me depressing for the masses, I can have no opinion about music connected to this spectacle.

—Vincent d'Indy

The illustrious composer of Mârouf, *Henri Rabaud,*[20] *member of the Institut Français, is more favorable to us:*

It is quite obvious that the accompaniment to a cinematographic spectacle can provide a composer with the occasion to write excellent music. As to how this music will distinguish itself from incidental music, that is a question about which I have hardly thought and on which I would not be able to say anything interesting.

—Henri Rabaud

His colleague at the Académie des Beaux-Arts, Théodore Dubois,[21] *who just celebrated his fiftieth year as organist of La Madeleine, who for a long time directed the national Conservatoire, who is the author of so many masterpieces of sacred music, and who achieved so much success with* Xavière *at the Opéra, looks favorably on music for the cinema:*

I believe that musicians should adapt their composition to the subject, as it unfolds in the films. Obviously, themes will not be made of the material for grand symphonic development, but the intelligent composer can find in them an interesting variety of color, if he has some talent and an appropriate technique. It is all a question of taste, tact, and experience. It seems to me no less apparent that scores made specially for films, if they are worth something, will always be preferable to those arbitrarily taken and adapted, however well or poorly.

—Th. Dubois

Henri Maréchal,[22] *recipient of the Prix de Rome, with his eternally young mind and broad views; author of* Les Amoureux de Cathérine, *who asserted himself as a remarkable writer in his memoirs, is a devotee of the cinema.*

From the beginning I believed in cinema, and its rapid development has not proven me wrong. It seems opportune, however, for our country to step up in this regard and for us to no longer be condemned to foreign films, of which some, it is true, are ingenious and deftly produced, but of which a very large number are continual repetitions of the same effects.

The intervention of real music [*vraie musique*] is something to be desired; but here we need patience. Several years ago, some large establishments in Paris offered to the public some veritable masterworks, which should be considered as such first by the subject, then by the musical adaptations taken from the greatest masters and remarkably performed, and finally by a sense and surety of direction that brought great credit to the enterprise. However, this project had to be withdrawn because of the public's disinterest! That is hardly encouraging! But we can insist—we should even—and this would not be the first time that we saw the public adore what it had previously disdained!

We still need to find a practical means of closely linking all of these combined arts. I have often dreamed of that and, keeping my complete faith in a point of arrival, I do not hide from the difficulties to be overcome. How to combine an orchestral score, patiently and precisely created, with the fidgetiness of that which *rolls* [*tourne*]?[23] One day—if there is plenty of time!—the film maintains one speed and the next day—if pressed for time!—it maintains another; the score remains immutable; from that comes the discrepancy between what we see and what we hear.

Once again, we can and should be able to reconcile these two opposed elements and it is in applauding in advance this reconciliation that I send you my best regards.

—H. Maréchal

André Messager,[24] *who has triumphed in all countries as conductor of the Concerts du Conservatoire, former director of the Opéra, composer of delicious comic operas (*La Basoche, Véronique, Fortunio, *etc.) whose success is far from being exhausted.*

In response to your letter of June 30, I hasten to give you my opinion about the music applied to cinematographic films. I do not think that this represents a newly opened path. But I see in it the opportunity to make incidental music— not as it has been used, but continuous and amplified and being, in sum, very similar to the music for pantomimes, since it should follow as closely as possible the movement of the scenes and the expression of the acting.

The inconvenient thing is that symphonic development will always be restrained, the rapidity of the scenes forcing the composer to change tempos, rhythms, and styles in a fashion hardly compatible with themes of a certain proportion.

But it is very much to be desired that films, whether their plot is tragic or comic, be accompanied by music composed expressly for them, instead of using more or less well-adapted fragments, which generally just barely follow the plot and abruptly break off in the middle of a motive due to the necessities of film.

—A. Messager

Gabriel Pierné,[25] *winner of the Prix de Rome, conductor of the Concerts Colonne, whose harmonious melodies are on everybody's lips, the author of* Ramuntcho, Saint-François d'Assise, Les Cathédrales, La Coupe Enchantée, Vendée, *etc. . . .*

Music is as indispensable to cinema as wind in the sails is to a fisherman.

The improvisation of a resigned pianist is sufficient for the presentation of the 'news'; a mechanical instrument can grind a perforated box to accompany the regrettable films that gratify the public on a daily basis; these noisy contraptions—economical!—are largely sufficient for the current spectacle of our neighborhood cinemas and some other sumptuous establishments. I think that it is necessary that when a play performed with incidental music is then projected on the screen, it is best to use the music written for the play and not to use, for example, the "Farandole" from *L'Arlésienne*[26] to accompany a skating competition in Norway or kittens eating; all of that depends on the intelligence of the pianist (an improviser who is always resigned) or on the taste and quality of the music director.

'Appropriate' music is everything! And I believe that it would be especially interesting and *new* to write a score for a *special* and truly artistic film; such a thing has been tried before, and it could have succeeded with money and a performance worthy of the work that was performed. Now, it needs an orchestra of sixty to seventy performers *in the hall* and a second smaller orchestra and singers *behind the screen*; we can only hope that a director will agree to such costs . . . couldn't the formidable profits made during the war encourage directors to make some sacrifices?

—Gabriel Pierné

Claude Terrasse,[27] *who does not look down on operetta, with* Les Dragées d'Hercule, *and who triumphed at the Opéra-Comique with* Télémaque, *a relatively young musician who is not afraid of being cheerful and clear.*

I am absolutely convinced that there is a new path in the association of film and music. The 'cinematographic opera' [*lyrique cinématographique*] will be created. I am very concerned with this question at any given moment, but I have found such incomprehension and hostility with our principal film producers that I am resigned to wait for a better time to realize this project.

In France, most artists have excellent ideas, which they are incapable of realizing themselves; each has a part to play. Unfortunately, producers do not want to try to understand or adapt those ideas; this is especially true for the specialty that interests you, the film opera [*cinéma-lyrique*].

It is not a question of writing whatever music for whatever film script to produce a lasting work. The film must be a musical film. I possess several worthy scripts for which I have tried to compose a new type of music. I used clever spotting [*des repères faciles*] so that there was not any imprecision between the image and the music. This is an easy process to use. I am certain that the practical directing of several films will give the best impression to the audience. I am equally convinced that very soon someone will create a true musical library and new movie theatres, with *repertory*.

This all remains to be seen, as I told you, since our current producers understand nothing or do not want to understand, which is the same in the end. The idea, as always, will be exploited by foreigners and will bring to us the greatest successes from England, America, or elsewhere.

—Claude Terrasse

Camille Chevillard,[28] *who masterfully succeeded Lamoureux at the head of his own orchestra, author of classical symphonic variations for piano:*

I essentially believe in the future of the musical film, which was also the view of the late Claude Debussy, on the condition that we forever spurn what has been attempted up until now.

It is necessary to conceive of films that can be translated by a score that adapts itself to each gesture and each expression of the character. Without this, we will have random creations instead of the proper union of two art forms.

—Camille Chevillard

The question even interests art critics. Here are the opinions of Le Gaulois, *dearly collected from Louis Schneider,*[29] *whose articles ring with authority.*

It seems to me that as things stand, people commit veritable heresies by forcing certain pages of music to accompany cinematographic scenes with which they can have no relationship.

But if you pursue the idea of scores that are specially written for specific films, the mutilation—and I will even say debasement [*dénobilisation*]—of the music appears to me no less inevitable. The primary condition of cinema is the process, the cleverness, the artificiality—I do not mean, of course, the documentary scenes whose realism excludes all formal inspiration. The primary condition of music, on the other hand, is sincerity, interior emotion, and also meditation. How to reconcile two such diametrically opposed means of expression, one aiming only for the eyes of the spectator and the other being made only for the listener's soul?

Perhaps certain composers, who are insufficiently gifted to endow the operatic tradition with lofty works, will nevertheless have enough talent to compose in view of improving the musical level of certain cinemas, thereby raising the public taste. This would be some sort of musical wallpaper, which would contrast with the tapestries that we owe to the great genius of masters.

—Louis Schneider

Albert Mangeot,[30] *the eminent director of* Le Monde Musical:

It is not uncertain that the cinema could offer excellent librettos for music, but I wonder how a composer, however clever he might be, can actually comment on films, which are cut into little pieces that follow one another on the screen at such a vertiginous speed?

Wouldn't the real solution consist of making films on pre-existing symphonic poems, which lend themselves particularly well to visual representation?

Among these, and drawing on very different types, I am thinking of Charpentier's *Impressions d'Italie*, Paul Dukas's *l'Apprenti Sorcier*, Debussy's *l'Après-midi d'un faune*, and above all Ernest Fanelli's *Thèbes*, which evokes in such a striking manner the Egypt of Gautier's *Roman de la Momie*.[31]

But it would be necessary for the film directors, if not musicians themselves, to at least be partnered with musicians. Such a thing should not be impossible.

—A. Mangeot

René Doire,[32] director of the Courrier Musical *and composer of a recent sonata for piano and violin:*

We do not, I think, have to fall back on the cinema's need for music. Despite the powerful interest that attaches itself to the rich invention that is cinematography, a film without music demonstrates the need. This was recognized without discussion. It is agreed to look for what should be 'the absolute adaptation.'

Cinema certainly opens the door to a new formula for music. It is high time, in my opinion, that people stop borrowing various pages that accompany the film with more or less . . . fantasy.

Some special music for each film, a special orchestration (with new effects and new instruments), a special cut, perfect timing, tempos that are immutable once agreed upon—that is what we need to wish for, but that requires so many studies, so many rehearsals, such a huge amount of work in this period of vacations, leisure, and strikes![33] Rehearsals . . . there is the secret of all creations of proper art. Unfortunately—not more in cinema than elsewhere—people 'blast' through rehearsals in order to save time, i.e., to reduce costs. As long as this regime persists, we cannot claim to have any profitable collaboration in the film-musical art.

—René Doire

The author of Le Père La Victoire, *of* La Tsarine, *and of* La Marche Lorraine *and of so many other compositions that have carried his name to the ends of the earth, is really too modest:*

Excuse me for not being able to respond to your question, since I have no competence in cinematography and so little in music! However, I suspect that the good art films deserve a score specially composed without conventional theatrical conceptions, and I ardently hope that we find there a new and productive outlet for young composers!

—Louis Ganne[34]

Paul Vidal,[35] conductor at the Opéra, where his marvelous ballet La Maladetta *has so often been applauded:*

I think that people can make excellent film music, either by adapting pre-existing music or by creating new scores. It is not impossible to closely follow the action as it unfolds, one can also sometimes write rather long pieces, and finally the cinema could become an excellent school for theater composers. It would be necessary to combine solo and choral songs, which would diminish the terrible competition with operatic presentations.

—Paul Vidal

André Wormser,[36] *pianist and professor of the most famous, who will not be forgotten thanks to his music for* L'Enfant Prodigue, *a pantomime that enjoyed hundreds of performances.*

I believe that for the presentation of great films, a special, adequate, and so-to-speak plastic music would particularly enhance the strength of the impressions produced, principally in picturesque, passionate, and dramatic scenes, by reinforcing the visual sensation with auditory emotion.

I am not disguising the difficulty of the task, the greatest challenge of which will be to establish synchronization of the extremely variable projection speed with the necessarily fixed duration of the orchestral performance.

Nevertheless, I believe that there is there a fertile path and a new form that could become a beautiful expression of art.

—André Wormser

Shortly before the war, Reynaldo Hahn[37] *was successful at the Opéra with* La Fête chez Thérèse. *You know the exquisite art with which he sings his delicious, delicate songs; he offers here a piece of advice that would be urgent and easy to heed:*

I do not believe that cinematography can open new paths for music. But it seems to me that people should strive to heighten the interest in cinematographic spectacles through the choice and precise adaptation of the accompanying music. People will be able to succeed with the latter only by imposing an invariable projection speed for films accompanied by special scores. The employees charged with projecting films generally do so however they please and with a tendency to accelerate;[38] a score cannot accommodate itself to all of these caprices; a tempo is a tempo. All of the experiments by which people try to achieve absolute synchronization between what one sees and what one hears will be in vain as long as people do not project films with a precision and rhythmic invariability comparable to those achieved in musical performance.

—Reynaldo Hahn

Henry Busser,[39] *winner of the Prix de Rome, conductor of the Opéra.*

There is certainly a very interesting experiment to attempt in the domain of cinematography for musicians who will have the patience to treat a 'musical film' like a *pantomime*, of which the least details will be underlined by the orchestra. But the musician must be the humble servant to the 'gesture' so that the collaboration of the two arts, 'film and music,' will be perfect. I see there a great future for French musicians, who are so numerous and so little played!

—Henry Busser

29

Gustave Doret,[40] *the famous Swiss composer, who achieved great success with* Les Armaillis *and who is one of the most erudite writers on musical subjects:*

Without hesitation, I am responding to your question: yes. But I add that only when the cinematographic art wants to resolutely search for a means of expression completely separate from traditional theatrical forms, then the intimate collaboration of music will become more clearly original.

And who knows if music won't be the very reason for a complete transformation in the conception of films? Since the form has not yet been realized, it would be childish to deny it.

—Gustave Doret

The idea is one of those that can tempt youth: such as Albert Roussel,[41] *the composer of* Les Evocations, Le Poème de la Forêt, *and* Le Festin de l'Araignée.

I am convinced that music is called to take an increasingly important part in the presentation of films, and that for composers this is a new path on which they will have the opportunity to create truly interesting works.

Until now, the music that has accompanied films has been too often taken, without proper judgment, from here and from there among familiar songs, fashionable waltzes, and fragments of operas and operettas, each having no relation with what is happening on the screen. And it is necessary to recognize that it was difficult to do otherwise, since there existed no special repertoire for the cinematograph. There were, however, laudable efforts by some conductors to play works having a real musical value, adapted as well as possible to the subject of the film. I remember the shock that I experienced in a large establishment on the outer boulevards of Paris, where I heard difficult modern works performed with an attention to detail that, unfortunately, could not make up for insufficient rehearsals.

Music written for cinematographic presentations, if it wants to be heard, should adorn itself with simple lines and very clear textures, should express itself clearly, and should not encumber itself with superimposed motives or complicated counterpoint. This will not prevent new and incisive harmonies, or colorful orchestrations. It should go straight to the point, underlining the diverse reversals of the plot, even suggesting the emotions, all the more free to sing since it need not fear burying the voices or making the audience miss a line of dialogue. In the theater, incidental music is either heard too much or too little: either way, in most cases it is an unclear and vague noise of muted violins, a sort of unexpressive and anemic drone, or the predictable rhythm of a military march. In the cinema, music will have the most elbow-room and its conception will be infinitely larger and more varied; the composer will be able, in certain films, to create veritable symphonic poems to which the public will lend an increasingly attentive ear. And this last consideration seems to me, from the musician's point of view, one of the most interesting, since the cinema can do so much for the music education of the crowds. Music written specially for a film, if it combines all the qualities I mentioned above, will be heard and understood; the spectators will discuss its merits during the intermission or as they leave, their tastes will form or refine little by little. And who knows if such laymen, who since their childhood have only known more or less inane refrains from the café-concerts, will not one day have the curiosity to go hear what is being played at the Concerts Pasdeloup,[42] for example?

Who knows if our grand symphonic associations, if they don't otherwise harm the cinema, might thus gain some regulars? And frankly, it would be wonderful if music was, in our beautiful country of France, a little better understood and loved.

—Albert Roussel

Gabriel Grovlez,[43] *conductor at the Opéra, author of the most highly thought of songs, erudite writer on music:*

I think that there is a new path for composers to follow in linking themselves to the cinematograph. For modern musicians, therein lies a complete and new means of expression to use, but it will be necessary to completely abandon the bad habits of the past—theatrical art is one thing, cinematography [*cinégraphie*] another. The day when the musician can see on-screen the stylized visions of his mind and when an artist can discover how to present to us a transposition of the musical idea in, say, *Ride of the Valkyries*, then a new form of art will have been created. This we can anticipate with the highest hopes.

But it seems to me that the new formula has not been found, since in my humble opinion, *La Suprême Epopée*, which you mentioned, was still written under the influence of theatrical composition. And I very much fear that this formula will not be evident in M. Mascagni's film, which undoubtedly will be a cinematographic adaptation of his opera *Iris*.

We need to create a new art and I think that French artists are just the ones to do it.

—Gabriel Grovlez

Armande de Polignac,[44] *the charming composer of* Bazar d'Orient, La Princesse Lointaine, Judith:

Yes, I heard Camille Erlanger's very interesting score for *La Suprême Epopée*, and I was satisfied with this effort to revive cinematographic music. Essentially, I believe that this genre, which really interests me, has a great artistic future. There are certainly many new things to do with the almost unlimited means offered by cinema, and music that is in line with the plot seems to me an absolute necessity.

—Armande de Polignac

Georges Hüe,[45] *the composer of* Chansons printanières, Les Croquis d'Orient, *and* Le Miracle, *which was performed at the Opéra:*

It is very difficult for me to respond to your question in just a few lines. Everything that tends to expand the domain of symphonic music can only be of interest to me. Certainly, a film is improved when presented with a score that is precisely adapted to the dramatic situations, as if it were made for a pantomime.

The realization [of film music] seems to me more difficult, given the number of films and the very frequent changes to cinematographic programs.

—Georges Hüe

Francis Casadesus,[46] *renowned conductor, of which we had a good taste last July 14, with a cantata performed under his baton by eight hundred singers and instrumentalists:*

Up until the present time, it has been the cinema that solicited (if I may use that word) the collaboration of music, and I believe that it [music] has rendered some real services, but I am absolutely certain that the contrary will soon be produced and will give very new and very moving results.

Pardon me for not saying any more on this subject that interests me to the greatest degree. As in everything, actions speak louder than words, and so what I said today would spoil an idea without helping it.

—Francis Casadesus

Guy Ropartz,[47] *the commendable author of* Retour *and* Le Poème de la Maison, *who was recently appointed Director of the Strasbourg Conservatory:*

To offer a slightly useful response to your question, I would have to be more competent than I am, having never collaborated on a cinematographic work: but it seems to me that the score destined to accompany a film should be close to that which a composer used to write for a pantomime. And only the cinematographic libretto will guide the musician in choosing this or that expressive formula.

—J. Guy Ropartz

Léon Moreau and Henry Février,[48] *whose successful endeavor was interrupted by the war, naturally demand only to recommence a new experiment:*

The question that you ask is fascinating to me:

Perhaps you know that, with M. Henry Février, I presented at the Gaumont-Palace a true opera in three acts entitled *L'Agonie de Byzance* (1913). This was a grand success. But unfortunately, this film portrayed the victory of the Turks over Emperor Constantine and it is this very triumph that I think prevents the re-release of this very important work.

I am certain that the cinema has opened a marvelous new path for music. And this music will be as different from that which exists as the cinema is from the theater; for example, the theater cannot show a continuous journey. It can only express the arrival or departure of the characters and their ever-so-short stop on the stage, no matter how large that [stage] might be.

Musicians who wanted to express a continuous journey needed to write concert works, like "La Course à l'Abîme" from *La Damnation de Faust,*[49] which can be shown only by the cinema.

However, one observation from a man informed about the subject: *The music must be written before the film is edited*. It is easier for the director to adapt his ideas to the music than for the music to adapt its tempos and length to the editing. The opposite situation obliges the conductor to continually change tempos, the composer to make cuts and adjutoria[50] that are often hardly artistic.

—Léon Moreau

I am one of the first to have dreamed of writing dramatic music for the cinematograph. In 1913, in collaboration with Léon Moreau, we composed the music for *L'Agonie de Byzance*, a true opera that was given by the Maison Gaumont at the Hippodrome—and it was magnificently presented! The distinguished M. Costil[51] brought to it all of his attention. Since this time, there have been many improvements in this genre of adaptation, which I am convinced can only continue to develop.

—Henry Février

Félix Fourdrain,[52] *to whom we owe* La Légende du Point d'Argentan *and* Les Maris de Ginette*:*

Yes, there is a new path for music associated with film, so long as the score faithfully follows said film and, consequently, the composer writes an adequate score. If it is a question of an operatic work adapted to the screen, the composer should not haphazardly tack the music on, but should extract from it the developments demanded by the film. But to protect the production of cinematographic music, the rental of a film must include the rental of the score. Thus a publishing house for filmed music. In addition, the orchestrator or the author should compose his score in such a way that it can be performed by both the minimal ensembles of the smallest theaters and the orchestras of the largest.

There is much to do and the most beautiful future is reserved for artistic films accompanied by scores of real value.

—Félix Fourdrain

Sylvio Lazzari,[53] *whose* La Lépreuse *created a considerable stir and whose* Le Sautirlot, *premiered last year in New York, will be performed next season at the Opéra-Comique.*

In response to your letter of July 1, I should admit to you that, until now, I have not concerned myself with music for the cinema. Thus I am hardly competent to speak to you about it. However, it seems to me that therein lies a new and vast field to exploit; a field where, from the point of view of sonority, the music could be deployed more freely than in the theater or in vocal music.

So-called incidental music is inevitably a slave to the words. So that people can hear these, it is necessary to moderate and even, as much as possible, to erase the sonorities of the orchestra.

To a lesser degree, it is the same in opera [*le drame lyrique*]. There, too, the essential thing is to understand the words and to orchestrate with this in mind. Thus, the music is subordinated to the drama. In a purely visual art like the cinema, this preoccupation with sonority would not exist. You could freely handle the orchestra, just like in the concert hall. In contrast, the free development of the music would still be hindered by the length of the scenes. It would also be slave to precise synchronization, a little like in ballet or pantomime. In sum, there is no true freedom for music, except in the concert hall.

But finally, since incidental music is necessary in the theater, it seems to me that music for films will enjoy a great future. It will subordinate itself to the special demands of the cinema, as it has always subordinated itself to the needs of the sung and spoken theater.

—Sylvio Lazzari

Jane Vieu,[54] a woman of taste and intelligence, who wrote delicate songs and exquisite incidental music, established an important publishing house:

I think that 'films' would benefit from being supported by a music that conforms to whatever they represent, following the action of the libretto at all times, and that is written specially for the play!

It is irritating to hear, say, a gigue à la Charlot[55] following the beautiful funeral march by Chopin—and this without transition or link—simply because the characters are happy! It is really a brutal awakening for sensitive ears!

If some films can support any old 'song,' there are others for which the incidental music, linked to the subject, should play its full role! There is much to be done with the cinema!

Incidental music is always too dependant on the plot of a play to seek expressions beyond those of the libretto ... and that should suffice for the musician.

—Jane Vieu

The famous Polish composer and pianist, Moszkowski,[56] author of piano works and the opera Boabdil:

The cinema is, in fact, just a pantomime fixed by a photographic process. I do not see very well in what fashion this could influence the composer's technique or open a new path in the theatrical art.

—Maurice Moszkowski

Fernand Le Borne,[57] brilliant music critic for L'Avenir, *whose opera* Les Girondins *had a certain success and which is keeping him actively occupied with the question that interests us:*

When for six months *Film d'Art* gave screenings in the offices on the rue Charras, I took advantage of the opportunity given to me by the management. As musical director for the studio, I asked our great Saint-Saëns to write the music for *l'Assassinat du Duc de Guise*, written by Lavedan.[58] In addition, MM. Hüe, Vidal, Erlanger, and others accepted the screenplays that I offered them. For my part, I composed a rather lengthy score that was intended to accompany a film entitled *L'Empreinte*.[59] Unfortunately, I think we were wrong to not demand that the theater owners who rented or bought these films also perform our scores that, although printed, have fallen into oblivion.

Despite not having your letter before me, it seems to me that based on what I just wrote, you will be able to draw the conclusion that seems obvious to me.

—Fernand Le Borne

Marcel Samuel-Rousseau,[60] winner of the Prix de Rome, distinguished professor of harmony and composition:

The experiment by Camille Erlanger is most interesting ... It should finally convince the large film studios [*maisons d'éditions cinématographiques*] to commission French composers for important scores, written in intimate collaboration with the director.

Thus could be born new and unusual operatic works. Thus could surely disappear the musical infamies currently played before all screens.

—Marcel Samuel-Rousseau

Stan Golestan,[61] among the best of Romanian composers, who showed to us the songs of his country and whose violin playing was a great success in the Red Cross concert given in 1917 at the Théâtre Sarah-Bernhardt:

There is certainly a new path to follow by making a specially adapted and written score for the cinematograph—this music could definitely evoke and better imprint fleeting scenes in spectators' memories. In this case, it will likely expand its range of expression, since the cinematograph is one of the newest manifestations of today's spirit. In the past, however, symphonic music, dramatic and comic music, picturesque and descriptive music were full enough of inspiration and examples to allow a composer to write an adequate score for this new theatrical conception.

What I find uncalled for is to hear a famous symphonic passage, adapted to a film scene that is often completely antagonistic to the subject [of the symphonic work.]

—Stan Golestan

Georges Auric,[62] ultramodernist, could not remain indifferent to an experiment that will mark a step forward:

I think that we will soon know something that, despite various attempts, we can as yet only imagine: *film music.*

The young musicians will be the ones to create it—those who have a taste for life, fresh air, and whose art aims to be plain and stripped-down, like a good film. I am certain that this would be a very interesting project to do—and perhaps it would be enough to dare to do so boldly and with a new spirit [*un esprit nouveau*].

'Film music' will not be anything like the genre called 'incidental music'—a bastardized genre, without resources of any depth, that uses the orchestra to fill in silences, to underline the play, to accompany the moonlight, or to garnish interludes. Its success will demand a serious collaboration between the filmmaker and the composer. The latter will also need a precise knowledge of the resources offered by cinema orchestras.

35

I hope that we don't have to wait too long for the score that will unite, better than in some clever 'adaptations,' the technique of music with that of the screen.

—Georges Auric

We are pleased today to publish two very interesting responses that we received too late to include in the August issue, from MM. Jean Nouguès[63] and Michel-Maurice Lévy.[64] Our readers will also see the portrait of M. Albert Roussel, from whom they read a brilliant page in our last issue.[65]

The cinema—alone—is the cause of this response's delay. I was in the Scottish countryside to study a film project (non-musical, this time) and your letter, sent to my studio in London, had to await my return.

Since authors and—I hate to say it—especially composers have rendered the theater *boring*, it is not surprising that the majority of the public—who do not want to be *bored* at the theater, no matter what good arguments are given to convince them—report themselves to the cinema, of which it would be childish to deny its dominance at the current moment.

The reaction against *boredom* was inevitable: it was expressed in operetta's takeover of our premier opera theaters and in the popular vogue for cinema. It would be wonderful if, in France, one or the other were of the quality that they are in other countries, such as America and England, where in this regard I have spent some interesting and instructive years.

Music *should* be the collaborator that enlivens, comments, and animates the decidedly too-cold images on the screen.

Didn't people understand this necessity from the beginning? But there we touch on a sensitive point, since what has been done until now is far removed from what should be done. The producer, worried about a good profit [*exploitation cinématographique*] should address himself to the composers, just as he does to the actors, librettists, and directors. The current fashion of playing anything is deplorable. In a large cinema, I recently heard "Aase's Death" accompany the pirouettes of Charlie Chaplin; you can judge as well as I that this good Charlie (who, parenthetically, is an excellent musician in his private life), would not have desired at such a moment the beautiful and poignant page of Grieg.[66]

There are exceptions and, in passing, I am rendering homage to the conductor at the Gaumont-Palace, who knew how to ingeniously and artistically edit the choral and orchestral score for the sumptuous film *Quo Vadis*—but—the process is, in itself, wrong and hardly recommended.[67] *Above all, a film requires the music of its subject.*

For their part, composers should abandon the processes, intransigencies, and prejudices to compose a music that is essentially simple, clear, quick, and clean, which adapts itself to cinema and serves its cause—and, in this case—it is not a question of *intention*, but rather of *ability*.

For my part, I am very happy to be engaged in this new path with several interesting projects—but, naturally, all are overseas.

And I am delighted in advance of several sunny weeks that will deliver me this winter to the Gulf of Naples, for the filmed version of *La Danseuse de Pompeï*.[68]

—Jean Nouguès

Musical adaptation in the cinema is possibly only for those films shown in exclusivity.

In the 'weekly' presentations, the Conductor—having only a ridiculously short period of time (just one rehearsal on Friday afternoons) to prepare the first screening of the evening—cannot compose adhesives [*béquets*] to hold together this passage from César Franck's *Symphonie fantastique* to that passage from *La Marche des Titis*, and must of necessity stop to change the piece.[69] These pauses permit the public to hear the "tatatatatata" that merrily escapes the camera booth.

But it is not a question here of the accompaniment of a film, rather of *adaptation*. In my mind, IT IS ESSENTIAL.

Although one says, "He loves me not" or "Matador, *en ga-a-ar-de*," it will never fit with a young Hindu woman who picks the petals off a daisy or with Rio Jim taking aim at Andréas.

It requires a *completely new* score IN PERFECT SYNCHRONIZATION with the film to move us. This is inarguable and the future will prove it.

It also requires that the film is worth the trouble of being adapted for, alas, a fortnight of presentations. You can hardly find one or two films of this much interest and that is why the filmmakers, fearing presentations in exclusivity and wanting *above all* to 'direct,' abuse the notorious gullibility of spectators by substituting quantity for quality. Let us first remedy our authors' and directors' poverty of imagination.

A new score requires several fees; but in France, and especially in the cinematographic industry, to demand to be *paid* is to ask the impossible. They waste ten times more and skimp on the loans that are necessary to do their work.

Let us suppose, however, that a musical work was produced, what would result from it?

I composed the music for the fourth part of Gance's beautiful film, *La Dixième Symphonie*.[70]

For several months, I had followed the shooting of the film and that inspired me; but the payment for my efforts was very mediocre.

My work was performed at the premiere in deplorable conditions. Because the studio, the owner of the film, had decided to cut some scenes *without alerting me*, the music was no longer in the right place. In addition, still in the name of economy, there were not enough rehearsals of the orchestra, and this was the most beautiful of cacophonies.

The theater owners could rent the score for 150 francs.[71] Seven or eight made this "difficult sacrifice"; the authors (including the director of a company that made ten thousand francs and more in daily receipts) refused to disburse the enormous sum, judging it useless to "throw money out the windows."

There still remains the question of royalties: to declare a musical adaptation at the society on rue Henner, is to see it taxed at 2%. Now, with the current conditions, a theater owner never gives this percentage. The work should be declared at the Society on the rue Chaptal.[72] This society, which distributes a global sum amongst all of the composers played at each performance—and believe me, they [the performances] are numerous—the personal share of the composer varies FROM FOUR CENTIMES TO ONE FRANC, sums that are approximately what I think the music of *La Dixième symphonie* is worth.

A project should be undertaken in which some propositions should be made to the two societies: in the first, a maximum should be established; in the second, a minimum.

For the moment, the artistic interest of cinema is found in presentations IN EXCLUSIVITY. Only there can the public find a complete film, without untimely cuts, prepared with a maximum of effort, a disciplined orchestra comprising worthy artists, under the direction of a well-informed conductor, and a new musical adaptation as interesting as an operatic work.

The French Cinema can, at that point, think of competing with the largest foreign firms and the composers, stepping out of their usual apathy, will find new prospects.

Until then, our cinematographic productions will be without interest.

—Michel-Maurice Lévy

From *Le Film* 162 (August 15, 1919), 9–16, 66–70; and 163 (September 15, 1919), 86–89. (Translation by Colin Roust)

3

PRACTICAL ADVICE IN THE HEYDAY OF THE SILENT FILM

In terms of what reached a filmgoer's ears, there were enormous differences between the piano playing that supported one-reel nickelodeon films during the twentieth century's first decade and the orchestral or organ accompaniments that supported multi-reel feature films between the time of World War I and the late 1920s. There were also enormous differences between the recorded soundtracks that began to prevail c.1933 and *all* that had come before. Notwithstanding these obvious sonic and technological differences, one can nevertheless note in the foregoing comments numerous ideas consistent not just with the best advice offered by nickelodeon-era columnists but also with the conventions, adopted almost universally by the late 1930s, of the so-called classical-style sound film.[1] Realization of these ideas during silent film's heyday of course varied from venue to venue, and the results likely were not always of the highest artistic order. But there can be no denying that the general approach espoused here, in terms of the intended effect on audience members, seemed to work.

The authors represented in this section were all major players during silent film's heyday. By the time his *Encyclopedia of Music for Pictures* was published in 1925, the Hungarian-born Erno Rapee had already headed music departments at four of the largest cinemas on the United States' eastern seaboard; like Rapee, the Canadian-born Victor Wagner had logged years of work conducting opera and operetta before taking positions with various large "movie palaces"; in Germany, Hans Erdmann since 1922 had been director of the music department at the prestigious UFA studio. With film accompaniment in the 1920s having settled into a more or less standard *modus operandi*, these writers have relatively little to say about aesthetics or multimedia theory. Instead, they offer practical advice for musical directors at cinemas hither and yon who might seek to follow in their own obviously successful footsteps.

Echoing the trade-journal columnists and foreshadowing remarks that later would be issued by many of Hollywood's "star" composers, these writers note, for example, the dramaturgical utility of musically depicting a film's geographic or national locale and of fitting each of a film's main characters with a distinctive theme. Like those who came both before and after them, they recommend selecting music that catches a scene's overall mood and then changing this mood only at dramatically significant moments, and they caution strongly against the temptation to overdo precise synchronization of music with filmed action. And as teachers of film-music composition tell students even today, they inform their readers that music should indeed help clarify a film's plot but should never give away too much of that plot in advance, and that— except in special instances that call for music to rise to the fore—the accompanying score should for the most part remain subordinate to the on-screen story telling.

In addition to such enduringly useful tips on the concoction of a viable film score, the writings gathered here contain a wealth of detailed information specific to how film music in fact was successfully managed at the peak of a long-gone but surely glorious period during which responsibility for film accompaniment rested by and large in the hands of musical directors engaged by individual cinemas. Certainly unique to the situation of the 1920s is the role of a cinema house's music library, optimally vast in its holdings and staffed by savvy personnel who at a moment's notice could pull from the shelves whatever material the musical director requested. Also unique to the heyday of silent film is speculation as to how off-stage choruses or "special" sonic effects might contribute to a film score and, on a much more down-to-earth level, thoughts on how accompaniments in general might be made smoother if the materials on the players' music racks were arrayed with consideration for page turns.

3.1 MUSICAL ACCOMPANIMENT TO THE FEATURE PICTURE

Erno Rapee

After studying piano and conducting at the National Conservatory in his native Budapest, Erno Rapee (1891–1945) worked as an opera conductor in Germany and Poland before emigrating to the United States in 1912 to serve as director of New York's Hungarian Opera Company. In 1917 he was named music director of New York's 1,900-seat Rialto Theater, the United States' first "movie palace" to employ a full-time symphony orchestra;[2] he took up similar posts at New York's Rivoli Theater in 1918, at the same city's Capitol Theater in 1920, and at Philadelphia's Fox Theater in 1923. From 1924 to 1926 he pursued an independent conducting career in Europe, but in 1927 he returned to New York and a position at the new Roxy Theater. Between 1920 and 1929 Rapee composed original scores for more than two dozen silent films, most of them big-budget features released by Fox.[3] After the advent of the sound film he relocated briefly to Hollywood to head the music departments of both Warner Bros. and First National Pictures. In 1932 he was appointed music director at New York's Radio City Music Hall, and he remained in that position—famously leading the weekly radio broadcasts titled "Music Hall of the Air"—until his death.

Rapee remains best known today for his authorship of two large compendiums of music designed as practical resources for motion-picture accompanists. The first of these, published in 1924, was Motion Picture Moods for Pianists and Organists: A Rapid Reference Collection of Selected Pieces, Adapted to 52 Moods and Situations;[4] *the thick book contains almost 300 pieces, some of them simplified keyboard arrangements of staples of the "classical" repertoire but most of them original works by composers who specialized in creating generic music for film accompaniment. That* Motion Picture Moods *was truly intended to be a "rapid" reference is evidenced by the fact that all fifty-two of the "moods and situations" are listed alphabetically, along with their locations within the book, in the outer margins of each and every pair of pages.*

Lest a mere fifty-two dramatic pigeonholes seem too limiting, Rapee in 1925 authored an Encyclopedia of Music for Pictures *that itemizes copyright-free music for tenfold more categories.[5] Whereas earlier film-music anthologies might have been content with a simple "exotic" category, Rapee's* Encyclopedia *lists compositions that qualify "distinctly" as "Abyssinian, Arabian, Argentine, Armenian, etc.," and it sorts pieces of an "agitato" nature that previously might have been lumped together into groups characterized as "light, medium and heavy."[6] Significantly, the* Encyclopedia's *careful listings of specific pieces are prefaced by a series of tutorial chapters—like the one reproduced here—in which Rapee explains, in clear and simple terms, how musical directors at theaters both large and small might best go about concocting a proper accompaniment for the films at hand.*

A great deal has been written on how to arrange music to feature pictures. Experience and observation have taught me that the simplest procedure is as follows:—Firstly—determine the geographic and national atmosphere of your picture,—Secondly—embody everyone of your important characters with a theme. Undoubtedly there will be a Love Theme and most likely there will be a theme for the Villain. If there is a humorous character who makes repeated appearances he will also have to be characterized by a theme of his own.

It will happen quite often that two characters, each having a theme will appear together in which case it will be necessary to write original music, that particular scene treating the two themes according to the rules of counterpoint.—After your atmosphere is established and your characters are endowed with their respective themes determine if either the playing of atmosphere music of the individual theme will suffice in portraying happenings on the screen or if the psychologic conditions are such that the emotional part will have to be portrayed in preference to atmospheric or characteristic situations. Now you can start setting each scene: if you have a picture playing, for instance, in China, you will have to find all your accompaniment material in existing Chinese music, both to cover atmospheric situations as well as to endow your characters. If there happens to be two Chinese characters and one English you will of course cover your English character by English music for the sake of contrast.

The choice of the Love Theme is a very important part of the scoring as it is a constantly recurring theme in the average run of pictures and as a rule will impress your audience more than any other theme. Special care should be taken in choosing the Love Theme from various angles. If you have a Western picture dealing with a farm-hand and a country girl you should choose a musically simple and sweet ballad. If your Love Theme is to cover a relationship between society people, usually portrayed as sophisticated and blasé, choose a number of the type represented by the compositions of such composers as Victor Herbert or Chaminade.[7]

It will often happen that the situations on the screen require the Love Theme being used for an extraordinary length of time in which case you may have to play four or five choruses. This situation should be handled by varying your orchestrations, play one chorus as a violin solo, then have all the strings play it; the next one can be played on the Oboe or Cello and so forth. If you have exhausted all variations and particularly if the situation is of a dramatic sort have your men play that same chorus 1/2 a tone higher or lower. As long as you vary your instrumentation or your tonality it will not get tiresome. The danger of monotony is often encountered playing an oriental picture, as the playing of oriental music for an hour or longer will naturally get on the nerves of almost any listener, more so as oriental music is of very specific type. In that case grasp every opportunity the picture will afford and play some English, French, Italian or American music to break the monotony.

The Villain ordinarily can easily be represented by any Agitato of which there are thousands. Distinction should be made between sneaky, boisterous, crafty, powerful and evil-minded villains. A crafty villain who does not exhibit any physical villainy in the course of the picture can be easily described by a dissonant chord being held tremolo and very soft. If the Villain happens to be of the brute type who indulges in lots of physical activities, a fast moving number would be more apt. Sometimes you have a villain whose power to do evil is mighty but he achieves his evil deeds without any physical activities in which case chords slow and heavy should be a proper synchronization.

The portrayal of humorous characters seems to be rather hard as there is very little music written which in itself sounds humorous and you very often will have to fall back upon your own ingenuity for the creation of such themes. Emotional and dramatic characters and situations are the hardest to fit, firstly because it requires that the music should swell and diminish in accord with the emotional moods portrayed on the screen and it is a rare good luck to find a piece of dramatic music which will rise and fall simultaneously with the action; secondly because that very dramatic music we have reference to ought to play around the themes which are identified with the characters and within whom the emotional or dramatic situation exists. This also very often necessitates the writing of original music. The use of Silence will prove very often highly effective in situations like the appearing of an unexpected person, committing a crime, in fact all unexpected happenings which are followed, as a rule, by stillness. The recitativo, to be effective, should also be built on the theme or themes of the characters. Very often the arranger of the music for the picture will not have time to cover every little detail in the manner here suggested, but he can help a great deal by shaping the orchestra's playing. A good musician can take an ordinary 4/4 Andante and as readily make it into a misterioso as into a recitativo. This is purely a case of ingenuity and adaptability on the part of the leader.

The flash-backs seem to be a continuous source of trouble to the inexperienced leader. If the flash-back is not of extreme length and the scene preceding the flash-back is of such character that it will hold attention even during the flash-back, I would not advise changing the music but would advise bringing it down to "PPP." Another source of trouble I found is the making of musical endings. The brutal procedure of breaking your music no matter where you are just because the cue for the next number is flashed on the screen is an antiquated procedure not in use any more in first-class theatres. If you train your orchestra sufficiently and arrange for some kind of a signal for your men, you will not have to go more than 8 or 10 bars in most compositions before you can come to a tonic close. The finishing of most numbers during a feature picture should not be in a decisive cut-off manner but more of a dying-away effect. The more segues you can arrange between your numbers the more symphonic the accompaniment will sound.

The turning of pages in the orchestra is a comparatively easy matter, if you have more than one man to each instrument. It is important that the outside men religiously stick to playing only and have the turning done by the inside men. In theatres where you have time to prepare a score most of your numbers will not start at the beginning, but with certain passages which you think will fit particular scenes. The number on your music and the place where it should start should be marked very plainly by an arrow so that the eye can grasp it in a second. If you have more than one theme it will be an easy matter if you will carry out the following suggestions:—If theme No. 1 is also 7–13–18 and 24 put all three numbers on top of the page and have the music sticking out in the center of your stand above your other music; if theme No. 2 is also 3–14–29 and 34 put that number also on top of your music and have that piece sticking out of the right or left side of your stand. If you will then mark on the bottom of No. 6 that the next number is Theme No. 1 I think you will find no difficulty in handling two or more themes. If your film breaks, which nowadays is a rare happening, I advise keeping on playing the number and if necessary make a D.C. If you were playing your number soft and with strings only, bring in your brass and wood-wind and play the number in concert form. Fortunately these breaks never last more than 10 or 15 seconds. Should there be a fire in the booth, which may necessitate a wait of several minutes, I advise bringing up the houselights and having the men play any popular hit of the day which they may know by heart. It is advisable to keep in mind some such selection for use in case of emergency. The main object is to prevent the audience from getting nervous and to keep them entertained.

The effects in the percussion section and back stage can be made very effective if used judiciously. I only advise the use of effects if they are humorous or if they can be made very realistic. The shooting of the villain, unless a real shot can be fired back stage and can be timed absolutely, will be much better handled by stopping your orchestra abruptly and keeping silent for a few seconds than if the attempt of a shot is made with a snare drum. In one of the foremost theatres in New York City, I saw a picture in the course of which the villain jumped through the window and immediately after was slapped on the face by the heroine. The effect-man back stage was supposed to drop some glass at the proper moment to imitate the breaking of the window. As it happened the man was asleep on the job and the dropping the glass occurred when the heroine slapped the villain, so what would have [had] a tolerably descriptive effect turned out to be the cause of hilarious laughter on the audience's part.

Effects which can be worked most satisfactorily are storm effects, obtained by the use of batteries of large square head drums and wind machines back stage.

In theatres where singers are available, vocal selections back stage will occasionally prove very effective. The most effective incident of such type I remember was applied in the Capitol Theatre in New York City during the presentation of the "Passion" where during the scene of the funeral of the French King a mixed chorus chanted the Funeral March from *Madame Sans Gene*.[8] The effect was almost uncanny as outside the death chamber there were a multitude of people assembled.

It is the Vaudeville theatres throughout the country which commit the grossest insults to feature pictures for reasons I was never able to quite understand. If the musicians are too tired after having played the vaudeville to play music to the feature picture, then there should be an organist who is alive to the possibilities. If it is ignorance on the leader's part it is up to the management to see that the accompaniment to the feature picture is placed in proper hands. Happenings like one I witnessed where Dvorak's "Largo" was played from beginning to end with frightful tuning and wrong tempo during a reel of snappy events depicting dancing cannibals, Italian Army, Streets of New York, etc. indicated a condition which ought to be remedied if for nothing else but for the sake of music and its masters.

In choosing your orchestrations I would advise the use of arrangements which are so cued that if necessary they can be played with strings alone and will sound full, for in three quarters of the average feature picture music of very soft quality is required. The "Over-playing" by which is meant playing so loud that it attracts the ear more than the picture attracts the eye, has killed many a good picture. Careful study of the various headings and the numbers contained therein of Chapter 16[9] will prove a very useful asset to the person arranging music for the feature picture.

From *Encyclopedia of Music for Pictures*
(New York: Belwin, 1925), 13–16.

3.2 SCORING A MOTION PICTURE

Victor Wagner

Victor Wagner (1875–1939) was born in Toronto and studied cello at the Vienna Conservatory of Music. His first orchestral experiences were as a cellist, first in the orchestra of the Royal Opera House in Vienna and the Vienna Philharmonic and, beginning in 1906, in the orchestra of New York's Metropolitan Opera. While still a member of the Met orchestra, he conducted operettas at New York's Irving Place Theater. His work with film began in 1908, when he was appointed musical director at both the Rialto and Rivoli Theaters in New York.

At the invitation of film-stock manufacturer and philanthropist George Eastman, in 1921 Wagner moved to Rochester, New York, to lead a newly formed ensemble that served both as resident orchestra for the Eastman Theatre and, in a concert-giving capacity, as the Rochester Philharmonic. In 1927 he was named musical director of radio station WHAM and in 1929 conductor of the broadcast orchestra sponsored by radio station WGY in Schenectady, New York. Wagner took over conducting duties at Loew's Theater in Rochester in 1930, and for the last four years of his life also served as conductor of the Eastman Kodak Company Employee Chorus.

Perhaps because of his close relationship with the Eastman Kodak Company, Wagner in 1926 was well aware of the latest developments in motion-picture technology. He gives no indication that he thought the obviously approaching sound film would upset the practice, by this time well established, of silent films accompanied by fully professional orchestras. Although the paper reproduced here is addressed to an audience of engineers, its focus is almost entirely on the artistic aspects of music in a cinematic context.

Following the advice offered by the early film-music columnists, Wagner favors the linkage of music with a scene's overall mood, not its specific action. Anticipating the common practice of composers who in the 1930s and 1940s created original scores for so-called classical-style films, he notes that carefully chosen music can suggest a film's ever-shifting moods in a way that keeps audience members always "mentally sympathetic" to the dynamics of the narrative. Significantly, he cautions that information-laden music be used sparingly so as not to spoil the narrative's elements of surprise. Especially in the case of "genre" films that feature stereotyped characters and turns of plot, he says, "the difficult thing is not so much to know what to play as what not to play."

It takes years to accumulate a fund of musical knowledge before one is able to synchronize the music with the picture. A musician who through ignorance or whim chooses music which burlesques a serious scene commits an offense, he destroys the science and art of musical presentation of motion pictures. One has to have at his command a musical library of a thousand different numbers and a sensitive feeling for their different moods to be able to classify the numbers properly. The well known operatic melodies are not very useful, as they fit only the scene for which they were written and which scene the public visualizes on hearing the music. It is therefore important to consider the key in which each number is written to make a smooth musical bridge from one selection to another. In selecting the most appropriate music, one has to be careful not to anticipate the development of character so as not to stamp immediately the man with the cigarette as a villain; or, when a particularly beautiful girl enters, not to draw too hastily the third line of the triangle. Again, if one sees a man walk into a room wearing a derby and having a cigar in his mouth, one does not play mysterious music at once, because he may not be a detective after all. Not only is a knowledge of high-class music necessary but also a knowledge of most of the popular and national music with their characteristics of practically all the civilized and uncivilized nations.

There is one task laid on the musical director who arranges a musical program of accompaniment for motion pictures which is seldom appreciated. This is the task of making music supply in a measure the spoken word—the missing dialogue, the play on the speaking stage—where this is not provided in action and in subtitles. The musical adapter has thirty, forty, or more scenes instead of a series of three or four acts. This I mention, because it must be remembered that no scene of any great length will maintain the same emotional key throughout. In the spoken play, there is a constant shift of emotional appeal as the incidents of the scene progress. But in the motion picture the play breaks up, not into acts, but into scenes, and scenes so arranged that a much closer sympathy of emotional suggestion may be obtained scene by scene, than is possible act by act. Thus it is that musical accord with the poetry of action and mood can be made scenically unified, and can really produce a more concise and closely correlated emotional suggestion than any other form of union of music and action. Now, I have said that it is one business of the adapter to make the musical accompaniment supply the motion picture with an important part of what the speaking stage gets from dialogue. I mean that while the picture vividly gives to the eye the story, the characterization can suggest constantly a mood to make the spectator mentally sympathetic. It follows that one preparation which the musical director must make is careful study of the picture, sufficient to bring to him definite and vivid impressions and emotions derived from it; he must himself feel the need of the music which he will later select and arrange.

The appropriateness of selection of motion picture accompaniment depends largely on this preparation. Scenically, the motion picture is a great inspiration; no speaking stage can in completeness, in gorgeous realities, and in generous detail approach the scenic richness of the motion picture. So, the musical director is always under the inspiration of an art kindred to his own. And so adept are good motion picture actors and actresses becoming, that careful observation of their pictured pantomime is all the inspiration needed for an impression that readily suggests music best suited to express it. It is therefore the study of the musical director of the picture with special regard to opportunity to make the music aid in its emotional suggestion of something truly felt and appreciated that counts most for the success of his work.

45

We speak of accompanying motion pictures with music. Now the accompaniment of song, the expression by means of music of a beautiful idea or of a dramatic idea is a province of art; if the song or the idea or scene or story has strong elements of beauty, the art of accompaniment becomes really akin to the poetic art. The poet takes ideas and thoughts and gives them beautiful word forms; the accompanist, given this sort of material to inspire him, can add beauty to his work. Now, turning to motion pictures, the arrangement of a musical accompaniment for pictures in which there is definite mood, a central idea, a real emotional element that is consistent, makes a congenial task for a musician, and in the majority the arranger does find pictures inspirational; he does find opportunity for a musical accompaniment that is really expressive of the appeal which the picture makes.

But there are kinds of motion pictures which present difficulties. Take, for instance, the detective story picture, the adventure story, or the farce comedy. In each story the interest centers in the plot. There may be excitement of emotion in looking at the picture, but the emotion is not in the picture itself. Here the difficult thing is not so much to know what to play as what not to play. Music that strikes any hearer as incongruous will do much to spoil that picture for him. Then, too, the action is rapid, and this causes the change in mood of the onlooker and hearer to be abrupt—too abrupt to be successfully followed in music. The point made is that it is awkward and impracticable to accord intimately with the incidents of such pictures. For instance, picture a scene in which two men are struggling in a cellar while a dance is going on above them. I suppose for realism we should have a dance orchestra off-stage playing dance music steadily while the regular orchestra plays dramatic music according in mood with the fight. This is an extreme illustration perhaps but one which the motion picture adapter will recognize as within his experience.

The film play is a form of art and is analogous to the ballet in that it necessitates, for its adequate presentation, the synchronization of action with music. Thus, in its right development, we find a new art form in music, the possibilities of which are practically limitless. In film play we see one art-form which is dependent upon another—music— for its completion, and it is still incomplete and imperfect for presentation to the public without its musical counterpart accompanying it, just as is the case in the ballet, where dance and action are synchronized with music to ensure a perfect whole. The time has come when the motion picture theater orchestra is receiving universal recognition as an organization of artists who are working to achieve and maintain a high standard in a distinct art.

Many times the question has been brought to me, "How do you synchronize the music with the picture?" When we come to the screening room to work on our next pictures, the most important part from the very start is to make a title sheet, which lists the first few words of each main and subtitle and indicates the beginning of each new reel. These titles are used as milestones in the music score as well as descriptive cues. A piano part or a full orchestral score of each orchestration is filed on shelves in the screening room, classified according to mood, nationality, etc. We have one hundred thirty-five such classifications all the way from "Airplane Music" to "Funeral Music" and from "Wedding Music" to "Happiness Music." The next important move is to find the music best suited to the action and mood of the picture without allowing the music to dominate the play, in which event it would distract the attention of the onlooker from the picture to the music. It is mostly the sensitiveness of the adapter which enables him to balance the action on the screen with the music in the orchestra pit. Of especial assistance is the up-to-date motion picture machine which allows the film to run in either direction. If the music which has been selected does not fit the scene, the film may be reversed without taking it from the machine, and another selection tried.

Scoring a good picture is just as fascinating as composing. When a picture is scored, one has the satisfaction of knowing that he will have at least twenty-one orchestral performances the first week which is more than a well known composer of fame can ever expect. It may be interesting to know that no music is furnished with the film. Our library consists of about 15,000 different selections with separate parts for each instrument of our large orchestra. The original orchestration cannot always be used exactly as bought from the publisher. In order to make it of the proper length for a scene, endings or modulations are written which must be technically correct. Many times when we are unable to find a suitable selection, we cover the action with music which is originated in our department for this particular scene. In selecting a musical theme for a leading character, the principal aim is not only to be consistent with the atmosphere or period but to portray and intensify characteristics through music. One morning last week, when we were screening our next week's picture, a young singer entered the screening room just as we had reached a touching scene of *Stella Dallas*.[10] In the dark silence of the room, interrupted only by the buzz of the projection machine, the singer sat down at the piano and sang a tender melody. The effect was spontaneous; each of us realized what new intensity had been given by the song to the fine acting on the screen.

From *Transactions of the Society of Motion Picture Engineers* 27
(September 1926), 40–43.

3.3 THE ARTISTIC FEATURE FILM AND MUSIC: ITS GENRES

(Der künstlerische Spielfilm und die Musik: Seine Gattungen)

Hans Erdmann

Hans Erdmann (1882–1942) was born in Breslau and earned a Ph.D. in musicology at that city's university with a dissertation of the history of Catholic church music in the Prussian province of Schlesien. He had studied violin since childhood, and his first full-time job was as concertmaster of the Breslau opera house. After military service during World War I he was a theatrical conductor first in Riga, Latvia, and then in the German cities of Jena, Brandenburg, and—significantly—Potsdam.

The small town of Babelsberg, near Potsdam, was the Hollywood of Germany, the site first of Studio Babelsberg, then Decla-Bioskop (formed through a merger of Deutsche-Bioskop and the German branch of the French Eclair Decla studios), and then, beginning in 1921, the ultimately dominant German studio known as Universum Film AG (UFA).

47

It was at the UFA studio that Erdmann entered the film business; after being invited to compose a score for Wilhelm Murnau's 1922 Nosferatu—Eine Symphonie des Grauen *he became the studio's musical director, and it was in this capacity that he made the acquaintance of Giuseppe Becce.*

Becce (1877–1973) was an Italian musician who in 1906 relocated to Berlin in order to study composition with Ferruccio Busoni and Arthur Nikisch. He earned his first film credits in 1913, not just providing music for but also playing the title role in Carl Froelich's Richard Wagner.[11] *In 1919 Becce published the first of numerous volumes of generic film music collectively titled* Kinothek; *at about the same time, he was appointed head of the music department at Decla-Bioskop. After the merger with UFA, he served the large studio primarily as a composer, contributing original scores for such silent-film classics as Robert Wiene's 1920* The Cabinet of Dr. Caligari, *Fritz Lang's 1921* Der müde Tod (Destiny), *Michael Curtiz's 1922* Sodom and Gomorrha, *Wilhelm Murnau's 1924* Der letzte Mann (The Last Man), *and Georg Wilhelm Pabst's 1926* Geheimnisse einer Seele (Secrets of a Soul).[12] *In 1920 Becce founded a periodical called* Film-Ton-Kunst; *in 1926 Erdmann joined that publication as a contributing editor,[13] and the next year Erdmann and Becce came out with their monumental* Allgemeines Handbuch der Film-Musik.

Erdmann and Becce's 1927 General Handbook of Film Music *is every bit as comprehensive as the* Encyclopedia of Music for Pictures *that Erno Rapee published in the United States two years earlier (see p. 40, this volume). And it has a similar format. The second part is a voluminous "Thematisches Skalenregister" (thematic catalogue) that lists thousands of titles of musical compositions categorized according to their appropriateness for filmic scenes whose emotional content ranges from calm (for example, "Wiegenlied," or lullabies) to creepy ("unheimliches Agitato"), whose depicted action ranges from confrontationally martial ("Kriegerisch / Militärisch") to pleasantly marital ("Hochzeitszeremonie"). The first part is labeled a film-and-music "Verzeichnisse" (literally, an "index"), but in fact it is a collection of short essays—authored by Erdmann—that, like the chapters that introduce Rapee's* Encyclopedia, *explore various theoretical aspects of film music but also offer practical advice to those in charge of music at venues where films are exhibited.*

The fifty-eight pages that make up the introductory text are divided into ten sections. In the first seven sections Erdmann explores film in relation to all the temporal arts, the history of how film music came to be and the question of whether or not "silent film" can exist without music, the function of musical "illustration" and its relationship to genuine musical composition, the possibility of there ever being a truly artistic linkage of music and filmic imagery, and the use of music not just in "artistic" films but also in educational films and newsreels.[14] In the final two sections Erdmann gives a realistic explanation of how film music as conceived at the studio is likely to be changed by the time it reaches an exhibiting theater and then, in a concluding intellectual flourish, offers a deeply philosophical reflection on music's dramaturgical functions.[15] In the eighth section, presented here, he offers still apt insights on the music that seems most appropriate to various genres of the feature film.

In the genres of the feature film, the music is usually an obedient servant; however, certain decisions still need to be made regarding the music's construction.[16]

If the feature film is indeed the quintessential art of our time, an art capable of expressing the spirit of modern times, and if it is indeed a truly new art form, one might expect to find a deep contradiction between it and music. The idea is often expressed that while the music of our time has struggled to grow out of music of earlier periods—that even though it seems absolutely modern, it nevertheless has roots in an age-old tradition—film, on the other hand, seems to be somehow devoid of tradition. Such an idea carries some weight, especially if one considers the numerous differences that seem to separate film and music. But perhaps the art of film,[17] in its deepest sense, is not without tradition. Humankind can hardly forget its history and origins when it makes leaps forward; indeed, humankind continues to be tradition incarnate. By the same token, very little in film's artistic conception is actually new, for the idea behind it lived a long while in the dreams of artists before it could be even modestly realized.[18] Today, those dreams have become reality.

It might be argued—as it often is—that artistic form first and foremost, in order to be truly artistic, depends upon its medium. It might be argued as well that the form of film is so truly new that perhaps it is an expression of our "unmusical" modern times. But is our time really so unmusical?

The external tempo of modern life is certainly faster than that of earlier periods. And since musical questions today are for the most part questions having to do with this accelerated time, it stands to reason that many persons today do not find in contemporary music the overall peacefulness offered by classical-style music. We have indeed lost the musical sensuousness of earlier times, but this is not to say that musicality today is in decline. We are simply living in an age of faster rhythms and more urgent tempos; contemporary music expresses this, and so—to no little extent—does film. The grandest and most expansive scenes of a rich screenplay,[19] for example, can be depicted in much less time than would be the case in staged dramas or in opera.[20] And with this we get to the essential question of [film-music] style.

The music [for a film] conceivably holds to clear stylistic principles, has a uniquely built architectural form, and—at least in exceptional works—gives voice to genuine expressiveness. But all this seems to mean little if the audience does not perceive, immediately, that the film itself bears similarities [to certain other films].

Let us be the first to state this directly: Most everyday feature films do not involve the sort of production effort that will even begin to raise the average level of filmmaking; the unfortunate consequence is that, like all the dozens of other mass-produced things that go on and on in the same mundane way, the repertoire will start to shrink, and this will greatly affect film's artistic development. We still have no [official] Film Theater devoted to the cultivation of the cinematic arts,[21] and thus the opportunity to study film is available only to a very small group of artists and critics.

If we seriously reflect on how these circumstances relate to style in cinematic art, we find ourselves in a rather difficult position.[22] Indeed, [this position] seems directly contrary to what by and large is our current inability—one could almost speak here of "impossibility"—to form judgments regarding stylistic correspondences between film and music.[23] Thus far, the relationship between film and music has been persistently confused and disordered, and this has had the inevitable effect of separating music and film, not—almost never—of uniting them. It is a curious fact that the literature that seriously addresses the aesthetics of film carefully avoids the "hot potato" of music.[24] On the one hand, it seems not strange at all that some pose the idea, perhaps with a great sigh of relief, that, after all, "the feature film is a new art form"; on the other hand, there remains the simple fact that this new art form has always limped along in public on rather poorly managed musical crutches. Is it surprising, then, that film music should so often be misjudged?[25]

So long as film was just a concern of the show-booth,[26] there was no real reason to think seriously about its [accompanying] music;[27] whatever conversations transpired had no real [intellectual] thrust, and they concerned only the fact that show-booths, no matter what they had to offer, would also somehow have "made music." We have by no means negotiated [the obstacles] of these early periods. [We can see that] film itself, in terms of what its art would or might yet become, began to defend itself against musical mishandling; nevertheless, it seems that the undisciplined relationship between film and music will always demonstrate how it is the more systematic 'moving picture on the white screen'[28] that has expanded the boundaries of art.

As for the main issue of the combined style of music and film, however, we are still without guidelines; from the past almost nothing remains except for a few bits of methodology that must be collected and which perhaps can be brought together, in a mosaic, as a modest signpost for later work. But before this can be undertaken we should make several general remarks about the different genres of feature films and how they relate to music. For this, too, we fall back on earlier thinking.

A language of sentimental fantasy, music is for most people a rational, ordinary, and even trivial thing, so long as the sentiment and fantasy are kept in balance. That being the case, it seems that music has only two primary colors—joy and pain, which correspond to major and minor—with which to express the countless shades that make up the full range of life's emotions. One can see, then, that the often-posed question as to whether music in and of itself can be humorous or comic cannot be answered without considerable qualifications. (One can certainly speak of comic musical effects, but these typically have to do with gestures and the sound of particular instruments, and with the workings of tone-paintings. But it seems laughable to speak of absolute music having comic or humorous attributes.)

But to follow up on the idea of music as [a language of] fantasy, in this music has tremendous possibilities. It should be obvious, for example, that the very same music that accompanies the commonplace can sometimes be borne aloft into some sort of deeply meaningful, exalted sphere. And in this music finds nourishment or, at the very least, room in which to move.

This brings us to a complex of problems surrounding a general principle of film-music style, a principle by which film scenes might be classified according to their musicality.

For the most part, all scenes are unfavorable for music unless they are artificially animated by sentimental or fantastic stimulation. Generally speaking, such scenes are of the basest sort, for in terms of subject matter they are not at all like reality; they belong to the category of dime-a-dozen commercial entertainments. Such pieces have no strong emotional line—at best they are melodramatic[29]—but they do lend themselves to fantasy; they remain bogged down in contrived sensationalism for its own sake.

It turns out that the first level of genuine musical possibility is to be found in scenes where the borders of reality overlap with those of fantasy. So long as these borders are barely perceptible, comic play of all sorts is possible. Since these films are not "real" and belong in the realm of humorous fantasy, the musician has room to move about; he simply assists the prevailing cheerful mood, and he can indulge himself without restraint. The extent to which it might be advisable for him to step down from this neutral bridge of basic sentiment will be addressed later.

But first we should consider the so-called "style films" that purport to portray events either historical or legendary.[30]

There is no compelling necessity for music in such films, yet music here has real artistic possibilities; it can help, and enliven, the drama. If nowadays we speak in general of "musically fruitful" films, we are referring to films that involve a particular type of situation. A higher degree of "musical fruitfulness," of course, would occur in situations where the music actually controls the film's "line of feeling,"[31] or brings the fantasy to life. Films of this sort would keep the musician very active, indeed, but they are few and far between.

But now we move on to some of the deeper connections between film and music; there are few generally effective classifications of these connections, because it is impossible to compare all the elements of film with those of music.

Ben Hur is a blockbuster historical film, a wonder of cinematography, yet it lacks artistic momentum and an overall "line of feeling."[32] The same can be said of *The Thief of Baghdad*, a fairytale of great pageantry but a film with very little soul. Then there is *The Bear's Wedding,* a film not half so important in terms of its technical means but nevertheless one that almost seems to be a reproach to music;[33] the same could be said for *The Student from Prague*[34] and, most notably, *The Volga Boatman.*[35]

The Violinist of Florence is a film set in modern times that requires very little music,[36] and it could even be said to be a rebuke to music. This is also the case with the Chaplin film *A Woman of Paris: A Drama of Fate,*[37] but it does not apply so conveniently to *The Last Man.*[38]

Then again, there are films with entirely definite artistic tendencies, but which still are thin when it comes to their real need for music. In this category we could place both *The Gold Rush* and parts of *The Battleship Potemkin.*[39]

And here lies the true problem of the connection between film and music.

Again we hark back to opera as an object of comparison. It is said that opera is an "eternal hybrid" that will always produce works that are limited to their own time. And we can concede that the number of operas that might retain their value for centuries, compared with all the operas that have ever been produced, is indeed very small. Opera, of course, is an artistic union of words, actions, and music, and of course it exists at those basic elements' precise point of intersection. But this constraint does not really apply to film, and in film one can at least hope for a loosening of the bonds. Yes, film has its limitations, but they are not so severe as those of opera, for in film there remains the possibility of genuinely *musical* action.

All things considered, it seems that the film with music[40] may well have its best chances for success only in certain genres, but the success will be measured only on a case-to-case basis. In actual practice, no one wastes time or money by first considering the music; that would be hopeless, or at the very least not very important. Instead, one considers first and foremost the film; so long as the musician can sympathize with the film, and feel its spirit, his work will be worthwhile. But only the musician himself can decide which films are truly deserving of music. Unfortunately, the filmmakers seem far too willing to write and shoot[41] whatever happenstance throws into their laps, and they seldom end up with films of the sort we should expect from them. And it is the same, alas, for the musician. The current practice of film music seems to correspond to that of the filmmakers: it is a methodical hindrance to success.

From *Allgemeines Handbuch der Film-Musik* (Berlin-Lichterfelde und Leipzig: Schelsinger, 1927), 11–14. (Translation by Abby Anderton and Andrew S. Kohler)

Part 2

EARLY SOUND FILM

4

TRANSITIONAL CONCERNS

Efforts to combine motion pictures with recorded sound had begun even before December 1895, when the Lumière brothers in France entered the annals of history by being the first to exhibit films on screen before a paying audience; as early as 1891 the American inventor Thomas Edison at least attempted to synchronize a brief film of a boxing match displayed via his peephole-like Kinetoscope with sounds played via a phonograph, and sometime between September 1894 and June 1895 his assistant William Kennedy Laurie Dickson successfully coordinated a sound recording with a film that shows two men dancing while Dickson plays the violin.[1] The first decade of the twentieth century witnessed numerous colorfully named contraptions, among them the Chronophone, the Cameraphone, the Graphophonoscope, the Kinematophone, the Phoneidograph, the Synchroscope, and the Vivaphone.[2] All of these involved the mechanical linkage of two separate reproduction devices, one for sound and one for image, and all of them were limited by the fact that their sonic components could be projected only with a purely acoustical megaphone. And all of them, significantly, were concerned not with providing recorded musical support for narrative films but only with presenting "documentations" of actors, musicians, and other performers whose offerings depended to a large extent on sound.

Two important scientific developments unfolded in the years surrounding World War I; when more or less perfected and eventually merged, they would completely transform the relationship between film and music.

One of them involved a method of transcribing sound not by Edison's method (that is, by means of a vibrating needle into a soft surface carved with grooves whose "hills and valleys" were analogous to sound waves) but, rather, by an optical method that allowed the vibrations of a sound-stimulated diaphragm to be photographed by a motion-picture camera. Experiments on the optical recording of sound had been initiated in England by the French-born engineer Eugene Augustin Lauste in 1904. After 1910 such experiments were conducted widely in both the United States and Europe, but they came most fully to fruition, after the war, in the laboratories of a trio of German scientists;[3] so-called because it was "the work of three," the Tri-Ergon process of sound-on-film recording *c.*1930–31 would become the worldwide industry standard.

The other development that would forever change the nature of film music had to do with the amplification of recorded sound. Concerned at first only with the possibilities of amplification for the sake of radio broadcasts and telephonic communication, the American engineer Lee de Forest began to address the problem in 1906, and a year later he patented a gas-filled "audion tube" that allowed sound-provoked electrical signals to be increased at least slightly. De Forest's invention immediately caught the attention of Western Electric, the manufacturing division of the American Telephone and Telegraph company. During World War I, largely for reasons of national security, Western Electric invested heavily in expanding on de Forest's ideas; after the war, the privately owned corporation sought eagerly for ways to capitalize on its efforts. The first public display of electrically amplified sound took place during a "Victory Day" parade in New York in September 1919; the next summer the national conventions of both the Republican and the Democratic parties featured addresses delivered via electrically powered "public address" systems, and by November 1921 the newly elected American president, Warren G. Harding, was able to speak, in real time, to large audiences gathered in amplification-equipped auditoriums as distant as New York and San Francisco. By the mid-1920s the technology for the electrical amplification of sound—live or recorded—was already quite sophisticated.

The first film studio to capitalize on the possibilities was the small but successful Hollywood-based Warner Bros. After contracting for exclusive rights to the Western Electric technology and then experimenting for more than a year, Warner Bros. in August 1926 exhibited a program of films that utilized a patented sound-on-disc method it called Vitaphone. Following the model established earlier in the century, most of the films were "shorts" that featured vaudeville of concert-hall performers; unremarkably, in terms of critics' reactions, the program also included *Don Juan*, a feature-length silent film retrofitted with an orchestral score presented not via orchestra but via phonograph.[4] In October 1926 Warner Bros. exhibited a second Vitaphone program, similarly comprising a group of "shorts" followed by a feature-length film (in this case *The Better 'Ole*, a comedy whose recorded materials included not just orchestral music[5] but also songs and sound effects).

Warner Bros. launched a third Vitaphone program in October 1927, by which time more than 130 American theaters had been "wired" for sound. This third program, too, began with a selection of documentary "shorts" of the sort that to date seemed to intrigue the public far more than did "silent" movies accompanied by phonograph recordings. Momentously, however, the 1927 program concluded with a feature film titled *The Jazz Singer*.

To be sure, most of *The Jazz Singer*, like *Don Juan* and *The Better 'Ole*, amounted to a "silent" film with conventional, albeit recorded, orchestral support.[6] But crucial moments of *The Jazz Singer* involved diegetic songs performed by the title character (played by Broadway star Al Jolson[7]), and some of these moments included interjections of spoken dialogue. Cinema audiences up to this time had heard accompanimental music aplenty, but never before had they been exposed to songs and dialogue that serviced a film in a dramatically significant way. Frances Goldwyn, the wife of MGM mogul Samuel Goldwyn, exaggerated only slightly when she stated that the Hollywood premiere of *The Jazz Singer*, in December 1927, was "the most important event in cultural history since Martin Luther nailed his theses on the church door."[8]

In the two years that followed *The Jazz Singer*'s sensational release, filmmakers not just in Hollywood but worldwide invested heavily in the equipment and the license fees that would allow them to follow in the lucrative footsteps of Warner Bros. Fortunately for studios as well as exhibitors, the sound film's expensive infrastructure was already solidly established by the time the international stock markets crashed in October 1929. There was still much to be debated in terms of aesthetics, but there was no question that sound film—that is, film accompanied either by disc recordings or, beginning *c.*1930–31, by sound-on-film recordings—was the way of the future.

The authors whose comments are gathered in this section address the sound film from various perspectives. Only Dmitry Shostakovich, writing from a country whose scientists were aware of developments in the West yet stubbornly resisted technological imports, holds to a silent-film aesthetic that was rapidly becoming out-moded. The others—the English critic Edwin Evans and the French composer Darius Milhaud—approach the new medium hopefully yet skeptically. They agree that there is much to be gained from modern technology that allows for a precise linkage of filmic image with recorded sound. At the same time, they collectively regret that technology's forward march marks the end of a relationship between film and music that, throughout most of the 1920s, was often quite glorious.

4.1 MUSIC AND THE CINEMA

Edwin Evans

Edwin Evans (1871–1943) was an English critic who paid particular attention to contemporary British and French music and to music for the theater. Along with regular reviews for the Pall Mall Gazette *and the* Daily Mail, *his publications include many articles for scholarly journals, program notes for London concerts, and monographs on Tchaikovsky, Stravinsky, and—published posthumously—the relationship between music and dance. At the time he penned the comments reprinted here, Evans served as editor of a periodical called* The Dominant.

Coming as it does on the cusp between the periods of silent film and sound film, the article is interesting at the very least because it demonstrates how a keen and perhaps snobbishly opinionated observer of film music could be, on the subject of mechanically reproduced sound in a filmic context, of two minds.

On the one hand, Evans early in 1929 acknowledges the importance of the movie theater as a place of employment for musicians. On the other hand, Evans rails against the typical film accompaniment that, with its haphazard synchronization and frequent borrowings from pre-existing repertoire, fairly "savours of barbarism." The remedy, he suggests, would be original scores not just written for but also somehow mechanically linked to specific films. Evans was certainly aware of recent developments in sound-on-disc (Vitaphone) and sound-on-film (Movietone) technology. But he was sensitive to the rather obvious difference between "live" sounds coming directly from musical instruments and recorded sounds pouring forth from loudspeakers, and thus he championed the fruitless idea of film accompaniments sounded by means of player-pianos or pneumatic organs.

Significantly, Evans comments at length on the perceived low status of cinema musicians c.1928–29. This situation would change markedly in the ensuing decade, when British filmmakers, like their counterparts in France, sought to acquire scores from the ranks of top-flight concert-hall composers.

Speaking at a recent dinner of the Musicians' Club of London Dr. Malcolm Sargent referred to certain words of disparagement pronounced against brass bands. 'If they played bad music,' he said, 'it was largely because the better class musician had not tackled the problem of giving them good music.' In other words, for the shortcomings of that popular institution the better class musician must bear his share of responsibility.

How much greater is that responsibility if the argument is transferred to a still more popular institution, with vastly greater potentialities, the cinema. It is estimated, on the basis of union statistics, that picture theatres, great and small, are now providing between three-quarters and four-fifths of the paid musical employment in the country. It is further estimated, though on data less subject to verification, that the cinema is the sole, or at any rate the chief, avenue by which music reaches three-quarters of the potential audience in the population. For about fifty-nine hours weekly, music is being performed in upwards of three thousand cinemas, and for shorter periods in perhaps a thousand isolated halls. Setting aside all aesthetic considerations in favour of a purely objective view, one may say that the cinema is at present the most important musical institution in the country. Yet, whenever 'better class musicians' find occasion to refer to cinema music, it is invariably in terms of disparagement compared with which those recently applied to the brass band were the mildest expostulation. And, ever more than in the case of the brass band, a large share of responsibility for the undisputed evils of cinema music rests upon the class of musicians from whom these facile denunciations usually emanate. Had they not, as a class, been so anxious lest they defile themselves by contact with the despised institution, there might have been a different story to relate.

It is not disputed that, like many other modern inventions, the cinema was kidnapped in its perambulator, or that its early tutors were of a type scarcely susceptible to aesthetic influences. Unfortunately, so far as music is concerned, it was abandoned to its fate. Not only was the potentially fertile ground yielded without a struggle but it was treated as a plague spot. Professors warned their students against the contamination of the cinema, remonstrated with them, or even dismissed them from their colleges if they were tempted to accept an engagement in a picture theatre though the motive might be—and in some instances was—that of providing for the continuance of their studies. To this day organists are told that they lower the high standards of their profession if they seize the opportunity of appealing to a larger audience,[9] despite the obvious possibility that they may, with discretion, help to spread the light. The undeclared policy has been to place the cinema out of bounds, and then reprove it for being there—to put obstacles wherever possible in the way of 'better class musicians' who were tempted to enter this field, and then point to it as being peopled by those having no claim to be thus described—to hold aloof, making no attempt to meet any of the needs engendered by this new form of entertainment, and then deride it on the ground that those needs have been met by musicians of less lofty pretensions. Better class composers made practically no attempt to provide suitable music, and they or their friends are now virtuously contemptuous of that which they find doing duty instead. It would, of course, be absurd to infer that better class music would have entered the cinema by the simple process of knocking at the door. Not without a struggle would it have forced its way into a sphere so beset, from its inception, with meretricious influences. That the struggle need not have been a hopeless one is proved by the remarkable amount of good music that has, in spite of all, found its way into the cinema. But it was allowed to go by default.

One consequence of this abstention has been the creation of the most conservative of all vested interests, that inherent in an established mode of procedure. Like all new inventions, the cinema began with adaptation. Just as the earliest railway carriages adapted the shape of the stage coach, the earliest motor cars that of other horse-drawn vehicles, and both only gradually evolved the now familiar types, the cinema began by adapting almost everything that lay within reach. Yet even its earliest sponsors were fully aware that it must inevitably develop on its own lines and create an independent technique such as has now emerged from the crudities of early efforts. Though adaptation still clogs the progress of the film, so much has been accomplished that the existence of an 'art of the screen,' with an independent future before it, is no longer questioned. It was, or should have been, obvious that in the music of the cinema the stage of adaptation was similarly primitive, and that a new form corresponding to music drama was the goal towards which, however remote it may have then seemed, the efforts of pioneers must tend. But, in the absence of musical pioneers, adaptation has developed a technique of its own which, crude as it may seem to its outside critics, nevertheless demands no inconsiderable skill on the part of those who exercise it, especially when the conditions of their vocation are considered. In the 'fitting' of a film which is the principal item in a cinema programme it is nowadays usual to draw upon more than a hundred compositions, some excerpts being recurrent, more or less after the manner of leitmotive—and even, in some instances, subject to analogous metamorphosis—whilst the others are employed to accompany passing incidents or moods. In dealing with important productions there is now a growing tendency to have this done before marketing the film, in which case the musician may have reasonable time to collect his thoughts. But this course is still exceptional. Usually the question is deferred to the 'trade show,' when the publicity manager, in whose province this preliminary exhibition falls, bethinks himself of the need of music and appoints someone to provide it, commonly at a few days' notice. This gentleman sees the film once, and is given no orchestral rehearsal. Latterly it has become customary to pass his suggestions on to the eventual exhibitors, whose own conductors may or may not have the music in their libraries. Even this is not a general practice, and the musical director of a picture theatre must still be prepared to improvise at a few days'—sometimes a few hours'—notice, a pot pourri of a hundred ingredients that shall more or less fit incidents occupying from an hour to an hour and a half. It is a task demanding first of all a capacious memory, the time being insufficient to ransack the library; then an alert sense of dramatic effect, rapid decision, resourcefulness and ingenuity, and a sense of humour that can be summoned or silenced at will. And in this intricate task the leading cinema musicians have developed an almost uncanny slickness. Of course, judged by any aesthetic standard, it savours of barbarism. But any impartial observer, reviewing the cinema from its own angle as a popular entertainment, must cheerfully admit that these men make the best of what is, seen from any other angle, a bad job. The trouble is that this practical slickness, constantly exhibited, and satisfactory to the audience for whom it is intended, is now an established craft, with, as stated above, that form of conservatism which appertains to technical experience. Years ago the cinema community might have been impressed with the views uttered by eminent musicians upon the possibilities of this new field. To-day, confident in their own technical experience, their retort to any outside musician, however world famous, is 'What does he know about it?' He does not share that experience, and therefore his views are irrelevant. It was difficult enough, when the cinema was in its infancy, to convince its sponsors that it should develop its music at first hand. To-day any suggestion of the kind—such as Richard Strauss recently put forward—is promptly met with the reply that original music would prove, not more, but less satisfactory, for a variety of reasons, the first of which is that the method would lack the skill of the present adaptors, and the substance would lack the appealing quality of the music which is their present stock in trade. There are other reasons, but as they arise from the routine of film making, which after all is not as the laws of the Medes and Persians, they need not detain us here.

There is, however, one obstacle that may yield to the pressure of mechanical competition. Hitherto a powerful objection, not only to original music, but even to a carefully considered and skillfully joined adaptation prepared at the source of the film has been that, after all the trouble involved, it was still at the mercy of the exhibitors, a large proportion of whom were impervious to any consideration not directly measurable by the box office returns. They would reduce the best intended efforts to naught by failing to provide adequate means of performance, and generally refusing to regard the music as other than an irksome tax upon their business. The advent of the sound film confronts them with the only argument likely to affect them: that of reduced trouble and expense. To-day we have already adapted film settings, synchronized with the films, and reproduced by such devices as the Vitaphone or the Movietone which, with all their obvious shortcomings, are even now preferable to inferior playing by an incomplete team, and may be improved beyond expectation before we are much older.[10] Moreover, the circumstances attending the preparation of the music ensure a degree of skill that is not otherwise available to every exhibitor. For the present the vested interest of the adaptor monopolises the new devices, but their dissemination necessarily creates a vehicle, such as has not hitherto existed, for the eventual music drama of the screen, should it ever triumph over the other obstacles in its path. Nor are these the only developments that make for progress in the direction of original film music. At Baden-Baden, in the summer, a film was shown with original music by Paul Hindemith which was performed by means of a perforated roll, synchronized with the projector, upon an instrument of the piano-player type.[11] The pneumatic mechanism operated by the perforated roll is also capable of being installed in organs, a recent type of which has become an almost indispensable adjunct to the cinema. This mode of mechanical reproduction has over the other the advantage that it performs upon an actual musical instrument, and therefore produces a first-hand tone. And there is the Duo-Art to prove that its results need not aggressively evoke the robot.

It may seem a counsel of despair to look to mechanical aids for the reclamation of the cinema as a field of creative musical effort, but the other alternatives appear less promising. True, we have had a few films provided with original music. There was the one based upon the Nibelungen-Lied—though, to be sure, a well known film critic remarked how well Wagner's music fitted it!—and we have had *Metropolis* and *Berlin*, the latter being conceived as a film symphony, the result of direct collaboration between producer and composer.[12] But, with all deference to the musicians responsible for these attempts, they were not of a nature to carry such conviction as would break down the present barriers. *Berlin*, for instance, was so completely lacking in the lyrical element that it actually estranged as many as it converted. It is not by such means that the lost ground can be reconquered. The public—which in this sphere is almost identical with the population—knows the music it wants, though it may be incapable of describing it, and in that music the lyrical element is indispensable. The film music drama that will eventually throw open the gates to original composition must obviously be one that appeals to the public for which it is intended. At this point we may echo a passage which Harvey Grace has already quoted in a similar connection from Chesterton. Writing upon Dickens the latter asks leave to examine the fashionable statement that the public likes bad literature, and proceeds thus: 'The public does not like bad literature. The public likes a certain kind of literature and likes that kind of literature even when it is bad better than another type of literature even when it is good.'[13] The successful pioneers in this field will be those who, accepting this wise observation as applicable to all art, will give the cinema public music of the kind it likes, but of a better quality and a more complete fitness than that to which it is accustomed. Despite the constant—and sometimes bathetic—use of familiar classics, to which the adaptors point with pride, the task should not be one of insuperable difficulty. And if it should appear an irksome one, may one offer a reminder that it took many generations of opera makers to prepare an audience for *Tristan*, although theirs was an aristocratic patronage?

From *Music & Letters* 10, no. 1 (January 1929), 65–69.

4.2 ABOUT THE MUSIC TO *NEW BABYLON*

(O muzïke k "Novomu Vavilonu")

Dmitry Shostakovich

Dmitry Shostakovich (1906–75) published his first essay on film music during the Cultural Revolution, a time when all the arts in the Soviet Union were experiencing significant change. Film in particular was targeted because of its potential to carry propagandistic messages. Many film-related conferences were held, and among the most discussed topics was the new role of sound in the cinematic product.

As evidenced by numerous articles in the popular press—most famously the 1928 "Statement on Sound" authored by directors Sergey Eisenstein, Vsevolod Pudovkin, and Grigory Alexandrov[14]—Soviet filmmakers expressed the need for a cautious and thoughtful approach to synchronized sound and music. Amidst the debates, the Leningrad Film Studio, also known as the Lenfil'm studio, set out to hire "art music" composers with established reputations to write "specially composed" music for their silent films.[15] By this time the young Shostakovich had already gained an international reputation with his First Symphony (1924–25), and he had become infamous for his grotesque opera (1927–28) based on Nikolay Gogol's story "The Nose." Having caught the attention of directors Grigory Kozintsev and Leonid Trauberg, in December 1928 Shostakovich was selected to write a score specific to their forthcoming New Babylon; *he worked quickly and met a series of deadlines set for January and February of the following year. In March 1929 the 23-year-old composer wrote an article ("O muzïke k 'Novomu Vavilonu'") for the weekly magazine* Sovetskiy Ekran *in which he responded to contemporary Soviet thinking about how sound should behave with filmic image and explained how he sought to write music that would actively participate in the creation of meaning.*

With flair, Shostakovich discussed a pair of "principles" that guided his approach. One of these was the "principle of the shot/scene," and the other was the "principle of contrast."[16] Each of these was a response to and a critique of the modes of film accompaniment (ranging from compilations of pre-existing repertoire and generic pieces drawn from film-music manuals to improvisations by so-called pianist-illustrators) that during the 1920s were prevalent as much in the Soviet Union as in the West. Shostakovich had been a pianist-illustrator since the mid-1920s for such Leningrad cinema houses as the Bright Reel, the Splendid Palace, the Aurora, and the Piccadilly, and this experience undoubtedly provided him with an insider's view of the problems of film accompaniment.

Shostakovich's article on his music for New Babylon, *translated here in full,[17] pre-empted a complex response to the film and its score that eventually became known as a scandal.[18] A resurgence of interest in* New Babylon *began in 1976, thanks in part to Gennady Rozhdestvensky's discovery of musical manuscripts in Russian archives and libraries. Since then, conductors and enthusiasts such as Rozhdestvensky, Omni Hadari, Marek Pytel, and Frank Strobel have produced various synchronized versions of the score and the film. These versions were created from European and Russian copies of the film and from the extant orchestral suite (1976) and the more recently published extant score (2006).[19]*

There is no part of the Soviet community that is more forgotten than the musical illustration to the *kino-film*.[20]

The majority of musicians who work in the capacity of cinema illustrators regard this labor as if it were in a swamp that sucks in this or that musician and kills the talent within him, making him into an "inspired" machine, obliged to improvise under the film every evening for so many hours, and superimposing a heavy indelible stamp on his compositional talent.

For conductors the situation is no better. Despite the heroic efforts of some conductors to raise the quality of musical illustration, they cannot do it. In most cinema-theaters[21] the orchestras are more or less qualified. But while on the qualitative side the orchestras are not so bad, on the quantitative side orchestras in the majority of cinemas are of no use at all. The number of string players is scandalously small (two, maximum three, stands of violins). It is good if an orchestra has woodwind instruments, but very often those instruments are lacking. And yet such orchestras play the works of Beethoven, Schubert, Schumann, Tchaikovsky, and so forth.

Conscientious working conductors occasionally use the existing personnel to compensate for the missing instruments. But usually this is simply impossible because of lack of time. For the most part, the limited orchestra and the pianist just play "a bit louder," pounding out the parts of the missing instruments. Instead of trombones, there is a piano.[22] Tchaikovsky in his grave is probably spinning like a top because of such interpretations.

There are often cases where the conductor "successfully" adjusts the music. On the screen there is a trumpet, and at that same moment in the orchestra a trumpet also sounds.[23] The result is marvelous. So marvelous that, they think, this is precisely why the public flocks to the halls of cinema-theaters. "Aha, the public likes it," thinks the manager, and gives the order to the projectionist to crank the film faster, in order to have four *séances* in an evening instead of three.[24] [But then] the trumpet [playing] does not coincide [with the film]. And the result is offensive.

In a word, this is *khaltura*,[25] a most shameless *khaltura* that is firmly rooted in cinema's musical accompaniment.[26] The most annoying thing is that this *khaltura* is completely legitimized. No one screams or protests.

Once I had occasion to visit a musical conference that took place at the Leningrad Film Studio. Many good words were spoken. Everyone agreed, and seemed reconciled. But there were many [interesting] words offered by a representative of the [theater] managers, a comrade Sokov. He said:

"If the picture is pleasing, then of course I order the projectionist to crank it in order to handle more *séances*. If it is not pleasing, then I order the projectionist to crank it slower. If the theater is empty, then sometimes we can not justify the use of electricity."

It was said, quite convincingly, that once when I objected [to this sort of thing] there was a resolution passed by Glavrepetkom[27] to the effect that a film should always go at the same tempo (I have not seen this resolution, but I have discussed it with comrade Fayer). Everyone [at the conference] then listlessly started to talk about the fact that, apparently, there may or may not have been such a resolution.

If there is no such resolution, then it absolutely must be made; if there is a resolution, then it should be displayed in a prominent place in the offices of all cinema managers. Unless this happens, *khaltura*—with the blessing from comrade Sokov and his kind—will thrive in the cinema. Indeed, no one in his or her right mind would ever agree to an opera that is driven at high speed just so that instead of presenting it once in an evening it can be presented twice!

Most of the repertory of cinema-music is incredibly monotonous. It gets hardly any rehearsal time. And if even one hour is allotted, that hour is paid back in time, not in money: each musician may delete an hour from his or her assigned work hours. Time is money. Therefore orchestras in the cinemas play only worn-out pieces that are well known and of which everyone is tired. It is time for the musical community to take hold of music for the cinema and rid it of *khaltura* and anti-artistry, and to clean the local Augean stables.[28] Lack of space does not permit me to write more about the so-called film music manuals, [which contain generic] pieces for tears, for uprisings, for the corrupt bourgeoisie, for love, and so forth. About them I will say just one thing: this is such *khaltura*, if not worse.

The only correct path is to write special music, as has been done, if I am not mistaken, in one of the first instances with *New Babylon*.[29]

When composing the music for *New Babylon*, I was guided least of all by the idea of obligatory illustration of every shot. Mainly, I began with the principal shot in each sequence of shots.

Take for example, the end of the second part.[30] The primary action here is the attack of the German cavalry on Paris. The part ends with a [scene in a] deserted restaurant, [which suggests] total silence. But the music, despite the fact that the German cavalry is no longer shown on the screen, comes from the cavalry just the same, reminding the viewer of the cavalry's impending, menacing force.

[Another example is] the music for the seventh part. The soldier ends up in a restaurant filled[31] with the bourgeoisie, who are having fun after the crushing defeat of the Commune; despite the restaurant's cheery atmosphere, the music emanates from the somber emotions of the soldier as he searches for his beloved, [who has been] sentenced to be executed by a firing squad.

Much [of my score] is constructed according to the principle of contrast. For example, the soldier (a Versaillais) who met his beloved (a Communard) on the barricades[32] [eventually] enters into a state of gloomy desperation. [Yet when this happens] the music becomes more and more jubilant, until finally it culminates in a frantic and "obscene" waltz that represents the victory of the Versaillais forces over the Communards.

Another interesting example [of contrast] can be found in the film's fourth part, which depicts the rehearsal of an operetta. The music offers a rather well-known exercise by Hanon,[33] but this takes on different nuances in relation to the action: sometimes the music has a gay mood, but sometimes it seems boring, and sometimes even terrifying.

The film's music makes use of a great number of dances from the epoch being depicted (waltzes, for example, or cancans), and it even features melodies borrowed directly from operettas by Offenbach. Beyond that, the film score makes use of French folk and revolutionary songs (for example, "Ça-ira" and "La Carmagnole"[34]). The primary theme assigned to the Versaillais is [of course] "La Marseillaise," but sometimes this appears in unexpected contexts, for example, in counterpoint with cancans, waltzes, and so forth.

Even when the amount of musical material is great, the score strives to maintain a continuous—and symphonic—tone. The primary goal here is that the music holds to the film's [overall] tempos and rhythms, and that it serves to intensify whatever impression the film itself seeks to make.

I tried to give the music novelty and unusualness (especially for film-music that has been available up to this point), dynamics, and to convey the *patetik*[35] of the *New Babylon*. . . . But if the Sokovism[36] [see above] will continue to crank films at any tempo he wants, then surely the music will completely disappear.

From *Sovetskiy Ekran* [*The Soviet Screen*] no. 11 (March 1929), 5.
(Translation by Joan M. Titus)

4.3 EXPERIMENTING WITH SOUND FILMS

Darius Milhaud

Darius Milhaud (1892–1974), one of the group of French composers famously known as "Les Six,"[37] *came relatively late to film scoring. Although during the World War I years he gained considerable recognition for theatrical work as manifest in his 1919 ballet* Le boeuf sur le toit *and his incidental music for various plays by Paul Claudel (*Agamemnon, *1913–14;* Protée, *1913;* Les choëphores, *1915;* Les euménides, *1917), Milhaud was conspicuously not among the participants in the film-music survey conducted in 1919 by the Paris-based journal* Le Film.[38] *Indeed, Milhaud did not engage with the cinema until 1929, when he concocted music first for a newsreel and then—as described in this article—the Cavalcanti-directed short feature* La p'tite Lilie.[39]

Between 1933 and 1959 Milhaud composed music for more than two dozen films, most of them French productions. Milhaud's only direct involvement with Hollywood came on the heels of his 1940–47 American sojourn, during which time he served on the faculty of Mills College in northern California: he wrote the complete score for Albert Lewin's 1947 fictional The Private Affairs of Bel Ami *(United Artists) and music for a segment of Hans Richter's 1948 documentary* Dreams That Money Can Buy *(Films International of America).*[40]

Writing early in 1930, Milhaud presciently favors the sound-on-film technology as developed in Germany (but soon to be adopted by filmmakers worldwide) over the distinctly American sound-on-disc technology with which the "talking picture" first made its great international splash. Specific technologies notwithstanding, Milhaud in 1930 clearly embraces the idea of the sound film in general. He disparages the industry's penchant for filling the newly available "soundtrack" with songs, but he encourages the use of originally composed "underscore" music that in some cases might be tightly synchronized with cinematic action.

From the moment I first heard the Vitaphone in New York in 1927, I was convinced of the great possibilities of this new way to use music for the movies. The film, a long one of Sidney Chaplin's, had an accompaniment, played by the Philharmonic, which deluged our ears with a dull confused sound, a sort of tonal fog, which, though full of the best intentions, kept us restless and irritated.[41] It was followed by a demonstration—some jazz music, a singer accompanied by an organ, a flight of shrieking sea gulls, the roaring of an airplane motor, a string quartet—and relief settled on us, we breathed more easily; for the sound of the solo instruments and the piano, the human voice, the various noises, all came over. The purpose of the operation was achieved, namely the faithful reproduction of the sound. The mistake with the long film had been the use of the full orchestra, an impression which the experiments made in the Baden-Baden festival of 1927 and 1928 with the "Tri-Ergon" confirmed.[42]

The talking pictures have since definitively arrived, with their good qualities and bad, their menace, their promise, and their snares. And with what a sudden avalanche of elementary, superficial methods. It is impossible to resist synchronizing the twelve strokes of a clock with the image showing the hour, or the sound of an automobile, a train, a passing airplane, a crowd in tumult. What nonsense! An actor with a good voice is found and a thousand excuses are dug up to have him sing, retarding the action in the most tiresome fashion. There is always the temptation to blindly abuse a new invention. It is so wonderful to be able to make some one sing on the screen, it seems a waste of opportunity not to have him render ballad after ballad; just as, before the war, actors were made to move violently and excessively to show that movement could be photographed, that here was no magic lantern. It was up to the actor, expressing himself only by pantomime, to demonstrate that his gestures were eloquent enough to replace words.

Sound movies are in their infancy, it is true, but their application has already become important. What was the condition formerly, when a composer wrote special music for a film? Only a few theatres had orchestras large enough to execute it. In the provinces any sort of accompaniment was used and the score disappeared without a trace. Thanks to talking pictures, the music will be recorded forever and will be heard everywhere, simultaneously with the view of the film. For records of folklore the sound movies will be invaluable. Worse music than is used to accompany the dances of Africa or any other exotic country is hardly conceivable. Now it is possible to join the authentic music to the dances which the screen has long shown us. It is so easy to imagine the application of sound movies in education. Scientific courses with experiments, lessons by conservatory professors, all sorts of lectures with demonstrations, photographed simultaneously for the eye and ear, can be presented to the schools of a whole nation at once.

In the relation of music to the movies, the primary problem is synchronization. There are two existing methods. The writer can create a film—as the choreographer does a ballet—for an existing musical work, and the picture is, of course, no worry to the composer. Or a musician can write for an already existing film, and here he must work out a new technique. In Germany synchronization has in the main been solved by the chronometer of Dr. Karl Blum.[43] This apparatus unrolls two spools on a plate, one with the film, the other with two blank staffs. The latter unrolls much more slowly than the first. The starting points once marked, it is only necessary to divide the second into equal divisions, spaced more or less according to the metronomic movements used (which allows as frequent change in measures as the music requires). All that is needed is to let the imagination flow and fill the prepared spaces. Making my own experiment with this device, I wrote music for a German newsreel (*Wochenschau*), and found it possible to make as many little pieces of different character as there were events, and to relate them with absolute synchronization. On reproduction, the photographic images on one spool are thrown on the screen, the other spool unrolls on the conductor's desk under a little glass window. It is possible to have the time of each measure exact, since it is mechanically determined by the composer's spacing.

A step further is to make real sound films by registering the music on records or films, and then sending it through a loud speaker while the action unfolds on the screen. By making several recordings, it becomes possible to select the most exactly synchronized. I don't know for what mysterious reason the great German sound studios of Tobis, on the Ufa grounds, do not use this device, which gives maximum precision. In these studios I recorded the score I composed for *La Petite Lilie* of Cavalcanti.[44]

For this composition, I used a technic especially adapted to the present requirements of the microphone: suppression of the oboe, which is poorly heard, a moderate, often faint use of the flute, as also of the cymbals and the percussion. It is probable that the microphone will soon be sufficiently perfected to record all different sounds equally well, so that musicians will not have to consider these difficulties. But I, on the contrary, had to use the most empirical methods to match the music to the picture. I measured the film with a ruler and took notes; made all kinds of calculations on the relations of the number of images per second and per meter; composed gropingly with my eyes on the second hand of my watch. Because of the absence of scientific method, the music runs the risk of varying in the time of the measures and of following the interpretation of the orchestra leader.

There was a similar difficulty in the recording studio. A hundred meters were recorded at a time—about three and a half minutes of music. Several recordings of each hundred meter section were necessary to afford an opportunity for selection. The orchestra leader had only approximate synchronization marks and was compelled, in spite of all the precautions taken, to speed up or slow down in order to exactly accompany a certain image with the corresponding music.

Having tackled this job, one can appreciate the ease of a transcription on films. Several versions of different parts of each section may be interchanged. It is just a question of cutting and pasting. I remember a false cornet note which was replaced by a correct one, sounded after the recording was over. This of course means a great advantage over disks, where the least error, the slightest sound—makes it necessary to start again from scratch. This happened to me with a record I was making for Columbia when a dog barked in the street.

Once the final choice of the different pieces of film is made, they are joined. The work is over, but alas, not all one's troubles. The tone quality depends on the projection. Poor projection may make the music sound as if it came through a layer of wadding. *La Petite Lilie* was perfectly recorded through the efforts of the orchestra leader, Zeller, and the technicians, who were supervised by a young composer, Wagner Regeny.[45] When I heard it in the Tobis Studio in Berlin it was perfect but when presented at the Baden-Baden festival a poor projection resulted in an unfortunate audition, muffled and dull. It is not encouraging to think of one's film making the rounds of German cities with no guaranty as to the quality of the reproduction.

We must remember that sound movies are just beginning. Methods of synchronization, recording and reproduction will be perfected. Meanwhile, for our personal entertainment, why does not some one construct a small device that will enable us to record the voices of our friends, the laughter of the children who surround us, street noises, etc., to synchronize with the amateur movies we can take?

From *Modern Music* 7, no. 2 (February–March 1930), 11–14.

5

ACCOUNTS OF THE SOUND
FILM'S EARLY YEARS

Embellishing one of his musical numbers in *The Jazz Singer* with a spoken declaration, in effect addressed not just to his on-screen partner but also to the audience, with a gleeful twinkle in his eye the character played by Al Jolson says: "You ain't heard nothin' yet!" And that by and large summarizes that attitude that studios worldwide took to the new medium of the sound film.

Indeed, within months of *The Jazz Singer*'s premiere virtually all of Hollywood was scrambling to jump on the sound-film bandwagon. Although it would take a few years for the dust to settle on the fierce technological competition between the sound-on-disc Vitaphone system used by Warner Bros. and the sound-on-film Movietone system being promoted by Fox,[1] the first half of 1928 nevertheless witnessed the quick expenditure of millions of dollars on the construction of Hollywood sound stages. During the same period, hundreds of movie theaters not just throughout the United States but in the major European cities invested in the Western Electric amplification equipment that could accommodate both Vitaphone and Movietone releases.

Vitaphone enjoyed an early success not just because it had a head start in the marketplace but also because its audio quality, at least at first, was superior to that of Movietone. But Vitaphone was cumbersome and, in exhibition, often unreliable; it entailed both a film projector and a phonograph, the mechanical connection between which was subject to disastrous break-downs.[2] In marked contrast, the self-contained Movietone apparatus practically guaranteed exact synchronization between sound and image. Its single camera was equipped with both an "eye" that watched the movements of actors and an optical "ear" that listened to whatever sounds those actors made; photographed simultaneously on a single strip of celluloid, whatever visual and aural data a scene contained were indissolubly linked. Movietone's practical advantages over Vitaphone seemed obvious to almost everyone. All that remained was for Movietone's developmental engineers, affiliated for the most part with the Radio Corporation of America (RCA), to raise the system's audio fidelity to the level set early on by Vitaphone. By the middle of 1930 this was a fait accompli, and within the next year or so virtually all sound films—whatever their origin—utilized the new sound-on-film technology.

Filmmakers c.1930–31 no longer had to be concerned with how the sonic components of their products might be recorded. But they were very much concerned with what those sonic components should be, and with how they should function within a filmed narrative. With few localized exceptions, during the heyday of the "silent" film in the 1920s there was international agreement as to how supportive music, and assorted "live" sound effects, might service the exhibition of a narrative film. Almost immediately upon the introduction of sound-film technology, however, this once-comfortable consensus gave way to rampant confusion.

Spurred by what seemed an obviously favorable response to the musical numbers in *The Jazz Singer*, Hollywood in the earliest years of the sound film produced an extraordinary number of pictures that centered on more or less elaborate song-and-dance routines. For a while this indeed satisfied the public's appetite, but the novelty of lightweight "musicals" quickly wore thin. Hollywood *c*.1930–31 was certainly capable, as it had been throughout the 1920s, of delivering more dramatically substantial products. But now, in the early years of the sound film, Hollywood faced the perplexing question of how those products might be musically accompanied.

After the fad for musicals ended, some Hollywood filmmakers opted starkly for no music at all, except during title sequences and build-ups to on-screen statements of "The End." Others chose to lather long sections of their films with orchestral music—much of it drawn from the familiar classical repertoire—whose chief purpose seems to have been to add variety to an otherwise quotidian mix of dialogue and naturalistic sounds. Still others, representing a small minority, made liberal use of diegetic music that in canny ways foreshadowed "modern" film music's narrative and structural functions. Not until 1932–33, when pre-existing orchestral music gave way to entirely original material, and when "underscore" began to be used with discretion, did the classical-style film score start to emerge.[3]

The three writers whose commentaries are gathered here were journalists who closely observed developments in Hollywood during film music's transitional years. Helen Louise Walker's article, originally published in a magazine geared toward movie fans, easily and breezily conveys the excitement generated by the urgent question of whether Hollywood would or would not continue to supply fans with star-studded musicals. The articles by Philip K. Scheurer and Edwin Schallert, both of them reporters for the *Los Angeles Times*, take more serious approaches to the matter of film music. Along with his own well-considered views, Scheurer's piece includes differing opinions from the heads of music departments at various Hollywood studios; Schallert's piece, penned just before the dawn of the "modern" film score, not only points prophetically to the future but also succinctly reviews the sound film's brief history.

After 1927's *The Jazz Singer*, audiences worldwide seemed delightedly convinced that the best of the new sound-film's offerings was yet to come. But as these reportorial articles suggest, it took at least a few years before the film industry collectively settled on what the "best" might be.

5.1 MUSICAL PICTURE QUIETLY UNDERGOES RENAISSANCE

Studios Recognize Inability Wholly to Dispense With Score When Interpolation Logical

Philip K. Scheurer

Philip K. Scheurer (1901–85) was a long-time movie critic for the Los Angeles Times, *and the writer of his obituary noted that Scheurer at the time of his death "was believed to be the last of the critics who had reviewed both silent and talking films."*[4] *His close involvement with films began when he was still a teenager. Born in Newark, New Jersey, he first visited Hollywood as the result of winning a high-school essay contest; "after that," he reminisced, "there was simply no chance that [he] would ever go into any other line of work."⁵ Scheurer settled in Hollywood immediately upon graduating from high school and began working in the* Times' *entertainment section. In 1927 he became the paper's second assistant film and drama critic, and until his retirement forty years later he prolifically covered the Hollywood scene, writing not only reviews but also, for many years, an almost daily column ("A Town Called Hollywood") of industry news.*

As a critic, Scheurer expressed his views freely, yet his unbiased reporting of artistic trends and technological developments in filmmaking earned him the continued respect of studio insiders. Reflecting this, the article reproduced here is remarkable for its candid comments from executives in charge of music at no less than four of Hollywood's largest studios.

Early in 1931 the very concept of film music was perhaps more in flux than at any other point in the twentieth century. Scheurer notes with unbridled optimism that the major studios—after a few excited years that had them focused mostly on song-and-dance numbers—were at last starting to take a serious look at the role that mood-generating music might play in their productions. Yet as Scheurer reports, opinions as to precisely how *dramatically potent "background" music might find its way into films still varied from studio to studio.*

While everybody is trying to outshout his neighbor with the news that the musical picture is dead, several of the major companies are making quiet preparations to revive it in a big way. The fact of the matter is, if one stops to think, that the abortive musical picture of recent passing never had a really fighting chance to live—spawn of a helter-skelter attempt to unite the artificial theater with the realistic screen, it was murdered in its cradle by the very producers who were nursing it along.

The genuine musical picture will not have a legitimate birth until someone with genius and foresight enough to create it comes along. But that does not mean that sweet sounds are taboo; temporarily, at least, we shall have "the picture with music."

There is a distinction here. Four musical leaders in Hollywood studios were unanimous, when consulted, in declaring that interpolated music, whether incidental or part of the action, is assuming more importance daily in their respective plants. The trick lies in applying it where it will do the most good.

Music, points out Nathaniel Finston, able general of Paramount's West Coast clef forces, is too much a part of our lives to be ignored in our cinema. He recalls that in those halcyon days when he, along with Hugo Riesenfeld, Erno Rapee, David Mendoza, William Axt, and the late Josiah Zuro were arranging scores for New York's Capitols and Rialtos, these musical accompaniments were regarded as a good 50 per cent of the success of any picture. He asks who can deny the enhancing power of the scores for such spectacles as *Way Down East, The Birth of a Nation, The Big Parade,* and the rest; and adds that all this was forgotten over night with the astounding discovery that voices could be made to come out of the mouths of babes. On that day, he says, the work of twenty years went for naught.

Recovery is only now beginning.

Summed up, these truths become self-evident:

A majority of filmgoers acknowledge their susceptibility to the influence of music accompaniment. They find it an emotional stimulus, tending to increase reaction to the scenes portrayed on the screen.

But the instant music is made the object of attention, and the visual movement halted for emphasis on the aural, the eye becomes fatigued, the ear conscious that it is listening to a mechanical reproduction.

This, I think, is the whole story of the success and failure of the musical movie. There are, of course, other factors: the nature of the story, the degree in which a mood is evoked from the listener, and the quality of performance, recording and reproduction. But most vital of all is the proper use of a medium which, no matter how much the producers may deny it, is still aimed squarely at our eyes.

Finston used a 100 per cent musical "underscore" for *Fighting Caravans*, a recent release. For *Rango*, current jungle film, he did the same thing.[6] He says that he is not altogether positive that a complete musical underscore is advisable for a talkie, certain episodes lending themselves better to silence; but he is convinced that no music at all is infinitely worse.

"We have a surprise in store for Hollywood in *Dishonored*, the new Von Sternberg production," the conductor asserts.[7] "In this picture we have made a piano an integral part of the plot, so that the music played on it becomes important to the actors involved; and as the result of this piano-playing is made visually apparent, a full symphony orchestra develops the original themes to terrific proportions.

"We were able to do this because allowance for the music was written into the script and planned by the director—the only way in which music can be successfully developed in pictures. Ernst Lubitsch did the same thing in mapping out *The Love Parade* and *Monte Carlo*, and that is why they were real musical films."[8]

First National and Warner Brothers, which have used underscores intermittently in talkies since their inception, will continue to do so. Arthur Franklin, in charge of music at these studios, states that the usual 40 per cent underscore will be increased to 60 or 70 per cent in many forthcoming Vitaphones.

"We must be careful, however, not to 'overload' an audience," he explains. "As it is, the spectator can no longer relax at a talkie as he used to in the silent days. It takes greater effort to listen than to look. And we cannot use music that is too familiar, or the hearer will lose track of the picture and concentrate on what its title is, and where he has heard it before."

The danger of "overloading" is stressed also by William (Dr. Billy) Axt, veteran composer and arranger, now with Metro-Goldwyn-Mayer. This studio is apparently still opposed to any sort of music which has no "legitimate" place in the film, believing in a "literal" interpretation of the action, except in the case of a frankly musical picture like *Jenny Lind* or *The Rogue Song*.[9] Dr. Billy, however, sees no reason why dialogue should not have a musical obbligato. Because it has been done badly in some instances proves nothing, he says.

"Naturally, people resent an accompaniment that drowns out the dialogue," Axt remarks. "I know cases of arrangers using woodwinds in the upper register to accompany the actors' voices, when they ought to know that even one flute will do the dirty work. Nobody ever heard of strings in mid-register ruining a speech. It's all a matter of common sense."

Typical of their methods, Axt says, was the way in which the studios rushed out and hired Tin Pan Alley in its entirety as soon as the musical talkie was invented. Now they have gone to the other extreme, loudly declaiming that their motto is "Millions for production, but not one cent for music." They still, Dr. Billy notes, cannot tell a songwriter from a composer.

"Eventually," he adds, "a man will come along who can combine the screen, the drama and music into one harmonious whole. Today, nine-tenths of our directors—and I don't care how expert they may be at camera angles or dialogue—arc 'tone deaf.' "

Following Metro-Goldwyn-Mayer's lead, Radio Pictures announces that no music will be introduced in its products "illogically," Max Steiner, the company's baton chief, says. "When music is found in Radio films, it will be secondary to the plot action and the movement of the story itself." Steiner does not believe in the abstract underscoring of a picture by an orchestra, differing in this respect from Franklin, Axt and Finston.

"Music will be largely incidental, and often atmospheric," he amplifies. "It will not come into a picture from some mysterious source (the orchestra pit?) but by some logical, and, if possible, visual means—such as the turning-on of a radio or a phonograph in a scene, or a glimpse of an orchestra or chorus."

And so, though they may not agree on the means of presentation, most of the studios recognize the present need for music with their movies. No chance need, this, but a definite force that once aided immeasurably in lifting the once lowly nickelodeon to the pedestal of an eighth lively art, and made our great film palaces dignified as the homes of good orchestras. The screen can part with dialogue, if the time ever comes when it must, but it can never wholly dispense with music.

From *Los Angeles Times*, February 22, 1931, B9, B20.

5.2 MUSICAL PICTURES ARE HERE AGAIN

Helen Louise Walker

About the career of Helen Louise Walker little is known other than that she was born in Pleasantville, New York, and that at the time of her marriage (in 1938, to J. Edward Schipper Jr.) she was affiliated primarily with Readers Digest. *But the frequent appearance of her by-line in* Motion Picture Magazine *between 1929 and 1932 suggests that earlier in her career Walker fairly reveled in reportage on the lively movie scene.*

Motion Picture Magazine *was a slickly produced fan-oriented periodical that enjoyed a prosperous run from 1912 to 1959. Apropos of the monthly magazine's focus, most of Walker's contributions are feature stories that somehow celebrate the "behind the scenes" lives of established or emerging actors and actresses. In marked contrast, the article reproduced here is a commentary on what Walker perceives as a drastic shift in the film industry's attitude toward music.*

Walker's comments here are not at all on extra-diegetic film music. Her concern, rather, is with musical "numbers" of the sort that in 1929 and 1930 fairly glutted Hollywood production but which since early 1931 had been all but abandoned.[10] *"The big comeback news of 1931," she writes approvingly, has to do with songs. Her account is breezy and, of course, studded with the names of movie stars; at the same time, it is filled not just with facts but also with insights as to how the studios—suddenly and en masse—were reconsidering the use of music in films.*

You want musicals—I want musicals—All God's Chillun Want Musicals. Maybe you don't know it. Maybe I don't know it. But it must be so. For every single studio in Hollywood—except one—either has a musical picture in production or is getting one ready. And Universal admits that it is just waiting "to see what happens to the others."

Pola Negri may be staging a big comeback, like Dolores Del Rio, and Clara Bow may be planning one—but you haven't heard anything yet. Musicals, which everybody thought had gone forever, are coming back. In fact, they're here. THIS is the big comeback news of 1931.

The romances of Gaynor and Farrell are going to be rhythmic again. Ramon Novarro will serenade his lady loves one more. Lawrence Tibbett will keep right on thrilling millions of women with that powerful, passionate voice. Gloria Swanson is even now playing the role of an opera star in *Tonight or Never*—and that means that she is practicing her scales. You will even hear Marlene Dietrich sing—and maybe play the violin (or even her musical saw).[11]

The first time that music rushed at you from the screen, it brought you such new stars as Al Jolson, Maurice Chevalier, Jeanette MacDonald, Lawrence Tibbett, Irene Dunne, John Boles, Eddie Cantor, Marilyn Miller, Winnie Lightner, Joe E. Brown, Wheeler and Woolsey and Dorothy Lee, Marjorie White, Eddie Dowling, Fifi Dorsay and Cliff Edwards. They stayed when music went—but it was music that brought them to you. It gave such old-time favorites as Gloria Swanson and Bebe Daniels a new lease on screen life. Will the comeback of musicals bring us still newer faces and favorites—and bring back still other old-time stars?

Maybe you have felt it coming—this return of music to the screen? Maybe you remember that Marlene Dietrich sang a subtle little ditty in *Morocco*? Maybe you recall that Charles Farrell was a composer in *Merely Mary Ann*—and there had to be music to make things real! Maybe you remember that Adolphe Menjou was an opera star in *The Great Lover*—and not just a stage star, mind you, but an *opera* star? And did you notice that Winnie Lightner put across two songs (no less) in *Side Show*?

A year ago Hollywood would have had a violent attack of the shudders if you had so much as mentioned musical pictures. Especially musical comedies or revues. "Musical pictures are OUT!" the movie magnates chorused. "The public simply won't have 'em. They may revive in ten or fifteen years. But we doubt it." Everybody doubted it.

Now Maurice Chevalier in *The Smiling Lieutenant* has just packed them in all over the country. Eddie Cantor has just finished *Palmy Days* (verra, verra musical) and it promises to be a hit. Al Jolson, whose last picture was a pretty discouraging affair, has arrived in Hollywood to rest his poor throat, all tired and rasped from singing on Broadway, and to prepare for his next singing effort in pictures.[12] Marilyn Miller is back in town, amid much ballyhoo, to contribute her bit to the revival.[13]

The first musical pictures made money. Whereupon the studios flooded a gasping world with more and more and *more* musical pictures. These, hastily made, with new

73

personalities in the leading roles, grew worse and worse until the public, which has been pretty patient when you consider all it had had to bear, finally expressed its protest by staying sulkily away from the theaters where these offerings were showing.

Then a strange thing happened. Just when all the song writers were selling their pretty, pink Beverly Hills houses and all the little, rompered chorus-girls who had brightened up the Hollywood landscape were sadly packing their suitcases and all the voice teachers were closing their ornate studios—along came *Whoopee*, a rollicking musical comedy, with Eddie Cantor.[14] *Whoopee* made money—just when everyone was saying, bitterly, that there *was* no more money in musicals.

Producers scratched their heads and thought and thought. After a lot of concentration they reached the surprising conclusion that maybe this phenomenon was caused by the fact that *Whoopee* was a *good picture!* But even then they were doubtful. Most of them had taken some bad lickings with musicals.

And now several more surprising things have happened. Bing Crosby, who used to be one of Paul Whiteman's "Rhythm Boys" (as well as Dixie Lee's husband), was crooning over at the Cocoanut Grove (one of the Swanker places where our dancing daughters dance). He left and went to making "crooning shorts" for Mack Sennett.[15]

Musicals! They're what the public wants—in moderation.

RKO, at the recent convention of its salesmen, took a vote as to whether *Girl Crazy* (with Wheeler and Woolsey and Dorothy Lee) should be made as a musical comedy or not. To everyone's enormous astonishment, the answer was almost unanimously in favor of a musical comedy! It is now being made with music and choruses—and all the trimmings.[16] *Marcheta*, with Richard Dix, Irene Dunne and Ricardo Cortez, will also be a musical, and after that will be *Bird of Paradise* with Dolores Del Rio.[17] RKO is *that* surprised.

Fox Studios was all a-twitter this summer when *Sunnyside Up*, one of their old musicals, was revived at Roxy's in New York City. The picture played to miserable business. Considering that Gaynor and Farrell usually pack this world's largest theater, but the studio can hardly wait to get started on its new musical, *Delicious*, which George and Ira Gershwin and Guy Bolton have written for America's Two Favorite Sweethearts. The piece was dashed off several months ago when the Gershwins were on the Coast—and it has been bidin' its time ever since.

Janet is practicing her singing and dancing again and things begin to look a good deal as they did two years ago. Fox is still cautious, however—and mindful of those lickings. They describe the new piece, timidly, as "a comedy with music."

Warners have been taking votes in their theaters as to their patrons' preferences in re-issues of old pictures. At least half of them have voted for *Hold Everything* and *Gold-Diggers of Broadway*—both musicals. The other half are in favor of *Disraeli* and *Son of the Gods*. From which Warners have concluded that a *good* musical will vie with a *good* dramatic picture any day.

They have released the musical *Children of Dreams* and *Men of the Sky*, after holding them back for months.[18] And they are going busily and happily to work on *Her Majesty, Love* with Marilyn Miller—just to mention one of their musical projects.

M-G-M, all encouraged by these things, reached up to the top shelf the other day and took down their *Old-Timers' Revue*, made a year or more ago with lots of bright luminaries of former days, and they are now in the process of dusting it off and refurbishing it for the winter trade.

They are also concocting *Flying High*, from a New York musical show, with the inimitable Bert Lahr, Charlotte Greenwood and bevies and bevies of little darlings capering about in satin shorts and gauze.[19] (Not very much gauze.)

These are to be real musicals with no excuses made for them. Up to now, people have been apologetic about singing on the screen. "Remember that little song I used to like so well?" the lady would say to the leading man. "Sing it for me now." Thus having made it "logical" for a song to be introduced, the gentleman was free to go ahead and sing his little ditty.

All of which brings us around to the question of what all this will mean to our favorite actors. For there is no doubt about it—if one or two of these pictures are successful, we shall certainly have another avalanche of singing and dancing. And why not? Isn't the field just as ripe for this type of entertainment as it is for the heavy dramatics?

If this comes to pass, will it mean that Paul Whiteman, Rudy Vallee, Morton Downey, Helen (Poop-a-doop) Kane, the Duncan Sisters, the Sisters G, Dennis King, Grace Moore, Lillian Roth, Jack Whiting, Charles King, Alexander Gray, Stanley Smith, Bernice Caire, Vivienne Segal and the scores of others who came and sang their ditties, played their bands or danced their dances and then went away again, will be returning to the screen?

Maybe that's why Paramount would not release Buddy Rogers to go East and play with his band. Maybe that's why they were so anxious to keep Ruth Chatterton. For even our Ruthie essayed a couple of jazz numbers in *The Magnificent Lie*! While John Boles was waiting for Universal to okay his idea of a new contract, offers poured in from other studios.

Bebe Daniels made a spectacular comeback when she proved that she could sing in *Rio Rita*.[20] Of late there have been whispers that Warners would be just as happy if they had not signed her on that long-term contract.—Will musicals let Bebe make a *second* comeback?

Is that why M-G-M re-signed Ramon Novarro when all the reports had it that they would let him go when his contract expired?

Pictures are certainly much nicer for the singer than the stage. Al Jolson's throat gave out while he was appearing night after night in *Wonder Bar* in New York. In pictures he can sing a song once and then sit back at his ease (and at a large salary) while the thing goes all over the world. Eddie Cantor has had a bit of throat trouble—but the California climate seems to agree with him. And Chevalier suffered from rasped vocal chords [sic], 'tis said, after his triumphal tour of Europe.

Well—we shall see. Meanwhile, it will be pleasant to have our wave of stark realism broken by a song or two. *All Quiet* ushered in this cycle of stark realism—and gosh, how stark most of it has been, too;[21] with a parade across the screen of soldiers and gangsters and racketeers and ladies of the late afternoon and evening.

People writhed and died from being (1) hanged (2) electrocuted (3) poisoned (4) slashed (5) stabbed (6) shot with (a) machine guns (b) revolvers (c) sawed-off shotguns (d) rifles (e) cannon (f) et cetera. The writhes the average actor has writhed while dying in pictures the past year, would reach from San Quentin to the Sing Sing death-house and back. It must have been *terribly* hard on them.

From *Motion Picture Magazine*, November 1931, 52–53, 88.

5.3 FILM MUSIC EXPERIENCES ITS SANEST DEVELOPMENT

Orchestral Background Finds Niche in Pictures; Original Scores Becoming More Popular

Edwin Schallert

Edwin Schallert (1890–1968) was a staff writer for the Los Angeles Times *from 1912 until his retirement in 1957. After initial assignments in the newspaper's business section, his duties at the newspaper involved coverage of not just theatrical events but also of purely musical activity. Beginning in 1919, after his return from military service in Europe, Schallert regularly reviewed concerts presented by the recently founded Los Angeles Philharmonic; at the same time, he commented professionally on virtually all the "dramatic" products issued by Hollywood. While his journalistic work after 1930 focused primarily on quotidian reviews of films, Schallert never abandoned his affiliation with music; like Scheuer's, his writing is sprinkled with insightful commentary on the effectiveness of music in specific films and observations on how film music in general, especially in the 1950s, was undergoing shifts in both style and approach.*

The article reproduced here is noteworthy for its tidy summary of film music's short albeit turbulent history from the advent of the song-oriented Vitaphone productions of 1926–27 up to the most recent experiments with accompanimental music. The very first word of the article is "underscoring," and its inclusion in quotation marks suggests that early in the era of the sound film the concept of extra-diegetic music (notwithstanding the important role such music had played throughout the heyday of the silent film) still seemed radically new.

"Underscoring" of pictures is a new and progressive activity in the motion-picture studios. It is seeing its sanest development today. Not only are excerpts from published works being used, but more and more original melodies and harmonies are being added to the tapestry of film tone.

This optimistic sentiment is vouchsafed by the men in charge of the musical work at the various motion-picture plants of Hollywood. They are making steady headway in securing a place for the orchestral background. Indeed, it often becomes an intimate factor in the scene.

Such pictures as *Grand Hotel, Street Scene, Symphony of Six Million, Letty Lynton* and others disclose its importance, as quite dissociated from mere jazz. Many other pictures are being made, in which music is something more than a mere incident, but a real feature. There are no concertos, symphonies and solo performances by great artists to be heard as stellar events of an entertainment, but all concerned with music in the studios hold hopes for the future.

Three stages in the history of the melodious excursion might be described to date:

(1) The frantic, feverish, frenzied time when everybody went crazy on the subject of music, and little or no discrimination prevailed in its use.
(2) The natural follow-up. No music at all.
(3) The gradual recovery from the first two eras of insanity. The "creeping in" of music where it really helped.

Mostly, this third stage has been distinguished by the use of the melodic theme as supplementary to the scene. It is a harking back to the days when the theater orchestra accompanied the picture.

A year and a half ago the director of music in the studio found little opportunity, except in contriving a few bars to be played while the main title of the picture was flashed on the screen, and a few more measures swelling to a sort of finale when all the "shooting was over." In between most of the music was furnished by the rat-tat-tat of machine guns, which did not happily associate itself with truer harmony.

Now the percentage of orchestral backgrounding in pictures is variously estimated at 25 to 50 per cent. In *Symphony of Six Million* it is reputed to be even higher.

While *Grand Hotel* seems to exude the atmosphere of music, there is—according to Dr. William Axt, in charge of Metro-Goldwyn-Mayer's music department—just about 15 to 20 per cent. He figures a very close net on this, and it will be noted by those who either have seen the picture, or who are planning to see it, that the music is constantly justified. The impression exists that it is coming from an orchestra playing in the hotel.

Letty Lynton and *Huddle* from the same studio have more music, but in *Huddle* this is, in part, college songs rather than background. Orchestras of various sizes are used in recording. Generally the small orchestra is favored. "Much more of an effect can often be obtained with a violin solo than with a full orchestra," said Dr. Axt. "In fact, we are, I believe, gradually working toward the small ensemble."

Original music is being much aimed for, provided there is sufficient time allowed for its composition. Both Dr. Axt and Max Steiner, at R.-K.-O. Radio, are active in creating the original score for the picture. Steiner is credited with no end of industry in this direction. He was educated in Vienna in the art, and had an active association with the theater in London and New York. The score of *Symphony of Six Million* is the result of his efforts.

One thing accomplished by original scores is the avoidance of complications due to the much-entangled foreign copyright laws. It veritably takes a whole legal department to solve the perplexities of obtaining permission to use certain tunes abroad, and some compositions are under an almost absolute ban as applies to motion pictures.

Orchestras, as such, are not kept under regular contract at the studios. Leo Forbstein, in charge of Warner activities, seems to seek considerable variety in this field. He arranges for various jazz organizations as they are needed for pictures, and according to their own special qualifications. Then besides he batons his own groups, especially when the need is for serious atmospheric accompaniments.

Outstanding among musical effects was the accompaniment to the transition from night to morning in *Street Scene*, and this attracted especial attention to Alfred Newman, as head of the United Artists department, even though a very brief episode. It showed deftly and surely how much music could mean in creating an effect. Much music of the lighter order is, of course, in prospect in the Eddie Cantor feature, while Al Jolson's picture may have a well-nigh continuous score.[22]

Nathaniel Finston at Paramount has received great credit for his supervision of the music in film. In *This Is the Night* many unique effects were also created, which played an integral part in the action of the Chevalier pictures, which have been admirably scored.[23]

From *Los Angeles Times*, May 22, 1932, B16.

6

DEBATES ON THE FUTURE OF
MUSIC IN SOUND FILMS

As was neatly summarized in Edwin Schallert's article for the *Los Angeles Times*,[1] film music experienced a number of "sea changes" in the few short years between 1927 (when the new medium of sound film was generally embraced by the public) and 1932 (when the first glimmers of classical-style scoring practice appeared on the horizon). But even as certain landmark scores by Max Steiner were in effect establishing the model for what was soon to come,[2] many film-game participants in the mid-1930s not only wondered about what the future might be but also argued about what that future *should* be.

The first two pieces gathered in this section represent differing Western points of view. On the one hand, there is the American-born but Paris-trained composer/critic Virgil Thomson, reminiscing wistfully about the apparently good old days of silent film and snidely remarking—in what is likely his first public comment on film music—that the only "worthy" film music he had lately experienced came almost exclusively from the pens of European composers. On the other hand, there is Clarence Raybould, a British musician whose reputation never ascended to the heights of Thomson's but who nevertheless—doubtless owing to his years in the recording industry—has wise things to say about the film industry's need to improve the audio quality of its recorded music.

The third and fourth pieces in this section come from the Soviet Union, where sound-film technology moved at a pace quite different from that experienced in the West and where film's narrative content was typically concerned with matters that went far beyond mere entertainment. The 1935 article by critic Azary Azarin sheds light on the often troubled Soviet mode of production and at the same time illustrates how importantly Soviet filmmakers took the role of music. The 1936 article by composer Nikolai Kryukov boldly charts a path for Soviet filmmaking's immediate future, some of whose elements—the dramatically provocative use of pre-existing music, for example, and the purposeful incorporation of "noise" into a soundtrack—did not begin to figure into Western films until the 1960s and 1970s.

6.1 A LITTLE ABOUT MOVIE MUSIC

Virgil Thomson

Virgil Thomson (1896–1989) was an American composer who not only wrote prolifically for the concert hall and the opera house but also provided scores for several documentary

79

films. These were the 1936 The Plow That Broke the Plains *(a short commissioned by the U.S. government's Resettlement Administration and directed by Pare Lorentz), the 1938* The River *(likewise a short sponsored by the Resettlement Administration and directed by Lorentz), and the 1948* Louisiana Story *(a 78-minute quasi-documentary narrative film commissioned by the Standard Oil Company and directed by Robert J. Flaherty); despite the fact that* Louisiana Story *was obviously a public-relations vehicle designed to muster support for the oil company's environmentally unfriendly drilling in the Mississippi delta, Thomson's contribution in 1949 became the first—and thus far only—film score to be awarded the prestigious Pulitzer Prize for Music.*

Quite aside from his occasional scores for documentary films, Thomson looms large in the discussion of film music because of his outspoken and influential written commentaries. In 1933, at the time he penned the article for Modern Music *that is reproduced here, Thomson was still a relatively young composer struggling to find an identity that meshed his evolving Americanist sentiments with all the European refinement that he had learned, beginning in 1921, at the feet of Nadia Boulanger and other Paris-based teachers. In 1940, after having resided for the previous fifteen years more in France than in the United States, Thomson accepted the position of chief music critic for the New York Herald-Tribune. He held this bully pulpit until 1954, over the course of his tenure becoming—by dint not just of the sharpness of his opinion but also the sheer brilliance of his writing—the preeminent figure in American music journalism.*

As a critic, Thomson on several occasions addressed the matter of film music. The most positive of his accounts took the form of an article headlined "Hollywood's Best" that appeared in the New York Herald-Tribune *on April 10, 1949;[3] in it, Thomson deigned to heap praise on Aaron Copland (for his score for Lewis Milestone's 1949* The Red Pony*) but for the most part focused on "worthy" film music by such European and Russian composers as Georges Auric, William Walton, Dmitry Shostakovich, and Sergei Prokofiev. His most negative appraisal came not in a newspaper article but in a portion of a chapter of a 1939 book that Thomson published just before (and which perhaps led to) his appointment to the* Herald-Tribune's *music desk; in the "Music and Photography" section of a chapter titled "How to Write a Piece, or Functional Design in Music,"[4] Thomson not only attacked what he felt was Hollywood's essential insincerity but also argued that the underscore of a Hollywood-style narrative film, so long as it was made subservient to dialogue and was constantly being interrupted, could not possibly have any real musical value.*

Thomson's bitter comments about Hollywood aesthetics were perhaps prompted by the fact—as reported by George Antheil—that "from the Hollywood point of view" his score for The Plow That Broke the Plains *seemed distinctly "amateurish."[5] But even in this early article Thomson's bias toward the European approach is clearly apparent.*

The trouble with most movie-music is its lack of continuity. The cinema is naturally a discontinuous medium. Narrative or dramatic continuity is achieved therein only by effort and much care, against the grain, as it were, like playing *legato* on the trombone. Musical accompaniment should be an aid to continuity. It should establish and preserve an atmosphere, a tone of augmenting or unrolling drama. It should envelope and sustain a narrative the cinematographic recounting of which is after all only a series of very short incidents seen from different angles. To break the music with every shot or change of scene is an error and ineffective.

Curiously enough, the best union of movies and music that has ever been made, so far as I know, is a work in which this "ineffectiveness" is committed so systematically that it is not ineffective at all but a strong procedure. I mean *Entr' acte*, film by Francis Picabia and René Clair, music by Erik Satie.[6]

This is not, however, a narrative film. It is pure dada and *jeux d'esprit*. The successive incidents are of similar or progressively changing length. The accompaniment is made up of little musical blocks, each of which is a repeating-formula continued without any change till time for the succeeding one which accompanies a succeeding incident. Each of these musical units is stationary within itself and goes nowhere. The succession of them is, as in the case of the film-incidents, the continuity and the form. The whole is like a train of dominoes. A very brilliant success is thus achieved, as in cubist painting, by the elimination of a major difficulty, in this case that of narrative continuity.

The Russian film *Odna*, on the other hand, tells a simple and continuous story. Shostakovich's musical accompaniments, most of them quite pleasing in themselves, tend by their abrupt changings to break up the drama rather than to continue it.[7]

I have often felt that the playing of movements from the better-known symphonic repertory, as was commonly done for the pre-talkie pictures, and as is still done in small theatres where a gramophone is the only available music, I have often felt that the artistic result of that habit was superior to that achieved by the most expressive and competent modern music. Honegger has made movie music.[8] So have Ibert and Rivier and many others.[9] With the exception of Auric's music in the court-yard scene of Cocteau's *La Vie* [sic] *d'un Poète*,[10] which is very fine music, I have never heard anything especially written for the films which seemed to be as beautiful and as appropriate as those tremendously dramatic, intimately dramatic (like close-ups), narratively dramatic movements from the symphonies of Beethoven and Mozart that used to envelope us and carry us along through the sorrows of Lilian Gish, the epic adventures of Fred Thompson and of Buck Jones. If any one piece deserves the palm for services to cinematographic art, it is easily, I should say, Schubert's *Unfinished Symphony*, which year in and year out has provided an appropriate dramatic continuity for a larger number of stories than any other single piece classic or modern.

Another trouble with movie-music is the tendency to introduce song-numbers into talking-plays. The trouble rather is not the tendency, which is legitimate like any other tendency, but the way of doing it. Songs add to entertainment, but they break up the show unless the incident of the singing has some real place in the story. Even then, the change of medium is very expensive to the story. The problem of the film-with-songs is one which the French talkies have made peculiarly their own and for the solution of which they have come nearer to providing a good working-formula than have any other group of studios. I except isolated successes like Mae West's *She Done Him Wrong* and Kurt Weill's *Dreigroschenoper*. (Personally, I find the songs in the latter film interminable, very heavy, and quite over-powering to the effectiveness of the rest of the film.)[11]

The films of the French Paramount and of René Clair are, however, somewhere close to an effective dramatico-musical form. The integrating center of that form is always a scene in a night-club. The night-club is just as important and as rigidly *réglementaire* to the French talkie as the ballet is to the French opera. In Clair's films it occasionally takes the less conventional form of a *fête de famille*, a wedding, or a household celebration of some kind; but it is always there. It occurs about three fourths of the way through the picture. It shows dancing and singing, the throwing of confetti and the drinking of champagne. It is the moment when the story and the music become really coordinated.

A third movie problem and one that has been very little worked at is the making of films to accompany music. Animated cartoons are usually made this way. At least the writing of the music usually preceded the actual drawing of the pictures. The result is a closer collaboration than is possible by the reverse process. As in choreography, the story is determined first of all and outlined into its main sections with appropriate timing. Then the music is written. Finally, the visible thing is made to fit the details of the musical inspiration.

There is no reason, in fact, why movies should not be made to accompany all sorts of classic pieces, as ballets have been danced to music of Schumann and Chopin and even Bach. Schumann's *Carnaval*, Rimsky's *Schéhérazade*, Weber's *Invitation à la Valse*, Debussy's *Afternoon of a Faun*, have been in no way demeaned, rather enhanced in all eyes, from having provided inspiration for some of the most agreeable choreography of our century.

Henwar Rodakiewicz's *Portrait of a Young Man* was made on a musical inspiration, Dvorak's *New World Symphony*, if I mistake not. The failure to tie up the musical basis and its visible expression into a single sound-film, a procedure impracticable to amateurs at the time of the film's making, removed from the film its *raison d'être* and left the spectators confused before a series of very beautiful but empty shots of movement in natural scenery.

The other kind of movie-music I wish to note is the case of music used not as accompaniment but as part of the drama. The quotation of familiar hymns of popular tunes to accentuate or to comment on a situation is of course an old and very useful device. Here the music becomes more than tune. The most remarkable usage of this kind that I know is the playing of *Tristan and Isolde* in *L'Age d'Or* of Bunuel and Dali. In a film containing nearly every subversive gesture imaginable, there is, curiously, no attempt made to violate the bourgeois ideal of simultaneous love. On the contrary, that ideal as represented by the music of *Tristan and Isolde*, is the one element of bourgeois civilization that remains intact. Its frustration provokes the catastrophe of revolution. *Tristan*, as the form and model for sexual desire and experience, is played all during the scene of erotic frustration. It does not express the drama that is taking place. It is there as an actor or a chorus calling attention to what is not taking place, or rather to what is taking place in a very different way from that depicted by the music. The music is there for its associations and its prestige as well as for its character. It is the official, the impressive, the impotent god. A god, nevertheless, whose desecration provokes disaster. It is heard in close-up and at a distance. Through ten minutes of shifting scenes it continues unimpeded, only giving place at the final frustration to the drums of revolution.

From *Modern Music* 10, no. 4 (May–June 1933), 188–91.

6.2 MUSIC AND THE SYNCHRONIZED FILM

Clarence Raybould

Clarence Raybould (1886–1972) was a British musician known throughout his long career as a pianist, conductor, and composer of works for the concert hall. His contribution to film scoring is limited to a handful of documentary films made around the time he wrote the brief article by which he is represented here; all dating from 1933, these include Paul Rotha's Contact *and* Rising Tide *(about airplane manufacture and international shipping, respectively) and, for the Steuart Films studio,* Flight to India *and* Where the Road Begins *(about international air travel and automobile manufacture).*

From 1927 until 1931 Raybould worked as an accompanist for the Columbia Graphophone company, and from 1936 until 1945 he was an assistant conductor for the BBC. In both capacities, but especially as a conductor, he made a prodigious number of recordings. It seems hardly surprising, then, that he was keenly attuned to recordings, not just to evolving studio techniques but also to the final results.

Some of what Raybould offers in this article for an early issue of the trade journal Sight and Sound *echoes admonitions that had circulated since the days of the nickelodeon-era columnists, to the effect that films are served not so much by musical accompaniments in general as by music carefully selected—and likely composed afresh—for the purposes of supporting specific scenes. But most of the article concerns what Raybould perceives as the relatively poor audio quality projected by the sound-on-film recording technology that, in England in 1933, was still primitive. He rightly observes: "There has as yet been no film recording of an orchestra, or even a part of one, to my knowledge which can stand comparison with the standard tone-quality of the best gramophone records." Also rightly, as though he were predicting what would transpire later in the decade, he advises: "There* must *be expended the care and research on sound-film recording which the gramophone companies have already devoted to their task."*

In view of the public revulsion against the flood of dialogue in so many films of the last three or four years and the consequent tendency to enlist again the aid of music, sometimes even to the exclusion of the spoken word or at least retaining only an intermittent commentary, the comparatively new art of synchronized musical accompaniment or description may perhaps be discussed with equal interest to both sides of film production—the commercial and the artistic.

When, at the end of 1932, I was asked to undertake the task of supplying music for the then forthcoming film *Contact*, it was with considerable diffidence that I accepted the invitation.[12] This was not due to lack of interest. On the contrary, the theme of the film appealed strongly to my imagination. But I was fearful of being unable to put into practice certain ideas on the subject of the marriage of picture and sound which I had been considering for some little while. Naturally, I had hoped to be able to write new music for the complete picture, but in the end, for various reasons, the time available was so short that it became necessary to select already existing music and, on the score of economy, non-copyright music. That the result, though largely a compromise, has been favourably received reveals the interest displayed by the public in orchestral music. But at the same time it clearly proves that any attempt to adapt already existing music to a new conception in terms of film cannot of necessity produce a wholly satisfactory result.

Apart from the difficulty of finding existing music of the right nature for any particular film sequence, it is infinitely harder to satisfy artistic standards which should hold good in this alliance of sight and sound when, to meet the demands of the changing moods of the film, the unfortunate music must be left unfinished, hacked about, loose bars sewn up or otherwise maltreated. It is clear that the only successful method of setting music to a film, especially where there is no spoken commentary, is for the music to be specially composed. And it is here that our practical difficulties really begin.

Music, by comparison with action such as expressed by the visual images of film, develops slowly. A mere pictorialisation in music of a succession of film 'shots' will not result in a satisfactory musical phrase or movement. On the other hand, a reversal of the procedure, attempting to illustrate visually a definite piece of music, will slow down and govern the shot-construction of the film. The two jobs of construction must be undertaken together, with a certain elasticity on either side. So far, the elasticity has almost wholly been on the part of the musical composer.

The type of film, however, in which music is most required at the moment calls for a spoken commentary, in which case the music must provide only an unobtrusive background to the speaking voice. The suppressed nature of the music in such films, where it is constantly being faded-down or faded-up to accommodate the speaker, quite obviously gives the musical composer no opportunity at all, and it is quite frequent to find gramophone records employed in place of a living orchestra. This, despite the fact that in the process of 'dubbing' the intrinsic defects of the records are more than doubled. Some attempts are being made to construct the film so that the necessary commentary falls in blocks, separated by quite long intervals during which music alone is played. The results of the experiment will be watched with interest.

Few film producers so far reveal any real recognition of the value of good music to the cinema. The ignorance which exists among the executive powers regarding music is almost unbelievable. It appears to be their opinion that if a few hack musicians are supplied to a conductor, the resulting 'selections' constitute a 'special musical accompaniment.' They fail to appreciate that the visual appeal of the film can be doubled by the accompaniment of the right music. There must be at least a proper understanding on the part of movie producers and directors of the significance of film before the synchronized film can progress to a higher plane. The musician must be given time and opportunity to get 'into' the picture. He should be able to work out all his musical ideas step by step with the progress of the visual sequences and evolve from the tedious process of a mechanical measurement of feet and frames an accompaniment which will not only be an illumination of the camera's story but a musical entity in itself.

Assuming that this ideal has been achieved and the musical score, upon which so much time and thought have been expended, is ready for synchronisation to the picture, there still remains the problem of adequate recording on to film of the beauty of tone, balance and colour of orchestration upon which the score so much relies. In brief, the musician is at the mercy of a well-meaning body of sound-engineers who cannot yet reproduce the tone of a single violin adequately, let alone a mass of strings; whose idea of the characteristic tone of an oboe seems to be founded on tooth-comb and tissue-paper; and who, when criticised, think themselves unjustly abused because the banjo, the plucked string and the saxophone come off fairly well in recording. Research by sound engineers is badly needed on the recording of sound qualities for reproduction at high amplification. There has as yet been no film recording of an orchestra, or even a part of one, to my knowledge which can stand comparison with the standard tone-quality of the best gramophone records. It is of no avail to reply that film is not disc. There must be expended the care and research on sound-film recording which the gramophone companies have already devoted to their task.

From *Sight and Sound* 2, no. 7 (Autumn 1933), 80–81.

6.3 MUSICAL SURPRISES

(Muzïkal'nïye syurprizï)

Azary Azarin

Azary Mikhaílovich Azarin (1897–1937) was a son of Mikhaíl Borisovich Messerer, founder of the Moscow Art Theater; he was the first of his siblings to embark on a successful career as an actor, and he took on the new surname only so as not to be overshadowed by his distinguished father. His work as a dramatic actor was by and large limited to the stage, but he keep abreast of developments in film, and by the early 1930s he was regularly expressing opinions on film in such publications as the Moscow-based monthly Kino.

The short article reproduced here is remarkable for the large amount of pointed criticism it levels toward what at the time was not just the Soviet Union's largest film studio but also the designated showcase outlet for an agency, called Soyuzkino, that had been instituted in 1930 for the sake of monitoring the content of all *Soviet films. The Moscow studio to which Azary directs his attention dates back to 1915, when entrepreneur Mikhail Semenovich Trofimov launched a profit-oriented enterprise called "Rus'film." In 1924—after the revolution of 1917 and the 1922 election of Josef Stalin as General Secretary of the new Soviet Union's governing Communist Party, but more specifically after the death, in January 1924, of the Soviet Union's founding head of state Vladimir Ilyich Lenin—the studio changed its name to the "Russian Film Studio of the International Workers Relief Agency" (abbreviated, in Russian, as Mezhrabpom-Rus'). In 1928 the studio changed its name to the arguably more euphonious Mezhrabpomfilm, and eight years later it would change its name yet again to Soyuzdetfilm.*

Azarin's article is interesting at the very least for its account of the confusion that seemed to reign, regarding the use of music, at Mezhrabpomfilm in the early 1930s. But it becomes more interesting—quite intriguing, actually—when one considers that the article is a brazen attack not on individual film composers but on the organizational procedures of a newly established state-run agency. It is probably just coincidence that less than two years after the publication of this article Azarin died, quite prematurely, of what was diagnosed as a heart attack brought on by stress.

Recently at meetings and in the studios and corridors of Mezhrabpomfilm, there has been much talk criticizing music. Because of [music], films have not been released on time. In fact, the scores[13] for *In the Hero's Footsteps* and *The Month of May* were ready well in advance of the final editing, but for *At the Bluest Sea* the score was very much behind schedule.

It is not music, of course, that is at fault; the guilty parties are those who create the music. Apparently nobody wished for this, yet nevertheless it happened that the composer Pototsky was asked to compose music for these three films.[14] The directors—V[ladimir] Nemolyayev, I[gor] Savchenko, and B[oris] Barnet—all hoped that their films would press forward, and especially because of this the composer was allotted [what seemed to be] sufficient time. The same composer Pototsky hoped that the pictures would be filmed in the usual way, according to their schedules, and that there would not be revisions to the scripts.

The opposite happened. Three times the thematic plan of *The Month of May* was revised. And because the music had been written before the start of filming, it was necessary to change it significantly. The other two films were delayed in production. All [three] were supposed to be released in time for the anniversary of October.[15] But they were not released on time, chiefly because their scores had not yet been finished. The composer could not simultaneously complete music for three films. He managed only to finish the music for two of them: *The Month of May* and *In the Hero's Footsteps*, both of which were released in December [1934]. For *At the Bluest Sea*, music had to be re-ordered from a different composer, Z. Feldman, who was required to fill the order by 15 December.[16] So because of inattention to music, all three films were late.

Indeed. Is it conceivable to order at one time three scripts from one writer? It would seem that the answer would be: "no." And yet it occurred to no one at Mezhrabpomfilm that it might be just as inconceivable to order music for three films from a single composer. This is not just an accident. Although sound films are now filled with music, much less concern is given to the music than to the scenarios. This can be illustrated by many examples.

At Mezhrabpomfilm the composer has little contact with the director. Film doubtless would benefit if the composer took part in the preparation of the script. And as far as the [value of] a musician's contributions to the sonic aspects of a director's script is concerned, that should be self-evident. But these are rules that more often than not go completely unobserved.

There are exceptions. At the very same Mezhrabpomfilm studio, D[avid] Blok and director Y[akov] Protazanov worked together on the script for *The Strangeness of Love* and *The Dowryless Girl*.[17] V[ladimir] Kryukov together with K[onstantin] Eggert worked on a sound portion of the director's script.[18] But these exceptions simply prove the point that the composer can, and should, get involved in a project even before filming begins.

We are used to the idea of a scenario being discussed among various artistic workers long before a film actually goes into production. Often this results in practical, and significant, changes that only benefit the common cause. But typically these discussions do not involve those in the musical circles, and they seldom concern sketches or even finished scores destined for one film or another. Might not involvement in the process be of benefit not just to the composer but also to the film?

Mezhrabpomfilm attracts prominent composers. Among them are M. [*sic*] Shostakovich, V[issarion] Shebalin, Yu[ri] Shaporin, S[ergey] Vasilenko, and others. But not once has the artistic administration of Mezhrabpomfilm brought together these fully competent people to discuss the musical design of the most important films, to talk about the quality of production, about the correspondence of music to a film's images, about the place of musical phrases in this or that episode, about recording technology, about the perception of sound, and so on. And it is necessary to do all of this on a daily basis.

To become more closely involved with cinematography, to grasp its creative and technological processes, is an honorable duty for Soviet composers. All of these matters should be subjects for discussion at the All-Union conference on film production.

From *Kino 57* (December 11, 1935), 3. (Translation by Kevin Bartig)

6.4 THE EXPERIENCE OF THE COMPOSER

(Opït kompozitora)

Nikolai Kryukov

Nikolai Nikolayevich Kryukov (1908–61) was born in Moscow and like his older brother Vladimir[19] studied at the Moscow Conservatory, where his composition teacher was Sergey Vasilenko. Although Kryukov produced numerous arrangements of Russian folksongs and orchestral suites based on themes native to various of the Soviet republics, his career was devoted primarily to the production of music for films. His initial projects were scores for the 'silent' films Battleship Potemkin *and* The Heir to Genghis Khan.[20] *Kryukov's first recorded film score was for the 1932* Business and People *to which he alludes here; after that, he composed music for some three dozen Soviet films. For his efforts in film-music composition, Kryukov was twice awarded the Soviet Union's prestigious Stalin Prize.*

For the politically minded student of film music, Kryukov's brief article for the monthly periodical Kino *is noteworthy not just because Kryukov writes for the most part in the first person plural but also because—in effect speaking for all Soviet composers of film music—he daringly offers a set of "demands" for general artistic improvements. For readers who opt to focus only on techniques, the article is remarkable at the very least for its prescient exploration of the possibilities of what Kryukov calls "noise-music" and for its description of the "three paths" by which pre-existing music might be put to dramatic use in the context of a film score.*

We must work on examining the musical and sound design of our films. Sound is the most important part of our work. Because of this, I would like to share [my] experiences of working with sound on the film *We Are from Kronstadt*.[21]

Our first demand concerns the organic nature of sound and image. The matter here is not simply the relationship between sound and image but, rather, their equality and their indivisibility. Often a director, in filming a picture, does not take into account the specific details of sound; he does not consider that sound makes its own demands on the behavior of the actors and, indeed, on the compositional substance of the entire film. This being the case, [those of us who work with film sound] have to make special efforts to ensure that the final results indeed feature a union of sound and image.

Our second demand concerns simplicity and economy of means. For us this is not simply a worn and empty phrase but a concrete problem of production. Our general principle has to do with a reduction, to a minimum, of the quantity of a film's sonic elements. [In other words, we seek to] cast off everything that is superfluous.

Our third demand is for the motivation for sound in film. We categorically object to the idea of illustrative music.[22] We must always have an answer to these questions: for what reason does sound enter the film, what is the sound's function? The variety of motivations for filmic sound of course is inexhaustible, yet it is [precisely] here that we find the secret of the dramatic composition of sound.

The following is [also] necessary: that every sound be directed. The presence of indifferent, unnecessary little sounds is intolerable. Each sound must have a logical and emotional direction.

[Vis-à-vis this,] especially important is the idea of [so-called] noise-music, that is, the practically inconspicuous mixing into an accompanying score of the [potentially] musical elements (rhythm, timbre, intonations[23]) of a realistic sonic backdrop. Noise-music offers a huge range of emotional expressiveness, and it colossally widens the arsenal of sound techniques. Work on noise-music was begun by me in *Business and People*, *Petersburg Nights*, and others—I would suggest even in *We Are from Kronstadt*.[24]

Working on musical-historical folklore, we strove to reformulate it. It seems to us that *We Are from Kronstadt* outlines three paths toward the refashioning of folklore. The first path involves the rethinking of musically inviolable songs through a sound-image complex, through the function of the song in the general [filmic] composition; examples include the use of the "Internationale" during the attack scene and the use of "Bravely, Comrades, In Step!" at the start of the film.[25] The second path involves the musical reworking of existing songs, as it is done [in *We Are from Kronstadt*] with the old revolutionary navy song "The Sea Groaned in Anger."[26] The third path involves the use of intonations and rhythms characteristic of the old revolutionary music as the foundation for entirely new compositions.

This is how the infantry march to the entrenchment was done. I did not use specific musical quotations; [it was sufficient for me simply to refer to] the spirit—to the overall melodic-rhythmic essence—of the old revolutionary songs.

For it was on this [spirit, and essence] that we based all our sonic work for *We Are from Kronstadt*.

From *Kino* 79 (April 6, 1936), 3. (Translation by Kevin Bartig)

Part 3

MUSIC IN THE CLASSICAL-STYLE FILM

7

PRACTICAL ADVICE AS FILM MUSIC'S "CLASSICAL STYLE" TAKES SHAPE

By the mid-1930s the technical problems that had plagued pioneering film composers had for the most part been solved. The cumbersome and unreliable sound-on-disc method of synchronizing music with the filmic image, so revolutionary in the late 1920s, was now a thing of the past. Multi-channel mixers that allowed engineers complete control over the balance of a soundtrack's three components—dialogue, sound effects, and music—were in wide use. The audio fidelity of sound-on-film recording, while still noticeably inferior to that of commercial phonograph discs, nevertheless represented an enormous improvement over what the new optical recording technology had offered just a few years before.

Just as significant, by this time the film industry—at least in the West, where news of what seemed to "work" with audiences circulated even more quickly than did news of technological developments—had settled on a more or less standard way of handling underscore in the context of a narrative film. Filmmakers no longer argued over whether films should or should not have supportive music, or whether such music should be drawn from a familiar repertoire or be newly composed. Likely impressed by the box-office success of a handful of films released in 1932 and 1933 by RKO under the supervision of producer David O. Selznick and featuring music by Max Steiner,[1] studio executives throughout the West concurred almost simultaneously that their products could indeed be well-served by the discreet use of freshly composed underscore. Just as narrative film in general in the mid-1930s was fast approaching its state of "classical perfection," so was film music moving rapidly toward its classical-style conventions.[2]

The producer and three composers represented here contributed to the formulation of the never "official" yet generally adopted conventions of the classical-style film score. These conventions called for, among other things, music that in most instances played a role subordinate to both dialogue and visual imagery, music that in more or less obvious ways supported the film's action and emotional situations, music that regularly identified certain filmic entities by means of memorable themes, music that provided continuity between scenes, and music that, with its use of an overall style and just a few recurring themes, lent a sense of cohesion to an entire film.[3]

It is hardly surprising that the three composers—one based in England, the others based in Hollywood—went about their business in their own ways and complained vociferously about problems unique to their particular situations. Nor is it surprising that they harbored conflicting opinions regarding not just how certain local problems might be solved but also how film music might, presumably in the near future, be bettered. Indeed, the differences in these accounts by Arthur Benjamin, Franz Waxman, and George Antheil strikingly prove the point that as late as 1940 film music was still just *on the verge* of settling into an international norm that, once accepted, would prevail for the next decade and a half. But more remarkable than the accounts' spirited differences are the several themes they hold in common.

In contrast to producer Selznick, the composers seem to be in staunch agreement that films are best served if their musical support consists, for the most part, of originally created material. In the late 1930s Waxman and certain other composers, such as Max Steiner and Erich Wolfgang Korngold, were well on their way to becoming film-industry "stars," and it was thus very much to their personal advantage—and to the advantage of all composers whose names around this time began to appear in ever-larger type in opening-credit sequences—to promote the notion that a potent film score was for the most part the work of a single artist/craftsman.

At the same time, all four of these writers suggest—albeit sometimes only in subtle ways—that the music in their films depended upon effective collaboration among production personnel and the yeoman work of a veritable army of orchestrators, recording engineers, and film-music editors. Their comments on time constraints and technological limitations often project a negative tone, yet it is precisely with their quibbles and complaints that they affirm the undeniable fact that the creation of film music has long been a collaborative process. The late 1930s was indeed the period of ascendancy of the "star" film-music composer, but it was also the period that witnessed the establishment of the efficient and thoroughly professionalized studio music department.

7.1 FILM MUSIC

Arthur Benjamin

Arthur Benjamin (1893–1960) was born in Australia but studied, and for the most part based his career, in England. In the 1920s he established himself as both a composer and a concert pianist. Although he produced more or less "serious" works in virtually all the classical music formats, he was best known during his lifetime—and likely remains best known today—for the orchestral version of his jaunty 1938 Jamaican Rumba.

Benjamin made his film-music debut in 1934 with Alfred Hitchcock's The Man Who Knew Too Much, *whose Albert Hall sequence (featuring the diegetic "Storm Cloud Cantata") he calls attention to in this article without naming himself as composer.[4] The next year he provided music for Bernard Browne's documentary* Wharves and Strays *and the feature-length films* The Clairvoyant *(dir. Maurice Elvey),* The Scarlet Pimpernel *(dir. Harold Young), and* The Turn of the Tide *(dir. Norman Walker). In 1936 and 1938 he scored a few more British films (*Lobsters, Wings of the Morning, The Return of the Pimpernel, Under the Red Robe*) and then emigrated to Canada, where he spent the wartime years writing concert music and, influentially, organizing and hosting radio broadcasts of contemporary British music. Upon his return to England, Benjamin wrote scores for Walter Forde's 1947* The Crowthers of Bankdam *and Alexander Korda's 1948* An Ideal Husband, *but most of his post-war energies were focused on operas, chamber music, and orchestral works.*

The article that Benjamin wrote in 1937 for The Musical Times *is notable both for its expression of aesthetic attitudes toward film music, and film sound, in general and for its detailed description of the process of composing and recording film music. While the aesthetic attitudes are staunchly European, the techniques—arguably in the England of 1937 still somewhat behind the times—are thoroughly American.*

If music be the Cinderella of the arts, cinema music is one of the Ugly Sisters.

Although some composers well known in the concert-world have written for the films—an entirely new aspect of their art—their efforts have so far met with little appreciation from the makers, and none at all from the critics.

Film directors and producers in England (one excepted) show little feeling for the music in films. But to them Publicity is God and the box-office the Ark of the Covenant.

So this article is written to suggest that the film-music of such composers as Richard Addinsell, Arthur Bliss, Benjamin Britten, John Greenwood, and William Walton should be criticized seriously.[5] Their work has been almost entirely ignored by the press. Surely it should be recognized as a primarily emotional and organic force?

It cannot be denied that the music in any film of quality is becoming of more importance every day. The intelligent film-goer will remember the use of music in the opening sequences of *The Informer*, the Albert Hall sequence in *The Man Who Knew Too Much*, the discord when the murdered man fell on to the organ keys in *Secret Agent* (Hitchcock understands music in films), the tinkling of the glass luster which became some rather strange chords in *My Man Godfrey*, the episode of the drum-taps in *La Kermesse Héroïque* (what spiciness this gave!), and the almost unbearable tenseness of the music which accompanied the end of *Mayerling*.[6]

In what way should one regard and judge music for films?

Outside cartoons (with what perfection Disney uses music!), film-music is mainly of two kinds, realistic or background; and background-music can be either dramatic or emotional.

It is unnecessary to say that realistic music happens where the sound synchronizes with an actual visual musical episode and that background-music happens where there is no reason for music other than that of heightening the emotion of an episode.

An example of the first kind occurs in the scene in *Henry the Eighth* where one of his wives sang to her own accompaniment on the lute.[7] For the second kind, look at the end of *Mayerling*. Unfortunately, realism is not always strictly sought, for in *Henry the Eighth* all but two of the lute-strings were broken and the song was accompanied by a harp (quite legitimate!) with some wood-wind.

Now the wood-wind was too loud, so we are led on to the question of how to combine realistic and background music. No aesthetic harm would have been done had the song been accompanied by a full orchestra used, very softly, to portray the emotions of the scene while the harp and voice were placed well in the foreground realistically—very good microphone technique.

Again, in a film about Nell Gwynne, Nell was dancing on the stage of Drury Lane to a little orchestra of about four antique instruments; but, booming forth from the loudspeaker, the Edward German Dances were heard on a full orchestra![8] This was a place where realism was ruined without excuse on the pleas of emotional background. It was simply bad art.

Let me quote from an article by Louis le Sidaner in the *Mercure de France* on 'L'importance du Cinématographe':

Talented composers such as Jacques Ibert or A. Honegger have not disdained to write music according to classical procedure, writing music on incidental lines, so to speak; whereas the true cinematographic music of the future will be made of quite other elements, such as the noise of flowing water; the grinding of carriage wheels; the stridency of a policeman's whistle; the languorous voice of a "vamp"; the chug-chug of a motor; the irregular tic-tac of a typewriter; the barking of a dog; even silences; a man sneezing; church bells; the caustic laugh of a "boulevardier"; the cry of a child who suffers or is frightened; the song of the nightingale; the grunts of a pig or the tender murmur of happy lovers. Up till now we have hardly touched on these things.[9]

Some of these items have been successfully done (the old tug-boat engines in that charming short film *Wharves and Strays*,[10] for example); but to try and imitate a languorous 'vamp' or a grunting pig would carry realism to an absurdity of use only in a 'comic.'

Background-music also can be (indeed, it too often is) ridiculous. There still are produced American films in which one sees a tender love-scene in the depths of a wood where, suddenly, an orchestra breaks in with a jazzy waltz!

It should be a rule that background-music should take the colouring either of the surroundings or the emotion of the scene. Concurrent with this one can superimpose realistic orchestral noises. An example is *Wings of the Morning* at the moment where the lovers walk through the gardens.[11] The feeling of the background is tender and pastoral, but at those points where they pass the weir and waterfall suggestive orchestral sounds are added. Utmost care should be taken to ensure that the background be psychologically apt. In spite of the general excellence of the score of *Mayerling*, Honegger made a great mistake in one scene—that sequence where Marie goes to the palace for her very first meeting with the Prince. She has worshipped this man as a sort of 'Prince Charming.' Surely the mood should be one of youthful, innocent expectancy as she goes through the long corridors of that rococo palace. Instead, the music has a rather sinister quality suggesting the tragic future (of which she was, of course, quite ignorant) rather than the expectant present.

For sheer delight one turns to the French films of René Clair. Here, as in the opening sequence of *The Informer*, is the closest co-operation between director and musician *before* the 'shooting' of the film begins.

That co-operation is sadly lacking in this country. Often the composer has not met the film-director. Yet of the finest films, one American (*The Informer*), one British (*The Man Who Knew Too Much*), and one French (*Le Million*) have absolutely depended for their best scenes on the accompanying music.[12]

Now for the actual making of music.

'Flair' is essential. That is, the successful film-composer must have the gift of summing up the atmosphere of a scene quickly. He will then find that the rhythm of any scene will get into his subconscious memory, and so when the music is recorded, the rhythms fall to certain actions in the picture where, had he consciously tried, he would have failed.

The composer should put away any idea of using an orchestra in the Straussian, Elgarian, or even in the Debussian sense. Concert scoring and microphone scoring are vastly different. And although the latter would 'come off' in the concert-room, the former would often be muddy and dull through the 'mike' (Americanisms are *de rigeur* in the film studios!).

Composers have had to sit up all night rescoring work which the microphone refused to take—waste and expense for the producing company.

Elaborate counterpoint or 'symphonic' writing is entirely lost. Counterpoint, if used, should be extremely simple and clearly scored. The composer has not much time, as a rule, for the music is the last thing thought about by the producers. As much as thirty-five minutes (almost the length of a symphony) of music has been composed *and* scored for full orchestra in six days! So a symphonically complicated score is out of the question. The composer must be quick in the uptake.

If the composer is capable (and if the contract is signed!), here is the usual procedure.

Of any scene to be 'shot' to music, the composer is given the length in film footage. This he converts into seconds—90 feet to 60 seconds. The composer may well say, 'This is ideal'; but he lives in a fool's paradise, for often, after recording, the director decides to cut some action. A wily composer is careful that in his film work a bar or two can be cut here and there at a moment's notice.

For the most part, the music is written to the film. This is how it is done.

When the film is rough-cut, the composer and the music-director (sometimes with the film-director) see it through as often as they wish until they can decide where the music should go and the exact points where it should start and stop.

The composer should take some MS paper with him, for those ideas which come in a flash, inspired by the first sight of the film, are often the best. Also, film-directors are liable to be impressed if a composer looks as though he has been suddenly touched by Apollo's finger!

The composer has now a few days until the film is finally cut, during which he can jot down tentative ideas. Then he can ask to see his special sections repeated on the screen. The chief cutter gives him the actual footage and his music must keep rigorously to that length.

While composing he is constantly in touch with his metronome and stop-watch, as sometimes scenes come to such figures as 2 minutes 27 2/3 seconds.

The music written and scored, the parts are copied; and then the fun commences.

Recording sessions last for three hours, usually 10–1 and 2–5, with two ten-minute breaks. But often with a rush job the recording goes on until the early hours of the morning. The difficulties are enormous. It needs but little imagination to understand that it is no easy matter to record a scene lasting four or five minutes with, perhaps, points 'en route' which have to be perfectly synchronized in music and action. The whole job is an extremely 'nervy' affair. Tempers become a little frayed.

A perfect 'take' is being made, balance perfect, everything going swimmingly; and then, a few bars from the end, a player makes a mistake, or a chair creaks. The whole thing is spoiled.

But here it must be said that (even to those foreign artists who make so many of our British films) the orchestral player in this country is a sort of miraculous being. Not only are his sight-reading and accuracy astounding, but also his ready understanding and his never-failing good humour, under most trying conditions.

'Balance' is made during rehearsal by either the music-director or the composer in the soundproof recording-room; the other conducts in the recording-theatre. They are in touch either by signal through the windows or by telephone. Often it is necessary to place certain instruments nearer to or farther from the microphone for the sake of balance. When balance is perfect and the music has been adequately rehearsed, it is decided to try a 'take.'

The lights in the theatre are lowered and the film is thrown on to a screen behind the orchestra where, of course, the conductor can see it. Suppose it is a 'gypsy scene.' The conductor says 'O.K. Turn 'em over.' That is a signal for the film and sound film to be speeded up. Someone announces 'Gypsy scene; Take 1 (or 2, or 3).'

The conductor waits until a certain number of flashes, each at one second's interval, appear on the screen. This gives him the exact moment to begin conducting and also allows for the exact synchronization of sight and sound at the final 'dubbing.' (Dubbing is that process where speech, natural sound, and music are all balanced on to the one film which acts as the eventual negative.)

If the 'take' is good, the conductor's 'O.K.—cut' comes as a relief. But if it has been spoilt, the language rises from American to a very succinct Anglo-Saxon.

And at least two 'takes' must be made of every scene for safety's sake.

The music being all recorded, the film is sent to the laboratory to be developed, where work goes on all through the night; and the next day the music-director, the composer, and the film-director hear all the 'takes' played back in order to choose the best. Sometimes a director (if he is not certain about his job) will cut a scene even after the music has been recorded. This leads to some unpleasant shocks to the composer, who finds that a bar or so of his music is missing and the resultant modulations rather surprising! But he need not worry. The public does not notice such little mishaps.

Good film-music must never unduly obtrude, but should be missed if it were absent.

The dubbing, as has been mentioned, completes the film. Dubbing, in this country, is not yet good. There seems to be a timidity lest the music should cover up any other sound. But they have mastered this abroad.

Walton's lovely pastoral music in *As You Like It* was almost completely lost every time a sheep said 'Ma-a-a.' One day it will be an essential part of a sound-engineer's training to be able to read a music score.

An amusing story is told of a film-director who, on hearing the music-director turn to the composer and say, during a 'play-back,' 'That was a lovely modulation!', broke in with: 'O.K., boy, If you like that one, get a lot like it and have 'em put in the library.'

From *The Musical Times* 78, no. 1133 (July 1937), 595–597.

7.2 ON THE HOLLYWOOD FRONT

George Antheil

With an outpouring of works in the most extreme modernist style, the American composer George Antheil (1900–59) after his move to Paris in the early 1920s quickly gained the attention, and affection, of critics affiliated with the musical avant-garde. Along with such colorfully titled piano pieces as Mechanisms, Sonata Sauvage, *and* Death of Machines, *Antheil's 1926* Ballet mécanique—*scored outrageously for an ensemble that included airplane propellers, electric bells, and sixteen player pianos, and intended to accompany an experimental silent film by Fernand Léger[13]—gave the composer an impressive reputation as an enfant terrible. Although his music took a turn toward the conservative after his return to the United States in 1927, Antheil capitalized on his early reputation and titled his 1945 autobiography* Bad Boy of Music.[14]

Antheil's autobiography remains of interest at least in part because of the considerable light it sheds on the relationship of music to filmmaking during the formative years of Hollywood's so-called classical style. After struggling for almost a decade to establish himself as an East Coast composer of concert music, Antheil in the mid-1930s gravitated toward Hollywood. His first assignment was for Paramount's 1935 Once in a Blue Moon *(dir. Ben Hecht), and the next year he provided the score for the same studio's lavish production of* The Plainsman *(dir. Cecil B. DeMille). Over the next two decades Antheil provided music for a dozen and a half Hollywood films, none of them especially remarkable yet all of them lucrative enough to provide the composer with a decent living. And through this entire time, even as he enjoyed Hollywood's financial rewards, Antheil complained bitterly about what he perceived as Hollywood's low artistic standards.*

In articles that at the same time reflected his own biases and reported more or less objectively on industry doings, Antheil in 1935 began writing on film music for the journal Modern Music. *The article presented here, which starkly measures European and Soviet film scoring against its American counterpart, is remarkable both for its harsh diatribe against Hollywood's "action-crazy" film music and for its hopeful predictions of an intelligent "movie music of the future."*

Film music—at least in Hollywood—may be roughly divided into three different categories. The first is synchronized to the action of the film, the second to the mood, and the third to the locale, that is, it attempts to show whether or not the action is going on in a bistro, Mexico, Atlantic City, or down in the South Seas with Dorothy Lamour.

The first category belongs to the very infancy of film music. Whenever a screen man would fall downstairs in the nickelodeon of yore, he was almost sure to be accompanied by a down-into-the bass glissando on the piano. When a close-up of a birdie signaled "Came the Dawn," birdie trills in the treble were *de rigueur.*

This first movie music, however, has had the direst of effects. As most Hollywoodian directors cut their teeth upon it, it has for them a certain sentimental allure; they cannot stop asking composers to write music that ties up inanely with every bit of the picture's action. In fact Hollywoodian music is "action-crazy."

Much, however, as I detest the literalness of most of Hollywood's movie music, I detest the European method of scoring even more. For European music usually plays so completely "against" the film to which it is "set," that one cannot imagine why it was placed there, except, perhaps, for the very good reason that the film composer had an octet, a symphony, and a couple of string quartets tucked away, and so decided that this sound track was as good an occasion to get them heard as any other.

That, alas, is also the impression this commentator gets when he hears most "art" films. I have looked at and listened to these long and pretentious pictures, and I have been confused. This, certainly, is not the movie music of the future, any more than the ridiculous "action music" of present day Hollywood is the movie music of the future.

I do believe, however, that there is a movie music of the future, and that it is already beginning to take form. A method and an esthetic for criticizing it has come to be born, not from Hollywood, but from the combined reasonable critical opinion of the world.

Having pondered over this matter for some four years, I come to the following conclusions about motion picture music:

(1) It must always have the sense of the picture at heart; after all it is picture music and not a demonstration of the composer's virtuosity in the various orchestral forms. This does not mean that music must only play *with* a picture; it can also play against it; in fact I believe that very often indeed it should play against it. But this "against" should be a definite and intended contrast, heightening the drama and the effect of the picture instead of merely drawing attention to the queer non-matching music.

(2) Motion pictures, whether made in Hollywood or Moscow, are made for audiences of millions. Therefore one of the principal problems of motion picture music is *simplicity*, plus telling effect. Please notice that it is not stipulated that this simple music be ultra-melodic. On the contrary, it can be as cacophonous as one likes, but wherever that cacophony occurs, it should be stirringly simple. The *intention* of all movie music must be unmistakable. Movie audiences only see a picture once; they have no time to analyze the composer's intentions.

(3) Motion picture sound tracks live in the world of the microphone. Orchestrations should be made for that microphone, and not for any either banal or trick arrangement of orchestral instruments. Oftentimes one single instrument, "stepped up" in volume, produces a much more magnificent and sweeping effect than a whole symphony orchestra playing fortissimo; such fortissimos must always be dubbed down anyway, and they often sound very feeble indeed.

These are what I consider to be the fundamental principles of motion picture music criticism.

During the past year I have seen two remarkable films; neither of them came from Hollywood. They were *Spanish Earth* and *Alone*. Two American colleagues—Virgil Thomson and Marc Blitzstein—wrote the score of the one in 1937;[15] the Russian Shostakovitch wrote for the other in 1931. Both scores go completely anti-Hollywood for they play against their films throughout. But the *Spanish Earth* score plays against its picture in an odd way. Before I go into that I would like to say that I have nothing whatsoever against a picture composer scoring a war scene in gay or lilting music. As a matter of fact I believe that such music is much more true to war than the heavy Straussian groans that issue from the scores of most Hollywoodian wars. Soldiers, certainly, march into battle over the major, rather the minor tonalities. Curiously enough, they are also more apt to three-four rather than four-four when they go over the top—one need only think of "La Cucaracha," or of any of the songs our doughboys sang in 1918, to remember that.

But *Spanish Earth*'s score does not build. It is not really dramatic. It is not motion-picture-music-for-the-motion-picture. Frankly, it does not play either for or against any specific ideas; it merely strings along. And it is difficult to string music along for any protracted length of time without a definite sag—unless that music has a specific plan. The plan of the *Spanish Earth* score is, apparently, to fill up the time allotted to the film, and that creates neither a musical nor a dramatic form. This, in my opinion, and according to the principles of motion picture musical criticism above outlined, is what the *Spanish Earth* musical score is, whether or not it was *intended* to be so. Still, it should be noted that many intelligent persons liked the music.

The fact of the matter is this: every intelligent human being is well fed up with the literal method of Hollywood underscoring. In fact many persons cannot bear the Hollywood method at all, and anything that attempts to turn this method upside down rates about one hundred percent with them.

Shostakovitch is one of these persons. Every score presents us with a clear picture of his positive hatred for Hollywood methods, and I am the last to take issue with him. In fact I should like to put myself on record as saying that although the Russian *Alone* is not a good picture and full of incredible "Russian-lengths," nevertheless its score is one of the best I have ever heard.

Hollywood, of course, would look askance at his technic of playing hurdy-gurdy music every time the young lady school teacher thinks of marriage. We should write some sentimental bit; moreover we (as a class I mean) disapprove of inflicting hurdy-gurdy music upon any public if there is not a hurdy-gurdy in the picture—visible constantly and intimately connected with the plot.

Hollywood, too, would be utterly and completely confused by his technic of playing hideous marches (bourgeois confusion) whenever the Siberian sheep herders stare at the camera in unashamed non-comprehension. Marches, for us, mean soldiers marching and we have always thought that it meant just that to all the rest of the world, too.

Hollywood would never understand the long screeching flute and clarinet solos floating over the Mongolian wastes; we should have written (or rewritten) a patch or two out of *Rossignol* and considered that we had done something quite smart.[16]

I believe that the entire "composition" of the Shostakovitch score is magnificently and completely articulate. I am also sympathetic to the attempt made in *Spanish Earth*.

The authors have said to themselves frankly, "Hollywood music smells; we shall do the opposite, and, in so doing, shall achieve a freshness and an atmosphere that will be ultra-striking." So they did, and the atmosphere was striking, although not quite in the way they had expected. They had thought far—farther than most American screen composers, but not far enough. Not so far, for instance, as Shostakovich, although the latter had written his "against" many years before.

Shostakovitch comes as near as solution of the problem of movie music as anyone. His brittle "sound track" score bristles with striking tunes, striking discords, striking orchestral effects usually upon one or two instruments, and many striking "againsts." But it builds and builds right up to the end when the Soviet airplane takes off and the music does likewise.

From *Modern Music* 15, no. 4 (May–June 1938), 251–54.

7.3 HISTORY OF MOTION PICTURE MUSIC

Franz Waxman

Franz Waxman (1906–67) was already a seasoned film composer and arranger when he arrived in Hollywood in 1934. During his studies at the Berlin Conservatory in the 1920s he had made extra money playing music for silent films. Later he began orchestrating and arranging music for early sound films, including the music that Friederich Holländer had written for Josef von Sternberg's Der blaue Engel *(1930). After suffering assault from Nazi thugs in the early 1930s, Waxman left Berlin for Paris. There he quickly distinguished himself as the composer for Fritz Lang's* Liliom *(1934) and Billy Wilder's* Mauvaise Graine *(1934). Shortly after arriving in Hollywood, Waxman composed one of his best-known scores, the colorful and thematically dense music for* Bride of Frankenstein *(1935).*

Over the ensuing years Waxman worked under contract to Universal, MGM, and Warner Bros. Prestige pictures with independent producer David O. Selznick secured Waxman's reputation as one of Hollywood's premiere film composers. Waxman's humorous music for Selznick's The Young in Heart *(1938) stole many scenes and received praise from critics. After this promising start, Waxman joined Selznick again on* Rebecca *(1940) and* The Paradine Case *(1947), both directed by Alfred Hitchcock.*

As in The Young in Heart, *Waxman's music for* Rebecca *enjoys a prominent place. Most notably, the sinuous "Rebecca" theme wafts through the film's most suspenseful scenes, trailing unease in its wake. When Waxman's Oscar-nominated score lost to the music that Leigh Harline, Paul Smith, and Ned Washington wrote for Walt Disney's* Pinocchio *(1940), Selznick sent a conciliatory note to the composer: "I am sure you know how much I was rooting for you to receive an award, which your score truly merited. But I'm sure that you'll be winning many awards in the years to come."[17] Selznick was right. Waxman would become the first composer to win the Best Score award for two consecutive years—for* Sunset Blvd. *(1950) and* A Place in the Sun *(1951)—an accomplishment that mirrored Selznick's back-to-back triumphs with* Gone with the Wind *(1939) and* Rebecca.

Waxman delivered the speech reprinted here to a women's club about a month after Rebecca's *general release. Production manager Raymond Klune reported an attendance of two hundred, noting "that every one of them had seen REBECCA once and better than half of them had seen it twice."[18] Although in his speech Waxman describes his work for* Rebecca, *he broaches many central aesthetic debates: music's psychological impact in film, audiences' awareness of the score, and the withholding of music for dramatic effect. The composer also offers insight into his manipulation of the "Rebecca" theme, which represents a character never physically present in the film. Interestingly, Waxman focuses his discussion not on melody or harmony but, rather, on orchestral color and the inclusion of an electronic instrument, the novachord.[19] The use of timbre as an expressive device is often overlooked in film music analysis, but Waxman's emphasis here evinces great sensitivity to it.*

Madam President, Madam Chairman, Members of the Federation:

I wish first to tell you that I am sincerely grateful for the opportunity to speak to you. I welcome this occasion to speak to you about music—that is, one branch of music that only in the recent years has won the appreciation of the general public.

By this time you have no doubt noticed my accent—I would like to explain that—five years ago I entered this country, and just the other day I celebrated the happiest day of my life by receiving my final papers as a full-fledged American citizen. However I was not so successful in adapting myself to the language as I was in adapting my heart to the accent of my new country—America. So if I speak to you with the help of a few notes of mine, I ask your indulgence.

The history of motion picture music is a march from ragtime to symphony. Hammering away on pianos, it was designed first to help audiences concentrate on the films by emphasizing the action on the screen. As the theatres grew in luxury, the music likewise increased in lavishness. Huge orchestras were substituted for the old piano. During the period of great war pictures the rattle of machine guns, the whine of shells, the march of soldiers to band music was given life by the orchestra. Complete musical scores often accompanied films whose dialogue was still conveyed to the audience by means of written titles.

The novelty of talking pictures gave screen music its first set-back. It was feared that the score might interfere with the speech of the characters. And for a period music played a minimum part in pictures.

But finally tiring of the all-dialogue films, the audiences again demanded music—for music and drama seemingly are inseparable. The pendulum swung the other way. Dialogue was dethroned during an era of musical comedies. Both speech and plot were sacrificed for light melodies of the musical comedy type.

When the pendulum swung in the opposite direction a balance between music and dialogue had been achieved. Its importance in creating and sustaining dramatic moods now clearly recognized, music today has a permanent place in film production. The composition of film music has become an art of its own.

As a composer of motion picture music, I hear much debating over the actual purpose of a film score. One theory defended by many, claims that music should not violate the realistic factors of a scene. It should only be used if there is a logical explanation for it. Now what is realism on the screen? Does it mean that if a picture is captivating its audience, the people in the seats are actually living the scene? If that would hold true, I would expect to see an audience turn up their collars the moment it started raining on the screen. But since they are not doing that I believe that it is only the emotion within them which makes them laugh or cry, or react in any way. If I can cause the proper reaction by means of photography, sound effects, music, or any other device of showmanship, I have achieved my purpose.

In scoring various films I had discussions about the placing of music in a particular film, and I did from time to time encounter the theory that this or that scene could not be underscored by music, because it took place, let us say, in a little boat out on the ocean.[20] Well, to me it would not matter where the scene took place or what its pictorial effect was—to me there was only one problem—can this scene be improved in its emotional value by music. Will the audience react differently if the proper music is written to that scene?

For example, you who remember the picture *Fury* done a few years ago with Spencer Tracy, will remember the Vigilante scene in which the mob, caught in an emotion beyond the control of any individual, marched upon the jail—it was one of the highlights of the picture—it was Fury.[21] The tremendous aspects of mob psychology had in some way to be revealed to the audience, and the task of revelation was thrown on the music. I could see nothing so well expressed—that spirit of frantic frenzy—as strains of dissonant martial band music, although there was at no time any band visible on the screen. So we sacrificed the realistic principle for the emotional revelation. Wherever there is a good story told, you will find emotion—therefore I believe that any scene revealing emotion justifies music.

101

Incidentally, the best proof to my mind that music and realism go perfectly together is the fact that all modern newsreels—(and certainly there is nothing more realistic than a newsreel)—are today given a complete music background.

At this point I want to mention an exception to this rule—the motion picture *Grapes of Wrath*—where the absence of a stimulating musical score, and the only occasional entrance on a lonely accordion emphasized the sadness and gripping simplicity of the story.[22]

I read a statement in one of the musical papers the other day where somebody said that a good motion picture score should be of such nature that you don't notice it—in other words it should be unobtrusive and so much in the background that on leaving the theatre one wouldn't be sure that there was any music in the picture at all. This of course is a very flexible statement, because I do think that music should not distract the audience's attention from the drama—but on the other hand, if it is so subdued that its only virtue lies in the fact that it is not noticeable, it can hardly be effective.

A motion picture score should be noticed just as much as you notice the other elements that make up a motion picture—like dialogue, camera movement, sets, costumes, etc. All these elements should form an harmonious effect to deepen the scenes and to intensify the characters and their conflicts. The audience should be fully aware of not only the existence, but also the virtues of each of them. Balancing these contributing elements is a delicate and artistic process. They at no time must become distracting factors while achieving their fullest effects, for drama and characterization are after all the primary functions of motion pictures.

One of the most talented men for balancing these various elements of a motion picture is David O. Selznick, producer of *Gone With the Wind* and *Rebecca*.[23] His interest and painstaking work for the most minute detail in the production of a motion picture is stimulating to the creative artist. When Mr. Selznick assigned me to write the musical score for [*Rebecca*], I was faced with a peculiar problem. The complexity and nature of the plot made it necessary to lean heavily upon music. As you who have seen the picture, or read the book, know Rebecca, the really dominant character of the story, is dead—in actuality she never appears in the scenes, yet the entire drama revolves around her. Through the speech and action of others, and particularly through the use of music, her character with all its powerful effects, had to be revealed to the audience. For this reason in composing the film score I first wrote the main theme for the picture representing Rebecca. It had to be a theme of sophisticated and haunting quality, which could be adapted to the various dramatic situations created in the story. Whenever a scene involving Rebecca appeared on the screen, it was up to the music to give Rebecca's character life and presence.

Since there was accompanying dramatic music through almost all the scenes of the picture, I had to invent something that would make Rebecca's theme stand out over the living characters. I achieved the effect in this manner: I set up a normal orchestra playing the accompanying music for the living characters on the screen—whereas for the dead Rebecca I set up an individual group of mechanical instruments—a ghost orchestra, so to speak. It consisted of three instruments—an electrical organ and two novachords. A novachord is a newly invented instrument which produces its sound by means of radio tubes. It has a peculiar sound of unreality—of something that you cannot define. So in reality there are two orchestras playing at the same time whenever the story called for the overshadowing spirit of the dead Rebecca. I used this technique of scoring up to the scene where Rebecca's successor learns about the true character of the dead mistress of Manderley—at this moment the theme, which so far has been given a haunting and almost lovely interpretation, turns suddenly vicious, revealing the true character of Rebecca, now played by the real orchestra in a dramatic and almost sinister form, ascending to the climax of the picture.

The treatment of the music from there on is powerful and symphonic, showing the destruction of Rebecca's shadow which is symbolically shown on the screen through the burning down of Rebecca's home, at the same time optimistically forecasting the beginning of a new and happy life for our living characters.

I have been asked to write a condensed version of my music to *Rebecca* which will be broadcast by the Los Angeles Philharmonic orchestra on the Standard Oil Hour next week. This short version is based entirely on the various developments of the Rebecca theme only.

In conclusion I want to thank you again for your kind attention and I hope that the efforts of the film composers of today will be rewarded by the growing appreciation of motion picture music.

I thank you.

A speech addressed to the Local Federation of Women's Clubs in
Hollywood, California, May 1940.

7.4 MEMORANDA

David O. Selznick

David O. Selznick (1902–65) was in his teens when he began working in the moving picture business with his father, Lewis J. Selznick. He later thrived as a producer at MGM, RKO, and Paramount studios before becoming an independent and making one of Hollywood's most famous films, Gone with the Wind *(1939). That film's success continues to overshadow many other distinguished Selznick films, including* King Kong *(1933),* David Copperfield *(1935),* Prisoner of Zenda *(1937),* Rebecca *(1940),* Since You Went Away *(1944), and* Spellbound *(1945).*

As these two documents indicate, Selznick was a committed advocate for film music. In addition to supporting Max Steiner's early and influential scores at RKO in the early 1930s, he later promoted film music through radio broadcasts and the nascent soundtrack industry of the 1940s. Selznick also personally advised composers working on his films. The letters reproduced here pertain to film music practice and preservation. The second letter, written to the film curator of the Museum of Modern Art, reveals Selznick's abiding interest in music for the silent cinema and includes a suggestion that important sound film scores be preserved for study and research, a remarkably prescient idea in 1941.

The first letter is written to Selznick's story editor, Katherine Brown, who was in contact with New York-based conductor and composer Walter Damrosch. Damrosch had been approached to write music for Gone with the Wind, *and he had asked several questions about the film scoring process.*[24] *Brown passed these questions on to Selznick, who offered the response reprinted here. The letter demonstrates both Selznick's acute attention to music in film and his limited understanding of musical composition. His assertion, for example, that film scores ought to be composed from the script would strike most composers as grossly counterproductive. Nevertheless, Selznick's ruminations offer an important perspective from a filmmaker who worked closely with many of Hollywood's finest composers, including Miklós Rózsa, Max Steiner, Herbert Stothart, Dimitri Tiomkin, and Franz Waxman. After receiving Selznick's response to his questions, Damrosch marveled: "I am amazed at the study which Mr. Selznick has given to this part of moving pictures."*[25]

August 30, 1937
To: Mrs. Katherine Brown
From: DOS

Answering your questions, and so that you will know about these matters for the future, the usual method of scoring pictures is for the arranger and scorer not to come near the picture until the editing is completed. The producer then turns the picture over to the music people, usually with the injunction to do a great job cheaply in a couple of weeks. This, on the face of it, is silly, and I have tried to avoid working this way as well as to minimize the delays which are involved to get a picture released because of the time it takes to write, arrange, and record a score. Usually I have had the score in well ahead and I have tried to get these men to do the score from the script, having the weeks and months of production for the job—so that they are in a position to keep up with the changes as we edit the picture and to go with the least possible delay into the scoring, at the same time having had sufficient time during the shooting of the picture to do a good job, instead of being rushed into doing it in a week or so when the picture is finished. Incredibly, I have met resistance on this, particularly from Max Steiner, who found it difficult to do the work in this fashion, claiming that he had to have a finished picture. This was one of my long-standing arguments with Max, and his point in turn was based upon something else which was the root of our decision to get a divorce, which was my objection to what I term "Mickey Mouse" scoring: an interpretation of each line of dialogue and each movement musically, so that the score tells with music exactly what is being done by the actors on the screen. It has long been my contention that this is ridiculous and that the purpose of a score is to unobtrusively help the mood of each scene without the audience being even aware that they are listening to music—and if I am right in this contention, why can't the score be prepared from the script even though the cuts and rearrangements may be necessary after the picture is edited—for the basic selection of music and general arrangement would not be affected by these cuts. I could go into this with you at further length but it would develop into an essay on musical scoring, about which I feel very keenly. I don't think there is another producer in Hollywood that devotes ten per cent as much time to the score as I do—and it may interest you to know that I was the first producer to use dramatic scores. Max Steiner argued with me at the time, as he has since readily admitted, that musical scoring could not be used without the source of the music being explained to an audience.

I feel now that musical scoring is due for great improvement. Among other things, I feel that we have not had topnotch composers and conductors. I feel too that our pictures have been used as an exploitation ground for the second-rate talents of the composers who have been out here, and who have seen fit to substitute their own compositions for the practically untouched library of the world's music—which in my opinion is a gold mine for emotional effect that requires intelligent and educated selection and arrangement for our purposes by a man who has learned which music plays with most effect upon the emotions of the public. I am not certain that I would argue so much about the use of the world's classical and even non-classical music if I had as an alternate really fine original composition. But too much of what has been composed for my pictures, and everybody else's pictures, has been second-rate—and I say this even though I am grateful for what I regard as the excellent composition in some of my pictures, notably Stothart's work in *Viva Villa!* and Steiner's work in *The Garden of Allah*.[26]

Newman has been much more reasonable about working from script than Max was, but he too resisted the use of standard music that I thought could be used effectively and even help in achieving subconsciously a nostalgic mood. On occasion, notably in the score of *Anna Karenina*, I was able to force standard music. In the case of *Karenina*, Tschaikovsky selections—and with good effect.[27]

February 19, 1941

Mr. John Abbott
Film Library; Museum of Modern Art
11 West 43rd Street
New York City, N.Y.

Dear Mr. Abbott:

I had a thought the other day about an extension to your Film Library's activities which I discussed with Mr. Whitney, and which he seemed to think was an excellent one. He agreed that I should write you concerning it.[28]

As I think you will agree, the scoring of pictures is becoming increasingly important. The amount of time and effort devoted to these scores is increasing all the time; important musicians are finally coming to recognize their importance; and more and more, really fine musicians are recognizing that scoring is a new form of musical art. Why, then, would it not be a good idea to start to collect important scores, including those of real quality and those which have an effect upon the art as a whole?

You showed me some of the scores that were written for the early silent pictures, including cue sheets for some of the early short subjects, and I believe you also have the score of *The Birth of a Nation*.[29] I think that without too much effort, you might accumulate scores of other important pictures up to the time that sound was introduced. From the time that sound came in, I would suggest inclusion of the score of *Tabu*, which I believe was originally made as a silent picture;[30] and the scores of early RKO pictures written by Max Steiner, such as *Bird of Paradise* and *Symphony of Six Million*.[31]

I am under the impression, and I hope I'm not wrong, that it was I who was responsible for the first scoring under dialogue. I remember a discussion with Max Steiner in which he protested that the audience might ask where the music came from, for up to that time it was felt that scoring under dialogue was not possible unless it was first shown in action that a radio or Victrola had been turned on! I insisted there was no more reason for explaining scoring than there was for indicating the source of music that accompanied silent pictures.

More recent scores in the collection could include those for *The Informer*, *Gone With the Wind*, and Stokowski's adaptations for *Fantasia*.[32]

I think that scores written since the inclusion of sound might be accumulated by the Library both in their written parts and in sound tracks, which I believe could be obtained with all their dialogue and sound effects omitted.

I believe that it is high time that someone gave encouragement to the training of musicians for the express purpose of scoring; and that many musicians and musical students would be delighted to study the written scores, and to hear them played in your theater.

Sincerely yours,
David O. Selznick

8

AESTHETIC SQUABBLES

In keeping with the unofficial dictum of "if it bleeds, it leads," newspapers have long enjoyed reporting the details of intellectual tiffs that involve well-known persons.

One of the juicier accounts transpired in the pages of the *Los Angeles Times* early in 1952, just after the famously contentious British conductor Thomas Beecham arrived on the West Coast for an engagement with the Los Angeles Philharmonic. Fishing for "good copy" in the midst of an otherwise bland interview session, a reporter suggested that surely there must be something about which Beecham would like to complain. In an uncharacteristically congenial mood, Beecham had to pause for a moment to think. Then, perhaps because the climate and palm trees reminded him that he was in the vicinity of Hollywood, he casually took a shot at film music. It seems quite ridiculous, Beecham said, to have a full symphony orchestra "sawing away while some such actress as Lassie disports [herself] upon the screen." Beecham granted that recent improvements in recording technology had made the experience of movie-going somewhat more tolerable to sensitive ears, but in almost all cases, he said, film music is "not only useless" but "highly distracting."[1]

While the largely unremarkable story on Beecham ran inside the newspaper's A section, the next day a bold response appeared on the front page. Headlined "Film Music Composer Hits Back at Beecham," the article featured comments by Dimitri Tiomkin that had been forwarded to the newspaper by Tiomkin's press agent. A few months later Tiomkin would have the chance to wax reflectively in the form of lengthy quotations incorporated into an overview article on current trends in film music penned by the *Times*'s film critic Philip K. Scheurer.[2] Tiomkin's well-considered later thoughts are valuable, to be sure, but they are not nearly so colorful as those contained in his knee-jerk reaction to Beecham's slight. Tiomkin wondered why the maestro did not find it equally "ridiculous and distracting to have a full symphony orchestra sawing away in the pit [of an opera house] while an Oklahoma City tenor with an assumed continental name sings an old German song in Italian," and he called Beecham, among other things, "a chronic sourball" who indulged in "a crusty and hidebound type of thinking."[3]

Comparable but generally more polite dialogue appeared later in the decade. In 1957, for example, the *New York Times*'s chief classical music critic Harold C. Schonberg triggered a flurry of retorts when, in a column about recent soundtrack recordings, he suggested that "if Hollywood wants good movie music it had better think of engaging good composers to write it."[4] Similarly, after *Los Angeles Times* music critic Albert Goldberg in 1958 casually decried the "cliché-ridden" scores that lately seemed to be the Hollywood norm, his counterpart from the film desk fired back a lengthy rebuttal the very next day.[5] And there would be more to come, especially as—in the 1960s and 1970s—the aesthetic and dramatic issues of film music came into conflict with purely commercial considerations.

But aesthetic squabbles over film music have a history that pre-dates the 1950s and 1960s. Two of the grandest early debates are reproduced here. Neither of them was triggered by off-the-cuff responses to an interviewer's deliberately provocative question; rather, each of them started with the publication in the popular press of a serious and apparently unsolicited commentary on film music from a prestigious conductor of opera and/or symphonic music. While the responses vary considerably, it is worth nothing that in both tone and content the initial statements—from Gianandrea Gavazzeni in Italy in 1943, from Erich Leinsdorf in the United States in 1945—are remarkably similar.

The long and deeply thoughtful rebuttal to Gavazzeni came from Fedele d'Amico, who in the years following World War II would become Italy's most respected music journalist. The quick reaction to Leinsdorf came from Bernard Herrmann, a composer who was still years away from becoming a Hollywood icon, and accompanying Herrmann's brief yet heated response was a "mediation" by a supposedly disinterested third party.

Quite unlike the colorful Beecham–Tiomkin exchange described above, neither the in-print dialogue involving Gavazzeni and d'Amico in Italy nor the one involving Leinsdorf, Herrmann, and film critic Bosley Crowther in the United States amount to a fracas. The conversations were conducted with dignity and respectfulness, and their collection of differing points of view simply represents the peculiar position in which film music—vis-à-vis music in general—has long found itself.

8.1 MUSIC AND CINEMA: AN IMPOSSIBLE MARRIAGE

(Musica e cinema. Un connubio impossibli)

Gianandrea Gavazzeni

Gianandrea Gavazzeni (1909–96) was one of Italy's foremost opera conductors, holding for almost half a century—from 1948 until his death—the title of principal conductor at La Scala in Milan. Before taking up the La Scala post, however, he was known not just as a conductor but also as a composer: his successful works include the oratorio Canti per Sant'Allessandro *(1934), the one-act opera* Paolo e Virginia *(1935), the ballet* Il furioso nell'isola di San Domingo *(1936), and a violin concerto (1937). In addition, Gavazzeni was a scholar; by the time he wrote this brief article for the monthly magazine* La Ruota *[The Wheel] he had already published book-length biographical studies of Donizetti, Pizzetti, and Mussorgsky, and in 1974 he won Italy's prestigious Viareggio Prize for a book of essays on Beethoven.*

Gavazzeni's stance vis-à-vis film music bears comparison with that of Erich Leinsdorf (whose comments from 1945 are presented on p. 117 of this volume). Whereas Leinsdorf admits that documentaries and certain other films had occasionally been well served by good music, Gavazzeni more radically attests that music that aspires to high artistic quality has an aesthetic completely alien to that of cinema. He grants that bits of popular music might serve as useful "props" in a filmic scene, but real *music—that is, "artistic" music of the sort that is written by genuine composers and intended to be heard in the concert hall—has no place in film. Indeed, he seems to feel that even to attempt to recreate "artistic" music for filmic purposes amounts to an abasement.*

Years after film music began, the topic remains relevant. There has been no change or evolution in the fundamental purposes of music,[6] no change or evolution in music's geologic, primitive, or most radical poetic existence. In contrast, the art of cinema, just like any other creative and composite element of our culture, has often changed its purposes and systems, adjusting itself carefully to match the passing of the seasons and the passing of the years.

It is therefore not easy to know how to frame the argument, how to discuss the problem of film music.[7] The fact that cinema uses words has never given birth to a poetry problem in relation to film. And the fact that cinema relies on sound does not mean that, simply for this reason, music must be a part of it.

We approach cinema in particular moments of our days. We are drawn to it by different stimuli, such as a futile, nervous, or sensual desire for images, faces, bodies, landscapes, or motions. We follow the shadow of a woman among the shadows of many other shapes that move on the screen. When the film features something that we recognize, the echo of a landscape dear to us, for example, this has a subtle effect on us. This same principle applies to sound, especially such sounds as the 'pedal'[8] of wind, of rain, of the sea, of the forest. The pealing of bells, the noise of walking, the rustling of clothes. Screams, fragments of songs. There is a full emblematic vocabulary that does not acquire the status of music and absolutely must not reach that status. To support this idea it is enough to consider the [lowly] phonic position into which film music is cast: usually the music has a remoteness that misrepresents its timbres, that diminishes and dissolves its acoustic facts, that empties out all its harmonic, contrapuntal, and instrumental substance. Or sometimes it is brought into the foreground in a way that focuses on only one of its elements—usually its timbre or rhythm—in a way that serves the film but not the music: such featured elements have little to do with music, because they arise from a text, or from a page of a text.

The techniques of music have of course experienced change; musical genres have evolved; forms of music have been killed and then reinvented. But the differences between the development of music and the development of cinema are enormous! In a film that uses state-of-the-art technology we are likely to encounter, at a [dramatically] appropriate point, a citation of an old Viennese waltz, for example, or the stanza of a generic lullaby, or a sequence of simple chords such as might be invented by the organist at some rural church. I will never be able to forget the few measures of a little song that, in a short film by Allegret that I saw years ago,[9] accompanied the night run of a locomotive. These few measures did not really exist as music, but they existed wonderfully as a sonic prolongation of the image. Amidst all the hissing and sizzling noises coming from the locomotive there was still room for the song and its burlesque, irreverent flavor. I would say that this episode has remained, for me, one of the best examples of film music. In this little song there was just the right amount of sentiment that—to get back to the idea of music in cinema—perhaps you will never find in a composition with high aesthetic value, written in a masterly way by some great musician.

Such is the nature of things, of both cinema and music. The former does not need from music anything more than a sentimental affinity; the latter represents the spirit that is embedded in the history and blood of humankind, in its places of memory, in all its terrestrial and metaphysical landscapes. To propose an arbitrary and cerebral argument on film music is to attempt an aesthetic brew, a bastardized cross-fertilization of things that ought to be kicked back into their natural boundaries. The matter in question, quite aside from its applications to art, is simply one of logical coherence.

Music has an aesthetic integrity, a language all its own, and it behaves the way it does (forming shapes, representing actions, and so on) because of its aesthetic nature. Cinema offers us the faces of beautiful women, images that give us goose bumps, the larva-like development of landscapes and other things. Cinema satisfies curiosity and feelings of restlessness. It occupies its own space, between audience members' nerves and senses. And there it should stay, without intruding into [the space of] music.

From *La Ruota* 4, no. 1 (January 19, 1943), 20–21.
(Translation by Stefano Mengozzi)

8.2 MUSIC AND CINEMA: A DIFFICULT MARRIAGE

(Musica e cinematografa. Un connubio difficile)

Fedele d'Amico

Fedele d'Amico (1912–90) during the second half of the twentieth century was Italy's leading music critic. After earning a degree in law he briefly studied composition with Alfredo Casella before turning to full-time music journalism; based for the most part in Rome, he regularly contributed reviews and opinion pieces, in turn, to Il tevere, L'Italia letteraria, Sette giorni, Voce operaia, Vie nuove, Il contemporaneo, The Musical Quarterly, Italia domain, La fiera letteraria, and—most famously—L'espresso.[10] In addition to working as a music journalist, d'Amico taught music history at the University of Rome, translated into Italian numerous opera librettos (for works by, among others, Hans Werner Henze, Paul Hindemith, Leoš Janáček, Dmitry Shostakovich, Igor Stravinsky, and Kurt Weill), and authored monographs on such varied topics as the operas of Rossini and Puccini, the role of the virtuoso in classical music, and the intertwined aesthetics of Jean Cocteau and Stéphane Mallarmé.

D'Amico was just beginning his journalistic career at the time he penned this extended rebuttal to Gianandrea Gavazzeni's brief dismissal of film music in general (see p. 108), and it is worth noting that his article was written not for the popular press but for a specialized music journal. He argues here that the fruitful combination of music and film is not, as Gavazzeni bluntly stated, "impossible" but only problematic, and by citing numerous examples he demonstrates how the problem over the years has, in fact, been dealt with quite effectively.

110

The article makes philosophical points that seem as relevant to film music today as they were in 1943, when the Italian film industry was struggling to survive amidst the ongoing turmoil of World War II. Quite aside from the strength of its argument, the article is interesting at the very least because of its frequent use of terms (for example, colonne sonore, binario, inquadratura, *and* musica 'di commento'*) that for all their apparent foreignness nevertheless have direct counterparts in English-language film jargon.*

"Such is the nature of things, of both cinema and music. The former does not need from music anything more than a sentimental affinity; the latter represents the spirit that is embedded in the history and blood of humankind, in its places of memory, in all its terrestrial and metaphysical landscapes. To propose an arbitrary and cerebral argument on film music is to attempt an aesthetic brew, a bastardized cross-fertilization of things that ought to be kicked back into their natural boundaries." Thus wrote Gavazzeni in *La Ruota* (January 1943) in an article titled "An Impossible Marriage," where in a few words—very brief and concise and epigrammatic—he once again makes the case for the unpopular truth just cited.

Unless I misunderstand it, the argument does not pretend to delegitimize film music. In fact, Gavazzeni writes: "I will never be able to forget the few measures of a little song that, in a short film by Allegret that I saw years ago, accompanied the night run of a locomotive. These few measures did not really exist as music, but they existed wonderfully as a sonic prolongation of the image. Amidst all the hissing and sizzling noises coming from the locomotive there was still room for the song and its burlesque, irreverent flavor. I would say that this episode has remained, for me, one of the best examples of film music. In this little song there was just the right amount of sentiment that—to get back to the idea of music in cinema—perhaps you will never find in a composition with high aesthetic value, written in a masterly way by some great musician." It is clear, therefore, that for Gavazzeni music on the screen can serve a purpose. But this music is not there for its autonomous values, for its real interior rhythm; it exists only as generic evocative matter, no more and no less than any noise, independent of what properly speaking might be called its artistic signification. In short, it offers no more than an "emblematic vocabulary," as Gavazzeni puts it.

We know how it works. In the most humble case, the musician is asked to provide some generic music for a specific scene. Some notes of any kind, something that will open up the dead areas of the visual field, something that will hint at the full scale of a dangerous situation, something that will gently put the spectator into a trance, into a painless and harmless ecstasy that will lead him to a bird-like flight, something in which he can indulge the way he might indulge in a good glass of wine. Let's all love one another, in other words. We can see a return, with its catalyzing function, of silent film's dear old out-of-tune upright piano. (And then, in Italy, we also have the urgent task of ironing out the technical flaws of our very dented soundtracks.[11])

Then there is the more noble case. This is the one in which we ask music, as we say, to make a "comment." In fact, more than a comment or a poetic prolongation of the action, the music in these cases in effect provides a caption;[12] it has the task of narrating what the represented and spoken action does not tell, or of recalling memories, or of providing an anchor for certain situations that are figuratively elusive. Everybody has the impression that this happens through some kind of magic, a magic that from the beginning of time has been attributed to musicians. But we should know that music, after all, is an art like all the other arts, with its rhetorical methods, its symbolic mechanics, with—in a word—its prose. Who would not be able to write a little tune conveying pain rather than joy, anxiety rather than languor? Or who would not be able to tack on Leitmotifs,[13] the use of which, our directors believe, is all there is to musical architecture? To do those things is in essence no more difficult than to advertise a film as "a strong drama" as opposed to "a devilishly funny comedy."

One does not need to be born a poet in order to do this. There is a conventional way of expressing oneself in sounds, as unmistakable and precise as the language of flower-arranging or the standard lines of the flirtatious office worker.[14] Everybody understands him, even—and perhaps especially—his prey.[15]

It is not my intent, in saying this, to belittle the individual musicians [who contribute to film]. There is no doubt that they are able to perform the function of transmitting encrypted messages (but the encryption is always a friendly one, designed to safeguard nothing more than Pulcinella's secret[16]). They do this more or less with taste, and sometimes with a great deal of taste, so much that it meets the highest expectations of their art. But I should add that this taste, which may well be the mark of genuine creativity, is as a rule considered to be something extra, a gracious gift to the musician, not a necessity; at times it may even be a liability. It is not a part of music's regular function [in film], and the composer is almost never paid for it.

So far, so good. But to this I would like to add two observations. The first has to do with the [apparent] motivations that bring Gavazzeni to his conclusions; the second involves an attempt to clarify these motivations, at least on one point in particular.

* * *

The argument that Gavazzeni makes to support his thesis of the organic irreconcilability of music and cinema does not rest on a distinction of expressive means that are postulated as being irreducible, and straightaway he discusses the different natures, purposes, and results [of the two art forms]. His argument rests on the idea[17] that whereas cinema brings us "the faces of beautiful women, images that give us goose bumps, the larva-like development of landscapes and other things," that it "satisfies curiosity and feelings of restlessness," that it "occupies its own space, between audience members' nerves and senses," music is a precise reality. His argument rests, in other words, on the idea that cinema is not an art but music is.

Such an allegation seems to me in its premises to be not just altogether mistaken but also superfluous. It is not that I believe that cinema is absolutely an art (along the lines of "Chiare, fresche et dolci acque," or *Tristano*[18]); such a proposition would be futile to discuss here. But I cannot see, not even from the perspective of someone open to the idea, how or why it would be impossible for a non-art to rely on the assistance of an authentic art. The rationale of Gavazzeni's thesis makes sense only if we interpret it in a purely psychological sense. Indeed, it is almost impossible for anyone who pays attention to a film's on-screen action to really listen to the music. From the music the audience member gets only the most obvious signals that support the film's narrative line and [perhaps compensate for] its shortcomings, and these signals (not so much as music *per se* but as symbols that in some way relate to the action) reach the audience member very quickly. In opera the situation is exactly the opposite. Operatic music pushes both words and scenarios into the background; to the operagoer (although it might not seem this way to the librettist) it is irrelevant whether the text is poetry or not because the rhythm of the text is inevitably governed by the music.

Why does this happen? In other words, why does the psychological impossibility of following two things at the same time lead the audience member to concentrate, instinctively, on just a single medium (in the case of film, on the on-screen imagery; in the case of opera, on the music)? It is because the spectator is immediately drawn to whatever source demands the greater investment of his formal attention. One can see a thousand things in a concert hall, but anyone who is not deaf is likely to be drawn more to listening to the music than observing the color of the necktie of his neighbor; even from an exclusively visual point of view, he will be more likely to watch the violinists' bows or the conductor's baton, which in some ways behave in an organized and 'formal' fashion, rather than the purely casual expression in the faces of the other listeners. Likewise, when one is in the theater, noticing not the merely partially organized movement of opera but the entirely conscious movement of ballet, what occupies the foreground is the overall scene; assuming equal levels of formal elaboration, a scenic narrative is infinitely more evident and comprehensible than musical syntax; the music in this case becomes a caption, a rhythmic or atmospheric track[19] (if the choreography is pleasing, the ballet is successful no matter the music: if the choreography is not pleasing, the ballet is unsuccessful no matter the music). In order to really listen, it is advisable to close your eyes.

To an even greater extent, this is the case of cinema.[20] From a psychological standpoint, the simple facts of photography and montage give at least the appearance of an absolute formal elaboration, and therefore everything that one listens to, for the same reasons that we have mentioned in regard to ballet, inevitably moves to an auxiliary position. (The exception would involve complete photographic indifference for the sake of concentrating on a speaking voice. For example, a sustained shot[21] of a speaking person, visually monotonous and inexpressive, is made comprehensible only through the language. But this, in any case, is an alternative between photography and the spoken voice, hardly one between photography and music.)

All this is common experience. Ask a musician, upon his exiting the movie theater, for his opinion of the music; if he is sincere he will confess not to have paid any attention to it. If he seems to be not sincere, test him as follows:[22] ask him "how much" music was in the film. He will likely answer that the film featured at most ten minutes of music, whereas in fact the music amounted to perhaps three quarters of an hour, and the ten minutes he remembers are precisely those in which the music stood out (on this point I have noticed a curious thing: the majority of people judge a film on the basis of only one piece of music, the underscore[23] for the titles, and this is precisely because their intention of listening to the music vanishes with the film's very first scene[24]). For me, personal experience has always provided the ultimate proof of this phenomenon. Being a musician, sensitive to the figurative arts and to all visual stimuli only in an unsophisticated way, and long being of the opinion that the motion picture is hardly the most interesting spectacle this world has to offer, I nevertheless find that I am able to listen to film music[25] only at the price of a constantly renewed effort, and [even when I try] I do not always meet my goal. The cheapest movie seems more attractive than the

113

most beautiful music, and in this can be found yet another good reason for my basic antipathy toward the cinema.[26]

So-called scenic music—in other words, music that is part of action and which you can "see" being performed on the screen, in the face of the singer, or in the playing of the violinist—is not really an exception.[27] Granted, in some cases the dramatic relevance of music of this sort—because it is so integrated with the photographed narrative—is incomparably greater than that of "commentary" music.[28] The "commentary" music nonetheless can have value, but only to the extent that it meshes with the narrative's dramatic rhythm.

For a famous example, consider the use of Ibert's song at the end of Pabst's *Don Quixote*.[29] The piece is very much in the film's foreground, since in an interminable shot[30] the screen shows nothing but the re-assembling of the burned pages of a book, and the story at this point is almost finished. All spectators in effect hang on to the vocal cords of [Fyodor] Chaliapin,[31] which give meaning to the otherwise indecipherable arabesque of crumpled paper. And this is precisely my point: what matters here is Chaliapin's throat and voice, not the music *per se*, which after all is just a song that in terms of decorousness is no more than average. All that matters here is the suggestion of the grand narrative, the suggestion of the grand character who transforms himself, ultimately, into song. And this is communicated not through an individualized aria by the likes of, say, Bellini[32] but through a song that on paper seems most generic, one that takes on character only because of the fascinating inflections of "that voice," the voice of "that" personality, which we already know through other avenues, a song that for this very reason immediately alludes to the story. The dramatic masterstroke at the end of *Don Quixote* is not the doing of Ibert, even if—as happens very seldom in film—his music here seems to be the absolute ruler, and even if the octave leap that closes the song is destined never to escape our memory.

And thus we find common ground, for the case of the Ibert song is perhaps no different from that of the little song mentioned by Gavazzeni. I only seek to clarify the reasons why, considering how different are the media of the two songs, given the diversity of the two media, Gavazzeni's conclusions are indeed legitimate.

* * *

And here I come to my second observation, which does not so much oppose as expand upon the ideas proposed by Gavazzeni. As I have argued before, the denial of the contribution [to film] of music as an autonomous art does not imply denial of contributions that might be made in other ways; that is to say, music—at least, what little of it emerges—can be used as a material component of cinema's goals. In other words, we can indeed rely on the musician's work, albeit more or less marginalized, and more or less modest, as is dictated by each individual case.

Even the marginal job, however, will be relatively large when we assign to music the task of comic caricature—that is, of following in detailed ways virtually all of the on-screen action (this, as should be clear, would approximate the situation in ballet, or in the animated cartoon)—or of parodying a musical style that seems inherent to a cinematic scene (consider, for example, the parody of melodrama in Clair's *Million*[33]). As we can clearly see, these are cases in which the musician needs to have a higher than usual amount of intelligence, but it does not mean that what has been requested of him amounts to 'good music' in the absolute sense.[34] The music in the sound films of Chaplin is marvelously suited to its purpose, yet it consists by and large of third-rate material.[35] A Stravinsky was not needed to write the unforgettable score[36] of *A Nous la liberté*; an Auric was enough.[37]

But I wish to point to another type of case, that in which music for the sake of sonic unity creates a continuous background that, without completely monopolizing the attention of the spectator, penetrates the senses imperceptibly and forms a stable point of reference for evocations. In practice, this is something that can hardly be ignored [when considering] the economy of film; even more important, this is something that is attainable only when a certain stylistic foundation has been laid, through values that to an extent are strictly musical.

We might cite, to stay with our own cinema, the score[38] by Achille Longo for *Via delle Cinque Lune*,[39] an excellent filter through which the musician passed all the popularizing material and the "local color," a filter steadily maintained, with exemplary control of taste, throughout the film, and which created some very precise atmospheric elements. But even more remarkable is Longo's achievement when the film, abandoning for the most part spoken words[40] and consigning its drama only to images, or, even without reducing the dialogue, concentrates the narrative interest only in a scenic arabesque; this offers the possibility of greatly expanding the music, and of infusing the music with a stylistic consistency all its own.

These cases establish the basis for the two best scores[41] for Italian films that I know: namely, the one by Malipiero for Ruttmann's *Acciaio* and the one by Tommasini for Castellini's *Un colpo di pistola*.[42] About the first, a critic (a non-musician) once noted that the score had managed to confer to the film an Italian airiness, a limpid atmosphere of abandonment, a musical quality that translated directly yet imperceptibly—and thus with considerable impact—the film's playfulness. The second aimed at providing an historical evocation, that of Russia in the 1830s as seen through a late nineteenth-century patina. The unerring elegance with which Tommasini fulfilled his task will forever remain exemplary; even if he or she misses the details, the spectator need hardly wait for the moments of "source music"[43] in order to sense the rigorous continuity of atmosphere.[44] (It is worth noting that in both films this continuity of atmosphere comes about through a circumstance that is as rare abroad as it is in Italy; corresponding to the music there is a continuity of atmosphere in the photography, a sort of pictorial glue, which in both of these two very different films is absolutely flawless. Through significant coincidence, both films, although made ten years apart, are credited to the same cinematographer, Massimo Terzano.[45])

And now we come to the question that lies at the heart of the matter: Are the results attained by Malipiero and Tommasini due to pure musical values or to the fact that these two artists, with their intelligence and skill, adjusted to the needs of the task at hand without consideration of whether or not their music had artistic merit? It is a fact that, if brought into the concert hall, the music of *Acciaio* reveals a formal precision that is much inferior to that of other pieces by Malipiero from around the same time; as for the music for *Colpo di pistola*, it seems that one could extract from it a concert suite only with great difficulty. But to say this is really to say nothing, because one can hardly expect a work of art to retain its worth outside of the environment for which it was created.

Considering this music in its own place, it seems that for *Acciaio* Malipiero poured into an extremely simple form—in an enthusiastic and almost improvisatory manner—

the spirit and color that are typical of his taste and temperament; at least, [he brought to this music] certain particular aspects of [his style], namely, his feel for 'ancient Italianness' and, specifically, his melodic expansiveness. And for *Colpo di pistola* Tommasini did by and large the same thing, using methods just as simple as those for his autonomous compositions have been complex (in the entire score[46] it is just about impossible to find any harmonies that go beyond the style of Tchaikovsky); in any case, the prime input here is the exquisitely elegant tone that is one of the most positive attributes of Tommasini's art. I believe that from this I can draw the conclusion that [in this music] there is a genuine artistic quality that, even though sometimes it is absorbed by extraneous needs, in the final analysis has led to very positive results that could hardly have been matched by a faithful adherence to [film-music's] canon of genre and symbolism.

These examples, it should be understood, neither establish rules nor invalidate Gavazzeni's conclusions, so long as Gavazzeni's conclusions are interpreted only to mean that film music often exhibits rhythms, tempos, and meters that run counter to [what might be suggested by] the music itself. But these examples at the very least confirm the possibility that true musical values, even if occasionally they need to be somehow compromised, nevertheless *can* play a role in—to use the phrase that seems so dear to our film directors—"cinematographic function."[47]

*   *   *

From all this there might emerge still another question: What can musicians gain from the cinema? I am not speaking, obviously, in commercial terms, about which our composers need no advice, at least to judge from the enthusiasm and the appetite that has lately been awakened in them, and which indicates [for the business of film music] a clean bill of health. The question, rather, has to do with what an involvement with cinema might contribute to a musician's art?

To many, the very idea of cinema represents the ultimate sin, a prostitution and utter debasement of all that is artistically decent. Yet for those who believe that the true artist is not the one who yields to challenges but who rises up to meet them, the sins and indecencies of film music are apparent only when one compares film music to so-called absolute music. At least in principle, everyone—including the artists involved—can benefit from such an experience.

This would involve, first of all, an attempt at simplification. The results described above [i.e., the music for *Acciaio* and *Un colpo di pistola*] are possible only when one moves along this path, because of the already demonstrated difficulty that music has in reaching the spectator, among them multiple presences on the soundtrack[48] and technical imperfections in recording and sound reproduction. Impossible, therefore, are the fragments, the tiny details, the delicate or complex tone-colors, the abstruse harmonic relationships, the formal structures that go beyond the most elementary ones. Except in stylized situations that approach ballet, artistic results on the level of *Acciaio* and *Un colpo di pistola* are possible only with pieces with simple and immediate structure, with solid and simple orchestration, with simple and incisive thematic material, with simple and self-evident harmony. One needs to be able to grasp the essence of the piece just by hearing any particular moment of it, the same way one tastes the wine of an entire barrel with just one sip. In the most brutal and concrete sense of the word, the piece must be homogeneous.

Say what you want: I believe that taking on this task can be useful. This is not because one ought to behold in horror all the "modern complications." It is simply because any artist can profit from the experience of reducing his art to its most elementary ingredients. It is just as profitable as the other exercise, that of working on commission, which amounts to a most moral and humble act of obedience.

Then [if this task is taken on], perhaps film music[49] will no longer be that utter vacuity that ninety-nine per cent of the time we are forced to hear.

From *La rassegna musicale* [The Musical Review] 16, no. 2 (February 1943), 43–49.
(Translation by Stefano Mengozzi)

8.3 MUSIC AND THE SCREEN

Erich Leinsdorf

Leinsdorf (1912–93) has long been regarded as one of the most important figures on the US classical music scene during the second half of the twentieth century. Born in Vienna and trained as a pianist and conductor, he emigrated to the United States in 1937 to work as assistant conductor at the Metropolitan Opera in New York. In 1943 he succeeded Artur Rodzinski as music director of the Cleveland Orchestra, then from 1947 until 1955 led the Rochester Philharmonic; in 1956 he was named music director of the New York City Opera and a year later music consultant and principal conductor for the Met. Most significant, from 1962 until 1969 he was music director of the Boston Symphony Orchestra.[50]

There is no telling why someone so ensconced as was Leinsdorf in America's classical music establishment would, in the summer of 1945, feel the need to express himself publicly on the "lowly" art of film music. For whatever reasons, however, film music at this particular point in time appears to be something Leinsdorf took quite seriously. Along with this deliberately provocative article for the New York Times, *the conductor expressed comparable views a few months later in a journal geared largely to American music educators.[51]*

Leinsdorf's commentary is interesting at the very least because it gives official blessing to the opinion, long sustained by American academic writers in the 1950s and 1960s, that the only truly "good" film music was that created not for Hollywood fare but for decidedly non-commercial documentaries. At the same time, Leinsdorf's views are interesting because they seem almost pathetically out of touch—as film composer Bernard Herrmann would point out in his response—with what was happening on an almost day-to-day basis in Hollywood. Leinsdorf's opinions on theatrical music in all its manifestations are certainly deserving of respect, yet one has to wonder about how much time this prestigious maestro, in the 1940s, actually spent in the darkness of movie theaters.

For a professional musician it is always hard to accept any artistic communication which puts music in a subordinate and secondary position. A musician's work is centered in

117

the idea that music should be listened to, and, for all those who feel that way, it is hard to take any form of music which is incidental.

I have often found in discussions with people in the theatrical world that their reactions are utterly different: that, for them, music is another "prop" which ought to be used to the best advantage of the general effect. I will try to base my arguments on this assumption, and not on the attitude of the musician to whom the subordinate role of music is odious.

The use of music is obvious whenever anybody on the screen plays an instrument or sings a song. It is equally obvious in the dance sequences of musicals, because everyone realizes that in such instances music is necessary. Not so obvious, and often greatly misused, is the sound of music where it has no logical relation to the dramatic contents of a particular scene. In so-called realistic pictures one frequently hears an orchestra accompany a scene where absolutely no relation can be established between the music and the pictorial drama. In such instances, and they are too frequent for my taste, the music is used to replace the actual sounds which would be normally associated with such scenes. I remember some particular examples, but hesitate to mention them specifically, since I do not wish to single out certain pictures for specific criticism.

It is the style of an entire picture which ought to determine if music is to be used at all, outside of those moments when it is a logical necessity. Wherever the story and the treatment of it goes into the realm of fantasy, we can only criticize or praise the particular treatment. We can only say that in such and such a picture the music was well employed, because in the run of the fantastic any use of music can be justified through choice and treatment.

It is in the so-called realistic pictures where I take issue with the way music is used. When I see a scene in a railway terminal with the action centered around the information desk, with the porters running up and down staircases, with people milling about, the sound of a highly romantic piece of music played by a full orchestra is not only absurd but distracting; it draws the attention of the mind (at least of my own) from the actual scene to the music, which is usually too loud, out of place and out of style.

Music should not be used to help along actual sound effects. A skillful orchestra can produce, with our modern instrumental combinations, a great number of startling effects. But still this is out of place if we are dealing with a picture that endeavors to be realistic. It is a very nice trick to write some music which will give the impression of the sound of rain, but the actual sound of rain, as it can be produced by mechanical devices behind a microphone is more fitting for realistic treatment.

I may not have seen enough films to make a general statement, but as far as my experience is concerned, I have found satisfactory scores mostly in pictures of an unrealistic, fantastic nature. The reason for this may be that the composers who write for such films are less bound by the romantic style of last century's music. To me, the invariably lush sonorities which accompany most emotional scenes are unbearable, because they employ cold-bloodedly devices which have lost their originality, and which are meaningless as used according to a standard pattern.

Some of our contemporary composers have arranged scores which they had previously written for pictures to be used in concert. I find the most satisfactory ones those which have been written for documentary films, while those made for the so-called features do not stand up at all when detached from the screen.

Conclusive proof of the unsatisfactory status of music in the motion picture industry is the fact that some of our modern composers have given up working for pictures, while those who have stayed in Hollywood have subjected themselves to the demands for standardizations and pattern. Type-casting is deadly to a composer, and compulsion to write time and again identical scores for identical stories is bound to result in a lifeless pattern which no ambitious and honest musician will be able to stand for any length of time.

By and large, it is probably unfair to judge an "industry" on the terms of an "art." Art is an individual expression which is permitted only in cases when a motion picture is produced without the collaborations of dozens of individuals whose only aim is to fabricate another meal along the lines of a proved recipe.

The composers who have made their permanent residence in movieland have probably done the correct thing. From them we need not expect the impossible—which means, individual art born in industrial environment.

From the *New York Times*, June 17, 1945, X3.

8.4 MUSIC IN FILMS—A REBUTTAL

Bernard Herrmann

Bernard Herrmann (1911–75) is nowadays celebrated as one of the "canonic" composers of Hollywood film music. His much-deserved fame is linked largely to the scores he produced for films directed by Alfred Hitchcock,[52] but his work in Hollywood began more than a decade before he became involved with Hitchcock, and it was preceded by seven years of composing music for radio dramas.[53]

This brief yet intense response to Erich Leinsdorf's comments on film music, published the week before in the same newspaper, speaks easily for itself. Herrmann's main point of logic is that accompanimental music in films is no more "subordinate and secondary" than is a great deal of music in opera. His chief objection, however, is to Leinsdorf's claim that film music in general can be dismissed as being somehow "standardized." Just as conventions governed screenplays, acting styles, lighting, and costuming during the heyday of classical-style film production, so conventions governed the use of music. Speaking from his own experience but doubtless representing the opinions of many of his Hollywood colleagues, Herrmann argues forcefully that film music can indeed hold to these conventions yet still be of good quality and, in many ways, original.

In last Sunday's *Times*, Erich Leinsdorf indulged in a favorite sport current among many of our interpretive concert musicians—that of belittling film music. As one who is also a conductor of a symphony orchestra, besides being the composer of a considerable amount of film music, I would like to take issue with his criticisms. (Mr. Herrmann conducts the Columbia Broadcasting Symphony Orchestra and has composed the scores of several films, including *Citizen Kane* and *All That Money Can Buy*. Ed.[54])

119

In the first place, he seems upset by the fact that music in films must of necessity be incidental. He declares that music in any "subordinate" place is "odious" to a musician. I fail to see what he means by the word "subordinate." If film music is subordinate, so is music in the theatre and the opera house. Music in the films is a vital necessity, a living force. Had Mr. Leinsdorf ever seen a film in the projection room before the music was added, he would understand thoroughly how important the score is.

Music on the screen can seek out and intensify the inner thoughts of the characters. It can invest a scene with terror, grandeur, gaiety, or misery. It can propel narrative swiftly upward, or slow it down. It often lifts mere dialogue into the realm of poetry. Finally, it is the communicating link between the screen and the audience, reaching out and enveloping all into one single experience.

If this role is "subordinate and secondary," then so is the role of opera music, which, no matter how extended, is governed finally by the needs of the drama. So it is with the best film music. It identifies itself with the action, and becomes a living part of the whole. Obviously, few film scores could bear the scrutiny of the concert audience without being radically rewritten. But, similarly, even the Wagnerian excerpts which are performed by our symphony orchestras seem amputated when they are torn from their rightful places on the stage.

Film music is necessarily written to supply a particular moment of drama, and it is memorable only when it remains wedded to the screen. As such, the media has produced masterpieces. Aaron Copland's sardonic commentary on the monotonous supper of the bored married couple in *Of Mice and Men*; the father's hopeless search for work so eloquently expressed by Alfred Newman in *The Song of Bernadette*; the sound of the sinister jungle done almost entirely by percussion instruments by Franz Waxman in *Objective Burma*; Serge Prokofieff's terrifying Battle on the Ice sequence in *Alexander Nevsky*; and the coal delivery scherzo of Anthony Collins in *Forever and a Day*—all are classics of their kind.

Mr. Leinsdorf makes a great point, in his article, of criticizing the use of music in scenes of a so-called "realistic" nature. He is annoyed by the presence of an orchestra playing a "nineteenth-century romantic piece" during a scene showing a railway terminal, and feels that sound-effects would have sounded much better. He also objects to the use of a musical motif depicting rain in a storm sequence, when the real sound of rain falling could have been used.

Without knowing what scenes in what pictures he is discussing, it is a little difficult to answer this point. Certainly the music in the particular scenes he saw might have been ill-chosen. But again perhaps the composer was trying to achieve some psychological effect or atmospheric quality which could never have been attained through sound-effects on a dead screen. The examples of film music I have just mentioned above are all cases in point.

Contrary to all rumor, there is no such thing as the "standardization" of motion-picture music. The only "standard" for film music is that it be dramatic. Perhaps this is something Mr. Leinsdorf does not understand when he deplores the fact that many of our modern composers have given up working for the screen. Might it not be, simply, that these composers, though their talents are of startling quality, lack the dramatic flair?

The whole point I have been trying to make is that screen music is neither industrialized nor insignificant. Indeed the films and radio offer the only real creative and financial opportunities a composer has. He can write a film score for any musical combination

120

and hear it immediately performed. Moreover the film gives him the largest audience in the world—an audience whose interest and appreciation should not be underestimated. A good film score receives thousands of "fan letters" from intelligent music lovers everywhere.

From the *New York Times*, June 24, 1945, 27.

8.5 HEARD MELODIES[55]

Bosley Crowther

Bosley Crowther (1905–81) for twenty-seven years was the chief film reviewer for the New York Times, *and through most of his tenure—from 1940 until his retirement in 1968—he was generally regarded as the nation's preeminent newspaper-based movie critic. "Conscious of his power," observed his obituary writer, Crowther "rendered his judgments in scholarly rather than breezy language and conservative rather than raffish tones. His sober, resolutely nonpoetic style conveyed wit and the talent of a good storyteller, but it reflected his own fairness and sense of responsibility toward his craft. It also gave no quarter to cacophonous critical notices by some colleagues. There was, thus, an almost official quality to his writing."[56]*

Crowther's "official" but hardly officious stance made him the ideal intermediary for the dispute between conductor Erich Leinsdorf and composer Bernard Herrmann that erupted in the pages of the Times *in June of 1945. Although educated at Princeton and by this time a twelve-year veteran of serious criticism (he had worked on the paper's drama desk from 1933 until moving over to films), he claims here to be a "just plain Joe" who claims no special knowledge of music but who cannot help but notice, as someone who goes often to the movies, that some examples of film music seem to work better than others.*

It is regrettable that Crowther cuts his commentary so short. He admits to having thought often about the use of music in films, and to having much to say on the subject. For the full range of his insights into film music, alas, one has to peruse the tens of thousands of reviews and Sunday columns he penned for the New York Times *or—more easily—thumb through the several books in which his writings are collected.[57] Claiming limitations of space, here he gives only a most basic assessment, to the effect that if the "average person is conscious" of the score then likely "there's something wrong with [it]."*

This reviewer is constantly resolving to sit down some day and write a piece about the uses of music in movies as heard through a non-musician's ear. There's a lot to be said on the subject, from the strictly objective listener's point. But somehow, for reasons that are baffling, this writer never gets around to it. Maybe a fear of showing ignorance of musical techniques is the cause; maybe it's just the simple problem of finding the propitious time.

121

Anyhow, it is always gratifying when somebody else comes along to tackle this controversial subject with assurance and hardihood. And in that this section has been fortunate both last week and this. Last Sunday, Erich Leinsdorf of the Cleveland Orchestra had his say about what he considers the insufficiencies of music applied to films. This week, Bernard Herrmann of the Columbia Broadcasting Symphony and composer of many scores for pictures fires a spirited reply. Both of these seasoned musicians have made provocative points with which a lay listener to film music can more or less heartily agree. And both have propounded certain tenets which sound a bit firm to just plain Joe. The gentlemen have given their opinions as practicing professional musicians. They have covered the ground pretty thoroughly, pro and con, so far as esthetics go.

But Joe and the writer of this article, who pretend to no musical lore, would like to carry the subject farther along simple lines of taste—would like, indeed, to say a few things that we have long been meaning to say. And the first thing is that the best test of a musical score of a film is whether the average person is conscious of it. If he's not, then it has merit. If he is—if the incidental music or atmospheric music, as it is called, comes sharply and persistently to attention—then there's something wrong with the score.

If, for instance, two people are talking—a mother and her daughter, let's say (as we happened to hear two such talking in a silly little picture last week)—and, in the middle of their palavering, some sentimental music nudges in, very maudlin and very obvious, then that is definitely bad. The listener's ear is diverted by an immediately irrelevant set of sounds, the dialogue is cheaply supplemented by foreign music and the whole thing sounds nuts. (The picture we speak of, incidentally, was *Those Endearing Young Charms*, and the music which sneaked into the area was the sentimental song of that name.)[58]

This trick of "cheating" with music in a strictly conversational scene, the music having no validity other than to heighten an effect, is the one most flagrantly exploited by the writers of musical scores and is the one which the average moviegoer most frequently and consciously resents. It is one thing to have a scene with dialogue supported by a musical theme which comes from a source which is apparent, such as an orchestra, phonograph or radio. And it is likewise occasionally tolerable to have a musical theme thus justified carry on into a conversational sequence after the natural source of the music has been dismissed. A good demonstration of this usage was the scene in *The Grapes of Wrath*, wherein Tom Joad said good-by to his mother. The parting, you recall, took place on the platform where, just a little previously, the two had danced happily together. Thus it was reasonable and poetic that the hauntingly distant refrain of "Red River Valley," the dance music, should echo behind the scene. But it is quite something else to have music arbitrarily intrude without any physical justification into a natural exchange of dialogue.

The screen is indeed illusory, as Mr. Herrmann has pointed out, and music is a factor in illusion, even in a "realistic" style. A literal illustration of a destroyer racing through the water, say, such as the opening sequence of the film *In Which We Serve*, is made more effective by a thrilling, soaring musical theme that represents the stimulation of the spirit as one silently observes. In a case of this sort, the music is a commentator on the scene, an accompaniment to the exaltation which the observer inwardly feels. And even a scene such as the fine one at the beginning of *The Purple Heart*, in which the "Air Force Song" softly accompanied the American fliers into the hostile courtroom, was considerably helped by music. It came, as it were, from the audience's heart.

Now, there—you see—we're just beginning to say some of the many things about music that we long have intended, and already we've used up our space. We haven't even mentioned the virtues of silence, of natural sound effects, of a "thematic song" (such as in *Laura*) nor the nature of frankly musical films. As a matter of fact, we've probably done no more than agitate dispute. But that won't hurt anybody. Proper music will soothe our savage breasts.

From the *New York Times*, June 24, 1945, 25.

Part 4

THE POSTWAR YEARS

9

EUROPEAN vs. AMERICAN ATTITUDES

The years immediately following World War II were the most traumatic that the film industry, in general, has ever experienced. In Hollywood, a business that since the early 1920s had been consistently and fabulously lucrative was all of a sudden beset by such troubles as wide-spread complaints about the "moral" content of its products, a government order for the major studios to divest themselves of exhibition venues across the country, a precipitous drop in revenue from overseas markets, and—importantly—serious competition from the new medium of television. In Europe, where most human endeavors had been disrupted by the dangerously close-to-hand war, filmmaking was struggling simply to re-establish itself.

Doubtless some participants in European filmmaking were merely envious of the commercial success long enjoyed by their Hollywood counterparts who managed to muddle through the war years without fear of bombs, literally, falling on their heads. For others of them, perhaps the blessed calm of the post-war period simply offered them the opportunity to reflect—after years of wartime distraction—on what they regarded as fundamental differences between American and European filmmaking. In any case, and no matter to what it might be attributed—politics, economics, aesthetics—the European–American rift has probably never been wider than it was at the twentieth century's midpoint.

Vis-à-vis film music, the rift was spectacularly represented in the debate represented here. As volatile as an in-print exchange can be, it involved an American writer and two British writers, and it was triggered by reports on the proceedings of the International Music Congress held in Florence, Italy, in May 1950.

Although events officially or unofficially labeled "International Music Congress" had taken place in numerous cities under the auspices of various organizations during the preceding half-century, the Congresso Internazionale di Musica had been a more or less regular adjunct function of the Maggio Musicale Fiorentino since that festival was launched in 1933. The Congress did not start to become an annual affair until 1937 and 1938, after which time its intended pattern was broken by the outbreak of hostilities. The 1950 gathering—focused specifically on film music—was held in conjunction with Florence's thirteenth festival, but it was only the seventh in the series of congresses.

Along with general addresses by Fred Goldbeck, Wilfrid Mellers, and Boris de Schloezer, the VII Congresso Internazionale di Musica had on its agenda formal papers by Daniele Amfitheatrof ("American Film Music"), Yves Baudrier ("Realism and Lyricism"), Valentino Bucchi ("Cinema Plus Music"), Nicola Castarelli ("Audio-Visual Synthesis"), Alessandro Cicognini ("Author's Copyright"), Luciano Emmer ("Music in the Short Film"), Carmine Gallone ("The Value of Music in the Film"), Antony Hopkins ("Irony and Humor in Film Music"), Hans Keller ("Musical Quotation"), Roland Manuel ("Collaboration between Musician and Film-Maker"), Enzo Masetti

("Realistic Music"), Guido Pannain ("Music and the Film"), Fernando Previtali ("The Execution of Film Music"), André Schaeffner ("Musical Ethnology and Cinematography"), Hermann Scherchen ("Music and the Microphone"), Hans Strobel ("Musical and Cinematographic Literature"), Maurice Thiriet ("Problems of Music in the Historical Film"), Roman Vlad ("The Composer and Film Music"), and Max Vredenburg ("Music and the Documentary Film").[1] The only American delegate to the VII Congresso Internazionale di Musica was Amfitheatrof (1901–83), a Russian-born musician who emigrated to the United States in 1937 and, after a brief stint as assistant conductor of the Minneapolis Symphony Orchestra, between 1939 and 1955 provided scores for dozens of mostly low-budget Hollywood films.

Lawrence Morton, the American participant in the debate that follows, it is important to note, was *not* in attendance at the Florence event. His article was inspired largely by an allegedly biased report on the conference by one of the British delegates, and his argument in turn provoked a wonderfully colorful response by another of the conference's British attendees.

French composer Georges Auric, the fourth writer represented in this section of the anthology, also did not attend the 1950 conference, yet his essay from 1952 demonstrates that he, too, was actively participating in the debate circulating around European and American approaches to film music. Indeed, the point he raises about the different amounts of music in continental and American (and British) films is one that on several occasions provided Hans Keller with fodder for his own cannon.

9.1 MUSIC: CONGRESS AT FLORENCE

Antony Hopkins

Antony Hopkins (b. 1921) studied piano and composition at the Royal College of Music and soon after graduating established a reputation with his 1948 opera Lady Rohesia *and, even more solidly, with his incidental music for staged plays and radio dramas. Over the next several decades he continued to produce music for theatrical contexts, including scores for such British films as Hugo Fregonese's 1951* Decameron Nights *and 1957* Seven Thunders, *Noel Langley's 1954* The Pickwick Papers, *Lewis Gilbert's 1955* Cast a Dark Shadow, *Wolf Rilla's 1957* The Blue Peter, *and Peter Ustinov's 1962* Billy Budd. *But his talents as an engaging commentator—already evidenced in this report for the magazine* Sight and Sound—*led him to focus his energies primarily in the direction of broadcast journalism.*

*Beginning in the mid-1950s, Hopkins hosted a weekly program for BBC radio titled "Talking about Music." The program ran for almost thirty years, in the process generating a series of books (*Talking about Symphonies, *1961;* Talking about Concertos, *1964;* Talking about Sonatas, *1971) that remain popular as much for their substance as their witty literary style. Considering Hopkins's penchant for the light touch, it is hardly surprising that the paper he read at the 1950 International Music Congress in Florence, Italy, dealt with "Irony and Humour in Film Music."*

Possibly the general tone of Hopkins's report irritated and thus provoked the American writer Lawrence Morton to respond so vociferously in the article that follows in this anthology. Yet unbridled witticism seems confined largely to the report's opening paragraphs, which read more like passages from a travelogue or personal diary than a conference summary. The account of the proceedings per se *is not nearly so colorful; on the matter of film-score orchestration Hopkins readily admits to an anti-Hollywood bias, but likely it was just the content of what was reported—not its manner of presentation— that triggered Morton's heated response.*

I had never been to Florence. But then I don't believe that the disillusioned and bitter cynic who said "to travel hopefully is better than to arrive" had ever been there either. I stepped out of the plane at Milan airport after a breathtaking flight over the dazzling white snowfields of the Alps; the heat hit one like a tangible blow, cutting at once through the cloth of one's coat. My eyes were still blinking away the mirror-like reflection of the sunlight on Silvana Mangano's rice-fields, over which we had flown a minute or two before;[2] and as we sat in the long Italian bus, the unexpected North Country voices around me discussing, of all things, cranes, I felt again that strange feeling of disbelief that air travel always provokes in me. I am sure the traveler was never before so conscious of the essential sameness *within*; drop me suddenly upon the moon and still I will carry within me that small island of "myself" which does not change, wherever I may be.

My ears, still lethargic after the great height we had flown, scarcely heard the excited cries of my fellow Englishmen on seeing one of "their" cranes towering over a huge building project. I stayed the night near the incredible Duomo, most sublime standard-bearer of the Coca-Cola industry's banner; and my sleep, if sleep it could be called, was disturbed by the most refined piece of torture that I have so far met on the Continent— a repeating clock. At each quarter it chimed the full hour, and then one, two or three high-pitched tings according to which quarter it was. Thus between the hours of midnight and one a.m. it chimes a total of 55 times—enough to satisfy the most ardent Catholic.

The next day I was in Florence, and found in my hotel room a magnificent pile of travel leaflets, a vast programme of the Maggio Musicale, and a staggeringly beautiful volume of photographs of the great Baptistry doors, "the Gates of Paradise."[3] There were, however, no instruction as to where I was to go, or when I was required to be there, and inquiry at the hotel desk proved vain. Armed with my Italian phrase-book I sallied forth bravely: "Dore se trova il congresso internazionale di musica?" The police seemed ill-informed, and ultimately directed me to the Florentine equivalent of Keith Prowse[4] where I queued for some time, apparently to get tickets to Duke Ellington. Attempts to by-pass the queue were greeted with storms of protest that my phrase-book was ill-prepared to meet; and attempts to fraternize with an obviously American girl of remarkable beauty were chilled off in icy Florentine. So for two hours I walked alone in Florence, gazing in awe-struck wonder at one architectural masterpiece after another, till I arrived by chance at the Teatro Communale. Here I was received with open arms by a charming Italian, and informed that I was just in time for the first session. The Congress had begun.

I should perhaps explain that I had been invited to speak at an International Music Congress on "Irony and Humour in Film Music"; but during the week composers, critics and directors from many countries were due to read papers on a variety of subjects to do with music and the cinema. To attempt to deal with all these individually would take up more space than there is in the whole of this issue, but I will attempt to deal with some of the points I found outstanding. Once I had arrived there, the Congress was, in fact, extremely well organized. The delegates were able to illustrate their talks with films excellently projected and with good sound; also provided were a radiogram, piano and so on, and an extremely gifted woman interpreter. But what a thankless task she had; can there be anything more depressing to both parties than to have to sit through a translation into French of a speech one has just heard in Italian? Most speakers made the mistake of reading papers at a tremendous speed, trying to pack into their brief fifteen minutes material for an hour's lecture; and it was with some apprehension that I set a precedent by speaking *ad lib*. (I feel that if an audience has to listen to an incomprehensible tongue for a quarter of an hour, at least they might as well be edified by a lively expression on the speaker's countenance, rather than gaze fixedly at the top of his head.)

Twenty-three papers were presented to the Congress, of which I did not hear all. But outstanding among the examples of films were those showing the work of Yves Baudrier. He showed us in particular an extract from *Les Maudits* which for the underplaying of sadism with the maximum of effect would be hard to excel. Readers of SIGHT AND SOUND may remember my comments on Epstein's film *Le Tempestaire*, for which Baudrier also provided the score.[5] In both films, there is an incredible economy of musical resources. This composer can do more with one bass clarinet or a string quartet than most Hollywood composers can do with an orchestra of ninety. This economy, on which I commented in my own talk, was generally approved by the Congress: speaker after speaker attacked the principles of "too much music, too heavily scored." This mood reached its climax when Daniele Amphitheatrof[6] showed us fourteen examples of American film-music. These ranged from *Song of Bernadette* to *Sunset Boulevard*,[7] but Mr. Amphitheatrof apologised for a preponderance of scenes of violence, as the composers on the whole had preferred to choose passages showing their use of the full resources of the orchestra.

The Congress sat in stunned silence while reel after reel of high-powered music was blared out; only Copland's music to *The Red Pony* was vociferously applauded. To hear such a concentration of this type of music was frankly an appalling experience; and again we saw those extraordinary words "The music composed by ——, orchestrated by ——." I had already in my talk, publicly asked Mr. Amphitheatrof to explain this curious dichotomy so fashionable in America, but he dismissed my request in his introductory talk, as "involving too wide issues to be discussed here." However, after this shattering experience, the chairman, Pizzetti,[8] pinned him down on this very point; the explanation was, "on purely financial grounds." Mr. Amphitheatrof went on to explain that so many millions of dollars were tied up in a film, that producers could not wait while one man went through the arduous process of composing and scoring the music, and that a division of labour halved the time involved in waiting for completion of the score. He went on to defend this extraordinary course by expatiating on the virtues and talents of the arrangers. I do not think he realized that of this the Congress had little doubt; this music is orchestration run riot, but little else.

The next morning Benjamin Frankel opened a discussion on the American contributions.[9] With great courage and forthrightness he attacked in no uncertain terms the bulk of the music we had heard the previous evening. Brushing aside all chances of receiving a Hollywood contract, he spoke scathingly of the appalling taste shown in the music of *Song of Bernadette*, which he described as "in my opinion, a depth of vulgarity beyond which it is not possible to sink." The moment Frankel finished speaking, an

Italian composer leaped to his feet and demanded that these remarks should be struck from the minutes, as they were insulting to a great nation.[10] For the first time, a real vitality permeated the hall. Heated speeches were made by partisans of both sides, but the overwhelming majority supported Frankel in his denunciation. Your contributor ended the debate by giving his unconditional support to Frankel.

Unfortunately this was the only topic which really aroused the delegates' passions to any extent, and you must forgive me if I have devoted so much space to it. The general atmosphere of a congress such as this tends to become soporific as time passes. One after another the delegates read their papers, some of them with little variety of expression; there follows the inevitable translation into one or even two different languages, and it is hard to preserve throughout the same expression of unabated enthusiasm and interest however enthralled one may be by the film as an art. The relatively few moments when there was any real discussion or interchange of ideas were by far the most exciting and productive.

The Congress did not pass any resolutions or make any proclamations—that was not its purpose. But I think its general feeling may perhaps be crystallized in the following few statements:

1. That the composer can add immensely to the quality of a film—or mar it! And that consequently he should be entrusted with a say in the film's creation *from the beginning*.
2. That economy of means is more likely to succeed in film-music than overlavish scoring.
3. That the composer must be prepared to sacrifice his own personality in order to achieve the maximum integration with the film; the task is a challenge to his skill as a composer.
4. That the use of music in the cinema is still in a rudimentary state as an "art-form."

These decisions may not seem particularly striking or valuable; but on them at least there was a remarkable degree of unanimity. Besides this, papers were read on a very wide range of aspects of cinematic music, and I am certain that individual composers must have benefited considerably from the interchange of ideas over endless cups of coffee.

From *Sight and Sound* 19, no. 6 (August 1950), 243–44.

9.2 FILM MUSIC OF THE QUARTER

Lawrence Morton

Lawrence Morton (1904–87) distinguished himself, specifically in Southern California but with repercussions felt throughout the United States, for the most part as an entrepreneurial supporter of modernist concert music. In 1954 he took over directorship of Los Angeles's famed "Evenings on the Roof" series, holding to its cutting-edge artistic principles but shifting the presentations to a more conventional venue and changing the name to the "Monday Evening Concerts."[11] *In the same year, Morton helped launch the Ojai Music Festival at which members of the Los Angeles Philharmonic found late-spring employment, in a coastal town comfortably north of the city, performing not just tourist-oriented standard repertoire but also music of modernist, and even avant-garde, persuasion.*

Before he embarked on his full-time managerial activities, Morton was an outspoken critic who championed, among other things, what he considered to be the best efforts of composers working in Hollywood. Indeed, between 1945 and 1951 he wrote no less than nineteen articles on film music—most of them keenly focused on recent releases—for Hollywood Quarterly *and its successor,* The Quarterly Review of Film, Radio and Television. *In his ninth column for* Hollywood Quarterly, *Lawrence Morton responded with full force to reports from British writers Antony Hopkins and Hans Keller on the discussions of film music that had transpired during the summer of 1950 at the International Music Congress in Florence, Italy.*

Along with objecting strongly to what he took to be negative generalizations regarding the content and dramatic function of American film music as contrasted with its British and continental European counterparts, Morton took issue in particular with the British writers' apparently dismissive comments on the role of the Hollywood orchestrator. In assessing the diatribe printed here, one should of course note that Morton's younger brother Arthur had for years earned a living as an orchestrator before being engaged, c.1947, as composer for numerous low-budget Columbia films, and that Lawrence Morton himself served as orchestrator for his brother's score for Never Trust a Gambler *(Columbia, 1951), for David Raksin's score for* The Bad and the Beautiful *(MGM, 1952), and for Herschel Burke Gilbert's score for* Without Warning *(United Artists, 1952). But Morton's personal involvement with film-score orchestration ultimately seems less important than his logical argument that orchestration by hands other than the composer's is fairly demanded by Hollywood's production schedule and that the results—all things considered—are not necessarily bad.*

Morton's article—reprinted in Sight and Sound *under the provocative headline "Orchestration Run Riot?"*[12]*—prompted a vitriolic response from Keller (see p. 136) that in turn triggered yet more argument from Morton. Morton's formal rebuttal to Keller, in a column titled "Composing, Orchestrating, and Criticizing,"*[13] *was apparently the last "official" word in this particular debate. But as is evidenced by a wealth of post-1951 commentary, the forceful pronouncements by Keller and Morton hardly marked the end of the story.*

There is nothing in the current crop of film scores half so interesting as the discrepancies between Daniele Amfitheatrof's report on the reception given the exhibit of American film music at the International Music Congress at Florence and the reports of the British delegates. "We had a good hand at every entry," wrote Mr. Amfitheatrof, "and prolonged applause, verging on an ovation, at the end of the show."[14] Hans Keller, a British delegate and a critic, this time restrained his penchant for a metaphysical and Freudian vocabulary. Instead he indulged in invective, calling the exhibit a "repellent anthology" and noting that the assembly was composed of "musicians who could hardly be expected to like the stuff."[15] Antony Hopkins, another Briton and a composer, wrote that "the Congress sat in stunned silence while reel after reel of high-powered music was blared out: only Copland's music to *The Red Pony* was vociferously applauded."[16] Another British delegate, Benjamin Frankel, took the floor and "attacked in no uncertain terms the bulk of the music we had heard the previous evening," according to Mr. Hopkins. "Heated speeches were made by partisans on both sides," he continued, "but the overwhelming majority supported Frankel in his denunciation."

Obviously, strong national passions had been aroused, which, together with a long-standing bias against Hollywood, prevented any discussion of aesthetic matters on an aesthetic level. This was most unfortunate, for one would have expected, from an assembly only half so august as Mr. Keller deemed this one, a truly analytical and inquiring attitude toward at least two specific issues that came up for discussion. In both instances conclusions were apparently reached without consideration of all the facts concerned, proving once again that propaganda can best be made when ignorance is not allowed to interfere with the formulation of judgments.

The first of these issues was economy of instrumental resources in the scoring of films. Impressed by the sound of Yves Baudrier's music for *Les Maudits*, which called for a very small orchestra, the Congress was impelled to cry out, "Me, too!" and promptly went on record as favoring this kind of economy. But the larger issue of how and when to be economical appears to have been dodged. One would like to know, for instance, whether Baudrier's economy was dictated by aesthetic considerations or by a small budget, whether or not he had to underscore any earthquakes, chases, battles, or horse races, whether *Les Maudits* is a pastoral-scenic or an epic-historical drama, whether its love story (if there is any) is about high-flown purple passions or a sultry hall-bedroom amour.[17]

It may indeed be true, as Mr. Hopkins writes, that Baudrier "can do more with one bass clarinet or a string quartet than most Hollywood composers can do with an orchestra of ninety." Aside from the fact that Hollywood composers never have orchestras of ninety (thirty-five to fifty being even above average), while it is the British who employ the full resources of their great London orchestras—aside from this, it remains to be discovered precisely what Mr. Hopkins means by doing "more." One thing that can't be done with a string quartet is to equal the full sonority of an orchestral *tutti*, a noble and honorable sound that very few composers (even the most fastidious) and very few audiences (even the most snobbish) are quite willing to do without in dramatic music. The history of music gives no evidence that large sounds are inherently more vulgar than small ones. The crucial point, which the congress overlooked, is that economy is a matter of style rather than of numbers of performers. It is style that makes a Mozart quartet sound more economical than one of Schubert's, such as the great G-major. Stravinsky's *Symphony of Psalms* demands quadruple winds, yet it is a far more economical work than, say, Strauss' *Metamorphosis* which needs only strings.[18] And even Mahler's *Song of the Earth* is proof enough that some composers need very large orchestras to be economical with.[19]

Thus the congress' endorsement of economy was much like a politician's endorsement of virtue, an empty gesture. Attention to the real problem might have led to a consideration of what functions music is called upon to perform in films. So long as music is limited, as it is in both British and American films, to the performance of stereotyped functions, it is hardly likely to change very much from what it has been for many years. In the meantime, it will be no victory for music when Hamlet's funeral march is scored for a wind quintet or when Ben Hur drives his chariot around the

Coliseum to the accompaniment of a clarinet cadenza.[20] But it will be a real victory when, with the active collaboration of a composer, music gets itself written into the script of a screenplay, with appropriate opportunity for the intimate sound of a string quartet as well as the powerfully moving sonority of the full orchestra.

The other issue that the congress gave attention to, and scolded Hollywood for, is the custom of using orchestrators instead of allowing (or obliging) composers to score their own music. The solicitude of the Europeans for their American colleagues is indeed touching. It is also gratuitous. For the final judgment as to the correctness, style, and practicability of an orchestrator's work can only be made by the composer. Criticism may thereafter voice the opinion that it doesn't like the composition or the orchestration, but only the composer can say if it matches his conception of what he wants to hear. And it would seem to me that if the orchestration is proper to the music, it should make no difference who did it. On these grounds we accept as authentic Rabaud's orchestration of Fauré's *Dolly*, Koechlin's of *Pelléas et Mélisande*, Eustace's of *Prométhée*.[21]

Eager to condemn Hollywood, the congress did not pause to ask precisely what the orchestrator does. It asked "why"; but Mr. Amfitheatrof gave an inadequate answer, favoring only the chairman, Pizzetti, with a full reply in private.[22] There are some composers whose sketches are so complete and so detailed that the orchestrator performs, in effect, the duties of an intelligent copyist, as do the assistants who for a quarter of a century have been transcribing to the orchestral score page the contents of Prokofiev's fully worked out piano sketches.[23] One Hollywood orchestrator, asked to describe his job, said, "I take the music off the white paper and put it on the yellow." In such instances the orchestrator's discretion may be exercised only in such matters as assigning a phrase to the third clarinet instead of the second, spelling off the trombones in a lengthy passage requiring frequent change of position, making a practical division of labor between two percussion players, or deciding whether the harp part would be better notated in flats or sharps. There are not, to be sure, very many composers who execute their sketches in such detail, and no one can be expected to know who they are, since the list of credits does not tell. Neither does the absence of an orchestrator credit mean that the composer has orchestrated his own music. Aaron Copland, for instance, has always used orchestrators when working in Hollywood.[24] Yet their hands are never observable in the music for the simple reason that Copland's sketches are so complete that no other musical personality has an opportunity to intrude itself upon his music. Equally complete are the sketches of Adolph Deutsch, Hugo Friedhofer, David Raksin, and Miklos Rozsa, to name but a few. These composers are in fact responsible for every note in their scores, except in very rare instances when time pressures might operate against their usual practice.

Less well-known composers who work for small, independent producers do actually orchestrate their own music. The reasons here are economic: small budgets do not allow for orchestrators. In many cases the music is composed and orchestrated for the single orchestration fee, which has been established by the Musicians' Union. But since there is no wage scale for composition, many composers are obliged to "throw it in" for the price of orchestration in order to get the job. That is, they are paid very well for their drudgery, but not at all for their creativity. Here is a situation to which a congress somewhere, if only in Florence, might well give its attention.

By far the greater number of composers make sketches of varying degrees of roughness. Sometimes the association between a composer and his orchestrator is so intimate and of such long standing that they are in effect two aspects of a single mind, as Mr. Amfitheatrof pointed out to the questioning members of the congress. In these cases, if the composers accept the orchestration, criticism can justly make no separation between composition and orchestration, and the music must be evaluated as a unit. For all practical purposes, it would be identical if either of the collaborators had done all of the work.

In cases where the composer is totally unable or unwilling to orchestrate his own music, the orchestrator's responsibility is great and often amounts to composition. He may have to supply inner voices, change harmonies, invent accompaniment patterns, insert counterpoints, and disguise completely the keyboard origin of the music. He may also have to delete great handfuls of cluttering sonority. Criticism might very well say, on the basis of an examination of the composer's sketch, that he is simply not equipped for his job, that he is an ignorant hack. But criticism must also go on to say that the responsibility for the situation rests with the producers who hire hacks and not with the orchestrators who make the music viable and are at least honest and skilled workmen. And is there any valid reason why the inventive musician who lacks craft, and the capable workman who lacks inventiveness should not join forces to produce something for which there is a market? It is not the collaboration that should be condemned but the eventual output, if it is indeed *kitsch*. And if the collaboration should be able, by some chance, to produce a first-rate score, I see no reason why Messrs. Keller, Frankel, and Hopkins should not accept it on the basis of the sounds made, regardless of who made them.

The collateral charge, that all Hollywood music is orchestrated alike, is simply not true, except for persons who listen to scores with organs other than the ear. The scores that are orchestrated alike are the ones that have been composed alike. Composers are very fussy about who orchestrates their music, on the basis of such factors as treatment of bass lines, voicing of brass, thickness or thinness of texture, ability to make twelve studio fiddlers sound as full as the string section of the London Philharmonic Orchestra. If a composer has written a Straussian horn tune in the manner of *Don Juan*, it had better not be scored for an alto flute.[25] Such perversity, it so happens, thrives in the contemporary concert hall where it has been mistaken for a virtue. One is thought to be original if one gives an idiomatic string melody to a trumpet, a flute passage to an E-flat clarinet, a piccolo passage to a glockenspiel, particularly in arrangements of classical works for the ballet. This kind of perversity is little practiced in Hollywood studios, and novelty of effect usually results from a dramatic situation on the screen, the virtuosity of a particular instrumentalist in the studio orchestra, or the special characteristics of the microphone. On the whole, orchestration is remarkably conservative in its intent, for the obvious reason that the music calls for conservatism. There would be little point in dressing up such music in Stravinsky's late instrumental style. This is an error that many "serious" composers have fallen into, as though every one of their pieces had the parodistic intent of Stravinsky's *Pulcinella*.[26] Much "modern" orchestration has thus become "wrong instrument" orchestration, just as much "modern music" has become "wrong note" music. When these criteria become generally fashionable and are applied to situations where they are not relevant, it follows that almost anything can be weighed in the balance and be found wanting. Most Hollywood music gets the orchestration it deserves.

In an ideal world every film composer would be a master, and he would have time, energy, and the desire to compose, orchestrate, and conduct his own scores. The artistic purpose of every score would be calculated along with the planning of the film as a whole. But the industry is still a long way from granting music the status of a sovereign art cooperating with other sovereign arts toward the creation of a *gesamtkunstwerk*.[27] Meanwhile, any attack on the practice of using orchestrators is completely irrelevant to the real evils that exist. When composers operate like first-rate artists, their talents can never be watered down by orchestrators; and when the composers are hacks, their work is made viable, and sometimes even respectable, by the orchestrators.

If future congresses want to find out truly what is wrong with American film music, and resolve resolutions, they would do better to investigate Hollywood studios on the spot instead of waving divining rods in faraway Florence. Upon request, I myself would be happy to provide subject matter for dozens of resolutions that might be passed in an effort to secure a redress of grievances. The use of orchestrators would be near the bottom of the list.

From *Hollywood Quarterly* 5, no. 3 (Spring 1951), 282–88.

9.3 HOLLYWOOD ORCHESTRATORS: THE DRAGON SHOWS HIS TEETH

Hans Keller

Hans Keller (1919–85) was born in Vienna and emigrated to England in 1938. Trained as a violinist and violist, he found work in London first as an orchestral musician, but he discovered quickly that his gifts as a provocative commentator on music far surpassed his abilities as a player. He first expressed himself, in German, as a London correspondent for the Swiss Basler Nachrichten; *after quickly gaining fluency in English, he wrote prolifically for such British publications as* The Music Review, Music Survey, Musical Opinion, *and* The Musical Times; *in 1959 he accepted a full-time position with the British Broadcasting Corporation.[28] He wrote on a wide variety of musical topics (perhaps most important among them the "canonic" works of Mozart, Haydn, Beethoven, and Mendelssohn and the still controversial works of the twentieth-century composers Schoenberg and Benjamin Britten). Yet some of his most impassioned writing, beginning in 1946, had to do with the use of music—whether borrowed from pre-existing sources or originally composed—in films.[29]*

Keller had been fairly brief in his first comment on the 1950 International Music Congress at Florence, limiting his remarks to a single long paragraph appended to an extensive report on the Maggio Musicale Fiorentino festival into which the congress— which focused on film music—was incorporated.[30] Considering his penchant for self-expression, Keller also had been unusually reticent: instead of giving vent to his own opinions, he simply noted that his countryman Antony Hopkins in the course of his address on irony and humor in film music made "a successful attack on the Hollywood composer's obligation to entrust the scoring of his music to a time-saving 'orchestrator'" and that composer Benjamin Frankel, another countryman, "delivered ex abrupto *fireworks" on the particular American film clips shown at the conference and on "Hollywood music and orchestration in general." Barely hiding his gleefulness under a thin veneer of objectivity, Keller reported that Frankel "was not, in fact, polite" and that "practically everybody showed his gratitude" to him.*

Prompted by the American writer Lawrence Morton's impassioned response to his own terse account and Hopkins's more extended article on the congress,[31] Keller in the summer of 1951 published an uninhibited rebuttal. The article reproduced here is remarkable not just because it so colorfully typifies Keller's hyperbolic writing style but also—and more importantly—because it articulates fundamental differences between Hollywood and European film-music styles that would become increasingly apparent as the decade wore on.

Keller was perhaps on the mark when he wrote, dismissively, of postwar Hollywood's apparent fondness for "violin saccharine" and "tuberculous brass." It remains to be seen, however, if what Keller heatedly described as "the anti-artistic influence of Hollywood's music" was indeed "the most tenacious musical enemy of culture in the history of our civilization."

Not a Hollywood film title, but Hollywood itself. For long enough, Fafner has been watching in sleepy peace over that fatal gold he gained from the gods; at last Siegfried, in the disguise of three British delegates at the Florentine International Music Congress (1950), has made him spit venom from his nostrils.[32] In fact, Mr. Lawrence Morton, music critic of *Hollywood Quarterly* (Los Angeles), is annoyed. He devotes a whole article—reprinted from *Hollywood Quarterly* in *Sight and Sound*—to Siegfried's approach; Antony Hopkins gives his retort in *opere citato*.[33] Both articles should be read by everyone interested in music and uninterested in Hollywood music. The present article amends rather than doubles Mr. Hopkins's effort.

From the opening paragraph of Mr. Morton's piece:

> There is nothing in the current crop of film scores half so interesting as the discrepancies between Daniele Amfitheatrof's report on the reception given the exhibit of American film music at the International Music Congress at Florence and the reports of the British delegates. 'We had a good hand at every entry,' wrote Mr. Amfitheatrof, 'and prolonged applause, verging on an ovation, at the end of the show.' [Here Mr. Morton refers the reader to *Italy—Music and Films*, Academy of Motion Picture Arts and Sciences, Los Angeles, 1950.] Hans Keller, a British delegate and a critic, this time restrained his penchant for a metaphysical and Freudian vocabulary. Instead he indulged in invective, calling the exhibit 'a repellent anthology' and noting that the assembly was composed of 'musicians who could hardly be expected to like the stuff.' [Here Mr. Morton refers the reader to the *Music Review*, Vol. 9, No. 3, August, 1950, pp. 210–1, and goes on to cite Hopkins's report on the Congress, including a mention of Benjamin Frankel's denunciation of Hollywood music.] Obviously, strong national passions had been aroused, which, together with a long-standing bias against Hollywood, prevented any discussion of aesthetic matters on an aesthetic level. This was most unfortunate, for one would have expected, from an assembly only half so august as Mr. Keller deemed this one, a truly analytical and inquiring attitude towards at least two specific issues that came up for discussion.

Since Mr. Morton starts beside the point and ad hominem, I have to do likewise. I am not aware of having yet enlarged upon the metaphysics of music with which, at the same time, I cannot see anything wrong, except that it would be a curious undertaking to examine Hollywood music from this particular aspect. Mr. Morton may like to remind himself that Schopenhauer's metaphysics have enriched both Wagner's and Schoenberg's knowledge of the nature of music; I do not know whether *Hollywood Quarterly* has yet attempted a task of similar import. A 'Freudian vocabulary' I certainly do use in my capacity as musician-psychologist,[34] but again it is difficult to see what is wrong with the psychology of musical composition, except that Fafner is about the only one who has reason to be afraid of it. By his describing my all too reticent understatements as 'invective,' Mr. Morton appears to imply that my article on the Film Music Congress contained fewer details than he would have liked to see; if he will read some of my other writings on film music in general and Hollywood music in particular, he will perhaps find more musical facts than he will like to see.

His assumption of 'strong national passions' is silly nonsense. Frankel's stressedly international outlook is common knowledge; Hopkins has not yet given public expression to any kind of passion whatsoever; whereas the present writer—an Austrian-born, Jewish, naturalized Briton who during the short span of his life has been variously accused of (a) not being Austrian enough, (b) not being German, (c) being a Jew, (d) not being Jewish enough, (e) being German, (f) being too Austrian, (g) not being British enough, and (h) being too British—is hardly the most obvious type to go in for strong anti-rational national passions. He has in fact the deepest respect for American life and thought, but Hollywood music happens to contain neither.

Hopkins protests against Mr. Morton's accusation of 'a long-standing bias against Hollywood'; I enthusiastically confess it. My bias has developed from a conscientious study of Hollywood music—the most deadening task a contemporary musician can impose upon himself. Why, now, do I blame Hollywood instead of certain Hollywood composers? The overwhelming majority of Hollywood scores emit such a stench that one is forced to the conclusion that something is basically wrong with this film industry's musico-sociologico-economical set-up. I think I can foresee Mr. Morton's reply to this one, when I hasten to add that the purity of my heart and gall-bladder would satisfy the most perspicacious discoverer of un-American Activities. And even Aaron Copland, a kind being who does not readily dip his pen in gall and who, moreover, is not a completely independent observer inasmuch as (thank heaven) he contributes occasionally to Hollywood—even Copland has permitted himself the opinion that the music of the West Coast is 'artistically of a low order.'[35] He generously adds that, 'the best one can say about Hollywood is that it is a place where composers are actually needed.' I should say, the worst about Hollywood is that it is a place where composers are not needed. Copland's own observations hardly admit of a different conclusion. Writing of Ernst Toch's score for *Peter Ibbetson*, he points out that

> on the strength of this job, Toch should be to-day one of the best-known film composers. But unfortunately there aren't enough people in Hollywood who can tell a good score when they hear one. To-day Toch is generally assigned to do 'screwy music' (in Hollywood music is either 'screwy' or 'down to earth'— and most of it down to earth).

In short and mild,

> most [Hollywood] scores are written in the late-nineteenth-century symphonic style, a style now so generally accepted as to be considered inevitable.

At the same time, Toch has at least preserved his integrity. I have followed the musical envelopment of at least three European talents who haven't. They have gone so completely to the dogs in Hollywood that their stuff is now indistinguishable from that of their analphabetic colleagues, and untraceable to their own pre-Hollywoodian work. So much for my bias against Hollywood. There is only one thing better than an unprejudiced approach, and that is to have the right prejudices. Mr. Morton:

> The first issue was economy of instrumental resources ... the larger issue of how and when to be economical appears to have been dodged ... One thing that can't be done with a string quartet is to equal the full sonority of an orchestral *tutti*, a noble and honorable sound ... The history of music gives no evidence that large sounds are inherently more vulgar than small ones. The crucial point, which the Congress overlooked, is that economy is a matter of style rather than of numbers of performers. It is style that makes a Mozart quartet sound more economical than ... Schubert's ... great G-major.

It is quite true that Antony Hopkins has not analysed this question with sufficient precision. The sickening effect of empty extravagance which the typical, stereotyped Hollywood orchestration produces is not so much due to the strength of the forces employed as to their *disproportion*. That is to say, we hardly ever get that 'full sonority of an orchestral *tutti*,' that 'noble and honourable sound,' that 'powerfully moving sonority of the full orchestra' on which Mr. Morton rhapsodizes with Hollywoodian emphasis; what we hear on most of Hollywood's sound tracks is a perversely *restricted* full orchestra serving an obscene homophony. Almost every Hollywood orchestration is literally top-heavy. The upper part pesters you almost throughout, predominantly in the form of violin saccharine, and violently predominating, *ad absurdam*, over the vague fakes and fillers of inner parts—*in many cases there is no evidence at all of any 2nd violins!*—and over the tuberculous brass. The brass is used in the most elementary dialogic, chordal blocks, nor can the woodwinds be called differentiated: where they don't pad or double, they proffer one of those 'characterizations' that double the picture and centuplicate themselves. Mr. Morton's mention of 'the style that makes a Mozart quartet sound economical' reminds me that Fafner's harp not only explores his own imitations of nineteenth-century music, but even advances into the eighteenth century. In my paper, 'Featured Music: "Classical" Quotations,' which as it happened immediately preceded Amfitheatrof's exhibition at the Congress, I said:

> ... a rose thrown into a midden does not improve the smell, but rather starts to stink itself. Lionel Newman, for instance, Musical Director of last year's *Apartment for Peggy*, struck upon Mozart's Clarinet Quintet—not a popular proposition by Hollywood standards.[36] He (or his orchestrator) struck off the clarinet, and stuck on, so as to sound dead wrong, *flute and harp*, mindful maybe of Mozart's Concerto for Flute and Harp, if unaware that Mozart disliked these

two instruments throughout his life. The slow movement of the Quintet appeared *fully orchestrated*, and transposed to the key of the first movement, being thus used as suicide music. The minuet Mr. Newman first employed as background music to dialogue, and eventually, in its turn *fully orchestrated*, as 'end title music.' The second trio as streamlined by way of a hair-raising contraction . . . Every musician, and nobody else, should see this film.[37]

It seems that Hollywood does not altogether share Mr. Morton's respect for Mozart's economy of style. I put it to him that *outside Hollywood an equal outrage would be impossible.*
Mr. Morton continues:

> The other issue that the congress gave attention to, and scolded Hollywood for, is the custom of using orchestrators instead of allowing (or obliging) composers to score their own music . . . the final judgment as to the correctness, style and practicability of an orchestrator's work can only be made by the composer.

Again, it is true that by its fairly exclusive concentration on the question of orchestration, Hopkins's speech at the Congress was liable to give rise to misunderstandings: the impression was created that Hollywood's orchestrations were the root of most evil, whereas they are merely the symptoms of a simple though devastating disease. To some extent Frankel compensated for the defects of Hopkins's speech when, the day after the showing of Amfitheatrof's exhibits, he delivered a violent attack on them, suggesting (if I remember his exact words directly) that their musical substance itself 'reached the lowest imaginable depths'; but by that time the busy American delegate had left the Congress. The simple fact is that musically and creatively speaking there isn't such a separate thing as orchestration, and that the division of work between 'composer' and 'orchestrator' is only possible, in fact necessary, *where the composers can't compose, or can but don't.* A *posteriori*, of course, the symptom becomes in its turn a cause, by way of a vicious circle: the presence of the arranger or orchestrator makes it possible, indeed desirable, that an idiot should occupy the position of the composer. It is thus that Mr. Morton arrives at his shattering rhetorical opinion:

> Is there any valid reason why the inventive musician who lacks craft, and the capable workman who lacks inventiveness, should not join forces to produce something for which there is a market? It is not the collaboration that should be condemned but the eventual output, if it is indeed *Kitsch*. I see no reason why Messrs. Keller, Frankel and Hopkins should not accept it on the basis of the sounds made, regardless of who made them.

From the fact that a capable workman may lack inventiveness Mr. Morton derives the silent assumption that an inventive musician may lack craft and thus need an arranger; and while we do not 'accept' the musical products of Hollywood on the basis of the sounds made, it was our having to reject them on this basis that made us worry in the first place about what happened behind the scenes. As Hopkins points out, somewhat belatedly, in his reply to Mr. Morton:

> The point at issue at the Congress was never one of expressing a lack of
> confidence in the abilities of the orchestrators; their technique is unquestionable
> if at times their taste is not. The finger of suspicion was pointed at the
> 'composers.'

But it must be added that the unbearable standardization of Hollywood orchestrations
is undoubtedly more directly due to the good orchestrators than to the bad composers.

Scoring is an aspect of invention. It has remained for Hollywood to discover the talent
so pure and modest that it has not learned to express itself, to offer, at least, every
opportunity to the dumb genius, that the creator who gets ideas without having them,
to the thinker so abstract and transcendental that the power of his invention does not
make him, but on the contrary forbids him to learn how to write a score.

At the Congress, Hopkins did not point his 'finger of suspicion' with anything like
sufficient force and precision at the *composers*, but he makes ample amends in the
eloquent final paragraph of his reply:

> Who are these people, whose names never seem to appear on any concert
> programmes? What else have they written; what pages have they placed upon
> the altar of Art, rather than on the lap of Mammon? When we hear music that
> so depends on the artifice of the scoring, when we hear page after page of 'effects'
> with no development, no continuity, and little individuality, are we really being
> so impertinent if we are tempted to doubt the qualifications of the man behind
> it? I do not mind if Copland has a glorified copyist to do his dirty work for him,
> because I know from the concert world that he is a composer of stature, and a
> man whom one can trust.

This last in reply to Mr. Morton's reddest herring:

> Aaron Copland . . . has always used orchestrators when working in Hollywood.
> Yet their hands are never observable in the music for the simple reason that
> Copland's sketches are so complete that no other musical personality has an
> opportunity to intrude itself upon his music.

Exactly. In point of fact, Copland's film music shows how the cinema, far from being
legitimized to serve 'the inventive musician who lacks craft' as a lucrative playground,
can offer the real composer opportunities for original creative scoring, for novel functional sonorities. Copland's last (though, incidentally, by no means best) score to date,
for instance, i.e. that for *The Heiress* (Paramount Pictures, 1948–49), superimposes by
way of dubbing a string-orchestral over the orchestral sound-track, the string orchestra
being divided into the wood, brass and string parts of the underlying full orchestra. Mr.
Morton has not so far noticed how effectively the strongly national Copland paralyses
our strong national passions.

It is our artistic passion that makes us, now that Fafner has risen from his lair, draw
our sword and stand in defiance. The anti-artistic influence of Hollywood's music does
not merely extend far beyond the cinema, but is in all likelihood the most tenacious
musical enemy of culture in the history of our civilization. I shall regularly devote some
of the present feature's space to particularized criticisms of Hollywood and shall be the

first to praise where praise is musically due. Meanwhile the fight is on. Not, of course, against Mr. Morton as a person, nor even as an independent musician: certain remarks in both his present article and one of a year ago (where, if we remember correctly, he drew attention to the fact that Copland's title music for *The Heiress* was deleted and replaced by another composer's stuff, as well as to the need for musical film music criticism)[38] tend to show that if the Hollywood composers whom he appears to shield out of a mistaken sense of loyalty were as musical as he, he would have no reason to get annoyed with us.

From *Music Review* 12, no. 3 (August 1951), 221–25.

9.4 HOW FILM MUSIC WAS BORN AND HOW IT IS MADE TODAY

(Voici comment est née et comment se fait
aujourd'hui la musique de cinéma)

Georges Auric

Georges Auric (1899–1983) was one of the several dozen composers who responded to the 1919 survey conducted by the magazine Le Film *(see p. 23 of this volume), and the only one of them all who went on to have a long and fruitful career in film music. His first recorded scores were for Jean Cocteau's avant-garde* Le Sang d'un poète *(1930)[39] and René Clair's* À Nous la Liberté *(1931). He contributed prolifically to French cinema throughout the 1930s and, often in politically significant ways, during the Nazi occupation; after World War II Auric cultivated an international career, continuing to score French films but also working with studios in England—especially the Ealing Studio—and then, starting with William Wyler's 1953* Roman Holiday, *with various Hollywood studios. Although his music would continue to be heard in French films and television shows for another two decades, Auric in effect retired from film scoring in 1962 when he accepted both the presidency of the Académie des Beaux-Arts and the directorship of the Réunion des Théâtres Lyriques Nationaux that governed the activities of both of Paris's large opera houses; elected president of the organization that controls copyrights for French composers (SACEM) in 1954, Auric continued to serve in that capacity until 1977.*

As the first part of its title suggests, the article reproduced here has Auric recapitulating—from a decidedly French perspective—the history of film music. More significant, near the end of the article Auric explores questions that in the early 1950s were occupying the minds of filmmakers not just in France but throughout Europe and in the United States; echoing ideas that circulated in France and the Soviet Union during the earliest years of the sound film, he argues strongly for music that does not simply mimic whatever action or sentiment is being depicted on the screen, and he suggests that films in general might fare better with much less music than seems to be the current norm.

142

There is no doubt that from now on there will be musical works born from the cinema. I think that in order to understand how these works have come to be, we must return to the origins of sound cinema [*cinéma sonore*] and realize how extraordinary it was for musicians to be able to record a film score. Thinking of this, we can understand the early errors, which delayed the arrival of more interesting film music. Sound cinema demanded the composition of original scores; until then, all the music that accompanied silent films amounted only to adaptations.

There were, however, some precedents for music composed specially for films. Saint-Saëns even wrote a score, which nobody knows about and which it would be interesting to rediscover. I believe that it was written for *L'Assassinat du Duc de Guise*.[40] Then there was one from Rabaud for *Le Joueur d'échecs*,[41] and one from Florent Schmidt for the unknown film *Salambô*.[42] Of course, Saint-Saëns and Rabaud were unaware of all that the cinema could be.

The first person to pose this question was Honegger, because he worked with Gance for *La Roue*.[43] In Honegger's apartment, I remember seeing a little machine that measured tempo in relation to the length of the film strip; this seemed extraordinary back then. People got by on the idea that a film was accompanied by pieces chosen from a music library. Publishers printed pieces called pursuits, kidnapping in the moonlight, automobile races, etc. Thus people got by on a basic idea. From the beginning, sound films demanded specially written music, and composers were disconcerted.

I recall that, while I was writing the score for *À Nous la Liberté*,[44] René Clair strongly advised me to go listen to the music from *L'Opéra de quat' sous* [*Die Dreigroschenoper*],[45] which had just been released.

Music Brings an Original Element

Now, Kurt Weill, the composer of this film score, did not think about writing for the cinema. He had written his music for a play and it so happened that this music "stuck" admirably well to the film. I explain this by the fact that Pabst, the director, had a type of intuition before which we must bow down. Not being a musician, he could not realize the possibilities given to him by the score, but on the other hand, he knew how to pull the maximum from it. Without any doubt, this was not simply a stroke of luck. The music existed, it had a climate, an atmosphere, a character, and this character influenced the very atmosphere of Pabst's film. The proof of this is that you cannot find this character in any of Pabst's other films. Consequently, even though Kurt Weill's music was not written for the cinema, it brings to this film an element that belongs only to it. Remove the music from *L'Opéra de quat' sous* and the film is still very interesting for its time, but you lose fifty percent of its interest.

This was an indication and, when I saw this film, I dreamed about what I could do for René Clair. I found myself facing problems that at the time were excessively awkward. Indeed, from the beginning, the composer who arrived in a studio was faced with formidable, almost insurmountable difficulties. He met the sound engineer, who immediately declared that there were instruments that could never be heard; that if one wrote in such and such a fashion, it recorded poorly; that one couldn't mix words and this music.[46]

As it happened, the recording process had evolved a great deal. A musician like Maurice Jaubert, one of the best musicians to have written for the cinema, was very much concerned about these questions. He continually sought better instrumental combinations and orchestral arrangements than those in the theatres and concert halls.

As for the role of music in relation to the dramatic action, Walt Disney's marvelous sound cartoons were a very bad example for composers. The scores for these were written in a manner contrary to that used for a normal film. It is truly a music conceived note by note for precise movements and the cartoon is edited to the music, whereas for a normal film the composer writes his music after being shown a completed scene.

We are often asked if it would be possible and more interesting, from a musical point of view, to write a cue for certain scenes upon reading the script. People have tried it, but it is clear that it is necessary to see the manner in which the director has realized his subject.

But I strongly fear that I will never compose another score in the same conditions under which I composed for *À Nous la Liberté*. It was a period from the annals of cinema. René Clair had me sign a contract that nobody would make me sign again. I was to be present for every day of filming. I was to live at Epinay.[47] It taught me a great deal about what film music could be. Every evening I attended the screenings of the scenes that had been filmed that day; they were not yet edited, but right away that gave me a sufficient idea of the atmosphere. I could immediately sketch my music.

Music Should Not Accompany a Gesture, but a Complete Scene

It seems that the default for the earliest film scores was to begin from a principle analogous to that used in cartoons, and to seek an absolute synchronization with the movements. I myself committed this error in my first films. I believed that it was necessary to find this synchronization, if not by a manner as absolute as accompanying every gesture, then by a precise fashion like accompanying the steps of the characters.

On the other hand, now I believe that film music liberated itself from these shackles, which sometimes created comic effects in dramatic films. If you underline the tragedy of a film by a more precise accent, you make the audience laugh; it was even more striking during the silent era with the attempts at adapting classical music. When a hero killed somebody, some orchestra conductors thought it ingenious to strike a tremendous chord, which unleashed laughter. Thus, in film music, it is not a question of accompanying precise gestures, but the scene itself. The whole problem is there.

Personally, people give me the script and the editing script [*découpage*]. I try to find the passages that need music, and I talk about them with the director; when I can, I go see the film while it is being shot, to discover some of its elements. Then the moment comes when the rough cut is shown. I attend this and people give me the absolutely critical time indications. Obviously, it is impossible to not work with precision, it is necessary to know that this scene will last eleven minutes and five seconds, but without cutting said scene phrase-by-phrase or gesture-by-gesture. In my first films, I often asked for such indications. But the scores that I compose now seem to me better in the sense of what film music should be. I have since completely renounced this manner of working.

The Importance of Silence

In *La Belle et la Bête*,[48] for example, the music is simply adapted to each scene. And Cocteau had an excellent idea: I wrote a continuous cue to accompany certain scenes in the castle, and he had the stroke of genius to break it up with silences. I turned this to my advantage. Cocteau taught me the importance of silence.

In general, there is too much music in films. I am flattered when French directors that I really like ask me to write music for twenty out of twenty-five scenes, but I think that they are wrong. Regarding this, the English have an interesting sense of music. With them, I have made films where there is just a quarter-hour of music, but it is placed in such an obvious fashion that the spectators are struck by it, whereas I did other films where an hour of music passed unnoticed.

There is another important point, which is to know if the music should or should not be noticed in a film. A comment by Maurice Tourneur pleased me.[49] Long ago I made *Lac aux Dames* with him and, to somebody who had asked him what he thought about music, he responded: "It must be very good, I didn't notice it." This was reproduced in *Le Figaro*. And poor Tourneur thought he had to write to me, in the same newspaper, an open letter, in which he apologized. He believed I was angry; he was mistaken.

I believe moreover that people can make films without music. And you will see that these will happen in reaction against the excess of music. Certain directors, when they feel like a sequence isn't successful, believe that a little music will fix things. In fact, that only makes the failure stand out.

As for the belief that music superimposed on an action can transcend it, this is different, and the fact is known. As I said, you can't extract the music for *L'Opéra de quat' sous*, and I should even say, with much pretention, that you can't extract the music from *La Belle et la Bête*. There, the music is justified as a sonic setting [*décor sonore*].

But when Cocteau asked me to write a score for *Les Parents terribles*,[50] a filmed play, I caused for him some problems that I foresaw. He indicated to me the passages that seemed to him to suggest music. Then I had the idea for a theme that I arranged in six or seven different ways, with the possibility of cutting it or, on the other hand, repeating it when it was too short. They recorded the music without images, without being concerned about the duration, and Cocteau himself did a kind of musical montage work with that admirable sense of things that he has.

Sometimes a Musical Montage is Necessary

According to him, you can set anything, since chance is a great creator. Between you and me, this isn't true; there are miracles sometimes, but not always, and in the end it becomes a method. In *Les Enfants terribles*, Bach's music gives an effect so much more gripping than if there was general atmosphere music instead of a tune.

In *Orphée*,[51] there is a scene where the music has no relation to it; Cocteau took the music written for another scene and by an extraordinary chance it worked: the music fit the scene and fell perfectly, even in duration, with nothing added or cut. This is the scene where Orpheus must appear before the police captain and encounter Death, who has been following him. I wrote for this anxious scene a cue that Cocteau moved to the comic scene where Orpheus is afraid of looking at Eurydice. I should acknowledge that it works very well, which would seem to confirm his theory.

Gluck's intervention in the most realistic scenes of the film is also an idea that isn't filmed in the process. Indeed, for the majority of films, it is possible to find pre-composed music by searching through the famous classical works. That is a return to the processes of the silent cinema.

In conclusion, film music is still in a primitive stage; I am convinced that one day it will emerge from its hesitations. There will then be some series of commercial films like those with which we are familiar, for which people will write standard music; but apart from that the cinema will excite new musical experiments. However, for me, the problem is not just to take a lively tempo under a dramatic scene. People fall back into convention if they systematically make a slow gesture when the music is fast, and the inverse. A priori, it is more difficult to make a fast gesture over fast music than a slow gesture. It is easier to cross the stage of the Paris Opéra slowly while the orchestra plays "The Ride of the Valkyries" than it is to dance to "The Ride of the Valkyries."

From *Arts* (July 17, 1952). (Translation by Colin Roust)

10

FOREIGN IDEAS

This volume's original idea called for a collection of documents that covered only the first half of the twentieth century. The rationale for this had to do not so much with confinements of space as with the idea that up until the century's midpoint film music was somehow "all of a piece"; notwithstanding the diversity of its applications, film music worldwide developed along a more or less singular course from its tentative beginnings in the nickelodeon period through its blossoming in the silent-film heyday to its eventual establishment, in the late 1930s, as an international norm for the so-called classical-style film. It seems that regardless of their geographical location or their aesthetic stances, practitioners and critics at almost any time during the first half-century were able to think of—and vigorously discuss—film music "in general."

In the early 1950s, film music worldwide experienced an explosion of change. The reasons are many, not least among them being the healthy re-emergence of European film industries after World War II simultaneous with the rapid erosion, due as much to government regulations as the new competition from television, of Hollywood's hitherto highly efficient "studio system" of production and distribution. After that, it seems, film music moved not in a single mainstream but in numerous strong-flowing forks and branches. The extent to which these variously radical and conservative streams have influenced one another and perhaps served as tributaries for an as yet undiscovered film-music mainstream of the twenty-first century of course remains open to debate. Fuel for this ongoing debate, as readers will discover in the pages that follow, is abundant. The literary sources of extended film-music discussion are far more numerous than was the case before the 1950s; more intriguing, the sources are much more varied in approach and focus.

The articles included in this chapter represent ideas quite foreign to what remained of the film music mainstream in the years immediately following World War II.

American avant-garde composer John Cage was richly equipped with concepts that had little to do with conventional filmmaking; most of the things he suggests in his article likely would have been dismissed as absurd even by the most adventurous Hollywood types in the 1950s, yet in the twenty-first century the idea of film music flavored with the sound of out-of-tune pianos, or the noise of escaping compressed air, seems perhaps not strange at all. Although Pierre Schaeffer, founder of the style generally known as *musique concrète*, was involved only indirectly with filmmaking, his 1954 article nevertheless points very specifically to instances in the cinema where experimental sound techniques indeed make an impression; like Cage's ideas, Schaeffer's in the 1950s had very little influence on filmmakers, but today it seems as though Cage's and Schaeffer's influence is everywhere to be felt. The third writer represented in this chapter, Wang Yunjie, wrote music of a conventional sort, but in a sense he was doubly foreign to Western culture's film-music mainstream, for he lived and worked in a country whose cinema was severely pressed not just to be distinctly Chinese but also to be distinctly anti-capitalist; like his counterparts in the Soviet Union, Wang in the 1950s daily had concerns that went far beyond the merely artistic.

10.1 A FEW IDEAS ABOUT MUSIC AND FILM

John Cage

John Cage (1912–92) without doubt ranks as one of the twentieth century's most influential thinkers about the nature of music. But the extent to which he was, in fact, a "composer" remains open to debate. Certainly up until 1950 Cage was a creative artist who thought up particular combinations/sequences of sounds and then wrote down meticulous instructions for those sounds' realization by dutiful performers. After the century's midpoint, however, his focus shifted from the "putting together" of specific sounds to the devising of situations that accommodate virtually any sounds, so long as those sounds result from certain prescribed rules. Posterity has yet to cast its vote, but some today would say that Cage's conventionally scored works—including his fairly well-known pieces for prepared piano and percussion ensemble—count as minor contributions when compared with the ideas that gave birth to his so-called indeterminate music.

This brief article, which has gone virtually unnoticed in the increasingly extensive Cage literature, focuses on two film projects that in fact were Cage's only essays in film scoring. Although the actual sonorities of this music might strike some listeners' ears as unusual, the thinking behind them was quite conventional; more or less in consultation with the films' directors, Cage decided that certain combinations of sounds would be appropriate, albeit sometimes in ironic ways, for certain episodes of the films at hand. In his later works Cage would withdraw from the decision-making process, but even his most indeterminate efforts maintain a strong allegiance to structures of the sort described in the article's second and third paragraphs.

It is always a simple matter for someone who does not do it to know something about it, and that is my situation with regard to music for films. Of course I have done a little of it (the Duchamp sequence in *Dreams that Money Can Buy*, a miserable film in my opinion with the exception of this particular sequence—in which by a series of events the relation between music and pictures was botched up—and the Herbert Matter film, *Works of Calder*), but each time when I was working, I knew that I knew nothing about it.[1] The same was true when back in 1942, I did *The City Wears a Slouch Hat* for Columbia Workshop (not a film but a radio play).[2]

Not working, I know that music loses virtue when it accompanies. Nothing in life or art needs accompaniment, because each has its own center (which is no center). To bring about the state of no-accompaniment, there must underlie everything (whether words, pictures or what have you) a rhythmic structure. In my case, this is micro-macro cosmic.

If a film or play or dance is X minutes long, I take a pulse and then know how many measures of 2/2 there are in the work to be done. I let the major structural points in the film give me a particular structural articulation which is small in phraseology and is large in section-delimiting. (The numbers of measures must be capable of having a square root.) E.g., if there are 1600 measures in the film these will be divided into 40 x 40 measures and each 40 measures will be phrased in the same proportions that divide the 40 parts into large sections (e.g., 6, 7, 10, 5, 3, 9). This is a structural idea not distant in concept from Hindu tala (except that tala has no beginning or ending and is based on pulsation rather than phraseology), the work of Anton Webern and Erik Satie and hot jazz.

Given this structure, both film and music may proceed free of one another and everything works out beautifully. It is even possible to have several composers working independently of one another on the same music (the same part of the same music); what they do, when put together, becomes a polyphony anonymous by nature, but alive the way nature is. To understand this, one is obliged to give up harmony, melody, counterpoint, etc. (everything one has learned including genius and the three B's) and accept music for what it is: a way of life devoted to sound and silence, the only common denominator of which two is rhythm (not as pattern but as quantity, free to have or not have accents, for example). This accepted, one may have back, paradoxically, that much of harmony, melody, etc. (including genius and the B's and all else) one wishes to permit oneself.

It may seem artificial and forced (life often does) to clamp a rhythmic structure onto something that doesn't have it. It is of course artificial (so are the houses we live in; they don't, however, keep us from falling in love).

Another idea I have is that if there is a story or pictures, the sounds should be the noises and sounds characteristic of or relevant to what one is following or seeing. This is what I was thinking of in the Calder film and the *Slouch Hat* (Kenneth Patchen) radio play.[3] Not as sound effects but as organized sound (to quote Edgard Varèse). So that in the workshop part of the Calder film, what we hear are noises of mobiles and noises of the making of mobiles and the loudest noise comes when it is least needed. When the little boy smiles (a case of no-accompaniment) and no hammering when Calder is seen hammering, etc. (Opposed to the redundant—otherwise nonpartisan.)

I don't know what else there is to say, except that I love the idea of writing for films, but when I am doing it, it is not so good, because either the techniques one is always reading about are not available, or someone connected with it goes blank, when it comes to the imagination or something else. In the radio play, for instance, I scored a good deal of escaping compressed air, only to be told that each escape was worth five dollars and what with rehearsals, etc., "Please don't use it."

In the Hans Richter film [*Dreams That Money Can Buy*], the film was changed after the music was written and I was never informed (although, since I am in the phone book, it is the simplest thing in the world to reach me). And then in the Matter film, I had highfaluting ideas about superimposing inaccurate performances of a single prepared piano line with each time microtonal shifts of pitch and slight timbre changes (to be achieved by repositioning of screws and other mutes), all of this arising from the lovely accidents that mobiles by their nature of moving present to the eye. However, the machines necessary to do this were not available.

One more idea and then I am through. Music should not be recorded and film music should not be a recording of music. It should be a music which could not exist except as a recording, a music which comes into being by virtue of (and only by virtue of) the available contemporary (mechanical, electronic, film, etc.) means. (This is not the 18th century.)

More and more in my ears and those of younger composers (Boulez, Feldman, Wolff) are the sounds which radio and film means make available, and our imaginations run swiftly towards the *necessarily* "synthetic." We are in a real-life situation (not an academy, acoustically speaking) and it is impossible to say which is cause and which is effect (our ears or our sounds), which technic and which vision. Technic is Vision and vice-versa, the Sudden School.

What we desperately need in America is a laboratory for useless musical activity, devoted to failure rather than to success (research—A-1 in other fields—ignored in this one of art), and I record (shout) at this time that first Varèse tried to interest companies both in Hollywood and in New Jersey in such activity and then I myself spent a year (1940) trying to realize the same dream.

The dream is a simple one: a place for collaboration between composers and sound engineers replete with equipment—in Hollywood terms a simple get-together of the Music and the Sound Departments (in Canadian terms, an actuality; Norman McLaren and the National Film Board in Ottawa[4]).

Perhaps this has been accomplished in our United States and I am behind the times. However, if it has and there is such a place, lead us to it. We have work to do!

From *Film Music Notes* 10, no. 3 (January–February 1951), 12–15.

10.2 CONCRETE MUSIC

Pierre Schaeffer

Pierre Schaeffer (1910–95) was a French radio engineer who in the 1940s, while working in the studios of Radiodiffusion Française, morphed into first a theorist of sound and then a composer. His compositional efforts are limited in number and usually bear not just his own signature but also that of Pierre Henry, a conservatory-trained composer Schaeffer met in 1949 and with whom he collaborated artistically and co-founded, at the French radio station, the Groupe de Recherche de Musique Concrète. In 1953 Schaeffer left the GRMC but then, in 1958, re-established it under the name Groupe de Recherche Musicale (GRM); one of the students who worked with Schaeffer in the GRM was Michel Chion, a French composer who late in the twentieth century emerged as one of the leading theorists of film sound. Schaeffer's writings include À la Recherche d'une Musique Concrète *(1952), the* Traité des objets musicaux *(1967), and the recording-accompanied* Solfège de l'Objet Sonore *(1967); regrettably, these have yet to be translated into English.*

The article reproduced here was published early in 1954 in the Courier, *a magazine sponsored by the United Nations Educational, Scientific and Cultural Organization*

(UNESCO). An introductory paragraph mentions that UNESCO, in conjunction with a series of panel discussions collectively titled "Music and Film," will sponsor a same-titled exhibition at the upcoming International Film Festival in Cannes, France. The exhibition, the introduction states, will feature a section devoted especially to musique concrète, "a new form of sound creation in which composition and experiments are taking place in a number of countries, particularly France, Germany, the United States and Canada."

This article is clearly a translation, because Schaeffer never wrote in English; the translator, however, is not identified. The Cannes festival took place in April 1954; three months later a French version of this article—slightly longer, and with several sets of paragraphs presented in reverse order—was published in the journal Cahiers du cinéma *(no. 37, July 1954, pp. 54–56).*

Electronic music, music created by lines drawn on film,[5] concrete music—these are three new and astonishing kinds of musical creation which are being explored today. And their music should perhaps be named "Tapesichore," for all of them, despite their different purposes and methods, rely on a basic material—film—which brings them on common ground with the cinema.

Concrete music, for example, uses magnetic tape,[6] which is similar to the sound track of a film, for recording and recomposing its sounds. Its bars are traced by the scissors of the cutter who splices the different sections of tape. The sound itself is modified by phonogenic apparatus which by running the tape at greater or lesser speed can raise or lower the pitch of the original sound and greatly alter its tone quality.

Thus the tonality of the music comes not from normal musical scales but from the whole universe of sound. The composer chooses "concrete" sounds, those already existing in everyday life. From these raw materials an infinite variety of other sounds can be created so that identities are changed—a bell can become an oboe, a squeaking door is transformed into the sound of a violin, boogie-woogie into African tam-tam music.[7]

Composers of electronic music work differently. They compose their sounds in the abstract, since before the invention of the loud-speaker these sounds did not exist in the atmosphere, but were confined to electronic circuits. Unlike composers of concrete music, they make no use of pre-recorded sound. Instead the cunningly contrived components of this music are produced behind the glass of electronic tubes.

Then, there is the work of that interesting figure, the artist musician who "draws" sound, and, throwing harmony to the winds, jots down sound in its own frequency, rhythm, and approximate tone on the sound track of a film. The aim of men like Norman McLaren,[8] of Canada, eliminating at one stroke the conservatoire and all its instruments, is to blaze a sound track right over the film image.

What a wealth of methods we have here, all of them astonishingly prolific. And what a remarkable achievement all their different resources have been aimed at—the direct handling of sound colour. Here, sound ceases to be a fleeting thing; it is printed permanently on magnetic tape, and like movement itself, miraculously fixed on film.[9] It can be speeded up, slowed down, superimposed, contrasted, or its rhythm made irregular.

How should we regard all these new forms of musical exploration? The answer lies in a remark made by Professor Günther Bialas[10] of the Detmold Higher School of Music, during a heated debate broadcast by Munich radio. Faced by a group of musicians who could see nothing in all these novelties but formless noise, artistic decadence or even perversion of taste, he declared: "Who nowadays denies the infinite artistic possibilities of the cinema? Well, just as the film at the beginning, before it had acquired its own personal form of expression, was hardly more than filmed theatre, so electronic music, which was confined at first to the reproduction of existing sound forms, is only now, with the research of Pierre Schaeffer, Pierre Henry and doctor Meyer-Eppler,[11] beginning to create an entirely new musical material."

I should explain how I personally came across this possibility of creating new musical material. In 1948, at the Experimental Studio of the Radiodiffusion Française, I was carrying out research on noises. The idea of a "symphony of noise" haunted me, but I could not then see how to achieve it, and the word "symphony" at that stage did not seem to make any sense at all. For nothing is more realistic, more anecdotal and less musical than noise. Noise, the blind man's radar, calls things by their name. It is directly associated with objects one sees. Its emotional value lies in the effective associations it arouses: evening bells, birds at dawn, sirens in a port.

A symphony composed of such noises would take us into the theatre rather than the concert hall. And yet the gulf between a dramatic repertory of this kind and a piano keyboard or an orchestral score attracted me. How could I bridge it? As often happens, I hit upon the solution by accident. It was to abandon the complete noises, which were simply too expressive, and keep only fragments of them, and then to modify these fragments by all sorts of acoustic methods. A mass of sound objects thus came into being, quite unrecognizable, as remote from precise dramatic meaning as from musical structure.

These "sound combinations," isolated crystals of sound, that could be transformed, repeated, superimposed, became the complex "notes" of a generalized music. They also formed a language of their own, but instead of an alphabet of twelve recognizable sounds, there emerged what seemed like a profusion of Chinese characters. It was no good trying to make any sense of it in familiar musical terms, without immediately generalizing our ideas of notes, structure and musical form.

Thus the steps of composition took an opposite form to that of the usual notation, followed by execution. We began by sampling the sound material, and then composed by a series of attempts. In the same way as a painter or a sculptor, who can only work single-mindedly through his intuitions of matter and mass, and cannot assess the result until he has laid on his colour or his clay. That was when the name "concrete music" came to my mind.

The absolute parallel between concrete music and the cinema can easily be seen. Of course, a film director has an idea to work on and an exact method of cutting at his disposal.[12] Indeed, if he has not thought in terms of pictures, both as regards his inspiration and the landmarks, and if he has not seen his film beforehand, no scenario, and no production will save him. The film exists beforehand in his mind, as it does in the images fixed by the camera. A film is, therefore, the very opposite of an abstraction: it creates an absolutely specific world—that of a concrete language which borrows all its words from the real object, all its syntax from the continuity, and all its architecture from the sequences as a whole.

Although these ideas are more or less accepted nowadays, many enquiring and cultured minds are, nevertheless, disconcerted by the special technique of concrete music, and by the word itself. Our pursuit of sound upsets them: our huge sound-filing system exasperates them; composition based on cutting, instead of on a score in G, leaves them quite bewildered.

Unlike musicians who are conservative and easily shocked, artists of a plastic, dramatic or visual tradition and temperament are very amenable to concrete music and approach it with lively interest and a natural instinct. Painters are delighted to discover formal equivalences, stage designers to find a sound atmosphere discreetly and effectively in harmony with their sets. What might have been no more than a sort of realistic din is adjusted, its tone is heightened.

As for the cinema, it might well be said that this is the sort of music it has been dreaming of for years. Film makers did not wait for us before producing noises in the sound track that conveyed more than any cello could do. In *A man walks in the city*, to mention only one example, a "sound loop" accompanies the last sequence unforgettably. By prolonged repetition, a succession of street noises, suggestive enough in itself, is made into a "sound phrase." This phrase never loses touch with reality, yet is detached from it, like the theme of a symphony.

In this way Orson Welles, [Luis] Buñuel and many others have for years successfully sketched out their own natural concrete music. Max de Haas, in Holland, Fulchignoni for *Leonardo da Vinci*,[13] Allégret for special effects,[14] Grémillon for a poetic montage on a theme of Astrology,[15] Jean Rouch in order to reconstruct hundreds of feet of sound with the help of a few African fragments[16]—these were the first film-makers to join our team in its early stages.

Now, a technique, tested for nearly five years, offers every gradation from pure dramatic realism to abstract, plastic sound. From now on, concrete music makes it possible to incorporate into the image its sound accompaniment, drawn, so to speak, as Eve was from Adam, out of its own substance.

From *UNESCO Courier* 3, 1954, 18–20.

10.3 ON USING MUSICAL INSTRUMENTS IN FILM MUSIC

(Dianying yinyue de yueqi shiyong wenti)

(電影音樂的樂器使用問題)

Wang Yunjie

Wang Yunjie (1911–66) was one of China's leading composers in the decade preceding the adamantly anti-Western, anti-capitalist Cultural Revolution that lasted from 1966 until the death, ten years later, of Mao Zedong.[17] He studied piano and composition at the Xinhua School of the Arts in Shanghai and then, concentrating on composition, earned a degree at the Shanghai School of Music. Wang produced several symphonies and a string quartet, but most of his efforts focused on film scoring; in 1947 he became a staff composer at the Kunlun Film Studio in Shanghai and two years later, upon the establishment of the People's Republic of China, took a position in the music department of the nation's Central Film Bureau. His credits include more than forty film scores.

In this article, published in the short-lived journal Zhongguo dianying *[Chinese Film],[18] Wang addresses a question that has long bothered—and which continues to bother— cultures that proudly own indigenous musical traditions but nevertheless participate fully in an art form (i.e., cinema) whose technology and basic aesthetics are entirely Western.[19] In the case of Chinese cinema on the eve of the Cultural Revolution, the question of traditional vs. Western music in film scores transcends aesthetic debate and enters the often deadly serious arena of politics.*

On the issue of using musical instruments, the ways in which film directors hold their divergent views are quite concrete. There are different opinions on the issue. For example: "It is fortunate that I haven't used Chinese musical instruments in this film.[20] Those instruments are so incapable of expressing the content and style of the film." "This film has to use Chinese musical instruments completely. It doesn't matter if the musicians' performance level is poor, or if the musical instruments are out of tune." "This film has a section of music for *sanxian* [a three-stringed lute], and this makes the entire film sound dear." "This film has to use the symphonic technique, with only a Western orchestra." "Single-line melodies with percussion are good for the stage but not for film." "This film uses only Chinese musical instruments, so it would be great to have something that sounds like the music of the *yangge* plays."[21] "Only using Chinese musical instruments causes difficulties as well. One composer uses the *pipa* [a four-stringed, pear-shaped lute] for a battle scene, and another composer uses the *pipa* for a battle scene. It all comes out sounding the same." "Chinese instruments are not always necessary for expressing a national style. If, as some have said, only Chinese instruments have broad appeal to the masses, then why is our national anthem played not on Chinese instruments but on Western brasses?"

The director is the center of artistic leadership in the filmmaking process and thus holds the decision-making authority regarding musical usage. Since conforming to the director's intentions is the goal of the film-music composer, it is inevitable that we compose differently for different directors. For this film only Chinese musical instruments are used, but for that film only Western orchestral instruments are used. For yet another film, Chinese and Western instruments are mixed. It is true that this gives composers many opportunities, and much practical experience in using various instruments. But is every single demand of the director appropriate? This is worth some discussion.

Let's use music in *Well Wishes* (*Zhufui*) and *The Life of Lu Xun* (*Lu Xun de shengping*), two China-made films produced in 1956, as examples.[22] In terms of the use of musical instruments, composers have used different approaches. *Well Wishes* basically takes the expressive approach of [Chinese] opera, with single-line melodies played on Chinese musical instruments only. *The Life of Lu Xun*, however, takes the symphonic approach, using for the most part Western orchestral instruments. Regarding the content and expressive form of these two films, and the musical demands of their scriptwriters and directors, if we examine the score with the spirit of "Let a hundred flowers bloom" (*baihua qifang*),[23] it would seem that in both cases music is used appropriately. In terms of music, both films are representative of Chinese film production in 1956, and in each film the choice about musical instruments results from the film's content and expressive style.

But there is something else that arises. Some feel that music expresses our national identity *only* when it is played by Chinese instruments; our national identity is not nearly so prominent when the very same music—with exactly the same treatment of harmony and melody—is played on Western instruments. But this is not just a matter of instruments. When we write "Chinese" music, we adopt an entirely different approach not just to harmony and counterpoint but to melodic design and development; our compositional habits, and our ways of thinking, are completely different. Our instrumentation for Chinese music involves much more than simply choosing the "tools" for playing; it involves all the characteristics of intonation and melody, and modulation, that belong to our traditional style.

In film music, our traditional style needs to be united with characters' personalities, and with their dilemmas and conflicts. And thus we should expand the expressive capacity of our Chinese instruments; building upon our traditions, we should adopt whatever might be useful from outside our nation, including musical approaches to various dramatic situations.

So, in order to more prominently express the national style in our film music, it is fitting that the leaders in filmmaking ask composers to make serious use of Chinese instruments, and to try different approaches. In fact, more than 95% of film music composers today *have* taken the approach that combines Chinese and Western musical instruments, and it is the former that they favor.

Some have attempted to use only Chinese musical instruments. Regarding this approach, of course, what has been done in the past few years still has a long way to go before it meets the masses' demands. Although we gained some experience, we hit the wall a few times, and we suffered. On the one hand, composers themselves may not have a thorough understanding of Chinese instruments and therefore need to try hard to learn them; on the other hand, the players of Chinese instruments may be at limited performance levels. Also, tunings of Chinese instruments may contradict one another, or do not work with tunings of Western instruments. Practically speaking, the time it takes to record film music played only by Chinese instruments or by mixtures of Chinese and Western instruments could be double, or even triple, the time spent to record film music played by Western instruments only. Not only that, often the discrepancies of tuning among the various instruments simply cannot be overcome, and this affects the artistic quality of the recorded music.

As film music composers are trying hard to write music that uses Chinese instruments, we should not neglect the need to raise performance levels, and to improve the instruments' manufacturing. The accuracy of the instruments' tuning may be acceptable to our ears. But when [the recorded music is] processed through the overly sensitive sound recording machine, its defects surface easily. When the problem of intonation becomes truly serious, one has to—as the last resort—sacrifice the use of the [problematic] instrument. For example, someone has questioned why the *suona* [double reed wind instrument] is not used in the music of the choral piece "Let's Cross the Yellow River, or Die" in *Song Jingshi* (1955),[24] as the image of *suona* appears in the picture. The reason was that the *suona* was always out of tune during recording, and the time allotted for recording could not be extended. So, with no other better choices, the oboe was used as substitute *ad hoc*. The music of *Trouble about a Small White Flag (Xiao bai qi de feng*

155

bo, 1956) also originally had a section played by the *suona*. But during recording, the very competent *suona* player had to go to Beijing for personal reasons. So the instrumental part had to be re-written. In the music of *Garden of Youth* (*Qingchun de yuandi*, 1955),[25] I used the *suona* [for a while] as well. Someone asked me: "How come there is a strange sound in that section of your music?" That was the *suona*'s sound being out of tune. (Sometimes it is not so much being out of tune as being in a different tuning system.)

Thus far I have discussed the difficulties. But composers of film music have the confidence and patience to confront these difficulties, and to make greater efforts to learn.

But there is another issue, one that requires new breakthroughs in both composing and performing in order to be resolved. That is, in our nation's thousands of years of tradition, almost all musical compositions have expressed generalized emotions [or scenes], such as those of joy, mourning, high mountains, flowing rivers, a fisherman's singing, the flowery moon, and so on. Expressions of dilemmas and conflicts in real life (such as war, anger, etc.) are rare. And the expressive content of eighteenth-century classical music in the West was similar. The period of romanticism, however, developed the depth and breadth of emotional expression. Then the development of late romanticism, with realism, naturalism, and impressionism, and then neo-classicism, and then the twelve-tone serial method, and so on, further expanded the methods of expressing life and nature (these methods include thematic development, harmony, counterpoint, orchestration, musical form, etc.).

Over an extended period of time the development of Western music accumulated rich expressive methods. The useful ones among these are valuable tools for us as we compose music for feature films that have such diverse themes and forms. Borrowing these methods allows us to better express the character of our national style, the character of our own time, and the stereotypical character of stereotypical conditions. But national style and national musical instruments themselves are evolving concepts. Following what feature films demand in their music, which has undergone expansions in thematic expression and in the use of form, genre, and style, it is indispensable for us to gradually expand our application of musical instruments. In the past, quite a number of Chinese instruments, such as the *pipa*, the *erhu* [a two-stringed lap fiddle], and the *suona*, were originally foreign to our culture, and they became Chinese only through nationalization. It happened in the past, so why cannot we nationalize foreign musical instruments now? It is not right, of course, to ignore Chinese instruments. But it is narrow-minded to think that our national musical style can be expressed only by our national musical instruments.

From *Zhongguo dianying* [*Chinese Film*], July 1957.[26]
(Translation by Joys H. Y. Cheung)

11

STYLISTIC NOVELTIES

The music that accompanied classical-style film had one basic sound: that of the full symphony orchestra. According to their production budgets, different films of course had different-sized orchestras, but from the mid-1930s up through the early 1950s almost all film scores at least aspired to the sonic ideal of a full string section punctuated with percussion and colored with woodwinds and brass. To be sure, moviegoers in the 1930s and 1940s often encountered the sounds of, say, banjos or bagpipes or honky-tonk pianos, but invariably these were heard in the realistic context of a film's source music, not in a film's "commenting" underscore.

For reasons that have yet to be adequately explained, the same sonic ideal that governed film music's Golden Age—an ideal rooted in the concert-hall and opera-house traditions of the late nineteenth and early twentieth centuries—continues to be the norm for a great many films that seem to have in common only the desire on the part of their producers to appeal to the widest possible audience. For reasons that from a marketing point of view seem logical enough, just as many films nowadays feature scores whose overall sound seems quite specifically aimed; Internet search engines make it possible to identify films whose extra-diegetic scores can be pigeonholed—as surely their soundtrack albums are, or soon will be, in record stores—as 'heavy metal,' or 'hip-hop,' or 'retro pop,' or 'shoe-gaze indie.'

The diversification of film music's sound began in the 1950s, simultaneous with the break-down of Hollywood's long-entrenched "studio system" that included staff composers and staff orchestras, and also simultaneous with fundamental changes in society.

In the United States but especially in Europe, the horrific experience of World War II left many young adults feeling disenchanted with cultural 'illusions.' These intellectually vibrant persons were interested not in fantasy but in reality, dark as it often was, and the films that represented their concerns seemed to work better if their scores were somehow 'down to earth.'

The postwar years also saw the rise of a societal class that hitherto had never been acknowledged. Whereas before the global conflict human beings worldwide were either children or adults, after the war an in-between group was identified. Sometimes economically empowered and almost always carrying chips on their shoulders, 'teenagers' sought in every possible way to distance themselves from 'grown-ups.' As soon as filmmakers learned about the music that teenagers called their own, they fairly flooded the cinemas with movies that catered to young tastes.

A third category of novel sounds in film was spawned by fascination with the linked Arms Race and Space Race. At least in the United States, the first "official" sighting of flying saucers—near Mt. Rainier in the state of Washington—was reported in June 1947, and the famous Roswell incident took place the next year. Conflating interest in new technologies with fear of invasion or infiltration, or annihilation, by powerful and mysterious enemies, the public

157

seemed to find cathartic release in the science-fiction films that began to spew forth from Hollywood and other film industries c.1950. These films often had to do with alien creatures, and thus composers did the best they could to flavor their scores with appropriately alien sonorities.

The documents gathered together in this chapter deal in turn with jazz, rock 'n' roll, and electronic music, three categories that before 1950 were almost never heard in film scores but which after the century's midpoint contributed richly to film music's new norm.

11.1 SCORERS SKIP CLASSICS, SEEK NEW APPROACH

Philip K. Scheurer

Philip K. Scheurer (1901–85) wrote reviews aplenty during his long tenure at the Los Angeles Times,[1] *but usually he wore the hat of a reporter when he penned his regular "A Town Called Hollywood" columns. For the piece excerpted here, Scheurer's "nose for news" caught scent of a trend in film-scoring that would only grow as the postwar years rolled on.[2] Indeed, the tidbits of information Scheurer included in this particular column demonstrate that Hollywood's tendency toward jazz predated by at least a year the score for* The Man with the Golden Arm *that its composer, Elmer Bernstein, would often identify as the singularly influential "break-through" work.[3]*

It should be noted that for this column the term "classics" was chosen not by Scheurer but by the newspaper's headline writer. Scheurer mentions only film composers' "classical 'sources'," and he emphasizes his point by putting the noun, but not the adjective, in quotation marks. At first glance, Scheurer's opening remark likely seems cryptic. As his column from earlier in the month makes clear, however, the "sources" to which he refers are neither actual pieces from the so-called classical repertoire nor the medium—the symphony orchestra—through which both that repertoire and film music had long been presented. Rather, the "sources" that he suggests are on the wane are, in essence, fonts of inspiration.

Economically pressed though it was through most of the 1950s, Hollywood could still, when it felt the need, instruct its composers to churn out big orchestral scores that sustained the tradition of film music's Golden Age. But fewer and fewer films, it seemed, had narratives that warranted such scores; more and more of them, Scheurer noticed, were built on stories of the nitty-gritty sort.

Scorers of film music are beginning to reach out in new directions since, as I mentioned recently, their classical "sources" are drying up rapidly. This goes for type of music as well as method of presentation. In *Dementia*, an arty movie I caught some months ago, George Antheil contributed a score that was, as I recall, played at least in part by a small jazz aggregation under Shorty Rogers.[4]

Even earlier, of course, we have had the zither dominant in *The Third Man* and the harmonica in *Little Fugitive* and *Genevieve*.[5]

Alfred Hitchcock is mulling the idea of using a piano, solo, throughout his next comedy chiller, *The Trouble with Harry*.[6] And Leith Stevens has already composed a complete jazz score—"every note, including the main and end titles"—for Filmakers' *Private Hell 36* and will duplicate the feat for the same outfit's *Mad at the World*, which deals with juvenile delinquents.[7] Downbeat for dead beats.

"I began thinking along these lines with *The Wild One*, Marlon Brando's picture about cyclists, in which I incorporated some jazz sequences," Stevens told me.[8] "However, not all dramatic stories will stand this kind of treatment. *Private Hell 36* does; it's a story about two big-city cops, Howard Duff and Steve Cochran, and jazz works wonders for it.

"It's all background music, of course, but it always comes from legitimate and not an imaginary source—an apartment radio, a jukebox in a bar. A car crashes over a cliff, killing the driver, and out of the deathly silence we hear a jump tune." Appropriate, I'd say, if a bit grisly.

Stevens added that he is using contemporary jazz, bop or whatever, as well as blues and rhythm. It was recorded by that same Shorty Rogers and a group of "top-flight" side men.

Stevens employed jazz as long ago as 1942, in *Syncopation*—"about 50-50." His latter-day non-syncopated scores have included *Navajo*, *Destination Moon*, *War of the Worlds* and *The Bigamist*.[9]

The "new note" sounds fine to this moviegoer—as long as they don't go back to the pipe organ of the old movie house with all the tremolo stops pulled out.

From *Los Angeles Times*, August 29, 1954, D2.

11.2 THREE MOVIE SCORES ISSUED ON LP DISKS

John S. Wilson

John S. Wilson (1912–2002), on the staff of the New York Times *for more than forty years, was the first of that newspaper's music critics to write about activity and material outside the classical sphere. Equipped with a master's degree in journalism from Columbia University, Wilson joined the* Times *after military service during World War II; his "beat" included popular music of all sorts, but he made his lasting mark with his insightful commentary on music—both recorded and live—that emerged from the tradition of be bop.*

The column of record reviews reproduced here dates from only five years after Philip K. Scheurer observed, in his "A Town Called Hollywood" column for the Los Angeles Times, *that composers entrenched in the film business were leaning more and more frequently toward jazz-based scores. Wilson acknowledges that trend, but his focus here is not on veteran film composers who have appropriated jazz but, rather, on genuine jazz composers whose music had lately been utilized in films.*

Of the three jazz scores that Wilson discusses, the most enduringly famous and the most, arguably, "pure"—Miles Davis's contribution to Ascenseur pour l'échafaud—*is of French origin. The other two—John Lewis's for* Odds against Tomorrow *and Duke Ellington's for* Anatomy of a Murder—*are, for better or worse, the products of Hollywood. Wilson makes no overt predictions here about the future of jazz in film scoring, but anyone who reads between his lines can get a sense of what is to come.*

In the past year or two, the use of jazz on film sound tracks has advanced with unusual rapidity. From the pseudo-jazz contrived by Elmer Bernstein for *The Man with the Golden Arm* (a style since co-opted with a vengeance by the television private eye series),[10] which represented the deepest penetration of jazz into films three years ago, the scope has been expanded to such extent that three current films feature scores by genuine jazz musicians.

The scores of all three films—*Anatomy of a Murder, Odds against Tomorrow* and *Elevator to the Scaffold*[11]—have been transferred to record and, as it happens, they represent three different ways in which a jazz musician can create a film score.

The composers—Duke Ellington, John Lewis and Miles Davis—are all men who have established strongly defined playing and writing styles. Of the three, only Mr. Lewis has sublimated his familiar jazz personality to some extent in scoring *Odds against Tomorrow* (United Artists).

This is Mr. Lewis' second film score. His first, *No Sun in Venice*, consisted of a group of set pieces played by the Modern Jazz Quartet, which he serves as musical director and pianist.[12] But for *Odds against Tomorrow* his score is closely tied to the film in the customary fashion of movie underscore and it is played by a large orchestra, conducted by Mr. Lewis, which includes a sprinkling of jazz musicians.

Simply as documentation, recordings made from sound tracks that are subservient to the requirements of a film may have some value. But the music is usually so briefly episodic that the recording can rarely build or sustain interest. This is the difficulty with Mr. Lewis' score. There are several promising musical sequences but in most cases the incident is over before the promise can be developed. The bits and pieces that make up the disk show Mr. Lewis' facility for melodic invention but only occasionally does one find signs that suggest this is the work of a jazz musician.

However, Mr. Lewis has expanded several themes from his score in a thoroughgoing jazz vein, not as a composer but as an improviser, on *Music from 'Odds against Tomorrow'* (United Artists), played by the Modern Jazz Quartet. Mr. Lewis is almost always a highly disciplined pianist, so much so that the inherent swinging qualities of his playing seem sometimes to be obscured. On this disk, he is as disciplined as one would expect but his playing is also looser, more overtly and exuberantly rhythmic than on many of the Quartet's earlier recordings. With notable assistance from the group's vibraphonist, Milt Jackson, Mr. Lewis has turned his material for the film score into a set of unusually compelling jazz performances. The freedom and assurance shown by Mr. Lewis on this disk is also very evident on *Improvised Meditations and Excursions* (Atlantic), a set of beautifully structured, lean and loping piano solos on which he is accompanied by string bass and drums.

In writing the musical accompaniment for *Anatomy of a Murder* (Columbia), Duke Ellington has remained completely in character.[13] His score is unswervingly in the

Ellington idiom and is played by that uniquely personal extension of his pen, his orchestra. He has managed to avoid the "bits and pieces" problem by building several sequences on a central theme and, either by fortune or design, [managing] to have sufficient time to develop some of the sequences adequately.

His writing for the film is stronger and richer than it has been in many of his recent extended works and his orchestra has responded by playing with the mixture of polish, elegance and earthiness that has been the hallmark of the finest Ellington bands but which has been heard only sporadically in the last decade. Given the proper incentive, the Ellington well of creativity seems to be just as fresh as ever.

Miles Davis' backgrounds for the French film, *Elevator to the Scaffold*, which take up one side of *Jazz Track* (Columbia), are—in one respect, at least—the ultimate in jazz scoring. Mr. Davis and a group of French musicians created the score by watching sequences of the film and then improvising an accompaniment.[14] In view of the apparently spontaneous nature of this project, the score sustains interest remarkably well.

Mr. Davis makes extensive use of the lonesome, reflective sound that has become increasingly identified with his trumpet playing, but he employs it in such a variety of ways that it provides an element of continuity rather than of monotony. The musicians with him are cast almost completely in supporting roles except for the bassist, Pierre Michelot, who is a tremendous rhythmic spur to Mr. Davis and who builds a remarkable solo, which, unlike most jazz bass solos, makes a point and does it with tremendous impact. The disk is filled out by three pieces of minor interest by Mr. Davis' recent sextet.[15]

From *New York Times*, December 20, 1959, X15.

11.3 BRITISH RATTLED BY ROCK 'N' ROLL

Youths Go Wild in Theatres, Jive and Sing in the Streets and Attack Policemen

Thomas P. Ronan

While debates continue as to the precise musical origins of the genre known as rock 'n' roll, there seems little doubt that the genre's surge to the forefront of attention among youths worldwide began with the use of "Rock around the Clock" to underscore the main titles of MGM's 1955 Blackboard Jungle. *The film certainly made a hit out of a song that upon its initial release had been inconsequential; whereas in the summer of 1954 "Rock around the Clock" occupied the B side of a 45 rpm disk whose main attraction was an ill-fated novelty number titled "Thirteen Women (and Only One Man in Town)," after its post-*Blackboard Jungle *re-release in March 1955 it skyrocketed to the No. 1 position on* Billboard *magazine's pop chart, and it held that position for a full eight weeks.*

A dark and serious drama focused on the problem of inner-city juvenile delinquency,
Blackboard Jungle *was a film about teenagers but not geared specifically toward teenagers,*
and thus its contribution to the popularity of rock 'n' roll was perhaps accidental. The
breakthrough film that quite deliberately capitalized upon young persons' obvious
interest in the new music was Rock around the Clock, *a light-weight romp released by*
Columbia in April 1956. Unlike such earlier quasi-documentary efforts as Studio Films'
1954 Rock and Roll Revue *and* Harlem Variety Revue, *Fred Sears's* Rock around the
Clock *featured a semblance of a plot; more important vis-à-vis the film's box-office appeal,*
it featured performances by artists both black and white. Bill Haley and His Comets,
whose hit song from the previous year lent Rock around the Clock *its title, were the*
best-known 'stars,' but the cast also included The Platters, Tony Martinez, and Freddie
Bell and The Bellboys.

Whereas Blackboard Jungle *simply called attention to rock 'n' roll,* Rock around the
Clock *provoked reactions both in and around its exhibition venues that some*
commentators described as riots. There was indeed rambunctious behavior when the
film was shown in the United States, but it seems that the audience response was most
uninhibited—as reported here by veteran New York Times *foreign correspondent Thomas*
P. Ronan (1908–2005)—in the United Kingdom.

LONDON, Sept. 11—The rock 'n' roll craze is sweeping Britain and some of its teen-
age fans are jiving their way right into police stations.

Two cities already have prohibited showing of the American motion picture *Rock*
around the Clock and others are considering similar action. Newspapers are debating
the matter.

After listening to the rock 'n' roll rhythm to which the picture is devoted, teen-agers
have wrecked motion picture houses, assaulted policemen and danced in wild mobs
through the streets.

Hundreds of boys and girls danced and sang in the streets in the Elephant and Castle
section of London after having seen the picture last night. They stopped traffic, banged
on doors and roofs of cars and threw bottles.

It required thirty policemen, some with dogs, to break up a crowd outside another
theatre and to quell a disturbance inside it. They took about fifty youths along with them
when quiet had been restored.

One of the youths had been balancing on a rail in front of the stage chanting "rock—
rock—rock!" while others jived ecstatically in the aisles.

When Bill Haley's Comets, a rock 'n' roll band in the picture, was off-screen, the youths
kept shouting "We want Bill, we want Bill!"

At another theatre a 19-year-old soldier who was part of what the police described
as "a very excited crowd" was arrested for striking a policeman.

One of six youths arraigned in police courts here today was fined the equivalent of
$14. Two others were fined $2.80 each for "insulting behavior" toward the police. Three
were discharged.

London is by no means the only place where such things are going on. The police
were called out yesterday in Manchester and at Bootle, near Liverpool, to slow down
rock 'n' rollers at theatres showing the same picture.

In Manchester electric light bulbs and lighted cigarettes were thrown from theatre balconies. Youths sprayed part of the audience with water from fire hoses.

At Bootle, 500 youths from a similar audience were joined by 500 more who had gathered outside in a jiving, singing and shouting parade for a mile through the heart of town. A police escort kept it from getting out of hand.

Fireworks were set off in the Bootle theatre and in another at Welling, in Kent, where the same picture was being shown.

"Let 'em jive," *The Daily Sketch* said editorially this morning in opposing a ban on the film. It agreed that rowdies and "the wrecking parties" should be put down, but opposed being too hard on high-spirited boys and girls.

"Perhaps it is a case for the anthropologists to study, an echo in staider surroundings of tribal dances to the drum, or the slogans to which dervishes revolve," *The Manchester Guardian* commented, adding:

"One cannot help suspecting a certain amount of auto-intoxication, the dancers going to meet the rhythm halfway. It does not move them (or move them so powerfully) unless they go there with intent to be moved."

If one was arrested for smashing windows or obstructing traffic, it would be no excuse to plead that he was under the influence of rhythm, the paper said.

Rock around the Clock is a seventy-six-minute musical jamboree with a screen story about a dance band manager who tries to promote rock 'n' roll. It features Bill Haley and his Comets, the Platters, the Tony Martinez band, Freddie Bell and his Bellboys, Alan Freed, Johnny Johnston, Alix Talton and Lisa Gaye.

The Clover production, presented by Columbia Pictures, was released nationally in this country in April. It opened at the Fox Theatre in Brooklyn in May and subsequently played the Loew's circuit in the metropolitan area.

A spokesman for the Fox said, "It was very quiet here." A Loew's representative reported, "There was no trouble, but customers complained about annoyances—plenty of stomping."

At a showing in a Minneapolis theatre in April, youngsters marched out and snake-danced down a leading thoroughfare, breaking store windows. The police quelled the disturbance. Police intervention also was necessary to quiet disorderly juveniles in a theatre in La Crosse, Wis.

The movie has been shown in Ireland, Indonesia, the Philippines and Australia.

(In Singapore, an owner of a theatre where the film is to be shown Saturday said, "We are remaining calm—the Malayan temperament is not like that of the British or American.")

"Except for minor incidents, we've had no trouble thus far," a Columbia spokesman said, adding, "It's doing fantastic business."

From *New York Times*, September 12, 1956, 40.

163

11.4 A "REAL CRAZY" MANSFIELD IN RAUCOUS FILM

"The Girl Can't Help It"

Mae Tinee

Music of the sort featured in the 1956 film Rock around the Clock *enraged adult commentators, who variously characterized rock 'n' roll as little more than "primitive tom-tom thumping,"*[16] *a music that on the whole seemed merely "cannibalistic and tribalistic,"*[17] *and something that called to mind "the heathen rhythms of Africa"*[18] *or "the festive chorus of a tribe of Amazonians."*[19] *And this, of course, helped make it all the more popular with teenagers. Quick to capitalize on what seemed clearly to be a gold mine of opportunity, Hollywood responded with a flood of teen-oriented films in which the new music and its attendant controversy was the subject of a plot or films in more or less standard genres that somehow included rock 'n' roll in their diegetic soundtracks.*

*Some of the films that fall into the latter category were relatively sophisticated productions; the numerous films that starred Elvis Presley—*Love Me Tender *(1956),* Loving You *(1957),* Jailhouse Rock *(1957),* King Creole *(1958)—are spectacular examples. Films of the former sort were most often shot in black-and-white and delivered on a budget that made most contemporaneous B movies seem luxurious; they include such creatively titled pictures as* Don't Knock the Rock *(1956),* Shake, Rattle and Rock *(1956),* Mr. Rock and Roll *(1957),* Rock Baby, Rock It *(1957),* Rock All Night *(1957), and* Rock around the World *(1957).*

The documents reproduced here are reviews of two 1957 rock 'n' roll films whose storylines rise slightly above the average: Twentieth Century-Fox's The Girl Can't Help It *and Universal's* Rock, Pretty Baby.[20] *Interestingly, both reviews bear the by-line of Mae Tinee, who on first glance seems to have had the longest career (from 1914 until the late 1960s) in the history of film journalism. In his 1929 autobiography* My Life: East and West, *silent film actor William S. Hart claims to have actually met Mae Tinee; in a recent article, film historian Richard Abel states that Mae Tinee was in fact Frances Peck, a friend in the 1920s of Chicago-based gossip columnist Louella Parsons.[21] Mae Tinee probably was Frances Peck, but doubtless she was many other persons as well. In any case, the by-line of the* Chicago Tribune's *hugely prolific Mae Tinee disappeared only in 1969 when Gene Siskel became the newspaper's film critic.*

If you'd like a liberal education in the current jazz craze known as rock and roll, here it is. An even dozen of the most popular exponents of that raucous and repetitious music are presented. My nomination for the most moronic goes to a group of characters known as Gene Vincent and his Blue Caps.

The film also presents Jayne Mansfield, an unabashed imitator of Marilyn Monroe, even to the sticky speech affectations, with a bit of Mae West tossed in for good measure. She doesn't wiggle, she writhes, which may be due to the uneven distribution of her obviously ample weight. However, she's well cast in this brisk item as a dizzy blonde who doesn't want a career, just a home and babies.

Edmond O'Brien proves to be an excellent comedian as Fats Murdock, a beefy former gangster who misses the good old prohibition days when he rated headlines. He picks up Jayne, daughter of an old cellmate of his, and hires a cynical press agent to make her a "personality."

Tom Ewell is just right as this nervous character, caught between the ambitious gangster and his voluptuous girl friend.

The script, based on a story of Garson Kanin of *Born Yesterday* fame, has some echoes of that hit in this plot, and it has a ring of sophistication, belting out its sometimes slightly ribald humor deftly. It's a smart combination of worldliness and wit, spiced with sarcasm.

It's also quite an excursion into the world of rock and roll fans, with glassy-eyed youngsters jumping madly to the rhythms, and some otherwise presentable little girls stomping around a public dance hall in bare and dirty feet.

Definitely of little interest to old folks, but others will find it real crazy Mansfield.

From *Chicago Tribune*, January 28, 1957, B10.

11.4B FILM'S APPEAL IS BASED ON ROCK 'N' ROLL

"Rock, Pretty Baby"

Mae Tinee

Unless you're mad about rock and roll music, or amused by the antics of a group of noisy, undisciplined teenagers, I don't think you'll find much of interest in this film, which seems to make the point that if adults would just give the kiddies anything they want, everything will be all right.

While the two young principals are attractive, and better behaved than most of the other characters in the cast, the music seems endless and the story is a flimsy one.

John Saxon is cast as a high school boy who plays in a jazz combo, and resists his father's wish that he give up music for medicine. Papa won't buy him the electric guitar he wants, which proves, of course, that papa is a real square.

With the help of his friends and the sale of some books, our hero gets the guitar, but loses it again when he has to hock the instrument to pay for the damage he and some of his playful friends inflicted on his home and that of a neighbor.

All of this makes the young man very unhappy, at least until papa gives in, after mama points out that they've made the great mistake of treating a high school senior as an adult.

I guess I belong with the squares.

From *Chicago Tribune*, February 7, 1957, C9.

11.5 THE FIRST ELECTRONIC FILMSCORE— *FORBIDDEN PLANET*

A Conversation with Bebe Barron

Jane Brockman

Bebe Barron (1925–2008) and her first husband, Louis Barron (1920–89), are rightly credited as the co-creators of the first all-electronic score for a feature-length film. Their contributions to MGM's 1956 Forbidden Planet *of course had many precedents. In Europe and the Soviet Union, such electrically powered instruments as the ondes martenot, the theremin, and the Trautonium had been put to use in some of the earliest sound films,[22] and in Hollywood the theremin since 1945 had been a fixture of films dealing with psychological aberration and, beginning in 1950, of science-fiction films.[23] But in all these earlier cases electronic sounds functioned in a relatively conventional way, lending a special "color" to melodic materials that might just as easily have been assigned to standard orchestral instruments. In sharp contrast, the* Forbidden Planet *score was made up entirely of electronically generated sounds.*

In this interview with composer Jane Brockman (b. 1949), Bebe Barron explains how she and her husband—at the bold invitation of newly installed MGM executive Dore Schary—concocted the "electronic tonalities" that lent such a distinctive sonic character to the big-budget production.[24] Especially noteworthy is the light she sheds on the team's creative process. The Forbidden Planet *score, which often blurs the boundary between sound effects and extra-diegetic music, was hardly generated in the traditional manner; whereas most film composers "think up" and then prescribe music appropriate to various filmic situations, the Barrons responded to the film's scenes by rummaging through, and selecting from, a vast array of sounds already made by their "cybernetic" circuits.*

JB: Bebe, the late '40s–'50s were a time of extraordinary artistic excitement in New York. You and Louis were inventing methods of working with tape and electronics at a time where there were no models. In Paris, Mssrs. Schaeffer and Henry began experimenting with *musique concrète* in 1948, and later in 1953 Stockhausen began composing for electronics in Cologne, but you had no way of hearing their work.[25] Then Luening and Ussachevsky began experimenting with the tape recorder in Otto's basement in New York in 1952—but they were recording and processing pre-existing instruments, not building them.[26]

BB: Everything was just a matter of timing—including the equipment, which was just emerging. We couldn't wait to get our hands on it. And I think the time we worked with Cage was so wonderful because Cage gave you the feeling that there are no rules.[27] Then, Louis really was a technical genius. We were both musicians, but he was self-taught totally in electronics, and I think because of that he felt free to use electronics in a way that they'd never been used before. He didn't feel hampered by any formal knowledge. And Varèse, who used to hang out in our studio, defined music as organized sound. This had a great deal of meaning for us.[28]

JB: You and Louis were also tremendously influenced by Norbert Wiener's 1948 book *Cybernetics*—which he defined as the science of control and communications in the animal and machine.[29]

BB: Cybernetics was so appropriate to what we were doing—it *is* what we were doing. After working with Cage, and being totally imbued with his ideas on randomness and probability, Cybernetics gave a certain kind of authority to our tendencies regarding probability and randomness. That was the only thing our circuits could do.

JB: It allowed you to rethink the definition of music. It's difficult to grasp the revolutionary magnitude of this—prior to that time, music always implied performance of specific pitches. Did Cage know about Cybernetics?

BB: No, that was just his own personal philosophy based on the *I Ching* and the Oriental philosophies.[30] But there it all was in Cybernetics. For example, probability: Gibbs had just inserted probability into the whole physics realm.[31] Probability not only made random sounds O.K. in our minds, it also increased entropy—which was what we were trying for. Then, in Cybernetics there was also information theory: the more probable something is, the less information it transmits. Clichés, of course, are the least illuminating of all.

The extent of Cage's actual involvement with Eastern philosophies remains debatable. It is well known, however, that since the late 1940s Cage used the hexagram system of the *I Ching* as a method of generating random data.

JB: That had a crucial influence on the evolution of your musical style. I've often thought it historically fascinating that the acceptance of Schoenberg's idea of non-tonality was delayed by thirty years, until the advent of electronic music—where pitch priority was not an option.

BB: Yes, and then there were the fine points of entropy: all closed systems tend to deteriorate and lose their distinctiveness. Our circuits really did just that. Louis would invent a circuit and put it together. Then we would activate the circuit; it would come to life, and we would amplify it and start to tape it. And it would produce a burst of the most glorious kind of energy and electronic activity. That would level out a little bit—go on along a plateau. And then, in a moment of glory, it died—the electronic explanation would be that it overloaded in some way. But you could hear it climaxing, and the thing then would just give out, and run down to zero. At one point, a group of scientists came down to visit us from the Salk Institute. They were working on the origins of life and had heard about what we were doing, so they came down to investigate.

JB: Your circuits behaved like primitive organisms.

BB: That's right. And we never could get them to start up again after they died—each had a lifespan of its own.

Vacuum tubes were our main components. There were also resistors, capacitors, inductors and semiconductors. Semiconductors were very big with us because they were temperature sensitive and we didn't have air conditioning. So the things were always in a riot of activity.

Reverberation was also very big with us. We invented our own since there wasn't anything else. We used acoustical reverb and plate reverb. When we recorded sound at fifteen i.p.s. [inches per second] with acoustical reverberation and slowed it down a couple of generations, the reverb would give it a rhythmic beat—and that was extremely useful. It was one of very few ways we had for getting a regular rhythmic beat.

JB: I also hear quite a number of tape loops in *Forbidden Planet*. Did you invent the loop earlier?

BB: I think we did. I never heard of anyone else doing it at the time. In 1949, Stancil-Hoffman offered to make us a tape recorder to our specifications so we took advantage of it.[32] I believe it was the first commercial tape recorder ever made. The way the tapes were aligned vertically on the transport, it just kind of looked at you and said "Hey, I'm perfect for a tape loop." Then we had a voltage generator for varying the capstan speed, so were able to shift the pitch. This didn't work with our next deck, a stereo Ampex: we had to build up the capstan with splicing tape in order to vary the speed. Of course, we could play it at half speed also.

JB: Were you able to predict the sound of a circuit based on its design?

BB: We did have a pretty good idea of what kind of activity each circuit would have, whether the sounds were going to be pleasant or harsh, very active or passive and quiet. I was the one who was in charge of translating that into emotion. We relied on my ear for what sounds had possibilities that would make them worth processing. I would listen to the stuff. It came out of the circuits sounding like gibberish—harsh miserable sounds, and I got so that I could somehow hear the possibilities in them.

JB: A critical aspect of the work was identifying the effect these otherworldly sounds would have on human emotions. No one had the experiential references they have when they hear familiar instruments, an oboe or a solo violin.

BB: I had a universal mind, I think, because what sounded right to me usually sounded the same way to other people—like a love scene—I could tell what kind of circuit was going to be suitable, or the charge of the Ids/monsters.

JB: So those roaring Id/beasts were not sound effects: those were all your sounds?

BB: Yes, 95% of the sound in that picture was ours—everything except a couple of things like the computer blips. We were doing sound effects and scoring and source music. The author of an article in *Keyboard Magazine* a few years ago hit on the same thing.[33] I always wondered if that bothered people who were watching the film.

The roaring Id/beast came out of the circuit sounding not remotely like a beast. It was very high pitched, tinkling, with very complicated harmonic sounds. I would go through all the tapes and select things that had the most potential for further processing. When I heard all that high pitched activity, such complicated sounds, I said to Louis, "We've got to slow this way down." We probably lowered the frequencies sixty or seventy times [playing it back at half speed while re-recording at fifteen i.p.s.].[34] And each time we slowed it down, more of the sound would emerge to the foreground while other parts would disappear. But finally we got to what we thought was the optimum speed—the rhythm was all there. That's the way the monster sound came about.

JB: You intuitively knew the potential of this complex sound?

BB: More than that, all of our circuits were based on mathematical equations so there was an organic rightness about it. When you listen to the last cut on the soundtrack album, you can hear the monster sounds.[35] They have a unique attack—kind of a lumbering sound. The rhythm was absolutely organic to the circuit. In *Forbidden Planet*, when Morbius dies in the laboratory—that really was the Id/monster circuit dying at that point. And that worked especially well because Morbius *was* the monster; it was coming from his subconscious. That was the end of that circuit. It was the best circuit we ever had. We could never duplicate it.

And it was one of the more long-lived circuits. It must have gone on for several hours—it was full of variation, you would never know it all came from the same circuit. Of course, we recorded every second of it.

JB: Tell us about your method of scoring to film.

BB: We had several tape recorders and a little 16mm projector with a belt on it that made it always run the same speed. They were not tied together at all. They didn't have to be. We had this system of starting multiple tapedecks by hand, and we'd mark the film in such a way that we'd count 1, 2, 3, start. And we worked as one—we really were like a string quartet—fading tracks in and out. But we didn't have to be synchronized with the film that closely. It was a very time-consuming way of scoring.

We reserved all mixing until the very end. Thank God for fade-outs because we never could work out endings. I've never believed in real musical Beethoven-like endings for things. It's against my principles.

JB: And it was impossible for your circuits. I'm always cognizant of the personal nature of your timbres, your choices. You really established the sound of space music.

BB: I just knew instinctively that that's what it has to sound like when you're travelling through space. If our circuits started doing things that even remotely resembled existing instruments, we just tossed it out. We didn't even want to sound like any existing instrument. It was totally out of our realm.

JB: What was it like, working with the MGM music department?

BB: It was wonderful. They thought all the way up to the end that they were going to use Harry Partch's music for some of the scoring and our stuff for some of it.[36] They liked what we did for samples so much that they decided to let us do the whole score. One of the samples was the love scene in the garden. We came up with something that I thought was so beautiful and romantic. We played it for Johnny Green [head of the music department] and he said, "Oh my God, I didn't want the end of the earth, I wanted love." So obviously, it didn't sound like love to everybody, but it sure did to me. He was very clever, though. He said, "I want you to take it home and add all kinds of sweeteners to it."

We went back to our studio in New York, and at that time I didn't fly, so I had lots of time to think about it. We added sweeteners. In a conventional score, obviously, it would be like adding violins. But we didn't have anything like that. I found a little piece of tape that had just a single legato sound, several times at different pitches—I think there were only three of them that I could locate. And we tried adding it at random, and you know the amazing thing? It created a kind of harmonic relationship with the existing material.

JB: Tell us about the score's reception.

BB: The preview showing was one of our great experiences because they played the music directly off the magnetic tapes. They had synced up the projector and tape and they gave it so much volume it was embarrassing. It was so effective—they played it stereophonically, which they never did in those days. Then there was the landing of the space ship. That was one of the best cues in the picture—and the audience broke into spontaneous applause.

From *The Score* 7, no. 3 (Fall–Winter 1992), 5, 12–13.

11.6 ELECTRONIC STRAINS REINFORCE
ANDROMEDA FILM SCORE

Martin Bernheimer

Martin Bernheimer (b. 1936) served for thirty-one years—from 1965 until 1996—as chief music critic of the Los Angeles Times, *and since leaving that position he has contributed often to such periodicals as* Opera News *and the London-based* Financial Times. *Whereas his more recent writings have focused primarily on opera, his reviews and Sunday columns in Los Angeles addressed the full range of the city's "serious" musical activities. As might be gathered from the overt sarcasm and feigned naiveté in this article, Hollywood was not regularly a part of Bernheimer's journalistic beat; Bernheimer stepped out of his comfort zone, it seems, because the topic at hand—Gil Mellé's score for Robert Wise's 1971* The Andromeda Strain—*represented an apparently unprecedented mixing of commercial filmmaking with experimental electronic music.*

Notwithstanding the contributions that Louis and Bebe Barron made to the 1956 Forbidden Planet, *Mellé (1931–2004) insisted that he was "literally the very first electronic composer in films," and that his music for* The Andromeda Strain *was "the very first electronic [film] score."[37] Mellé's dismissal of the Barrons' efforts was based on the idea that whereas all their sounds resulted accidentally from electricity run through hodge-podges of store-bought equipment, all of his sounds resulted quite willfully either from manipulations of recorded noises or from electronic musical instruments of his own invention.*

Along with the Percussotron III mentioned in this article, these instruments included a "wireless synthesizer" and such colorfully named devices as the Electar and the Sound Gun. Mellé began developing these instruments in the late 1950s, when he worked primarily as a jazz musician in New York; upon his move to Hollywood in 1968, he put them to use first in the made-for-television film Perilous Voyage *and then in a theme that introduced Rod Serling's* Night Gallery *series.[38] Impressed not so much by these fledgling scoring efforts as by a demonstration tape, director Wise chose Mellé for his modern-day science-fiction film because, of all the Hollywood composers then experimenting with electronic music, he thought that Mellé could best deliver something that on the whole would function like a background score, with appropriate "edge and nervousness," but which in many instances would "be almost like sound effects."[39]*

Universal Studios are quiet at night. Eerily quiet.

As far as the outside world is concerned, movies are made in the daytime. But strange nocturnal things were happening recently, in a deserted recording studio on the Lankershim lot.[40]

The room is a tangled mass of wires, consoles, reels, buttons, charts, lights, levers and bizarre instruments, all of which seem ominously and independently mechanical. One wall is dominated by a screen on which an invisible camera rear-projects one fictitious-science sequence over and over again. And again.

170

A frantic gentleman in overalls, pursued by gas jets and lethal laser beams, is climbing a spiral ladder, searching it seems, for the elusive device which will cancel computerized destruction. That's the sequence on the screen.

Several technicians scramble about the studio to turn switches and nod approvingly at gauges. But the obvious chief protagonist, holding forth like some inspired mad scientist, in his cluttered, nefarious laboratory, is a cool, modish fellow with fashionably long hair and a sporty leather jacket.

He accompanies the filmed sequence in mysterious ways conjuring up some appropriately exotic, otherworldly sounds. The sounds—electronic sounds—illustrate the projected sights and automatically produce futuristic associations.

But they function, decisively as far more than sound effects, more than atmospheric devices. They also produce a fascinating network of rhythmic impulses, shifting textural patterns, repetitive timbre motives, even aggressive scraps of melody.

Music. Modern music!

In Hollywood, of all places.

Gil Mellé, a bright young composer-performer who knows his jazz as well as his Varèse and his way around a TV or movie lot, too, is preparing the score for *The Andromeda Strain*.

That, you may recall, is a best-seller by Michael Crichton about some deadly out-of-space organism which threatens fragile mankind. The movie version, soon to be released,[41] is the brainchild of Robert Wise, best known, perhaps, for *The Sound of Music*.

The *Sound of Music* was never like this.

Wise, it seems, is a man of considerable sophistication, even though he disclaims any advanced musical training or instincts. He felt the avant-garde subject matter demanded the reinforcement of avant-garde music. It was that simple.

Ergo. *The Andromeda Strain* may be the first major commercial film to utilize a bona-fide electronic soundtrack. The original-cast album might puzzle the collectors in Oshkosh, but they are bound to love it in Donaueschingen.[42]

Mellé, an intensely committed 37-year-old who likes to build ring modulators, synthesizers and oscillators—little things like that—regarded the commission as "a gift from the gods." He invented instruments—a powerful little reverberating banger called Percussotron III monopolized attention the day I visited—and he persuaded Universal to buy or borrow enough equipment to stock an electronic hardware sales convention.

The only serious problem facing our night-time Stockhausen was one of logistics.[43] The rooms at his command, it turned out, had to be used for more conventional recording purposes during normal working hours. So Mellé and his faithful attendants had to set up their super-ultra-complicated apparatuses every night at 6, only to tear it down again at 3 in the morning.

Only Penelope's weaving could have been more laborious, and equally frustrating.

Mellé was philosophical. "To be left alone to do a thing like this is fantastic," he mused, fondling a versatile little gadget he called the Planetary Controller. "Who cares about a little inconvenience?

"There's one great advantage to working at night," he added, we thought a little defensively. "It's quiet and there's no one around to disturb me."

Quiet seemed an odd word to describe a room vibrating with all manner of gurgles, rumbles, whines, drones, ripples, and explosions. But one man's crash is another's crescendo, one listener's coven of bleeps may be another's accumulation of arpeggios.

An observer asked Mellé the ultimate nasty question: "Doesn't it bother you that what you are writing won't have any validity without the movie it accompanies?"

The composer gulped. He began to deny that he was producing mere noise or simple effects. He insisted the offender listen to the music written to accompany the film titles. This, he claimed, was pure music, music with perfect validity of its own.

The tape supported its creator's claim. At least I thought it did (I cannot vouch for the undiplomatic skeptic who originally posed the question). The music created its own abstract logic, defined its own sonic dimensions, its own formal outlook and dynamic impact.

Mellé looked relieved.

The Andromeda Strain will utilize a multi-track score with its own built-in levels of "reality." There will be some traditional orchestral sounds as a point of sanity, intermingled and contrasted with pure electronic composition and *musique concrète* (electronic manipulations of non-electronic sounds).[44]

"The wonderful thing about this," enthuses Mellé, "is the flexibility of it all. I can improvise while I'm watching the film. I can combine materials and interpolate punctuation. It's all under my control right here, and, once we have the equipment, it all can be done with a relatively low budget."

The dubious observer got worrisome again. "But why," he wanted to know, "should a studio invest so much in all those machines when the resultant sounds are appropriate only for science fiction pictures?"

"Hell," responded our hero. "I'd like to write an electronic score for a western."

Mellé admitted that he might have some trouble selling that idea to the studio bosses. Still, he was reasonably optimistic.

"The young audiences won't have any trouble with electronic soundtracks. They are the best audiences. They don't bring any prefabricated prejudices with them."

We left Mellé twiddling his dials and pounding his Percussotron while the perspiring fellow on the screen continued to climb ladders and dodge lasers. It was midnight. For the composer and his crew the night was still young.

A few weeks later, the scene shifted to a dubbing (re-recording) studio. It was daytime business as usual: time to combine the music with the legitimate sound effects, the dialog and the finished print. The seat of power had shifted from Mellé to Wise. The attendant console technicians were regular studio engineers.

Ten weeks had elapsed since Mellé began working on the film. "It's still settling, and we're still finding quirks," he admitted. He seemed tired and content.

Also a little tense.

It was zero-hour, and it was becoming apparent that the music—so painstakingly accumulated—might be demoted to a force secondary to the words and the action. Everyone was polite. But the "mixing" experts obviously regarded Mellé's contributions as ornamental. And Wise, for all his musical sympathy, still had dramatic logic to worry about.

The fellow on the screen still was making his way up the familiar super-sterile underground structure with the seeing-eye lasers. But now his sweat was Technicolored. Now we heard him grunt. And now there was a sexless female voice on the soundtrack counting down the minutes and seconds to "self-destruct."

Before, with a mute film and a room full of electronic music, the climactic scene of *The Andromeda Strain* had been a marvelously otherworldly ballet. Mellé told us all we needed to know about the protagonist on the screen, his predicament, and his escape from it.

Now, with the addition of words and noises and colors, stylization gave way to some unexpected, unwanted but imperative realism. The ballet had become a movie.

The music, by natural default, had become less important.

It was Wise's job to tone down its impact. He suggested volume adjustments quietly, calmly, tactfully. Mellé winced, offered token resistance, ultimately acquiesced.

"I don't want my score to be something subliminal," he confided later. "I want people to hear the instruments. Each one has its own character. I want viewers to perceive the different textures and their psychological connotations.

"But these people know what they are doing. They know what they must do . . ."

The impression of a compromise was unmistakable. "Even if the word ultimately takes precedence over the music," he insisted, "everything I have written—some 40 minutes of music—is still there. I have had a chance to experiment, to create. It was all worthwhile."

A quarter of a century ago, Alfred Hitchcock requisitioned one embryonic electronic instrument called the Theremin to provide a weird sonic ambience for Ingrid Bergman's psychiatrics in *Spellbound*.[45] It was considered a daring innovation at the time. We have come a long way.

Or have we?

From *Los Angeles Times*, January 17, 1971, Y1, Y42.

Part 5

CHANGING TIMES

12

GLOOM AND DOOM

For many in Hollywood, the stylistic novelties discussed in Part 4 represented a source of the fresh air that American filmmaking so desperately needed after the suffocating onslaughts of the 1950s. But films whose scores were rich in 'weird' electronic sonorities, and especially films that drew from various pop repertoires not just for source music but for underscore, were not universally welcomed. Indeed, some in the industry felt that the infiltration of jazz and rock 'n' roll into film scores marked the beginning of the end of film music.

Not surprisingly, the warnings of barbarians at the gates came not from directors or writers, and certainly not from critics or audiences, but from composers whose relatively comfortable existence to date had depended upon their specialized ability to create wholly original orchestral music for narrative films of all sorts. For composers whose introduction to the cinema resonated with the sounds of film music's "Golden Age" and whose careers were built not so much on imitation of 1930s and 1940s style but on allegiance to that style's aesthetics and purposes, the very idea of 'scores' cobbled together from pre-existing pop song recordings was surely a bitter gall.

Composers schooled in the old ways by and large held their tongues as jazz-rock styles slowly infected film music throughout the postwar years. Dismay was loudly voiced, however, after the huge box-office successes of a pair of films released late in the 1960s. One of these was Mike Nichols's 1967 *The Graduate*, which supported its largely comic story of a hapless young romantic primarily with songs that before the film's release had been popularized by the duo Simon and Garfunkel;[1] the other was Dennis Hopper's 1969 *Easy Rider*, a gritty drama about motorcycle-riding drifters whose misadventures are accompanied exclusively by pre-existing rock songs.[2]

Executives of film studios in Hollywood and elsewhere could not help but notice that the substantial profits generated by *The Graduate* and *Easy Rider* were due less to box-office receipts than to sales of the soundtrack albums. Certainly not every film in the immediately ensuing years abandoned original music in favor of what would eventually be known as the 'compilation score.' But plenty of them did, or at least began to move in that direction. Soon enough it was clear that a trend had been started, and this grated seriously on the nerves of older composers.

Press clippings from the early 1970s abound with suggestions that more than a few film-music veterans felt that their storehouse of talent and skill was suddenly being ignored, that the industry had been overrun by money-minded young cretins who knew nothing of cinema's 'good old days' and thus cared not a hoot for filmic quality. Human nature being what it is, most of the quoted expressions of dismay are clouded in innuendo or veiled in humor, their articulators apparently being incapable of stifling themselves yet unwilling to bite the hand that likely might still feed them.

The two articles reproduced here are notable exceptions to that generalization. Famously feisty throughout their careers, and much more prone to extended verbalization than most of their colleagues, Elmer Bernstein and David Raksin in these similarly titled articles indeed pull some punches. But at the same time they offer logical reasons, and plenty of historical background, for their pessimistic thinking that film music—as they cared to define it—in the early 1970s had by and large reached the end of the line.

12.1 WHAT EVER HAPPENED TO GREAT MOVIE MUSIC?

Elmer Bernstein

Elmer Bernstein (1922–2004) was born in New York and trained both at Juilliard and New York University.[3] He began his career as a composer in 1943 by providing music for programs aired by the Armed Forces Radio Service; after postwar work in commercial radio, in 1950 he made his way to Hollywood. Likely in part because his liberal political sympathies had caused him to be 'grey-listed,' his early efforts in Hollywood were limited to a handful of decidedly low-budget films.[4] His first large-budget film was Philip Dunne's 1955 The View from Pompey's Head *(Twentieth Century-Fox), and in the same year Bernstein rose to prominence—and thereafter was an A-list composer—with his jazz-flavored score for Otto Preminger's* The Man with the Golden Arm *(United Artists).*

Bernstein refers to the Man with the Golden Arm *music near the end of the article reproduced here. Almost ruefully, he suggests that it was this score's very hipness that, along with the astoundingly popular theme song that Dimitri Tiomkin concocted in 1952 for* High Noon, *heralded the demise of 'great' movie music. But the thrust of Bernstein's sustained argument is simply that, for film music and for films in general, times seem to have changed for the worse. The reason for this has to do not with well-intentioned musical innovations by him or by others but, rather, with the apparent fact that Hollywood had been taken over by avaricious cretins.*

Be that as it may, Bernstein's career did not suffer as a result of this 1972 diatribe. While some critics might argue that all of Bernstein's 'masterpiece' scores[5] indeed predated this outpouring of negative sentiment, it remains that Bernstein was as much in demand in the next three decades as he had been earlier. In light of the bitterness that permeates this article that Bernstein wrote at the age of 50, it seems interesting that the most enduring of the films he later scored are comedies.[6]

The events of the past few years in the field of film scoring seem to indicate that any discussion on this great art may indeed have to be a historical summary at the end of its era of greatness. As a working film composer and an evolutionary product of the works of Aaron Copland, Bernard Herrmann, Max Steiner, Erich Korngold, Hugo Friedhofer, Franz Waxman, Alfred Newman, David Raksin, George Antheil, Miklos Rosza, Dimitri Tiomkin, and Bronislau Kaper, and a contemporary of Alex North, Jerry

Goldsmith, Henry Mancini, Lalo Schifrin, and André Previn, I find it inconceivable that this sophisticated art has in such a short time degenerated into a bleakness of various electronic noises and generally futile attempts to "make the pop Top 40 charts." Today the trend is most obviously to the nonscore, the song form, and General Electric. It appears that the king is dead and the court jester has been installed in his place. Before we consider the causes of death, let us first proceed to an examination of the corpus while its remains are still with us.

Music is the art that begins where words and images leave off—which is what makes it so effective in films. Sonic vibrations set part of the body in motion and touch the listener in an almost purely visceral manner. Music can stimulate the greatest possible range of moods, shades, and fantasies. Also, it is an art that envelopes the listener, who cannot escape it save by leaving the area. Unlike the written word or visual image, there is no need to intellectualize its existence. That its source is unseen and that it can enter and leave at almost imperceptible levels makes music an invaluable tool with which the skilled film composer can practice emotional seductions upon the viewer of a movie. Parenthetically, it is of interest to note that in the days of silent films David Wark Griffith used musicians to inspire his actors to passion on the set.

Some of us are old enough to remember the orchestras that accompanied the lavish first runs of silent films, or the inevitable pianists who created moods to help the neighborhood audiences hiss villains and applaud heroes. Many scores were composed and tailored to the films of their day, with written descriptions of the screen action so that the performer would know whether he was playing slow or fast enough to suit the image. The earliest piano scores for movies I know of—and which are still extant—were written for the films of Georges Méliès in the closing years of the nineteenth century. In these primitive scores, music was used to mimic the action on screen: fast music for fast action, lumbering music for lumbering action, low and menacing notes for the villain, trumpetlike themes for the hero, and so on. The music became a series of representative clichés rather than an emotional communication, and a whole set of conventions quickly grew up by which one could easily identify villain, hero, the chase, and love. Today one laughs at them, but in their heyday audiences looked forward to these conventionalized clichés.

It was quite natural, of course, that when sound came in audiences were more interested in hearing the voices of their favorite movie stars and musical performers. The earliest use of music in connection with nonmusical films seems to have been the filling of "dead spots" with some sort of sound. Today the results appear quite amusing—the music seems to drone on quite unrelated to the events in the picture. In this sense the lack of sophistication, integration, and skill is not unlike that of many contemporary motion pictures where the score functions merely to introduce popular material not often integrated into the film.

Max Steiner arrived in Hollywood in 1929. Very quickly his work educated the film colony to the possibilities of film music tailored to the needs of specific dramatic situations. Strange as all this may seem, it was in its time an original and thrilling concept. Steiner also pioneered musical authenticity. Nowadays we assume that a composer will research the music indigenous to the country in which a film story takes place. It is difficult then to remember how fresh and exciting was Steiner's attempt to create an Irish musical ambience for *The Informer*.[7]

During the following generation Hollywood sores, at least the best of them, developed into a sophisticated art for using sophisticated techniques. The techniques of course were not always apt. Take the leitmotif. The leitmotif—a specific theme continually used to identify a specific character, situation, or emotion—is a time-honored musicodramatic device raised to great heights by the genius of Richard Wagner. Its application in film scoring is obvious, but unless used well it can become another boring and trite device. My own score for *The Ten Commandments* made extensive use of the leitmotif. This score is in many ways the least characteristic of my works as it was written while working under the close supervision of the producer, Cecil B. DeMille.[8] DeMille believed the function of music in a motion picture to be an adjunctive story-telling device, with each character having a particular theme or motif to accompany his moments on screen. In *The Ten Commandments*, DeMille insisted upon identifying themes for Moses, Joshua, Ramses, Nefretiri, Lilia, Dathen. In addition, there were to be motifs for two opposing themes: the power of God and the force of evil. The motifs were heard whenever the characters were on screen and in cases where there was an interplay between two characters, a Wagnerian interweaving of the tunes was expected. Changes of mood created by the dramatic necessities of the story were accompanied mainly by changes of orchestral color. Thus when Moses is an infant in the bulrushes, his theme is performed by woodwind solo to a 6/8 lullaby accompaniment. Later, when he has become the prophet, his theme is announced by trumpets and horns in a martial tempo. And in this way one finds the score retelling the events on screen. This technique requires great skill in its execution to avoid extreme banality and is, I believe, one of the least attractive uses of film music since it serves merely to repeat what should be clearly evident in a good film. The leitmotif functions best in a film of epic proportions, for not many characters merit the grandeur of an accompanying musical theme. In other situations the constant repetition of a theme for a character becomes an unpardonable intrusion upon the dramatic integrity of the film. Besides, how many melodies have been created for films that one would want to hear twenty times in the course of ninety minutes?

Even more dangerous than the leitmotif device is the monothematic score. The single theme can designate a particular overriding emotion, as in Alfred Newman's *Love Is a Many-Splendored Thing* (85 per cent of that score is based on one tune), or it can even identify a character, as in David Raksin's eternal *Laura*. A technique that can be—and nowadays usually is—a boring cliché had its classic expression in *Laura*. The film portrayed a man falling in love with a ghost: The mystique was supplied by the insistence of the haunting melody. He could not escape it. It was everywhere. It was there when he was in Laura's apartment. It was there when he turned on the record player. It was never absent from his thoughts. We may not remember what Laura was like, but we never forget that she *was* the music and in that music she has of course come into our lives to stay. In that instance, the music and its insistence was the most compelling feature of the film.

For me, film music functions best when it is able to deal with that which is implicit but not explicit in a scene. It can thus add to the film art rather than simply ape another element in it. Here is another example from my own work: In *Men in War* one scene shows a group of soldiers walking through a Korean forest which they know to be mined. They are quite understandably terrified by the possibility of sudden death at every step. As I looked at that scene and considered what I wished to do musically, I thought of how many battles had been fought in the midst of beautiful country. As these men were making this walk their surroundings were a forest full of birds singing, leaves rustling, twigs snapping—sweet aural counterpoint that made the possibility of death even more terrible. I decided to emphasize this less obvious counterpoint in my music. While I called for an almost imperceptible tremolando in the basses, timpani and bass drum, I had the cellos gently guide the wind through the leaves in delicate pianissimo glissandos and trills, the woodwinds play quick, disjointed birdlike calls, the xylophone and other percussion play staccato woodsy figures, and I gave any sustaining lines to the ominous-sounding bass flute or the bass clarinet. This approach served to deepen the terror of the scene as it added an interesting subliminal note to it.

One of the surprising attributes of the film score is its ability to speed up or slow down the action. In my early career I believed that the accompanying music must have a kinetic energy equal to that of the scene for which it is written. Cecil B. DeMille changed my mind about that. In the Exodus scene of *The Ten Commandments* there is the moment in which the Hebrews begin their march out of Egyptian bondage. DeMille used approximately 8,000 people in that scene, with the effect that the start of their march was passive and lumbering. The first music I wrote for the scene was a ponderous Hebraic marchlike anthem. DeMille hated it. When I insisted that it had truly reflected the pace of the scene, he readily agreed, and stated that that was the trouble with it. If I would write music with a faster pace than that of the scene, the Hebrews would appear to move more brightly, the elation at their freedom would be more prominent. I was skeptical, but tried it. DeMille was right.

I remembered my lesson when I composed the score for *The Magnificent Seven*. The unhurried pace of the film as a whole was always a potential danger in a story that demanded tension and suspense. To help this situation I wrote the music in tempos always somewhat faster than those of the film's, and made considerable use of vigorous rhythmic patterns as well as repeated sixteenth-note figures. Again, I believe it worked.

The main body of a film composer's work is done after the editing is completed, though in some instances the composer may be called in for conferences even before shooting begins. This would be necessary for instance where musical material must be included in the shooting of a film. When the film is finally assembled, the composer and the producer or director view the film together and begin their general discussion about the character and use of music. In most cases the composer is left to decide such fine points as where the music should begin and end. The music editor then writes a description of every action and word of dialogue in the scene accurate to one-tenth of a second. The composer usually works from these descriptions, but some composers prefer to have the film and a Movieola in their homes. Since film is a medium locked in time, the composer must learn to compose music that falls naturally within the time confines.

In the recording session, the film is projected as the musicians perform. There are various visual metronomic devices such as streamers and punches[9] on the film to aid the conductor in his job of synchronizing the playing of the music to the action of the film. The final process is one in which music, sound, and dialogue are united into one soundtrack.

One of the problems besetting the film composer is the rapidity with which a device that seems fresh in one film so quickly becomes commonplace. One reason for this is the tremendous exposure afforded by motion pictures. The concert hall composer is lucky to expose his work to perhaps two thousand people at a time. But films are seen (and heard) by upwards of fifty million. It is very difficult for a fresh musical idea to stay fresh long under these conditions. The bass flute solo, which could be used to engender terror only a few years ago, is now part of the everyday language of the film composer. The once effective romantic "piano concerto" style has become banal almost to the point of the comic. To many second-rate movie composers, this phenomenon is terrifying and sends them to frantic searches for "new sounds"—which are also soon exhausted.

Two innocent events in the early and middle Fifties, it seems to me, signaled the beginning of the end of the golden age of film music. The first of these was the extraordinary commercial success of the title song by Dimitri Tiomkin for the 1951 motion picture *High Noon*.[10] How fresh and exciting that main title seemed then! But the free advertising resulting from the song—not to mention the enormous money that the song itself made—led to an instant demand by movie producers for similar title songs in almost every picture that followed. Lyric writers were beset with such problems as setting titles like *The Revolt of Mamie Stover* to music and the situation rapidly became ludicrous.[11] But the commercial attitude has remained. To hell with the score—let's get that title song on the charts!

The second event was the success of my own *Man with the Golden Arm* in 1955, which was compounded by Henry Mancini's TV success with *Peter Gunn*.[12] With the commercial bonanza of these "pop" sounds in two perfectly *legitimate* situations—my score was not a jazz score, but a score in which jazz elements were incorporated toward the end of creating specific atmosphere for that particular film—producers quickly began to transform film composing from a serious art into a pop art and more recently into pop garbage.

It is no secret that many title songs have made more money than the movies they came from. Movie companies suddenly became music publishing houses and recording firms so as not to allow any of the loot to slip by them. And in the process the serious composition of thoughtful film scores was given short shrift.

We live in times in which the soul must learn to live with the senseless killing of millions throughout the world; with the necessity of the double lock; with the knowledge of where not to walk after dark. We have learned to accept the philosophy that no person in public life can ever tell the whole truth, and that the future might hold annihilation either through man's brutishness or through his ecological selfishness. In such a world, art tends to become sensation, aesthetics becomes a belief that the way to protest brutality is to reflect it in art. In motion pictures we are treated to an onslaught of violence and sensation, without form, without art, and without humanity. In this atmosphere the quality of film scores is being strangled by the search for effect, for "new sounds" without content and form on the part of the artist, and by avarice on the part of the producer. Today the once proud art of film scoring has turned into a sound, a sensation or hopefully a hit. How ironic that in an era in which music enjoys its greatest popularity as an art, film producers are demonstrating the greatest ignorance of the use of music in films since the beginning of that medium's history.

From *High Fidelity*, July 1972, 55–58.

12.2 WHATEVER BECAME OF MOVIE MUSIC?

David Raksin

David Raksin (1912–2004) is likely more famous for his uninhibited and deliciously colorful commentaries on film music than he is for the prodigious amount of film music he wrote. At the expense of his contributions to more than a hundred other films between 1937 and his retirement in 1989, Raksin doubtless will forever be remembered for the monothematic score that haunted, like the spirit of the supposedly dead title character, Otto Preminger's 1944 Laura[13] and for the sarcastic parodies of genre music that illustrated behind-the-scenes Hollywood in Vincente Minnelli's 1952 The Bad and the Beautiful. But Raksin's enduring presence in film-music literature has less to do with his compositions than with his commentaries. Well known to the Hollywood community through his witty lectures on film music at the University of Southern California, and blessed with a voluble personality and an apparent love for the limelight, Raksin quickly became an A-list "go to" person for hurried journalists seeking to embellish their articles with quotations.

A perusal of the dozens of newspaper items in which his comments appear show Raksin to be fairly consistent both in his willingness to respond more or less directly to reporters' questions and in his preference to keep his own "two cents' worth" on the lighter side of various debates. Against that backdrop the article reproduced here stands in sharp contrast, for it resonates not with Raksin's characteristic levity but with bitter sarcasm and, sometimes, with what almost sounds like a heavy-hearted resignation.

Raksin, of course, has his own axes to grind. But like Elmer Bernstein in his 1972 "What Ever Happened to Great Movie Music?" Raksin in this similarly titled article attributes the perceived decline in film music largely to studio executives' changed attitude. Forgetting, perhaps, that in the United States filmmaking was right from the start a commercial enterprise, he bemoans the apparent fact that Hollywood in the mid-1970s is concerned not with music's contribution to a film's dramatic success but, rather, with music's ability to generate income.

The new director turned out to be an amiable roughneck, about my own age, bright and shrewd, talented, and still New Yorkish enough to need to let me know that he was not about to have "any of the Hollywood music" in his picture. What he wanted was "something different, really powerful—like *Wozzeck.*"[14] A string of three-frame cuts of the aurora borealis flashed in my head. To hear the magic name of Alban Berg's operatic masterpiece invoked by the man with whom I would be working was to be invited to be free! To hear it correctly pronounced was to doubt the evidence of my ears: here was a non-musician who was not only aware that *Wozzeck* existed, but actually thought of his film as one to which so highly expressive a musical style might be appropriate. It was too good to be true: but after all those years of struggling to be honest with people who couldn't understand why I was reluctant to compose pretty music for their violent and ugly movies I was ready to believe every word. I invited him out to my farm for dinner so that we could discuss the film, away from studio distractions.

So there we were in the living room, with drinks in hand, the phonograph playing and the conversation taking its time to get under way. I remember thinking that this was the way things ought to be: I liked his script, I admired him, and I couldn't wait to hear what he had to say and to get working on musical material for the score. Suddenly irritable, he said "What's that crap you're playing?" "That crap," I replied, "is *Wozzeck!*" That was twenty-five years ago, and if there is a story that tells more about why film composers sometimes despair of their profession, I have yet to hear it.

So here we are in 1974, and I am wondering what has changed. Having been invited to discuss the state of music in films, I find myself in the uncomfortable position of the tailor asked to give his opinion of the king's new clothes. If I am to be truthful, I have got to give up the neutralist, no-involvement copout that has enabled me thus far to avoid taking what is certain to be an unpopular stand. For there is no way to write about film music today without acknowledging the powerful current of revulsion toward many aspects of their own profession that is explicit in the words and attitudes of my most valued colleagues. I am not talking only of those who have been to some extent deprived of regular employment because of changing fashions in film scoring, and who might therefore be expected to look unfavorably upon present trends, but of leading figures who are as busy and successful today as ever they were—and yet seem to find the situation unacceptable: their talk is of getting out, somehow. Why?

The answer is not simple. To begin with, there is the state of the Industry; it should be news to no one that many people believe the Industry has been plundered, ruined by incompetence and left to twist slowly in the wind by men whose principal interests— whatever they may be—do not lie in film-making. The disastrous unemployment resulting from this circumstance has become worse as film companies have made more and more pictures abroad; American composers find it difficult to believe that the use of foreign composers is not related to the fact that they work for less money. As to the remaining available jobs, they are further curtailed by relegation of the film soundtrack to the humiliating status of an adjunct to the recording industry. In too many cases, the appropriateness of the music to the film is secondary to getting an album, or a single, and the voice of the A & R man is heard in the land.

All of this has become so much a part of the film music scene that anyone who challenges the propriety or, *perish forbid*, the artistic integrity of the process is sure to start heads shaking with concern for his sanity. Artists and Repertoire tycoons sit in the control rooms (how aptly named!) and freely render judgments upon the viability of film scores as commodities on record racks; these opinions are as freely transferred to apply (as though they were pertinent!) to the function of the music *in the picture*, and nobody seems to question the competence of these people to decide what is "right" for a sequence or for a film. Where are the proud directors and producers, formerly so zealous to ensure that all components of their films interacted to fashion the synergistic marvel that is a motion picture? (I suspect they are to be found in line at Tiffany's to ask, "Where do you keep your chrome?")

There are times these days when I suspect that my students at USC and UCLA[15] are trying to provoke me into "putting down" Rock or Pop film scores indiscriminately. And I feel absurdly virtuous when I ask them whether they can imagine pictures like *Easy Rider* or *The Last Picture Show* or *American Graffiti* with any other kind of music. The fact is that the music in those films was just what it should have been. But I do not find this to be equally true of all films in which such music is used. For unless we are willing to concede that what is essentially the music of the young is appropriate to *all* of the aspects of human experience with which films are concerned, we must ask what it is doing on the soundtracks of pictures that deal with other times and generations, other lives. It is one thing to appreciate the freshness and naivete of Pop music and quite another to accept it as inevitable no matter what the subject at hand. And *still* another to realize that the choice is often made for reasons that have little to do with the film itself. *One*: to sell recordings—and incidentally to garner publicity for the picture. *Two*: to appeal to the "demographically defined" audience, which is a symbolic unit conceived as an object of condescension. *Three* (and to my mind saddest of all): because so many directors and producers, having acquired their skills and reputations at the price of becoming elderly, suddenly find themselves aliens in the land of the young; tormented by fear of not being "with it," they are tragically susceptible to the brainwashing of Music-Biz types. What is one to think of men of taste and experience who can be persuaded that the difference between a good picture and a bad one is a "now" score that's "where it's at"?

As though that were not bad enough, the situation has deteriorated further because of an epidemic of *Griffithitis*, a term which I derive from the action of D. W. Griffith, who threw out the score originally composed for *The Birth of a Nation* and substituted a hodgepodge of mismatched pieces. My favorite boss, Alfred Newman, used to say that the trouble with Hollywood was that "everybody knows his own job—plus music!" These *plus-music boys*, as he called them, have never been more in evidence than they are today. Although I want to believe that an art of multiple components such as film should be guided by a single hand, and that that hand ought to be the director's, that belief has been sorely tried by the ignorance of music, as applied in films, and the uncontrollable willfulness which my colleagues and I so often encounter. When first I suggested that any composer who had not had at least one score thrown out was either a novice or a hack—or unbelievably lucky—even my friends thought I was merely setting up defenses. Now that so many of the better composers have suffered the humiliation of seeing their talent and experience defeated by the tin ear with the power behind it, they are beginning to wonder about the validity of an art that is at the mercy of so many untutored minds.

It would be ridiculous for me to contend that only we, and not the men who make the films—and who know, or ought to know what they require of the music—are always right. But it would be equally foolish to believe that the most talented and skilful composers who ever wrote music for films could possibly strike out as often as recent statistics appear to suggest. I think that what has happened is that we have fallen into the hands of some ungovernable men whose ability to comprehend the language of music and its function in film lags far, far behind their other, often substantial skills, and who are unable to see in this shortcoming a compelling reason for abstaining from judgment in an area in which their competence is minimal. Directors scream their pretty heads off about the imposition of raw power by insensitive men who alter the delicate balances and destroy the subtle rhythms of their precious footage; then they put on their Dracula hats and go to work on our music! What is especially disheartening about this phenomenon is the compulsion of such people to discredit what they cannot make subservient to their purposes. (Here I must pause to acknowledge gratefully those who were themselves free enough to grant me the freedom to do my best, and that would include the director who had second thoughts about *Wozzeck*.)

To repeat, I do not suggest that we composers are without fault. To the extent to which we have "bought" the propaganda of those who misconstrue the meaning and importance of our contribution to the art and business that is film making, to the extent that we have put up with the most consistently inhumane work schedules within the frame of film employment and accepted the appropriation of our right to legal "authorship" of our own music (would you believe that Twentieth Century-Fox Film Corp. is the "*author in fact*" of "Laura"?) we have only ourselves to blame. And we ought, among other things, to have been more persistent about reminding the studio barons that we are the *only* group among those who contribute to films who defray the costs of their own employment—by that portion of the royalties from the performance and sale of our music which goes into studio treasures.

It was withal a noble profession—by which I do not mean to suggest that the present situation is all bad or that movie music as we knew it is finished. For one thing, there are certain new, young composers in whose talents one can rejoice, and to whose future careers one can look—and listen—with hope. Even if one did not admire the more reserved kinds of musical utterances affected by some of today's brightest new lights, and more often than not I do, it would be necessary to concede that they are generally as appropriate in style to present modes of film making as some of the florid kinds of music would be inappropriate. But consider the apparent paradox that people who buy recordings of film scores are buying music—by Korngold, Steiner, Newman and others— that is the antithesis of what is for the most part heard on the soundtracks of current films. The smartest money seems to believe that it is more than "nostalgia" which impels new audiences to seek out films in the Hollywood tradition, with their concomitant musical lyricism, and to buy recordings of such music. Perhaps the audience is about to realize that it is not necessary to choose among different modes of filmic expression as though they were irreconcilable alternatives, that we are free to enjoy as much of the spectrum as the spirit can accommodate. If the process runs true to form, the Industry will be about half a generation in catching up.

It is just possible that (to quote Brahms) there is someone I may have forgotten to offend. Therefore, a few last shots from the hip. Today we are witnessing a disquieting situation in the Arts; in music this manifests itself through an abnormal polarization, in which the masses throng to the Inglewood Forum to enjoy the equivalent of finger painting, while the avant garde responds with ecstacies of anal retention. Nevertheless, valid and genuine musical languages are taking form, and it is up to those who aspire to leadership in the film arts to learn to understand these languages, so that our music is free to bespeak the substance of the film, instead of being forced by the ignorance of those in whom the ultimate control of the soundtrack lies to lag generations behind, aesthetically.

Finally, I will be surprised if this article does not provoke pious rebuttals from certain of my *Uncle Tom* colleagues, one of whom found it necessary to state for publication that, contrary to the notion that music can "save" a bad picture, it is good pictures that save bad music. Since that quaint notion originated in the abuse of music by film makers to attempt to repair *their* sins, music has too often been called upon to create miracles— and has come closer to achieving the impossible than anyone had a right to expect. Therefore, it was unseemly for a member of a proud profession to seek to ingratiate himself with prospective employers by being the first fellow on the block to demean his art. It is easy to see why some men who are deeply immersed in the process of *making it* feel compelled to rationalize away uncomfortable questions which threaten their continuing complicity in what is all too often a dirty game, because they see it quite correctly as the only game in town. However, to understand such behavior is one thing: to condone it is something else.

Composers (and others) of my generation have been reluctant to speak out for a number of reasons, not the least of which is that candor is a fine device for terminating one's "employability." And when one has reached that point at which, having finally learned something about the profession he has been practicing, he must come to terms with the fact that the largest chronological part of his work has been accomplished, it seems very poor grace to turn sour on that profession. To speak unfavorably of much that is currently being done—no matter with what wisdom, or forbearance, or inherent desire to appreciate what is worthwhile and disregard what is not—is certain to be interpreted in the worst possible light. Well, it may not convince any except those who know me (and who ought therefore to need little convincing), but I have always taken pleasure in the achievements of my talented colleagues, and I disavow envy—conscious or otherwise. (It is a matter of record that I have called to the attention of studio music executives certain film and television scores that might otherwise have been taken for granted.) And I would remind skeptics that the celebration of talent is traditional in our profession: said Robert Schumann on first hearing the music of Frederic Chopin, "Hats off, gentlemen, a genius!"

The gentlemen needed reminding and so do we; and, most of all, so do those men with whom and *for* whom we work. They need to be reminded that *they* need us quite as much as we need them, that it is time they abandoned their reliance upon the score that presupposes a jukebox as a human appendage and came to terms with the evocative power of dramatic music—and their fear of that power. We must (said the French politician, Jean Monnet) attack our problems instead of each other. While we are waiting for that to happen, we can do a lot worse than to keep an eye on the king's new clothes. Can it be that he is a *streaker*?

From *Film Music Notebook* 1, no. 1 (Autumn 1974), 24–28.
Originally published as "Film Music: Beauty and the Beast?:
Raksin Raps State of Art" in *Variety* 275, no. 1 (May 1974), 59.

187

13

PLENTY OF OPTIMISM

As composer Jerry Goldsmith pointed out in the 1967 interview with *Los Angeles Times* film critic Charles Champlin that opens this chapter, by that time "the whole style of film-making [had] changed." And for composers of a certain mind-set, this was reason for plenty of optimism.

The situation in Hollywood, and with it the manner in which many filmmakers approached their craft, was indeed quite different from what it had been during the so-called Studio Era.[1] Decisions on filmic content were increasingly made by independent producers rather than by executives of what remained of the major studios, whose still-valuable imprimatur often indicated not collective "authorship" but only distribution rights. Significantly, the aesthetics of commercial filmmaking in the United States had been radically transformed not just by such foreign influences as the Italian neo-realist style, the French "new wave," and the British "free cinema" but also by the bold statements of the iconoclasts who had banded together in 1960 as the New America Cinema Group. Even more significant, the narrative content of commercial filmmaking worldwide by the end of the decade was increasingly responsive—in ways both positive and negative—to the profound societal changes that various nations had recently experienced. In the United States, for example,

> the 1960s witnessed, to use the clichéd phrases, a sexual revolution and a rising drug culture, the women's liberation movement and the Hippie movement, the "British invasion" of American pop music and eventually the dominance of serious "rock" music over carefree rock 'n' roll. The decade's enduring icons include the Apollo moon landing and the Woodstock festival. Among its many driving forces, surely the most potent was wide-spread opposition, at least by young adults, to the United States' ever-escalating military involvement in Vietnam.[2]

For better or worse, the changes in the "whole style" of filmmaking that were clearly operational by the late 1960s involved the music that in one way or another figured into the typical film's soundtrack. One fairly obvious effect was the casting of originally composed "background" scores not in the form of symphonic music (as had generally been the case since the early 1930s) but, rather, in such popular genres as rock or jazz. Another effect was an increasing reliance on pre-existing music to serve not just as source music but as extra-diegetic underscore. Perhaps the most intriguing effect was the decision on the part of at least some directors to use music—or not use music—in ways that helped them deliberately thwart the conventions of the so-called classic-style film.

The classic-style film is one in which virtually all the elements of production (including the underscore) serve the single purpose of making the content of the narrative "excessively obvious."[3] The "classic" style of filmmaking of course endured well beyond the limited chronological period (approximately 1935–55) during which it was the international norm and which has coincidentally often been described, at least in part because it produced so many memorable scores that brilliantly made obvious even the most subtle nuances of their narratives' content, as film music's Golden Age; while it enjoyed its most notable resurgence in the late 1970s with action-packed features that took advantage of newly patented theatrical audio systems, the classic-style film and its concomitant orchestral music in fact never disappeared. Since the late 1950s, however, this once-dominant style has co-existed—comfortably or not— with styles of filmmaking that are in various ways, and to various extents, different.

For the composer respectful of tradition yet accepting of the fact that times had indeed changed, succeeding in post-classic Hollywood meant rising to enormous creative challenges. Those challenges, and the rewards forthcoming when the challenges were met, are the topic of the three articles collected in this section of the anthology.

13.1 SOUND AND FURY OVER FILM MUSIC

Charles Champlin

After working as a foreign correspondent for Life *and* Time *magazines, Charles Champlin (b. 1926) joined the staff of the* Los Angeles Times *in 1965; for almost thirty years, until his retirement, he served not just as the newspaper's chief film and book critic but also— and influentially—as its arts editor. In the 1970s he created the Public Broadcasting System's* Film Odyssey *program, and in later decades he hosted such interview-based cable television programs as* Champlin on Film *and* On the Film Scene. *Along with an autobiography and an anthology of film reviews from the 1970s, his books include* The Movies Grow Up: 1940–1980 *(Swallow Press, 1982),* George Lucas: The Creative Impulse—Lucasfilm's First Twenty Years *(Abrams, 1992), and* John Frankenheimer: A Conversation With Charles Champlin *(Riverwood Press, 1995).*

The article reproduced here dates from early in Champlin's tenure at the Los Angeles Times. *In terms of Champlin's output, it is relatively unusual in that it focuses not on film narrative but on film sound; at the same time, the article is representative of practically all of Champlin's critical writing, for it deals probingly not so much with the cinematic product as with the craft and consideration that goes into the product's making.*

Although the article takes as its cue a pessimistic quip issued a week earlier by Dimitri Tiomkin, in essence it is an interview with a younger film-music composer whose view of the current situation was entirely positive. Jerry Goldsmith was just a few years younger than Champlin, and at the time of this interview his career in Hollywood, like Champlin's, was just getting started.[4] In later decades Goldsmith would have plenty to say about how the film-music situation had, in his view, deteriorated. But here—interviewed at age 38, with his most important scores still to come[5]—he makes the telling point that "many of the older guys" simply haven't adjusted to the fact that "the whole style of film-making has changed."

The other Sunday Dimitri Tiomkin was saying that film music has gone to hell in a troika. "Is destroyed," he said. "Is in bad shape . . . . Today the tragedy is that there are new guys who can't write music."

Tiomkin was waving a red flag in front of a lot of fellows who are very bullish about today's film music. Jerry Goldsmith, who is up for an Academy Award for his score for Robert Wise's *The Sand Pebbles*, is as it happens one of the young composers (he is 38) Tiomkin admires. But Goldsmith nevertheless thought Tiomkin's reports of the death of film music were wildly exaggerated.

"The whole style of film-making has changed," Goldsmith said, "but many of the older guys haven't bridged the gap creatively or technically."

"The idea is not to bombard the audiences and beat them down with sound, not to fill the screen with as much music as there is picture. Composers have learned to save it for the right moments and make them count."

A Patch of Blue, for which Goldsmith did the score, runs two hours but he put music to only twenty-five minutes of it. The music won him an Academy nomination and the sound-track album has sold more than 100,000 copies (although this is another subject, as will appear).

The Sand Pebbles runs three hours and eight minutes, but contains only an hour and ten minutes of scoring, including the overtures.

"That's an unheard of small amount of music," says Goldsmith, "but Bob Wise realizes the old epic approach musically is no longer good. You look at the old epics and ask yourself how outstanding was the music. A lot of times it was carried by the picture. Aesthetically it was nothing.

"People always say music used to be used as a cosmetic to cover the bad spots in a picture. But I'll tell you this: there has never been a bad picture saved by a good score, although lots of bad scores have been saved by good pictures. Hollywood will never learn that but it keeps trying."

Goldsmith not only doesn't think film music is in bad shape, he is persuaded that "there's an abundance of young talent, people with new things to say and new means of saying it. They're revitalizing the whole art."

The most frequent complaint about present film music is that the post-Brahms, post-Wagner, post-Strauss sonorities of yesteryear have been drowned by jazz and rock 'n' roll type sounds. But Goldsmith's point about that is that you don't, can't, use late Beethoven to reinforce the mood of a very Mod film like, say, *Alfie*, for which Sonny Rollins' jazz score was singularly appropriate.[6]

"Music is a more potent force in society than it ever was before," he says, "and therefore it's a more potent force in the making of films. The young producers are much more aware of this. Some of them aren't yet aware how it works, but they know how it should work."

Since finishing *The Sand Pebbles*, Goldsmith has scored two more pictures, *In Like Flint* and *The Flim-Flam Man*, which he was dubbing last week. Both are different from each other and from *Pebbles*.

"They presented a whole different set of problems," Goldsmith says, "and that's what keeps me alive. *Flint* needed a jazzy, spoofing type of score. *Flim-Flam* is pure Americana, the simplest type of music. But not being locked in to a particular kind of film kind of recharges me."

For *Freud* some years ago Goldsmith wrote a score in twelve-tone form. "We recorded it in Rome with the Rome Opera orchestra. They'd played a lot of Schoenberg and Webern. The music didn't startle them, but they were amazed that a film producer would let you work in twelve-tone form. Some composers came by the sessions and they were envious. 'Here it's all Puccini,' they said."

Goldsmith is by no means unstintingly happy about present film music. "There's a lot of inadequate music," he says; "plenty I can't stand. But I'm a tough critic. To me, Alex North is superhuman. The rest I can find fault with now and again, but Alex has never stood still. He's always fresh."

Goldsmith hopes he'll be able to stay fresh himself. He has been at it for fifteen years. "People say I do too many films. Maybe I do; maybe I'll do less. But each one is a different kind of challenge. You're always learning. As a matter of fact, I've always thought that scoring movies is a very nice way to earn a nice living, while you're learning."

In terms of specific techniques, he has come to feel that the film, like an art form, depends on an interplay of tension and release. "Without this, there is no effect," he says. He likes to break the music, perhaps only for four or five seconds, and let the action, or the sound effects, carry on.

"The sound effects are part of the score; that's basic," Goldsmith says.

Like other young movie composers, Goldsmith feels that at its best film music provides a bridge from pop to serious music, which he thinks is borne out in the sales of sound-track albums and (in England and in Europe more than here) the fan-club-like attention film composers get. England has a Ben Hur Fan Club devoted to spreading the gospel of Miklos Rozsa.

If the album sales are a plus, Goldsmith admits to the mixed blessing of the title song. It can unquestionably be a promotional boon to the producer, as in the cases of *Born Free*, *Alfie*, "Lara's Theme" from *Dr. Zhivago*.[7]

But, he agrees, "Some producers are more interested in a hit than in the whole score." Wise had no such interest in connection with *The Sand Pebbles*, and the notion of putting a swelling romantic theme behind the main titles was abandoned.

Then again, the Wise experience was atypical. After two sneak previews of the film, Wise and Goldsmith agreed the music needed some changes. "Normally," says Goldsmith, "you juggle some music you've already recorded. But I was able to score two scenes from scratch and record them. Not very usual."

"It's been said," Goldsmith says philosophically, "that we who compose for films aren't that different from Mozart when he was commissioned to write *Don Giovanni* and the patron made him throw out one of the arias he'd written. (He preserved it because he knew it was better than the one he'd substituted.)

"Film music may not be great art, and it's probably not lasting art, but it's art. The film Mozart hasn't come along yet, but he may come along.

"If enough value is left to the creative aspects and not the exploitation aspects, who knows what will come out?"

From *Los Angeles Times*, March 12, 1967, C14.

191

13.2 NOTES FROM A SUB-CULTURE

Leonard Rosenman

Leonard Rosenman (1924–2008) was one of the relatively few successful Hollywood composers who in the second half of the twentieth century strived to maintain a strong presence in the world of "concert-hall" music. After military service in the Pacific during World War II, he first considered studying composition with Paul Hindemith at Yale University but decided instead on working with Roger Sessions at the University of California, Berkeley. In 1949, while still in the San Francisco Bay area, he wrote a score for five players for Frank Stauffacher and Martin Metal's short avant-garde film Form Evolution. *When he moved to Los Angeles shortly after that, however, it was not to pursue a career in film music but to study music theory with Arnold Schoenberg at the University of Southern California.*

Rosenman studied only briefly with Schoenberg. In 1950 he returned to his native New York, where he established himself as a composer with such works as a "Theme and Elaborations" for piano (1951), a Violin Concerto (1951), and a song cycle based on texts by García Lorca (1954). Although as a composer Rosenman was successful enough to win a fellowship at the Berkshire Music Festival in the summer of 1953 and a commission for an opera from the Koussevitzky Foundation, he supported himself primarily by giving piano lessons. One of his students was the actor James Dean, who after being cast in Elia Kazan's East of Eden *recommended his teacher for the scoring job. Rosenman's 1955* East of Eden *music brought him immediately to the forefront of Hollywood's attention, and his career as a film-music composer was virtually secured by his contribution later that year to Nicholas Ray's* Rebel without a Cause. *Significantly, in between these two James Dean features Rosenman contributed to Vincente Minnelli's psychologically fraught* The Cobweb, *the score for which is Hollywood's first to be crafted entirely according to the methods of twelve-tone serialism.*[8]

Launched in 1961, Perspectives of New Music *was and to a large extent still is an academic journal devoted to relatively esoteric forms of composition. It is extraordinary, to say the least, that in 1968 it deigned to publish an article on such a 'plebian' genre as film music. But Rosenman by this time had impressive credits not just in Hollywood but also in 'serious music' circles, and he was able to serve both cultures as an articulate go-between.*

The passage reproduced here is excerpted from a longer article. As originally published, the article begins with a "basic techniques" section that deals mostly with matters of film-music timing; this is followed by a section on film-music history, a history that Rosenman divides into the "literal period," the "catalytic period," and the "psychological period." After the excerpted material, Rosenman concludes with a discussion of the realities of the film-music economy and then a fairly optimistic statement to the effect that film offers a wealth of creative opportunity to "the concert composer who is dramaturgically aware."

Potentialities of Film Music

Aesthetic Considerations

Reality is, in films, an interpretation of naturalism. The image of the film, vastly larger than life, is by itself not real. For its reality it depends upon its cohesive intellectual and affective statement. It is often the musical statement in the film that gives it its reality. This is somewhat paradoxical because music is, within the filmic frame of reference, its most unnaturalistic element.

Considering the catalytic and psychological aspect of film music previously discussed it becomes increasingly clear that film music has the power to change naturalism into reality. Actually, the musical contribution to the film should be ideally to create a *supra-reality*, a condition wherein the elements of literary naturalism are perceptually altered. In this way the audience can have the insight into different aspects of behavior and motivation not possible under the aegis of naturalism.

Film music must thus enter directly into the "plot" of the film, adding a third dimension to the images and words. It is an attempt to establish the *supra-reality* of a many-faceted portrayal of behavior that should motivate the composer in the selection of sequences to be scored and, just as important, the sequences to be left silent. I cite a simple example of a specific use of music to illustrate this precept.

This image is that of a long shot of a large city, perhaps New York or San Francisco. The camera comes in for a closer shot of the city. Now we can see, in some detail, the crowds, moving vehicles, and the general hustle-bustle indigenous to this environment.

The composer has several choices in interpreting this scene. (1) He can elect to write one of those "big city" tunes most often heard as scoring to such scenes. The usual accompaniment to the Gershwin-like tune consists of an energetic ostinato, with a great deal of percussion, especially the xylophone. This kind of approach, often mingled with the naturalistic sound effects of the scene, does nothing to emphasize, improve upon, or say anything else about what the eye and ear already perceive, *naturalistically*. (2) He can elect not to score the scene, allowing sound effects to give the scene an aura of naturalism. (3) He can substitute composed and orchestrated "big city" noises for the sound effects, thus reverting to the old practice of *literalism*.

On the other hand, let us suppose that he elects to say something with music that will change the audience's perception of the image. Suppose he wants to make the statement that, "The city, for all its movement and activity, is actually a lonely place." Perhaps he would then score this sequence with solo instruments playing long lines, using disjunct intervals and phrases. In "playing against the scene" in this way he will have intruded into the plot of the film. He will have created that supra-reality in altering the naturalism of the image so that, as a work of art, the image can be perceived interpretively, and not merely actually.

The Contemporary Composer in Film Music

Throughout the mainstream of film music, there has been a parallel minority stream which, in my opinion, points toward a more creative and imaginative use of music in functional media. It is not coincidental that music of this minority was written by composers who wrote not only functional music but concert music as well. Concert composers who are awake to and interested in functional music are, by their training and interests, the potential possessors of that kind of original musical vocabulary and musico-dramaturgic syntax which constitute the culture, from which the sub-culture borrows and derives its driving forces. I use the word "original" not necessarily in terms of literal originality of compositional style, but rather in a larger sense; that of the very basis of descriptive comparison between the culture (original) and the sub-culture (derived).

It is the immediate and firsthand impact of a cultural force upon the sub-culture that imbues the sub-cultural industry with a deeper and more communicative spirit almost approaching "art." As it exists today, the big-studio film concept can only approach "art" but not achieve it. The closer to a concept of "art" we get, the more we observe that "art" is something of a one-man show. The achievement of a "cooperative art," as the film is sometimes called, is, as yet, a thing of the future. (By cooperative I mean film media using all the arts, including music.) Certainly an examination of the works of today's film "artists" will bear this out. The works of Fellini, Bergman, and Kurosawa are almost completely one-man shows. They exemplify that branch of the arts into which film aesthetically belongs, that of literature, of pictures, and verbal ideas. It is no coincidence that, in the works of the film makers mentioned above, very little music is used. And if and when music is used it is of a decidedly literal and/or naturalistic character. This does not mean that the concept of a "cooperative art" as applied to films is either false or impossible to realize. It does mean, however, that, by implication, in order to fashion a "cooperative art" one needs artists in *all* fields to do the fashioning.

In the musical realm the contemporary composer with a dramaturgical awareness can contribute greatly to this realization. He has a compositional technique superior to most, if not all, of the home-grown Hollywood film music producers. He has a greater sense of musical history and style which would enable him to adjust his articulation more imaginatively to the basic intent of the film, both in terms of variety and, if necessary, style. He has, besides, a more imaginative and articulate sense of musical interpretation of the potential *reality* of the image than a bandleader or jazz musician engaged in scoring a film demanding a more sophisticated symphonic treatment. Furthermore, in an age of economy, where studios want to get the most out of the least, the contemporary composer has that knowledge of the practice of chamber-music composition vital to the production of new scores involving small combinations of instruments.

Surely the great composers of musical history who dealt with opera and theater had these abilities. One can imagine (and composers in Hollywood often do!) that Mozart, Schumann, Hugo Wolf, Mahler, Strauss, Berg, Schoenberg, and Stravinsky (and the list merely begins here) would have written the kinds of scores to films illustrative of the material treated here.

An examination of the functional music of composers such as Copland, Eisler, Milhaud, and Prokofieff (to name but a few) will reveal that sense of musical-dramaturgical insight of which I speak. Today, [as several examples show], there are concert composers using contemporary compositional techniques in film music. Unfortunately, space does not permit a musical-dramaturgic analysis, and purely musical analysis here would be specious since the prime motivation of film music is literary. It is sufficient to say [that the examples] exemplify the existence of the minority film music stream which has functioned almost through its entire history.

A Potpourri of Musical and Stylistic Considerations, Reflections, and Advice

Stylist and Formal Problems

Previously I have discussed the catalytic ability of music to change the audience's perception of images and words. I now turn to the corollary: that of the effect of the image and words upon the music. There is a symbiotic catalytic exchange-relationship between the film and the music that accompanies it. I have personally had the experience of hearing musically unenlightened people comment positively and glowingly on a "dissonant" score after seeing the film. I have played these same people records of the score without telling them that it came from the film they had previously seen. Their reactions ranged from lukewarm confusion to positive rejection—no doubt their potential reactions on hearing a contemporary work of similar style in the concert hall.

It is therefore more than ever possible, in today's film of contemporary and even experimental images and words, for the composer to write stylistically the kind of music he would write for the concert hall. The important qualification to this statement is that the whole problem of musical style must be viewed strictly within the content of the functional field. Thus, the problems of form and style which arise in any serious approach to functional music must be discussed with a basically more complex definition of functional music than has been hitherto discussed here.

Within the strictest of musical definitions, most functional music is not music at all. This is not a critique of the *practice* of functional music but rather a musico-aesthetic statement about the circumscription of the field itself. For, while most of the elements of music as we know them appear to be present in the functional field, there is one element that is conspicuously absent. It is the propulsion of the score by means of *musical* ideas. As stated at the beginning of this article and implied throughout it, functional music is impelled by *literary* ideas. In an opera the composer can manipulate the image or the text to satisfy the demands of the music. In films, he must manipulate his music to express *literary* ideas. Thus any truly musical aspect of a film score comes as a by-product and not as a direct result of the marriage with the literary form. By this I mean that any potential concert music which may ultimately arise from the body of the functional score must be reconceived and rewritten *after the fact* of its original intent and creation in order that its *Gestalt* be that of a *musical* nature.[9]

Moreover, since the average musical sequence in a film runs from about one and a half to three minutes, with all the necessary literary cue-catching, most film music, regardless of style, tends to sound truncated, containing far too much material (or far too little) to be of value as a "listening" piece alone.

The contemporary concert composer reads the above and asks, "Why enter the field of functional music under these conditions?" In other words he asks, "What's in it for me, musically?"

The Laboratory

Imagine the idea of writing something for any combination of instruments and, as soon as it is finished having it performed by excellent professional players. In most cases, if it doesn't work it can be rewritten and re-recorded in a short space of time. This would include any combination of instruments imaginable: fourteen oboes, twelve pianos, electronic sounds, twenty tubas, etc. (please do not take seriously the specific combinations mentioned).

The functional field is a potential laboratory for the composer in which he can try out almost anything he wishes, provided it fits into the schema of the literary form. In today's film media, there are always opportunities for sequences in which experimentation and "serious" composition can be carried out.

[An example from Rosenman's score for the 1966 *Fantastic Voyage*] illustrates this point. In the film *Fantastic Voyage*, I experimented with *Klangfarben* and varied counterpoints of these kinds of sounds.[10] At that time, I was also writing a symphonic work in which this kind of texture played an important part. The opportunity of utilizing this particular technique in the film score enabled me to write certain sections of my concert piece with less speculation than if it had been otherwise.

Since the composer is usually given from four to ten weeks to write more music than is found in Beethoven's Ninth Symphony (I naturally speak quantitatively), several barriers exist to the composer's deriving any musical benefit from the assignment. But these can be overcome by a combination of attitude and experience.

Obviously, unless the composer is a Mozart, it is not possible for him to approach this kind of assignment with the same attitudes manifested toward the creation of a concert work of that length. It is mandatory, for both practical reasons as well as reasons of sanity, to approach the assignment with both limited and realistic compositional goals in mind. Usually, in a film which requires, say, forty-five minutes of music, the sequences in which the composer can treat somewhat experimentally are comparatively few in number. Besides, most film music consists of rather simple elements: long chords, repeated impacts, single long lines, ostinati, etc. These elements need not be complex to say whatever is needed.

Thus, if a time problem exists in carrying out the assignment (and it usually does), the composer, after much experience, will find that he devotes most of the time to the "laboratory" sequences. For the rest of the score the services of an orchestrator (the studio usually pays him) will help cut down the time of composition and enable the composer to devote more time to the sequences that "count."

As is shown by the indications for instrumentation [in three examples], the composer has complete control over the orchestration. In most cases the orchestrator serves as a kind of secretary, taking notes and ultimately writing the full-score version of the sequence. True, this process does not fully allow the composer to think orchestrally, to the extent of actually writing the lines on the score itself. But if the composer, in using the orchestrator, allows himself free time to write and orchestrate those sequences important to him, from both a musical and a dramatic viewpoint, the compromise is not so great. If the composer considers a ten-week compositional period, he would probably come up with anywhere from five to ten minutes of good concert material (depending upon how quickly one writes). There are films in which I chose to orchestrate the whole project. But these were films in which the time element was not crucial, and where the possibilities for more imaginative musical expressions were great.

Since, as I have pointed out, there is a two-way catalytic interaction between music and film, the serious musical intent of the composer in the context of the laboratory is of mutual benefit to both film and composer. If, throughout the pursuit of these realistic musical goals, the composer understands that his music serves a literary context, then he is giving both his audience and his employer their money's worth. The intensity and seriousness of the composer's musical intent will thus cause the image to be more vitally communicative.

To summarize this section: there is room for the contemporary concert composer in the functional field. There is also the opportunity for him to use, in his film music, any avant-garde compositional technique he may use in his concert work. But this is possible only if (1) he does not confuse what he does in the sub-culture with what he does in the culture, (2) he understands and accepts the literary-musical boundaries within which he must work, and (3) he clearly understands his compositional goals within his two fields so as not to suffer the frustration and creative-emotional debilitation of what he may feel to be a musical compromise. And it is on this later point that I feel it important now to fixate. For the question of "compromise" is ever present within the artist in the economic society.

From *Perspectives of New Music* 7, no. 1 (Autumn–Winter 1968), 128–33.

13.3 YOU MAY NOT LEAVE THE MOVIE HOUSE SINGING THEIR SONGS, BUT . . .

Charles Higham

In a note appended to this newspaper article, Charles Higham (b. 1931) is identified as "a freelance writer and author of Kate, a biography of Katharine Hepburn." Born in London and then established as a poet and literary critic in Sydney, Australia, by the time he contributed this piece on film music he had served both as a Regents Professor at the University of California, Berkeley, and a writer-in-residence at the University of California, Santa Cruz. In addition to his 1975 book on Hepburn, Higham had by this time authored a controversial study of the films of Orson Welles (1970) and biographies of Flo Ziegfeld (1972) and Cecil B. DeMille (1973); later, he would write biographies of Charles Laughton (1976), Marlene Dietrich (1977), Errol Flynn (1980), Bette Davis (1981), the sisters Olivia De Havilland and Joan Fontaine (1984), Audrey Hepburn (1985), Orson Welles (1985), Lucille Ball (1987), Cary Grant (1989), Louis B. Mayer (1993), and Howard Hughes (1993).

Writing just a year after the "doom and gloom" pronouncements by such veteran film composers as Elmer Bernstein and David Raksin (see pp. 178–183 of this volume), Higham here paints a distinctly rosy picture of music's situation in Hollywood, and he offers intriguing insight into the recent infiltration into films of relatively advanced techniques— exhibited in the work of such composers as Lalo Schifrin, John Williams, David Shire, and Jerry Goldsmith—that are borrowed from the world of concert-hall music.

Readers will perhaps be amused by Higham's generalized description of film-music composers as "a handsome, self-confident clan" whose members "dress very expensively, eat at the best restaurants, live in luxurious houses or apartments, drive costly cars, and mingle with the chic Hollywood set." Likely few will laugh, however, when they read the painful anecdotes about perfectly good scores that for various reasons were rejected and replaced almost at the last moment.

"Today, the film composer is a star. More than one third of a picture's success is due to the music. The audience doesn't know it is being turned on by the music, but a good score can grab an audience and hold it. I have seen weak performances helped enormously by music. I have seen it move weak stories forward. Music is the most underrated single contribution to pictures today."

The man talking is Robert Evans, former executive vice president in charge of production of Paramount Pictures and now an independent producer for that company. Evans's views on the crucial role played by the composer in contemporary films seems to be shared by the top executives at all the other studios. More than ever before, producers and directors are working closely with composers from the outset of a movie in an effort to underscore dramatic passages and to comment musically on the development of character and theme.

In the past, music for Hollywood movies was largely devised for the purpose of producing hit tunes which in turn would serve as valuable publicity for the movies themselves, or as a kind of narcotic to numb audiences into overlooking holes in the plot. There were notable exceptions, of course; one need only recall the forceful and sophisticated score written by Bernard Herrmann for *Citizen Kane*, or Aaron Copland's masterful music for *The Heiress*, or Bronislau Kaper's for *Gaslight*.

One of the most influential composers of Hollywood's past was Erich Wolfgang Korngold, who came out of Austria to work at Warner Brothers in the thirties. A distinguished alumnus of the Vienna opera, he continued to compose in the operatic vein, using leitmotivs for each character, place or emotional theme, drenching soundtracks with lush strings, establishing a whole romantic kitsch tradition in which such figures as Dimitri Tiomkin, Franz Waxman and Alfred Newman flourished in the forties and fifties. Another Austrian, Max Steiner, also a major presence on the Hollywood musical scene for over thirty years, had a similar style.

The transition from the Korngold-Steiner brand of lush, heavy film music to a more spare and selective orchestration came about very gradually, perhaps as a response to a tougher kind of moviemaking, as well as to the changes occurring in serious music and in musical tastes. At any rate, "wall-to-wall" music—scores crammed full of lilting melodies and emotional crescendos—are all but passé in Hollywood. The best composers working in films today use music far more sparingly than their predecessors, composing an average of twenty-five minutes of music for a 100-minute film instead of the eighty minutes which would have been typical of the past.

The most skilled of the current composers have managed to introduce elements of modernism and even twelve-tone procedures into pictures, and audiences have responded positively to the innovations. In violent films, arhythmic percussion effects are often used, although flowing, hummable melodies are still deemed advisable in romantic scenes.

Hard-pressed, often working eighteen-hour shifts and subject to the wills and whims of demanding executives, the leading composers in the field are few and on constant call. For those who can satisfy the top brass, the rise to success is swift. Perhaps the most gifted of the prominent music-makers today are Lalo Schifrin (*Enter the Dragon*, *The Four Musketeers*), John Williams (*The Towering Inferno*, *Jaws*) and David Shire (*The Taking of Pelham One Two Three*, *The Hindenburg*). They are resourceful composers, adept at contributing good music to films, along with the hackwork Hollywood inevitably requires.

Equally talented is Phillip Lambro, a dedicated composer who prefers to work in the documentary field, where more freedom is possible. Jerry Goldsmith, Jerry Fielding,

Marvin Hamlisch and Michel Legrand have also enjoyed huge success, but they are more conventional figures, content to work in a traditional romantic style. Goldsmith is probably the most accomplished of this group, having turned out compelling scores for *Patton*, *Papillon* and *Chinatown*.

Top-flight movie composers are paid $25,000 a score plus percentages of album sales, and earn $100,000 a year and up. A handsome, self-confident clan, they dress very expensively, eat at the best restaurants, live in luxurious houses or apartments, drive costly cars, and mingle with the chic Hollywood set. Unlike most "concert" composers, they are not struggling and anguished, fighting to achieve perfection; the secret of their success is speed, slickness and the ability to dash off scores in a week or two, with a minimum of fuss.

Of all the Hollywood composers who have achieved a compromise between traditionalism and modernism—while still managing to produce original, provocative effects—Lalo Schifrin, 39, is the most successful. An Argentinian, with dark eyes and hair and the romantic pallor of a latter-day Chopin, he began his career as an arranger—the customary route to full-scale composing. He seems proud of the fact that he not only studied with René Leibowitz and Oliver Messiaen, but did musical arrangements for Sarah Vaughan, Count Basie and Stan Getz and even conducted a jazz band.

"There are two kinds of composers," Schifrin says, "those who come from the conservatory and those who come from the street. I believe a film composer has to come from both. To use a literary analogy, he must be both poet and reporter."

Schifrin speaks for his contemporaries when he says, "We tend to work with the director from the very beginning of composition. Often, we play him a theme on a piano or—in cases where he can read a score—show him some sample work. In every case, we try to reflect the theme, or themes, of a film as dramatically as possible in simple motifs."

While respecting the work of old masters Korngold, Steiner and Waxman, Schifrin, like his confreres, has decisively rejected their use of ornate wall-to-wall music. Instead—in such films as *Bullitt* and *Dirty Harry*—he brought to scoring the somewhat austere approach of Schoenberg, Webern, and Penderecki.[11]

For *Cool Hand Luke*, a prison drama set in the south, Schifrin used a jagged banjo theme as his central motif; in *Enter the Dragon*, a Kung-Fu thriller, he rejected the usual windbells-and-tinsel approach of Hollywood composers to Chinese scores and instead based his score on an extensive study of Chinese music at UCLA. In Richard Lester's *The Four Musketeers* he effectively mirrored late Renaissance music, providing cunningly distorted sonorities with a very large orchestra in which the characteristic instruments of the period were wittily employed to reflect the acid, comic style of Lester's direction. Spirited gallops, triumphal marches, and muted pizzicati all create an impression of largeness undercut by a strong satirical sense.

John Williams, 43, may not be as consistently inventive as Schifrin, but he is every bit as popular with Hollywood producers. Subdued and self-effacing, with fair hair and a blond beard, he is known as one of the most cooperative composers in the industry. His first major feature was *The Reivers*, in which he supplied a cheerful pastiche of Stephen Foster tunes, and an attractive waltz theme expressing the romanticism of Steve McQueen's love for a car. His offbeat score for Robert Altman's *Images*, about a sexually disturbed girl's fantasies, was full of eerie, dissonant effects. In *The Towering Inferno*, he combined a series of water chimes and four Peking gongs to achieve atonal results one would not expect to find in a conventional "disaster" epic.

199

David Shire, 37, is a slight and subdued composer who has landed two big scoring jobs this year: *The Hindenburg* and *The Fortune*. A former television composer, he came to Hollywood to write the music for *Skin Game, Two People, Class of '44, Drive, He Said* and *Steelyard Blues*. His wife, Talia Shire, is Francis Ford Coppola's sister, a relationship which may have influenced Coppola's decision to hire Shire to write the music for *The Conversation*. His score for that film was written primarily for piano and Moog synthesizer (he played the piano himself). It created a jarring, unsettling mood which reflected the anguish of the central figure, a bugging agent played by Gene Hackman.

Shire's most ambitious score to date was for *The Taking of Pelham One Two Three*, in which he used serial techniques to suggest the disorganized and whirring sounds of a New York subway.

Despite the glamour and six-figure incomes, composing for films has its share of sour notes. "Film scoring may be very rewarding," John Williams says, "but it's also agony. Film composers are not their own masters. They are working for corporations. You accept that as part of the job." Studio executives have been known to replace or severely cut scores at the last minute. Musical arrangers, too, are subject to intense pressure: Peter Bogdanovich threw out Artie Butler's complete set of arrangements for his Cole Porter musical *At Long Last Love*, and the reworking of them by Butler cost a fortune, with musicians' fees averaging $32 an hour. And, at long last, the movie proved a box-office fizzle.

The replacement of scores has become a routine procedure in recent years. Robert Evans threw out Jimmy Webb's music for *Love Story* and replaced it with Francis Lai's, abandoning his duties at Paramount for months to work with Lai in the south of France. "Francis Lai saved the picture," Evans says now, and few would argue the point.

Evans also reconstructed much of Nino Rota's score for *The Godfather*, and he scrapped Phillip Lambro's elegant but occasionally harsh music for *Chinatown* when he felt that a preview audience was turned off by it. He replaced it with a more conventional but undeniably effective score by Jerry Goldsmith. Evans fought bitterly with Goldsmith all through the scoring session, but Goldsmith now feels Evans's decisions were right.

Phillip Lambro disagrees. "Evans knows nothing about music," he says. "I don't believe the preview audiences reacted against my score at all. I just think Evans was insecure. But the irony is that my theme for Faye Dunaway could have been a hit tune, and Jerry Goldsmith's could not."

Knowing that their work can be replaced or cut or transposed or otherwise tampered with at any moment, composers are very much in the same position as Hollywood writers, operating within a system which can rapidly corrupt them, forcing them to work too rapidly and superficially. A situation in which original ideas sometimes have to be sneaked into scores is not very healthy, and Lambro, for one, claims he will write only one score a year, and then only on condition that he is given complete freedom. Devoting himself with rigorous austerity to concert works, he is prepared to exist on a comparatively small income in order not to destroy himself as an artist.

But Lambro is atypical, not really a "Hollywood composer."[12] For the others, with their huge incomes, Beverly Hills houses, fast cars and well-dressed wives, it's still a question of placating studio executives, directors, critics, and the public. And, most difficult of all, their own artistic consciences, in Hollywood in 1975.

From *New York Times*, May 25, 1975, 119.

Part 6

THE BUSINESS OF FILM MUSIC

14

LABOR PAINS

Film historians have often noted that the very first showings of projected motion pictures—on December 28, 1895, in a basement room beneath the Grand Café on Paris's Boulevard des Capucines—seems to have featured the services of a professional pianist. No one seems to have a clue as to what the pianist might have done in support of a program of films that each lasted just a minute or so, and recent research has revealed that Emile Maraval in fact might *not* have played his Gaveau piano during the Lumière brothers' exhibition on that historic day; as the Norwegian writer Peter Larsen points out in his 2005 *Film Music*, an Italian scholar in 1991 fairly proved that the sole source of this information is an advertising poster that dates from 1896 or even later.[1]

In film's earliest days, musicians were engaged, as we know from numerous journalistic accounts, to provide 'ballyhoo' noise or fanfares or between-reel entertainment.[2] Accompanimental film music did not come about until c. 1902–03, when narrative films lasting upwards of ten minutes were first displayed. Whereas film accompanists during the nickelodeon period were typically lone instrumentalists or small ensembles, during the heyday of silent film they were members of large orchestras. It is not true, contrary to mythologies concocted in the 1930s by various misinformed writers, that film music *per se* dates back to the very origins of film itself. It is quite true, however, that almost right from the start the public exhibition of films represented a source of income for musicians. The new jobs for musicians were accompanied by calls for unionization. Initially, musicians in the film industry were represented by several unions, such as the American Federation of Musicians (United States), the Musicians' Union (United Kingdom), and the Confédération générale du travail (France).

In 1926 Hugo Riesenfeld, a Viennese-born conductor who by that time had served as music director for several of New York's large movie palaces, observed:

> The musician today is in demand as he never was before. Think of the army of them necessary to man the orchestras in our 18,000 [American] film theatres. ... In the larger of our motion picture theatres the minimum salary is eighty-three dollars a week, and almost half of the players get one hundred dollars. First stand players and concert masters usually are paid from $7000 to $10,000 a year. The organists get from $6000 to $20,000, depending on their individual performances. Is it any wonder with our American love of luxury that the ranks of musicians have increased so enormously during the last few years?[3]

The army of musicians that accompanied films in 1926, alas, was fairly decimated by the arrival of the sound film just a few years later. Riesenfeld was aware of the new technology, and he optimistically opined that recorded scores would simply make available to people in the provinces the musical glories that filmgoers in the big cities experienced almost on a daily basis; even though the audio fidelity of the new Vitaphone made it seem "as though the performers were in the same room as the listener," he wrote, it seemed to him highly unlikely that sound-on-disc Vitaphone recordings would ever "entirely replace the orchestra."[4] Riesenfeld was wrong. In the United States alone, some 22,000 music positions were eliminated as local theaters converted to sound-film projectors.[5] The American Federation of Musicians would spend the next several years campaigning against the film industry's use of "canned music," in an effort to ensure that live musicians were employed on all films produced in Hollywood.

Not just in the United States but throughout the Western world, first Vitaphone and then the more efficient sound-on-film technologies struck a hard blow at theater musicians. There were protests, of course, by the American Federation of Musicians and its international counterparts. Demonstrations and strikes, however, did nothing to stop the tidal flow. The economic boom of the 1920s enabled not just the development of technologies for sound recording but also the installation, in theaters around the world, of the sophisticated loudspeaker systems that allowed recorded soundtracks to be heard. The almost universal acceptance of the new technology came just before the boom's famous bust. Just four months after the start of the so-called Great Depression, the *New York Times* reported that "nearly all of those [musicians] who formerly found employment in [movie] theaters are now out of work."[6] With local variants, this sad story was repeated around the world.

Ironically, the Great Depression that for almost a decade wracked household budgets worldwide proved to be the most lucrative period that Hollywood, and its international counterparts, has to date ever experienced. It might have been that persons beaten down by the economy could scarcely put food on their families' tables, yet these same persons could easily afford what little it cost to go weekly to the movies, wherein they could escape—by means of larger-than-life romances, comedies, or whatever else they fancied—the miserable reality of their actual existence. Film industries worldwide in the hard-pressed 1930s became expert in providing audiences with escapist entertainment; such entertainment required lavish sets and glamorous movie stars, and by the middle of the decade it required as well sumptuous accompaniments. For the composers capable of devising the requisite scores, and for the orchestral musicians hired to realize those scores, the worst of times were in fact the best of times.

Cream-of-the-crop players employed by the major Hollywood filmmakers during film music's Golden Age may have been in clover, but their situation began to change with the breakdown, c.1950, of the long-established "studio system." Almost from the start the players were loyal members of the American Federation of Musicians, and so in their postwar distress they naturally appealed to their union for support. Union support was indeed given and in 1944 the American Federation of Musicians signed its first collective bargaining agreement with the major studios in Hollywood. However, the struggle for musicians' rights continued as unions worldwide sought to define what exactly constituted fair pay for musicians' work in the recording studio.

The documents presented here shed light on just a few of the many serious conflicts experienced by Hollywood musicians and their employers. Especially in the cases of the musicians' strikes of 1958 and 1980, the resolutions of the labor disputes had significant impacts on the nature of film music in the years that followed.

14.1A MUSICIANS TO PICKET TWO FILMS IN 20 U.S. CITIES

Vertigo and *Ten Frederick* Hit by Action

Howard Kennedy

The end of James Petrillo's eighteen-year reign as president of the American Federation of Musicians (AFM) came during a moment of crisis. On February 20, 1958, he called a strike by the union, after talks with the eight major Hollywood studios failed to yield a new contract. Many of the film musicians, however, were frustrated by the strike and chose instead to form a rival union, the Musicians Guild of America (MGA), led by trumpeter Cecil Read. On August 27, the MGA broke the strike when they agreed to a contract with the Association of Motion Picture Producers.

The strike was not the first one in Hollywood—the AFM had famously barred its members from making any commercial recordings from August 1, 1942, until November 11, 1944; a similar strike took place throughout almost the entirety of 1948, with the dawning of the television era. However, the 1958 strike had massive implications for the practice of making film music, as the MGA contract marked the end of the era when each of the major studios had a standing orchestra of thirty-six to fifty musicians on contract. But for this concession, the musicians won a better pay scale and a guarantee that every television program would feature live musicians, rather than "canned" music. In addition, the MGA's successful contract resolution marked the first time in fifty years that the AFM could not claim exclusive representation of all professional musicians in the United States.

The MGA, however, would have a short life. The film musicians' primary complaint against the AFM was that all royalties from their work went into one of Petrillo's pet projects, a trust fund used to pay musicians that played free concerts. Herman Kenin, who replaced Petrillo as AFM president during the strike, took action to address this complaint by establishing the AFM's Special Payments Fund, which paid royalties directly to the musicians. With this issue resolved, the MGA members returned to the AFM in 1962.

Nationwide picketing against two topflight Hollywood motion pictures was authorized by the American Federation of Musicians here yesterday as the union squared away for a fight to save its exclusive jurisdiction in the major film studios.

President Herman D. Kenin[7] and the union's five-man International Executive Board, meeting at the Hollywood Roosevelt in the first session of a two-or-three-day parley, said the picketing in twenty major cities would call attention to:

1—The eighteen-week strike called by the AFM against eight major studios after negotiations for a new contract for 1,200 studio musicians broke down in New York last Feb. 20.

2—The National Labor Relations Board election here July 9 and 10, at which a newly formed rival union, the Musicians Guild of America, supported by rebellious Hollywood musicians, will seek to wrest the studio jurisdiction from the federation.

Target of the informational picketing, said Kenin, will be the pictures *Vertigo*, a thriller produced for Paramount by Alfred Hitchcock and still on first run in Hollywood, starring Kim Novak and James Stewart, and *Ten North Frederick*, a 20th Century-Fox production with Gary Cooper and Suzy Parker.[8]

At the Hollywood Paramount Theater last night, where *Vertigo* was being shown, picketing was led by Eliot Daniel,[9] president of Los Angeles Musicians Local 47, and Kenin.

Because of the strike here, both studios sent the films outside the United States for their musical scoring.

Kenin attacked this as "an odious effort to defeat a lawful strike by resort to cheap foreign labor."

The federation has been careful to avoid picketing the struck studios here, however, because no support for such action could be obtained from other film unions and guilds. Thus the MGM, Allied Artists, Columbia, Walt Disney, Paramount, 20th Century-Fox, Universal and Warner Bros. studios have remained open since the federation called the musicians away from their jobs last Feb. 20.

Kenin and the International Executive Board said the AFM recognizes that studio employers cannot sign new contracts and settle the long strike until the NLRB election determines whether the studio musicians stay with the AFM or shift their collective-bargaining allegiance to the rival union, MGA.

As part of its campaign to whip MGA, the federation yesterday opened a supplementary West Coast office at 5903 Melrose Ave. under the direction of a traveling international representative, Ernie Lewis.[10]

Among matters to be taken up by Kenin and the IEB today and possibly tomorrow is the appointment of a successor to Kenin as head of the West Coast regional office.

Present for yesterday's opening session were IEB members Walter Murdoch, Toronto; Stanley Ballard, Minneapolis; Lee Repp, Cleveland; William Harris, Dallas; and E. E. Stokes, Houston; as well as Leo Cluesman, AFM secretary; George Clancy, treasurer; and Charles Lee Bagley, Los Angeles, the union's veteran vice-president.

Formation of the rival union is the outgrowth of a deep split within Los Angeles Musicians Local 47, whose rebel membership opposes AFM trust fund policies.

The Daniel administration appeared in solid control of last night's meeting by a two-to-one margin.

From *Los Angeles Times*, June 24, 1958, B1–2.

14.1B MUSICIANS GUILD WINS COAST VOTE

Breaks Federation's 30-Year Hold on Movie Industry—Strike at Studios Ends

Thomas M. Pryor

HOLLYWOOD, Calif., July 11—The American Federation of Musicians thirty-year monopoly in the film industry ended at 12:45 a.m. today.

That was when the National Labor Relations Board office in Los Angeles announced the Musicians Guild of America had won a bargaining representation election by a vote of 580 to 484.

This automatically terminated the strike begun last February by the A.F.M. against the eight major film studios. The guild announced that it would seek a meeting next week with the association of Motion Picture Producers, which represents the big studios, to negotiate an interim contract before discussing terms for a formal agreement.

The producers association would not make any statement.

"We have nothing to say," a spokesman reported this afternoon.

Cecil F. Read,[11] temporary chairman of the guild, declared it will seek to extend its jurisdiction to include the entire field of film music and phonograph recording as well.

Herbert C. Bumgarner, in charge of the local labor bureau office, has set July 22 for hearing the guild's petition to order an election among musicians employed by independent producers of motion pictures affiliated with the Society of Independent Motion Picture Producers and the Independent Motion Picture Producers Association.

With today's victory, the guild, which was organized last March, has also established a toehold in television since most of the major studios also make films for TV. The federation's contracts with television networks, television film producers and the record companies expire in December and January.

Mr. Read declared the guild would give the N.L.R.B. sixty days' notice of its intention to contest the A.F.M. in both fields.

Approximately 90 per cent of the lucrative over-all recording business is said to be concentrated in Los Angeles. The musicians are members of A.F.M. Local 47 here. Its 16,000 members form the second largest unit in the A.F.M. Local 802 in New York is the biggest.

Herman D. Kenin, who last month succeeded James C. Petrillo as president of the 264,000-member A.F.M., predicted "catastrophe" for the guild.

"Labor's history has shown that even short-lived technical victories, won by irresponsible splinter groups such as Cecil Read's guild, wind up in catastrophe for those who have followed the path of division," Mr. Kenin declared.

The guild has no card-established membership as yet. Besides Mr. Read, the organizers were Larry Sullivan, Ted Nash and Justin Gordon.[12]

A primary issue that started the splinter movement in Local 47 three years ago was the diversion to the union's performance trust fund of royalty payments from TV and record recordings. The musicians contend the money should be paid them as earned income.

The trust fund was the pet of Mr. Petrillo, who used it to sponsor performance of music union members who did not have regular employment.

Mr. Read, who was expelled by the A.F.M., said Mr. Petrillo used the trust fund revenues to perpetuate himself and others in power.

From *New York Times*, July 12, 1958, 16.

14.1C MUSICIANS GUILD WINS 14% HIKE IN STUDIO PAY

Newly Formed Union Reaches Agreement Subject to Approval by 1200 Members

Wage scale increases of 14% are included in an agreement reached yesterday by major Hollywood film studios and the Musicians Guild of America on a new contract for 1,200 studio musicians.

The contract, which must be ratified in the next five days by the rank and file of Hollywood musicians who compose the newly formed union, is to run for three years and three months starting next Wednesday.

On that day musicians will return to jobs in the eight major studios for the first time since last Feb. 20, when a strike was called by James Caesar Petrillo, then president of the American Federation of Musicians, after AFM talks with the Association of Motion Picture Producers broke down.

MGA, formed by Hollywood trumpeter Cecil F. Read after he had been expelled from the AFM for bucking Petrillo's policies, displaced AFM and its Los Angeles Musicians Local 47 affiliate as the exclusive collective bargaining agent for the major film studios' musicians. The guild won an NLRB election against AFM in July and has been negotiating with the AMPP ever since.

It is the first time in its fifty-year history that AFM has lost its claimed exclusive jurisdiction over every one of the 260,000 professional musicians in the United States and Canada. MGA has threatened to take other jurisdictions in the music field away from AFM.

Under the old AFM contract, the eight major film studios—MGM, Allied Artists, Columbia, Walt Disney Productions, Paramount, 20th Century-Fox, Universal and Warner Bros.—hired contract orchestras ranging in number from fifty at MGM, Warners and Fox to forty-five at Paramount and thirty-six at Columbia and Universal. The wage scale was $48.21 per musician per three-hour recording session.

AMPP members, long dissatisfied with the contract orchestra formula, refused to sign any agreement for extension of that formula, either in negotiations with the AFM last winter or with the guild this summer.

Instead, agreement was reached with MGA for the payment of higher wage scales for work actually performed in the recording of music for films.

Read and Charles Boren, AMPP vice-president in charge of industrial relations, issued a joint statement revealing the new pay scales to be:

1   When thirty-five or more musicians are called by a studio for work, they will be paid at the rate of $55 per man per three-hour session.
2   When thirty to thirty-four musicians are called, the scale goes to $57.75.
3   When twenty-four to twenty-nine musicians are called, the scale drops to $50.50.
4   When twenty-three or less are called, the scale jumps to $63.25.

The new rate for sideline musicians was boosted to $30.93 per day from the old rate of $27.13. Comparable increases will go to studio arrangers, orchestrators, copyists and librarians.

After MGA conceded on the issue of contract orchestras, the major film studio producers conceded on the use of live musicians on television film series.

For the first time, producers agreed to record a portion of a TV film series with live musicians instead of "canned" recordings. Each series of thirty-nine half-hour episodes will have a minimum nine-hour recording session at the $55 scale. Each series of thirty-nine one-hour episodes shall have a minimum eighteen-hour recording time at the same scale. Special provisions were made for ninety-minute programs, pilot films and spectaculars.

The new AMPP-MGA contract is expected to open up new work and more jobs for musicians in the studios and to eliminate gradually the recent practice by the studios of sending films abroad to have their musical recordings done.

Next MGA goal, Read said, is to oust AFM as the exclusive collective bargaining agent for some 800 musicians employed in Hollywood's independent studios.

From *Los Angeles Times*, August 28, 1958, B3.

14.2A MUSICIANS COULD BE LEFT OUT WHEN ACTORS SETTLE

Eric Malnic

The rise of the markets for pay television and home videos in the late 1970s set the stage for another round of strikes in Hollywood. In July 1980, the Screen Actors Guild and its sister union, the American Federation of Television and Radio Actors, went on strike. The American Federation of Musicians followed shortly thereafter with a strike of their own, beginning on August 1. However, when the actors settled their strike in October, the AFM found itself without any significant support for their strike—especially since the need for the strike was questioned by the Los Angeles chapter of the Recording Musicians Association, a group within the AFM representing those musicians working in the film, television, and recording industries.

The producers association found little incentive to discuss terms with the AFM, since they were content to re-use old soundtracks and to find musicians overseas for any new scores. The AFM lost the strike, with the most significant losses being the musicians' right to residual payments for work rebroadcast on television and the loss of any guarantee that live musicians would be used for all films produced by the major studios. In the wake of the AFM strike, the Composers and Lyricists Guild of America, a union independent of the AFM, went on strike in attempt to grant composers ownership rights of the music that they wrote for television and film scores. Unfortunately, it was poorly timed; since all of the other film industry unions had come to new contract agreements in 1980 and 1981, none could take action to support the composers. In 1982, after failing to gain any significant ground, the Composers and Lyricists Guild of America folded.

Musicians could be left alone and virtually unarmed in the continuing strike of performers against major motion picture and television producers.

With tentative agreement reached on the principal issues in the eight-week actors' strike against the producers, negotiators went back to the bargaining table Thursday to reach accord on the remaining issues.

But there have been no talks between the musicians and the producers since Local 47 of the American Federation of Musicians went on strike Aug. 1, and bargaining is not scheduled to resume until the actors strike is settled.

Should the actors settle soon and resume production within a few weeks, there is serious question how much support they would lend to the striking musicians.

A Screen Actors Guild official, who asked not to be identified, said he thought many actors would be reluctant to cross musicians' picket lines. But he conceded that contracts are expected to include clauses prohibiting a sympathy strike by actors, and even Michael Melvoin,[13] co-chairman of the musicians' strike committee, admitted that any help from actors would be "dependent on the support of individuals."

In addition, spokesmen for the producers association, the networks and the film studios have expressed little concern over the musicians' strike.

These men said privately Thursday that the producers could look elsewhere for musical scores—using overseas or domestic, non-union artists—or reuse existing sound tracks.

Nevertheless, the musicians union put an optimistic foot forward Thursday as more than 200 pickets representing the 5,000 AFM members demonstrated on the sidewalks in front of Universal Studios.

Marching to the accompaniment of a nine-piece band, the placard-bearing demonstrators expressed disappointment at the lack of progress in their dispute with the producers.

Melvoin said the AFM walkout began after producers refused to address the union's proposal that musicians be paid residuals for replayed films and programs.

"We currently are paid nothing for the reuse of our music," he said.

Actors have long received residuals for regular films and programs, and the tentative agreement reached Wednesday set up a formula under which they would receive payment for films made for the burgeoning TV and home video market.

From *Los Angeles Times*, September 19, 1980, A12.

14.2B TENTATIVE PACT REACHED IN MUSICIAN STRIKE

A tentative agreement ending the 167-day strike of the American Federation of Musicians against motion picture and television producers was reached Wednesday after an 11-hour negotiating session, a spokeswoman for the union announced.

Details of the settlement were not made public, and will be presented to the union's 5,000 members prior to voting on the new contract, AFM spokeswoman Kim Fellner[14] said.

But the ratification vote will be by mail, she said, and the musicians will be able to return to work immediately.

Wednesday's negotiation session, which began at 10 a.m., was the first between musicians and producers' representatives since December.

Last week, however, the musicians agreed to drop one of their key demands—payment for television film replays, and federal mediator Phyllis Cayse scheduled the meeting after delivering new proposals from the union to the producers.

The strike affected only those musicians who played scores for theatrical films and filmed television shows. Videotaped productions were not involved in the strike.

Producers have filled the musician gap during the strike by using old sound tracks in the case of television series production, or by scheduling music studio sessions in foreign countries where musicians did not support the American union.

From *Los Angeles Times*, January 15, 1981, A6.

14.3A AFM, FILM PRODUCERS REACH NEW THREE-YEAR PACT

The years since the 1980–81 musicians' strike and the 1982 composers' strike have been more stable from the perspective of labor issues. The driving issue for the American Federation of Musicians has been to keep control over the musical practices employed in Hollywood and other North American centers of filmmaking. Changing technologies have introduced the need for new types of musicians, and subsequently new union rules.

In the wake of previous strikes, technology-savvy musicians and music-savvy engineers played an increasingly important role in the creation of music for films. Some film scores from the 1980s—such as those by Vangelis for Chariots of Fire *(1981) and* Blade Runner *(1982), or by Michael Boddicker for* Flashdance *(1983) and the American version of* The Adventures of Milo and Otis *(1986)—were made entirely using synthesizers to produce sounds, samplers to record new sounds and to record bits of music, and sequencers to assemble all of those bits into the finished score. In terms of technique, all of this could be done without recourse to live performers. More significantly, according to the labor definitions of the time, this was considered to be music editing, not musical performance. During the 1990 contract negotiation with the Alliance of Motion Picture*

211

and Television Producers, the AFM successfully lobbied to extend their representation to those who created music via multitrack recording technologies, especially synthesizers and sequencers. Another concern during the 1990 AFM contract negotiation was the rising sales figures for soundtrack albums. This was again an issue of residual pay and "new use" fees for the re-use of music created for a different purpose. And, once again, the AFM stepped in to be sure that every contributing musician got his or her cut of the sales.

During the 2005 contract negotiations, attention was largely focused on the issue of film producers recording scores overseas, as in the second article here, written by AFM Secretary-Treasurer Florence Nelson for the "Official Reports" column of the AFM's journal, International Musician. *Since the fall of the Soviet Union, advancements in digital technologies and the global economy have made it increasingly practical and affordable to conduct recordings sessions in such cities as Prague, Moscow, Bratislava, and Sofia.*

The final article included here was written by Jon Burlingame, a prominent and prolific writer on music for film and television. His books include Sound and Vision: 60 Years of Motion Picture Soundtracks *(2000),* For the Record *(1997), and* TV's Biggest Hits *(1996). In this article, Burlingame highlights the periodic tension that exists amongst composers because of their lack of union representation. Since the collapse of the Composers and Lyricists Guild of America in 1982, film and television composers have been on their own to negotiate terms of their contracts for each film. The issue, at least for some, is whether or not they would be better off with a union.*

The American Federation of Musicians and the Alliance of Motion Picture and Television Producers (AMPTP) successfully concluded negotiations for a new three-year agreement that secured a 10 percent increase in wage scales over the life of the contract, continuation of the Special Payment Fund[15] and other improvements in the contract for the musicians. In addition, the producers agreed to withdraw their proposal to eliminate live scoring for prime time dramatic shows, which is an important source of income for musicians working under this agreement.

At the conclusion of the talks, AFM President J. Martin Emerson noted that "this agreement is the culmination of several hard-fought contract negotiations which the AFM has conducted over the last eighteen months in different areas of its jurisdiction with various management groups. We believe that we achieved the best contract possible in each of these negotiations." He added that this contract "provides a mechanism for ongoing meetings with representatives of the AMPTP for the purpose of addressing and resolving matters of mutual concern during the term of the agreement."

Nicholas Counter,[16] chief negotiator for AMPTP, commended the AFM's negotiators for their "forthright approach to the negotiations and their willingness to solve problems on a basis which addresses the needs of the industry as well as the musicians. This is yet another example of how enlightened leadership can achieve mutually acceptable bargaining goals without the necessity of confrontation. We look forward to ongoing discussions with AFM leadership regarding issues of mutual concern."

Negotiation with the AMPTP always presents a great challenge to the AFM since the AMPTP is considered the most hard-line group of negotiators the union faces. (They had previously won out on their proposals in three strikes by other unions in the industry.)

Therefore, the Federation begins gathering information for the film negotiations shortly after the previous agreement has been signed to insure that the AFM is fully versed in both how changes in the industry affect musicians and whether or not newly negotiated provisions are working in the best interests of the players.

For the latest round of talks with the AMPTP, AFM representatives began holding weekly meetings with Recording Musicians Advisory Committee musicians and Recording Musicians Association musicians six months prior to the start of these negotiations to get their input on the proposals the AFM would present at the table. The Federation also conducted research on possible proposals that might come from the producers. AFM General Counsel George Cohen and Presidential Assistant Dick Gabriel even traveled to each of the cities where musicians and their Local officers are active in the industry to get as much feedback on what was needed by the musicians as possible.

In addition to the significant gains made in scale wages mentioned above, the AFM was able to come out of these negotiations with several new provisions designed to enhance the Federation's ability to monitor and pursue the payment of residuals to members. As a result of these negotiations, all producers—including those who utilize signatory payroll companies—will be responsible for making Special Payments Fund payments and, if a producer enters into certain types of agreements to sell to distributors all of the worldwide market rights, that distributor must become responsible for making Special Payments Fund payments. The AFM's auditors believe that these changes will result in additional monies for musicians from supplemental market sales, which were difficult, if not sometimes impossible to trace in the past.

New provisions in the area of multi-tracking confirm that synthesizer players are musicians under the AFM definition and that sequencing pre-programming constitutes musical skills. This is particularly important since it will prevent producers from attempting to pay for synthesizer services under non-AFM union contracts and in some cases, particularly in the area of sequencing, it will deter attempts to make substandard payments. The new pact also confirms that musicians must be told up front whether they are to be paid at the real time or multi-tracking rate.

Michael Boddicker,[17] who is considered one of the finest synthesists in the music business, gave a practical demonstration during the negotiations to illustrate the AFM's proposals on multi-tracking to the AMPTP. Boddicker's appearance played an important part in the AFM's ability to achieve these new provisions.

Finally, the AFM and industry agreed to a two-year "experiment" that could generate an increase in the amount of soundtrack albums produced. Under the terms of the experiment, there will be a lower payment up front (50 percent of the regular amount) with an upgrade after 50,000 records to 100 percent (additional 50 percent) and an additional payment of 20 percent if the record sales exceed 100,000 records. If after the designated two-year period the AFM feels this new formula is not working in the best interests of musicians, the union has the right to terminate the provision. However, it is hoped that the new formula will spur soundtrack albums sales.

Once again in these negotiations, the AFM benefited from the input of a strong team, led by President Emerson and General Counsel Cohen. The Negotiating Subcommittee consisted of Vice President Mark Tully Massagli, Vice President from Canada J. Alan Wood, Secretary-Treasurer Kelly L. Castleberry II, Special Consultant Bob Crothers, Presidential Assistant Dick Gabriel and Rank-and-File member Dennis Dreith. The Advisory Committee consisted of Chicago Local 10-208 President Charles Guse, Los

Angeles Local 47 President Bernie Fleischer, Nashville Local 257 President Jay Collins, and New York City Local 802 President John Glasel, along with various representatives of those Locals and numerous members of the Recording Musicians Association.

From *International Musician* 88, no. 12 (May 1990), 1, 8.

14.3B KEEPING FILM SCORING ON OUR SHORES

Florence Nelson

Just in case there isn't much to do prior to the 96th AFM Convention,[18] the AFM enters into negotiations at the very beginning of June with the Alliance of Motion Picture and Television Producers for a renewal of the Motion Picture-Television Film Agreement. National negotiations are never easy to resolve, and this year will be no exception. As with all union negotiations, the discussions will most certainly revolve around our core concern, which is to keep AFM musicians employed.

This agreement covers several thousand AFM musicians each year who are involved with film scoring. On any day in Los Angeles, New York, Toronto, and San Francisco, to name some of the primary locations, perhaps fifty to 120 musicians work for approximately six hours a day for about a week to read and record the music that synchronizes with a film. In addition to the musicians, there are composers, arrangers, and copyists employed prior to the recording sessions and at the sound studio, prepared to make adjustments, write transpositions, and develop new music at a moment's notice. In 2004, AFM members earned approximately $24.5 million from work performed under this agreement, which is undeniably the most successful national agreement signed by the AFM. Along with the Sound Recording and Commercial Announcements Agreements, these three collective bargaining agreements establish national wages and working conditions for musicians throughout the U.S. and Canada.

The premise of these agreements is based on shared risk and shared reward. The AFM negotiated reasonable wages and working conditions for the initial recording sessions (the "risk"). Then, in the Commercial Announcements, if a "jingle" is successful, it is used for repeated cycles, bringing New Use payments to the musicians. And in the case of the sound recording or film agreement, if the recording or movie is successful, producers make a contribution to the Special Payments Fund (for sound recordings) or Secondary Market Fund (for film) based on a formula negotiated in each of the agreements. Annually, the funds then distribute this money to the contracted participating musicians ("the reward").

Understanding how these agreements operate doesn't necessarily answer the issue of maintaining work for AFM musicians. The words most frequently heard are "runaway productions" and "offshore recording." These are the films made overseas because it makes creative sense to someone in the movie industry to set the story in a certain location—or to record the film in Eastern Europe, where studios can offer much lower hourly scale wages to recording musicians.

Although the AFM cannot compete with Prague on a cash basis, we certainly have the talent and expertise necessary to produce great-sounding movie tracks in the shortest period of time. Just listen to the soundtracks for *Kinsey, Kill Bill 1* and *2, Heffalump, The Aviator, Spanglish, Million Dollar Baby, I, Robot, Hellboy,* and *The Incredibles* (just to name a few) to hear the quality and talent of our members. Further, film composers know that no other country can provide the experienced music prep personnel available to address production needs as efficiently and economically. And finally, the AFM has developed and negotiated a business model that works successfully with the film industry.

Time will tell if the decisions the negotiators make in our union caucus and then at the bargaining table help to retain the work here in North America. There will certainly be lively debate over the virtues of the "risks" we take in structuring the Film Agreement as it is currently established, and the "rewards" that come to musicians who participate on successful movies. As we proceed in these negotiations, it will be important to remember that our ultimate power will be achieved by working together with our colleagues throughout the Federation.

As allies working together under this strong, productive agreement, I am certain we will find the direction to enable us to address the discordant issues that naturally exist in a national agreement and develop a cohesive plan that assures that AFM members will continue to create film music on this side of the hemisphere.

From *International Musician* 103, no. 6 (June 2005), 4.

14.3C UNION DRUMBEAT'S GROWING

Health Care, Pension at Heart of Composers' Plan

Jon Burlingame

Music has long had a role in social activism, so it only seems fair that social activism is entering the dialogue among musicians.

Hundreds of composers and songwriters, including Hans Zimmer and Diane Warren, have jumped onto the union bandwagon by asking Teamsters Local 399 to represent them in negotiations with the Alliance of Motion Picture and Television Producers.

They've already received endorsements from the Writers Guild of America, the Screen Actors Guild, the American Federation of Musicians, the Recording Musicians Assn. (a group within AFM that reps most studio players) and the American Federation of Television and Radio Artists.

But the 1,200-member Society of Composers & Lyricists—the largest collection of composers and songwriters active in film and TV music—has not backed the effort, a sign that not everyone agrees unionization is a good idea, or that now is necessarily the right time.

Agents are divided, and it's not yet clear how unionization, especially given the current modest proposals for no more than medical benefits and a pension plan, would affect the bottom line of composer reps.

"We have the support of most of the composers, and many lyricists and songwriters," reports organizing committee chairman Bruce Broughton. "There has been unbelievable support for the idea of benefits-only. It's a fairness issue: Why in the world shouldn't composers and lyricists have benefits?"

That seems to be the single most unifying force in the movement. Backers of the move to unionize say composers are the last creatives left in Hollywood who have no collective bargaining agreement, and thus have no access to health care or a pension plan. (They did until 1982, when the Composers & Lyricists Guild of America was dissolved after battling the networks and studios for years over music rights issues.)

The movement to unionize has been brewing for some time now, and received a big boost April 19 when about 200 tunesmiths turned out for an organizational meeting at the WGA theater in Beverly Hills. By that time, such heavyweight film composers as Quincy Jones, Randy Newman, James Newton Howard and Carter Burwell had thrown their support behind unionization.

"What came out of that (April 19 organizing) meeting," says Teamsters business agent Steve Dayan, "was a renewed sense of hope and optimism, and a bit more solidarity from composers. That's a huge step forward."

But, most insiders admit, there is also genuine fear of unionizing on the part of many composers, who for decades have seen their wages plummet, their allotted time to write and record shrink, technology alter their methodology, and eager young composers who are willing—because there are no standard rates or minimum fees in place—to undercut the experienced veterans on pay, or even work for free.

The proposed Assn. of Media Composers and Lyricists does not endeavor to tackle those issues. Debating working conditions, *Law and Order* composer Mike Post[19] said at the meeting, is "a non-starter . . . the very thing that would put us out of work (and give) the producers and studios an excuse to use libraries"—the banks of cheap, generic music mined by many reality shows.

SCL president Dan Foliart[20] issued a statement to *Variety* that stops short of outright endorsement, noting that "the SCL applauds the organizing efforts of our peers (and) continues to monitor this effort, the impact that it will have on our profession, and assess the role that the SCL should play moving forward."

The AFM also has been silent on the issue. The organization, which already negotiates with the AMPTP, contractually covers orchestration, conducting, music preparation and performing, but not the act of writing music.

The process of unionization could take several years. The Teamsters needed more than four years to complete the unionization of casting directors and associates, who signed their first contract with the AMPTP in 2006.

Agent Richard Kraft, whose clients include Marc Shaiman and Alan Menken, believes the threshold for qualifying for benefits—both in terms of hours worked under union contracts, and the number of actual union (i.e., Teamsters) pictures composers are able to do per year—may be too high for many members, who work mostly on indie, low-budget or non-union films.

"The big, established composers are not the ones who really need these benefits," says Kraft, "and many are supporting this in the hopes of helping out those in a less-fortunate position."

But Kraft is also concerned that the move toward unionization could open up a "Pandora's Box of divisive issues," including working conditions, which few composers can agree on.

"If you talk to ten different composers about working conditions they'd like addressed, you'll get ten different answers," he says.

For example, the subject of demos, in which composers create music for free hoping to get a gig—now commonplace in TV—came up at the April 19 meeting when one composer cited an email from the Teamsters to the WGA that had been leaked to a popular Hollywood blog that day.

The email—which WGA West exec director David Young confirmed to *Variety* was never shown to the WGA board, much less "approved" as claimed—suggested the WGA ask its show-runner members to stop asking composers to write music for free. Since organizers for the proposed Assn. of Media Composers and Lyricists have decided to seek benefits only, the Teamsters memo is moot.

Family Guy composer Ron Jones is among the few composers publicly opposed to unionizing. "We haven't even explored other possibilities," he contends, suggesting that a group medical plan might be preferable, or even a class-action lawsuit over employers demanding intolerable hours.

Many composers "are not even getting minimum wage," he says. In fact, at the April 19 meeting, a casual reference to composers working a forty-hour week was met with loud guffaws from a crowd more accustomed to sixty- and eighty-hour work weeks. "They wanted something to really help these composers in dire need, and they're going to settle for a Twinkie from 7-Eleven," Jones says.

Broughton, however, suggests that the majority of working composers in Hollywood are ready to sign up with the Teamsters. "We're well on our way to establishing critical mass," he says.

From *Variety* 418, no. 12 (May 3–9, 2010), 65.

15

SOUNDTRACK ALBUMS

In an article published in 1976 in the magazine *High Fidelity*, Ted Wick describes his role in developing the concept of the movie soundtrack album.[1] He recounts the tale of how as a young man in the early 1940s he was engaged by independent producer David O. Selznick as "director of radio advertising and exploitation," and how in that capacity he struggled to come up with ways by which Selznick's successful filmic properties could be made all the more successful by means of promotion. Wick tells how with his first assignment—John Cromwell's 1944 *Since You Went Away*—he was attracted not so much by Margaret Buell Wilder's screenplay or the acting talents of Jennifer Jones and Joseph Cotten as by Max Steiner's score. Wick arranged to have some fourteen minutes' worth of Steiner's score recorded, by an orchestra of seventy-seven musicians, quite independent of what had been done for the sake of the actual film. More than a thousand pressings of the recording were made and subsequently distributed, in advance of the film's release, to radio stations throughout the United States. Executive producer Selznick was at first outraged at this unauthorized expense; he was appeased when he learned that radio stations were regularly airing bits of the recording, and even more so when Steiner for his contribution to *Since You Went Away* won the Academy Award for Best Original Score.

The recording of Steiner's music for *Since You Went Away* was not a commercial release, but the radio stations that aired the music received many inquiries as to where the disc might be purchased. Seeing an opportunity, Wick set about making a saleable album from the music for Selznick's next film, Alfred Hitchcock's 1945 *Spellbound*. All of the major labels approached by Wick rejected the idea as being "commercially unsound." Only the small company called ARA Records expressed an interest, but that was only if the Selznick studio covered all production costs. The deal accepted, ARA manufactured an album of five 10-inch 78 rpm discs, the last 'side' of which featured a *"Spellbound" Concerto* that composer Miklós Rózsa concocted especially for the album.

Whether the commercial success of the *Spellbound* album had anything to do with Rózsa's winning the Oscar for best score is difficult to say. But one thing led quickly to another, the most immediate of which was a bid from RCA Victor not just to re-record the *Spellbound* music but also to give album treatment to Dimitri Tiomkin's music for Selznick's forthcoming *Duel in the Sun*.

Like the made-to-order ARA albums, the RCA albums were bulky sets of 78 rpm discs. So was MGM Records' 1946 recording of music from the Jerome Kern biopic *Till the Clouds Roll By*. Although the 33 1/3 rpm 'long play' disc had been introduced by Columbia Records as early as 1948, it was not until the format evolved to accommodate twenty-six minutes of music on each side of a 12-inch disc, around 1952, that film scores regularly found their way onto single-disc packages. By the middle of the decade most of the major Hollywood studios either had close affiliations with equally major record labels or owned labels of their own; by the end of the decade the so-called soundtrack album had become a fixture of popular culture.

The items collected in this chapter are penned by writers for three different American newspapers, and they trace the story of the soundtrack album over a twenty-year period. It begins in the 1960s, at a time when the recordings were no longer regarded as mere after-the-fact adjuncts to the films that spawned them; the set of documents ends in the late 1980s, when projected sales of soundtrack albums sometimes had a huge influence on films that were yet to be made.

15.1 MUSIC IS NOW PROFIT TO THE EARS OF FILMMAKERS

Vincent Canby

Vincent Canby (1924–2000) was a member of the New York Times *staff for more than thirty years; for the last three years he reviewed theatrical events, but for most of his tenure—from 1969 to 1993—he was the newspaper's highly influential chief film critic. Whereas most of his New York newspaper and magazine colleagues sooner or later channeled their energies into books about the topics they covered, Canby spent his "spare time" writing novels and plays; his works for the stage include* End of the War *(1978),* After All *(1981), and* The Old Flag *(1984), and his published novels include* Living Quarters *(1976) and* Unnatural Scenery *(1979).*

The article reproduced here dates from shortly after Canby migrated to the Times *from* Variety, *where for six years he wrote for the most part not as a critic but as a reporter on the film industry. Canby's journalistic acumen is clearly evidenced in this short piece that ranks among the first acknowledgments that the relationship between film and music had already experienced a fundamental shift. The financial facts that Canby offers are in themselves breathtaking, but even more telling is the comment on the real "value" of film music that Canby elicits from a studio executive.*

The soundtrack album for *A Hard Day's Night*, the first feature film starring the Beatles, has so far made a profit estimated at $2 million for United Artists Corporation.[2]

This is more than three times the cost of the film itself ($580,000) and explains why film companies today place such emphasis on their music-publishing subsidiaries. It also explains why every film today, no matter what the subject, comes out brimming with theme music—not all of it appropriate.

Currently high on the best seller charts is MGM Records' soundtrack album for *Doctor Zhivago*, the film adaptation of the late Boris Pasternak's epic novel of revolutionary Russia.[3] The royalties from these records, from sheet music and from performing rights to the music, can play an important part in helping Metro-Goldwyn-Mayer recoup the huge, $11-million production cost of the film.

Film music, long a subliminal (some say insidious) advertising tool, has now also become a significant source for recurring profits.

In his office at 729 Seventh Avenue, Michael Stewart, president of United Artists' music and record divisions, yesterday dramatized both points. Marlboro Cigarettes, he said, paid U.A. "a sum which runs well into six figures" to use several bars of music from *The Magnificent Seven* in its current radio and TV commercials.[4]

To protect the music from being too loosely identified with some popular songs used in commercials, U.A. specified that no words be put to [the] *The Magnificent Seven* theme and that the theme would not be used as background music while words on the screen, or any off-screen voice, urged viewers to smoke Marlboros.

Not long ago, Mr. Stewart continued, the film company had turned down another advertiser's offer of $200,000 for the right to use, for one year, the title song from *Never on Sunday*.[5]

That song, he explained, has become what the trade calls a "standard," bringing in from $60,000 to $100,000 annually from records and performing fees. U.A. felt there was no reason to jeopardize that income by leasing the song to an advertiser.

By having their own music publishing and recording subsidiaries, the film companies share all royalties from film music with the composers, usually on a 50-50 basis.

The first consideration in film music, Mr. Stewart said, is that it "enhance the dramatic values of the film itself." Secondly, it is written with the idea that it can be "excerpted," perhaps as a title song that can be used as subliminal advertising for the film. Thirdly, with luck it will become a standard, returning money to the producer long after the film itself has been forgotten.

A classic example of the last is "Mona Lisa," a song used only incidentally in a 1950 Paramount film called *Captain Carey, U.S.A.*[6] The film has long since been forgotten, but "Mona Lisa" remains in popular music catalogues. According to one film executive, the song has probably made more money than the film itself.

From *New York Times*, May 24, 1966, 52.

15.2 THE SOUND OF (MOVIE) MUSIC: RE-RELEASES OF SOUNDTRACKS PAST

Tom Shales

Tom Shales (b. 1944) has occasionally reviewed films for National Public Radio in the United States, but most of his professional work has involved television. He joined the staff of the Washington Post *in 1972; after serving as a general assignment writer in the newspaper's "Style" section, in 1977 he took on the role of chief television columnist, and he remained in that position until his retirement in 2010. A collection of his columns was published in 1982 as* On the Air! *and another collection, devoted to lengthier appreciations of entertainment industry personalities, appeared in 1989 as* Legends:

Remembering America's Greatest Stars; *with James A. Miller, in 2002 he co-authored* Live from New York: An Uncensored History of "Saturday Night Live."

That Shales had a great deal of exposure to older films, presumably seen on television, is evident in the article reproduced here: he writes not just appreciatively but knowledgably of the music contained on the soundtrack albums he is reviewing, commenting often on the relationship of the music to dialogue, choreography, and mise en scène. *His remark on "movies they can't make like they used to" suggests a keen understanding of film industry economics, and the observation he makes in the concluding paragraph suggests real perspicacity.*

After mentioning that a recent compilation album had included excerpts from several of John Williams's scores for "disaster" films, he suggests that Williams's music in particular has reminded audiences of the "pleasurable manipulation" and "intimations of life larger than life" that used to be "an important part of what we got from the movies." Writing a year before Williams in effect changed film-music history with his epic score for the first of the Star Wars *films, Shales rightly notes that "there are many signs that many of us want [that sort of experience] once again."*

Where is Old Hollywood? It is everywhere. New Hollywood can't escape it. Television alone reminds us nightly in shows both late and late-late that many qualities within easy grasp of the old Hollywood are impossibly beyond the new. Movie nostalgia has become more than a disposition: it has turned into an industry, but beneath what seems to be just a grass-was-greener longing for anything previous to now, there is the fact that Old Hollywood had powers and capacities that very nearly were magical.

Thus should *That's Entertainment* really be called *That Was Entertainment.*[7]

You don't have to see old movies to realize the distinctions. You can just hear them. The best new movie music albums released in recent weeks are almost invariably records of old movie music. When the major studios maintained vast music departments, they produced music proportionate to the size of the screen and the enormity of the myths; it had style, melody, lushness, and it also had *importance*. The very fanfares that accompanied company symbols at the start of the picture (Franz Waxman wrote MGM's; Alfred Newman wrote 20th Century-Fox's) set you up for something great.[8]

John Green's score for MGM's *Raintree County*, now reissued after nearly twenty out-of-print years (Entr'acte Records, ERS 6503-ST), was everything a symphonic score could be; it struck immediate emotional responses, it used the leitmotiv technique to help advance the story and embellish the character studies; it provided enough strong melodies to fill a grand opera.[9] But the movie it was written for, a failed attempt to duplicate *Gone with the Wind*, didn't live up to the sumptuous setting Green made for it. As a result the score is a glorious landmark and the movie nearly a nonentity.

The new release is the first in stereo—*Raintree* got the official big treatment from MGM, including something called "Camera 65" (65 millimeter film instead of the usual 35)— and for a twenty-year-old, its sound (to judge from a test pressing) is magnificent. Green was head of the MGM music department at the time and he had revitalized the studio orchestra into a fairly flawless and versatile machine. The score also employs a forty-voice chorus.

The eighty minutes of music on this two-record set prove more than listenable; Green's score is cohesive, stirring and luminous, and it has a persuasive, unmistakable aura of

Americana. It was hardly unprecedented to use a solo harmonica to invoke that feeling, but Green has the harmonica meandering in counter-melody even when the chorus is at full-throttle, and the effect is one of the dozens in this score that make it a very clever sort of triumph.

RCA Records issued the original album, in both one- and two-record versions, but refused, once it was out of print, to reissue it, even though it became, to say the least, a collector's item. John Steven Lasher, who runs Entr'acte, finally talked the company into selling him the rights. The record is unfaithful in only one respect; Nat "King" Cole sang the main title but was under contract to Capitol Records, so he is replaced on the soundtrack album by the chorus. If one had to pick the ten best movie scores of all time, *Raintree* would be a certain candidate for the list. The record may be hard to find—Entr'acte is a small company and not every store will be carrying this album—but it is worth the search.

The second most auspicious event in the expanding annals of movie recordings this year is *David Raksin Conducts His Great Film Scores* (RCA ARL 1-1490), with the composer of *Laura*, *The Bad and the Beautiful* and *Forever Amber* conducting new stereo recordings of suites from those scores.[10] *The Bad and the Beautiful* was one of the juiciest potboilers Hollywood ever made about itself, and Raksin's music is full of expansive irony. *Amber* was a costume epic about a notorious woman that got a dignified assist from Raksin. But the best cut is the first, Raksin's variations on the theme for *Laura*, one of those very few musical themes that became not so much the embodiment of a character as a character itself.

Raksin only got to write the music for *Laura* on a fluke; 20th Century-Fox music chief Alfred Newman didn't want to bother with what he thought would be a minor film. Otto Preminger, the director, liked the idea of using a musical theme for the elusive lady of the title, but of all things, he wanted to use Gershwin's "Summertime" from *Porgy and Bess*.[11] Fortuitous interventions of fate resulted in one of the best-known themes in movie history.

On this recording, Raksin toys with the theme before stating it fully. At one point, a muted cornet floats in on a sea of strings, and this melancholy sound seems the absolutely definitive musical summation of '40s *film noir*, another genre from Old Hollywood that New Hollywood keeps trying to duplicate (David Shire's score for last year's *Farewell My Lovely* was a virtual, and rather successful, homage to *Laura*).[12] The quality of the recording is nothing less than super; Charles Gerhardt, who usually conducts on these RCA releases, produced this time and turned the baton over to the composer, whose liner notes are amusingly informative.

When it comes to movies they can't make like they used to, of course, nothing so graphically illustrates the difference between the Old and the New as the musical. There simply are no musicals any more. But movie revivals and soundtrack albums continue to revive the old ones—in the case of the albums, sometimes with dubious legality. A new double-soundtrack album of *Cover Girl* and *You Were Never Lovelier* is on one of those tiny labels (Curtain Calls CC 100/24).[13] But if this is the only way to secure a soundtrack album for old movie musicals, one can learn to endure the shoddy production and wretched recorded sound that apparently result.

This pairing is particularly appropriate. Both musicals were made at Columbia, a studio not noted for its musicals, during wartime, *Lovelier* in 1942 and *Cover Girl* in 1944. Each stars one of the movie musical's two leading men: Fred Astaire and Gene Kelly.

Each has a score by Jerome Kern. But most of all, each film is staged as a spectacular testimony to the beauty and talent of Rita Hayworth, who was in every discernible respect entirely worthy of the homage. Astaire has said Hayworth was his favorite dancing partner. She is certainly the only woman he danced with whom one feels was too good for him, rather than the other way around.

When we hear Astaire blurt, "Oh, you're terrific!" on the soundtrack of *Lovelier*, the snowed sincerity is wildly affecting. No love song, or worship song, seemed extreme for Hayworth, because in the early '40s she was the knockout of knockouts; she was what the boys fought for overseas. Astaire, of course, was such a masterful vocalist that he could get away with the gushiest stuff. Johnny Mercer's lyric for the title tune has Fred telling Rita, "Down the sky, the moonbeams fly, to light your face / I can only say they chose the proper place."

Moonbeams, hah. Rita was lit in every scene by all the voluptuous candlepower Hollywood could muster. Every shot of her in each of these films is as studiously composed as a formal portrait.

Hayworth didn't sing her own songs; they were dubbed by Nan Wynn, whose voice seems as ideal for Hayworth as Marni Nixon's was for Deborah Kerr.[14] The extension voice completes the illusion and Hayworth becomes merely and purely perfect, the kind of dreamy ideal only the Old Hollywood could really manufacture.

Cover Girl, on the other side of the disc, has Gene Kelly serenading the adored Hayworth. The film isn't a great musical, maybe, but it has great moments. Only recently has a print of the film in its original three-color Technicolor become available. (The American Film Institute showed it last year, and it is now playing at a small theater in Los Angeles). "Long Ago and Far Away" is the best-known song in the Kern score (with lyrics by Ira Gershwin), but the best number is Kern and E. Y. Harburg's "Make Way for Tomorrow," when Hayworth, Kelly and Phil Silvers, Mister Comic Relief, dance their way out of their neighborhood bar and out into the street.

It's the kind of thing that gives you a lump in your throat because it embodies not only the special exhilaration of the best movie musicals—the liberating spectacle of people singing and dancing on the very sidewalks of Everytown—but because it conveys what seems to be innocence. World War II was about to end, the nuclear age about to begin, and here are three amazing daffy people singing, "The sun is shining, make way for tomorrow . . ."

Many other albums of vintage movie music are appearing weekly. The small, classical Delos Record company is getting more heavily involved with movie music, and its latest releases include one sheer charmer, *The Film Music of Bronislau Kaper* (Delos Film Series DEL/F25421) with the veteran composer of *San Francisco*, *Lili*, *Green Dolphin Street* and *Auntie Mame* playing those themes and others on solo piano.[15]

Far less successful is *Classic Film Themes for Organ* (Delos Film Series DEL/F25411), with Gaylord Carter trying to be delicate and subtle at the keyboard of an instrument, the theater organ, that is anything but. He constantly shies away from the emphasis and bravado that would have made this recital representative of the moviegoing experience as it used to be, even though almost none of the films represented were silent.

Other releases include two on the "Classic International Filmusicals" label that have atrocious sound in a kind of appropriately tinny way: Busby Berkeley's *The Gang's All Here* (CIF 3003) and that zany antique *Flying Down to Rio* (CIF 3004), which has Astaire and Rogers dancing, though not singing, together.[16] "I'd like to try this thing just once,"

223

says Fred as the band strikes up "The Carioca," and Ginger says, "We'll show 'em a thing or three." And did they ever.

Henry Mancini has turned from grinding out such humdrum Muzakkian scores as the one he did for *The Return of the Pink Panther* to conducting an album of movie music by himself and other composers, *A Concert of Film Music* (RCA APL1-1379), with the London Symphony Orchestra. The "suites" on the album aren't really suites, just groups, but they include a "Disaster Movie Suite" of three worthy themes by John Williams, for the movies *Earthquake, The Towering Inferno* and *Jaws*.[17]

Williams has been highly instrumental in trying to bring back to the movies the full symphonic score, with all its potentials for pleasurable manipulation and its intimations of life larger than life. This was an important part of what we got from the movies once, and there are many signs that many of us want it once again.

From *Washington Post*, July 18, 1976, H1, H6.

15.3 MOVIE MUSIC: IS IT BECOMING HIT OR MISS?

Steven Smith

Steven C. Smith was still a graduate student in journalism at the University of California when, as an intern at the Los Angeles Times, *he penned the article reproduced here. At the time of this writing he had already been working for three years on the "large" academic project that would result, in 1991, in* A Heart at Fire's Center: The Life and Music of Bernard Herrmann. *In the years that followed he would continue to focus on Herrmann, earning his living primarily as a writer of scripts for documentaries on such Herrmann-scored films as* The Day the Earth Stood Still, The Trouble with Harry, Vertigo, Marnie, *and* Fahrenheit 451.

But Herrmann's music is not at all the issue under discussion here. Apparently equipped with the same "nose for news" that has served arts journalists since the early eighteenth century, Smith focuses on the palpable friction that in 1986 existed between film-music composers who wanted to do things their own way and film producers who had other ideas as to what sort of music might best serve not just a film's dramatic but also its commercial needs. Two of the three "items" with which Smith begins this article are indeed newsworthy, yet they are hardly the first instances of an authoritative filmmaker jettisoning a commissioned score in favor of something more to his liking: one thinks readily of Stanley Kubrick's rejection of Alex North's score for his 1968 2001: A Space Odyssey, *for example, and of Alfred Hitchcock's rejection of Herrmann's score for his 1966* Torn Curtain.

Perhaps out of a feeling of obeisance to film music's Golden Age, Smith here defers several times to veteran composer Elmer Bernstein, who minces no words in his condemnation of a society that seems to be "going through a plastic, corporate kind of culture." The facts remain, though, that film directors and producers have second-guessed composers' efforts since the beginning of the sound-film era, and that even during the nickelodeon era one of the driving forces of the industry has been the commercial potential of films' accompanying music.

Item: After disappointing previews, director Ridley Scott and Universal Studios drastically cut an hour out of his $30-million fantasy-epic *Legend* to suit American audience tastes. Universal also commissions a new score by synthesizer-pop band Tangerine Dream to replace *Legend*'s original symphonic score by Oscar-winning composer Jerry Goldsmith.

Item: In an apparent attempt to corral both "art" crowds and MTV-saturated youth audiences, Taylor Hackford's *White Nights* mingles pop rock, American ballet and Russian folk dance.[18] Critics aren't impressed, but first-week audiences made a hasty *jeté* to the box office. (As of last weekend, the film had sold more than $22-million worth of tickets.)

Item: Director Walter Hill tosses out James Horner's percussive *Streets of Fire* score in favor of Ry Cooder's more commercially exploitable music. Likewise, director Ivan Reitman sees visions of gold and discards portions of Oscar-winner Elmer Bernstein's tongue-in-cheek *Ghostbusters* score for potential hit records.[19]

The writing—make that composing—seems to be on the wall. As long as teen audiences shape the ways and means of studio executives, film scores increasingly will be heard in three-minute increments, with a steady techno-pop beat and co-vocal by Phil Collins.[20]

Ten years ago, the pulsating rhythm of cellos and orchestra helped send moviegoers screaming out of theaters in Spielberg's *Jaws*.[21] The commercial success of Williams's music was a timely reminder that the symphonic idiom had not worn out its welcome on movie sound tracks, sparking a widespread renaissance in film-music appreciation.

But in the wake of *Flashdance*, *Footloose* and MTV—all facets of the same demographic face lift from older to younger moviegoers—the second "golden age" of movie music is again becoming the platinum age.[22]

"The art of film scoring is in dire danger today, the greatest it's faced," said Elmer Bernstein, composer of scores for *The Ten Commandments*, *To Kill a Mockingbird* and more than seventy other films.[23] "The problem is one of pure ignorance. To the studios, film music is just a sort of wallpaper. If they don't like what they bought, they just paint over it.

"In the days when studios had music heads like John Green at MGM and Alfred Newman at Fox, composers had people who would fight for them if necessary, who would educate the executives. Today, the composer has no one to protect him. It's a very disturbing situation."

Bernstein feels that film music's ills are symptomatic of a larger problem in Hollywood: the mass-market movie maker.

"Socially, we're going through a plastic, corporate kind of culture; everything's very superficial. Mass media is great, but you can't have real progress in the arts if everything you make has to be liked by everybody. You tie yourself to the lowest common denominator every time. An art form can't survive that way."

A seeming majority of film makers would respond that numbers, not art, remains the target. With a teen-age audience worth millions at the box-office, the argument goes, what's so wrong about hit-oriented movie music?

"There's a cross-pollination between movies and records and MTV," lyricist/ screenwriter Dean Pitchford (*Footloose*) noted after his film's success. "If all the elements click, you have the most powerful marketing push imaginable."

Reaching the masses through movie music is hardly a new innovation. In the days of the silents, producers regularly incorporated well-known melodies into film scores; with the advent of talkies, movie musicals delivered the latest song amid highly secondary story lines.

But it was Dimitri Tiomkin's Oscar-winning score for *High Noon* in 1952, with its recurring use of the theme "Do Not Forsake Me Oh My Darlin'," that forcefully showed producers the commercial potential of songs in non-musical films.[24]

By the 1960s, with the explosion of pop groups like the Beatles and a growing awareness of the American teen-ager's buying power at the box office, the first wave of soundtrack mania struck. Soon, veteran composers like Bernard Herrmann (*Citizen Kane*), Max Steiner (*Gone with the Wind*) and Miklos Rozsa (*Ben-Hur*) found film offers on the wane as producers put their stakes on pop-oriented scores.[25]

After a brief return to the symphonic idiom in the mid-'70s with *Jaws* and Williams' hugely successful *Star Wars* sound track, the hit mentality has returned—with a subtle and disturbing new wrinkle, according to Bernstein.[26]

"In the '60s, it was strictly a matter of commerce," he said. "I think executives still knew what a good film score was. But now, we have a new generation of businessmen who are so used to synthesizers and electronic sounds that they've forgotten what real music sounds like."

Jerry Goldsmith is naturally frustrated by the rejection of his *Legend* score, but doesn't consider himself a victim. "I think the real victim is the picture," he said. "The entire concept of the film has been totally changed." (In a phone interview from London, director Ridley Scott said that *Legend*'s leisurely plot about fairies has been "toughened up" to emphasize the film's "action-adventure" aspects.)

Some good has actually come from the controversy, Goldsmith added: an album of his score will soon be released, in part because of the film's much-publicized troubles.

But Scott insisted that *Legend*'s re-cutting and re-scoring was entirely his own decision and Universal supported it. "Jerry's score is probably one of the best he's done," Scott said, "but I finally decided it was a bad marriage with the film. It just became too sweet."

After determining that Goldsmith was committed to other projects (Scott and Goldsmith both said they had not spoken since re-scoring), Scott said he chose Tangerine Dream: "I wanted a score that would still be appropriate to certain period elements of the film, but I wanted to use musicians that had a more contemporary connection."[27] Audiences can make up their own minds about *Legend* next spring after the film's domestic release.

Veteran screen composers are not entirely alone in feeling that studios are going too far. Taylor Hackford, whose *An Officer and a Gentleman* and *Against All Odds* each featured hit pop themes ("Up Where We Belong" and *Odds*' title song, respectively), is clearly not against "a synthesis of film making and record making."[28]

But "the film making has to come first. Some people don't approach it that way," he [said].

"The most important thing about songs in films is that they complement the emotional content of a scene. But when that approach meets with some success, other film makers throw in songs just to get a hit. A lot of music groups today are over-recording, with the idea that they can sell leftover songs to producers."

Film music's current state may not entirely be the fault of hit-hungry executives. "Perhaps, to a certain extent, composers are responsible," Bernstein noted, "because they haven't been tough enough by either rejecting jobs or asserting themselves more. It's difficult to get tough with people who have the power, but if you're going to be useful, you've got to stand up for what you believe in."

Movie music's current infatuation with pop hits may be only temporary but, in the meantime, Bernstein and others remain pessimistic.

"Film composing in a classical sense, I think, is disappearing," said the 63-year-old composer. "There's such a growing and pernicious disregard for it that the studios may wind up not having film composers anymore.

"Not every film score works, even when it's written by someone of experience. But if you're going to employ an expert in the field, your best decision is to trust the expert. If you're simply trying to hit the charts and make it with the 12-to-16-year-olds, there's no point in making a picture over that level in the first place."

From *Los Angeles Times*, January 5, 1986, S67.

Part 7

A WHOLE NEW WORLD

16

NEW INSTRUMENTS

Sonorities generated by such electronic instruments as the Trautonium, the ondes martenot, and the theremin found their way into scores for films of various sorts almost since the dawn of the sound-film era in Europe and the Soviet Union, and in the United States beginning in the mid-1940s electronic sonorities came to be especially associated with films whose narrative content was in one way or another "weird." The theremin was first heard in Hollywood films dealing with hypnosis (*Lady in the Dark*, 1944), dream interpretation (*Spellbound*, 1945), alcoholic dementia (*The Lost Weekend*, 1945), and murderous psychopathology (*The Spiral Staircase*, 1945); after the initial bustle of the Space Race, which coincided uncomfortably with the launch of the Arms Race and the first American "sightings" of Unidentified Flying Objects, the connotations of the theremin's tremulous sound shifted to the extraterrestrial, as evidenced in the scores of such science-fiction classics as *Rocketship X-M* (1950), *The Day the Earth Stood Still* (1951), *The Thing from Another World* (1951), and *It Came from Outer Space* (1953).

For better or worse, the characteristic sound of the theremin—and various oscillator-based imitations thereof—figured in dozens of sci-fi films from later in the 1950s and into the 1960s. An occasional effort stood apart from the crowd because of its use of sound-making technology concocted specifically for the film at hand; one thinks most immediately of Louis and Bebe Barron's score for the 1956 *Forbidden Planet* (see p. 166 this volume). But for a decade and a half most of the electronic music heard in films worldwide was of the blip-bleep-bloop variety; it was gimmicky and clichéd, and it is doubtful that sophisticated movie-goers missed it when the tide of sci-fi films finally ebbed.

Perhaps inspired by the 1969 landing on the moon of the Apollo 11 mission, science-fiction films—and with them electronic music—started to make a come-back in the early 1970s. One stellar example from Hollywood is Robert Wise's 1971 *The Andromeda Strain*, with music by Gil Mellé articulated on a panoply of instruments of his own invention (see p. 170); an example from the Soviet Union is Andrei Tarkovsky's 1972 *Solaris*, which features other-worldly atmospheres realized by Eduard Artemiev on a laboratory instrument called the ANS synthesizer.[1]

As significant as the above-mentioned efforts were, the film that likely clinched the relationship between electronic music and the cinema was Stanley Kubrick's 1971 *A Clockwork Orange*. Telling a futuristic but entirely earthbound story, Kubrick's film is rich in electronic arrangements of more or less familiar music by Beethoven, Rossini, and Henry Purcell; the arrangements were all by Walter Carlos, who in 1968 had released a chart-topping classical album titled *Switched-On Bach*. Like Carlos's treatments of Bach pieces on the album, his arrangements in *A Clockwork Orange* respected the pitches and rhythms of the original scores but colored the materials with sonorities that before this time were scarcely imaginable. The sonorities all

231

came from an electronic musical instrument that had been under development by the American physicist Robert Moog since the early 1950s and which—thanks to improvements in the transistor—in the mid-1960s entered the general marketplace. Although it attracted the attention of various rock performers when it was first exhibited at the 1967 Monterey International Pop Festival, it was only with *Switched-On Bach* that the so-called Moog synthesizer entered the popular culture. Kubrick's 1971 *A Clockwork Orange* marked the instrument's film debut, but by that time it had already been utilized profitably by composers of advertising jingles and mainstream pop songs.

The Moog synthesizer differed significantly from the theremin, which had been commercially manufactured in the United States since the late 1920s. With sounds generated by simple oscillators and controlled, in terms of pitch and volume levels, by interruptions of frequencies spewing from a pair of radio antennas, the theremin had a relatively limited range of sonorities and was extraordinarily difficult to play. With oscillator-based sounds channeled through a wide assortment of modulators and controlled from a conventional musical keyboard, the Moog synthesizer was at the same time infinitely colorful and quite simple to handle. The first marketed Moog synthesizer was monophonic, which meant that Carlos for both the Bach album and the *Clockwork Orange* score had to play the music's various strands one at a time. But the instrument quickly became polyphonic, and manufacturers other than Moog soon jumped on what was obviously a successful bandwagon.

By the end of the 1970s a wide variety of synthesizers had become available, each one seemingly more sophisticated yet less expensive than its predecessors. By the early 1980s synthesizers had grown digital—the various parameters that specified a particular sound's attack, decay, and so on were controlled not so much by knobs and sliders as by numbers punched into a keyboard, and all the information pertaining to a certain sound's "nature" was easily storable in a computer's memory. By 1982 the various manufacturers of electronic instruments cooperatively developed MIDI (Musical Instrument Digital Interface), a protocol by which signals generated by one device could be correctly interpreted by another. By the late 1980s competing software developers were marketing "sequencer" programs that allowed composers to write sequences of instructions (for pitch, duration, velocity of attack, etc.) that could be realized by sound-producing devices of their choosing.

One thing led quickly to another, and it is hardly surprising that the rapid developments in electronic music soon had an impact on composers who sought to create music for films. The documents presented in this chapter describe just a few of the many ways in which technology has lately been put to use in the making of film music.

16.1 SYNTHESIZER UPSTARTS CONQUER HOLLYWOOD

Jeff Burger

Jeff Burger (b. 1949) has had a long career as a freelance writer. His topics cover a wide range, but prominent among them are popular music in its own right and—especially relevant to this volume—the burgeoning use of technology by musicians of all sorts. For more than three decades his insightful articles on music have graced the pages of such publications as Circus, Creem, Melody Maker, Cash Box, High Fidelity, Electronic Musician, EQ, NewMedia, *and* Keyboard; *his technology-focused books include* The Murphy's Law MIDI/SMPTE Book *(1989),* The Desktop Multimedia Bible *(1993),* Multimedia for Decision Makers *(1994), and* Multimedia Studio for Windows *(1995).*

In this 1987 article for Keyboard *magazine, Burger interviews two musicians—Brian Banks and Anthony Marinelli—who in the 1980s shot rapidly to the forefront of Hollywood-based synthesizer specialists. Given the opportunity, Banks and Marinelli, as recounted here, readily composed original music for films. Far more often, however, the team serviced the needs of other composers either by electronically realizing scores for actual use on film soundtracks or by creating demonstration versions—what Marinelli calls "Polaroids"—of orchestral scores before final decisions about the music's length, placement, etc., were made.*

With ten years of Hollywood experience behind them at the time of this interview, Banks and Marinelli were veterans of the battles between studios who saw the economic advantage of using synthesized scores and orchestra musicians who feared they might be replaced by low-priced, non-union computer programmers. Significantly, Banks and Marinelli won the favor of orchestral musicians by proposing (and having accepted) a revision to the union contract that carefully defined synthesists' work and in effect put synthesists on a par with players of acoustic instruments.

Making film music is a crazy way to earn a living, but some people have it crazier than others. How many film composers are asked to produce techno-pop for Giorgio Moroder one day, create an ersatz orchestra for Steven Spielberg the next, and then mix the sound of mosquitos into Buffy Sainte-Marie's voice to make a string sound? Meet Brian Banks and Anthony Marinelli, a.k.a., Sonar Productions. In their ten years as partners, Banks and Marinelli have gone from being school pals to film industry staples. Lately, working on such big-budget extravaganzas as *Cat People*, *Clan of the Cave Bear*, and *The Color Purple* is all in a day's work at Sonar's Hollywood studio.

The two synthesist/composers met nearly twenty years ago as piano students under the same teacher. Independently, both graduated to ARP 2600 synthesizers in the mid-'70s, and eventually found themselves once again studying under the same teacher, studio synthesist Clark Spangler. In 1977, they joined forces to perform synthesized arrangements of classical music for live radio broadcasts from the Museum of Natural History in Los Angeles. During that period, the duo led six Yamaha CD-80s through such masterpieces as Beethoven's Eighth Symphony, Bach organ works, and Scott Joplin rags. After pooling their resources to buy an eight-track tape recorder and setting it up in Marinelli's parents' garage, the team started getting calls for commercial work. This led to their exposure to, and acquisition of, a New England Digital Synclavier—and things just haven't been the same since.

The Synclavier proved to be the calling card they needed to kick their careers into high gear. "FM was a major thing," Marinelli recalls. "That's what the system had to offer, and that's why we got into it. There was no terminal and no sampling, and the DX7 was still a good two years in the future. The Synclavier, coupled with our demo tape, which consisted of classical pieces, got us *Blue Thunder* over the name synthesists of the time. We could combine scoring, arranging, and making a big sound using FM to get new sounds. When we got *Blue Thunder*, everything took off."

After three months of work, they had transformed Arthur B. Rubinstein's musical sketch into one of the first scores realized on a digital synthesizer—and this time the orchestra was used to sweeten the synthesizers, rather than the other way around. The word spread quickly, and composers began turning to Banks and Marinelli as arrangers, orchestrators, and synthesists all rolled into one. Rubinstein called them back for *War Games* and *The Best of Times*, Larry Rosenthal hired them for *Heart Like A Wheel*, and Jack Nitzsche used the duo for *Starman*, *Stripper*, and *Stand by Me*. Then came Quincy Jones's score for *The Color Purple* and—well, their film bio alone is four pages long! And then there are the record credits, which include an obscure album called *Thriller* by a guy named Michael Jackson.[2]

Through it all, the two synthesists worked out of a garage. Two years ago, however, Sonar moved to a custom-designed studio in the heart of Hollywood. Banks says, "People would come to the garage and say, 'Gee, those kids are great.' Now they call us 'guys'!" The 'guys' have a 24-track room decked out with a video system and every imaginable piece of audio equipment, including two Synclavier systems. The off-line system has thirty-two M vices, SMPTE,[3] a touch-sensitive keyboard, a 20-Meg Winchester hard disk, and a Kennedy tape drive. Along with thirty-two FM voices, the on-line unit sports sixteen voices of sampling, eight megabytes of sampling memory, and eight individual outputs. Sonar's battery of support synths includes a Roland Super Jupiter, an Oberheim Xpander, a Prophet-5 with MIDI, a DX7, four ARP2600s driven by MIDI-to-control voltage converters, and more. Of course, there's also a Yamaha C7B grand, for those times when a sampled piano just won't do.

One of Sonar's most recent projects is Sylvester Stallone's *Over the Top*, with music by Giorgio Moroder, who originally called Banks and Marinelli for *Cat People*. "He had just bought a Synclavier," Banks remembers, "and, like many Synclavier owners, he thought it was great, but didn't have any way of getting into it. So we programmed it." *Keyboard* caught up with Banks and Marinelli at their studio, where they were taking a breather between sessions for the Stallone film and two new projects, *Nice Girls Don't Explode* and *Pinocchio and the Emperor of the Night*.

* * *

Do you rely on the Synclavier for most of your work?

Banks: As much as we may not like to tie our success to a hunk of hardware, having a Synclavier early on was really our calling card.[4] There wasn't any competition. DX7s were still a long way off, and even with thirty-two DX7 algorithms, there isn't one that sounds like a couple of the setups that are on the Synclavier.[5] We have a DX7 here, and it does some FM synthesis that the Synclavier doesn't, but they're different. Also, Anthony got very involved with consulting for the development of the Synclavier. A lot of things that are on the instrument are our fault! It's a nice feeling to be involved in the development of a musical instrument.

Why do you need two Synclaviers?

Marinelli: There are two of us! Actually, one Synclavier lives in the recording studio and is used almost exclusively for performance, and the other is in the B room. We use that one for composing and making our own sounds. We're trying to write music that's both idiomatic to the instrument and married to the video. Staying locked to picture all the time is really exciting. You can get such continuity. You can keep seeing the picture and reworking something, kind of like getting an orchestral performance the way Ravel might have.

You have floppy disk drives, Winchester hard disks, and Kennedy tape drives. Why so many different storage media?

Banks: Cost and convenience. Floppy disks are convenient, but they're more expensive per megabyte than Kennedy tapes, and the Kennedy is faster to retrieve from. We have a couple of hundred 15-Meg tape cartridges filled up. To keep that many floppy disks around is very time-consuming. Also, somebody has to sit there and feed them to the Synclavier. Just for a violin sound, we're into over thirty floppy disks. You're talking about a sample 50K long at 16-bit for every minor third across the range [of the keyboard].[6] We've got thirteen or fourteen [samples laid out] horizontally and up to three [layered] vertically. So you can have up to forty-five 16-bit 50K samples, and call that a violin.

Marinelli: Each sample, except for the hard down-bows, is between two and six seconds long. Manufacturers brag about seventeen seconds worth of sampling—we fill eight Meg of RAM with one instrument. At 50K, sampling with 16-bit words, you get roughly ten seconds per megabyte, so eight Meg is eighty seconds. That's how much we're using for one instrument. That's how you get great sounds.

Banks: Because of our training and background, we spend a lot of time trying to make a great-sounding orchestra. We've made it our business to get a lot of great orchestral samples. It's getting harder and harder as the players get hip to the fact that we can do a good job of imitating them.

Marinelli: Four years ago, they wanted to look at the [sampled] waveform [on the Synclavier screen]—they loved it! Now you can't get the good players. We were always straight about it. We told them what we were doing, and what it was going to be used for, and we tried to get people who were into it. If the players aren't into it, you're going to get rotten samples anyway. Part of our philosophy is to limit what we want to get in a night, because they'll blow themselves out and they won't get good tone on that many articulations in a night. We try to get three dynamic levels on everything. We go up in minor thirds, and then we try to get some articulations that we can stack vertically and bring in using velocity, pressure, pedals, breath control, and the control knob.

Banks: The sampling process is very laborious. You can assume that there are going to be takes that sound bad to your ear. Well, in order to guarantee that you've got one good take when you go to edit the samples, you'd better have two takes that you thought were good when they went down. There's no time, while a musician is sitting there, to listen to them all. You just keep rolling, and make sure that you have two. One of them is bound to be good, and if we're lucky enough to get two that are good, that's great, because now we have a double.

What do you use the double for?

Banks: For an *a due* part [a unison part played by two of the same instrument]. Doubling the same sample doesn't work. If you double samples, you get an awful, ugly, terrible phrasing. And if you delay the waveform or pitch-change it, all you do is make an ugly phase-shifter out of it. You don't get the sound of two instruments. You need two whole different samples. Psychologically and, sometimes, musically, it's nice if they're from different players, but at least they must be different samples.

Marinelli: We hand-play all the parts, because if you're playing the bottom guy and the top guy has the melody, you would do different things with vibrato and dynamics. We put in pedal information and all kinds of stuff to give us separate control.

Banks: Often, we'll play a whole bunch of lines into the Synclavier—we have a 200-track recorder here. Then I can roll all these takes in nonjustified time or in justified time.[7] I'll play both flute parts, or the first and second violins, into the sequencer, but with three passes of each. Then I'll spread them out in stereo to put them on the multitrack.

Marinelli: A lot of times the performances are done in the composing room, because, as you're composing, if you learn to think clearly and take a little extra time, you can get your performances done.

Do you find yourselves creating non-acoustic sounds on the Synclavier?

Banks: One of the more interesting things we did was for *The Color Purple*. There's a scene where Celie, the main female character, is in her house, which is a dilapidated place with a leaky roof. It's pouring rain, and she's got little tin cans and pails all over the living room. Her sister has been in Africa and sends her letters. Hearing the plink-plink-plink of the rain in the tin cans reminds Celie of the kalimba [African thumb-piano] music her sister has been telling her about. So we were asked to come up with a sequence that would go from raindrops to kalimba. They gave us a piece of kalimba music to segue into.

Marinelli: We also did some of the voices in *Pinocchio and the Emperor of the Night*. We did James Earl Jones.

What did you do to him?

Banks: Processed the hell out of him.

Marinelli: The amplitude of his voice gates a sound that's constantly changing, a whole twenty-four tracks' worth of sounds. The 24-track just runs, ticking off these sounds. Each track has up to ten different sounds laid on it—espresso machines blasting air into Sparklets bottles, mosquitos multi-tracked and taken down five octaves, low voices moaning, all kinds of windy, low rumblings. They all gate in along with backwards reverb when he talks. It's a great sound.

Banks: And all starting with his voice, which is one of the greatest instruments around.

Marinelli: For *Starman*, the string sounds came from one mosquito in a jar. We multi-tracked it loads of times, all out of phase—it was just five minutes of mosquito, so we'd record a bit of it, pick up at another point later on and dub it over the front part, and so on until there were thirty-six tracks of it. It was like thirty-six string players. A lot of the string sounds were mosquito mixed with Buffy Sainte-Marie's voice.

Banks: We wanted some good drum sounds for *Fast Forward*, so we went to a high school gymnasium, with all the horrible echo, and bounced balls on the floor. They made great kick drums. Unfortunately, there was an air conditioner going. So I looked at the recording on the Synclavier's SFM screen [Signal File Manager, one of the Synclavier's sampling software packages] and saw that there was a spike around 18K. Nobody would have heard that in the gymnasium, but when you isolate a sound and then play it in a lower range, even a perfect fifth lower, it's right there in your ear. So [using the software] I built a digital filter that removed a band between 17,950Hz to 18,050Hz. It worked just like a razor blade, removing just that frequency and leaving the rest of the sample untouched.

How much do you use the sequencing aspect of the Synclavier?

Banks: Extensively. We live and die inside of that sequencer. When we're doing an orchestral simulation, we play everything by hand into the sequencer. We use the sequencer because we can do editing in there that we could never do on tape.

Marinelli: Directors are always making changes at the last minute. We can just stick the floppy in, move some stuff around, and be done with it.

You compose while you watch the picture, with the Synclavier locked to SMPTE?

Banks: The Synclavier locks to picture with its own SMPTE interface. It'll track as slowly as one frame per second—you won't get any of those joyboxes to do that.

Marinelli: You hear your music at pitch, but it's slow.

Banks: You can tap a click track into the Synclavier. It's not just a sound reference for you to play against, but the justifying click track, so that if you want to do a justified [quantized] sequencer line against it, or if you're looking at it for beat reference on the screen, it's your actual click track. Or you can type in the click: I want eighty-seven clicks at this tempo, and then *accelerando* in the next twelve beats logarithmically to this new tempo, hang there for twelve beats, and then *ritard* down linearly in three beats to a new tempo.

Marinelli: The only movie we didn't use the sequencer for was *The Color Purple*, because we weren't doing the final score, except for that one cue with the raindrops. We did what we call Polaroids—we did the whole score, before it was recorded by orchestra. There were eighteen composers, each with one or two or three cues. Quincy [Jones] had the themes on lead sheets which would go to the composer who was to work on a particular cue. The composer would write a six-line sketch, the sketch would come to us, and we'd fill it out for the orchestra. We were just ripping through those cues. It was all hand-played directly to tape, with just two guys—one of us and our engineer, Mark Curry—recording up to six minutes of finished music a day. We did over 100 minutes of score like that. Those recordings went to Spielberg, he would look at them against picture, make changes, and send them back to the composer, who would send them back to us for a final version. Then we'd send them back to Spielberg. He was dealing with the real score as temp score [temporary score, an already-recorded, often well-known piece of music used until the actual score is ready]. We had to work fast, so it wasn't our best orchestra. Six minutes a day was hell.

Banks: Making orchestral Polaroids is a side business of ours. It's music insurance for directors and producers. A union orchestra is going to cost between $12,000 and $19,000 for a three-hour session, and if there are mistakes or changes to be made in the score, they have to call the orchestra back for a three-hour minimum call. They can hire us for three weeks for less money than it would cost them to hire a ninety-piece orchestra for a six-hour day. Very often in an orchestral score there are two or three cues that might be questionable; the director is really worried about the big love scene or the big chase. For $2,000 to $5,000, they can have a very representative orchestral demo and know whether or not the cues are happening.

How do you work together? What roles do you each play?

Banks: All of the above. Generally, we both write, play, do business, talk on the phone. But we each have our strengths and weaknesses.

Marinelli: We started out trying to do everything together, but there was more and more demand. Dividing up the tasks enabled the quality to get exponentially better as we increased our output.

Banks: Typically, we work together most when we're developing themes for a project, much more so than in the day-to-day work once the project gets started. The major conceptual stuff we really collaborate on. For instance, for *Nice Girls Don't Explode*, Anthony is doing the lion's share of the writing, while I'm doing the lion's share of production. It's faster that way because he's into the movie. He knows the characters and what's going to happen. I know what his floppy disk is going to look like when it gets to me.

Is it possible for you to collaborate that way if you're not working in your own studio?

Banks: One of the biggest reasons we put the studio together was the amount of software and hardware that had to be comfortably in place for us to be efficient. If we're going to have record producers, other composers, and advertising agents in here, we don't want them to feel like they're intruding on someone's backyard.

Marinelli: We were sidemen, too, and it was a drag to move all our stuff in and deal with a new engineer.

Banks: Giorgio Moroder has one of the finest studios in Los Angeles. When we did *Over the Top*, he gave us two days just to set up. We spent the better part of two days with [engineer] Brian Reeves setting up and getting the kinks out. The Synclavier lives in its own air-conditioned closet at our place. Giorgio didn't have that. We had to get special cables made, special MIDI cables with fifty-foot runs, to put the Synclavier in its own private space.

Marinelli: We wanted to stay out of the studio business, but we ended up studio owners. We had to. We couldn't do our work running around on dates.

Banks: Doing sessions was dissatisfying for us on another level, too—the creative level. If you're in there and there are sixty other guys sitting there waiting for you to finish, you don't get to take time to get a sound the way you want it. So you call up presets. The technology allows for a lot of presets these days, but when you use them, you're not creating anything new.

Marinelli: When you're in your own room, you can do five things at once. You can load a sample in, pick up the phone, and practice the part you're going to play. It's really an efficient way to spend your day, and it's more fun. When you go on a date, it's "hurry up and wait." That's going to change, I think. Even the Record Plant [recording studio] built a synthesizer room.

How much of the work you've been doing lately involves composing original music?

Banks: Right now, all of it.

Marinelli: *Pinocchio and the Emperor of the Night* is eighty-five minutes of orchestra that we're scoring now, and *Nice Girls Don't Explode* is twenty minutes, so we've got 100 minutes of orchestra to write in less than three months. Plus, we've got our clients: all the Suzuki Samurai commercials, KNBC News every week and—who knows? We might be getting into records next month.

Could you tell us about the Pinocchio *project?*

Banks: It's absolutely wall-to-wall music. Occasionally, we've been allowed to take a breath, maybe for one sentence. No kidding!

Marinelli: This is our best orchestra [simulation] to date. For the strings, it has five or six articulations—tremolos, off-of-the-string bowing, arcos, pizzicato, different dynamic levels—and it's all triple-tracked. If you were to take a sampled string sound and play a fast run, the attacks would sound mechanical. The way to avoid that is to use velocity to control volume, decay time, and attack time, so that your attack times are slightly different on each note. If you play it by hand and multi-track it, overlapping different string samples, you can eliminate that problem.

Banks: You can't get legato strings with fewer than three tracks. If we had a Mitsubishi 32-track [digital tape recorder] and tons and tons of RAM [in the Synclavier], I'd probably do it five or six times. The question that always comes up is, "If you have three 16-violin samples, aren't you making the most gargantuan string sample in the world?" The answer is no, because when you play from one note to another with a 16-violin sample, you still get only one gate per note. Part of the mass that you get when a string section moves is that all the notes change at different moments. Not only are there sixteen slightly different pitches, but the start times and the durations aren't all the same. In a real orchestra, you've got sixteen violinists doing it, so three [sampled tracks] is not a whole lot. But by the time you add a little reverb and a little DDL [digital delay line], it seems to work itself out.

Marinelli: We also have our own down-bows on velocity, so if you hit the key real hard, you've got a couple of different string sounds striking at once. We cheat that way. Also, the down-bows mixed with arco gives you more articulation. For every instrument, you've got to have a lot of tricks.

Do the various synthesizers in your setup play specific musical roles?

Banks: It's all in the variety. The reason you don't see a [Yamaha] TX816 here is that it would give us eight guys that sound the same. If I want five clarinets, I don't want five variations of a DX clarinet. I want a DX clarinet, a Roland clarinet, an Oberheim clarinet, a Synclavier clarinet, and a Sequential clarinet, because then I have five inherently different clarinets. A lot of pop record stuff, quick orchestra stuff, and quick synthesizer TV stuff has a very shallow sound because it's all one thing. There's enough of that kind of writing around. It's fast and easy to do with synthesizers. There are a lot of people who are using synthesizers as a convenience. Now they can have all these sounds in their bedroom. For us, the synthesizer is our instrument. We started studying young, and we play all different kinds of music with it. I don't ever expect to be satisfied.

Marinelli: We always argue, "Who's ahead, the manufacturers or the players?" I say the manufacturers are ahead, because we still aren't writing music for the instrument [idiomatically] the way Chopin wrote for piano.

Banks: But the artist is always pulling the technology. Artists aren't writing music that Anthony might call idiomatic to the instrument because the artist hears something else, and often has to fight with the instrument to get it. And then he'll have to settle for something in between. Drum machines like to go in loops, so you hear a lot of music that is segmented to a fault. Synthesizers have always been considered do-everything machines, but they've never lived up to it. Even old Moog synthesizers were supposed to be able to create any sound, and all you have to do is sit with one for a while and you'll know that that couldn't be further from the truth. The composer says, "Okay, now do this!" The machine says, "No." So the composer says, "Well, what will you do?" And it answers, "With this software update and that hardware, I'll do this." So the composer says, "All right, I'll write this, but I really wish I could write that."

Marinelli: What is a synthesizer for? Is it an instrument, or is it the do-everything box? New England Digital is saying the Synclavier is a recording studio in a box, but it's not really.

Banks: It's really a new kind of tape recorder, musical instrument, and signal processor all rolled into one. It's not really a recording studio in a box—yet—because it doesn't employ EQ, an array of faders for mixing, or a room to put a musician in.

Marinelli: We don't have the sample-to-disk option yet, but we will by August, and when we do, we'll use the 24-track for no more than reverb returns. We'll have as many as twelve great stereo reverb sounds, and let the Synclavier play back the whole thing, all digitally, and master to CD, number to number—if it works. If the multi-track is doing no more than playing back reverb, the noise floor will drop by a tremendous amount, because reverb doesn't have to be very loud in the mix.

Banks: We're going to be getting eight Winchester drives' worth of what NED calls direct-to-disk. They'll sample at up to 100K—no other digital recorder is even in that league—and you can get up to twenty-six minutes per drive. They're run by the Synclavier sequencer. Any number of those disks can be recording at any one time. Now, if you have a number of vocal takes for a pop song, you can take one phrase from take 17 and stick it on take 1, and the computer will very gently cross-fade from one to the other and back. It puts a Band-Aid over the joint between the two, but it's completely nondestructive, so if you don't like the way it sounds, you can go back.

Marinelli: The next software will be a CD algorithm that figures out the numbers so that you don't have to go back to the analog domain to make a CD. Who knows what that'll sound like?

Banks: We're also getting their optical disk storage system, which records to 12-inch laser disks—two-gigabyte random access disks. Our sample library will go on that. The cataloguing structure is so sophisticated that the catalog on your Winchester tells you, if you have more than one laser disk, which disk the sound you want is on. They're setting the whole thing up as a database management system. A laser disk will hold 10,000 entries, and there's no way you could ever flip through that many entries. So you ask it, "Tell me what I've got in terms of *pizz* violins," and it'll tell you.

Marinelli: That's the dream-come-true. For what we do, the library work is a real pain in the neck. If it's all in one spot, I'll be in heaven.

Banks: The Synclavier is an interesting instrument. The world knows it's a very expensive animal. We have always approached the Synclavier on two levels. First of all, it's the greatest musical synthesizer we've ever dealt with. But also, for that kind of money, you have to ask yourself, "Is this a good business venture?" Until now, the sample-to-disk option wasn't cost-effective, even though it's the funnest thing in the world. There is nothing more wonderful than working a tune with sixteen tracks of live stuff and 200 tracks of samples, and you say, "Okay, let's go to bar 12," and boom—you're right there! But remember, there's music, and there's the music business. You have to pay attention to the music business. Otherwise, you can't have a Synclavier.

Speaking of business, we understand that the American Federation of Musicians in Los Angeles recently accepted your proposal for a revision of the Union's wage scale for synthesists. What was your proposal, and why did you make it?

Banks: Usually, when you're doing a film score, every player is paid for a three-hour minimum, and they're also paid per overdub. The theory is that if you play one line, go back to the head of the tape, and play another line that goes over it, in the old days you'd have been two people. So ever since multi-tracking became standard, anyone doing an overdub has been paid twice, as though there were two people. Now, if you start at the beginning of a cue playing your DX7, and then at bar 17 you play your [Oberheim] Xpander, and then you play your [Sequential] Prophet-5, those are called doubles, rather than overdubs. That started with the woodwind doubler, who plays a variety of instruments during a cue. Doubles are paid as additional fractions of scale. With all the new synthesizers, computers, and sequencers, the number of tracks a synthesist has recorded for a cue no longer bears any relationship to the work that is done. Also, when you're a synthesist, you play arranger, orchestrator, engineer—everything. We came up with a proposal that synthesists should be paid by the hour at an inflated rate, with an unlimited amount of overdubs, doubles or anything else they're called upon to do. We needed a more standard way of doing things, so that we can all make money. Producers won't be afraid of us, because they'll know from the beginning how much it's going to cost. The scale that ended up being accepted was $200 an hour for one synthesist and $175 an hour for two or more synthesists. Scale for twenty-five or fewer orchestral players is $199.16 per player for three hours, so it's roughly triple scale.

Marinelli: We've seen the tables turn. We've been together for ten years, and in the beginning the Union didn't want any part of us. Using a synthesizer for a bass part was unheard-of. After a few years, we began to be treated like musicians. Then it got to the point where we were considered sidemen, but after a while we were doing bigger things than that—arranging, making sure the whole score got recorded properly. Now we can package the whole thing and deliver the finished product to the movie studio, and all they have to do is dub it.

Is this going to satisfy the acoustic players who are losing work to synthesists?

Marinelli: Whenever a new technology comes along, people get burned, and I'll do anything I can to help. It's like Social Security: You help the people who set it up for you. Well, those people set it up for us, and we owe it to them not to leave them out in the cold. But the realistic end of it is that it's going to be cooler than it has been in the past. Musicians have to stick together, though. There aren't very many people who really care about musicians in the business of film and recording.

Banks: To a greater or lesser degree, this stuff is inevitable, because film is a high-tech industry. Look at what they're doing in theaters, with six-track audio, all these computerized visual effects, and everything locked to SMPTE or VITC [Vertical Interval Time Code]. To have a computer-locked music system makes sense to people who are producing films because it fits right into what they're doing. If they can find composers who can make effective music with these systems—with whatever sounds they're capable of producing—it's bound to be less expensive, because it's tied more closely into the process of making the film. On one level you can say, "Why do I need eighty people, thirty microphones, six recordists, and a big soundstage when I can hire one or two people, and they can satisfy the picture and great sounds?" And I'm not even talking about orchestral simulation. I'm talking about new sounds, whatever they may be.

Marinelli: But it should be the composer's decision. I don't want to see us all get squeezed out. The producer's dream is to hire a programmer and say, "Get me a score that sounds like this temp score." They want to pay you as a programmer, not as a composer. That's why we got involved with all this Union stuff in the first place. The Union hated us in the beginning, and we weren't exactly loving it. But we realized that we had to form a coalition, we had to find out who our real enemies are—not our enemies, but the people who don't care about the music, who only care about product. Now, I'm really afraid of the people who go in and say, "I'm a programmer. I'll work for a low hourly rate," $25 an hour or something, and they end up composing, and people don't care. Not everybody cares about music.

Banks: Film studios and record producers want to hire people and call them programmers. That gets them off the Musicians Union contract and gets them in real cheap, but what it does is drag down the perceived value of the job to the degree that it's just like cleaning the toilets. When the perception of the value of the job drops to that level, then the musician has no leverage. There's someone around the corner saying,

"Yeah, I'll knock that out. I've got an [E-mu] Emulator," or "I've got a Synclavier." Synclavier guys tend not to be like that, because they've got so much money invested in their equipment that they have to make their money back.

Marinelli: Look at the claims made by the ads in the magazines. The producers read these things and believe them.

Banks: When we do what we do, we really have to stand firm and say, "We're doing music here. We're players if you hire us as players. We're composers if you hire us as composers. But we're never programmers. If you just want me to twist knobs, that's fine, but I'm still making musical decisions, and you're going to pay me that way. You're going to respect the fact that this is what I'm doing. That's why I've gone to the expense of getting the finest instrument that I can buy to do the art work that I do."

Marinelli: That's the only way to keep up with this. If you want to have this kind of equipment, you have to go through those politics in order to do it. If you don't, your art suffers, because it's a high-tech art. It's dependent on the instruments, and they don't get better with age. We're riding the wave. We're still on the surfboard, but it's rough water.

From *Keyboard* (September 13, 1987), 58–61, 64, 69–72, 77.

16.2 COMPUTERS IN THE MOVIES: HOW DESKTOP PCS HELP CREATE HOLLYWOOD'S AMAZING MUSIC AND SOUND EFFECTS

Lachlan Westfall

Lachlan Westfall (b. 1957) today works as a designer of computer-based graphic effects for television documentaries, but at the time he penned this article he was involved primarily with computer technology's musical applications. Part of the team that in the late 1980s significantly refined and expanded the original industry-wide specifications for MIDI (musical instrument digital interface), around the turn of the century he served variously as a member of the executive board of the MIDI Manufacturers Association, as president of the International MIDI Association, and as editor of the Roland Users Group *magazine.*

This 1998 article focuses on two active participants in the Hollywood scene who work out of relatively small studios equipped for the most part with store-bought computers. Westfall makes the telling point that in the waning years of the twentieth century "the line between sound effects and music is much less defined" than it had been in the first several decades of the sound film, and that lately "an entirely new term, sound design," has been created to describe the creative efforts of persons who contribute to the aural content of films by means of computer technology.

Even more tellingly, Westfall makes the point that Hollywood in 1998 seems to be much busier than it had been even in the most fertile years of its "classical" period. The quality of Hollywood's production is perhaps open to debate, but the fact remains,

Westfall observes, that "this town is [now] cranking out movies and TV shows at an amazing clip, and they all need sound." Much of the required sound, he suggests, is being generated by creative individuals whose resources are no more than what is available to them in their home studios. While the synergy between motion pictures and music/sound still resembles what prevailed in the 1930s, Westfall notes, it is obvious that the current means of production for picture-related music/sound are "completely different."

What do Tokyo-trashing monsters, an imperiled Nazi submarine, and talking green goo have in common? They're all made believable by the extensive use of computers in movie music and sound design. *Music & Computers* interviewed some of Hollywood's music and sound-effect wizards to find out how they do their magic. Grab a seat—you'll find some ideas here to stretch your own music-making, film-oriented or not.

Believe it or not, Hollywood is busier now than it was in its heyday in the 1930s. This town is cranking out movies and TV shows at an amazing clip, and they all need sound. While the concept is the same as it was back then—take moving pictures and embellish them with music and sound effects—the methods are completely different. Drop a composer from a generation ago into a modern scoring studio and he'll think he's sitting in a spaceship. (Actually, in some studios, today's composers might think that, too!) In Hollywood's new heyday, computers, software, and electronic musical instruments assist in virtually every aspect of sound production, from the initial creation of sounds to the final production of cues.

M&C spoke at length with composer Rob Arbittier of Noisy Neighbors and sound designer Scott Gershin of Soundelux about their use of computers and music technology. Rob, who has worked on albums by Stevie Wonder, Michael Jackson, and many others— as well as composing music for hundreds of TV commercials—was in the midst of scoring a trailer (preview) for Sony's blockbuster remake of *Godzilla*. Scott's credits include *True Lies, Flubber, Mousehunt, Das Boot*, and many more.

Both Rob and Scott jumped on the digital audio workstation bandwagon over ten years ago. Now the computer serves many purposes for them. "I use a *lot* of PCs," says Rob. "I've got twenty altogether in the studio. In the heat of a session I don't like to multitask on one computer, so I run a separate application on each one. I dedicate one each for sequencing, sound design, mixing, hard disk recording, and sound libraries."

That certainly sounds like a lot, but while Rob and Scott's systems are quite complex, they're actually built from some of the same components you probably have on your desktop. Let's begin where they do, with the initial creation of sounds.

Designer Sounds

Even just a few years ago, when it came to creating sounds for movies, the line between sound effects and the score was clearly defined. Synchronized sound effects, or Foley,[8] typically involved a couple of people, a room full of junk, and some microphones. There'd be a large screen playing the film, and the Foley artists would step, crash, boom, and shake right along with the actors on the screen. (Sound effect categories also include *ambience effects*, such as a recording of a busy intersection for a city scene; and *cut effects*, sounds such as airplane fly-overs that can't be performed in a room while watching a screen.)

When it came time for the music, an orchestra would set up in a similar room, where a conductor would watch the film and conduct the musicians, keeping them in sync with the film. Neither task was very easy, and it took significant time and talent to pull this off.

Today the line between sound effects and music is much less defined. In fact, an entirely new term, *sound design*, is used to define this new approach to creating sounds that will be used in a film. "Sound design has become something between music and sound effects," says Scott—a musician himself—of his role in creating many of the stunning audio effects we've heard over the years.

"We don't necessarily create melodies; we create cool whooshes, helicopters, etc.," he explains. "'But other times what we do would be considered music. In *Born on the Fourth of July*, we used a repeating heartbeat and a cell door slamming as the 'music' for a particular scene." This allowed director Oliver Stone to embellish a very dramatic moment with a subliminally evocative sound, where in the past a musical cue might have been used.

Scott continues, "Good sound design involves not always being literal but being emotional. Whether it's a harrier jet coming up and physically rumbling the theater in *True Lies*, or mixing the sounds of monks chanting with squealing pigs during a horrific scene in *Heaven and Earth*, the sounds aren't strictly representing the reality of the visual; they're conveying the emotion of the scene."

Sound designers use a variety of methods, some quite off the wall, to come up with these sounds. "On *Das Boot*, Michael Keller, Peter Sullivan, and I took a metal canoe and put it on our housing complex's swimming pool," Scott laughs. "We set up mics in the water, contact mics in the canoe, and used another mic on a boom pole. We needed to create the interior sounds of the submarine during a depth charge sequence and during normal running, so we started by slamming and shaking the canoe in the water.

"Next we took scuba tanks and did airbursts on the canoe. Finally we went into a Jacuzzi to get the sounds of the torpedoes and propellers, and we ended up using the scuba tanks and the blowers within the Jacuzzi itself. It's amazing what happens when you suddenly open up 3,000 pounds of air—we instantly emptied one third of the water. Everyone was soaked." But they got the sounds they were after.

Creating the sounds is actually just the first step, though. "We take those sounds and record them to DAT [digital audio tape]," Scott explains.[9] "Then we transfer them into one of three [computer-based] systems, the WaveFrame, Digidesign Pro Tools on the Mac, or Sonic Foundry's Sound Forge on the PC."

In each of these systems, the sound is stored on a hard disk as digital audio where it can be manipulated to form the final effect. "Once it's in the computer, we decide how we're going to use the sound," Scott continues. "Are we going to manipulate its pitch, its volume, or its filtering? Are we going to layer it with other sounds?"' With the computer and digital audio, the options are practically infinite. "It's a lot like sculpting," Scott says. "You start with a good piece of clay and then bend and shape it into what you need." Once the sound is tweaked, it can be loaded into a MIDI sampler such as the E-mu EIV, which Soundelux uses for further manipulation and playback.

The sampler and some outboard gear enable Scott to perform real-time changes to a sound's filtering and/or pitch, which makes the sound more dynamic and its creation more interactive. He often uses a motion-sensing device called the Dimension Beam (made by Interactive Light) to control samplers and outboard effects processors—the Beam emits a ray of infrared light and produces MIDI controller data when that light is disturbed.

Scott explains, "On *Flubber*, I used the Dimension Beam to control a Lexicon PCM 80 (effects processor), which I'd set up to manipulate my voice. That helped create the sound and personality of Flubber, the sound of Weebo's flight, and the flying car engine sounds. [Weebo is a small robot.] I could move my hand in the air and manipulate the sounds as Weebo banked and turned or as Flubber bounced and cooed." He records this real-time control as MIDI data into a computer running Steinberg Cubase sequencing software, where it can be further refined and manipulated.

Once all his sounds are recorded and fine-tuned, they must be synced to the actual movie. "We'll get the performances close with MIDI-synced stuff," Scott says, "but at the end we digitally record everything into Pro Tools and then fine-tune it from there."

Creating the Score

While Scott is busy emptying Jacuzzis, Rob Arbittier is up in the Hollywood hills waiting for yet another picture change to come for the latest trailer being used to promote *Godzilla* in theaters across the country. In one trailer, an enormous green foot crashes down through the roof of a natural history museum, crushing a Tyrannosaurus Rex skeleton; in another, Rob says, "a guy goes fishing and catches something really big—and everyone knows there's a new *Godzilla* movie coming out."

All the trailer music is done with the aid of Rob's computers. "I actually build all my own PCs from my favorite components, so they're all Arbittier brand," he says. Although he'll occasionally rent a large multitrack tape recorder to play back tracks recorded elsewhere, at his studio he does "hard disk recording exclusively." All the audio is converted into digital data by add-on cards for the PC; Rob is currently using the Lexicon Studio system. Like Scott, he also uses a WaveFrame system.

Computer-based recording systems give a film composer distinct advantages over tape-based setups. First, there's no waiting for the tape to rewind or fast forward; and second, since you're dealing with digital data, with specific software you can manipulate the sound in numerous creative ways. "I can take a drum groove that's straight and apply a swing feel to it,"' Rob enthuses. "You couldn't do that a few years ago; now I use it all the time."

In fact, these computer-based tools have had a hand in developing new styles of music. "I do a lot of dance remix work," Rob continues. "With these tools, I can take a drum loop that's at the wrong tempo and get it just right—without losing any sound quality."

In Rob's—and just about everyone's—studio in Hollywood, digital audio is only a piece of the puzzle. He also has a PC dedicated to running Cubase, which controls his museum-status collection of synthesizers. All these tools are needed because the scope of writing music for film is so vast.

"For the *Godzilla* trailers, we've been using live orchestras to play the music," Rob says. "We record them into a Sony 48-track digital tape recorder on the scoring stage and then bring the music back to our studio and mix it with synths and other stuff.

"We'll usually rent a 48-track recorder for the mix, though I do have four Sony PCM-800s [Sony's high-end version of the Tascam DA-88 8-track digital tape recorder], so sometimes I'll transfer the orchestral recording to those. I also have 64 tracks of disk recording, so I can transfer the audio to disk. It depends on the project and how many tracks we're really dealing with."

Rob also uses Cubase VST to record both digital audio and MIDI in the same program. "This lets me sync the MIDI to the audio as well as run lots of cool plug-ins," he notes. "I try to get every plug-in you can get for the PC—all the DirectX plug-ins, everything from tape simulators to vocoders to special EQs and compressors. There's quite a few available. Not as many as for the Mac, but the PC is catching up fast.

"I mostly use plug-ins as outboard effects toys," he continues. "The vocoder [Opcode Fusion: Vocode], for example, can do some really cool effects. I usually send a sound to it, make a new .WAV file out of it, and then use that file as an element in the Cubase sequence. I used to bring a sound in, manipulate it, and then send it back out to a sampler: now I can just do it all in my computer."

Noisy Neighbors

With the amount of impressive gear lurking in every corner, you'd think that Rob and his partner at Noisy Neighbors, Gary Adante, could create quite a racket. However, the entire system is amazingly organized. Rob is managing over 200 tracks of audio; the only way to do that is with computers.

"I have two [40-channel] Yamaha 02R digital mixers that I control from a PC running SEK'D Visualizer, which gives you an onscreen surround-sound joystick and all sorts of cool control," he reports. "I also have five [16-channel] Yamaha ProMix 01 mixers, and they're controlled by SAMM software from Innovative Quality Software.

"I don't usually record synthesizer audio into the computer until the last moment," Rob says. "It's silly to waste disk space recording synths, so I keep MIDI active down to the final mixdown. That's one of the reasons I have so many synths [he estimates 50] and mixer channels."

Even when you add in his computer-based MIDI sequencer, this incredibly complex system has everything within arm's reach. "If we did projects like this on a conventional mixer, it would have to be 30 feet wide," Rob laughs. "With all the computer control, I can sit in front of all these channels, yet it still feels like a unified user interface."

A self-proclaimed gear junkie, Rob confesses that while building such a complex system was exciting for him, all his clients really cared about was ending up with great-sounding music. "When you're doing TV and film music, things completely change every day," he remarks. "I could be doing a dance project in the morning and a symphony project in the afternoon. With traditional studios, that requires a huge amount of re-patching. It's a lot of work to reconfigure the studio between projects. With my system, I can switch between projects in about a minute. All the synths get their sounds from the librarian software [Sound Quest's MIDI Quest], my E-mu samplers get their presets from [Emagic] Sound Diver, and I'm ready to go."

Music for Film

Not only is scoring music for film done in ways that are quite different from those used even ten years ago, it's also quite different from recording standard songs. Music and sound for film must be synchronized with events that are happening on the screen. Sometimes it's quite obvious, like when a car crashes into a building, but the synchronization extends well beyond that. A film composer is given a section of the film for which he or she is to write the cue. In this set of visual events are "hit points," specific moments such as a door slam or a cut to a new scene that are important enough to have the music take them into account.

With computer control of the music, what happens next is quite amazing. Software such as Cubase can take a list of hit points and compute a specific tempo that will catch as many of the hit points as possible—even to the point of making subtle and practically imperceptible adjustments to the tempo so that all the strong beats of the music line up with the cuts in the film. The next time you watch a TV commercial, watch how well the music is synced to the visuals, and then imagine doing that by hand.

With the scores for the *Godzilla* trailers, Rob is dealing with this as we're talking.

"Right now we're in the middle of doing a trailer that keeps changing," he explains. "I've written music that's very rhythmic and driving but also has big orchestral sounds on top of it. Every time I get a new print, they might have added three frames or taken out five. There's no way I can just insert or delete a little extra time, 'cause it'll totally kill the groove. So what I have to do is finesse things, either by doing slight tempo adjustments or inserting an eighth note and turning a bar of 4/4 into a bar of 9/8— something to keep the *pulse* solid and yet open up more time to allow for the picture change."

Since this score is later going to be recorded by an orchestra, Rob has additional concerns. "I have to notate this in a way that an orchestra can later read," he remarks. "The computer can handle all kinds of odd time signatures, but if we're going to have 100 humans sitting on a sound stage reading it, I'll try not to throw them a bar of 1/8 because they'll all look at me like they hate me. If I'm doing something that will only be played by the computer, I'll happily toss in a bar of 1/8."

When done right, inserting an eighth note doesn't throw off the groove, Rob says. "It just makes it a little bit longer in one spot. It might seem kind of weird, but what you have to do is just smooth it over melodically or with some trick—that's when you always hope for sound effects.

"We have to take sound effects into account from the very beginning, because any place there's going to be a big sound effect, it's pointless for us to try to make too big a musical statement, since it's just going to be obliterated. It's much more practical to have the music crescendo before the effect, or play some kind of sound that echoes after the effect, or just do something to stay out of the way. A lot of times if it's a hard effect— which means it has to be in sync with something onscreen—the sound effects editor isn't going to have much leeway in where they put the sound. So music has to stay out of the way, because in that battle, the sound effect usually wins. Don't write your favorite chord to play under an explosion!"

Syncing to Video

The process of actually writing the score while watching the film has also changed drastically. Instead of sitting in front of an orchestra with the film being projected behind it, a modern film composer has yet another video monitor for displaying the film. Everything is synced up via SMPTE (Society of Motion Picture and Television Engineers) timecode and MIDI.

"There are two ways I can work," Rob explains. "One is to use a master controller to send timecode to the video deck and all the computers; that's probably the way I *should* work. But I actually work just like someone might at a small home studio: I take the timecode out of the video deck and patch it to the timecode input of the computer's MIDI interface."

Rob's primary MIDI Interface, an Opcode Music Quest 8Port/SE, reads in the SMPTE timecode and converts it to MIDI Time Code. Cubase then consults its tempo map and translates the incoming timecode into the bars, beats, and ticks (fractions of a beat) that tell the sequencer where it should be in the music. These calculations enable the sequencer to be precisely synced with the film.

Other Options

The changes that computers have brought to music and sound production are staggering, but they're not always what you might think. "Most of the time people think computers will make the job go faster, but I don't necessarily agree with that," Scott states. "The computer allows me to be more creative; it lets me try more things in the same amount of time. True, computers enable you to manipulate audio faster, but the way you work and think is not really sped up. You simply have more creative options now. In fact, sometimes using computers can add more time to a project, because the options are infinite."

But working faster also allows you to fix things that in the past might have caused a scoring session to crash and burn. "When we're doing TV commercials, I'll record a vocalist ten times," Rob says. "I can then go and edit together a perfect vocal in no time. On a thirty-second spot, that takes me about five minutes, whereas even in the most automated tape-based studio, it would take a huge amount of time to put together a great performance by muting and unmuting tracks syllable by syllable."

He offers another example of how the flexibility of computers can make or break a session: "On one commercial, the client had hired a big star to sing the main jingle. What they didn't realize was that the singer's style was very gravelly and sort of half-mumbled. It was a very soulful performance, but you couldn't understand a word of the jingle, and the clients were kinda panicking. Since I had recorded everything into the computer, I was able to go syllable-by-syllable and build an understandable vocal. That was the first time that my computer saved a session."

The computer also removes some of the bottlenecks in the production process. "Now we can generate a new version of the music almost as fast as they can generate new pictures," Rob says. "It's very easy to insert new measures and beats and adjust the tempo. There's such a huge advantage to using computers—I think everyone understands that now."

Computers are even being used as instruments themselves. "Now that the PC has been around for a while, there's lots of cool new software coming out," Rob says, excitedly. "I try to get all of it. I'm playing with Seer Systems Reality now. It's a really cool synthesizer, but exists entirely as software running on my PC. There are all these virtual environments on the computer now, for drum programming and other things, that are very cool." He cites Steinberg ReBirth as an example.

It's telling that someone doing such high-end work is so interested in software that runs on the most basic home computer. "I've been following the 'cheaper' technology (*i.e.*, stuff that is less expensive than your house) because it moves faster than the real high-end stuff," he reveals. "That's where the real innovations are."

The Right Attitude

Throughout this article we've talked about the gear that these two professionals are using to pull off amazing feats of sound design and music production. But in the end these devices are just tools. The secret of being successful in Hollywood is more than just having a bunch of great gear.

"We started Noisy Neighbors in 1990 because we'd done so much record work that we wanted to branch out into other things, like TV and film," Rob laughs. "We didn't realize how hard it would be to get started and that nobody would care how many records we had done or how much cool gear we had. We wanted to be on the cutting edge of technology, and hoped that that alone would bring in the business. It didn't at first, but once people got to know us, it certainly helped."

Scott also sees the gear as only a single piece of the puzzle. "The secret of success in this business is that you have to have a passion for what you do," he says. "If you have that passion, you can work sixteen hours a day and still have fun. If you're having fun, then sixteen hours won't faze you—much. You also must have perseverance. I've been told 'no' a lot, and even told I didn't have a talent for sound design. What that *really* taught me was to believe in myself." Clearly, for these two that approach has worked out quite well.

From *Music & Computers* 4, no. 4 (May–June 1998), 26–28, 30, 32.

16.3 THE UNREAL ORCHESTRA, PART 1: THE VIRTUAL FILM SCORE

Michael Prager

Michael Prager began his musical career as a guitarist but since the early 1990s has worked primarily as a developer of and writer on music-related software. Along with contributing to various technology-oriented magazines, he has authored several instruction manuals and tutorial DVDs; since 2003 he has been the main technical writer in support of Reason, *a music composition and hardware-emulation program for desktop computers marketed since 2000 by the Swedish company Propellerhead.*

This 2004 article for Keyboard *magazine is the first of a two-part series devoted to the intricacies of using synthesized and sampled sounds to create music that, to the casual listener, resembles music played by acoustic instruments. Whereas the second installment ("The Virtual Concert Hall") deals in general with electronic imitations of a standard symphony orchestra, the article reproduced here focuses specifically on the practical applications of an "unreal orchestra" to the needs of film and television scoring.*

Prager bases his article on interviews with three composers who represent different levels of experience and functionality within the Hollywood film-music community; whereas one of them is a veteran contributor to big-screen productions, the other two are relatively new to the scene and are involved for the most part with cable television programs and trailers. Interestingly, two of the interview subjects identify themselves as "pencil-and-paper" composers. While they regularly use samplers and synthesizers in order to realize their work, their thought processes—and their methods of cultivating a mere germ of an idea into a full-grown bit of music—move along traditional lines.

Whether comprised of racks of MIDI modules, stacks of samplers, or gigabytes of software instruments, virtual orchestras are an essential element of every composer's arsenal. With mind-boggling frequency, technological advances foster new sample libraries that offer ever-increasing control of expression and realism. You read about these in the pages of *Keyboard* every month: the Vienna Symphonic Library, Quantum Leap's Symphonic Orchestra, the Garritan Personal Orchestra, and other new virtual instruments let composers get much closer to the ideal of a highly expressive digital orchestra. They also make it easier to produce great-sounding orchestral tracks in a phenomenally short amount of time. As you might imagine, this comes in really handy in the world of film and TV music, where it seems nanoseconds can make the difference between a successful project and a missed deadline.

As fantastic as these new tools are, ultrarealistic orchestral tracks don't just flow out the minute you install them. And even if they did, there's a big difference between a track that sounds like a real orchestra and a cue that does its job in a film. There are many paths you can take to learn how to get the most from your digital orchestra and hone your chops at creating music for picture, but all of them combine the knowledge of traditional instruments and orchestration with a mastery of the technological resources available to you. We're here to help you figure out how to do it. We've interviewed several highly successful composers and orchestrators who make extensive use of virtual instruments.

Christopher Young is at the top of his game these days. Best known for forays into the macabre with the haunting themes for *Hellraiser* and *The Gift*, he has also covered other genres with his scores for *The Hurricane*, *The Core*, and *Swordfish*. Assisted by tech guru Jonathan Price, Young is hard at work on his newest scoring project, the upcoming prequel to *The Exorcist*.

Based in Northridge, California, Neal Acree is climbing the steps of film composing success with work that includes music for the TNT series *Witchblade* and cable feature films such as *Deadly Swarm* and *Project VIPER*.

Originally from the United Kingdom, Jane Cornish moved to LA in search of new challenges in film scoring, and has found them in a big way. Her current projects include composing for a series of ESPN biographies, as well as a steady flow of work from Ant Farm, one of the busiest movie-trailer music companies around.

Getting the Idea

Whether the score is orchestral in nature or not, the process begins with the same first step: watching the movie itself. This can sometimes include a temp score, which is a compilation of music that the director and music editor select to give the composer an idea of direction in which he or she would like to see the music go. In Christopher Young's case, his score to *The Fly II* served as the temp score to *Jennifer 8*, which subsequently resulted in his getting that gig, too. "The director heard my score and really wanted to hire me," he says. "But the studio wasn't keen on it, as I wasn't a big name. They ended up hiring someone else to do the score, but they didn't like it and threw it out. Then I came on board to replace that score.

"Before starting the scoring process, I like to see the film as many times as I can. That way, I'll have a better idea of what I'm trying to accomplish, and I can get a feel for where I think the music should and shouldn't be. Then I begin the process of writing the score out by hand on manuscript paper."

Like Young, Cornish is a pencil-and-paper composer, too. "I don't write at a keyboard when I'm working out themes," she says. "I go somewhere very quiet and compose the main themes sitting in a comfy chair, working things out completely in my head, and sketching the ideas out on manuscript paper, but fully orchestrated. I don't go to a keyboard or turn on any equipment until I've already composed the music. Then I need to rework the music to fit the picture precisely. I sync my sequencer to picture, make a note of where the hit points are and where changes should take place, then sequence the music."

In Acree's case, his approach involves a little emotion and being close to his keyboard. "The first step is watching the film and reacting to it as an audience member rather than a filmmaker," he says. "I take those emotions or ideas I get while watching and get to a keyboard as fast as I can to sequence stuff. I'll lay down as many thematic ideas as I can over the following two or three days. Once I start to get an idea that will work as a main theme, I'll develop that and play it for the director."

The next step is the spotting session, which involves the composer and director getting together to watch the film to decide where the music should be and what kind of emotion is required. Once that's done and some music is written or at least sketched out, it's time to create a mock-up of the score, which involves sequencing the score to make it sound as close to the real thing as possible. This is where a little tech savvy and a solid grounding in traditional orchestration comes in handy.

New Tools of the Trade

Jonathan Price, a film composer himself in addition to being Young's tech, describes how they approach the mock-up process. "MOTU Digital Performer [still under OS 9] is the hub of his studio," he says.[10] "It controls the MIDI, audio, and video. For mock-ups, we find our Gigastudio system running the Vienna Symphonic Library indispensable. For synth and sound design, Native Instruments Reaktor, Absynth, and Kontakt, as well as Spectrasonics Atmosphere, get used constantly.

"After Chris composes a cue in the upstairs studio, he photocopies the sketch and sends it downstairs to me with a tempo map. I'll mock it up with the Vienna Library. If there's a synth in the cue, I'll usually start with a patch from Absynth, D'cota, or Atmosphere and edit it until it sounds like something Chris would like. If it calls for designing a sound from the ground up, I'll turn to Reaktor."

Sitting in front of an impressive arsenal of computers and a large plasma screen, Cornish gives up the lowdown on her scoring rig. "I'm using Emagic Logic on a Mac G4 for

251

sequencing, with the built-in synth plug-ins and the EXS24 soft sampler," she says. "I use up to four Gigastudio systems as well, for orchestral samples. I have an orchestral palette template set up on the Gigas and in Logic. I make careful use of MIDI controllers to get the same kind of expression a well-trained musician would provide. I mix entirely in Logic."

Like many composers, Acree's studio is in a state of constant transition, but he maintains a distinctly retro edge, at least in terms of his sequencer. "I have a blue-and-white G3 that runs Opcode Studio Vision," he says, "and two PCs for Gigastudio. I have two E-mu E6400 samplers, which I use to handle some of the overflow from the Giga PCs, as I tend to max out the polyphony."

While having a great sample collection such as VSI or SO puts you on the road to capturing the realism of an actual orchestra, it can only get you halfway to your goal. Going the distance requires an intimate knowledge of what goes into orchestral writing, the characteristics of each instrument, and a few tricks of the trade.

"A common mistake that composers make is that they don't rely on real-world orchestration," says Acree. "You have to know the basic principles, such as voice leading, chord spacing, and the individual characteristics and ranges of each instrument."

Having spent much time performing as a classically-trained violinist, Cornish attains orchestral realism with a combination of her ears and her knowledge. "I rely on my ears, which is the most important part of scoring orchestral music in a MIDI studio," she says. "If a sample doesn't sound right, then I don't use it, even if I would score that instrument for live orchestra. I know in my head exactly how the music should sound when played by a real orchestra. So I use that as my basis and try to get as close as possible. I voice the instruments as I would if I were orchestrating the same piece for live orchestra, and keep all the instruments within their range.

"For a really massive string sound, I usually double the cellos and basses in octaves and leave the melody for just the violins, in octaves as well. I fill in harmonies in violas. Where synth players often go wrong is when they put in too much harmony in the middle; this tends to make things sound muddy. For brass I like to interweave voices, so I don't have each section by themselves. I might take a chord and alternate notes between horns and trombones for a more beautiful sound. It blends better. You need to be careful to not let low brass like the trombones get too close together—no interval smaller than a fifth between voices in the lower register. With a synth orchestra, I do a lot less doubling than I would with the real thing. For example, I don't double violins with winds on melodies, or it starts to sound very synthy."

Once your parts have been written and sequenced following the laws of orchestral physics, the next step is to add expression and dynamics into your work. This is typically accomplished using expression pedals, mod wheels, or MIDI sliders to control MIDI continuous controllers. "I'm a big advocate of capturing a real-time performance with MIDI," says Price. "I try to use controllers that are as expressive as possible. I use a Roland EV-7 foot pedal for volume. Since I play saxophone, it was easy for me to pick up the Yamaha WX-7 wind controller to play in wind and brass parts, or at least to add expression. I also use the Roland Handsonic to play in percussion parts in real time—it's an incredibly sensitive hand drum MIDI pad. The idea is that if you capture real-time performances, the result will sound musical. I play in every line of the score. If the strings are sustaining a chord, I play in each line separately, rather than play all the notes of the chord in one pass."

Pedal controllers figure heavily into Acree's orchestrations as well. "Ducking the attacks of samples is important. Most sample patches are created to be used universally for both fast and slow passages. But if you want to use a string patch in a slow passage, you have to compensate for the attack of the patch with the volume pedal.

"A lot of patches are programmed to attenuate the filter with the mod wheel, and that's certainly a useful way to control timbre and dynamics. But if you're already using both hands while playing a string or brass patch, you may want to consider re-assigning the filter to a pedal rather than the mod wheel. I use two pedals: The one on the right is the volume pedal, and the one on the left is set to control the filter or expression."

"If I want a dramatic crescendo in the trombones," says Cornish, "I raise the volume with MIDI, but also I use the mod wheel to crossfade to louder samples, which changes the timbre from light to aggressive—much more realistic."

Do Try This At Home

Learning the ropes and then finding success aren't steps that necessarily follow one another smoothly. But there are things you can do to give yourself the best shot possible. Young's outlook has always been very positive. "Becoming a film composer is a doable thing," he says, "if you have the willingness to go the distance. It takes a lot of desire to get there, but if you have the talent, it can be accomplished over time."

Cornish offers this advice: "As long as you have focus and develop your talent, there is no reason why you shouldn't pursue a career as a film composer. It's highly rewarding, though it requires a lot of hard work and sacrifice. Meeting good filmmakers and developing relationships with directors and producers is important. Scoring a good film, even if it's quite small, can lead to more scoring work. And you never know when the film or the film's director may do very well on the next one."

Acree agrees and adds, "You have to be strong-willed and thick-skinned. Being a talented composer is a prerequisite, but there's so much more that goes into getting jobs and dealing with criticism. You have to be prepared for the moment when what you think is the best thing you've ever written gets thrown out. You may often feel like you're working on product more than collaborating on an artistic endeavor. If you want to make a living at it, prepare yourself for the fact that it's a tough business to get into and just as difficult to stay in once you're in it. But if you're willing to fight your way to the end, then the best of luck to you. I can't think of anything I'd rather do."

From *Keyboard* 30, no. 2 (February 2004), 26–28, 30.

16.4 SOUND FOR PICTURE: HANS ZIMMER'S SCORING COLLECTIVE—COMPOSER COLLABORATION AT REMOTE CONTROL PRODUCTIONS

Matt Hurwitz

After training to be a civil engineer at the University of Maryland, Matt Hurwitz in the late 1980s embarked on what has proven to be a productive career as a freelance writer on various entertainment-related topics. His articles have appeared in such publications as the Washington Post, *the* Los Angeles Times, USA Today, Variety, *the* Hollywood Reporter, Videography, *and* American Cinematographer. *In 2009 he published two books:* The Complete X-Files: Behind the Scenes, the Myths and the Movies *(co-authored with Christopher Knowles) and* Reality Ends Here: The USC Film School—80 Years *(with Michael Goldman).*

The article reproduced here in many ways sets the record straight on the methods of the prolific German-born, London-raised Hollywood composer Hans Zimmer. Hurwitz offers no answer to the often-posed questions about Zimmer's musical "literacy"; when he quotes Zimmer as saying that he begins each new project by "sit[ting] in front of a blank page," the reader is left to wonder whether or not the expression is simply a figure of speech. The interview-based article sheds considerable light, however, on the progression of the typical Zimmer score from initial inspiration to orchestral realization. Clearly, Zimmer at almost every step of the way makes full use of a veritable army of skilled collaborators; just as clearly, the font of music in a Zimmer score is nothing less than Zimmer himself.

Film composer Hans Zimmer looks up from his computer monitor and keyboard to deal with an interruption. Although he's busy at work on a score, there is always time for this kind of intrusion: His small children have arrived for a visit and have brought dad some choice artwork to add to his collection.

Zimmer is master of his domain in the cavernous space known as "Hans's room" at Remote Control Productions in Santa Monica, Calif. With its exquisite wood paneling and flooring and plush furniture and accoutrements, the room "reminds me of a Viennese brothel," the composer jokes. While the fine-art books in the bookcases may say one thing about the space, the racks of vintage Moog synthesizer modules and patchbays and rows of other gear send a clearer message: If you come to this brothel, you'd better come equipped with a tune.

Comprising a dozen composing rooms, two state-of-the-art mixing studios and a recording space, Remote Control provides a home not only to Zimmer, but also to a great many other composers who have come up through the ranks to become some of the film and television businesses's top scorers. Harry Gregson-Williams, John Powell, Steve Jablonsky and James Levine are but a few who take refuge at the facility.

"Harry said to me, 'Do you know, in the summer, if you look at the box office, four out of the top five films were done by people from here?'" remarks Zimmer, who himself has written scores for such blockbusters as the *Pirates of the Caribbean* franchise,[11] *The Da Vinci Code*, *Crimson Tide*, *The Lion King* and so many others.

The facility began ten years ago when fellow composer Mark Mancina suggested the two share some space. "I wanted to build one room for me, and Mark, who's a friend, said, 'Wouldn't it be nice if we could share space or something?' It made it cheaper, but, at the same time, it seemed like a nice idea to have a sort of collaborative facility." Thus was born Media Ventures, which recently changed to its current name, Remote Control Productions.

The collaborative atmosphere concept stuck. Composers routinely pop their heads in to check out colleagues' work, tossing in the occasional idea. "I probably get more ideas from Heitor [Pereira, composer and Zimmer team member] than I give him," Zimmer says. "I've done 100-odd movies, but every time I start a new one I just sit in front of a blank page.

"The other day, Harry was mixing something, and after hearing it I just went straight back to my room and threw my stuff away and started again. We are competitive and there is a challenge, on an aesthetic level, which is really great. I heard his piece, and thought, 'Hang on a second—I better live up to that.' "

Another Set of Ears

One collaborator who can frequently be found alongside Zimmer is scoring mixer Al Clay (who alternates with engineer Alan Meyerson, depending on the project and schedules). The two met in London in 1983 at Trident Studios, where Zimmer was busy programming a Fairlight Series I sample sequencer for, as he describes it, "this horrible disco track."

"I was a tea boy," Clay recalls. "It was ten minutes into my first day, while I was being shown my duties. I walked in, sheepishly looking around the room, and saw this guy in leather pants and a flight jacket beating away on something."

It didn't take long for Clay to make an impression. "I had just spent three days programming on this little computer," says Zimmer, "and he came in and tripped over the mains cable—ripped it out of the wall. I hadn't saved and three days' work went up in smoke, and I went hysterical."

"He was screaming, 'It's crashed! It's crashed!' " adds Clay. "I was thinking, 'Crashed—obviously a bad thing. I don't know what it means, but I'll help you fix it.' " Zimmer adds, "He didn't seem too fazed by my screaming, so I thought, 'Whoa! Character strength. Guy can take a beating.' "

Not long after, Clay was hired by the composer, and the two began working long hours at Zimmer's tiny studio, Little Yard, in West London. "We used to do tons of commercials, which was a great way for Hans to pay for the new equipment he wanted to use," Clay says. "We'd literally do two or three jingles in the morning, and then we'd be back on the film score in the afternoon."

Clay certainly proved his worth on Zimmer's first big film project, Chris Menges's 1988 film, *A World Apart*. "There was one scene that I absolutely didn't know how to write," Zimmer recalls. The composer put a picture up and simply played against the image. "I hated everything. And then about 9 o'clock, Al said, 'Well, come and have a listen to this.' He played me this really beautiful track, and I said, 'What's that? Where did you get that from?' He said, 'Oh, that's the first thing you played this morning.' He knew that I needed to go through the process, and he kept his mouth shut all day. He'd already done it."

Zimmer brought Clay with him from the U.K. for his first big American film scoring project that same year, *Rain Man*, recorded at the former Record Plant West on the Paramount Studios lot.

Writing to Pictures

While the workflow might vary from project to project, depending on the film and its director, Zimmer follows a fairly unique process for his scoring work. Avoiding traditional spotting sessions, Zimmer begins simply by meeting with the director to go over the film. At the same time, he sometimes can base his themes on something as simple as a photograph. While director Gore Verbinski was shooting his 2005 film *The Weather Man* in Chicago, Zimmer was trying to get a grasp of the film's emotional experience without seeing any footage.[12] "I said to him, 'I can't make heads or tails out of this. What is this going to be? Send me something.' And he sent me a photograph from the set, with those green hospital walls and with a clock in the corner. And I wrote pretty much the whole thing just from that photo."

The first thing Zimmer does is create a twenty-minute suite containing all of the dramatic and character themes. Once the demo suite is completed, Zimmer will play it for the director and producer. "Hans will explain the parts for each character and the overall feeling," explains Clay. "It gives the director a chance to say, 'Yes, I like that,' or, 'No, that could be even more . . . .' But what they hear, actually, isn't going to change drastically when they walk into the studio and hear the orchestra, so there are no surprises. Hans's 'demos' will be very, very close to the final product."

Once everyone is in agreement, Zimmer begins composing the film to picture, scene by scene, with director meetings continuing two to three times per week. "Some people work just writing it all out on manuscript and scoring three or four or five days," says Clay. "The director will come down and hear it for the first time in its finished state with a full orchestra, and they may not like what they hear. Doing it this way just saves you that big surprise at the end."

Even though he is not composing any of the music himself, Clay is involved in each of those meetings. Says Zimmer. "I don't see the recording engineer as being separate from the musicians. They can't do what they do in isolation; we're all part of the team."

The team also includes a handful of additional composers who help flesh out Zimmer's ideas after he's created his initial composition for each cue. Explains Clay, "Hans will have this great idea, and he'll pass it on. He'll rely on these people all around him to see it through."

"Hans gives you a road map of the cue," explains composer Henry Jackman. "He's written a 2:30 piano piece, with loads of key changes, the mood of the movement. So you've pretty much got all the ammunition, emotionally." Jackman will lock the cue exactly to picture and begin applying Zimmer's music to the scene. "If you don't do that by the frame and you start doing a massive orchestration, you might find yourself going, 'Hang on a minute. I'm missing all the cuts.' It's much better to apply the map first." Once completed, he can begin orchestrating the cue, with Zimmer dropping in every so often throughout the day to make sure Jackman's work maintains his original ideas.

Zimmer's own composing environment is made up of a mixture of state-of-the-art recording technology and vintage instruments and sources. Choosing which instruments will be used for which film depends on the project, he says. "And people constantly seem to mis-hear what I'm doing. They're criticizing synth sounds on *Pirates* when there are no synth sounds. All it is is an orchestra shoved through a big Marshall stack."

The composer has a great affection for analog synth equipment, including Moog modules recently used on *The Da Vinci Code*. "There just came one bit where I had to drag out the big old Moog because nothing else had that sort of resonance." He typically records to Pro Tools using a Cubase sequencer and GigaSamplers.

New equipment and software arrive fairly regularly at Remote Control, but it rarely is put to use straight out of the box. Upstairs in a loft space filled with cool old gear (like a Commodore 64 with its original ROM card and built-in MIDI interface), engineer Mark Wherry can be found taking things apart and making them fit. "[Wherry is] really a thinker and philosopher of musical technology," Zimmer says.

"Mark doesn't just screw around with stuff," Clay comments. "He actually has the ability to take the software and rewrite it."

According to Wherry, "There's a lot of things that Hans uses, like the touchscreen in front of him that has custom software that drives it. And we've customized things to allow the Gigas to work slightly better." He and his team also designed and built a custom network MIDI solution that can handle the facility's 14 GigaStudio computers with a large number of MIDI interfaces.

The mixing system includes three Pro Tools rigs—one for synth outputs of Zimmer's drums and percussion, etc.; one for orchestra; and a third to handle the mix. Clay says Zimmer remains quite involved down to the mixing stage.

"He'll have a definite plan of what he wants, and he thinks spatially," notes Clay. "For *Da Vinci Code*, he had a vision of the viols up in the gallery at AIR Studio, and as he was writing he knew that would be the case. So when it came time for mixing, he knew he wanted them in the surrounds, and we put them up there.

"A lot of people are either techno-heads or they're strictly composers and fumble with the technology," Clay says. "One of the great things about Hans is that he's got that technical head, but also the free composer head, and he somehow manages to marry the two."

From *Mix* 31, no. 9 (September 2007), 49, 53.

17

NEW METHODS

Along with a battery of new and ever-more capable electronic instruments for generating music for films, the 1980s witnessed an impressive rise of new methods for the selection of pre-existing music that is used in films.

The new methods, of course, were not altogether without precedent. The practice of the so-called music supervisor certainly reached a refined state after films such as *The Graduate* (1967), *Easy Rider* (1969), *American Graffiti* (1973), and *Saturday Night Fever* (1977) proved that a soundtrack album could be as crucial to profits as box-office receipts. As many of the documents in this volume demonstrate, the "compilation score"—that is, a score made up almost entirely of pre-existing music gathered for the purpose of serving a film's extra-diegetic as well as diegetic needs—grew increasingly common in the 1980s, and with it grew the importance of the person assigned the task of ensuring that all the compiled music was in fact legally available to the filmmaker. As Jeff Smith points out in his 1998 book on popular music in film, the role of the music supervisor in some cases has been creative, with the supervisor actively participating in "spotting sessions, the selection of preexisting musical materials, the organization of prerecords, the screening of dailies, and the preparation of 'temp tracks.'"[1] But more often the supervisor's job has been simply administrative, and in this respect it has a long history.

As long ago as 1917, when the heyday of silent film was still dawning, proprietors of movie palaces learned to be wary of using copyrighted musical material without first having obtained proper clearance. That was the year in which the United States Supreme Court ruled, emphatically, on a case that for several seasons had been working its way up a ladder of appeals. The case began when the composer Victor Herbert filed suit against a New York restaurant whose salon orchestra, he noticed without amusement, was entertaining the clientele with the title song from his 1913 operetta *Sweethearts*. No compensation had been offered Herbert for use of his song, and permission for its use had not been requested. Righteously miffed, Herbert—who in 1914 had been instrumental in the founding of the American Society of Composers, Authors, and Publishers (ASCAP)—with much publicity took his complaint to court; he lost on both the local and state levels, but he prevailed when the case finally ascended to the highest court in the land.

As a result of the 1917 Supreme Court decision, it was made patently clear to commercial enterprises of all sorts that fees needed to be paid for the use of copyright-protected materials. Their deep pockets made them tempting targets for anyone wishing to sue for breach of copyright, and thus the major exhibitors of silent films and later the studios that manufactured sound films trod carefully when it came to using pre-existing music. The silent-film movie palaces employed clerks to ensure that any material from the familiar classical and "light classical" repertoires was in fact in the public domain, and their musical directors indulged liberally in license-free pieces composed and marketed especially for use in the cinema[2]; the makers of early sound films followed suit, but the "stock" music that decorated their productions was less often store-bought than commissioned from composers on the studio payrolls.

Radically altering the nature of the game, the more ambitious West Coast studios—in response to what they perceived as the public's insatiable hunger for songs in films—simply bought up many of the East Coast music publishers. Fans of vintage movies will doubtless have noticed that certain popular songs are heard fairly often in films from the early 1930s; what they may not have noticed is that these songs are heard only in films produced by the studio that, after fast-paced high-stakes wheeling and dealing, suddenly *owned* those particular songs' copyrights.

The idea of film studios being somehow "in bed" with music publishers has been around for a long time, but it fairly dominated industry reportage in the 1980s. In her 2004 *Music and Film: Soundtracks and Synergy*, Pauline Reay noted that in that decade of upheaval most of the major Hollywood studios were absorbed by larger concerns that included music among their properties: Rupert Murdoch's News Corporation bought Twentieth Century-Fox in 1985, Sony bought Columbia in 1989, Matsushita bought Universal in 1990, and so on.[3] A writer for the *Los Angeles Times* reported in 1986 that the Hollywood studios' sudden search for profitable soundtrack albums amounted to "a feeding frenzy."[4]

In that dangerously hungry environment, the music supervisor—charged sometimes with selecting but always with managing the songs that make up a potentially lucrative compilation score—truly came to the fore. Through interviews with persons who participate in "music supervision" on an almost daily basis, the documents gathered here shed light on the often misunderstood process that has shaped the scores of many recent films.

17.1A MAKING SOUNDTRACKS, PART 1: THOSE PESKY SONGS THAT SHOW UP IN BETWEEN YOUR CUES—WHO PUTS 'EM THERE, ANYWAY?

Jeff Rona

Jeff Rona (b. 1957) began his musical career as a performer with various bands in the New York City area, then returned to his native Los Angeles to work variously as a performer, a composer of music for high school bands and orchestras, a software developer for the Roland corporation, and a technological assistant for high-profile pop artists. His expertise in synthesis and music-related computer programming soon brought him into contact with such established film composers as Mark Isham and Hans Zimmer; his scoring debut came in 1993 with Barry Levinson's television series Homicide: Life on the Street, *and three years later—with Ridley Scott's* White Squall— *he realized the first of his many feature-film assignments.*

The articles reproduced here are two successive installments of "The Reel World," a column that Rona since the mid-1990s has penned for Keyboard *magazine and whose choicest bits were published in 2000 as* The Reel World: Scoring for Pictures—A Practical

Guide to the Art, Technology, and Business of Composing for Film, TV, and Video. *While Rona's columns typically deal with the composition of film music, these two columns focus on the use in films of pre-existing music. Songs of course have figured into film ever since 1927's* The Jazz Singer, *but as Rona states in his introduction, "songs have never been as important as they are to today's soundtracks." Through probing interviews with music supervisor Chris Douridas, these columns explore both the artistic logic and the commercial motivations behind "placement" of songs in films.*

Those pesky songs that show up in between your cues—who puts 'em there, anyway?

Any discussion of film scores and film soundtracks would be incomplete without coverage of at least some of the aspects of song usage. Songs have never been as important as they are to today's soundtracks.

As the composer of the film score, you're usually not part of the selection or production process for any songs that may also appear in a film you're working on, though there are exceptions. The producers may want you to arrange a song that is used elsewhere in a film, to base a cue on a theme from a song used in the film, or to create a score that integrates carefully with songs.

Film music budgets are often broken into two parts, one for the score and the other for the licensing of songs. For a song to be acquired for a film, the producers must approach the song's publisher and negotiate a deal. When you start talking about putting songs on a film soundtrack album, things can get quite political. As a composer you're not always insulated from this, but you can coexist peacefully.

The chores of song placement fall upon someone called a music supervisor. I had the opportunity to talk about the process with Chris Douridas, an emerging talent in the world of film soundtrack supervision. He's worked on projects such as *Austin Powers* (*1* and *2*), *American Beauty, One Eight Seven, Grace of My Heart,* and many others.[5] Here's what Chris has to say about his work.

Is choosing songs for films experimental, or is it a more planned-out process?

I'm sure everybody has their own system. For me, I just start. You know, you can talk about music all day long, but until you're actually hearing ideas and getting on the same page creatively with the people you're working with, you're not really going to get anywhere. So the first thing I do is to start feeding the director tapes—tapes of things that have come to me or tunes that have occurred to me as possibilities that fit within the world of a particular movie. I'll try to collect a broad range of things so I can outline what I understand about this movie. So the first tape might have ten songs that really stake out the parameters of this film's world, story, and characters. I ask the director to avoid thinking of specific scenes and to come back with feedback as to whether or not these pieces fit in the film's world as he understands it. Then I'll take that feedback, keep the ideas that were good, and discard the ideas that didn't fit. On the next tape I'll hone the selection further, so that by the fourth or fifth tape we're starting to really define the musical world of this movie. We're still not talking in terms of specific scenes or characters. Usually by the third or fourth tape, the director will have hit on some of those songs as being right for a certain scene or character. So without knowing it, we're starting to get the job done.

Do any of the directors you've worked with come to you with specific songs in mind?

It's great when a director has some musical ideas at the start. Often they'll have that from their own reading of the script. If they wrote the script, then they often have musical ideas in their head that may be undeveloped, but essential to what the film is going to be. I use those as hunching points to build a musical world around myself and the film.

Do you ever find yourself in disagreement with the director?

I don't think any creative participant in a film project should be shy about challenging the director's preconceived notions. Film is a collaborative medium, so that's part of what I'm there for. Every creative contributor to a film has to speak out and be prepared to challenge ideas they feel are inappropriate or in the wrong direction.

How did you get started doing music supervision in film?

My story is unique—as I'm sure most are. Music supervisor is not something you study to become in school. I was a radio disc jockey for about fifteen years—the last nine years in Los Angeles—which gave me a great forum. I did a daily morning music show that presented new music from all around the world. It was only natural that a lot of that great music might find its way into film projects. So I started getting called upon because of the variety of music with which I was familiar.

What was the first film you worked on as a supervisor?

I worked on a film with Kevin Reynolds called *One Eight Seven*, starring Samuel L. Jackson. Prior to that, I was a consultant, first on the TV show *Northern Exposure*, and then on Michael Mann's film *Heat*. In both cases, the directors were fans of my radio show.

What's the difference between a supervisor and a consultant?

A consultant will usually be brought in as a contributing element to the musical vision of the film. They work with the music supervisor to contribute ideas in the pre-production, production, or post-production of the film. It's a more limited role, and it may be focused on a single aspect of the soundtrack.

Tell me a little bit about the interaction between you as a music supervisor and the composer who's writing the underscore for the film. There are certainly situations where it's a toss-up whether a scene will be scored with underscore or a song. Who makes those decisions, how do you get involved, and what sorts of interactions do you have with a film's composer?

It's always a diplomatic process, especially with regard to the relationship between the film composer and the music supervisor. Both essentially provide the necessary musical ingredients for the film. There's a limited amount of space available, and the film composer will want to have the opportunity to get his or her vision across in as many moments as possible. The music supervisor might have other ideas for the same reasons, but initially it's the director's decision. The film composer is usually brought in late in the process, unfortunately. This can make the process even more difficult, since decisions get made before the composer is even on the job.

From *Keyboard* 26, no. 3 (March 2000), 118.

17.1B MAKING SOUNDTRACKS, PART 2: MORE ON THE DIFFERENCES BETWEEN THE SCORE AND THE SOUNDTRACK

Jeff Rona

Last month, I spoke with music supervisor Chris Douridas about his role in the creation of film soundtracks. In the second part of this series, Chris talks about how he handles temp scores and the inner workings of soundtrack albums—often a politically charged area. Soundtrack albums can be as lucrative as the film itself or even more, so a lot of attention is paid to them. Composers will frequently put a clause in their contract that guarantees a cut will appear on the soundtrack album. And most score aficionados know that feeling of buying a soundtrack album only to find none of the film's score on it.

Let's see what Chris has to say.

Have you ever been involved with putting together temp music on films, or have you influenced the choice of composer?

It's a different story with every film. Sometimes the composer will already be in place when the supervisor is hired. There are a lot of composers who work with directors consistently, and they have a history together. If a director sees eye to eye with the composer and they have a great working relationship, then that may continue over the course of the director's career.

One of the biggest difficulties in the process of film music is the temp score. Often the director will fall in love with a temp score, and sometimes it will be nearly impossible to sway him from using the temp. Composers are routinely asked to emulate temp scores, sometimes even to do a blatant rip-off. This can be a thorn in the side of both the composer and the music supervisor. Temp scores can, however, be very helpful in getting an idea across to a composer or director where words fail.

A music supervisor should help guide the director to the options that are available to him or her. Ultimately, it is the director's choice as to who will compose the score. It's incumbent upon the music supervisor to work closely with the composer to establish the musical personality of the film. The songs and musical elements that aren't part of the score should enhance the score.

From time to time there are film scores with a preponderance of songs, seemingly to ensure a successful soundtrack album and not necessarily to support what a director might want for the film. Do you specifically get asked to try to make a hit record?

I've been really lucky. I haven't had to work on many films that demand that of me. But, yes, it has come up. On the films *Austin Powers*, *Austin Powers 2*, and *Forces of Nature*, I was involved as an A&R person.[6] *Austin Powers 2* was building on a franchise that had been a little burned by the lack of commercial success of the first soundtrack album. So from the very beginning, it was clear that it was important to sell records with *Austin Powers 2*. I was a consultant in pre-production to help build on the musical personality that I helped develop for the first film. It was my role to come up with the theme of the film, that Quincy Jones soul bossa nova thing, as well as all the kitschy '60s pop, such as the Bacharach and Sergio Mendes stuff. So I staked out that part of the job, and left the hit-making part to the music supervisor on the second film, Danny Bramson. He was working on behalf of Warner Bros. Records as their film person.[7]

That said, sometimes there can be a conflict between the musical needs of the film and the needs of the soundtrack album. That's just a symptom of the fact that film is at the heart of our pop culture and therefore stands to generate a tremendous amount of cash.

Do you see it working to the detriment of some films?

Absolutely. It gives films a disposable quality. Look at the Giorgio Moroder version of *Metropolis*, with his new soundtrack.[8] It became a very dated version of the original, which was heralded at the time as being cutting edge. The new version is like a piece of candy compared to the original. I think it's very shortsighted of filmmakers, because over time the songs aren't going to remain current.

You're saying the pop status of the film can last a lot longer than the pop status of some of the songs?

In the case of DreamWorks' *American Beauty*, we were very careful not to date the film with a slew of contemporary bands. If you watch the film, it doesn't sound like 1999.

What's the budgeting process for a film score with songs, and how involved do you get with that? Are you given a budget to work within?

Usually when I get a script, the writer has peppered it with song choices with no regard to the budget. I'll read scripts that have songs by the Beatles, Rolling Stones, or Led Zeppelin, only to come to the budgeting point and realize that the cost is prohibitive. Even with *American Beauty*, the original script had "Fixing a Hole" by the Beatles at the front of the film. There were also Pink Floyd and Led Zeppelin references. While they were helpful to the filmmakers as they built that cinematic world, when it came time to lay out the song budget, we were dealing with a relatively small independent film with a total budget of around $15 million. A sliver of that is earmarked for music. When we started *American Beauty*, the music budget was about $200,000.

As a project gets rolling, it builds momentum. The director jumps onboard, there are stars attached, and you have the filmmaking crew put together. Then the film studio producing the film can get a sense of where the picture is headed. As the dailies [the scenes as they come out of the camera, prior to editing][9] start coming in, we see the performances that the director is getting, and a buzz starts to build around the film. People start to see there is something serious happening here; it's a real film in the making. Then I can make a case for more money, and the producers are more likely to go along with it. When we were done, we got [film composer] Tom Newman to come in for a fraction of his normal fee. Because the script was so attractive to all the creative people involved, everyone took lesser fees because they wanted to be associated with a "golden" project. All of these money-saving tactics go a long way to getting more funds from the studio. It's about timing and seeing what the market can bear.

Do you get involved in the negotiation of song fees?

If it's a studio project, they'll have an in-house department that handles those negotiations. I'm happy to push it off on whoever wants to take it. I think most supervisors prefer to stick to the creative side of it, because it's your relationships with these artists and these record labels that help grease the wheels of your career. If you get too involved with the negotiations, it hinders your relationships with the musical creative people you want to work with in the future.

What if it's an independent film: Do you find a lawyer to do it or do you do it?

You can always find someone who will do clearances outright for set fees—they are clearance specialists. I would advise any supervisor to extricate themselves from the process of clearances if possible. It's easy to find somebody to come onboard on a consultant or freelance basis to do clearances for somewhere around $1,000 per track.

Do you have a vague sense going in of what a song will cost? Do you have a sense of what a Beatles song would cost? How flexible are those prices?

You go to publishers to get a ballpark figure when you're budgeting the film. If the script calls for certain songs, you have to allow for those or be prepared to make changes later on. In the case of *American Beauty*, we ended up with a Beatles song. We didn't use "Fixing a Hole" as the script called for, but for the end credit song we used a Beatles song covered by Elliot Smith.

It's cheaper to use somebody else's recording of a song than the original?

Sometimes. There are no rules. In the case of this one, the Beatles committee (the part of a publishing company that determines permissions and prices) was fond of the script, the idea, and the project. While it was still very expensive, they did come down in price for us. This is where people pull out whatever relationships they have. We had a Who track that we wouldn't have been able to afford had the director not been a friend of Pete Townshend.[10] That's why I like to work on great scripts. A great script can change a lot of people's minds and help you tremendously in the negotiation process. If you're working on a crappy film, nobody wants to be a part of it unless you pay full price. But if you're working on a great project, everybody wants to be a part of it, and the rules change.

From *Keyboard* 26, no. 4 (April 2000), 139.

17.2 MUSIC IN MOVIES AND TV: FILLING THE BILL

Nick Krewen

Toronto-based freelance journalist Nick Krewen writes about topics ranging from books to the environment, but since the early 1980s most of his work has focused on the music industry. Along with Words & Music, *the quarterly journal of the Society of Composers, Authors, and Music Publishers of Canada (SOCAN), publications that have presented his work include the* Toronto Star, Billboard, Songwriters Magazine, Country Music, Chatelain, *and* Maclean's. *In 2010 Krewen co-authored (with Karen Bliss, Larry LeBlanc, and Jason Schneider)* Music from Far and Wide: Celebrating Forty Years of the JUNO Awards, *an account of the prizes given annually by the Canadian Academy of Recording Arts and Sciences.*

In this article, Krewen sheds valuable light on the process of how music supervisors sort through huge amounts of songs, select those they feel might be viable in a television program or motion picture, and then negotiate deals to have those songs actually used. Many of the details he offers are specific to the Canadian entertainment business, but the principles and methods described apply generally to music supervision in film industries worldwide.

Scott Komer has felt the power of music supervision first hand. After a handful of songs by his punk rock band The Pettit Project was placed in the popular teen TV show, *Radio Free Roscoe*, by Toronto-based Arpix Media Inc. during the program's initial season, he noticed a fundamental impact. "It got our name and music out to thousands of people who otherwise wouldn't have heard of us," says Komer, who has fronted his Oakville, Ont.-based sextet for five-and-a-half years. "We wouldn't have the new fans, the non-underground punk ones, without it."

Ron Proulx is happy to oblige. As founder and president of Toronto's Arpix Media Inc., one of Canada's two leading music-supervision companies (the other being S.L. Feldman & Associates, with offices in Vancouver and Toronto), he notes that his profession can—and does—make a tangible difference. "We're one of the few businesses that will put money into the hands of the artist," says Proulx, author of the how-to-license guide, *Get Your Music into Movies and Television*. "Music in film and TV is one of the greatest parts of the music game, from a creative and economic perspective, for artists, songwriters and publishers. With retail, radio, international boundaries and CDs going through massive changes, one of the constants has been film and TV. It's become one of the great cornerstones of the business."

It's also one of the few areas of the music business enjoying consistent growth. During an interview with *The Hollywood Reporter* last year, Martin Bandier, chairman and CEO of EMI Music Publishing, mentioned that his company's "synchronization area has had double-digit compound annual growth for the past 10 years."

In its latest financial report, SOCAN also acknowledged that income from commercial television increased to $45.5-million, while cable-television proceeds were up 17.1 percent from a year earlier, bringing in $28-million, both of which make up a significant portion of SOCAN's record $151-million revenues distributed in 2004. Excluded from those SOCAN figures, derived from a bundle of source licences including master use, synchronization and performing rights, is money generated by film, advertising-spot and video/computer game placements, another sizable chunk of change.

But as Sarah Webster, S.L. Feldman & Associates' Vancouver-based music supervisor, points out, money isn't the only benefit from song placement. Currently on the lookout for tunes to insert into *Falcon Beach*, a new 13-episode Global Television series she describes as "the Canadian O.C.," she says the prime-time exposure for the act that gets the series theme song could sky-rocket its popularity. "Securing the opening song for *Falcon Beach* will be an incredibly lucrative move for some band," says Webster, who will place an average of ten songs per episode in the upcoming series. "Having their song played over the title sequence once a week will jumpstart their career."

So what exactly is the function of a music supervisor? Hired by producers or directors, Proulx and Webster find, research, clear and license music for film and television productions, although those duties are increasingly expanding to embrace the advertising and video-game worlds.

"The parameters are quite specific when you get down to it," Webster explains. "It's got to fit creatively, it's got to fit within budget. The director may want a specific vocal. He may say, 'For this scene where she's walking down the street, I definitely want to hear a strong female voice.' So it gets narrowed down."

And if a producer wants, but can't afford, to use Shania Twain's "Up!" for a key scene? "You find perfect replacements," Webster replies. "Being Feldman, our ties are deep in the music industry. After you've done this for a few years, you get in touch with all the publishers and the record labels around the world and you know who has what."

Proulx notes that when it comes to film and TV, Canadian production budgets are usually much more limited than their U.S. counterparts and need to be subsidized by government funding, adding further restrictions when allotting funds to music. "It's hard to produce film and television in this country," says Proulx, a 2005 Genie recipient for "Pantaloon In Black," a song he co-wrote for the movie *Twist*.[11] "In Canada, you're doing things where it's 10 cents on the dollar. Obviously, government funding has been very important to the film and TV industries."

Webster says that producers and directors often rely on a supervisor's wealth of musical knowledge for support. "Some directors and producers are clear down to the specific songs they're after. Others don't have any idea about the music they want for a cue. In those instances, we have complete creative control, and we pitch the genres of music we think will work for different themes or cues."

As a result, both Webster and Proulx spend a good portion of their days listening to music, with MP3s replacing CDs as the preferred method of moving sounds around. "The Internet has really revolutionized this business," Proulx admits. "I'm always on the lookout for new stuff because the lifeblood of what we do is music. That said, I'm always looking forward to receiving slip-through-the-cracks music. It's very easy to find the major-label and independent versions of Sum 41. Finding an independent Loreena McKennitt is a lot more difficult."

Dealing with songs isn't a music supervisor's only responsibility. "There's two completely different streams in the film and TV music game: there are the songs, and then there's the composer world of the underscore, which is completely separate ninety-nine times out of a hundred from the songs that are used," Proulx says. Webster agrees. "We also have a roster of score composers," she says. "I pitch them for projects and negotiate the deals for them."

Despite the numerous win-win scenarios in attaching songs and performers to popular visual media, both Proulx and Webster are often mystified when they run into resistance—and in some cases, outright rejection from major record labels and music publishers they've contacted for a piece of music. "There's fear, especially with record labels, that their music is going to be magically extricated from its audio track and somehow placed onto some device by an end user," says Proulx. "The strange thing is, ninety-nine percent of the time I'm not licensing the whole song anyway. I'm licensing thirty seconds to a minute of it."

Proulx, whose *Get Your Music into Movies and Television* covers practical tips ranging from copyright issues and deal points to sample negotiations, suggests that a long-term vision may be more prudent than a short-term stalemate. "Whatever money the artists are getting paid, what's worthwhile is that eyeballs are seeing and ears are hearing it," says Proulx. Nonetheless, he says the independent sector has picked up the ball dropped by the multinationals. "We license so much more to the independent sector as a direct consequence of record companies not wanting to take the money."

For Webster, preferring to deal with independents rather than majors comes down to logistics. She notes that film directors and producers often contact her for song availabilities when the film is near completion, requiring a quick turnaround. "Independent songs are much easier to clear," Webster says. "Whenever you go to a major publishing company or a major record label, there are so many people and so much red tape involved, it's virtually impossible to turn an approval around in under a week or two. With independent labels, your phone calls get answered. The deal is usually one-stop—they can sign off on the publishing and master in one telephone call. You're answered, you're looked after. You ask for the sign-off and it's faxed right back to you, so you can call the director and tell them, 'We're good to go on this cue. Next?'"

Webster says the music business isn't the only industry guilty of misunderstanding the role of music supervisor; film directors and producers also have their moments. "I don't think people have any understanding of how much work goes into getting one song cleared," says Webster, who, along with *Falcon Beach*, is working on the music for two motion pictures currently being filmed on the West Coast, *Slither* and *Fido*. "When I call to pitch our services, I'll be told by the producer, 'No thanks. We don't need a music supervisor. We'll have our office p.a. negotiate any licences we need.' Later, I see these people at film-festival parties saying, 'Oh, we could only afford one song for that film because of the expense.' And I have to tell them, 'If you had called us, it would have been a tenth of the price. I know the licensing rep because I buy tens of thousands of dollars a year worth of music from her.'"

Harmony between the film and music industries is important, and Proulx says nothing gives a musician better exposure than song placement: "Artists like Sarah McLachlan and Loreena McKennitt can show the correlation between the use of music in film and television and the growth of their careers."

As for Komer and The Pettil Project, the *Radio Free Roscoe* placement not only substantially increased the band's fan base but also added some much needed cash to their coffers—enough for them to purchase some new touring gear—and an unexpected bonus: a second-season appearance on an episode specifically written around the group. "It was great," says Komer enthusiastically. "It was basically a half-hour commercial for our band."

The Fine Print

When it comes to licensing your music to film or television, Ron Proulx suggests you think of it in terms of a van rental. "Are you renting the van for unlimited mileage, or are you renting it for 250 km?" he asks. "After 250 km you have to rent it by the kilometer." That, in essence, is what a music-licensing deal is for film and TV. Proulx says producers usually require "unlimited mileage" for their distribution agreements, represented by specific terminology in licensing agreements. "The catch-all phrase is 'all media now known or hereafter devised in perpetuity for the universe,'" he says. And that terminology is what gives major record companies and music publishers conniptions. It's a concern for lost revenue streams.

However, such avenues as videogram buyouts—which cover DVD and other similar formats that consumers purchase or rent—allow for additional "kilometer" options, especially if they are based on unit sales. "Say your deal calls for a residual of 10 cents per unit on a 10,000 rollover," Proulx says. "So you pay me $1,000 now, go off and manufacture 10,000 units. When you've sold your 10,000 units, you pay me another $1,000 and go manufacture and sell another 10,000 units."

Whether you negotiate for unlimited or restricted licensing options, Proulx says, the constant development of new technologies is causing media to be redefined on almost a daily basis, clouding previously outlined interpretations. "People are getting real antsy about it," he admits. He says other deal-point expressions that licensees should know include "most favoured nations," "in-context" and "out-of-context" use.

- Most favoured nations: This stipulation ensures you will receive equal compensation to all other licensed music secured for a particular film or TV episode, but Proulx warns it will be adjusted to your stature. "If I have a Steppenwolf track in the movie and you're an indie band, you probably won't get it," Proulx says. "But it's not uncommon to have three MFN tiers in a single licence. Tier one includes platinum-level acts. Tier two includes major record companies' developing acts. Tier three includes independent stuff."
- In-context/out-of-context for promotional and trailer uses: "In-context is the idea that you can use the music as it's contained in the scene," Proulx says. "Out-of-context dictates that you can use it in the trailer in any manner to promote the movie."

Although he doesn't reference licensing rates in his book *Get Your Music into Movies and Television*, Proulx says independent artists, labels and publishers can expect anywhere from "several hundred dollars" for placement in Canadian TV shows to $100,000-plus for major artists licensing their music to Hollywood blockbusters. "Performing rights are the gift that keeps on giving," he says. "That is probably the single most important reason to do any deal. Regardless of what area of the business you're in, some day, this is going to make you or someone you love some money."

From *Words & Music* 12, no. 3 (Fall 2005), 12–14.

17.3 MUSIC BUSINESS INSIDER:
Q&A: JACK RUDY

Mike Levine

Along with being editor of the magazine Electronic Musician, *Mike Levine is a composer and a performing musician. His creative work has enlivened productions for The History Channel and television commercials for such products as Days Inn, Advil, and Lysol; as a guitarist and mandolin player he has been a session musician for numerous recordings and television productions, and he currently works with two bands—the Reticents and the Sarlin/Levine/Ganz trio—in the Los Angeles area. Levine is the author of five books, including* How to Be a Working Musician: A Practical Guide to Earning Money in the Music Business *(1997) and, with Warren Haynes, a* Guide to Slide Guitar *(2005).*

The article reproduced here is a question-answer interview with Jack Rudy, who has maintained an active career as a music supervisor over the past decade and who also has a long career as a senior producer for various advertising agencies. Levine's conversation with Rudy touches not only on the practical and commercial aspects of music supervision but also on its aesthetics; of particular interest here is Rudy's idea of what he terms a song's "credibility."

In the music-for-picture world, composers get most of the glory. But there's another group of professionals who have a big impact on which music gets into a film or TV show: music supervisors. While film composers write custom instrumental music to set moods and fit with the action in various scenes, music supervisors choose their music from songs and compositions that have already been written. Music supervisors are therefore a conduit for songwriters and independent composers who are trying to get their music on the screen.

For a better understanding of what music supervisors do, I recently spoke with Jack Rudy, who has supervised the music for feature film, sitcom, *Comedy Central*, and more.[12] Rudy brings plenty of musical skill and experience to his job, having worked as a professional harmonica player for years, playing with artists such as Dave Alvin, the Blasters, and John Lee Hooker.

What is the role of the music supervisor in a production?

I complement the work of the composer by providing cues that come from outside of the composer's brain—so band cues, rock music songs, preexisting songs. That's why my specialty as a music supervisor is to stay on top of the music of all current bands: bands that have albums, bands that don't have albums, bands that are playing in clubs.

In the rock world, mostly?

Not necessarily just the rock world—the whole world of music. Anybody who is playing music live for people is at the top of my list. And not just because those songs work well in movies. It's also because those musicians and I have a similar self-interest in a project. What will work for me and my film will also work for those artists in their careers.

Obtaining a film placement or a television placement is a very valuable and positive step in a live musician's career. It's kind of like what getting on the radio meant in 1955. So with a film or TV show, does the audience focus on your music less than it would if it were on the radio?

Yes, but a lot of shows are music driven. A huge percentage of the people who are of record-buying age buy their music based on what they've seen on television. The people who are selecting music for television shows are trusted; their taste is trusted by the watchers of those shows. So in a weird twist of fate, I am able to function in much the same way that, say, Wolfman Jack did back in 1970—by finding songs and helping people discover new music.[13]

What types of scenes require songs rather than music written by the film composer?

There are certain obvious places where we put songs from bands. Source music is one of them—every time a character in a film or show turns on a radio, walks into a bar, sits in a waiting room, or turns on a jukebox. Then there are the cues in which the composer and the music supervisor must work together to decide whether a composed piece or a song from a band would work best. Things such as a musical montage segment sometimes work great with a band and sometimes it works great with a composer's own work.

Can you generalize about what particular attributes of a song make it useful for a film or TV show?

What you're looking for first in a particular scene is credibility (as opposed to musical innovation), and everything follows after.

By "credibility" do you mean that the song has authenticity from a stylistic standpoint?

You're getting there. But I actually mean it more literally than metaphorically. What I'm saying is that you as a listener need to believe it. Forget that it's music for a second.

If it were a person talking to you and telling you something, would you believe them, or would you think that they were not credible, not believable?

Based on the lyrics?

Just ask yourself if the music captures an emotional component of a scene that needs to be there. Because the component is emotional, it can't ring false. An example of a song that lacks credibility would be one in which the composer tries too hard to be literal with the lyrics and what's going on in a particular scene and ends up with something that's too matchy-matchy.

What happens when a noncredible song is used?

If there's one insincere note in the song, the actors will look like bad actors. One song in the background that's baloney can wipe out the hard work of an actor, a lighting designer, or a set director.

Do you ever go to music libraries for material?

Yes, I absolutely do. Mostly for instrumental tracks, and mostly if a particular scene requires a style of music that my composer isn't familiar with.

For a song to be considered for a movie, I assume that it has to have a certain level of quality, production-wise.

Yeah, absolutely. These days, everybody has to have high-quality production. Nobody is walking around with a four-track cassette tape anymore.

There's a big variation in quality on independently released CDs.

That's true. But practically speaking, if the mix is okay, the music is fine by the time it gets compressed and pushed into the background of a TV show. In fact, we've run with MP3s on TV shows and haven't had a problem. What makes the interests of the band musicians align with the music supervisor's is that the guy who's playing in a band has rehearsed and performed these songs in front of people repeatedly. And he has had the benefit of what—to an ad agency, for example—would be a very expensive focus group. He's playing the songs over and over again, and that's why he's getting a crowd to come and see him. That's the reason a well-placed band track will leap off the screen, compared to a custom-composed song for that particular scene. Now that is my own personal taste; that's subjective. And a band benefits from having its song on a TV show or in a film in ways that a composer sitting at home doesn't. Even though they both get performance-rights royalties and some sort of a license fee.

What's a typical licensing fee that an artist would get for use of his song in a movie or TV show?

Some TV shows pay less than $500 for an up-front license fee.

How can artists maximize their exposure to music supervisors?

If your band is successful locally and you are playing a great gig that gathers a large crowd, and you look out into the audience and ask yourself if there might be someone in that audience who might help your career, it's more likely that a music supervisor is out there scouting than a record company executive.

Is it only in L.A. and New York that this happens, or can it happen in, say, Lubbock, Texas?

It could happen to somebody in Lubbock. I'm not going to fly to Lubbock to see a country band perform, but I am going to pick up the phone and I'm going to call someone who knows country music and ask them to tell me who is out there right now playing, and who is good.

Do you require people to get permission from you to submit something?

That's an interesting question. Oftentimes with record companies you can't even find their address. There's all that crazy, weird secrecy. That's not true at all for me—not one bit. If I solicit for a song through a network, I give an address. Whoever answers is submitting based on my solicitation.

So music supervisors are generally more accessible than record company A&R people?

We're on the ground. We're where the rubber hits the road, where music meets film. We are actually interested in finding new music, and we aren't motivated in the way that so many record companies are: by profit and sale of the album. We're seeking out and searching for songs that fit scenes. So when you submit your work to us, we'll truly listen to it. We don't have prejudice between a known band and an unknown band.

From *Electronic Musician* 23, no. 2 (February 2007), 80, 82.

Part 8

TODAY, TOMORROW

18

FIN DE SIÈCLE

Almost as soon as film music had evolved from its hit-or-miss beginnings during the "cinema of attraction"[1] period into something resembling an actual practice for the accompaniment of narrative films in the nickelodeon period,[2] persons who for one reason or another cared about the incipient art argued intensely for the use of music somehow appropriate to the on-screen drama. They argued about the artistic merit of music that was heard, or *should* be heard, in the filmic context, about whether it was even possible for truly "good" music to work in a situation where the audience's attention was most likely not on the music itself. And they argued about the utility in film of music that had a life of its own quite apart from the cinema and which, for most audience members, would—for better or worse—immediately ring the proverbial bell.

At the end of the twentieth century, many of the same concerns still circulated. Film music is of course different from what it was during its formative years, but it is also very different from what it was during its so-called Golden Age. In the 1930s, when the making of sound films in Hollywood and Europe began to approach its state of "classical perfection,"[3] film music similarly settled into a standardized mode of operation that allowed for a "classical" style of both production and content. But the Golden Age of film music lasted only as long as the studio system that supported it.[4] Around 1950 the studio system for various economic and political reasons started to dissolve, and with it went its infrastructure of staff orchestras, composers, and music editors. Around 1950, too, filmmakers in Europe and later in the United States began responding more and more overtly to what they perceived as profound societal changes. The postwar world, it seemed, wanted a new type of narrative film; thus was born a new type of film music—rather, thus was born a variety of new types of film music, each of which subsequently moved along its own path.

The practice of film music today is every bit as eclectic as it was a hundred years ago, and its very diversity has prompted echoes of the debates that flare in the earliest film-music literature. The documents collected in this section of the anthology all come from the pens of journalists; based on observation of the scene, they represent as wide a range of opinion about film music's purposes, qualities, and formats as one can imagine.

———————————

18.1 FILM MUSIC HAS TWO MASTERS

Donal Henahan

Donal Henahan (b. 1929) worked for the Chicago Daily News *first as a general news reporter and then, beginning in 1957, as a music critic. While based in Chicago he contributed often to such publications as* Saturday Review, *the* Musical Quarterly, Stereo Review, *and* High Fidelity. *In 1967 he joined the staff of the* New York Times *and in 1980 succeeded Harold C. Schonberg as the paper's chief music critic.*

The issue that Henahan addresses here is one that bothered filmmakers during the heyday of the silent film and came especially to the fore in the early years of the sound film. Music drawn from the canon of masterpieces, or from the lesser known works of composers who count among the great masters, is indeed often highly suited to whatever mood a filmmaker might be trying to establish. But what happens when an audience member is intimately familiar with that music? Does the music in fact enhance the filmic experience in the way that the filmmaker presumably intended, or does a previously existing relationship with the music prove distracting?

Filmmakers in the early 1930s solved the problem quickly enough by instructing their contracted composers to concoct scores that mimicked the emotive content of certain types of classical music but which were, in fact, completely original. A half-century later many filmmakers—several of which are mentioned in Henahan's article—were seeing value in appropriating for their purposes bits of classical music which clearly would be recognized as such even by relatively unsophisticated audiences. Henahan begins his article by protesting loudly against the use in films of classical music that he knows and loves; he ends the article—tellingly—by admitting that, if sensitively handled, classical music in films can indeed be highly effective.

Oh, the power of music to stir the coals of memory—and, *pace* Noël Coward, it needn't be cheap music, either.[5] Although twenty years must have passed since I saw Bo Widerberg's *Elvira Madigan* for the first and only time, the mood of that sweetly pathetic, sun-dappled Swedish film came stealing back the other evening as I sat listening to Alicia de Larrocha play the Andante from the Piano Concerto No. 21 at a Mostly Mozart concert.[6] This has happened to me before during especially sensitive performances of this work, and I invariably feel guilty. No doubt I should, a little.

My generation of music critics was taught to be uncompromising in such matters. I was therefore not surprised to see the evening's program notes ticking off the film as usual: Widerberg is unforgiven, it seems, for having "brutalized" Mozart's poignant piece in the pursuit of cinematic gain. That certainly has been the conventional wisdom among us serious Mozartians ever since Widerberg excerpted the Andante from Geza Anda's recording of the concerto and turned it into a soundtrack back in 1967.

However, I have found my own righteous disdain softening in recent years. It still bothers me when certain deeply cherished pieces of music are merged with visual images in such a way that the sounds take on a film master's specific meanings, thereby depriving me of my own—or at any rate trying to. In that respect, Ingmar Bergman has a lot to answer for in the next world. I can't pinpoint which of his films to blame, but whenever

I hear a recording of Casals playing a Bach suite I am trapped in a dark room with a morbidly depressed woman. Outside the window, I believe, large black birds flap menacingly. It is hard for me to believe that Casals is somehow not to blame.

But directors are not going to abandon the practice of stealing from the classics, and why should they, when a few bars of, say, the "Moonlight" Sonata can quickly establish the atmosphere they need. Rather often, of course, the fit is not so perfect. For his *Jean de Florette*, a notable film in so many ways, Claude Berri uses themes from *La Forza del Destino*, probably as a literary device to point up the doomed hero's struggle.[7] However, Verdi's music adds little to the film beyond the ironic humor of its title.

For *Elvira Madigan*, on the contrary, the choice of music was clairvoyantly right. The innocent sentimentality of the film was both tempered and refined by the pathos of the Mozart melody, with its pained, throbbing accompaniment. It did not hurt, of course, that the camera work was memorably beautiful, offering painterly images that the music helped imprint on the memory.

Such a perfect match between filmed drama and music does not happen often, but when it does, it ought not to be scorned. I can think offhand of only a few similar examples, though you may have a dozen of your own. It is difficult to imagine, for instance, what Werner Herzog's *Fitzcarraldo* might have been without its Caruso records weaving in and out of the dramatic fabric.[8] It will be a long time before I lose the sound and sight of that crank-up phonograph on the prow of the obsessed opera lover's steamer, croaking its siren songs at unseen natives in the Amazon jungle. Caruso was not dishonored by being shanghaied into this film, far from it. In a sense, he was its true hero and moving force.

Luchino Visconti, whose use of music in his films is often heavy-handed, could hardly have chosen more sensitively in his *Death in Venice*, which opens with a motor launch carrying Aschenbach toward Venice while the Adagietto from Mahler's Fifth Symphony murmurs its message of resignation. Perhaps less strikingly right but memorable enough is the scene in the salon where the dying writer watches as the beautiful boy Tadzio haltingly picks out with one finger the first few measures of *Für Elise*. The innocence of the tune is thrown into contrast with the old man's guilty intimations of desire.[9]

There is excellent music whose use in films somehow does not bring charges of brutalization. Nobody, as I recall, thought that Ligeti and Johann Strauss Jr. were degraded when Stanley Kubrick grafted recordings of their works onto his *2001: A Space Odyssey*.[10] Some Bizet admirers certainly did tear their garments over *Carmen Jones* and probably not all Verdians thought *A Night at the Opera* did *Il Trovatore* justice.[11] But generally music lovers tolerate such plundering of the classics quite well. George Balanchine was not accused of brutalizing Tchaikovsky's *Serenade for Strings* when he made one of his greatest ballets of it. His *Scottish Symphony* was also greeted without much rancor, although it dispensed with the first movement of Mendelssohn's score. There was indeed a certain amount of dismay registered over the potpourri of Mozart served up in *Amadeus*, perhaps because most critics believe, with some justice, that he is the composer who most deserves to be protected from pop-cult exploitation.[12]

Still, guilty as charged. I would have to admit that I found myself enraptured rather than outraged by the strains of "Soave sia il vento," the trio from *Così fan tutte* that recurred throughout John Schlesinger's *Sunday, Bloody Sunday*.[13] Here, I think, a director happened upon the ideal piece to sum up and dramatize the tangled emotions of his three characters. It is hard to begrudge him his triumph, even if I find that I listen to Mozart's brief but potent trio at the opera nowadays with some ambivalence, reminded of the film's allusive mood and yet a bit irritated at the distraction.

All I am saying, your honor, is that I find it possible to love the slow movement of Mozart's Piano Concerto No. 21 for its musically pure, unspecific self alone, while still permitting memories of *Elvira Madigan* to steal upon me when I hear it played well. So, jail me.

From *New York Times*, July 19, 1987, H1, H23.

18.2 IN HOLLYWOOD, DISCORD ON WHAT MAKES MUSIC

David Mermelstein

David Mermelstein is a prolific freelance writer whose work has appeared regularly in such publications as The New Criterion, *the* Wall Street Journal, Variety, *the* New York Times, *and the* Los Angeles Times. *Most of his articles have dealt with mainstream classical and, in particular, opera. The relationship between opera and film music is of course a close one, and it is hardly surprising that Mermelstein, when he relocated from New York to Los Angeles around the time this article was written, was drawn to the latest film-music brouhaha.*

To put this piece into perspective, readers might want to refer to the comparably headlined Los Angeles Times *article from 1967 (p. 189 of this volume). In that article, composer Jerry Goldsmith is quoted as saying that "many of the older guys" on the film-music scene seem not to have understood that "the whole style of film-making has changed." In this article from three decades later, Goldsmith himself speaks as one of "the older guys," bemoaning—as Elmer Bernstein and David Raksin did in the documents from the mid-1970s included in Chapter 12 "Gloom and Doom" of this volume—that in current Hollywood there seems to be "a preponderance of dilettantes and sophomoric people" and, as a result, "now is certainly not the greatest time for film music."*

But at least Goldsmith admits, hopefully, that "filmmaking is a cyclical thing."

LOS ANGELES—At a time when loose collections of pop songs increasingly displace integrated orchestral scores in motion pictures, it makes sense that composers and cinéphiles alike are nostalgically looking back to an era when film music was a vibrant and respected art.

But beyond objecting to the use of songs, many people in the movie business insist that film scores themselves have declined in quality. These people rhapsodize about a golden age of film scoring, a time when rigorously schooled composers like Bernard Herrmann (*Vertigo*) and Franz Waxman (*Sunset Boulevard*) wrote music that not only amplified a film's dramatic action but also possessed considerable artistic merit in its own right.

With the proliferation of electronic editing and other computer-driven habits, many of today's younger film composers never develop the basic musical skills that were once essential in fashioning a score. And it's the absence of those skills that many movie professionals believe is the primary reason for a paucity of good film music now.

"I think it's shocking the number of so-called composers who can't even read music," says Jerry Goldsmith, 68, one of Hollywood's most distinguished composers and an outspoken critic of how the film industry currently seems to devalue the talents of skilled musicians. His more than 170 scores include music for the recently released *L.A. Confidential* as well as for classic films like *Planet of the Apes*, *Patton*, *Papillon*, *Chinatown*, *The Omen* and *Basic Instinct*.

David Raksin, who at 83 is generally regarded as the dean of American screen composers, shares Mr. Goldsmith's view. "There's no doubt about it: quality in this sort of work hardly exists anymore," he said. And he certainly has the credentials to comment. He received his start in cinema arranging Charlie Chaplin's music for *Modern Times* and went on to compose benchmark scores of the 1940s and '50s like those for *Laura* and *The Bad and the Beautiful*.

Not all members of the Hollywood musical establishment so bemoan the situation. The conductor John Mauceri has lately made something of a career resurrecting old film scores and presenting them, but he finds value in the new way of doing things as well. "I'm not sure that if a composer has vision, the absence of training is as important as it used to be," he said. "All this wailing and moaning about training can be countered by the machinery we have now, which allows people to accomplish what they otherwise could do only through musical notation. Is this a bad thing? Only if the machine breaks."

In any case, the appreciation of classic film scores has never been higher. And thanks to an increasing number of compact discs, even people unfamiliar with the movies that inspired the scores can acquaint themselves with the music.

Where classical-music labels once held up their noses at such material, they now see good business and stock their catalogues with newly realized versions of old film scores. Nonesuch, for example, has just started a series of collections of scores performed by major orchestras and well-regarded conductors like John Adams, David Zinman and Hugh Wolff.

"It's not the classical music of our time, as some people insist," said Robert Hurwitz, the president of Nonesuch and the executive producer of the film-music series. "But this music is part of the fabric, part of the panorama of music in the twentieth century. If you refer to Benjamin Britten and Dmitri Shostakovich, you must also make mention of Alex North and Toru Takemitsu."

Mr. North, who died in 1991, scored classics like *A Streetcar Named Desire*, *Spartacus*, *The Misfits* and *Who's Afraid of Virginia Woolf?* Mr. Takemitsu, who died last year, created the music for *Black Rain* and *Woman in the Dunes*, among many other films.

For the most part, it's these old scores, not newer ones, that attract the interest of connoisseurs. According to Mr. Goldsmith, it's easy to figure out why. "I blame it on all the high-tech stuff we have: the synthesizer and MIDI and computers," he said. "Some guy puts three knuckles together and thinks it sounds like film music. It's sad that mediocrity is so readily accepted today."

Not everyone involved with film scoring agrees that it is in a tailspin, however. One of the younger composers Mr. Goldsmith most admirers is David Newman, a son of Alfred Newman. The elder Newman, who died in 1970, was a legendary figure in

Hollywood. A music director for Twentieth Century-Fox from the early sound days, he wrote more than 250 scores and won eight Academy Awards.

David Newman, with his brother Thomas and his well-known cousin Randy, is carrying on in the family tradition. At 43, he has composed the scores to films like *The War of the Roses*, *Hoffa*, *The Flintstones* and the forthcoming *Anastasia*. A classically trained musician who holds degrees from the University of Southern California, he insists that a solid musical education provides the best foundation for a career as a film composer, but he also sees other legitimate paths to success. "Many people believe that what matters is the product, not how it is achieved," he said. "And a lot of people have different kinds of training these days. They approach film scoring more like a record producer would."

He points out that Hollywood composers have long depended on a host of assistants to carry out time-consuming chores like orchestration. The difference now is that the assistants must assume greater responsibilities. "In the past, these people copied short scores into full scores," he said. "These days, they take ideas and transform them into digitalized scores."

Ask about composers who have prospered despite a lack of formal musical training, and the first name to come up is Danny Elfman's. Mr. Elfman, who is 44 and was the leader of the rock band Oingo Boingo, has composed scores for hit films like *Men in Black*, *Batman*, *Beetlejuice* and *Edward Scissorhands*. His forthcoming scores include Gus Van Sant's *Good Will Hunting* and Disney's *Flubber*.

Mr. Elfman is yet another admirer of classic film music; he even cites it as an inspiration for his work. And he, too, notes a decline in the quality of music in movies. "The older film scores had more individual voices," he said. "And the style of those voices was clearer. It's very disheartening to hear a mishmash."

Even Mr. Elfman admitted that a traditional musical background made a career in film composition easier. But he added: "Just having a great classical education doesn't make you a great film composer. Ultimately, it's all about storytelling, and it doesn't matter whether you come from a film or music background."

Is film scoring really mostly about storytelling? Mr. Goldsmith thinks it is. "Writing good music is only part of the process," he said. "It's writing the right music for a given dramatic situation that matters. When I was just starting out, David Raksin told me that music needs to work with the picture and without the picture. That's still true today."

One of the most respected film composers of the so-called golden age was Mr. North. His widow, Anna, well remembers his feelings about music's role in movies. "Story content was the most important thing for Alex," she said. "He was very selective when it came to his work and so admired the written word. He saw his craft as a way to amplify that."

The composer Elmer Bernstein, 75, considers himself lucky to have entered the film world when he did. In the early 1950s, Mr. Bernstein, who like Mr. Goldsmith is among the most sought-after film scorers in the business, is responsible for the music in films like *The Sweet Smell of Success*, *The Magnificent Seven* and, most recently, *Hoodlum*. "I've always perceived the purpose of a good score to be to support a film," he said.

In the past, it was common for directors to share Mr. Bernstein's view. They, too, saw scores as a means of furthering a film's emotional reach. Elia Kazan, for instance, had very specific ideas about what the scores for his films would convey. When he chose Mr. North to compose the music for *A Streetcar Named Desire*, for example, the director knew what he was looking for. "I wanted Alex North for *Streetcar* because he knew jazz, and jazz was New Orleans," the director recalled.

Mike Nichols also worked with Mr. North, on *Who's Afraid of Virginia Woolf?* He said that the work between director and composer, which usually takes place toward the end of the filming process, was above all a matter of chemistry. "Alex's approach was gentle and collaborative," he said.

Perhaps the most famous music in a Mike Nichols film, however, isn't a score at all; it's the series of songs written by Paul Simon for *The Graduate*. Nowadays, it's common for a string of songs to replace the traditional score in a film, but in 1967, when *The Graduate* had its premiere, this was not the case.

Mr. Nichols decided to break with tradition because, he said, the songs reflected the subconscious voice of the film's protagonist. But he acknowledges that employing songs instead of an orchestral score presents certain problems. "Using songs is wonderful, but it's difficult," he said. "It should never sound like someone's just flipped on a radio. Songs and dialogue generally don't go well together, and when you have a lot of dialogue, it gets complicated."

Many film composers believe that too little care is taken when directors use songs instead of scores in their movies. Moreover, it is now generally felt that the decision to use songs is less an artistic choice than a financial one. David Newman was blunt in his assessment. "I think there's a huge push for the studios to do cross-promotion with the record labels they're affiliated with," he said. "It makes money for them, and money is a big factor."

Yet film composers appear to remain hopeful about the future.

"Now is certainly not the greatest time for film music," said Mr. Goldsmith. "There's a preponderance of dilettantes and sophomoric people in the business, but filmmaking is a cyclical thing. Those who have talent will grow regardless of the circumstances. And those who don't will ultimately fall by the wayside."

Mr. Raksin put it this way: "Film scoring is too vital a part of movie-making for there to be no hope. The necessity of a score is what will rescue it."

From *New York Times*, November 2, 1997, AR17, AR30.

18.3 KEEPING SCORES: GOOD OLD-FASHIONED MOVIE MUSIC IS AS HEALTHY AS IT EVER WAS

James Hunter

James Hunter is a freelancer who writes about not just music but also books. He maintains a strong interest in vintage music, as is evidenced by his contributions to Nostalgia *and* The Journal of Country Music. *At the same time, he keeps his finger on the pulse of contemporary popular music, as is evidenced by his work for* Rolling Stone, Vibe, US Weekly, *the* New York Times Magazine, *and—perhaps most impressively—the Manhattan-based weekly* The Village Voice.

Contrary to what might be gathered on first impression from its headline, the article reproduced here deals not all with a resurgence of scores along the lines of those that animated films during film music's so-called Golden Age. Rather, it deals with late twentieth-century music that, while its sound is obviously different from that of film music in the 1930s and 1940s, nevertheless functions in ways that hold to the model of the classical-style film score.

The adjective "old-fashioned," readers might note, appears nowhere in Hunter's text; it is a creation of an anonymous headline writer, who surely deserves credit for perceiving that the recent music that attracted Hunter's attention indeed has much in common—in terms of its function within the filmic narrative—with film music from "the good old days." Hunter refers to film music as "that knowing mongrelization of European concert music or jazz or whatever" that, somehow, serves a film's dramatic purposes. With that definition, probably most composers from film music's Golden Age would readily agree.

A decade ago, bestselling multi-artist compilations and their smash singles redefined how millions of people use movie soundtracks. *Flashdance*! *Beverly Hills Cop*! *Vision Quest*! Reacting against the incursion of Bombay procedures into the American entertainment industries, film-music buffs—as well as those who despised multi-artist compilations, those crass sources of the distressingly K-Tel[14]—cranked up their violins and deplored the fast-impending death of the film score. In fact, although Irene Cara and Eddie Murphy and Patti LaBelle could do many things, they couldn't quite murder scoring. If anything, the decade-long pop triumph of their soul songs only helped nourish and strengthen smaller parallel markets for other creative and business enterprises. With regard to what rings in your ears or haunts your head when walking out of theaters, it's still a big country.

International dance music's heroic reclamations of Burt Bacharach and the equally resonant James Bond scorer John Barry started a buzz. Last year, when David Arnold scored *Tomorrow Never Dies* (A&M), he turned it into an outright homage to the Barry-written and -orchestrated 007 soundtracks of the '60s and '70s, affectionately shading everything with a taut quotational air aimed, wryly if perhaps unintentionally, at the sampling generation. Right now, as Rykodisc reissues Bacharach's *After the Fox* and *What's New Pussycat?*, Elvis Costello and Bacharach, in their *Painted From Memory* collaboration, tap not only the New York Californian's songwriting facility but also his scoring genius for Florentine swoops and coloristic strings.[15]

A lot of other action surrounds those transatlantic titans. Komeda, texture-mad popheads from northernmost Sweden, name themselves after Roman Polanski's '60s scorer, Christoph Komeda.[16] Rialto, from London, project their guitar-rock tunes onto sonic canvases fashioned from cool old cinematic ambiences. Rykodisc also reissues scores from *Some Like It Hot*, *Elmer Gantry*, *Never on Sunday*, and many deluxe others. Repertoire-minded Nonesuch entered the game in 1997, commissioning stark new recordings, under the direction of John Adams and others, of film music by Georges Delerue (*Music From the Films of François Truffaut*), Alex North, Leonard Rosenman, and Toru Takemitsu.

Indie-rock kids, meantime, smirk along to the swingy music written for '70s German porn—Gert Wilson & Orchestra's *Schoolgirl Report* on Crippled Dick is a popular title—and the seven crowded volumes of Easy Tempo (Right Tempo import) that collect vividly pointed scorings from predominately '60s and '70s Italian curiosities. For retroists, and what remains of the art-film crowd, there's *Cannes Film Festival: 50th Anniversary Album* (Milan), which features things like Herbie Hancock's strolling theme from *Blow-Up* and Nino Rota's seaside-boulevard rhapsody from *La Dolce Vita*,[17] as well as *The Music of Rainer Werner Fassbinder Films*, which collects the shivering brocades of Peer Raben.[18] In 1996, even Motown got hip, squaring film music and hip-hop iconography with its reissue of Willie Hutch's 1973 *The Mack*, the kind of nonstop accumulation of juicy beats and riffs the Chemical Brothers can't get enough of.

Film music has always had its international franchises, like Rota, whose zesty yet considered music for Federico Fellini yielded the Hal Willner produced 1981 collection by American jazz musicians, *Amarcord Nino Rota* (Hannibal), not to mention the Elvis Presley of the field, Ennio Morricone, the apparently indefatigable old Roman whose hearty woodwinds for 1997's *U Turn* leapt with the rich spring of a recent conservatory grad's. And from Bill Conti's '70s *Rocky* extravaganzas (a Puff Daddy fave) to James Horner's '90s *Titanic* hominess, the odd scoring megaseller does occur.[19]

Yet they're often a personal thing, scores, and not a little screwy. For a moment, Christopher Young's sizzlingly contrasted negotiation of Bernard Herrmann's symphonic moodiness and his own edgy piano élan convinced me that *Jennifer Eight* (Milan) was the most stylish thriller ever. The soundtrack to Joseph Conrad's *The Secret Agent* (Nonesuch), where the English Chamber Orchestra romanticizes Philip Glass's pointillistic writing with blood-and-guts intensity, worked a comparable magic on a film I no longer believe synthesizes twentieth-century panic and nineteenth-century dread quite so perfectly. Other times, everything clicks: the silvery, occasionally sad cool-jazz Mark Isham put together for *Afterglow* (Columbia) is like a meditation on Miles Davis praising both leading ladies, Julie Christie and Lara Flynn Boyle. And my vote for the coolest piece of recorded music ever released in the United States would go to a vinyl album from the '60s on Columbia. The black-and-white cover shows a head shot of John Barry, looking for all the world like a member of Traffic. *Ready When You Are, J.B.: John Barry Plays His Great Movie Hits*, it's called.

So, while some may prefer Ry Cooder smuggling retooled rock vibes onto the screen, four instrumental soundtracks this year stand out because they do, in fact, seem like movie music, that knowing mongrelization of European concert music or jazz or whatever, the calculated yet never dry stuff that allows only, in the words of the Art of Noise co-founder and Oscar-winning scorer Anne Dudley, "the good bits." Gavin Friday and Maurice Seezer's lush score for *The Boxer* (MCA) isn't all Irish Film Orchestra; it also includes morsels of industrial noise and even a few guitar stylings in the Cooder mode. But the orchestral stuff is momentous: long lines falling into hushed dips, often fortified by piano, with full harmonies luxuriating in space, occasionally answered by Monteverdi-like chorales in, naturally, minor keys.[20]

In their aggressive beauty, Friday and Seezer recall the peerless Ryuichi Sakamoto, who wrote the symphonic parts for *The Last Emperor*, and whose latest classic is *Love Is the Devil* (Asphodel).[21] Electronicism and Debussy-like chord clusters have long compelled Sakamoto, and on this very scene-dictated score, twenty-eight pieces with titles like "Museum" and "Toilet," he mates his interest in both, placing borderline-static electronic soundscapes alongside more-frenetic passages, alternating these with a percussive piano melodicism that itself often discusses immobility, entrapment, and suffocation.

The most striking score of 1998, though, does something else entirely, sustaining, with a lot of shifting around, one unshakable mood that sounds brand-new. For *High Art*

(Velvel), the rock band Shudder To Think put velvety basses on top of slowed-down, crummy-toned techno grooves, accenting everything with brief guitar outbursts, stray keyboard notes, and occasional Middle Eastern figures.[22] The result is movie music as imagined by rockers tired of rock, expansive and Miles-like in bluesy places, abrupt and Eno-fed in others. The tone—unremitting Downtown rattiness—stays put as the tempos pick up ("Mom's Mercedes"), go flat ("Photographic Ecstasy"), or stretch out ("The Gavial"). This is cinematic grandeur as conceived by channel surfers, tranced-out and insomniac.

But the slightly earnest novelty, the realized creative striving of *High Art*, is a fluke right now. What's really happened to film music is that, like everything from new shoes Petula Clark could have bought thirty years ago to bicycles whose thick fenders might have excited Beaver Cleaver, it's discovered the comforts of the neoclassic, the notion that a certain kind of mood and composition and approach can seem not only timeless but completely modern. "Tony's brief to me for the music was 'big and elegiac,'" Anne Dudley writes of director Tony Kaye in the liner notes to her dizzyingly intense score for *American History X* (Angel). "He felt the score should somehow stand apart from the events on the screen and underline the deeper implications." So Dudley and her orchestra do their hugely symphonic interknittings of nineteenth-century gravitas, sacred concentrations, and personal tragedy. It's not how John Barry did it when his flugelhorns elaborated on the cut of James Bond's dinner jacket. But these days, things move on, even as they don't.

From *The Village Voice*, November 10, 1998, 43, 45.

18.4 MANY WAYS TO SCORE

New pop, old-school scorers go to the movies together

Catherine Applefeld Olson

Catherine Applefeld Olson is a freelance journalist based in Alexandria, Virginia. Over the past two decades she has written for numerous publications, including Home & Design, Teaching Music, Child Magazine, *and* Time Out New York. *Most often, however, her reportage has appeared in* Billboard, *which began in 1894 as a broadsheet announcing performance events in the New York area, later expanded to cover virtually all other aspects of the entertainment industry, and since the 1990s has focused—as it did in the years surrounding World War II—on the music industry.*

In contrast to some of the articles on popular music in film that appeared earlier in this anthology, the document reproduced here lists no sales figures. Indeed, its topic is not the financial 'scores' that often result from a top-selling soundtrack album but, rather, the challenges encountered by directors who look to rock for their underscores and the synergy that sometimes results from mixing rock with film music of a more conventional sort. Along with a recording company executive who sees the situation from all sides, the subjects of Olson's interviews are a pair of rock musicians fairly new to the film scoring business and a pair of seasoned mainstream film music composers who have cooperated—apparently productively—with rockers.

Although some degree of change is a constant in the world of moviemaking, an influx of "new" composers from the pop, rock and R&B communities has rendered the classic art of film scoring anything but the same old song these days.

Film's [attraction] to non-traditional film composers is not a new scenario, but it recently has gained enough strength to bump it from the category of phenomenon and create yet another potentially lucrative avenue for soundtracks.[23] Artists such as David Byrne, Peter Gabriel and Tom Waits have been joined by Shudder To Think, Mark Mothersbaugh, Wyclef Jean and a host of others who have placed their distinct stamp on scores to recent movies.

Smashing Pumpkins' front-man Billy Corgan, who wrote a portion of the score to *Stigmata*, says he had been trolling around for a film gig as far back as '94 but had never found the right opportunity. "There were different things floating around, but no one took me seriously, or I didn't take them seriously," he says. Virgin released the *Stigmata* soundtrack last month.

Meeting of Minds

Expecting his meeting with *Stigmata* director Rupert Wainwright and producer Frank Mancuso Jr., a fan of the Pumpkins, to follow a similar path, Corgan says he was surprised by the support he received for his artistic vision. "The music I described to them was dark and brooding and atonal. I told them what I wanted to do was way too dark for a Hollywood movie, but they said, 'Don't be so sure.'"

Yet, despite his own positive experience, Corgan believes Hollywood filmmakers still don't pay much attention to the rock and pop worlds. "I don't think an opportunity like this would have come to me in '94," he says. "Now I am at a place where people recognize who I am, and certainly you can't disregard the commercial aspect of it. It's a fact that attaching my name to something like this gives a certain feel. As filmmakers look for other ways to bring music to movies and other ways of advertising and reaching other people, it makes sense to branch out. I'd like to think it was all musical, but I know that's not necessarily the case."

To show they are taking their filmscoring duties seriously, many of the new school of composers are establishing their new identities from the outset. Rocker Chris Vrenna, who used to play with Nine Inch Nails and has remixed songs for several soundtracks, including *Godzilla*, recently signed as a film composer client at Creative Artists Agency and is shopping around for a project.

"The kind of music I've fallen into making for myself is instrumental and electronic music, and that's kind of how I see film scores," Vrenna says. "And Hollywood is starting to move into that world as well. As Hollywood becomes younger and is looking at different approaches, this kind of music makes sense."

Vrenna says he has had meetings with several filmmakers and is encouraged by their interest in seeking out nontraditional film composers. "Some of the most successful movies are directly targeted to younger crowds, and those younger crowds listen to heavy metal and dance music, so it seems a natural crossover to be able to have music more set up for that kind of audience."

Souvenirs to Films

Russell Ziecker, senior VP/GM at BMG-distributed Milan Entertainment, says he has noticed heightened buzz surrounding recording artists wanting to make their mark in film. "I create souvenirs to films, and, if that souvenir comes from a rock artist or a composer that's traditional, it doesn't matter to me," he says.

Nevertheless, Ziecker says film composers who "cross over" from a rock background tend at least initially to be burdened with stereotypes. "Legit composers tend to look at rock guys or ex-rock guys as not legit," he says. "Billy Corgan temporarily has a career in both worlds, but he is a rock musician. Composers like Danny Elfman and Michael Kamen to some extent turned their back on their rock career in favor of being film composers. It is a rare exception to bridge both."

Elia Cmiral, who wrote the score portions of *Stigmata* that Corgan did not, says that, although he and Corgan had little interaction, the existence of two composers on one film—particularly composers from such different worlds—pushed him to excel.

"To have another composer from a completely different field working on the score requires even more sensitive writing and processing of the music," Cmiral says. "Working with Billy was extremely inspiring. And there is no doubt it was the right decision; the result is great."

Classically trained John Debney, whose credits include *I Know What You Did Last Summer* and *Dick*, says his score for the upcoming Arnold Schwarzenegger actioner *End Of Days* likely will include a counterpart from the rock world. "We have a number of songs from really great bands, and the idea was to make the songs and the underscore not seem like two separate elements, to somehow blend the songs with the score," Debney explains. "I think we can all agree that one of the things that's a little bothersome is when a lot of songs are thrown into a film just for a record. To have them all integrated and flow into each other is a much more elegant way to do it."

Debney says he believes there will be more instances of schooled film composers working with rock artists as time goes on. "It only makes sense. In the past, film composers and music supervisors have lived in two worlds. It is so much better for film if we can all be on the same page and communicate and collaborate together," he says.

In the case of *Days*, he says, "I've written all the themes, and I'd like to give them to an artist who would take them and do what he does so well: produce or remix a new piece from a theme of mine that is cutting-edge and contemporary."

From *Billboard* 111, no. 43 (October 23, 1999), 22.

19

ONWARD AND UPWARD?

The headlines introducing the four articles in the preceding chapter perhaps tell film music's entire story. Any bit of handiwork that puts itself at the service of a multimedia art form is in the difficult position of serving, at the very least, two masters; in Hollywood and everywhere else that movies are made there is—as there has always been—discord regarding what type of music best serves any film's needs; for all the variety of music that today's films offer, the fundamental and essentially old-fashioned idea of music as a support to filmic narrative seems as healthy as it ever was; film itself being so wonderfully diverse in its genres and styles, there are of course many ways, and many idioms, in which films can be scored. The articles bearing those apt headlines date from the 1990s; with adjustments for detail, they could have been written in the 1980s or the 1960s, or they could be written tomorrow.

Readers inclined to make prognostications for film music's future might profit by reviewing this volume's darkest statements, in particular the similarly titled articles by Elmer Bernstein and David Raksin (pp. 178–183) in Chapter 12, "Gloom and Doom," and also the comments from Jerry Goldsmith in the just-mentioned article about discord in Hollywood (p. 189) and the various news items cited by Steven C. Smith in his "Hit or Miss" article (p. 224). It is easy to see how a composer who for decades had honed a specialized craft might be miffed by the overnight success of a young upstart who seemed not to know the first thing about that craft. It is easy, too, to understand the bitterness of a composer who had worked hard to create exactly the score a director wanted only to have his work tossed out at the last minute because the director suddenly changed his mind. For composers who have nourished a life-long respect not only for the instruments of the orchestra but also for the talented human beings who play them, the mere idea of a "sampler" must make the blood run cold; for composers who know that a scene of action or romance or suspense can be controlled as much by nuanced underscore as by acting and lighting, it is probably not much fun to experience such a scene washed over by a store-bought pop song.

The negativity expressed in those documents is worth reviewing, because it puts into perspective the overwhelmingly positive attitudes evidenced in so many of this volume's other documents. In style and content, film music has *never* been static; regardless of its time period or nation of origin, it has been part of the always-moving flow of culture. Now and then film music has settled into something resembling a mainstream, and its enthusiasts have certainly created a pantheon of Great Men against whose canonized Great Works the efforts of everyone else seem hardly worth measuring. But experiments took place regularly even during film music's Golden Age, and the 'good old days'—whenever they occurred—were constantly enlivened by new ideas.

The articles that comprise this final chapter muse on film music's present state and, by implication if not overtly, on film music's future. A theme that runs through all the documents is the seriousness of it all. This is not to say that the writings give the impression that current film music is especially serious in tone, or that the persons who comment on film music are of a dour sort; rather, the collected writings suggest that almost everyone in the film music community takes the art form seriously.

Whether critics or composers, classicists or rockers, the commentators remind readers that film music—in all its dimensions and manifestations—is something that matters.

19.1 TAKING MOVIE MUSIC SERIOUSLY, LIKE IT OR NOT

David Schiff

A former student of John Corigliano at the Manhattan School of Music and Elliott Carter at the Juilliard School of Music, David Schiff (b. 1945) is a composer whose works have been commissioned by such ensembles as the Oregon Symphony Orchestra, the Seattle Symphony, the Minnesota Orchestra, and the Chamber Music Society of Lincoln Center. He has written prolifically on music of many types; his books include The Music of Elliott Carter *(1983) and* George Gershwin: Rhapsody in Blue *(1997), and his articles have appeared in the* New York Times, *the* Atlantic Monthly, Opera News, *and numerous other periodicals. Since 1980 Schiff has been a member of the musical faculty of Reed College in Portland, Oregon.*

Prompted by an up-coming program by the American Composers Orchestra, Schiff in this article muses on the idea of an artistic division between film music and music designed for the concert hall. "The opposition," he states early on, "is a phantom of the last century," and then he proceeds to give a summary account of film music at the dawn of the new millennium. His optimism stands in sharp contrast to commentators who, at various times over the decades, expressed the view that 'good' film music had in effect been displaced by a crass pandering to commercialism. Indeed, Schiff's idea that at least some film music belongs in the category of high art calls to mind the "dreams of the future" represented in Chapter 2 of this volume.

For two years in a row, the Academy Award for best film score has gone to a classical composer, first John Corigliano for *The Red Violin*, then Tan Dun for *Crouching Tiger, Hidden Dragon*. While cynics claim that this is the film industry's way of advertising its high-art pretensions, Hollywood may really be ahead of New York in acknowledging that the opposition between film music and concert music is a phantom of the last century. Today the two styles constantly interact, John Williams's scores for George Lucas's *Star Wars* movies and for Steven Spielberg's *Jaws* and *Close Encounters of the Third Kind*, which resurrected the symphonic style for film in the '70s, have also exerted a huge influence on the work of young concert composers.[1] Philip Glass's music for *Koyaanisqatsi* made Minimalism an essential component of any film composer's stylistic vocabulary.[2]

Now the American Composers Orchestra is catching up with the Motion Picture Academy, presenting a "Hollywood" concert this afternoon at Carnegie Hall that culminates a two-week series of small concerts and film screenings. The program, conducted by Dennis Russell Davies, includes music for two camp classics, the Hollywood "exposé" *The Bad and the Beautiful* (David Raksin, composer) and Alfred Hitchcock's Freudian whodunit *Spellbound* (Miklos Rozsa), the cult sci-fi thriller *The Thing* (Dimitri Tiomkin), and Hitchcock's unavoidable *Psycho* (Bernard Herrmann). Except for *Psycho*, none of these is a pinnacle of cinematic art, but each score is a milestone in film music.

The orchestra's warm embrace of Hollywood may be a deceptive sign of a thaw in the longstanding cold war between the musical cultures of the two coasts. Last year, when Washington had other scandals to think about, a minor Beltway drama—call it Kamengate—erupted around a concert by the National Symphony Orchestra that included the premiere of Michael Kamen's *New Moon in the Old Moon's Arms*. Mr. Kamen is a Juilliard-trained composer of many film scores, including *Mr. Holland's Opus*. But for Philip Kennicott, the music critic of *The Washington Post*, he represents everything wrong with music today.

Mr. Kennicott dismissed Mr. Kamen's symphony as "pretentious and pernicious tonal tripe . . . scored in the usual sodden and overripe Hollywood manner." And he blasted the National Symphony for commissioning a "well-remunerated Hollywood hack" who "doesn't need to be dipping into the paltry amount that's available to composers of serious music." Mr. Kennicott seemed to assume that commissions, like welfare payments, should be based on need. And he was nearly as harsh on works by non-Hollywood composers, criticizing Richard Danielpour's *Voice of Remembrance* as "a succession of familiar moods and feeling." In other words, it sounded like film music.

Mr. Kamen's mediocre score hardly deserved so much ink, but Mr. Kennicott's bile, like Mr. Kamen's music, sounded recycled. The classical world's anti-Hollywood bias goes back to the dawn of film music in the 1930s, when Max Steiner established the genre with *King Kong*. During the Depression, New York and Hollywood contrasted starkly. Economically, New York was broke, Hollywood was rich. Politically, New York was left, Hollywood was right.

But sound movies were new, and Hollywood needed composers; a musical gold rush was on. As lights dimmed on Broadway, Irving Berlin, Jerome Kern and the Gershwins headed west, as did Copland, Herrmann, Alex North and Jerome Moross. While the tunesmiths happily adjusted to life in paradise, modernist composers like Copland were put off by the power politics of the studio system and the lush late-Romantic style of established studio composers like Steiner and Erich Wolfgang Korngold.

In a sense, Hollywood was the new Versailles or Esterhaza. The studio moguls were princes of patronage, but composers had grown used to neglect and forgotten the advantages and disadvantages of steady employment. Every composer who got close enough to dance with the devil had a Hollywood horror story to send back east.

Disney's *Fantasia* (1940) turned Stravinsky's *Rite of Spring* into "an unresisting imbecility," in the composer's phrase, with drastic cuts and *Jurassic Park* animation. Since the score lacked copyright protection because of the Russian Revolution, Stravinsky had no choice but to accept Disney's modest remuneration and immodest editorial insults.[3] Still, he continued to seek out film projects, with little success. (Music he wrote for *The Commandos Strike at Dawn* in 1943 ended up as *Four Norwegian Moods*, also to be played by the American Composers Orchestra.)[4]

Stravinsky's archrival, Schoenberg, fared no better. Irving Thalberg hoped that Schoenberg's name would lend intellectual cachet to *The Good Earth* (1937), the MGM prestige epic based on Pearl Buck's novel. Whether in a state of delusion or merely seeking an escape hatch, Schoenberg wanted to compose pitches and rhythms for the actors' lines and demanded final editing rights. He claimed to be relieved when the collaboration fell through, saying, "It would have been the end of me."[5]

For the later *Duel in the Sun* (Vanguard, 1947), David Selznick demanded that Tiomkin whistle first a love theme, then an orgasm theme.[6] William Wyler replaced Copland's title music for *The Heiress* (Paramount, 1949) as soon as the composer left town. There are more stories, and worse.

In a 1940 *New York Times* article on film music, Copland praised the new genre but attacked Steiner's nineteenth-century style, his use of leitmotifs and his dependence on "mickey-mousing."[7] Although Copland continued to work successfully in Hollywood through 1948, his writings confirmed the East Coast view that the industry was dominated by studio hacks working in a reactionary idiom. By contrast, Hollywood honored Copland with an Oscar (for *The Heiress*, despite its non-Copland title music) and quickly appropriated his lean, modernist style for psychological dramas and the grander horse operas.[8]

Composers who remained in Hollywood were given the cold shoulder by New York. Paul Chihara said recently that Herrmann and Rozsa bitterly resented the refusal of the concert world to take their music seriously. But Mr. Chihara, whose *Clouds (. . . from out of the past)* receives its premiere in the American Composers Orchestra program, exemplifies the way times have changed.[9] A student of Nadia Boulanger with a doctorate in composition from Cornell, he has won numerous prizes and commissions for his classical scores. He has also composed for more than eighty films, including *Crossing Delancey* and *Prince of the City*, and television series, including *China Beach* and the current A&E series *100 Centre Street*.[10]

The smoky, sinuous title trumpet solo for *100 Centre Street* begins like a film noir cliché but takes a series of surprising harmonic turns that sound more like the devices of a concert composer. "I used to think I was writing in two different styles, but now they have come together," Mr. Chihara said. "Things changed for me when people told me I wasn't weird but postmodern."

Mr. Chihara, who teaches at UCLA, is in constant demand as a guest lecturer at university music departments and conservatories that used to ignore film music. For either artistic or economic reasons, the old stigma against commercial music has disappeared. "Today composition teachers want to make sure their students know how to write for movies," Mr. Chihara said.

Film music and concert music are converging in style and technology. Postmodernism, a style that emerged in the early 1970s, dominates American concert music today, but it took a while to be properly understood. George Crumb, David Del Tredici and Mr. Corigliano were, like Mr. Chihara, postmodern before the term was invented. They all mixed styles fearlessly and experimented with amplification. In his Clarinet Concerto (1977), Mr. Corigliano, whose East Coast credentials were just recertified by a Pulitzer Prize for his Symphony No. 2 for String Orchestra, placed instruments around the hall, less in imitation of Gabrieli and Ives than in anticipation of THX and surround sound.[11]

Whereas modernist music emphasized structural and stylistic integrity, postmodern music is a polystylistic hybrid, mingling and matching incongruous elements with a heavy dose of irony—just like film music. Listen to Franz Waxman's title track for *Sunset Boulevard*, and then listen to John Adams's *Chairman Dances*; they are not just stylistically similar; they are virtually the same piece.[12]

Mr. Raksin's score for *The Bad and the Beautiful* (MGM, 1952) shows how much composers today have learned from the Hollywood masters. The film itself is a couple of tall steps below such behind-the-scenes sagas as *Sunset Boulevard* and *Singing' in the Rain*, though not without its gripping moments. Teetering between conscious and unconscious self-parody, it shows a brutish genius director, played by Kirk Douglas abusing his closest friends and lovers to make "great" movies.

Pauline Kael described *The Bad and the Beautiful* as a "spangled, overwrought piece of Hollywood self-analysis" but also wrote that the director, Vincente Minnelli, gave it a "hysterical stylishness." A lot of that stylishness and hysteria is Mr. Raksin's doing. He captures the studio's seductive glamour with a romantic theme not far below his classic "Laura"; then, as the film tours the backlots, he serves up fifteen-second pastiches of B-movie scores. How many "serious" composers could evoke a cardboard cowboy-and-Indian film or a Saturday morning science fiction potboiler in such a fleeting window of opportunity?

Mr. Raksin's underscore itself is a series of ironic allusions: here a little Gershwin, there a little Ellington. In one scene, Mr. Douglas carries a limp Lana Turner in his arms against a backdrop of stormy skies. The music surges with passion in the grandest Steineresque manner. Then Mr. Douglas drops Ms. Turner into a swimming pool to sober her up, and we realize that Mr. Raksin has been parodying Hollywood's dream-factory style to sober us up as well. Interestingly, the most dramatic scene in the film, Ms. Turner driving off in terror from Mr. Douglas's ultimate act of cruelty, has no music, the ultimate form of musical irony.

Mr. Raksin's ironic juxtapositions of style make him the grandfather of current postmodernists like John Zorn and Michael Daugherty. But the collapse of the wall separating film music and art music may be a question of technology more than of style. Because it depends on recording, Hollywood has always been in the forefront of musical science, sculpturing and styling performances through microphone placement, overdubbing and editing. Both Rozsa's *Spellbound* and Tiomkin's *Thing* feature that quintessentially eerie electronic instrument, the theremin. Gregory Peck's amnesiac character in *Spellbound* seems to be suffering from theremin on the brain as well as what Ingrid Bergman keeps calling his "guilt complex."

Sixty years ago Copland enthusiastically reported on the technology of film scoring, the fine art of coordinating music and image. But today only a few composers—notably, John Williams—fit their music to the screen action in the time-honored way. The artistry with which Mr. Williams's Oscar-nominated score for *The Patriot* minutely matches the action proves the value of the traditional method, but both the artistry and the method may already be anachronistic.

"There really is no such thing as Hollywood music anymore," Mr. Chihara said. "It's all done in a garage in North Hollywood." Composers are now expected to produce the music, not just write it. Most of the music you hear on television and at the movies uses sound synthesis instead of live performers or in addition to them. The blend of live and synthesized sounds is a signature of Hans Zimmer, whose Electronica-does-Holst score for *Gladiator* was nominated for an Oscar this year. Synthesized music is cheaper, and young people, the target audience, prefer its sound.

Today the audio and video components of a film come together not on a soundstage but on a computer screen. Editing software allows composers to stretch or compress the music as needed. The new technologies may reinforce the old prejudice, resurrected by Mr. Kennicott, that film composers lack traditional musical technique. Although composers like Mr. Kamen and James Horner (*Titanic*) have full conservatory credentials, it is quite possible these days to compose and produce film music with little traditional musical training. The industry is full of notorious "hummers," whose careers depend on armies of unnamed technical assistants.

But synthesizers and computer editing are transforming concert music as well. Music publishing in its older form has virtually disappeared. Every composer today is expected to produce scores at home; all you need is a computer and a printer. And performers routinely ask composers to provide computer playback along with a score; conductors no longer even pretend to be able to imagine a score silently.

The next step is for the computer playback to begin to replace some or all aspects of live performance. As in film music, this development is spurred by economics and aesthetics. Recent scores like Mr. Adams's *Gnarly Buttons* depend on a synthesizer to give the music a sound that younger listeners will recognize as contemporary.[13] Perhaps concert music will have its share of hummers before long, if they're not out there already.

Still, there remain fundamental differences in the functioning of concert and film genres, which cause problems when composers try to cross over. The central difference is one of speed. Concert music has to fill a lot of time, but most film music cues are brief. This difference became important only with the advent of talkies. Silent movies required continuous music to cover the sound of the projector and create continuity in a flickering medium. Concert composers had room to stretch without skirting around dialogue, so they did not have to change their musical habits.

Copland's first film, *The City*, was a documentary, with a voice-over but no on-screen speech, and most of the music he used for the Suite from *The Red Pony* comes from nondramatic parts of the film.[14] Because *Crouching Tiger, Hidden Dragon* uses subtitles rather than dubbed dialogue, it works like a silent movie with broad swaths of music; a lot of it feels like a Yo-Yo Ma video.

With the talkies, film music became more fragmentary and film composing more specialized. In Mr. Raksin's *Bad and the Beautiful* score, for instance, most cues after the sustained opening are less than a minute long. This imposed brevity made film music seem irreconcilable with the concert hall. Concert composers keep their music going by a strategy of postponement, setting up expectations and delaying their fulfillment, but a film composer has to deliver the goods quickly.

A good example of instantaneous evocation comes in Copland's score for *The Heiress*. The heroine waits for a lover who will never arrive. When preview audiences laughed at Olivia de Haviland's predicament, Copland added a sudden gust of whirling woodwind music, which perfectly captured her state of nervous expectancy. The music feels like a muscle spasm. (Did anyone ask Copland to whistle a muscle spasm?) The film creates suspense by keeping us waiting to see if the caddish Montgomery Clift will ever show up; the music makes the woman's agony real, and in a matter of seconds.

Herrmann said he did not have time for an eight-bar tune; he built his film scores from two-second motifs that could do their job no matter how brief a musical cue might be. But for concertgoers used to waiting twenty minutes for Beethoven to answer his own musical questions, a succession of cues does not add up to a symphonic experience, especially when they are detached from the images they serve to amplify.

The concert hall automatically gives its own composers an edge. Some, when they cross over, conceive the concert version of their music simultaneously with the film score, as Copland did with *The Red Pony* and Mr. Corigliano did with *The Red Violin*.[15] Herrmann's *Psycho* Suite is a more complicated example, for the film score made use of a previously composed symphonic composition, but most listeners are just waiting for the shower scene anyway.[16]

Blame postmodernism or technology, but our expectations of symphonic structure have diminished; we live in an age of short attention spans and sound bites, after all, and delayed gratification is so nineteenth century. We also live in an eye rather than an ear culture. Many orchestras are talking about using some kind of video even for their classical concerts: the MTV-ization of the concert hall. When that happens, and it won't be long, everything really will be film music.

From *New York Times*, April 22, 2001, AR1, AR36.

19.2 THE SOUNDTRACK GAME IS ATTRACTING FRESH AND EDGY ARTISTS

Dylan Callaghan

Dylan Callaghan has written about almost all aspects of the filmmaking process, including the development of scripts and the adaptations of novels for the newsletter of the western division of the Writer's Guild of America. For the most part, however, his efforts since the turn of the century have focused—both in Billboard *magazine and its sister publication,* The Hollywood Reporter—*on film music.*

In contrast to the preceding article by David Schiff, Callaghan's reportorial piece focuses almost exclusively on film music's commercial side. His interviews with various industry insiders reveal that considerations of the popular music used in films include such things as the possibilities of prestige, opportunities for publicity, and even solely artistic matters. But as he observes near the end of the article, "ultimately, though, money still matters most."

In reaction to flaccid record sales, format-choked radio and a seeming glut of quick-score compilation albums, the soundtrack business today appears to have graduated to a new aesthetic high-water mark.

Increasingly competitive markets and burnout from the slapdash needle-drop records that dominated the late 1990s have conspired to make today's soundtracks artistically deeper and more relevant to the films they represent. In addition, industry figures say they are luring much more original music from an edgier, more diverse collection of pop,

293

rock, metal and hip-hop's new generation of recording artists. The game has changed and the players have shuffled their seats.

Writing original soundtrack singles—even hit mainstream titles—is no longer the exclusive domain of such iconic superhitsters as Bryan Adams and Phil Collins. Today's exclusive movie tunes are as likely to come from bad-ass hard rockers like Godsmack—whose lead singer Sully Erna wrote "I Stand Alone" for the nearly platinum-selling soundtrack to Universal's hit spring/summer actioner *The Scorpion King*—as they are from Brit-rock darlings Travis, who penned the lead single, "Love Will Come Through," for Buena Vista's film *Moonlight Mile*.[17]

"We've seen a feeding frenzy over the last few years, to the extent where every TV show and film has soundtrack," says Danny Bramson, who oversees soundtracks for Warner Music Group, a Goliath that includes, among others, the Elektra, Atlantic, Warner Bros., Lava and Maverick labels. "The one good element to this plethora of 'soundtracks' is the fact that it's allowed a variety of new and fresh faces it wouldn't have allowed before. The ones they were doing at the peak of the frenzy a few years ago—those kind of 'hits collections'—they really feel a little worn now."

Miramax head of movie music Randy Spendlove, who worked for a decade in the record business, agrees. "Nowadays, the making of these albums is more thought out and focused on original songs made specifically for a movie rather than lesser album tracks," he says. "There was a time when people were making soundtracks to movies that didn't warrant them; today, the use of more original music and the quality of the music is part of a correction. What happened before is you'd get the three throw-away tracks from the artist's record; that's not the case anymore."

Fresh, exclusive tracks also have become a must because audiences, spoiled by an enormous array of entertainment options, keep expecting more from movie albums, Universal Music Group soundtrack chief and industry titan Kathy Nelson says.

"It's not so much a lack of attention span as it is greed and demand," she says. "They want and expect so much; you have to give it to them."

Says veteran music supervisor Maureen Crowe, whose hit soundtracks include 1992's *The Bodyguard* and *Wayne's World*: "If it's original material and they can't get it anywhere else, (customers) are gonna want the soundtrack. We're further away from just cramming songs on soundtracks."[18]

In addition to containing original songs, Crowe says, soundtracks must be edgy, hip and very much part of contemporary youth culture. "Today, it's not just about being on the curve but ahead of it," she says. For their part, musicians are finding film projects not only a hipper thing to do but more necessary than ever.

"It's considered airtime now," Crowe says. "For the sophisticated artists today, any exposure is considered good exposure."

Agrees Dawn Soler, who recently supervised the soundtrack to Buena Vista's romantic comedy *Sweet Home Alabama*, which includes first-time covers by Jewel, the Calling and Sheryl Crow and an original track by Ryan Adam: "I think we're seeing a lot more artists getting involved in film because of radio and this Napster thing. . . . Record labels are so busy fighting about how to do business; they need to start promoting bands properly again. Plus, bands just like to be active creatively and be heard regardless—they're artists."[19]

Crowe also believes that "soundtracks have put artists under much less pressure than their own records—they offer more freedom." Gavin Rossdale, frontman for multiplatinum-selling alternative rockers Bush, represents a new type of recording artist being drawn to film work. His first foray into film was the track "Adrenaline," which has helped propel sales of the soundtrack to Sony's hit summer actioner *xXx* to nearly 250,000 units.[20]

"I love film so much that to be part of it has always been an interest of mine," Rossdale says. The experience of taking a fresh approach to songwriting for a different medium—and in league with famed producer-songwriter Glen Ballard—was creatively enlivening for the musician.

"Writing for film feels like a natural process, but at the same time I've never collaborated before," Rossdale says. "It was really interesting. Bush is great, and making our records is great; you don't complain, but you always want to look to broaden yourself. I love the idea of sustaining Bush, and I think this is ultimately good for that as well."

Revolutionary Devo leader Mark Mothersbaugh, whose extensive film music credits run the gamut from last year's *The Royal Tenenbaums* and both *Rugrats* movies to the upcoming Warner Bros. Pictures comedy *Welcome to Collinwood*, sums up the trend with point-blank bluntness.[21] Artists today, he says, are more interested than they used to be in soundtracks, partly because pop music is just an unpleasant arena right now. "Film music is more enjoyable and creative; you get a lot more freedom. The MTV/Home Shopping Network mentality just doesn't cut it."

But to Pharrell Williams, a young hip-hop wunderkind and member of the Neptunes producing team—whose movie credits include the tracks "Work It Out" and "Boys" from the soundtrack to the hit summer comedy *Austin Powers in Goldmember* and the soundtrack to Sony's upcoming animated film *Lil' Pimp*—movie music is no different from album music.[22]

"Music is music," he says, adding that film is "no different than what we do now. Hello—music videos?"

But for all of the talk of creative opportunity and artistic consideration, movie studios and record companies remain bound by the same bottom line. Nelson says the diversified array of music acts in the soundtrack game has made target marketing an even more precise endeavor.

"How do you show a demographic that they will like a movie? A soundtrack can be a great way," she says. "We already do demographic testing and can attract audiences based on the ad or the poster. . . . You can't make somebody like something, but (a song or soundtrack) can help show them what it's about."

Awards also motivate moviemakers and musicians, Spendlove says.

"Original music has surged quite a bit, and the reason is that there's an opportunity to win an Oscar," he says. "There's a real elite group of people who've won Oscars, and there are so many benefits for the studio to having an original song work in a film; it creates an awareness for the movie, but beyond that, a great song can put a stamp on a moment in time for a great film."

Ultimately, though, money still matters most.

"Soundtracks are fueled by a capitalistic structure," Mothersbaugh says. "The soundtracks that you're allowed to buy will continue to be based on what sold last week; that's the way it's always been."

Says Bramson of the struggle to make artistically winning soundtracks while still turning a profit: "I guess it's the ultimate dance. Look, you never want to lose anyone's money; for all the talk of purity, face it—you've got to be able to make those numbers, as they say, to be able to continue playing the game."

From Billboard 114, no. 41 (October 12, 2002), S3–S4, S6.

19.3 WHEN IS FILM MUSIC CLASSICAL?

Jed Distler

Jed Distler (b. 1956) is a composer and pianist whose works range from song cycles to full-length operas and whose recorded output features music by Virgil Thomson, Richard Rodney Bennett, Alvin Curran, Frederic Rzewski, and many others. He has been a member of the keyboard faculty at Sarah Lawrence College in Bronxville, New York, and since 1987 he has been artistic director of the New York presenting organization called ComposersCollaborative, Inc. For several decades he has contributed reviews of recordings to such publications as Piano & Keyboard, Pulse, Soundscapes, Classics Today, *and—most prolifically—*Gramophone; *through articles published in* Gramophone, *Distler in 2007 was one of the main revealers of the facts behind the Joyce Hatto hoax.[23]*

In this article Distler deals not with keyboard music but, rather, with music for films. His interlocutors are John Corigliano and Philip Glass, two composers with a presence not just in the concert hall and opera house but also in the cinema; Corigliano is best known for his scores for Ken Russell's Altered States *(1980) and François Girard's* The Red Violin *(1998),[24] and Glass has provided music for almost a hundred film and television projects.[25] Among the subjects discussed is the suspicion with which representatives of film music and so-called classical music regard one another; this was a common theme in the film-music dialogue of the 1930s and 1940s, and apparently it continues to resonate into the twenty-first century.*

With film soundtracks promoted by recording companies' classical divisions, and with the sweeping orchestral scores of the likes of John Williams, Hans Zimmer and from an earlier age Bernard Herrmann and Elmer Bernstein, debate continues to rage as to whether—or when—film music counts as classical. Philip Glass and John Corigliano are both regarded as classical composers first and foremost despite their work for the cinema. But both, as Jed Distler found out, find that the lines between classical and film music are by no means clear-cut.

JD: People often think about film and classical music as two different things. But isn't there in fact a tenuous relationship between those two worlds? You have each, to different degrees, straddled both.

PG: Well, in the twentieth century many so-called classical composers made their livings writing film music. Take the Russians, people like Shostakovich, Prokofiev. There has always been an attraction in film music; it's the only place in our world where there is some actual money.

JC: And even in film music's beginnings, you've got people like Korngold and Rósza, who originally were symphonic composers. But even after they wrote for film, they still created symphonic repertoire.

PG: Today film is what opera was formerly, it's the popular art form of our time. Now John and I are both film composers and opera composers, and it may be easier for people who are experienced in theatre to work in films than for people who only work in concert music, because both theatre and films are about subject matter.

JC: I think also you can see the difference between concert music, theatre and film if you work in all three genres. You relate to the projects differently; it's like a balancing act. When I write a symphonic piece, the orchestra, the conductor, and the soloist, no matter how famous or important they are, all try to express my artistic vision. When you write an opera, it's in the middle. They sort of want to honour your vision, but the diva wants this, the director has his or her ideas, the stage designer wants such and such. When you get to film . . .

PG (laughing): You've lost it completely and utterly!

JC: It's the director who's in charge and you're supposed to write music that makes that director happy and the studio happy.

JD: I guess whomever pays the piper the most gets to call most of the tunes! But aside from who has more artistic control in a given situation, does it follow that the music is necessarily different?

JC: When you see a film, the music reflects what's happening on the screen. The music comes out and in, for one minute in one sequence, or maybe six minutes and twenty-two seconds somewhere else. When you're sitting in a concert hall on a wooden chair watching a bunch of people saw away at instruments, your entire concentration is only on the sound and that's the difference. For example, I took themes from *The Red Violin* and used them for my Violin Concerto. There's also the *Suite for Violin and Strings*, and those are about twenty-five minutes of music cues for the film sequenced together.[26] To me, the suite is not as satisfying, because a lot of them are short cues, and they don't build a structure abstractly that one can sit and listen to in the concert hall in the same way that the concerto does.

PG: You miss the expanse of time that you have in the concert hall.

JC: When I'm writing for the concert hall I'm thinking about shaping long arches or sustaining a fifteen- or twenty-minute movement. When we're writing film cues, we don't think that way, because we have to work within much shorter time limits that are given to us.

PG: Six minutes would be considered a long cue. Although when I'm working on a film score that's also going to be a commercial recording, I plan ahead to see which cues I can combine. And then I'll write transition pieces specifically for the recording that never will be in the film.

JD: Do you consciously adjust your style when you score films?

JC: I don't like the word "style" so much as "techniques," because generally I think that the style of a composer is the unconscious choices that he makes, not the conscious ones. A film composer who takes whatever job he can get has to master techniques that are very, very varied, from pop music and jazz to symphonic idioms. Yet if you listen closely to their scores, you find that the film composer's personality eventually comes out, because their signatures are not in moments that are highly stylized, but the little things: the way you jump to a note, the way you gravitate to certain harmonic ideas, the way you do things instinctively. That's style.

JD related the story of being asked by some film-makers to compose the score to an airline video. Having heard him give a piano recital which included some of his own compositions, they gave him a VHS cassette with "images of trees and flowers, all underscored by the sappiest new age music." Assuming he was to follow that model, he wrote a trio of bland tunes and one that was more harmonically complex for his own enjoyment. They wanted the complex piece, saying it was more true to his own voice. Personal style, suggested JD, was clearly not dead in the visual world. PG expanded.

PG: What I learnt from studying with Nadia Boulanger was that personal style was a special case of technique, the predilection one has to voice chords or manipulate instrumentation in certain ways. But this predilection lies within a larger framework of technique, and I tell young composers that without learning technique, they'll never have a style. So one of the interesting things about being a concert composer working in film is that we can get into larger areas of technique that we generally don't work in.

JD: So it stands to reason that your film scoring experiences might inform how you write for the concert hall.

JC: Oh, sure. For example, when I was working on the Ken Russell film *Altered States*, I had these nine- and ten-minute scenes with no words, and I had to write a lot of busy music, but didn't want to use millions of notes. So I took simple symbols that you use for what I call "motion sonorities" like trills and tremolos, and, for about a week, developed my own versions of them. I'd give a symbol, say, to a section of cellos, to make them play agitatedly, between certain notes as fast as possible. And eventually I brought these techniques into my concert music.

JD: A friend of mine was listening to the original soundtrack to a James Bond film, and was swept away by the big crescendos and percussion effects, all happening so fast, which is the nature of short cues. Does this follow that composers who mainly write for film would find it a challenge to deal with symphonic forms and larger scales of time?

PG: Not that many of them have the opportunity. People who are exclusively film composers usually don't get concert hall commissions.

JC: I think there's a prejudice that creeps into this matter. When someone primarily is a film composer, and then composes for the concert hall, certain critics will point out how that composer is limited in what he or she can do. But when a classical composer comes into a film, we tend to be treated very well.

PG: It's a lot easier to make your reputation in the straight music world first, and then walk into the entertainment business if you can. But there's another side to that. It took years before people in the film world (I'm talking about mainstream, commercial films) were convinced that I could actually write film scores, long after I had been writing them. For example, a couple of composers who had been hired to do *The Hours* were fired for some reason. The producer was going around Hollywood asking, "can anyone around write music like Philip Glass?" And someone said, "well why don't you call him up?" Which he did, eventually. But it doesn't occur to these people to go to the source!

JD: That just proves how elements of your style have permeated the "Hollywood" sound today, just as Rachmaninov did in movies of the '30s and '40s.

PG: Actually, my harmonic language usually is more adventurous in my film scores than in my concert music. It's much more dissonant. I'm more liable to sound like other people who write modern music.

JD: Is that because most people accept dissonance more readily in a cinematic context? Listeners who couldn't sit through Schoenberg's Second Chamber Symphony in concert wouldn't have trouble if it was the soundtrack to *Attack of the Killer Tone Rows*?

PG: Absolutely. After all, wasn't it John Williams who made Stravinsky a popular idiom?

JD: In fact, many people nowadays first experience orchestral music not through Beethoven, not through Mozart, but John Williams . . .

JC: . . . who uses more French horns than any symphony orchestra can ever afford . . .

PG: . . . more than Wagner!

JD: Will audiences who respond to John Williams use that as a steppingstone into starting to appreciate concert music?

JC: Well, the sounds of an orchestra might provide this kind of bridge. But there's a very great difference between listening to something without any words, story or picture, and a piece of music that's basically accompaniment to words and pictures.

PG: But John, in *The Red Violin*, you used music to articulate the film's structure, and I tried to do that too in *The Hours*. This is something not generally done. And I'm sure you've heard some people in Hollywood say that this is not "real" film music, that it violates some unwritten law that film music must be decorative. Yet we've seen how music has the potential to articulate and formulate the structural emotional point of view of the film. That's a great contribution that we, and I mean the larger "we" of concert, opera and ballet composers, have brought to the film world, and it's an important one.

From *Gramophone* 84, no. 1014 (January 2007), 28–29.

19.4 HOLLYWOOD COMPOSERS TUNE IN FOR RARE GATHERING

Kevin Cassidy

Kevin Cassidy trained in journalism at the University of Washington in Seattle; for more than a decade he has been on the staff of The Hollywood Reporter, *and he now serves that publication as senior features editor.*

For this extraordinary article, Cassidy gathered together all five of the composers who were in the running for the Academy of Motion Picture Arts and Sciences' 2009 award for "Best Original Score." The extent of these composers' experience is considerable, and the range of their backgrounds says much about the richly eclectic nature of film music today.

Toronto-born Howard Shore (b. 1946) is the group's senior member; after studying at the Berklee College of Music in Boston he steadily ascended the ladder of popular music, very visibly serving as musical director for the Saturday Night Live *television show before embarking on a career in film scoring in 1979. Jan Kaczmarek (b. 1953) began writing music for live theater in his native Poland in the late 1970s and since then has scored more than fifty documentaries and feature films. Danny Elfman (b. 1953) gained fame as the singer and songwriter for the rock group Oingo Boingo before being invited in 1985, by director Tim Burton, to try his hand at film scoring; although his formal training in composition is nonexistent, Elfman nevertheless in 2004 completed a suite of pieces collectively titled* Serenada Schizophrana *for the American Composers Orchestra. Alexandre Desplat (b. 1961) studied composition in his native Paris with the ultra-modernists Claude Ballif and Iannis Xanakis; he has scored more than a hundred films, most of them produced in France and dating from the past ten years. Allah Rakha Rahman (b. 1966) is the youngest member of the set convened for this collective interview; born in India, he studied composition in London at Trinity College of Music and then set up a high-tech recording studio in his native Madras;[27] he has been scoring films since 1992 and, in a 2005 article in* Time *magazine, was declared to be "India's most prominent movie songwriter."*

Cassidy describes the fruits of his reportorial labor as "a frank, passionate discussion of the past, present and future of film music." Readers will note that in the article the current state of film music, and film music's possible future, are never explicitly addressed. But from the composers' comments—and from the actual music that these A-list composers are producing—readers can easily draw their own conclusions about the art form's today and tomorrow.

Film composers aren't exactly the most social creatures in Hollywood.

But when five of this year's Oscar front-runners—A. R. Rahman (*Slumdog Millionaire*), Howard Shore (*Doubt*), Danny Elfman (*Milk*), Alexandre Desplat (*The Curious Case of Benjamin Button*) and Jan Kaczmarek (*The Visitor*)—sat down recently with *The Hollywood Reporter*, they seized the opportunity for a frank, passionate discussion of the past, present and future of film music.[28]

The Hollywood Reporter: Film is a collaborative art, but composers work in relative isolation. Is it strange to get together like this?

Jan Kaczmarek: We tend to socialize very little. Much less than writers or directors.

Danny Elfman: Any part of the industry really. In fact, directors and writers tend to seek each other out. God knows actors all seem to know each other. It is the weirdest field for sure.

Howard Shore: Let's change that.

Alexandre Desplat: We should set aside a week or so during the year and meet. Or at least try to . . .

Shore: Like a retreat.

Elfman: Somewhere in the Himalayas.

Desplat: With a studio of course.

THR: If you had to name one score that has influenced your work the most, what would it be?

A. R. Rahman: (Vangelis's) *Chariots of Fire*, because it was all electronic and it was fascinating. I used to listen to orchestral scores, but this one was completely new.[29] It interested me to get into synthesizers and explore the feeling and emotions (of electronic scores).

Kaczmarek: This needs a disclaimer: There are a number of great scores. But because I have to answer: *The Mission* by Ennio Morricone. If you ask why, I don't know. Maybe it's because I'm coming from a Catholic country (Poland) and I prefer a certain amount of spiritual emotion or passion. I love ethnic elements and, for me, it was deeply moving—and deeply moving is the ultimate compliment.

Shore: I would say Toru Takemitsu's work. Especially *Woman in the Dunes*. His use of silence, I thought, was interesting. Takemitsu also did *Ran*. He used music in an epic way. I think that I was interested in how other composers from different countries expressed their ideas in film.

Elfman: (1951's) *The Day the Earth Stood Still*. Bernard Herrmann. Probably because of the age. A lot of the bigger influences have a lot to do with what age you were exposed to something. I must have been 12, and it was the first time that I became aware that there is a personality behind music. Until then, I just thought music rolled out of a machine. It was that movie that I noticed the music, and I noticed the name, and I realized that somebody did this. (After that) I started looking for Herrmann's name every time I would go to the movies.

THR: Do you ever listen to your past work and think, "I could have done that better?"

Shore: I try not to. It's too painful because, of course, you are always trying to rewrite music you've done. You are always trying to achieve something greater than what you've done. You're rarely ever satisfied.

THR: Rephrasing the question, do you ever think you really nailed it?

Shore: No. Never. I was at a screening of *Lord of the Rings: Return of the King*, and I kept trying to rewrite it as I was watching it—still trying to fix certain bars.[30]

Desplat: I can't even play a CD of mine. I can't look back, because you remember how on that particular day you could have achieved something better, or how it was in the studio that day, or how the sound engineer wasn't there. I don't think a creator should look back—not only for your work but for everything. Looking back captures your history, but you should continue to look forward.

THR: Can it help being on a schedule with such tight deadlines?

Elfman: I think this is critical when I talk to young composers. If you can not adapt to work under, sometimes, excruciating deadlines, then you really are not going to last in this industry—because that is, most of the time, a reality. It's an exception if a movie has no particular time limit.

Desplat: Sometimes when I wake up in the morning I feel like I'm in a film noir, with my back up against the wall and there is a gun. But I have no gun.

THR: Do you like where film music is at now in its evolution?

Kaczmarek: Well, there is this great era of composers that we always cite, like Herrmann and (Erich) Korngold. But as much as I like bold strokes and the great scope of that era, it is, in a sense, useless today because we can't write that way. As much as I admire that craft, we are living in different times. There is a much more subtle language being used now.

Rahman: I am so much in love with scores that have great melodies, but nowadays if you have a great melody they say, "Oh, it's distracting from my film."

Shore: Film music is changing all the time. From year to year, the styles are changing, and frankly, they are all of interest. I find it an interesting, fascinating process seeing this art form evolve over a hundred years. I think this year is the 100th anniversary of

301

film music. If you look at the history of it, and where we are in it, it's such a young art form steeped in music tradition. It started with classical music and then opera and then evolved into the great scores of the '30s, the experimentation of the '50s and '60s. It has just been an interesting process. Film music is a fascinating art form and there is still great work to be done. We have the benefit of all these great works of the past to build on, and there is a future ahead.

Desplat: The field is so wide open in front of us. That's why I like to create music for movies, because you can try anything.

THR: *It does seem that these days the music can easily get lost because the sound effects are so loud.*

Elfman: There's a trend for films in general to be louder and louder each summer. I noticed this for the last ten, twelve years. There is a point where it can't go any louder.

Kaczmarek: It also depends on the type of film. Some films require huge electric energy. But it's very good to discuss. I believe it is in a critical situation. On the other hand, we cannot start complaining all the time because this is also unwise. Of course it's critical because of what you all said and what Danny said: There is less space for our creative contribution. There are some directors who are very sensitive to music and who understand music, who know that music can create a miracle. But there is a second part to this: the studios.

Desplat: I think the director is crucial. Sometimes he can have power over the studios.

Kaczmarek: Sometimes, but it's very rare. I worked one time with this director who had final cut, and even then it wasn't that great because the studio said, "Yes, you can have your final cut, but we will only open you in five theaters instead of 2,000."

THR: *How are shrinking budgets affecting film music?*

Elfman: The best music is often done on the lower budgets. Look at the dozen best scores of the year. Very often—not always, but often—they are the little films that tend to come out at the end of the year where the music is allowed to shine.

Shore: I tend to disagree with that, I must say. I think the quality of recordings is being affected by the budgets. There are budgets that are required to achieve a certain quality in the studio. We shouldn't be trying to do things with less and less money.

Elfman: We both just finished relatively low budget movies.

Shore: Yes, but the music budgets should bear a relationship to the overall cost of the film—and that's not quite happening. I don't like to see that. I'd like to see the budgets maintain a certain percentage of the overall cost.

Kaczmarek: I think it's very dangerous. I think it's romantic to think things can happen with no money, but if there is no money in our profession, we cannot afford the best orchestras. If we don't hire orchestras, they have no income, they lose their instruments. In my country, the film business deteriorated to a miserable level. Under communism, Polish filmmaking was stronger. Even with censorship, it was much better because there was money in the system so people could make good movies.

Desplat: I think the debate is more about different types of cinema. We are talking more about art movies. That's what they are called here. In France, they are just called movies. (Laughter.) We don't have big studio movies. So I think, yes, when you do an art movie, everyone has the same kind of energy. They're all trying to create something different, something that explores, something that takes chances. There's more freedom. If you don't need a big orchestra and only need a few players, you can have that and make a very good score.

Shore: To make good films you need a good balance between all parts—the cinematography, the production design, the postproduction, the preproduction. Music has to maintain a quality of the overall design of the film. I see that shrinking. I don't like the fact that it's shrinking. It should maintain a level that it had maybe five to ten years ago. To make good films, there should be a balance. Music shouldn't get short shrift.

THR: What is the least enjoyable part of the composing process?

Rahman: Deadlines and pressure. That happens every time.

Desplat: It's when I can't find what I am looking for, day or night. One day goes by. Then it's a week. Then it's ten days. When the ideas aren't coming, I sleep.

Kaczmarek: I go for a walk. An intense one. Speed-walking helps.

Elfman: Like Alexandre, needing to find something that I feel like I haven't found, feeling the ticking of the clock. Trying to be relaxed enough to not panic, because if you panic, you will never find what you are looking for.

Shore: I asked an illustrator how he creates so much, and he said, "Just keep the pencil moving." Just toil. Keep the pencil moving. It's so simple. As long as your pencil is moving, you are working. If it's moving, you feel a sense of accomplishment. Even if it's not very good, you feel it's moving.

Elfman: Do you ever feel like you are working on an equation?

Shore: It's a cumulative process, writing music. The *Lord of the Rings* scores took almost four years to write, but it felt like forty years because it took a lot of time for me to learn how to write that much music in that time frame, to be able to do it and orchestrate it. It's a cumulative effect that allows you to write and open up under pressure, under deadlines. It's just the experience and the cumulative energy of doing it all those years.

Elfman: What do you do when you put that bucket down the well and you don't hear the water?

Shore: You keep the pencil moving.

From *The Hollywood Reporter*, December 22, 2008, 92.

19.5 *127 HOURS* AND OTHER FILMS TAKE EXPERIMENTAL TURNS IN MUSIC[31]

Composers like Trent Reznor (*The Social Network*),
A. R. Rahman (*127 Hours*) and Carter Burwell (*True Grit*)
Dig Deep into Movies' Moods to Conjure Up Matching Melodies

Todd Martens

Todd Martens has been a staff writer for the Los Angeles Times *since 2007; before that he wrote about popular music, especially recordings produced by independent labels, for* Billboard, *and as a freelancer his work has appeared in such publications as* Punk Planet *and the* Alternative Press.

303

In this article Martens considers the broad range of the past year's film scores. He calls attention to films featuring original music by artists rooted in the rock and disco genres, but he devotes most of his space to what he considers to be innovative methods on the part of well-established composers.

Two of his interview subjects, A. R. Rahman and Alexandre Desplat, were among the Oscar nominees featured in the roundtable discussion that made up the previous article. By 2010 Rahman and Desplat surely belonged to Hollywood's new film-music pantheon, and high-ranking among their assets were the trademark styles they had brought to previous projects. Nevertheless, the approaches they describe here—a rich mix of electronically processed guitar sounds in the case of Rahman's score for 127 Hours, *the use of vintage recording equipment in the case of Desplat's score for* The King's Speech— *suggest that they were hardly satisfied with holding to routine.*

Plenty of filmmakers took non-traditional routes this season, turning to the world of rock to bring an immediacy to their stories.

Trent Reznor of Nine Inch Nails scored his first flick in the Facebook drama *The Social Network*, and French disco purveyors Daft Punk anchored Disney's high-concept reboot in *Tron*.[32] Digging deeper, former Smiths guitarist Johnny Marr brought a human element to *Inception*, LCD Soundsystem leader James Murphy distilled the anxiety of *Greenberg* and Radiohead producer Nigel Godrich experimented with electronics for *Scott Pilgrim vs. the World*.

Not to be outshined, veteran composers also did some experimenting. Carter Burwell grappled with how to make a western not sound like a western, while A. R. Rahman had to set the tone for a film in which the camera is largely static, focused on just one character. Clint Mansell, meanwhile, riffed on Tchaikovsky in *Black Swan* and John Powell had a colorful canvas to decorate for *How to Train Your Dragon*.

Here's a sampling of just a few of 2010's film music standouts:

A. R. Rahman

For those who felt squeamish during Danny Boyle's *127 Hours*—or those who have avoided it after hearing war stories—know that composer A. R. Rahman could have made things far worse for the audience. Not often, after all, is an artist charged with providing the musical accompaniment for a man cutting off his own arm.

Make no mistake, there are times Rahman's score is harsh. Yet when it comes to the completion of the deed itself, when James Franco as trapped climber Aron Ralston is in a near-delusionary hopeful state, Rahman toned it down. At that moment, the more metallic aspects of the score become awash in calming atmospheres.

"At first, it felt a little bit too harsh, but I went to the computer and went for something meditative rather than harsh," Rahman says. "It was a very difficult scene. I had to see it more than forty times. We started pulling things out of the score. We wanted to make it more human."

The Bollywood megastar and musical architect of Boyle's Oscar-winning *Slumdog Millionaire*, Rahman tapped into his Western influences for much of *127 Hours*. Ralston is often seen sporting headphones, with upbeat rock and dance bleeding out of them. Rahman's score feels very much like something the cinematic Ralston might be listening to, a mix of heavily layered acoustic and electric guitars, and it's all brightened with digital effects.

"My thing was to have one instrument, one instrument that was very close to this character," Rahman says. "He was single, he was very confident and young. So I thought the guitar would be perfect."

Carter Burwell[33]

The opening few moments of Joel and Ethan Coen's take on *True Grit* are designed to make it clear that this is not going to be standard western fare.[34] A significant portion of that task would fall on composer Carter Burwell, working here on his fourteenth collaboration with the Coen brothers. Ultimately, Burwell settled on interpreting a hymn, "Leaning on the Everlasting Arms," with a solitary piano.

"We use the hymn in the very first scene and gradually lead the viewer away from it," Burwell says. "So where you expect a western to be grand, we wanted it to be the exact opposite. It's very specific to time and place, and there are a lot of different traditions to call upon or ignore. Mostly we chose to ignore them."

Following the young Mattie Ross (newcomer Hailee Steinfeld) on her quest for retribution, Burwell's score gradually escalates. The piano eventually gives way to a full orchestra, but Burwell never fully loses the influence of the hymn.

"One of the things I liked about the hymns, and the general concept that we used, was the idea of call-and-response," Burwell says. "A soloist sings, and the congregation responds. There are places in the score where we use that. We have an enormous landscape and a solo clarinet, and it is answered by the whole orchestra. There's all this land, and you sense this enormous unfeeling country with the orchestra."

Burwell does note that he and the Coens weren't simply trying to toy with audience expectations. Two scenes—a shootout and a river crossing—receive the triumphant horns and adventurous grandeur of western scores of yore.

"I'm not saying I'm Dimitri Tiomkin, but it references that kind of approach," Burwell says of the famed western film composer. "We debated how much we should have the classic feel, but for those two scenes, it seemed to be right. It seemed like the characters were enjoying being in a western."

Alexandre Desplat

The drama in *The King's Speech* stems from the inability to communicate. The challenge, then, for French composer Alexandre Desplat, was to keep his score from saying too much.

"This is a film about the sound of the voice," Desplat says. "Music has to deal with that. Music has to deal with silence. Music has to deal with time."

First, the score to the Tom Hooper-directed film could not sound too perfect. The sleuthing skills of Abbey Road's chief engineer, Pete Cobin, helped Desplat find the tone he needed.

Digging through the EMI archives, Cobin recovered vintage microphones owned by the royal family, Desplat says.[35] "At that time, the royal family had microphones made to order. We recorded the score with these microphones. It allowed the sound to have a dated feel—a purely dated feel."

For someone who averages seven to ten films a year, *The King's Speech* may be Desplat's warmest and most restrained effort to date. Much of the score centers on a piano, chosen to match the film's use of Beethoven and Mozart. As string melodies drift and cascade in the background, the piano tends to lag just behind, save for the romantic swing that accompanies Colin Firth's King George VI as he rehearses in Westminster Abbey.

Says Desplat, "The king stammers, so how can you say that in musical terms without being didactic or obvious? I suggested to Tom that we could maybe give this idea that music is not going forward. How do you do that? I suggested one note, repeated . . . It's almost like a sad movement of a Schubert quartet."

Trent Reznor and Atticus Ross

For his first film score, Trent Reznor was eager to try his hand at leading an orchestra. Yet it was Reznor's Nine Inch Nails work, namely the 2008 atmospheric collection *Ghosts I–IV*, that more closely aligned with what *The Social Network* director David Fincher was after.

"There was a part of me that was really disappointed," says Reznor, who composed the score with longtime collaborator Atticus Ross. "The orchestral route was a challenge that I thought would be fun to address."

But with no string section, Reznor and Ross began modifying their initial ideas to fit into a "world of modular synthesizers and an acoustic piano." The latter became the key, as the hissing electronics indicated tension, and the sorrowful piano melody, with notes patiently spaced measures apart, hinted at what Ross described as the "serious human shortcomings on display."

The down-and-out piano-draped electronic piece scored the film's opening title sequence, a move that surprised Reznor.

"There's a level of tension, a level of reserve and a level of anger," Reznor says of the piece. "It's not a bombastic title scene. It's not a comfortable rock song. Seeing David had the taste and insight to try that in that spot defined how the rest of the score would go. We realized that Fincher was ready to break some rules."

Some initial tendencies, such as an overuse of 8-bit video game sounds, were largely abandoned. Instead, the score is one with fraught rhythms and sometimes uncomfortable synthetic landscapes.

"The music kind of goes along with the idea that 'you take this, and you make your own decisions,'" Ross says. "The music is not one of those ones where you see someone sad, and this sad music goes along with it."

From *Los Angeles Times*, December 7, 2010, S22.

NOTES

Preface

1   Louis Reeves Harrison, "Jackass Music," *Moving Picture World* 8, no. 3 (January 21, 1911): 25.

2   Roy Prendergast, *Film Music: A Neglected Art* (New York: New York University Press, 1977), xiii, quoted and discussed in Martin Marks, "Film Music: The Material, Literature, and Present State of Research," *Notes*, second series, 36, no. 2 (December 1979): 289.

3   The author of the quip is Jean-Baptiste Alphonse Karr, a Parisian journalist who in the 1840s edited a magazine called *Les Guêpes* ("The Wasps"); his famous line first appeared in an article in *Les Guêpes* in January 1849.

Chapter 1

1   See Charles Merrell Berg, *An Investigation of the Motives for and Realization of Music to Accompany the American Silent Film, 1896–1927* (New York: Arno Press, 1976), 6; Martin Miller Marks, *Music and the Silent Film: Contexts and Case Studies, 1895–1924* (New York: Oxford University Press, 1997), 3; Roy Prendergast, *Film Music: A Neglected Art*, 2nd ed. (New York: Norton, 1992); James Wierzbicki, *Film Music: A History* (New York and London: Routledge, 2008), 1–22.

2   See Rick Altman, *Silent Film Sound* (New York: Columbia University Press, 2004), 119–32.

3   Tim Anderson, "Reforming 'Jackass Music': The Problematic Aesthetics of Early American Film Music Accompaniment," *Cinema Journal* 37, no. 1 (Autumn, 1997), 8.

4   Though not represented in this collection, Ernst Luz contributed an important column on musical accompaniment to *Moving Picture News* and vehemently opposed Martin's improvisatory methods: "Mr. Musician, in repertoire lies your salvation, for it is only fair to suppose that the advanced player cannot only use a larger repertoire to better advantage than the amateur or student, but he can also render it more effectively, and this alone will bring him into demand. Positively no one can hope to render satisfactory musical setting for a picture by the sole means of what some would like to call improvising and which I know to be faking pure and simple" (Ernst Luz, "Picture Music," *Moving Picture News* 6, no. 19 (November 9, 1911), 24).

5   Louis Reeves Harrison, "Managerial Stupidity," *Moving Picture World* 7, no. 25 (December 17, 1910), 1400.

6   Clarence Sinn, "Music for the Pictures," *Moving Picture World* 8, no. 5 (February 4, 1911), 235.

7   Clyde Martin, "Playing the Pictures," *Film Index* 6, no. 18 (October 22, 1910), 13.

8   Louis Reeves Harrison, "New Fields," *Moving Picture World* 14, no. 11 (December 14, 1912), 1057.

9   Louis Reeves Harrison, "Jackass Music," *Moving Picture World* 8, no. 3 (January 21, 1911), 124–25.

10   For a more comprehensive listing of film music standards espoused by the trade presses, see Altman, 246.

11 While these columns are still frequently overlooked, several studies dedicate substantial attention to them. See especially Altman, 231–48; Berg, 112–22; and Wierzbicki, 33–36.

12 Clarence E. Sinn, "Music for the Picture," *Moving Picture World* vol. 7, no. 22 (November 26, 1910), 1227. Appropriately, this statement follows a mere six pages after one of Harrison's diatribes: "Over and over again, while trying to get the full benefit of the pictures shown, we hear the pianist deliberately practicing a song accompaniment, as if we were giving time and money to hear playing far worse than that of the street organ on wheels. The orchestra does not stop to tune up while the opera is in progress, and humble patrons of the little opera deserve something better than such intrusions on their limited pleasure." Louis Reeves Harrison, "The Pictural Drama As a Fine Art: It Is Your Turn, Mr. Exhibitor," *Moving Picture World* 7, no. 22 (November 26, 1910), 1221.

13 Ibid. Harrison once described opera as "not much more than a grand pantomime," although this comparative gloss does little to bring the two distinct genres closer together (see Harrison, "Managerial Stupidity," *Moving Picture World* 7, no. 25 (December 17, 1910), 1400).

14 See Rick Altman, *Silent Film Sound* (New York: Columbia University Press, 2004), 372; Scott D. Paulin, "Richard Wagner and the Fantasy of Cinematic Unity: The Idea of the *Gesamtkunstwerk* in the History and Theory of Film Music," in *Music and Cinema*, ed. James Buhler, Caryl Flinn, and David Neumeyer (Hanover: Wesleyan University Press, 2000), 70, 82; Melvyn Stokes, *D.W. Griffith's* The Birth of a Nation: *A History of the Most Controversial Motion Picture of All Time* (New York: Oxford University Press, 2008). Sinn's views on Wagner are better clarified in James Buhler, "Wagnerian Motives: Narrative Integration and the Development of Silent Film Accompaniment, 1908–1913," in *Wagner and Cinema*, ed. Jeongwon Joe and Sander L. Gilman (Bloomington, IN: University of Indiana Press, 2010), 27–45. See also Sinn, "Music for the Picture," *Moving Picture World* 8, no. 2 (January 14, 1911), 76; Sinn, "Music for the Picture," *Moving Picture World* 8, no. 3 (January 21, 1911), 135; and Sinn, "Music for the Picture," *Moving Picture World* 8, no. 5 (February 4, 1911), 235.

15 Deagan bells were advertised in the pages of *Moving Picture World*; the reference here is a convenient exercise in cross promotion. J. C. Deagan of Chicago, Illinois, manufactured many types of bells, including xylophones, orchestra bells, chimes, and tuning forks. Deagan's patent electric bells were said to "create great enthusiasm in Moving Picture Houses," and could be played "from a keyboard as a solo instrument, or as an accompaniment to songs." The entire package, which included twenty-five bells, resonators, magnets, and keyboard cost $75.00. See "Music," *Moving Picture World* 7, no. 17 (October 22, 1910), 937.

16 The initials are John M. Bradlet's, the Chicago-based western representative for *Moving Picture World*.

17 "I Love My Wife; But, Oh, You Kid," by Harry Armstrong and Billy Clark, was published in 1909. While there are a number of early silent films depicting the life of Moses (including a 1903 Gaumont production titled *Moses in the Bullrushes*), the date of the song suggests that Sinn may have been thinking of *Life of Moses, Part I of V* (Vitagraph, 1909) or perhaps *Pharaoh* (or *Israel in Egypt*) (Gaumont, 1910).

18 Sinn is referring here to several classical selections that would have been familiar to musicians and audiences of the day: "Träumerei," Op. 15, no. 7 (1839) by Robert Schumann (1810–56); The "Flower Song" from *Carmen* (1875) by Georges Bizet (1838–75); and "La Serenata," or "Angel's Serenade," by Gaetano Braga (1829–1907).

19 The ballad of "Auld Robin Gray" was written by Lady Anne Barnard (*née* Lindsay, 1750–1825) in 1771 and published anonymously. The authorship remained a mystery until 1823, when she admitted to Sir Walter Scott that she wrote the poem. Rev. William Leeves (1748–1828) set the text to music in the 1770s and kept his authorship secret until 1812. See S. J. Adair Fitz-Gerald, *Stories of Famous Songs* (London: John C. Nimmo, 1898), 119–125.

20 Commonly played by regimental bands with Scottish affiliations, this martial tune is based on the folk melody, "If thou'lt play me fair play."

21 Sir Francesco Paolo Tosti (1846–1916) spent the first half of his life in Italy where he worked as a song composer and singing teacher. He moved to London in 1880 and spent more

than thirty years there before retiring to Italy. "Goodbye" represents one of his early efforts at setting English verse and was composed in London during the summer of 1880. The lyrics are by G. T. Whyte-Melville. See Francesco Sanvitale and Andreina Manzo, *The Song of a Life: Francesco Paolo Tosti (1846–1916)*, trans. Nicola Hawthorne (Burlington, VT: Ashgate, 2004).

22   Clyde Martin, "Playing the Pictures," *Film Index* 6, no. 19 (November 5, 1910), 6.

23   Martin, "Playing the Pictures," *Film Index* 6, no. 17 (October 22, 1910), 13.

24   Ibid., 13.

25   Martin, "Playing the Pictures," *Film Index* 7, no. 13 (April 1, 1911), 13.

26   Vitagraph released *The Legacy* on October 15, 1910.

27   It is unclear why Martin does not include the title of the film to which he is referring. The Edison release of October 11, 1910, was *The Song that Reached His Heart*. A review of the film specifies the role of the phonograph in the narrative: "A story that will touch the hearts of many because it brings back long forgotten, or only dimly remembered scenes wherein some old and favorite song has played an important part. . . . The phonograph, too, has an important part, and as the familiar strains of 'Annie Laurie' pour from the instrument the man's visions are all of the long ago." See "The Song that Reached His Heart," *Moving Picture World* 7, no. 17 (October 22, 1910), 936.

28   Pathé Frères released *An Indian's Gratitude* on October 8, 1910. The film starred George Larkin and Lucille Younge.

29   Vitagraph released *Francesca Da Rimini* on November 19, 1910. The film was directed by J. Stuart Blackton and starred Edwin R. Phillips and Florence Turner.

30   Martin's belief that the film in question was produced by Biograph has political ramifications. *Film Index* was strongly allied with the Motion Picture Patents Company (MPPC), an organization that sought to limit competition in film production, distribution, and exhibition through its control of camera and projector patents. Not coincidentally, all but one of the films that Martin discusses in this column were produced by MPPC companies (Edison, Vitagraph, and Pathé Frères) and exhibited in MPPC theaters. Martin makes an exception when he cites an example of substandard musical accompaniment. In this case, the film was made by Biograph, an "independent" production company, and presumably was shown at a non-MPPC theater.

31   See Madeline Matz, "Louis Reeves Harrison," *Encyclopedia of Early Cinema*, ed. Richard Abel (London: Routledge, 2005), 295.

32   Louis Reeves Harrison, "Melodrama," *Moving Picture World* 8, no. 20 (May 13, 1911), 1058.

33   Louis Reeves Harrison, "The Pictural Drama as a Fine Art," *Moving Picture World* 7, no. 21 (November 19, 1910), 1163.

34   In addition to drawing the pictures for Harrison's article, H. F. Hoffman also contributed articles to *Moving Picture World* on the use of sound effects for accompaniment.

35   See especially Tim Anderson, "Reforming 'Jackass Music': The Problematic Aesthetics of Early American Film Music Accompaniment," *Cinema Journal* 37, no. 1 (Autumn, 1997), 3–22. (Reprinted in *Movie Music: A Film Reader*, ed. Kay Dickinson (London: Routledge, 2003), 49–60.) See also Rick Altman, *Silent Film Sound* (New York: Columbia University Press, 2004), 236, 239.

36   Louis Reeves Harrison, "Jackass Music," *Moving Picture World* 8, no. 3 (January, 21, 1911), 124.

37   Ibid., 125.

38   See Louis Reeves Harrison, "The Pictural Drama as a Fine Art," *Moving Picture World* 7, no. 21 (November 19, 1910), 1163; "The Pictural Drama as a Fine Art: It Is Your Turn, Mr. Exhibitor," *Moving Picture World* 7, no. 22 (November 26, 1910), 1221; "Managerial Stupidity," *Moving Picture World* 7, no. 25 (December 17, 1910), 1400; and "Is 'Vodeveal' Necessary?" *Moving Picture World* 8, no. 14 (April 8, 1911), 758.

39   *Non compos mentis* translated directly from the Latin means "not in control of the mind;" *le diable au corps* is a more familiar French phrase (not to mention book and film title) that translates as "the devil in the flesh."

40   Two letters written in response to Harrison's "Jackass Music" were printed in subsequent issues of *Moving Picture World*. The first letter heartily affirms the problems Harrison had identified and offers further evidence; the second letter is an indignant response to the first. Together, they offer a revealing—albeit conflicting—account of musical practices in the moving picture theaters of Allentown, Pennsylvania. Both letters are reproduced here in their entirety.

"Jackass Music," *The Moving Picture World* 8, no. 4 (January 28, 1911), 176.

Dear Sirs—I have just seen the article on "Jackass Music," by Louis Reeves Harrison, in the issue of January 21, 1911, and I am sure Mr. Harrison has not exaggerated his views, as far as music in moving picture houses is concerned. For I, also, have heard some jackass music, as he describes it, and wonder how on earth managers can expect anyone to come into their theaters, and sit down, and listen to such unappropriate [sic] music, as I was obliged to listen to while there. The week commencing January 2, 1911, I had business in Allentown, Pa., and on the evening of the same day, with another traveling man, I went to see some picture plays. The first house we entered was a small one, in which there was only a piano to furnish music, and I will say the music at that house was quite fair. The young girl presiding, played music in harmony with the picture, in fact, it suited the pictures quite well, and she kept the piano going from the time the picture started until it was ended, when she took a short rest, or until the next picture was shown on the screen, when she again started to play, which is more than I can say for the larger house, to which we went afterward, and where we found they had a six-piece orchestra. But oh! such torture as we were obliged to suffer while in that place was indescribable. The orchestra was there all right, but very little music was rendered, for they never started to play to a picture until it was almost over, and when the end of the picture appeared they shut off the music abruptly, not even waiting to get to the end of a line, and worse still, we noticed that when a comic picture was on the screen; they did not play at all, not a sound of music during the entire reel, instead of that, they got up and scattered through the audience. When the next picture appeared, which was dramatic, entitled "The Refuge," the musicians reappeared, and by the time this picture was almost, or more than half over, the leader of the orchestra had at last found some music, which, no doubt, she thought was appropriate for this particular picture (judging from the length of time it took her to find it), imagine our surprise and disgust, when they struck up the strain of "John Took Me Home to See His Mother," when the scene appeared in which the drunkard's child was dying, and the poor mother, beside herself with grief, is left to fight the battle against the world without the only treasure that had given her strength to go forward. Then, they switched off to the strain of "Meet Me Tonight in Dreamland," and it seemed as if the pianist was trying to race with the rest of the orchestra. Finally, we could stand the torture no longer, so we left the theater in disgust, vowing we would never enter it again, to be made to endure such torture—for torture it certainly was to be obliged to sit and look at pictures to which there was no music. One might as well listen to a singer unaccompanied by music as to look at pictures without music, for it would detract all the beauty from the song and singer, same as it did from the pictures which would otherwise have been good.
—WM. H. McCRACKEN

"Jackass Music," *Moving Picture World* 8, no. 5 (February 4, 1911), 258.

Sirs—I would like to say a word or two in answer to the letter entitled, "Jackass Music," which appeared in your paper, the Moving Picture World, January 28, 1911.

The person who wrote that article is entirely in error as regards the music which he says he heard played in the largest picture theater in Allentown, Pa. I am the leader of that orchestra, and in justice to myself and the other musicians, I must contradict his statement.

Firstly—he says that I do not start the music until the picture is nearly over, and that I end abruptly when the picture is through, not even ending the strain; both of which are absolutely untrue. I, as a professional pianist, would not be guilty of such gross carelessness, and as to not playing the comic pictures, that is the rule of the house, as those pictures have a better effect without music. As to his remarks about the length of time in finding suitable music, the picture he referred to was a sad one, entitled "The Refuge;" the house was dark, the music plaintive, and the only conclusion I can come to, is that he must have fallen asleep, and woke up in time to see the end of the picture.

The selection in which the song occurs, "John Took Me Home to See His Mother," was played for a Thanhouser comedy, called "Looking Forward," and "Meet Me Tonight in Dreamland," was played along with "You Taught Me How to Love You, You Now Teach Me How to Forget," for a Reliance picture, called "A Woman's Way," which was not shown on the day mentioned, which proves the traveling man must have been to the theater more than once.

When a man writes an article to a popular and reliable paper, he should take lessons before posing as a critic. He has unwittingly paid me a compliment, when he praised the young lady who played the piano at the small picture house which he says he went to. I would like him to know through your valuable paper, that the lady piano players at the two picture houses were my pupils, and were taught the business by me.

—MRS. BUTTERY

41   This illustration was not actually included in the original article "Jackass Music"; it was published in the following issue of *Moving Picture World* and was printed on the same page as another music column, even though it clearly did not go with that article's subject. It certainly appears to have been drawn for "Jackass Music."

Chapter 2

1   One of the earliest Italian epics accompanied by an original orchestral score was the five-reel *Dante's Inferno* (1911), followed in short order by such films as *Homer's Odyssey* (1912), *Quo Vadis?* (1913), *The Last Days of Pompeii* (1913), *Antony and Cleopatra* (1914), *Spartacus* (1914), and *Cabiria* (1914). Early French features released with original scores include *Camille*, *Mme. Sans-Gêne*, and *Queen Elizabeth*, all from 1913. Early American features similarly fitted with original scores include *The Prisoner of Zenda* (1913), *Tess of the D'Urbervilles* (1913), *In the Bishop's Carriage* (1913), and—perhaps most famously—D. W. Griffith's *The Birth of a Nation* (1915). For details, see Martin M. Marks, *Music and the Silent Film: Contexts and Case Studies, 1895–1924* (Oxford: Oxford University Press, 1997).

2   With a seating capacity of 2,460, New York's Regent Theatre opened in 1913 and billed itself as the city's "first de luxe theatre built expressly for showing movies" (quoted in John Belton, *American Cinema/American Culture* (New York: McGraw-Hill, 1994), 16). But the Gaumont Palace, with 5,500 seats, had opened in Paris as early as 1907.

3   The first theater organ—a pipe organ equipped with various sound-effects devices—was the Unit Orchestra designed by Robert Hope-Jones and distributed in the United States by the Rudolf Wurlitzer Company in 1910. Although Wurlitzer remained the dominant American manufacturer of theater organs, by 1913 comparable instruments were being sold by more than a dozen European companies.

4   The quoted phrases are from Maurice Moszkowski (p. 34, this volume) and Vincent d'Indy (p. 24, this volume).

5   World War I, generally known at the time as "the Great War," began in the summer of 1914 with Germany's invasion of Belgium. Germany did not surrender to the Allied Forces until 1917; the conflict did not end until Austria surrendered in November of the following year.

6   All published in New York by Knopf, these include *Peter Whiffle* (1922), *The Blind Bow-Boy* (1923), *The Tattooed Countess* (1924), *Firecrackers* (1925), *Nigger Heaven* (1926), *Spider Boy* (1928), and *Parties* (1930).

7   Harley Granville-Barker was a British actor and director who championed an "ensemble" approach as opposed to a "star-based" approach. Van Vechten here refers to the production of Shakespeare's *A Midsummer Night's Dream* that Granville-Barker presented at London's Savoy Theatre in 1914.

8   Mendelssohn's incidental music for a Berlin production of Shakespeare's *A Midsummer Night's Dream* was composed in 1843 on commission from Friedrich Wilhelm IV; Beethoven's overture and nine pieces of incidental music for *Egmont* date from 1809–10; Arthur Sullivan's incidental music for Shakespeare's *The Tempest* served as his graduation exercise from the Leipzig Conservatory in 1861; the 1823 "romantic drama" *Rosamunde, Fürstin von Cypern* is by Helmina von Chézy, better known today for writing, in the same year, the libretto for Carl Maria von Weber's opera *Euryanthe*; Grieg's incidental music for Henrik Ibsen's *Peer Gynt* was first performed, as part of a production of the play, in 1876.

9   Camille Saint-Saëns's music for Eugène Brieux's *La Foi* was composed for the play's London premiere in 1909 and was published in 1912; Pietro Mascagni's music for Hall Caine's play *The Eternal City* was featured with the October 1902 premiere in London and again two months later when the play was performed in New York. Although Van Vechten likely knew about Strauss's music for *Le Bourgeois gentilhomme*, it is doubtful that he had actually heard any of it; the music was composed in 1911 for a translation by Hugo von Hofmannsthal of the Molière play, but the production never materialized; in 1917 Strauss reworked the music into an orchestral suite that was not premiered until 1920.

10 The references are to Oscar Wilde's *Lady Windermere's Fan: A Play about a Good Woman*, premiered in London in 1892; John Hartley Manners's *Peg O' My Heart: A Comedy of Youth*, premiered in New York in 1912 (the song of the same title, with lyrics by Alfred Bryan and music by Fred Fischer, was published in 1913); Shakespeare's *The Tragedy of Cymbeline* (*c*.1610); and Edmond Rostand's *La Samaritaine*, a Bible-based play written in 1897 as a vehicle for Sarah Bernhardt and presented in New York, with Bernhardt in the title role, in 1910.

11 Lincoln J. Carter (1865–1926) was a playwright who specialized in touring melodramas laden with spectacular "special effects" for the stage. A few of his scripts were adapted for film; he wrote the scenario for *The Slow Express* (1918) and the screenplay for *The Cyclone Rider* (1924).

12 Van Vechten here refers to the films produced and directed by Mack Sennett and featuring an ensemble of comedians known as the Keystone Kops. The Keystone Kops films were made between 1912 and 1917.

13 Filippo Tommaso Marinetti (1876–1944) was one of the founders of the so-called Futurist movement that flourished between 1909 and *c*.1918. Marinetti was a poet, not a musician; composers active in the Futurist movement included Francesco Pratella and Luigi Russolo, both of whom championed the making of music with various noise effects.

14 Before Van Vechten's book chapter, the Italian novelist and poet Gabriel D'Annunzio (1863–1938) had written scenarios for the films *Francesca da Rimini* (1910) and *Cabiria* (1914); films based on his novel *La Gioconda* were made in 1910, 1915, and 1916; other films based on D'Annunzio's works include *Sogno di un tramonto d'autunno* (1911), *La Figlia di Iorio* (1911), *La Nave* (1912), *Giovanna Episcopo* (1916), *Forse che sì forse che no* (1916), and *La Crociata degli innocenti* (1916).

    Although Richard Strauss's music has often been used in films, the composer's only direct involvement with film came in 1925 when he helped arrange the score that was to accompany a filmed version of his 1911 opera, *Der Rosenkavlier*.

15 Pietro Mascagni (1863–1945) in 1914 signed a contract with the Italian Cinés studio to write music for *Rapsodia satanica* (dir. Nino Oxilia) and a never produced biography of Garibaldi; in 1916 he supervised film versions of his 1890 opera *Cavalleria Rusticana* (dir. Ugo Falena) and his 1905 opera *Amica* (dir. Enrico Guazzoni); in 1918 he supervised a film (dir. Giuseppe De Liguoro) of his 1898 opera *Iris*. Mascagni's only other film activities involved a cameo appearance in the 1937 *Regina della Scala* and contributions (with Salvatore Allegra and Umberto Giordano) to the 1942 *Voglio vivere cosí*.

16 Stravinsky never wrote music for films, but many critics have cited "cinematic" influences in such of his early works as *Petrouchka* (1911), *Les Noces* (1914), *Renard* (1916), and *L'Histoire du Soldat* (1918).

17 Camille Erlanger (1863–1919) composed principally for the stage after winning the Prix de Rome in 1888. Strongly influenced by Wagner and Massenet, his only big successes were with *Le Juif polonais* (1900) and *Aphrodite* (1906).

18   Robert's asterisked footnote reads: "Messrs Ricordi and Co. tell us that this film is only an adaptation of the opera that Mascagni composed several years ago."
      Pietro Mascagni (1863–1945) was one of the most popular opera composers in Europe at the turn of the century. A number of productions by Pathé's Films d'Art company during the silent era were screen adaptations of operas accompanied by live music. Mascagni was involved in at least two such projects, the cited one involving his 1898 opera *Iris* and an earlier one, in 1909, involving his 1890 opera *Cavalleria rusticana*. In both cases the film scores were adaptations of Mascagni's original operatic scores.

19   Vincent d'Indy (1851–1931) was known primarily as the composer of such works as the 1889–93 opera *Fervaal* and the 1886 orchestral *Symphonie sur un chant montagnard français* and as the co-founder and long-time director of the Schola Cantorum.

20   Henri Rabaud (1873–1949) conducted at l'Opéra from 1914 to 1918, was elected to the Académie des Beaux-Arts in 1918, and was director of the Conservatoire from 1922 until 1941. He composed scores for the first two films produced by the Société des Films Historiques—*Le Miracle des loups* (1924) and *Le Joueur d'échecs* (1927), both directed by Raymond Bernard. *Mârouf, savetier du Caire* (1914) was his most popular opera.

21   Théodore Dubois (1837–1924) won the Prix de Rome in 1861, replaced Gounod in the Académie des Beaux-Arts in 1894, and was the long-time organist at la Madeleine (his fiftieth anniversary there was celebrated in 1919). Principally a composer of religious music, he composed eight stage works in various genres; his opera *Xavière* dates from 1895.

22   Henri Maréchal (1842–1924) shared the Prix de Rome with Charles Edouard Lefebvre in 1870; he was principally known for his 1876 opera *Les amoureux de Cathérine* and other stage works.

23   The sentence ends with a play on words. The verb *tourner* is here used to describe both the shooting of a film and the motion of the reel when projecting a film.

24   André Messager (1853–1929) was a successful composer of operas, ballets, operettas, and incidental music. He also served at various times as conductor of the Paris Opéra, the Concerts du Conservatoire, the Paris Opéra-Comique, the Folies-Bergère, and, in England, at Covent Garden.

25   Gabriel Pierné (1863–1937) won the Prix de Rome in 1872 and was elected to the Académie des Beaux-Arts in 1925. Because he was such an active conductor (giving at least forty-eight concerts per season), he composed only during the summers.

26   Alphonse Daudet's play *L'Arlésienne* was first presented in 1872, with incidental music by Georges Bizet. Two suites of the incidental music were extracted and ever since have been performed regularly in the concert hall. The "Farandole" is the final movement of the second suite.

27   Claude Terrasse (1867–1923) was known primarily as a composer of operettas. Among his most successful works were *Les Travaux d'Hercule* (1901), the title of which Robert gives incorrectly, and *Le Mariage de Télémaque* (1910).

28   Camille Chevillard (1859–1923) was best known as a pianist and as the conductor of the Concerts Lamoureux, a position given to him by his father-in-law, Charles Lamoureux. Robert here seems to refer to Chevillard's *Thème et variations*, op. 5 (1888).

29   Louis Schneider (1861–1935) was a music, theater, and art critic for several newspapers, including *Le Gaulois*, *La Paix*, *The New York Herald*, and *La Revue de France*.

30   Albert Mangeot was a publisher primarily associated with the journal *Le Monde Musicale*. His son, André (1883–1970), was a prominent violinist and impresario in London after World War I.

31   The references are to Gustave Charpentier's 1887–89 orchestral suite *Impressions d'Italie*, Dukas's 1897 "symphonic scherzo" *l'Apprenti Sorcier*, Debussy's 1892–94 tone poem *Prélude a l'après-midi d'un faune*, and one of the six *tableaux symphoniques* that Fanelli composed in 1912 in response to Théophile Gautier's 1882 prose-poems. The Debussy music had been famously choreographed by Vaslav Nijinsky for Serge Diaghilev's Ballets Russes for performances at Paris's Théâtre du Chatelet in 1912; just as famously, but not nearly so controversially, the Dukas music would later be used to accompany a sequence of Walt Disney's 1940 animated film *Fantasia*.

32 René Doire (1879–1959) was a composer, conductor, and the editor-in-chief of *Le Courrier Musical*.

33 The phrase "this period" refers not to the times in general but only to France's typically relaxed summertime, when Doire and the others were asked to respond to *Le Film*'s questionnaire.

34 Louis Ganne (1862–1923) was a composer and conductor who studied with Théodore Dubois and César Franck. He is best known for salon pieces and dance tunes, including the three mentioned in Robert's introductory note.

35 Paul Vidal (1863–1931) won the Prix de Rome in 1883, conducted at the Paris Opéra, and taught at the Paris Conservatory. His score for *La maladetta* dates from 1893.

36 André Wormser (1851–1926) received the Prix de Rome in 1875 and was best known as a pianist and as composer of the music for the 1890 pantomime mentioned in Robert's introductory note.

37 Reynaldo Hahn (1874–1947) was most famous for his songs, which enjoyed considerable success in *fin-de-siècle* Parisian salons. The ballet *La Fête chez Thérèse* was premiered at the Paris Opéra in 1910.

38 Hahn refers here to the operators of manually cranked cameras.

39 Henry Busser (1872–1973), whose name was sometimes given as Henri Büsser, was a composer, organist, and conductor who won the Prix de Rome in 1893. He was particularly noted for his supervision, in 1902, of the premiere of Debussy's opera *Pelléas et Mélisande*.

40 Gustave Doret (1866–1943) was best known for conducting the premiere of Debussy's *Prélude a l'après-midi d'un faune* and for promoting French music in Switzerland. As a composer, his greatest success was the operetta *Les Armaillis*, which premiered at the Paris Opéra-Comique in 1906.

41 Albert Roussel (1869–1937) taught counterpoint at the Schola Cantorum from 1902 to 1914. His compositions—including the 1904–06 *Poème de la forêt* and the 1910–11 *Evocations* for orchestra and the 1912 ballet-pantomime *La festin de l'araignée*—were critically acclaimed throughout Europe and North America.

42 At the time, the Concerts Pasdeloup, named for founder Jules Pasdeloup, were one of the four main Parisian orchestras, along with the Concerts Colonne, the Concerts Lamoureux, and the Société des Concerts du Conservatoire.

43 Gabriel Grovlez (1879–1944) maintained a successful conducting career in Europe and the United States, in addition to composing and teaching at both the Schola Cantorum (from 1899 until 1909) and the Paris Conservatory (from 1939 until 1944).

44 Armande de Polignac (1876–1962), the niece of Prince Edouard de Polignac, was known for her songs and was the first female conductor of French professional orchestras.

45 Georges Hüe (1858–1948) for the most part composed vocal works, including the two song albums and the opera mentioned by Robert. He also arranged the score for the 1909 film version of *The Return of Ulysses*, produced by Pathé's Films d'Art.

46 Francis Casadesus (1870–1954) was a prominent composer, conductor, violinist, and critic. His works demonstrate a particular interest in such dramatic genres as opera, radio, and film. He played a central role in the establishment of the American Conservatory in Fontainebleau.

47 Guy Ropartz (1864–1955) was a conductor and composer who self-consciously eschewed both modernism and academicism, despite teaching at the conservatories in Nancy (from 1894 to 1919) and Strasbourg (from 1919 to 1929). Premiered in Lyon in January 1919, *Le Poème de la Maison* is a secular oratorio with a text by Georges Witkowski.

48 Léon Moreau (1863–1946) and Henry Février (1875–1957) were composers who collaborated with director Louis Feuillade on the 1913 film-opera *L'Agonie de Byzance*. Février also composed for several silent films throughout the 1920s.

49 Hector Berlioz's 1854 "dramatic legend" *La damnation de Faust* was originally conceived as a "concert opera" and relied on the audience's imagination to provide the visual elements that a traditional opera would present on the stage. In particular, the harrowing "Ride to the Abyss" musically depicts Faust's descent into Hell.

50 Moreau's invocation of the word "adjutorium" is a reference to Psalm 70, the first verse of which, in Latin, is: "Deus in adjutorium meum intende; Domine ad adjuvandum me

festina." The translation in the King James Bible reads: "Make haste, o God, to deliver me; make haste to help me, o Lord." According to Frederick G. Holweck's 1907 *The Catholic Encyclopedia*, this verse is "the introductory prayer to every Hour of the Roman, monastic, and Ambrosian Breviaries, except during the last three days of Holy Week, and in the Office of the Dead."

51   This perhaps refers to Edgard Castil (18??–1943), a composer of French *chansons* who, in 1927, became production director of the newly formed Franco-Film production and distribution company.

52   In addition to composing the operas cited here and many songs, Félix Fourdrain (1880–1923) taught orchestration and composition at the Paris Conservatory.

53   Sylvio Lazzari (1857–1944) was widely regarded for his songs and a few successful operas. His *La Tour de feu*, composed in 1925 and premiered in 1928, was the first opera to use motion-picture projection as an integral element of its staging.

54   Jane Vieu (1871–1955) was best known for the opera *Arlette* (1904) and for her songs, some of which are published under the pseudonym Pierre Valette. C.1910, with Maurice Vieu she established the publishing house named for the two of them (i.e., Maurice Vieu et Jane Vieu).

55   Charlot was the affectionate name given by the French to Charlie Chaplin. It most frequently refers to Chaplin's popular tramp character.

56   Moritz Moszkowski (1854–1925) was an internationally renowned piano virtuoso who composed almost exclusively for his own instrument. By 1910, he had faded from the public eye, living as a recluse in poverty for the remainder of his life. His opera *Boabdil* was composed in 1892.

57   Fernand Le Borne (1862–1929) was primarily known as a critic and as the musical director of the Film d'Art studio established by Pathé in 1907. His opera *Les Girondins* premiered at the Théâtre de la Gaîté in January 1912.

58   Premiered at Paris's Salle Charras on November 17, 1908, Henri Lavedan's *L'Assassinat du Duc de Guise* is arguably the first feature-length film to be accompanied by an original score (earlier candidates for "first original film score" might include the anonymously composed music that accompanied a 1900 Salvation Army film titled *Soldiers of the Cross* in Melbourne, Australia, and music by Herman Finck that accompanied a London showing of *Marie Antoinette* in 1904). In any case, Camille Saint-Saëns's music for the eighteen-minute *L'Assassinat* in 1908 shared a bill with Gaston Berardi's music for *Le Secret de Myrto* and Le Borne's music for *L'Empreinte*.

59   *L'Empreinte* was not a narrative film but, rather, a brief series of tableaux featuring traditional French pantomime characters.

60   Marcel Samuel-Rousseau (1882–1955) won the Prix de Rome in 1905 and then went on to a career as a professor at the Paris Conservatoire and as music director for the Pathé studio.

61   Stan Golestan (1875–1956) was a prominent composer who served for twenty years as music critic for *Le Figaro*.

62   Georges Auric (1899–1983), the survey's youngest respondent, in 1919 was just emerging as a prominent figure in the Parisian avant-garde. His later career focused largely on ballet, songs, and—significantly—film music. In the course of his long career he would score more than 120 feature-length films.

63   Jean Noguès (1875–1932) was a successful opera composer who during his lifetime enjoyed more than 8,000 performances of his works. He adapted several of his operas into films produced in London and Naples.

64   Michel-Maurice Lévy (1883–1965) composed operas, operettas, and vaudevilles, most of them under the pseudonym Bétove.

65   The August 15, 1919, article was illustrated with photographs of all the contributors except Auric, Doire, Février, Ganne, Golestan, Hahn, Hüe, Le Borne, Mangeot, Moszkowski, Polignac, Schneider, and Terrasse.

66   "Aase's Death" is one of the pieces contained in the suite of incidental music that Norwegian composer Edvard Grieg wrote in 1874–75 to accompany a production of Henrik Ibsen's play *Peer Gynt*.

67 Based on Henryck Sienkiewicz's 1896 novel, Enrico Guazzoni's eight-reel *Quo Vadis?* (Cinès) was released internationally in 1913.

68 *La Danseuse de Pompeï* (*The Dancer of Pompeii*) is an 1899 novel by Jean Bertheroy. Working with librettists Henry Ferrare and Henri Cain, Nouguès had composed music for a five-act ballet version for the Paris Opéra-comique in 1912; it is not known if a film version of *La Danseuse de Pompeï* was ever made, but it is possible that Nouguès here refers to *La fanciulla de Pompei* (*The Girl of Pompeii*), an Italian film directed by Giulio Antamoro and released in 1925.

69 Lévy presumably is referring to the 1830 *Symphonie fantastique* of Hector Berlioz and, perhaps, to a popular *bal musette* song entitled "La Marche des titis parisiens."

70 Abel Gance's *La Dixième Symphonie* (Le Film d'Art) was released in 1918.

71 According to the Institut National de la Statistique et des Etudes Economiques, one French franc in 1919 had purchasing power of US $1.82 in 2010.

72 The societies mentioned here are, respectively, the Société des Auteurs des Arts Visuels (which at the time managed royalties related to film) and the Société des Auteurs, Compositeurs, et Editeurs de la Musique (which at the time managed royalties related to art music).

Chapter 3

1 For details on the musical conventions of the "classical-style" film, see Chapter 7, note 2, this volume.

2 The Rialto was neither the first nor the largest of the new "movie palaces" that sprang up in New York in the middle of the twentieth century's second decade. The 2,460-seat Regent Theater opened in 1913, followed by the 3,500-seat Strand in 1914, the Rialto and the 2,100-seat Rivoli in 1917, and the 5,300-seat Capitol in 1919. Although billed as "movie palaces," all these venues were in fact multi-purpose venues that hosted both filmed and "live" entertainments.

3 Silent films that Rapee scored for Fox include *Over the Hill* and *A Connecticut Yankee in King Arthur's Court* (1920), *The Queen of Sheba* (1921), *Nero* (an Italian film, but released in the United States by Fox in 1922), *If Winter Comes* (1923), *The Last Man on Earth* and *Iron Horse* (1924), *The Man Without a Country* (1925), *What Price Glory* (1926), and *Sunrise* and *7th Heaven* (1927). Among the sound films that Rapee scored for Fox are *Four Sons*, *Mother Machree*, *Street Angel*, *The Red Dance*, and *Mother Knows Best* (1928), and *Making the Grade* (1929).

4 Originally published by Belwin, *Motion Picture Moods* was reprinted in 1974 by the Arno Press (New York).

5 Likewise originally published by Belwin, Rapee's *Encyclopedia* was reprinted by the Arno Press (New York) in 1970.

6 Erno Rapee, *Encyclopedia of Music for Pictures* (New York: Belwin, 1925), 25.

7 At the time of Rapee's writing, Victor Herbert (1859–1924) was well known as the composer of such popular operettas as *Babes in Toyland* (1903), *Naughty Marietta* (1910), *Sweethearts* (1913), and *Angel Face* (1919); within the film industry, Herbert was also well known as a co-founder, in 1914, of the American Society of Composers, Authors, and Publishers (ASCAP), an organization that after a strained legal battle effectively forced film exhibitors to pay license fees for the use of music whose copyrights were owned by ASCAP members. Cécile Chaminade (1857–1944) was a French composer who to this day remains best known for her salon-style works for various chamber ensembles.

8 *Madame Sans-Gêne* tells the story of the life of Cathérine Hubscher, a washerwoman who became the influential wife of Napoleon's French field marshal François Joseph Lefebvre. The story began in 1893 as a play by Victorien Sardou and Émile Moreau, then was furthered in an 1898 novel by Edmond Lepelletier, a 1911 French film directed by Henri Desfontaines, a 1915 opera by Umberto Giordano, and a 1925 film (Famous Players-Lasky) directed by Leonce Perret and starring Gloria Swanson in the title role. The funeral march referred to by Rapee—and used by him in his score for the 1920 film *Passion* (an American release of a German film titled *Madame DuBarry*)—comes from the Giordano opera; the 1925

Madame Sans-Gêne, which premiered at New York's Rivoli Theater after Rapee's book had gone to press, featured a score by Hugo Riesenfeld.

9 Chapter 16 is the "Encyclopedia Section" of Rapee's book. Almost 500 pages long, it contains a list of topic headings that range from "Abyssinian Music" and "Aeroplanes" to "Zanzibar" and "Zoo"; under each heading there appears a list of appropriate musical numbers and information regarding their publishers.

10 Produced by the Samuel Goldwyn Company and released by United Artists in November 1925, the first film treatment of *Stella Dallas* (directed by Henry King and starring Belle Bennett in the title role) was fitted with music by Herman Rosen. It was Wagner's prerogative, of course, to come up with a score of his own.

11 Froelich's *Richard Wagner* was produced by the Berlin-based Messter-Film, a studio that was absorbed by UFA in 1918.

12 After the introduction of the sound film, Becce composed a memorable score for Fritz Lang's 1933 *The Testament of Dr. Mabuse*. He worked for UFA until 1957, but primarily as a conductor for musicals and films with opera- or operetta-based subject matter.

13 Before signing on with Becce's *Film-Ton-Kunst* (Film-Sound-Art) Erdmann, beginning in 1924, was a columnist for *Filmtechnik* (*Film Technique*) and *Reichsfilmblatt* (the *National Film Newspaper*).

14 The headings for the first seven sections of the *Allgemeines Handbuch der Film-Musik* are (1) "Der Film im Rahmen der Zeitkünste," (2) "Wie kam die Musik zum Film?," (3) "Kann der stumme Filme ohne Musik sein?," (4) "Von der musikalischen Illustration," (5) "Illustration, Autorenillustration, Komposition?," (6) "Ist eine künstleriche Bindung zwischen Film und Musik möglich?," and (7) "Lehrfilm, Kulturfilm, Tagesschau."

15 The headings for the last two sections are "Vom Atelier zum Theater" and "Zur Musikdramaturgie des Film."

16 Throughout the *Allgemeines Handbuch der Film-Musik*, Erdmann uses the term *Spielfilm* (literally, "play film," or "performance film") for what is here translated as "feature film."

17 For "art of film," Erdmann uses the word *Filmkunst*.

18 The *Allgemeines Handbuch der Film-Musik* features neither footnotes nor endnotes but, rather, fine-print comments in right-hand margins of the pages. The marginal note aligned with this sentence reads: "One thinks here of the proper artistic precursor of the film, the age-old shadow-play, which played an especially large role in the Orient. The shadow-play was later adopted by the West and for a long time figured importantly in public entertainment. See Georg Jacob, *Geschichte der Schatten-theaters* [*The History of Shadow Theaters*] (Hannover: Heinz Lafaire)."

19 For "screenplay," Erdmann uses the word *Filmhandlung* (literally, "film plot").

20 The rather lengthy marginal note that Erdmann aligns with this paragraph has to do with the markedly different scales of time afforded to composers for film and composers of operas and symphonic music. Whereas the opera or symphonic composer often has as much as a half-hour in which to build toward a moment of peak tension, the film composer typically must accomplish the same effect in a matter of minutes.

21 Erdmann's phrase is: "Wir haben auch noch keine Filmtheater die sich der Pflege der Filmkunst widmen . . ."

22 The marginal note aligned with this paragraph suggests that, among other things, one of the primary difficulties confronted by anyone embarking on a serious systematic or theoretical study of film is the lack of archival material. Erdmann wonders if film is, after all, merely an ephemeral art form, just an "apparition of the day" (*eine Erscheinung des Tages*). But then, with pointed questions, he compares film with venerable examples of painting and sculpture. He asks: Why should such a time-rooted work as Da Vinci's *Last Supper* retain its artistic value over centuries while the impact of a well-made film—perhaps just as thoughtful, arguably just as artistic—fades so quickly? Erdmann wonders how much the widespread idea of film's ephemeral nature is connected with the equally widespread idea that film, in general, lacks artistic value.

23 Erdmann's phrase is: "Stilbeziehungen zwischen Film und Musik."

24 "Hot potato," meaning an issue so problematic that most persons would prefer to pass it along to someone else rather than deal with it themselves, is a distinctly English cliché.

Setting off the phrase in quotation marks, Erdmann here uses the German equivalent *"das heiße Eisen Musik"* (literally, "the hot iron"—e.g., a horseshoe or sword fresh from a blacksmith's anvil—"of music").

25 Erdmann in this sentence does not mention film music in particular. He refers only to the "artistic situation" (*die Kunstsituation*) that he has described.

26 The sesquipedalian noun that Erdmann uses here is *Schaubudenangelegenheit*, which perhaps refers not just to nickelodeon-era exhibition spaces but also to the peephole-like Kinetoscope machines that *c.*1893 introduced motion pictures to the public.

27 In the marginal note aligned with this paragraph, Erdmann takes serious issue with what he calls "uninformed" statements regarding the earliest uses of music in conjunction with film made by Hungarian film theorist Béla Balázs in his 1924 book *Der sichtbare Mensch, oder die Kultur des Films*. Erdmann quotes, and ridicules, a "remarkable" passage in which Balázs states, in effect, that each and every scene in early film exhibition was accompanied by music whose expressiveness was brazen and shameless ("brutal und irgendwie schamlos"). But Erdmann misrepresents Balázs, for the quoted passage refers not to whatever music might have sounded in conjunction with the "show-booth" cinema of the 1890s but, rather, to the music that genuinely accompanied, for better or worse, the nickelodeon-era narrative films made throughout the twentieth century's first decade. It is worth noting that Erdmann (1882–1942) and Balázs (1884–1949) were contemporaries, and that both of them in the late 1890s would have been old enough to have acquired first-hand experience with the earliest public combinations of music and film.

28 Erdmann uses the phrase "bewegte Bild der weißen Wand," and he does not set it off in quotation marks.

29 The original phrase within the em-dashes is "sie sind höchstens lamoryant," doubtless a problem for translators because "lamoryant" is a typographical error. The word should be "larmoyant," an old-fashioned German adjective derived from the French and meaning "weepy" or "tearful."

30 In his marginal note, Erdman cites as prime examples of "style films" (Stilfilmen) such American swashbucklers as *The Mark of Zorro* (1920), *Robin Hood* (1922), and *The Thief of Baghdad* (1924). As German examples, he mentions *Ein Sommernachtstraum* (1925) and the Ernst Lubitsch romantic comedies *Die Ehe im Kreise* (1924) and *Küß mich noch einmal* (1925).

31 Erdman uses the word "Gefühlslinie," literally, "line of feeling."

32 In his marginal note, Erdman describes *Ben Hur* (MGM, 1925) as an episodic film that culminates in its overblown "sea" and "chariot race" scenes. The "small German film *Derby*," he notes, also culminates in a "race" scene, but this is "handled properly" ("aber mit Recht").

33 Erdman gives the title *Die Bärenhochzeit* for this 1926 Soviet horror film (originally titled *Medvezhya svadba*) based on a novel by Anatoli Lunacharsky and directed by Konstantin Eggert. In his marginal note, he describes the film as a "potboiler" ("Räuber-romantik") yet one adequately enough made; the film simply does not need music, he claims.

34 *The Student from Prague* (*Der Student von Prag*), also known in English as *A Bargain with Satan*, was made by Deutsche Bioscop GmbH; its co-directors were Stellan Rye and Paul Wegener, and it was originally issued with music by Joseph Weiss. In his marginal note, Erdman says that it is a "tidy fantasy" that accommodates music in a natural way. In the same category, Erdman says, belong *The Cabinet of Dr. Caligari* (Decla-Bioscop AG, 1920), directed by Robert Wiene, with original music by his colleague Giuseppe Becce; and *Das Wachsfigurenkabinett* (*The Wax Museum*) (Neptune-Film A.G., 1924), directed by Leo Birinsky and Paul Leni.

35 *The Volga Boatman*, whose German title is *Der Wolgaschiffer*, is an epic set in Tsarist Russia, directed by Cecil B. DeMille and produced by DeMille's own company in 1926; its Los Angeles premiere featured original music by R. H. Bassett and its New York premiere featured original music by Hugo Riesenfeld. In his marginal note, Erdman describes the film as being structured along the lines of an opera and thus very suitable for a "musical flow"; the film's use of the famous "Volga Boatman" song, he says, is a model of effectiveness.

36 *Der Geiger von Florenz*, sometimes known by the English title *Impetuous Youth*, was made by the German UFA studio in 1926; directed by Paul Czinner, it featured original music by Giuseppe Becce.

37 For the 1923 Charles Chaplin film, Erdman uses the German title *Die Nächte einer schönen Frau*; the film was also known in Germany as *Eine Frau in Paris*.

38 F. W. Murnau's *Der letzte Mann* (known in English both as *The Last Man* and *The Last Laugh*) was released by UFA in 1924; it featured an original score by Giuseppe Becce and Florian C. Reithner. In his marginal note, Erdman writes that the "worlds" of the three films mentioned in this paragraph lend themselves only to "tangible," i.e., diegetic, music.

39 Erdman's marginal note observes that while Chaplin's 1925 *The Gold Rush* (*Goldrausch*) is a comedy of great significance, it nevertheless poses problems for music. Also problematic, and in similar ways, is Soviet director Sergei Eisenstein's *Battleship Potemkin* (*Panzerkreuzer Potemkin*), a 1925 epic about the early years of the Russian revolution which, for its German release, featured original music by Edmund Meisel; *Potemkin* "begins in a difficult place," Erdman writes, and "from then until the end the music is simply left running."

40 Erdman uses the word "Musikfilm."

41 Erdman uses the verb "zu drehen."

Chapter 4

1 Although it was reported in 1895, it is now generally regarded as "a myth" that Dickson, in 1889, presented Edison with a sound film that had Dickson saying: "Good morning, Mr. Edison, glad to see you back. I hope you are satisfied with the kineto-phonograph." See Douglas Gomery, *The Coming of Sound* (New York and London: Routledge, 2005), 159.

2 For more on these, see Rick Altman, *Silent Film Sound* (New York: Columbia University Press, 2004), 158–75, and James Wierzbicki, *Film Music: A History* (New York and London: Routledge, 2009), 74–76.

3 The Berlin-based trio consisted of Josef Engl, Joseph Massolle, and Hans Vogt.

4 The score for *Don Juan* was composed for the most part by William Axt, with contributions from David Mendoza and orchestrations by Maurice Baron. The film's opening credits indicate that the recorded music was performed by the New York Philharmonic.

5 The score for *The Better 'Ole* was by Herman Heller, with contributions from Maurice Baron, Fred Heff, and Edward Kilenyi. Clifford McCarty, in his 2000 *Film Composers in America: A Filmography*, credits the score only to Baron.

6 The score for *The Jazz Singer*, which included numerous quotations of pre-existing music, is the work of Louis Silvers.

7 The songs performed by Jolson's character include "Toot Toot Tootsie," "Dirty Hands, Dirty Face," "Blue Skies," and—most famously—"My Mammy."

8 Quoted in A. Scott Berg, *Goldwyn: A Biography* (New York: Knopf, 1989), 173.

9 Evans here inserts an asterisked footnote: Several 'better class musicians' were recently invited to become honorary presidents and vice-presidents of the newly founded British School of Cinema Organists. Most of them answered with transparent evasions, from which it could be inferred that they were afraid of compromising their authority.

10 England's first exposure to the Vitaphone came in late September of 1928, when Warner Bros.' *The Jazz Singer* opened—with great acclaim—at London's new Piccadilly Theatre.

11 The Hindemith player-piano score that was premiered in July 1928 at the Baden-Baden festival accompanied a short animated film directed by Hans Richter and titled *Vormittagsspuk*; the film survives but the music does not.

12 All the fully scored silent films to which Evans refers were German. Fritz Lang in 1924 directed two films based on the Nibelung legend—*Die Niebelungen: Siegfried* and *Die Niebelungen: Kreimhilds Rache*—both of them featuring Wagner-based scores by Gottfried Huppertz. Huppertz also wrote the music for Lang's 1927 *Metropolis*. The music for Walter Ruttmann's 1927 *Berlin: Die Symphonie der Großstadt* was by Edmund Meisel.

13 Harvey Grace (1874–1944) was a British organist and choirmaster who in the 1920s served as editor of *The Musical Times*. The quotation is from G. K. Chesterton's introduction to a 1906 edition of Charles Dickens's 1826–37 serialized novel *The Pickwick Papers*.

14   The "Statement on Sound" was first published in the Leningrad magazine *Zhizn' iskusstva* on August 5, 1928. A translation by Jay Leda is available in *Film Sound: Theory and Practice*, ed. Elisabeth Weis and John Belton (New York: Columbia University Press, 1985), 83–85; a translation by Richard Taylor is in *The Film Factory: Russian and Soviet Cinema in Documents 1896–1939*, ed. Richard Taylor and Ian Christie (London: Routledge & Kegan Paul, 1988), 234–35.

15   For details, see chapter three of Joan M. Titus, "Modernism, Socialist Realism, and Identity in the Early Film Music of Dmitry Shostakovich, 1929–1932" (Ph.D. dissertation, Ohio State University, 2006).

16   These phrases are invented by Joan Titus but are based closely on Shostakovich's language throughout the article. For a full discussion of how Shostakovich employed these principles throughout his score, see the sources cited in note 15.

17   Shostakovich's article has been fully translated into English once before—Marek Pytel in *New Babylon: Trauberg, Kozintsev, Shostakovich* (London: Eccentric Press, 1999), 26— but this translation is quite liberal and contains misinterpretations of specific words. Sections of the article have also been translated into English in an editorial note for the *New Collected Works of Shostakovich*. See Manashir Yakubov, ed., "Muzïka D.D. Shostakovicha k nemomu kinofil'mu 'Novyi Vavilon'" [Dmitry Shostakovich's Music to the Silent Film *New Babylon*] in *Dmitry Shostakovich: Novoye Sobraniye Sochineniy, Tom 122, "Novyi Vavilon,"* [Dmitry Shostakovich: New Collected Works, Volume 122, *The New Babylon*] (Moscow: DSCH, 2004).

18   For more on the press, the studio, and the film's reception, see chapter three of Titus, "Modernism, Socialist Realism, and Identity."

19   D. Shostakovich, *Novyi vavilon, syuita iz muzïki k kinofil'mu partitura* [The New Babylon, Suite from the Music to the Film Score] Gennady Rozhdestvenskiy, ed. (Moscow: Sovetskiy kompozitor, 1976); and Yakubov, Dmitry Shostakovich: New Collected Works, Volume 122, *The New Babylon*. Both Sikorski and Boosey & Hawkes published the suite in the West, but the editions differ from one another. See the interview with Mark FitzGerald in John Riley, "The New Babylon in Rotterdam," *DSCH Journal*, January 16, 2002, 50–51. For a brief history of the extant recordings of the film, see Titus, "Silents, Sound, and Modernism," forthcoming.

20   The term *kino-film* ("cinema-film") was used in the Soviet Union for a particular type of film, one categorized as somehow more "artistic" than the run-of-the-mill motion picture.

21   Shostakovich uses the term *kino-theater*, which perhaps suggests a cinema oriented toward a relatively high level of artistic presentation.

22   Here Shostakovich uses the word *royal* ("grand piano"). In the previous sentence he used *klavier*, which suggests simply an upright or spinet piano.

23   Referring to what the orchestral trumpeter on such occasions might do, Shostakovich uses not the word *igrat* ("to play") but, rather *trubit* ("to sound").

24   In this case, Shostakovich is using the French word *séances* simply to mean "showings" or "screenings" of the film.

25   *Khaltura* is best translated as "hackwork," but it can also mean "trash" or "garbage." For alternative translations, see Yakubov, 542, and Pytel, 26.

26   Shostakovich uses the word *soprovozhdenniye* ("accompaniment") in the most general sense, meaning both the compiled orchestral scores (in large theaters) and the playing of pianists (in small theaters) that in the 1920s were common throughout Soviet Russia.

27   *Glavrepetkom* is the standard compound word for the "Main Repertory Committee," to which film scenarios as well as musical scenarios needed to be sent for advance approval.

28   To clean the stables of King Augeus of Elis in a single day was the fifth of the twelve "labors" assigned by the gods to the Greek mythological hero Hercules as penance for hubris. The Augean stables were legendary not just for being the largest in all of ancient Greece but also for—until Hercules's assignment—*never* having been cleaned.

29   As noted in the introduction, *Novomu vavilonu* (*New Babylon*) was directed by Grigory Kozintsev and Leonid Trauberg; it was produced by the Sovkino studio and released on March 18, 1929.

30   Shostakovich uses the word *chast*, which here is translated as "part" but which can also mean, in the filmic sense, "reel."

31   The translated word "filled" is here gleaned from the context of the sentence and just three letters (*pol*—), the rest of the word in all existing copies of the article being smudged out.

32   At this turbulent moment in French history, a Versaillais was someone loyal to the regime whose seat of government was still the palace at Versailles; in marked contrast, a Communard was a supporter of the hopeful but short-lived socialist movement whose leaders took control of Paris for just a few months in the spring of 1871.

33   Shostakovich is referring to the piano exercises of French composer and pedagogue Charles Louis Hanon (1819–1900). This phrase has been misrepresented by Marek Pytel in his English translation (Pytel, 26) and by Hélène Bernatchez in her German translation of Shostakovich's article in *Schostakowitsch und die Fabrik des Exzentrischen Schauspielers* (Munich: Martin Meidenbauer Verlagbuchhandlung, 2006), 123 and 252. Both Pytel and Bernatchez translate the phrase as a "well-known galop" instead of a "well-known exercise" by Hanon. The mistranslations may have arisen because of the degraded and difficult-to-read extant copies of the article.

34   "Ça-ira" (French for "that will do") is the title of a song, usually attributed to a street singer named Ladré, that dates back to the days of the French revolution. The title of "La Carmagnole" refers to a garb—in essence, a short jacket—traditionally worn by working-class residents of the Piedmont village of Carmagnola; the song that celebrates both this humble dress and the spirit behind it likewise dates back to the days of the French revolution.

35   *Patetik* can be translated as "pathétique" or "pathos."

36   Shostakovich uses the word *Sokovshchina*.

37   The name "Les Six"—describing a group of young French musicians whose generally insouciant style was championed both by composer Erik Satie and writer–filmmaker Jean Cocteau—was conferred by the music critic Henri Collet in a January 16, 1920, article in the magazine *Comoedia*. The other members of the group were Georges Auric, Louis Durey, Arthur Honegger, Francis Poulenc, and Germaine Tailleferre.

38   For the survey, see p. 23 of this anthology.

39   Insistent upon cataloguing virtually everything he wrote, Milhaud affixed the label Op. 104 to his music for the generically titled *Actualités / Wochenschau* and the label Op. 107 to his music for the Cavalcanti film.

40   Milhaud's contribution underscored the segment titled "Ruth, Roses, and Revolvers," which focused on the work of avant-garde photographer Man Ray. Other segments of Richter's decidedly non-commercial "art house" film, which explores the work not just of Man Ray but also of Alexander Calder, Max Ernst, and Marcel Duchamp, were scored by the American composers Louis Applebaum, Paul Bowles, John Cage, and David Diamond.

41   The film to which Milhaud refers is likely *The Better 'Ole*, a wartime comedy that starred Charles Chaplin's half-brother Syd and which was first presented in New York in October 1926. Warner Bros.' second feature-length Vitaphone film, *The Better 'Ole*, was a retrofitted silent film featuring only music and sound effects, without any dialogue. According to the printed program—reproduced on p. 84 of Donald Crafton, *The Talkies: American Cinema's Transition to Sound, 1926–1931* (Berkeley: University of California Press, 1997)—the music was "by Herman Heller, assisted by Maurice Baron, Fred Heff and Dr. Edward Kilenyi." Clifford McCarty, in his generally reliable *Film Composers in America: A Filmography, 1911–1970* (Oxford: Oxford University Press, 2000), credits the score only to Baron (35).

42   Tri-Ergon—so-called because it represented the efforts of three workers (Josef Engl, Joseph Massolle, and Hans Vogt)—was a technology that involved the optical recording of sound waves on motion-picture film. It was patented in Germany in 1919, the same year in which the American inventor Lee de Forest patented his Phonofilm process for sound-on-film recording.

43   Berlin-based music theoretician Carl Robert Blum had been working on synchronization devices since 1920. For details, see Michael Wedel, "Vom Synchronismus zur Synchronisation: Carl Robert Blum und der frühe Tonfilm," in *Weltwunder der Kinematographie. Beiträge zu einer Kulturgeschichte der Filmtechnik*, ed. Joachim Polzer

(Berlin: Polzer Media Group, 2002), 97–112. For more comments from Milhaud on his use of Blum's Musik-Chronometer, see Darius Milhaud, *Notes without Music*, trans. Donald Evans (London: Dennis Dobson Ltd., 1951), 174 (orig. *Notes sans musique*, 1949, and later published as *Ma vie heureuse*, 1974).

44 Alberto Cavalcanti's *La P'tite Lili* (Studio Films, 1929) was a fifteen-minute film during which Milhaud's music for the most part embellished the Gravel-Benech title song.

45 The conductor Milhaud mentions is Wolfgang Zeller (1893–1967); the technical assistant is Rudolf Wagner-Régeny (1903–69), a Leipzig- and Berlin-trained musician who during the 1930s and 1940s composed more than a dozen operas.

Chapter 5

1 Fox's first public demonstration of the Movietone system, in New York in May 1927, involved only a newsreel-like film set at the West Point military academy. The second demonstration took place in Los Angeles in September 1928; along with newsreels and various shorts, it included the feature-length romance *Mother Knows Best*, with music by William Kernell, Erno Rapee, and S. L. Rothafel. Likely the most impressive early demonstration of the Movietone system was the premiere, in November 1928, of Walt Disney's animated cartoon *Steamboat Willie*.

2 MGM's 1954 *Singin' in the Rain*, a musical comedy set in Hollywood in the late 1920s, features delightfully humorous depictions of what could—and likely often did—go wrong in Vitaphone exhibitions.

3 The decision to use original orchestral music in dramatically purposeful ways likely originated with RKO executive producer David O. Selznick. The trio of landmark films in which Selznick developed his film-music ideas comprises *Bird of Paradise* (1932; dir. King Vidor), *The Most Dangerous Game* (1932; dir. Ernest B. Schoedsack and Irving Pichel), and—most famously—*King Kong* (1933; dir. Merion C. Cooper). The scores for all three films were by Max Steiner.

4 Ted Thackrey Jr., "Philip Scheurer, Times Film Critic for 4 Generations of Movies, Dies at 82," *Los Angeles Times*, February 19, 1985, SD A5.

5 Ibid.

6 The music for Paramount's 1931 *Rango* (dir. Ernest B. Schoedsack) was primarily by Karl Hajos, but contributing composers included Max Bergunker, Gerard Carbonara, Herman Hand, W. Franke Harling, Sigmund Krumgold, John Leipold, and George Steiner. See Clifford McCarty, *Film Composer in America: A Filmography, 1911–1970* (Oxford: Oxford University Press, 2000), 125.

7 McCarty lists only Karl Hajos as composer for Paramount's 1931 *Dishonored* (dir. Josef von Sternberg), but the online International Movie Data Base mentions Herman Hand as an uncredited musical contributor.

8 Paramount's 1930 *The Love Parade* (dir. Ernst Lubitsch) featured music primarily by John Leipold, with contributions from W. Franke Harling, Oscar Potoker, and Max Terr. The same studio's 1930 *Monte Carlo* (dir. Lubitsch) featured a score primarily by Harling, with contributions from Hajos, Hand, Leipold, and Krumgold.

9 MGM's *Jenny Lind* (dir. Arthur Robison) was a 1931 re-make—for release in France—of a 1930 film titled *A Lady's Morals* (Cosmopolitan; dir. Sidney Franklin); both versions starred Grace Moore in the role of the nineteenth-century singer popularly known as "the Swedish nightingale." Along with library "tracks," the 1931 film featured music by William Axt.

   Directed by Lionel Barrymore, MGM's 1930 *The Rogue Song* was a treatment of Franz Lehár's 1859 operetta *Zigeunerliebe*; it starred baritone Lawrence Tibbett and featured Lehár's music as arranged, and supplemented, by Axt.

10 Responsive to Hollywood's intense but short-lived interest in popular songs, between April and August of 1930 *Motion Picture Magazine* ran a regular feature—titled "Theme Songs of the Movies"—that included facsimile reprints of sheet music. The inaugural article showcased "Happy Feet" (lyrics by Jack Yellen, music by Milton Ager) from *The King of Jazz* and "It Happened in Monterey" (lyrics by Billy Rose, music by Mabel Wayne) from

the film of the same title. Subsequent issues showcased Irving Berlin's "Tango Melody" from *The Bad One*; Charles Wakefield Cadman's "Song of the Sword" from the film of the same title; "As Long As We're Together" (lyrics by Ben Bard, music anonymous) from *Reno*; and "With My Guitar and You" (lyrics by Mort Harris and Edward Heyman, music by Ted Snyder) from *Swing High*.

11 Best known as a sultry voiced singing actress, Marlene Dietrich (1901–92) was indeed an accomplished player of the musical saw, and she made a point of including saw performances when she famously entertained American troops in Europe during World War II. Trained in childhood as a violinist, Dietrich learned to play the musical saw in 1927 when she was in Vienna making the film *Café Electric*; her teacher was the Bavarian music-hall artist Igo Sym.

12 Walker seems to be referring here to *Mammy*, a 1930 Warner Bros. feature that had Jolson singing such songs as "Across the Breakfast Table Looking at You," "Let Me Sing and I'm Happy," "My Mammy," and "Yes! We Have No Bananas." In 1931 Jolson's voice—singing "Sonny Boy"—was featured in MGM's *The Two Barks Brothers*, but this was an animated short about a pair of dogs. Jolson's much-anticipated comeback would not occur until 1933, in *Hallelujah I'm a Bum*, produced by Lewis Milestone and released by United Artists, with a large number of pre-existing songs coupled with original music by Alfred Newman.

13 Broadway star Marilyn Miller had played the title roles in First National's musicals *Sally* (1929) and *Sunny* (1930); she returned to Hollywood for Warner Bros.' *Her Majesty, Love*, released in December 1931, and this was the last of her films.

14 Produced by Samuel Goldwyn and released in September 1930 by United Artists, *Whoopee!* was an adaptation of the highly successful Broadway show (music by Walter Donaldson, lyrics by Gus Kahn) mounted by Florenz Ziegfeld in late 1928. The film, featuring a two-color Technicolor process, marked the Hollywood debut of choreographer Busby Berkeley.

15 The "crooning shorts" that Crosby made for Sennett are limited to *I Surrender Dear*, and *One More Chance*, both from early in 1931.

16 This statement is worthy of special note. Released in March 1932, RKO's *Girl Crazy* was an adaptation of the highly successful 1930 Broadway show of the same title that featured a "book" by Guy Bolton and—much more famously—songs by George and Ira Gershwin. So enduring are the Gershwins' *Girl Crazy* songs (which include "Someone to Watch Over Me," "Bidin' My Time," "Embraceable You," and "I Got Rhythm") that it is hard to imagine that the film adaptation could have been conceived as anything other than a musical. Yet apparently this was a matter upon which RKO executives, in the anti-musical climate of 1931, seriously needed to reflect.

17 RKO's remake of Colorart Pictures' 1928 *Marcheta* was released not under that title but, rather, as *Waiting for the Bride*, *Waiting at the Church*, and then, finally, *The Runaround*. *Bird of Paradise* indeed features songs performed by the Mexican-born actress Dolores Del Rio, but in film-music annals it lays claim to fame for being the first RKO film to feature an almost continuous "underscore" by composer Max Steiner. For more on Steiner's involvement in "underscoring," see pp. 88–93 of this volume.

18 Both of these films were indeed "musicals," the one by Sigmund Romberg and Oscar Hammerstein II, the other by Jerome Kern and Otto A. Harbach. Additional music for Alan Crosland's *Children of Dreams* was provided by David Mendoza; additional music for Alfred E. Green's *Men of the Sky* was by Mendoza and Erno Rapee.

19 *Flying High*, which opened in November 1931, featured music by Ray Henderson and lyrics by Buddy DeSylva and Lew Brown.

20 Making a telling point about the difficulty of musical attributions for the earliest Hollywood sound films, Clifford McCarty notes that "the full orchestral score" for RKO's *Rio Rita* "bears no name or even initials, although studio documents identify the arranger as Roy Webb." McCarty, *Film Composers in America: A Filmography, 1911–1970* (Oxford: Oxford University Press, 2000), 10.

21 The reference is to Universal's *All Quiet on the Western Front*, directed by Lewis Milestone and released in August 1930; aside from opening and closing music by Heinz Roemheld, the famously "stark" adaptation of Erich Marie Remarque's novel about World War I is quite devoid of music.

22   The Eddie Cantor feature to which Schallert refers is most likely *The Kid from Spain* (dir. Leo McCarey), produced independently by the Samuel Goldwyn Company but released by United Artists in November 1932; the score was largely by Alfred Newman, with additional music by Bert Kelmar and Harry Ruby. Al Jolson at the time of Schallert's writing was making *Hallelujah, I'm a Bum* (dir. Lewis Milestone), an independent production likewise released, in February 1933, by United Artists; the film was built around songs by Richard Rodgers and Lorenz Hart, with additional music by Newman.

23   Paramount's 1932 *This Is the Night* (dir. Frank Tuttle) featured a score primarily by W. Franke Harling and Ralph Rainger, with additional music by Rudolph G. Kopp, Arthur Lange, and John Leipold. The film did not involve actor-singer Maurice Chevalier, who at the time of Schallert's writing had starred in such Paramount "musicals" as *Innocents of Paris* (1929), *The Love Parade* (1929), *The Big Pond* (1930), *The Playboy of Paris* (1930), *The Smiling Lieutenant* (1931), and *One Hour with You* (1932).

Chapter 6

1   See p. 76 of this volume.

2   All of them released by RKO and produced by David O. Selznick, the films with which Steiner laid the foundations for the classical-style film score were *Bird of Paradise* (1932), *The Most Dangerous Game* (1932), and—most famously—*King Kong* (1933).

3   The article is included in the collection *Music Reviewed, 1940–1954* (New York: Random House, 1967), 277–279; it is reprinted in *A Virgil Thomson Reader*, ed. John Rockwell (Boston: Houghton Mifflin, 1981), 324–26.

4   "How to Write a Piece" is Chapter Ten of *The State of Music* (New York: William Morrow, 1939), 155–92. The chapter is reprinted in the above cited *A Virgil Thomson Reader*, 148–70.

5   The remark comes from George Antheil, "Breaking into the Movies," *Modern Music* 14, no. 2 (January–February 1937), 86.

6   First presented on December 4, 1923, at the Théâtre Champs-Elysées in Paris, *Entr'acte* was a twenty-minute intermission feature separating the two parts of a ballet (choreographed largely by Jean Börlin, with sets by Picabia and Clair and music by Satie) titled *Relâche*. Like the ballet, the film in both imagery and accompanying music is representative of the then-fashionable Dada aesthetic; the imagery conveys no narrative, and the music consists of what Martin M. Marks has described as a series of "brief repetitive patterns strung together in units of four or eight measures" (169). In part because it was so deliberately untypical of 1920s practice, *Entr'acte* has generated considerable scholarly commentary. See, for example, Douglas W. Gallez, "Satie's *Entr'acte*: A Model of Film Music," *Cinema Journal* 16, no. 1 (Fall 1976), 36–50; Noël Carroll, "*Entr'acte*, Paris and Dada," *Millennium Film Journal* 1, no. 1 (Winter 1977), 5–11; and the final chapter ("Erik Satie's Score for *Entr'acte*") of Marks's *Music and the Silent Film: Contexts and Case Studies, 1895–1924* (Oxford: Oxford University Press, 1997), 167–85.

7   Directed by Grigori Kozintsev and Leonid Trauberg, *Odna* was originally conceived as a silent film, then retrofitted, shortly before its release in October 1931, with music by Dmitry Shostakovich; the score, which the composer published as his Opus 26, is remarkable for both its use of Mongolian "throat singing" and its various episodes that employ the relatively new electronic instrument—named after its Soviet inventor—called the theremin. For more on Leonid Theremin's instrument and its use in film scores, see James Wierzbicki, "Weird Vibrations: How the Theremin Gave Voice to Hollywood's Extraterrestrial Others," *Journal of Popular Film and Television* 30, no. 2 (Fall 2002), 125–35.

8   The French composer Arthur Honegger (1892–1955) had by the time of Thomson's writing provided music for two silent films and two sound films: the silent films were *La roue* (1923) and *Napoléon* (1927), both directed by Abel Gance and both upwards of four hours in length; the sound films were Gance's 1931 *La fin du monde* (for which Honegger—along with Maurice Martenot, Michel Michelet, Robert-Lucien Siohan, and Vladimir Zederbaum—was just one of five credited composers) and Berthold Bartosche's 1932 animated short *L'Idée*. Over the next twenty years Honegger composed music for more than thirty additional sound films.

9   Jacques Ibert (1890–1962) famously contributed four songs to Georg Wilhelm Pabst's 1933 *Don Quixote* (for Fedele d'Amico's comments on these, see p. 110 of this volume); the film was released in Germany, and it is not likely that by the time of this writing Thomson would have seen it. Thomson seems to be referring here to the score that Ibert composed for Julien Duvivier's 1931 *Les cinq gentlemen maudits* (1931); possibly he is referring as well to music that Ibert (along with Marcel Delannoy) wrote for Maurice Tourneur's *Les deux orphelines*, not released in the United States until February 1934, but shown in France in March 1933. After these early efforts, Ibert composed some two dozen more film scores.

A contemporary of Ibert and Honegger, Jean Rivier (1896–1987) in fact produced very little music for films.

10   In light of how celebratory his comments are, it is rather spectacular that Thomson gets the film's title wrong. He refers here to Jean Cocteau's 1930 *Le sang d'un poète* (*The Blood of a Poet*), a decidedly avant-garde film that uses the music by Georges Auric (1899–1983) in ways that the composer had not anticipated. *Le sang d'un poète* marked Auric's film debut, after which he composed prolifically for films not just in France but also in England and the United States; among the enduringly famous for which Auric provided scores are Cocteau's 1946 *La belle et la bête* (*Beauty and the Beast*), Charles Chrichton's 1951 *The Lavender Hill Mob*, John Huston's 1952 *Moulin Rouge*, William Wyler's 1953 *Roman Holiday*, Otto Preminger's 1958 *Bonjour tristesse*, and Jack Clayton's 1961 *The Innocents*. For details on Auric's music for *Le sang d'un poète*, see chapter two of Colin Roust, "Sounding French: The Film Music and Criticism of Georges Auric, 1919–1945" (Ph.D. diss., University of Michigan, 2007).

11   This is an odd comparative pairing. Paramount's 1933 *She Done Him Wrong* (directed by Lowell Sherman, with a relatively small amount of original music by John Leipold and Ralph Rainger) is a comedy during which Mae West, playing the part of saloon singer Diamond Lil, offers in-character renditions of the songs "Easy Rider" and "Frankie and Johnny." Tobias-Klangfilm's 1932 *Die Dreigroschenoper* (directed by Georg Wilhelm Pabst), on the other hand, is an adaptation for the screen of the 1928 Kurt Weill/Bertolt Brecht music-theater work of the same title. Whereas *She Done Him Wrong* is simply a movie that features a bit of diegetic singing, *Die Dreigroschenoper* is in essence an operetta.

12   The documentary film *Contact* was commissioned by Imperial Airways.

13   Here and throughout his article, instead of "score" Azarin uses the term *muzïkal'noye oformleniye* which means "musical design."

14   This refers to Sergei Pototsky (1883–1958), who studied with Sergey Vasilenko at the Moscow Conservatory.

15   This refers to the seventeenth anniversary of the Bolshevik Revolution, which had taken place in October 1917.

16   Most probably the composer was Zinovy Petrovich Fel'dman (1893–1942). Barnet's *At the Bluest Sea* (*U samogo sinyego morya*; known in English also as *By the Bluest of Seas*) was not released until April 20, 1936, yet Azarin may be citing incorrect information, as the film's credits list Pototsky as composer. *The Month of May* (*Mesyats May*) was released under the title *A Chance Encounter* (*Sluchaynay vstrecha*) in 1936. Igor Savchenko was the director. *In the Hero's Footsteps* (*po sledam geroya*) premiered on January 19, 1936.

17   Protazanov and composer David Blok worked together not just on the scripts but also on the final production for both *The Strangeness of Love* (*O strannostyakh lyubvi*; known in English also as *About the Oddities of Love*) and *The Dowryless Girl* (*Bespridannitsa*; known in English also as *Without Dowry*). *The Strangeness of Love* was released in 1936 and *The Dowryless Girl* was released in January 1937; both films were made at the Mezhrabpomfilm studio.

18   Eggert (1883–1955) was a silent film actor who in the 1920s turned to directing. Identified only by the initial of his given name, the Kryukov named here is Vladimir Nikolayevitch Kryukov (1902–60), a composer who studied with Myaskovsky, Grechaninov, and Catoire at the Moscow Conservatory; although best known for his operas and many works for the concert hall, Vladimir Kryukov did compose occasionally for both cinema and radio, and

at the time of Azarin's writing he served as music director for the Moscow-based Theater of the Revolution. Vladimir Kryukov should not be confused with his brother, Nikolai Kryukov (1908–61), who for his entire career worked primarily as a composer for Soviet films.

The film to which Azarin refers is *Nasten'ka Ustinova*, which premiered on August 29, 1934. Kryukov composed the score for the film.

19   For details on Vladimir Nikolayevitch Kryukov, see the preceding note.

20   Sergei Eisenstein's 1925 *Battleship Potemkin* (*Bronenosets Potyomkin*), nowadays more famously associated with a contemporaneous score by German composer Edmund Meisel and a later score by Dmitry Shostakovitch, was made at the Goskino studio. Vsevolod Pudovkin's 1928 *The Heir to Genghis Khan* (*Potomok Chingis-Khana*) was made at Mezhrabpomfilm.

21   Based on the 1919 naval defense of Petrograd against counter-revolutionary forces, Yefim Dzigan's *We Are from Kronstadt* (*Mï iz Kronshtadta*; known also in English as *The Sailors of Kronstadt*) was released in May 1936. The film was produced by Mosfilm studios.

22   It seems that with the phrase "illustrative music" (*illyustrativnaya muzïka*) Kryukov is referring to music that is excessively synchronized with filmic action. The Soviet Union in 1931 drastically reduced the number of foreign films imported each year, so it is not likely that Kryukov in 1936 would have had knowledge of such highly synchronized scores as those that Max Steiner, working in Hollywood, produced for such films as *King Kong* (1933), *Of Human Bondage* (1934), and *The Informer* (1935). But in the sound film's early years the temptation to synchronize music with on-screen action was surely as great in the Soviet Union as it was in the West.

23   "Intonation" (*intonazia*) is a standard Soviet-era film theory term. Malcolm H. Brown writes: "The concept of 'intonazia' is defined in its primal sense as any phonic manifestation of life or reality, perceived and understood (directly or metaphorically) as a carrier of meaning. In other words, an 'intonazia' in its simplest form is a real sound produced by something, be it creature or natural phenomenon (the moaning of a sick child, the ululation of the wind, a bugle call) with which meaning is associated or to which meaning is ascribed. Thus, a musical 'intonazia' results when some 'intonazia' from life experience is transmuted into a musical phrase; as such, it retains from the original intonational source that quality, property, or characteristic essence which expresses meaning and therefore possesses the power to quicken man's emotions and touch his sensibilities." Malcolm H. Brown, "The Soviet Russian Concepts of 'Intonazia' and 'Musical Imagery,'" *The Musical Quarterly* 60, no. 4 (October 1974), 557–67.

24   Aleksandr Macheret's 1932 *Business and People* (*Dela i lyudi*, known also in English as *Men and Jobs*) is the first sound film to which Kryukov contributed music; it was produced by the Soyuzkino studio. *Petersburg Nights* (*Peterburgskaya noch'*) is a 1934 film produced by the Moskinokombinat studio and directed by Grigory Roshal and Vera Stroyeva; it was the first film scored by Dmitri Kabalevsky (1904–87), who continued to compose for films until 1959.

25   The original French text of the "Internationale" was written by Eugène Pottier during the worker-dominated regime that governed Paris (known as the Paris Commune) during the spring of 1871; intended to be sung to the melody of "La Marseillaise," Pottier's text in 1888 was fitted with new music by Pierre De Geyter, and it was in De Geyter's setting that the song moved beyond the borders of France. Associated from the start with the ideals of communism, between 1922 and 1944 the "Internationale" served as the national anthem of the Soviet Union. The "Internationale" was featured in the score that Edmund Meisel composed for the 1925 premiere in Berlin of Eisenstein's *Battleship Potemkin*, and it is precisely because of the song's ability to stir communist sympathies that Meisel's score was squelched by Germany's fascist-leaning government. The lyrics and music of the enormously popular "Bravely, Comrades, In Step!" ("Smelo, tovarishchi, v nogu!") were written by L. Radin.

26   "The Sea Groaned in Anger" ("More v yarosti stonalo") was a popular revolutionary song written by Grigory Rivkin.

Chapter 7

1   The Selznick-produced, Steiner-scored RKO films that seem to have led directly to the industry-wide reconsideration of the role of originally composed accompanimental music were Gregory La Cava's *Symphony of Six Million* (1932), King Vidor's *Bird of Paradise* (1932), Ernest B. Schoedsack's *The Most Dangerous Game* (1932), and—most spectacular of the lot—Merian C. Cooper's *King Kong* (1933). For details on these early Steiner scores, see chapter two of Nathan R. Platte, "Musical Collaboration in the Films of David O. Selznick, 1932–1957," Ph.D. diss., University of Michigan, 2010.

2   The notion of the "classical-style" film sprang up in the 1970s in response to the observation by French critic André Bazin that "by 1938 or 1939 the talking film, particularly in France and the United States, had reached a level of classical perfection" (André Bazin, "The Evolution of the Language of Cinema," in *What Is Cinema?* vol. 1, trans. Hugh Gray (Berkeley: University of California Press, 1967), 30). The idea was solidified—perhaps institutionalized—by film historians David Bordwell, Janet Staiger, and Kristin Thompson in their 1985 *The Classical Hollywood Cinema: Film Style and Production to 1960* (London: Routledge & Kegan Paul). Bordwell et al. identified the "classical style" as a mode of filmmaking in which virtually all elements of the narrative were somehow made "excessively obvious" (1). Embellishing that idea, and perhaps with the intention of making sure that the phrase "excessively obvious" is not read as a pejorative, a recent dictionary of film terminology explains that the "classical style" is a mode of cinematic story-telling whose myriad technical devices, including musical accompaniment, serve primarily "to explain, and not obscure, the narrative" (Susan Hayward, *Cinema Studies: The Key Concepts* (London: Routledge, 2000), 64).

3   The conventions of the classical-style film score are described in detail, in an often quoted seven-point list, in Claudia Gorbman, *Unheard Melodies: Narrative Film Music* (Bloomington, IN: Indiana University Press, 1987), 73, and they are conveniently summarized in Kathryn Kalinak, *Settling the Score: Music and the Classical Hollywood Film* (Madison: University of Wisconsin Press, 1992), 113–14.

4   For details on this miniature cantata and its reuse in Hitchcock's same-titled 1956 film, see James Wierzbicki, "Grand Illusion: The 'Storm Cloud' Music in Hitchcock's *The Man Who Knew Too Much*," *Journal of Film Music* 1, nos. 2–3 (Fall–Winter 2003), 217–38.

5   In 1933 Richard Addinsell (1904–77) spent six months in Hollywood writing "stock" music for the RKO studio; his first feature-film score was for Alexander Korda's 1936 *The Amateur Gentleman*, and his 1937 work includes scores for *Dark Journey*, *Farewell Again*, *South Riding*, and *Fire over England*; between 1938 and 1962 Addinsell composed music for numerous British films, and he remains best known for his scores for *Goodbye, Mr. Chips* (1939) and *Blithe Spirit* (1945) and for the "Warsaw Concerto" that figures into his music for *Dangerous Moonlight* (1941). Arthur Bliss (1891–1975) composed relatively little for films, but at the time of this article he was solidly ensconced in the British film-music pantheon because of his score for William Cameron Menzies's *Things to Come* (1935). Benjamin Britten (1913–76), who as a youth studied piano with Arthur Benjamin, in 1936 and 1937 provided music for a number of documentaries (including *Coal Face*, *Night Mail*, *Line to Tschierva Hut*, and *The Calendar of Time*); his only score for a feature-length film accompanied Rowland V. Lee's *Love from a Stranger* (1937); his best-known film music—albeit most often heard in concert settings—is the *Young Person's Guide to the Orchestra* that was written for a 1946 educational film directed by Muir Matheson. John Greenwood (1889–1975), likely the least well known of the composers that Benjamin mentions, between 1933 and 1947 wrote music for dozens of mostly low-budget British films. Like Bliss, William Walton (1902–83) over the course of his long career wrote relatively little music for film, but at the time of Benjamin's writing he was already quite famous for his scores for Elizabeth Bergner's *Escape Me Never* (1935) and Paul Czinner's Shakespeare-based *As You Like It* (1936).

6   The music for RKO's 1935 *The Informer* was by Max Steiner. Benjamin himself provided the music for the 1934 version of Alfred Hitchcock's *The Man Who Knew Too Much* (the cantata in the Albert Hall sequence of which was re-used by Bernard Herrmann in the 1956 same-titled remake). The organ discord in Hitchcock's 1936 *Secret Agent*, arguably not

music at all, is an example of diegetic sound; no composer is credited for *Secret Agent*, but the musical director for all six of the "thriller" films that Hitchcock made for Gaumont-British between 1934 and 1938 (*The Man Who Knew Too Much*, *The 39 Steps*, *Secret Agent*, *Sabotage*, *Young and Innocent*, and *The Lady Vanishes*) was Louis Levy. *My Man Godfrey*, an American film released by Universal in 1936, featured music by Charles Previn. *La Kermesse Héroïque*, directed by Jacques Feyder and released in 1936, had music by Louis Beydts; the 1936 French film *Mayerling*, directed by Anatole Litvak, had music by Arthur Honegger.

7 Benjamin is referring to *The Private Life of Henry VIII*, a 1933 film starring Charles Laughton and directed by Alexander Korda; the music was by Kurt Schröder.

8 The film to which Benjamin refers is Herbert Wilcox's 1935 *Nell Gwyn*. The music for the film was by Philip Braham, but it incorporated pre-existing material by Edward German (1862–1936), an English composer who specialized in incidental music for the London theaters. One of German's best-known efforts was the music for Anthony Hope's 1900 *English Nell*, later known as *Nell Gwynn*.

9 Louis le Sidaner was a Paris-based art critic.

10 *Wharves and Strays* was a short documentary produced by Alexander Korda and directed by Bernard Browne; the music was by Benjamin.

11 Released by New World Pictures Ltd. early in 1937, Harold D. Schuster's *Wings of the Morning* starred American actor Henry Fonda and counts as England's first film to use Technicolor. Along with songs sung by tenor John McCormack, the film features accompanimental music by Benjamin.

12 The music for René Clair's 1931 *Le Million* was by Armand Bernard, Phillipe Parès, and George Van Parys.

13 Due to synchronization problems, Antheil's score during the composer's lifetime was never performed "live" in conjunction with Léger's film. With a substantially reduced orchestration, Antheil's *Ballet mécanique* received its premiere in a Paris auditorium on June 19, 1926.

14 George Antheil, *Bad Boy of Music* (Garden City, NY: Doubleday, 1945). The book was reprinted by Samuel French in 1990.

15 For details on the Thomson/Blitzstein score for *Spanish Earth*, see Carol Hess, "Competing Utopias? Musical Ideologies in the 1930s and Two Spanish Civil War Films," *Journal of the Society for American Music* 2, no. 3 (August 2008), 319–54.

16 The reference is to Igor Stravinsky's 1914 three-act opera, based on a story by Hans Christian Andersen, *Solevey* ("Le rossignol / The Nightingale").

17 Letter from David O. Selznick to Franz Waxman, March 6, 1941, Franz Waxman Papers, Special Collections Research Center, Syracuse University Library, Box 8.

18 Letter from Raymond Klune to David O. Selznick, May 3, 1940, David O. Selznick Collection, Harry Ransom Humanities Research Center, The University of Texas at Austin, Box 172, Folder 3.

19 The novachord was invented and patented by Laurens Hammond (inventor of the Hammond organ) and was manufactured between 1939 and 1942. The instrument had a six-octave range and could play chords as well as individual notes.

20 Waxman's statement here is oddly prophetic. Several years later Alfred Hitchcock would direct *Lifeboat*, a film that has no underscore (aside from the main and closing titles) and is set entirely on a lifeboat in the middle of the ocean. As Jack Sullivan notes, "Hitchcock jokingly explained this absence by asking his production crew, 'Where would the music come from?' . . . The famous retort was 'Where does the camera come from?'" See Sullivan, *Hitchcock's Music* (New Haven: Yale University Press, 2007), 104.

21 MGM released *Fury* on June 5, 1936. Produced by Joseph L. Mankiewicz and directed by Fritz Lang, the film starred Sylvia Sidney and Spencer Tracy. Waxman composed the score.

22 Twentieth Century-Fox released *The Grapes of Wrath* on March 15, 1940. Produced by Darryl F. Zanuck and directed by John Ford, the film starred Henry Fonda. Alfred Newman served as music director.

23 Selznick International Pictures (in association with MGM) released *Gone with the Wind* on December 15, 1939. Produced by Selznick and directed by Victor Fleming, the film starred

Vivien Leigh and Clark Gable. Max Steiner, assisted by Hugo Friedhofer, Adolph Deutsch, Joseph Nussbaum, and Heinz Roemheld, composed the score. Selznick International Pictures released *Rebecca* on April 12, 1940. Produced by Selznick and directed by Alfred Hitchcock (it was the British director's first American film), the film starred Laurence Olivier and Joan Fontaine. Waxman, assisted by Russel Bennett and Joseph Nussbaum, composed the score. Both scores were nominated for Academy Awards.

24 Negotiations with Damrosch did not go far. Although hiring Damrosch would have contributed publicity to the already over-publicized *Gone with the Wind* production, Selznick ultimately hired his trusted collaborator, Max Steiner.

25 Letter from Walter Damrosch to Katherine Brown, September 9, 1937, David O. Selznick Collection, Harry Ransom Humanities Research Center, The University of Texas at Austin, Box 1237, Folder 3.

26 MGM's *Viva Villa!* premiered on April 10, 1934. Produced by David O. Selznick and directed by Jack Conway, the film starred Wallace Beery. Herbert Stothart composed the score. Stothart's selection and incorporation of traditional Mexican melodies was assisted by Juan Aguilar, who served as music consultant. Selznick International Pictures' *Garden of Allah* premiered on November 15, 1936. Produced by David O. Selznick and directed by Richard Boleslawski, the film starred Marlene Dietrich and Charles Boyer. Max Steiner composed the score.

27 MGM's *Anna Karenina* premiered on August 30, 1935. Produced by David O. Selznick and directed by Clarence Brown, the film starred Greta Garbo and Frederic March. Herbert Stothart composed the score and incorporated passages from Pyotr Tchaikovsky's "None but the Lonely Heart" (from op. 6) and "Humoresque" (op. 10, no. 2). The film also features other Russian works on the soundtrack, including the "Valse Caprice" of Anton Rubenstein, a mazurka by Mikhail Glinka, a choral work by Dmitri Bortniansky, and Tchaikovsky's "Polonaise" from *Eugene Onegin*. It seems unlikely that Selznick had to "force" Stothart to use concert works in *Anna Karenina*, as Stothart himself advocated the incorporation of classical works into Hollywood film scores.

28 John Hay "Jock" Whitney served as the chairman of the board for Selznick International Pictures. He was a longtime friend of Selznick but was based in New York, not Hollywood. He therefore assisted Selznick with networking on the East Coast, including this correspondence with John Abbott. Whitney later became the United States Ambassador to Great Britain and the editor-in-chief of the *New York Herald Tribune*.

29 The David W. Griffith Corporation released *The Birth of a Nation* on February 8, 1915. Produced and directed by D. W. Griffith, the film starred Lillian Gish. Joseph Carl Breil assembled the musical score, which included passages of original music interspersed with arrangements of popular and classical works.

30 Golden Bough released *Tabu* on March 18, 1931. Produced by David Flaherty and directed by F. W. Murnau, the film starred Matahi and Reri, two native Polynesians who were hired when budgetary problems forced Murnau to forgo his original cast, which included Lotus Long. The score was arranged by Hugo Riesenfeld. Selznick is correct in remembering that the film was shot as a silent picture. Music was added to the soundtrack during postproduction.

31 RKO's *Symphony of Six Million* premiered on April 14, 1931. Produced by David O. Selznick and directed by Gregory La Cava, the film starred Ricardo Cortez and Irene Dunne. RKO released *Bird of Paradise* on August 12, 1932. Produced by David O. Selznick and directed by King Vidor, the film starred Dolores Del Rio and Joel McCrea. Max Steiner composed the music for both films and touted *Symphony of Six Million* as his first film to receive substantial underscoring.

32 The scores for John Ford's *The Informer* (1935) and Victor Fleming's *Gone with the Wind* (1939) are by Max Steiner. Walt Disney's *Fantasia* (1940) was a series of animated shorts inspired by classical concert works; the music on the soundtrack was performed by the Philadelphia Symphony Orchestra and conducted by Leopold Stokowski, who arranged and in some cases orchestrated the works for performance in the film.

Chapter 8

1 Thomas Beecham, quoted in "Beecham Arrives Minus Acid Speech," *Los Angeles Times*, February 27, 1952, A5.

2 See Philip K. Scheurer, "Tiomkin Soft-Pedals Fortissimo Fanfare in Film Music Scores," *Los Angeles Times*, August 17, 1952, D1.

3 Dimitri Tiomkin, quoted in "Film Music Composer Hits Back at Beecham," *Los Angeles Times*, February 28, 1952, A1.

4 Harold C. Schonberg, "Records: Background Music for Films," *New York Times*, July 14, 1957, 88.

5 Albert Goldberg, "The Sounding Board: Shostakovitch's New 11th Symphony a Tragic Decline," *Los Angeles Times*, August 31, 1958, D5; and Philip K. Scheurer, "How Important Is Incidental Score?" *Los Angeles Times*, September 1, 1958, B33.

6 Gavazzeni uses the phrase *misure fondamentale di musica*.

7 Whereas in the first paragraph Gavazzeni used the term *musica per film*, here he uses the term *musica cinematografica*.

8 He uses the word *pedale*, set off in italics; this refers to the musical 'pedal point,' a single pitch that is sustained (originally by means of a depressed organ pedal) throughout a passage in which the other parts are relatively active.

9 Gavazzeni is referring to *Attaque nocturne*, a 25-minute comedy made in 1931 by the Swiss director Marc Allégret (1900–73).

10 A three-volume collection of d'Amico's writings for this influential Rome-based newspaper —more than seven hundred articles—was published as *Tutte le cronache musicali: "L'espresso," 1967–1989*, ed. Luigi Bellingardi (Rome: Bulzoni Editore, 2000).

11 Instead of "soundtrack," d'Amico uses the term *colonna sonora* ("column of sound").

12 D'Amico uses the word *didascalia*, which might be translated not only as "caption" but also as "subtitle."

13 D'Amico uses the German *Leitmotiven*, and he sets off the word in italics.

14 D'Amico here uses the masculine form of "secretary," which in 1940s Italy would have meant simply a male office worker. The original phrase is "*il formulario del segretario galante.*"

15 D'Amico uses the word *cascherini*. This is a variant of the more common *cacciarini*, a plural—and decidedly feminine—word meaning the target of a sporting hunter of fowl.

16 Pulcinella is a stock character from Italy's seventeenth-century tradition of *commedia dell'arte*. Known in French as Polichinelle and in English, mostly by way of puppet shows, as Punch, Pulcinella is clever yet often pretends—for the sake of manipulating his social superiors—to be stupid. Although not common in English literature, the phrase 'Pulcinella's secret' (or, as d'Amico puts it, *il segreto di Pulcinella*) refers to a theatrical cliché that involves information clearly known by the audience yet unknown by whatever officious characters Pulcinella seeks to dupe.

17 In both this sentence and the next d'Amico uses the word *fatto* for what is here translated as "idea." Most literally, the Italian *fatto* means "fact," but other meanings—appropriate, it seems, to this context—include "point," "concept," and "idea."

18 These are references to lyrics by the fourteenth-century Italian poets Francesco Petrarch and Giovanni Boccaccio, specifically, to Petrarch's Canzona No. 126 from his *Canzoniere* collection and to Boccaccio's *Lamento di Tristano*. In the context of the point that d'Amico seems to be trying to make, the quoted line from Petrarch is perhaps more clear than the mere reference to Boccaccio. The Petrarch poem begins: "Chiare, fresche et dolci acque / ove le belle membra / pose colei che sola a me par donna" (in the translation by William Dudley Foulke that first appeared in his *Petrarch: Some Love Songs* (Oxford: Oxford University Press, 1915): "Clear, fresh and sweet waters where she who alone to me seems woman rested her lovely limbs"). For sophisticated Italian readers of d'Amico's article, the well-known phrase "Chiare, fresche et dolci acque" doubtless had, and still has, implications that resonate far beyond the words' literal meaning; for the anglophone editors of this volume, it seems that d'Amico quotes Petrarch only for the sake of emphasizing that his opinion of cinema as art is definitely *not* as uncompromising as Petrarch's opinion of his love object.

19   D'Amico uses the word *binario*, which means 'track' in the railroad sense.

20   At this point D'Amico adds a footnote: "It goes without saying that music in the cinema occupies a far more disadvantageous position than it does in the ballet. This is so because in ballet every rhythmic accent that corresponds to a gesture is part of a musical scheme, even if the scheme is not always apparent. In terms of details, a good deal of synchronization between music and cinematic action is purely casual. Except in the obvious case of the animated cartoon, which is clearly identical to ballet."

21   He uses the phrase *inquadratura lunga e uguale*, literally, "a frame, long and steady."

22   D'Amico uses the phrase *fate la prove per nove*, literally, "cast out nines." To 'cast out nines' is to perform a numerical procedure whereby additions, subtractions, and other computations can be quickly checked for accuracy. Known in Latin as "abjectio novenaria," the procedure was used as early as the third century AD. It is regularly taught to Italian schoolchildren, to the extent that *"fate la prove per nove"* has long been a cliché whose modern American equivalent is "do a reality check."

23   He uses the term *commento musicale*, literally, "musical commentary," which has long been the Italian equivalent of the English "underscore" or "extra-diegetic music."

24   D'Amico uses the phrase *primo fotogramma scenico*, literally, the "first scenic photographic image." In Italian film jargon, both *fotogramma* and *inquadratura* are equivalents of the English "shot."

25   Here D'Amico uses the term *la musica cinematografica*, literally, "cinematographic music."

26   D'Amico is clearly being disingenuous here. At the time of this writing he was a musical consultant for the Italian production company Lux Film, and for years he had been a close friend of both the Italian film composer Nino Rota and the German film theorist Rudolf Arnheim; even more noteworthy, since 1938 he had been married to Susanna Cecchi, who for decades to come would rank as one of Italy's foremost screenwriters. One suspects that D'Amico here professes an *antipitia per il cinematografo* only for the sake of making a rhetorical point.

27   Here, of course, d'Amico is referring to what in Hollywood has long been known as "source music" and which, in the Anglo-French language of recent film theory, is called "diegetic music" (the former term refers to the fact that the music's source is explicitly depicted or at least implied; the latter term refers to the fact that the music in some way belongs to the film's "diegesis," or "narrative world"). At the beginning of the sentence d'Amico uses the self-explanatory term *musica di scena* (meaning music that is somehow *in* the filmic scene). Curiously, to describe the finger movements of the hypothetical violinist he uses the decidedly German verb *musizieren*.

28   Interestingly, d'Amico sets off the descriptor in quotation marks. In this sentence he compares *musica di scena* to *musica 'di commento.'*

29   For German director Georg Wilhelm Pabst's 1933 film *Don Quixote* the French composer Jacques Ibert wrote four songs ("Chanson du départ," "Chanson à Dulcinée," "Chanson du duc," and "Chanson de la mort"). It is to the last of these songs that d'Amico here refers.

30   Again, d'Amico here uses the tem *inquadratura*.

31   D'Amico gives the surname of the famous Russian basso, who in the film not only sang Ibert's songs but enacted the part of Don Quixote, as *Scialiàpin*; some English-language sources, including the lofty *New Grove Dictionary of Music and Musicians*, give the name as "Shalyapin."

32   The reference is to Vincenzo Bellini (1801–35), one of the chief representatives of early nineteenth-century Italy's "bel canto" style of opera and famous for arias that convey specific aspects of individual dramatic characters.

33   The reference is to René Clair's 1931 *Le Million*, a French film whose music—by Armand Bernard, Philippe Parès, and Georges Van Parys—in many scenes indeed evokes the spirit of nineteenth-century melodrama.

34   The emphasizing quotation marks have been editorially added; D'Amico here writes simply of *buona musica in senso assoluto*.

35   Charles Chaplin, internationally famous since c.1920 as a comic star of silent films, as a director sustained the aesthetic of 'silent' film well into the 1930s, and in most cases the

recorded orchestral music that accompanied his quasi-silent films was composed by Chaplin himself. For more on this, see Eric James, *Making Music with Charlie Chaplin* (Lanham, MD: Scarecrow Press, 2000) and the review of same by Dan Blim in the *Journal of Film Music* 1, no. 4 (Winter 2006).

36 For "score," d'Amico here uses the word *partitura*, which means the pages that contain the musical notation.

37 The reference is to René Clair's 1931 *À nous la liberté!* For details on how the music by French composer Georges Auric contributed substantially to the film, see Colin Roust, "Sounding French: The Film Music and Criticism of Georges Auric, 1919–1945" (Ph.D. diss., University of Michigan, 2007).

38 In this case, for "score" d'Amico uses the word *commento*, meaning the film's musical 'commentary.' See note 23 above.

39 *Via delle Cinque Lune* is a 1942 film directed by Luigi Chiarini and released by the Centro Sperimentale di Cinematografi. It is the third of seven films scored by Achille Longo (1900–54), an Italian composer known mostly for his chamber music and for serving, from 1944 until his death, as director of the Naples Conservatory. Before *Via delle Cinque Lune*, Longo provided music for *La fanciulla dell'altra riva* and *La bella addormentata* (both 1942); afterwards, he scored *Non mi muovo!* (1943), *La Locandiera* (1944), *Patto con il diavolo* (1949), and *L'ultimo amante* (1954).

40 D'Amico adds a footnote: "On the difference between the talking film [*film parlato*] and the sound film [*film sonoro*], and on the musical implications raised by the question, it is useful to consult the interesting essay by Rudolf Arnheim titled 'Nuovo Laocoonte' (in *Bianco e nero*, August 1938), in which, despite a few overly rigid schemata, the problem of the limits of the various arts in film (and occasionally elsewhere) finds neat and compelling solutions. Also worth mentioning in regard to this and other of the topics discussed above is Massimo Mila's very sensible article 'Musica e cinematografo' (in *Pégaso*, February 1933); this was written at the dawn of the sound film but it is still useful."

 Differences between the "talking film" and the "sound film" (i.e., the film in which recorded sound for the most part focused on spoken dialogue in contrast to the film in which all sorts of recorded sounds, including music and noises, are used to artistic effect) were discussed as early as May 1929 by the French filmmaker René Clair. In "L'Art du son" ("The Art of Sound"), originally written as a letter and not published in essay form until 1951, Clair distinguished between the "film parlant" and the "film sonore."

 Rudolf Arnheim (1904–2007) was a German aesthetician and film theorist who lived in Italy from 1933 to 1939 and then, after a brief sojourn in England, settled in the United States. The essay mentioned by d'Amico first appeared in Italian and was not translated into English until 1958 (as "The New Laocoön: Artistic Composites and the Talking Film" in the collection *Film as Art*). Both the essay's title and its content take inspiration from a 1766 essay ("Laokoon oder Über die Grenzen der Malerei und Poesie," or "Laocoon: An Essay on the Limits of Painting and Poetry") by the German playwright Gotthold Lessing.

41 Here, d'Amico uses the term *commenti musicale*.

42 As much as d'Amico celebrates them, these two films—and their scores—are likely not much known in the English-speaking world. The 1933 *Acciaio* ("Steel"; released by the Società Italiana Cines) was German director Walter Ruttmann's only Italian film; aside from Goffredo Allesandrini's 1935 *Don Bosco*, it was the only film for which Italian composer Gian Francesco Malipiero (1882–1973) provided music. The 1942 *Un colpo di pistola* ("A Pistol Shot"; released by Lux Film) was one of a great many Italian films directed by Renato Castellini between the early 1930s and the late 1980s; aside from Gianni Franciolini's 1946 *Notte di tempesta*, it was the only film for which Vincenzo Tommasini (1878–1950) provided music. Although only Malipiero's music remains in circulation today, at the time of d'Amico's writing both Malipiero and Tommasini were known primarily as composers for the concert hall.

43 For "source music," or "diegetic" music, d'Amico uses the term *musica di scena*, and he sets off the phrase in quotation marks.

44 Here and in the parenthetical sentence that follows d'Amico uses the phrase *continuità di tono*.

45 Massimo Terzano (1882–1947) began his cinematographic career in 1915 with Adelardo Fernández Arias's *Più forte della verità* and before 1930 worked on more than two dozen other silent films.

46 D'Amico uses the word *partitura*.

47 In d'Amico's article, the phrase—enclosed in quotation marks—is *cinematograficamente funzionare*.

48 For "soundtrack," d'Amico uses the standard Italian term *colonna sonora* ("column of sound").

49 Here d'Amico uses the phrase *musica cinematografica*.

50 Leinsdorf colorfully recounts his life story, especially as it involves his work with the Metropolitan Opera, in *Cadenza: A Musical Career* (Boston: Houghton Mifflin, 1976).

51 See Erich Leinsdorf, "Some Views on Film Music," *Music Journal* 3, no. 5 (September–October 1945), 15, 53–54. In this article Leinsdorf simply expands upon his opinions, albeit only slightly, as expressed in the *New York Times* article.

52 These are *The Trouble with Harry* (Paramount, 1955), *The Man Who Knew Too Much* (Paramount, 1956), *The Wrong Man* (Warner Bros., 1957), *Vertigo* (Paramount, 1958), *North by Northwest* (MGM, 1959), *Psycho* (Paramount, 1960), and *Marnie* (Universal, 1964). Herrmann was involved as a "sound consultant" with the electronically scored *The Birds* (Universal, 1963); he composed numerous cues for *Torn Curtain* (Universal, 1966) before being replaced, at Hitchcock's request, by John Addison. For details on the break-up of the Herrmann–Hitchcock relationship, see Steven C. Smith, *A Heart at Fire's Center: The Life and Music of Bernard Herrmann* (Berkeley: University of California Press, 1991), 267–74, and Jack Sullivan, *Hitchcock's Music* (New Haven: Yale University Press, 2006), 276–87.

53 Between 1934 and 1939 Herrmann composed prolifically for the CBS radio series "Secone Sketchbook," the "Columbia Workshop," and the "Mercury Theater on the Air," and he returned to the radio genre in 1942 (for the series "Suspense") and 1952 (for "Crime Classics").

54 Aside from his work as a composer for radio dramas, Herrmann had been associated with the CBS Symphony Orchestra—originally as an arranger and rehearsal conductor, then as on-air conductor for the concert series "Music in the Modern Manner"—since 1934.

He made his film scoring debut in 1941 with Orson Welles's *Citizen Kane* (RKO), and later that year he scored William Dieterle's *All that Money Can Buy* (RKO; alternately known as *The Devil and Daniel Webster* and *Here Is a Man*); both scores were nominated for Academy Awards, with the score for *All That Money Can Buy* winning. By the time the *New York Times* editor made this comment, Herrmann had also scored Welles's *The Magnificent Ambersons* (Twentieth Century-Fox, 1942), Robert Stevenson's *Jane Eyre* (Twentieth Century-Fox, 1944), and John Brahm's *Hangover Square* (Twentieth Century-Fox, 1945). *Hangover Square* had been released in February of 1945.

55 The headline borrows from John Keats's 1819 poem "Ode on a Grecian Urn," which features the lines: "Heard melodies are sweet, but those unheard/Are sweeter; therefore, ye soft pipes, play on." Claudia Gorbman uses these lines as the epigraph for 1987 *Unheard Melodies: Narrative Film Music* (Bloomington: Indiana University Press).

56 Robert D. McFadden, "Bosley Crowther, 27 Years a Critic of Films for Times, is Dead at 75," *New York Times*, March 8, 1981, 36.

57 These are *The Great Films: Fifty Golden Years of Motion Pictures* (New York: Putnam's, 1967), *Vintage Films* (New York: Putnam's, 1977), and *Reruns: 50 Memorable Films* (New York: Putnam's, 1978). Crowther's other books are *The Lion's Share: The Story of an Entertainment Empire* (1957), a history of the MGM studio, and *Hollywood Rajah: The Life and Times of Louis B. Mayer* (1960). For a scholarly assessment of Crowther's work, see Frank Eugene Beaver, *Bosley Crowther: Social Critic of the Film, 1940–1967* (New York: Arno Press, 1974).

58 *Those Endearing Young Charms* was a 1945 RKO film directed by Lewis Allen. Along with the title song, the film featured original music by Roy Webb as orchestrated by Gilbert Grau. The title song ("Believe Me, If All Those Endearing Young Charms"), with both word and music by Thomas Moore (1779–1852), was first published *c.*1810 in one

of the volumes of Moore's serialized *A Selection of Irish Melodies*; it had been popularized in a recording by soprano Anna Case in 1912.

Chapter 9

1   Martin Marks writes: "As far as the seventh ICM is concerned, although the bibliography under "Film Music" in *Grove*'s 5th edition lists a volume of *Proceedings*, I have been unable to locate such a publication. However, in conjunction with the congress, *Bianco e nero* published a special double issue on "La musica nel film," ed. Luigi Chiarini & Enzio Micocci, 11, nos. 5–6 (1950), issued the same year in book form. The 1959 anthology on *Musica e Film*, ed. S. G. Biamonte (Rome: Aeteneo) also includes some papers read at the congress." "Film Music: The Material, Literature, and Present State of Research," MLA *Notes*, second series, 36, no. 2 (December 1979), 305–06.
     In addition, Bianca Becherini reported on the congress in "A Firenze, il VII Congresso Internazionale di Musica," *Rivista musicale italiana* 52, no. 3 (July–Sept. 1950), 296–99.
2   Silvana Mangano (1930–89) was an Italian actress known *c.*1950 largely for her physical beauty and later for her prolific marriage—resulting in four children—to Italian film producer Dino De Laurentis. Hopkins's reference is not to rice fields actually owned by Mangano but, rather, to fields of the sort depicted in her 1949 film *Riso Amaro* ("Bitter Rice").
3   Hopkins here refers to the pair of bronze doors, on the east entrance of Florence's Church of San Giovanni, designed and cast by Lorenzo Ghiberti *c.*1430–50. The doors were dubbed "The Gates of Paradise" not by their designer but by Michelangelo.
4   Keith Prowse was a British "travel guide" firm, geared toward musically oriented English citizens who wished to tour continental Europe, founded by music publishers Robert Keith and William Prowse in the 1780s.
5   Jean Epstein's *Le Tempestaire* (France Illustration) was released in 1947; it is a "short" that lasts only twenty-two minutes.
6   Daniele Amfitheatrof (1901–83) was born in Russia and immigrated to the United States in 1937. After working as a conductor in Minneapolis he settled, in 1941, in Southern California, where for the next twenty years he contributed prolifically—although never famously—to film and television productions.
7   Henry King's *The Song of Bernadette* (Twentieth Century-Fox, 1943) featured an Oscar-winning score by Alfred Newman; Billy Wilder's *Sunset Blvd.* (Paramount, 1950) featured a similarly lauded score by Franz Waxman.
8   The chair of the sessions was Ildenbrando Pizzetti (1880–1968), an Italian composer esteemed for his operas and symphonic works in the 1920s and 1930s but never directly involved with film music.
9   The British composer Benjamin Frankel (1906–73) had been involved with film music since 1934. By the time of Hopkins's writing he had produced more than two dozen film scores.
10   There is no record, alas, that identifies the outspoken Italian composer.
11   The "Evenings on the Roof" series was launched in 1939, with a chamber-music program devoted entirely to the music of Béla Bartók, presented literally on the roof of the modernist Silver Lake residence (designed by Bauhaus architect Rudolf Schindler) of critic Peter Yates and his wife, the pianist Francis Mullen. Throughout the 1940s the concert series often shifted its venue but never veered from its stated goals of presenting, to a small and elite audience, the "best" of modern music. The concerts under Morton's seventeen years of leadership were given, for the most part, in the Los Angeles County Auditorium in West Hollywood Park.
12   *Sight and Sound* 20, no. 1 (May 1951), 21–23.
13   Midway through 1951 the *Hollywood Quarterly*, without interrupting its series of volume numbers, changed its name to *The Quarterly Review of Film, Radio and Television*. Morton's follow-up column appears in the renamed journal's vol. 6, no. 2 (Winter 1951), 191–206.
14   The original footnote cites the source of Amfitheatrof's article and summarizes the conference's agenda: "Daniele Amfitheatrof, *Italy: Music and Films* (Los Angeles: Academy

of Motion Picture Arts and Sciences, 1950). The exhibit included excerpts from Amfitheatrof's *The Capture* [RKO, 1950], [Aaron] Copland's *The Red Pony* [Republic Pictures, 1949], [Adolph] Deutsch's *Mask of Dimitrios* [Warner Bros., 1944], [John] Green's *The Inspector General* [Warner Bros., 1949], [Lennie] Hayton's *Battleground* [MGM, 1949], [Bronislau] Kaper's *Act of Violence* [MGM, 1948], [Alfred] Newman's *The Snake Pit* [Twentieth Century-Fox, 1948] and *The Song of Bernadette* [Twentieth Century-Fox, 1943], [David] Raksin's *Force of Evil* [MGM, 1949], [Miklós] Rózsa's *Brute Force* [Universal, 1947] and *A Double Life* [Universal, 1948], [Max] Steiner's *Johnny Belinda* [Warner Bros., 1948], [Franz] Waxman's *Objective, Burma!* [Warner Bros., 1945] and *Sunset Blvd.* [Warner Bros., 1950], [and Roy] Webb's *Hitler's Children* [RKO, 1943]."

The footnote for the reprint in *Sight and Sound* gives only the source of the Amfitheatrof article.

15   The original footnote cites comments by Keller that appeared in *The Music Review* 11, no. 3 (August 1950), 210–11. Keller's report is reproduced in Hans Keller, *Film Music and Beyond: Writings on Music and the Screen, 1946–59,* ed. Christopher Wintle (London: Plumbago, 2006), 34.

16   The original footnote cites the article by Hopkins reproduced on pp. 129–131 of this anthology.

17   With a screenplay by Jacques Rémy and directed by René Clément, *Les Maudits* (Spéva Films, 1947; released in the United States as *The Damned* in April 1948) is a psychological drama about a diverse group of Nazi officials attempting to escape Germany by means of a submarine during the final days of World War II.

18   Igor Stravinsky's *Symphony of Psalms,* for orchestra and chorus, dates from 1930; the orchestration features large wind and percussion sections, but no violins, violas, or clarinets. Richard Strauss's *Metamorphosen,* for twenty-three strings, dates from 1945.

19   Gustav Mahler's *Das Lied von der Erde,* for orchestra and vocal soloists, dates from 1908–09.

20   MGM's first version of *Ben-Hur,* a silent film with original music by William Axt, had been released in 1925. The same studio's second version of the film, directed by William Wyler and featuring a score by Miklós Rózsa, was not released until 1959.

21   At this point Morton, or the editor of *Hollywood Quarterly,* gives a citation: "Charles Koechlin, *Gabriel Fauré* (London: Dennis Dobson Ltd., 1945), pp. 69–70." Fauré's *Dolly* was a suite for piano, four hands, composed between 1894 and 1897; it was orchestrated by Henri Rabaud in 1906. Fauré's Op. 80 incidental music for *Pelléas et Mélisande* dates from 1898 and was adapted by the composer into an orchestral suite in 1901; Charles Koechlin's arrangements of various sections of the suite date from 1898 and 1936. Fauré's Op. 82 *Prométhée,* a *tragédie lyrique,* dates from 1900; the original score, for strings, harps, and three groups of winds, was orchestrated by the composer in collaboration with Charles Eustace; a second version, orchestrated by the composer in collaboration with Jean Roger-Ducasse, was issued in 1917.

22   The chair of the sessions was Ildenbrando Pizzetti (1880–1968).

23   At this point there is another citation: "Israel V. Nestyev, *Sergei Prokofiev* (New York: Alfred A. Knopf, 1946), pp. 67–68."

24   Copland's orchestrators include George Bassman (for *Of Mice and Men,* 1940); Gilbert Grau, Jerome Moross, and Arthur Morton (for *The North Star,* 1943); Nathan Scott and R. Dale Butts (for *The Red Pony,* 1949); and Nathan Van Cleave (for *The Heiress,* 1940). Arthur Morton (1908–2000) was Lawrence Morton's brother.

25   Richard Strauss's tone poem *Don Juan* dates from 1888–89.

26   Igor Stravinsky's *Pulcinella,* a ballet based on themes by Giovanni Battista Pergolesi and other early eighteenth-century composers, dates from 1919–20.

27   Originated by Richard Wagner in the 1870s to describe operas for which he wrote not only the music but also the librettos, and significantly influenced the stage design, the German word *Gesamtkunstwerk* means "total art work."

28   For a brief biography of Keller, see the introduction to *Hans Keller: Essays on Music,* ed. Christopher Wintle (Cambridge: Cambridge University Press, 1994). For an extensive

account of Keller's work in broadcasting, see Alison Garnham, *Hans Keller and the BBC: The Musical Conscience of British Broadcasting, 1959–79* (Aldershot: Ashgate, 2003).

29 Keller's more or less complete writings on film music are anthologized in *Film Music and Beyond: Writings on Music and the Screen, 1946–59*, ed. Christopher Wintle (London: Plumbago, 2006).

30 Keller's initial comment on the congress appeared in *The Music Review* 11, no. 3 (August 1950), 210–11; it is reproduced in Hans Keller, *Film Music and Beyond: Writings on Music and the Screen, 1946–59*, ed. Christopher Wintle (London: Plumbago, 2006), 34.

31 Hopkins's article, published in *Sight and Sound* in August 1950, is reproduced on p. 129 of this volume; Morton's rebuttal, published in *Hollywood Quarterly* in the spring of 1951, is reproduced on p. 132.

32 The references are to characters that appear in three of the four operas that make up Richard Wagner's *Der Ring des Nibelungen* cycle. In the first opera—*Das Rheingold*—Fafner (sung by a bass) is a giant who kills his brother Fasalt in a struggle over the empowered golden ring; as punishment, the gods transform him into a dragon who guards the treasure of the dwarf-like Nibelungs. In the second act of the third opera—*Siegfried*—the title character (a tenor) confronts Fafner and kills him with a specially forged sword.

33 Hopkins's response, quoted several times in course of Keller's essay, appears on pp. 23 and 30 of *Sight and Sound* 20, no.1 (May 1951), immediately following the reprinted version of Morton's article.

34 For Keller's writings in the capacity of musician-psychologist, see *Music and Psychology: From Vienna to London, 1939–52*, ed. Christopher Wintle and Alison Garnham (London: Plumbago, 2003).

35 The quotation comes from the chapter on film music in Copland's 1941 *Our New Music* (New York: McGraw-Hill) that Keller cited in the 1947–48 *Sight and Sound* article that is reproduced on p. 136 of this volume.

36 The title music for George Seaton's *Apartment for Peggy* (Twentieth Century-Fox, 1948) was by David Raksin, with additional music by Earle Hagen, Cyril Mockridge, and Alfred Newman and orchestrations by Maurice De Packh and Herbert Spencer. Lionel Newman (Alfred Newman's brother) served the production as musical director and conductor.

37 Although delivered at the conference in English, Keller's article was translated into Italian and eventually published as "Citazioni di musica classica nel film" in *Musica e Film*, ed. S. G. Biamonte (Rome: Dell' Aeteneo, 1959), 223–26.

38 Without naming the replacement composer, Morton made the observation in "Film Music of the Quarter," *Hollywood Quarterly* 4, no. 3 (Spring 1950), 291. The title music for *The Heiress* is by Nathan Van Cleave, who also served as the score's orchestrator; it involves three measures of Copland's original title theme followed by an arrangement of the song "Plaisir d'Amour" and then, as Copland's name appears on the screen, Copland's original cadential measures. For details, see Howard Pollack, *Aaron Copland: The Life and Work of an Uncommon Man* (Urbana: University of Illinois Press, 1999), 433–37.

39 *Le Sang d'un poète* was the first installment of what eventually came to be known as Cocteau's "Orphic" trilogy; Auric wrote the score for *Orphée* (1950) but contributed only the title music to *Le testament d'Orphée, ou ne me demandez pas pourquoi!* (1960).

40 French composer Camille Saint-Saëns (1835–1921) composed the music for André Chalmette's 1908 *The Assassination of the Duke of Guise*, which was released by Pathé's Films d'Art studio. While the film may not have been well known in 1952, it has since come to be celebrated as having the first original film score.

41 *The Chess Player* was directed by Raymond Bernard and released in 1927 by the Société des Films Historiques. Henri Rabaud (1873–1949) composed two film scores, but he is best known as a conductor (and briefly director) of the Paris Opéra and as the long-time director of the Paris Conservatoire.

42 Auric misspelled both the title of the film and the last name of Schmitt (1870–1958). *Salammbô*, based on Gustave Flaubert's novel, was directed by Pierre Marodon and released in 1925.

43 Arthur Honegger (1892–1955) composed the music for Abel Gance's *The Wheel* in 1923.

44 Clair's *À Nous la Liberté!* was released in 1931 by Films Sonores Tobis. This was Auric's second film score, following his work on Cocteau's *The Blood of a Poet* the previous year.

45 G. W. Pabst's *The Three-Penny Opera* was released by Films Sonores Tobis in 1931, with the music that Kurt Weill (1900–50) had originally composed for the stage version of Bertolt Brecht's play.

46 This seems to have been exactly the situation that Auric faced when composing his first film score, for Jean Cocteau's *Le Sang d'un poète* (1930). See Auric, "Préface," in Jacques Bourgeois, *René Clair* (Paris: Roulet, 1949).

47 Epinay-sur-Seine, just north of Paris, was the site of one of the most important film studios in France, Studios Éclair.

48 Jean Cocteau's *Beauty and the Beast* was released in 1946 by DisCina.

49 Tourneur (1873–1961) was a prominent French director from the silent era through World War II. He was not, however, involved in the production of Marc Allégret's *Lac aux Dames* (1934).

50 Cocteau's *The Terrible Parents*, based on his play, was released in 1948 by Les Films Ariane.

51 Cocteau's *Orpheus* was produced and released in 1950 by André Paulvé. The score is mostly by Auric, but also includes the "Dance of the Blessed Spirits" from the 1774 revision of Christoph Willibald Gluck's opera *Orphée et Eurydice*.

Chapter 10

1 *Dreams That Money Can Buy* was an hour-long film directed by Hans Richter and released by Films International of America in 1947. Louis Applebaum was the film's music director and also wrote the music for the segment titled "Narcissus." Along with Applebaum and Cage (whose sequence was titled "Discs"), other composers involved in the project were Paul Bowles (for the segments titled "Desire" and "Ballet"), David Diamond (for "Circus"), and Darius Milhaud (for "Ruth, Roses, and Revolvers").

   Works of Calder was a short produced independently by Herbert Matter in 1950; Cage, who provided a score for prepared piano and tape, was the sole composer.

2 With music by Cage, Kenneth Patchen's radio play *The City Wears a Slouch Hat* was broadcast by Chicago radio station WBBM on May 31, 1942; the score is for narrator and six percussionists.

3 In the original article, a caption under a still from the film says: "*Works of Calder*, filmed in color and directed by Herbert Matter, and produced and narrated by Burgess Meredith, has been acquired for exclusive 16mm non-commercial distribution by the Museum of Modern Art Film Library. The music was written by [myself]; narration by John Latouche. Rhythmically composed sequences suggest a parallel between familiar forms and movements in nature and the movements of Calder's mobiles. Between these two sequences, Calder is seen at work in his studio, surrounded by his magical world of moving objects."

4 The Scottish-born McLaren (1914–87) was an animator who emigrated from the United Kingdom to New York in 1939 and then to Canada in 1941. His invitation to settle in Canada came at the request of documentary filmmaker and fellow Scotsman John Grierson, who had moved to Canada in 1938 to establish that country's National Film Board.

5 In the French version of this article, Schaeffer uses the term *musique dessinée*, literally, "drawn sound."

6 In the French version of the article, Schaeffer uses the term *bande* and then adds that "tape" is an English word.

7 Schaeffer indeed uses the word "tam-tam," but clearly he means "tom-tom."

8 In the original English version, Schaeffer misspells the name as "Norman MacLaren"; in the French version he misspells it as "Mac Laren." Norman McLaren (1914–87) was a Canadian animator and filmmaker who was pivotal in the development of "drawn sound," in which he would paint directly onto tape with magnetic ink.

9 In the French version, instead of "film" Schaeffer uses the term *la commode pellicule*.

10 Günther Bialas (1907–95) was a German composer who taught at the Hochschule für Musik Detmold and later at the Hochschule für Musik in Munich and at the Bavarian Academy of Fine Arts.

11 Werner Meyer-Eppler (1913–60) was a Belgian-German physicist and acoustician who taught at the University of Bonn and in 1949 published a book on the possibility of generating music entirely by electronic means. In 1951 he collaborated with engineer Robert Beyer and composer Herbert Eimert to establish an electronic music laboratory at the studios of Nordwesdeutscher Rundfunk in Cologne.

12 In the French version, Schaeffer refers to a *découpage précis*, that is, a "precise editing script."

13 The reference is to Enrico Fulchignoni (1913–88) and his 1953 film *Leonardo da Vinci, or, the Tragic Pursuit of Perfection*.

14 It is unclear whether Schaeffer is referring to Marc Allégret or his younger brother Yves. By 1954, both were successful film directors. It is probably Yves, who had collaborated with Schaeffer on a radio adaptation of Léopold Chauveau's 1930 novel *Monsieur Lyonnet*.

15 The reference is to Jean Grémillon (1898–1959) and his 1952 short *Astrologie, ou le miroire de la vie*.

16 Jean Rouch (1917–2004) had worked as a civil engineer in French West Africa during World War II. Between 1947 and 2002 Rouch made dozens of documentary films, most of them focused on African topics.

17 Mao (1893–1978) had been chairman of the Chinese Communist Party, and thus leader of the People's Republic of China, since 1949.

18 The journal existed only from 1956 until 1959.

19 Donald Richie, for example, has written on the curious fact that whereas Western cinema draws from only one musical tradition, Japanese cinema—his personal area of expertise—is always placed in the difficult position of having to choose between Western and Japanese musical approaches. He notes that even in costume dramas set in medieval Japan the accompanying music, reflecting the overall style of acting and *mise en scène*, most often holds to Western models. See Donald Richie and Joseph L. Anderson, "Traditional Theater and the Film in Japan," *Film Quarterly* 12, no. 1 (Autumn 1958).

20 Instead of "Chinese musical instruments," throughout the essay Wang uses the term "national musical instruments" (*minzu yueqi*).

21 The word *yangge* means, literally, "rice-sprouting song." The *yangge* play, which developed in rural regions in northern China, is a musical play that features local folksongs and dance; *yangge* plays are performed at major festivals around the year.

22 *Well Wishes*, which also goes by the English title *New Year Sacrifice*, was released by the Beijing Film Studio; directed by Hu Sang and featuring music by Ruzeng Liu, the film won a "special prize" in 1957 at the Karlovy Vary International Film Festival in Czechoslovakia. *The Life of Lu Xun*, a biography of the Chinese writer who lived from 1881 until 1936, was written and directed by Sun Yu; Sun began work on the film in 1950, but his screenplay was severely criticized by Mao Zedong, and the preponderance of evidence (including letters from Lu Xun's widow and son) suggests that the film was never, in fact, finished (see Zhou Haiying zhu, *Lu Xun yu wo qi shi nian* (*Lu Xun and Me, Seventy Years*) (Haikou Shi; Nan hai chu ban gong si, 2001), 303–04). It is not known who the composer for *The Life of Lu Xun* might have been.

23 This refers to the spirit of the "Hundred Flowers Campaign" (1956–57), a short-lived movement of criticism initiated by the Communist Party itself, guided by the slogan: "Let a hundred flowers bloom together, let the hundred schools of thoughts contend."

24 Also known as *The Rebels*, *Song Jingshi* was directed by Zheng Junli and Sun Yu.

25 Produced by the Shanghai Film Studios, the film was directed by Weiyi Wang.

26 The article was reprinted in Wang Yunjie, *Lun dianying yinyue* [*On Film Music*] (Beijing: Zhongguo dianying chubanshe, 1984), 110–13.

Chapter 11

1 For biographical information on Scheurer, see p. 62 of this volume.

2 After the paragraphs reproduced here, the column goes on to discuss the involvement of jazz musician Shorty Rogers with composer André Previn on a ballet project, and album for MGM Records, titled *Collaboration*; changing the subject, Schuerer then offers notes on MGM's new *Prodigal* and in-progress *My Sister Eileen*.

3   For an example of Bernstein's claims, see p. 182 of this volume.

4   Completed in 1953 but not released until late in 1955, *Dementia* was an independent film directed and produced by John Parker.

5   In *The Third Man* (British Lion, 1949; dir. Carol Reed, music by Anon Karas), the zither was played by composer Karas; in the scores for both *Little Fugitive* (Little Fugitive Production Co., 1953; dir. Raymond Ashley, music by Eddie Manson) and *Genevieve* (Arthur Rank Organization, 1953; dir. Henry Cornelius, music by Larry Adler), the harmonica player was Larry Adler.

6   *The Trouble with Harry* (Paramount, 1955) eventually was fitted with an orchestral score by Bernard Herrmann.

7   *Private Hell 36* (1954) was directed by Don Siegel; *Mad at the World* (1955) was directed by Harry Essex.

8   *The Wild One* (Stanley Kramer Productions; 1953) was directed by Laslo Benedek.

9   The references are to *Syncopation* (RKO, 1942; dir. William Dieterle), *Navajo* (Lippert Pictures, 1953; dir. Norman Foster), *Destination Moon* (George Pal Productions, 1950; dir. Irving Pichel), *The War of the Worlds* (Paramount, 1953; dir. Byron Haskin), and *The Bigamist* (Filmakers, 1953; dir. Ida Lupino).

10   Otto Preminger's *The Man with the Golden Arm*, which Bernstein discusses in the essay included on p. 178 of this volume, was produced independently by Preminger and released by United Artists in 1955.

11   Louis Malle's *Ascenseur pour l'échafaud* has been titled in English as not just *Elevator to the Scaffold* but also *Elevator to the Gallows* and *Frantic*.

12   *No Sun in Venice* (Carol Film and Iéna Productions, 1957; dir. Roger Vadim) is better known by its original French title, *Sait-on jamais . . . .*

13   Duke Ellington is "in character" not just on the album but also in the film, in which he portrays a pianist-band leader named Pie Eye.

14   Along with Davis on trumpet, the ensemble included the American drummer Kenny Clarke and French musicians Pierre Michelot on bass, René Urtreger on piano, and Barney Wilen on tenor saxophone.

15   The sextet for the recording included, along with Davis, alto saxophonist Julian "Cannonball" Adderley, tenor saxophonist John Coltrane, pianist Red Garland, bassist Paul Chambers, and drummer Philly Joe Jones.

16   Malcolm Sargent, conductor of London's BBC Symphony Orchestra, in "Queen's Curiosity Aroused, Her Kingdom Much Upset by Rock 'n' Roll Film," *Variety*, September 26, 1956.

17   Francis J. Braceland, director of the Institute of Living, in "Rock-and-roll Called Communicable Disease," *New York Times*, March 28, 1956.

18   Attributed to an anonymous Canadian minister, in "What You Don't Need to Know about Rock 'n' Roll," *Maclean's*, July 7, 1956.

19   "Rhythm and Rumble," *Washington Post and Times-Herald*, June 6, 1956, 14.

20   Directed by Frank Tashlin, *The Girl Can't Help It* starred Jayne Mansfield and featured— along with some original music by Leigh Harline, Hugo Friedhofer, and Lionel Newman—songs performed on-screen by the likes of Fats Domino, the Platters, Little Richard and the Upsetters, Gene Vincent, Eddie Fontaine, the Chuckles, and Eddie Cochran. Richard Bartlett's *Rock, Pretty Baby* featured Fay Wray, Sal Mineo, and Shelley Fabares, but only in supporting roles; along with Sonny Burke's title song and Bill Haley's "The Saints Rock 'n' Roll," the film teems with bongo-flavored songs written for the most part by Henry Mancini.

21   Richard Abel, "Fan Discourse in the Heartland: The Early 1910s," *Film History: An International Journal* 18, no. 2 (2006), 150.

22   The Trautonium was used as early as 1930 in Paul Dessau's score for the German film *Stürme über dem Montblanc*; the ondes martenot was used in 1932 by Dmitry Shostakovich in his score for *Counterplan* and in 1934 by Arthur Honegger and Franz Waxman in their scores for, respectively, *L'Idée* and *Liliom*; the theremin was used by Shostakovich in his score for *Odna (Alone)* (1931) and by Gavreil Popov in his score for *Komsomol: The Patron of Elecrification* (1934).

23 The theremin made its Hollywood debut in 1944, in Robert Dolan's score for the screen adaptation of Kurt Weill's and Ira Gershwin's musical *Lady in the Dark*; more famously, the theremin was used by Miklós Rózsa in his scores for Alfred Hitchcock's *Spellbound* and Billy Wilder's *The Lost Weekend*. The theremin's first use in a science-fiction film was in Ferde Grofé's score for *Rocketship X-M* (1950); in 1951 the theremin figured prominently in Bernard Herrmann's score for *The Day the Earth Stood Still* and Dimitri Tiomkin's score for *The Thing from Another World*, and after that its sound—or a similar sound generated simply by a tuned oscillator—became a sci-fi cliché.

24 For details on how Schary came to engage the Barrons, and on why the Barrons are officially credited not for music but for "electronic tonalities," see James Wierzbicki, *Louis and Bebe Barron's* Forbidden Planet: *A Film Score Guide* (Lanham, MD: Scarecrow Press, 2005), 1–17.

25 The references are to Pierre Schaeffer (1910–1995), Pierre Henry (b. 1928), and Karlheinz Stockausen (1928–2007). Schaeffer and Henry, a radio technician and a conservatoire-trained composer, respectively, in Paris in the years immediately following World War II experimented with recorded sounds and launched the genre soon to be known as *musique concrète*. Stockhausen, a German, studied with Schaeffer in Paris and then established a synthesizer-based electronic music studio in Cologne.

26 The references are to Otto Luening (1900–96) and Vladimir Ussachevsky (1911–90), American composers who experimented—albeit with middling results—with electronic music throughout the 1950s.

27 Louis and Bebe Barron worked with John Cage (1912–92) on the realization of his 1952–53 *Williams Mix*.

28 The reference is to Edgard Varèse (1883–1965), the French-born composer who spent most of his career in the United States and who, famously, explored electronic music in *Poème électronique* (1958) and sections of *Déserts* (1959).

29 The American mathematician Norbert Wiener (1894–1964) remains best known for his 1948 book *Cybernetics: Or Control and Communication in the Animal and the Machine*. His other important books include *The Human Use of Human Beings* (1950), *Nonlinear Problems in Random Theory* (1958), and *Invention: The Care and Feeding of Ideas* (1994).

30 The extent of Cage's actual involvement with Eastern philosophies remains debatable. It is well known, however, that since the late 1940s Cage used the hexagram system of the *I Ching* as a method for generating random data.

31 The reference is to J. Willard Gibbs (1839–1903), an American physicist who, from his base of operations at Yale University, conducted pioneering research in probability theory as applied to chemistry and thermodynamics.

32 The Stancil Corporation was founded by Hollywood sound engineer William V. Stancil in 1946; it was renamed the Stancil-Hoffman Company in 1948. Originally based in San Carlos, California, Ampex was founded in 1944 by Alexander M. Poniatoff; its first commercial tape recorders were marketed in 1947.

33 The referenced article is Ted Greenwald, "The Self-Destructing Modules behind the Revolutionary 1956 Soundtrack of *Forbidden Planet*," *Keyboard* 12 (February 1986): 54–60, 65.

34 The bracketed material is the author's.

35 Although advertised as the "original MGM soundtrack," *Forbidden Planet: Electronic Music by Louis and Bebe Barron* (Planet Records PR-001) in fact features mixes different from those used in the film. The vinyl disc was issued in 1977 and then re-issued as compact disc in 1989. For a comparison of the music in the film and on the album, see James Wierzbicki, *Louis and Bebe Barron's* Forbidden Planet: *A Film Score Guide* (Lanham, MD: Scarecrow Press, 2005), 63–153.

36 The idea to use music by Harry Partch was never more than wishful thinking on the part of *Forbidden Planet* producer Dore Schary.

37 Mellé's bold statements date from 1983, when he was interviewed by Randall D. Larson for the purposes of Larson's *Musique Fantastique: A Survey of Music in the Fantastic Cinema* (Metuchen, NJ: Scarecrow Press, 1984). The entirety of the interview was published in *The Cue Sheet—Quarterly Journal of the Film Music Society* 20, no. 1 (January 2005), 23–46.

38   Directed by William A. Graham and produced by Universal in 1968, *Perilous Voyage* was not aired until 1976. Serling's *Night Gallery* aired from 1970 until 1973.

39   Sergio Leemann, *Robert Wise on His Films: From Editing Room to Director's Chair* (Los Angeles: Silman James, 1995), 198.

40   Lankershim is the old name for the neighborhood in Southern California's San Fernando Valley that since 1927 has been known officially as North Hollywood. Lankershim Boulevard forms part of the area's northeast border.

41   The film was released on March 12, 1971.

42   Based in the town of Donaueschingen in Germany's Black Forest region, the Donaueschingen Festival of Contemporary Music, internationally famous as a venue for daring experiments in concert-hall music, began in 1921. The festival continues to this day, although in the 1930s and 1940s its activities were often suspended.

43   The reference is to Karlheinz Stockhausen (1928–2007), the German composer who in the 1950s created several important works in the still new field of electronic music.

44   The genre of *musique concrète*, whose name implies rather more than simply the use of sounds recorded from the real, or "concrete," world, was started by French radio technician Pierre Schaeffer in the years immediately following World War II.

45   Miklós Rózsa's score for *Spellbound* (Selznick, 1945) is by and large a traditional orchestral score that uses the theremin as the principal instrument in iterations of its main themes.

Chapter 12

1   Only the film's 'trademark' song, "Mrs. Robinson," was written by Paul Simon and Art Garfunkel specifically for the film. Also written specifically for the film were pieces for one or two guitars—in the Simon and Garfunkel manner—by David Grusin.

2   Selected by film editor Donn Cambern and subsequently licensed for a total of more than a million dollars, the material included songs recorded by the Jimi Hendrix Experience, Steppenwolf, Little Eva, the Byrds, Fraternity of Man, the Electric Prunes, The Band, the Holy Modal Rounders, and the group called simply Smith.

3   Bernstein's primary composition teachers were Israel Citkowitz, Roger Sessions, and Stefan Wolpe.

4   These were *Saturday's Hero* and *Boots Malone* (1951); *Battles of Chief Pontiac* and *Sudden Fear* (1952); *Never Wave at a WAC*, *Cat Women of the Moon*, *Robot Monster*, and *Miss Robin Crusoe* (1953); *Make Haste to Live* and *Silent Raiders* (1954); and *The Eternal Sea* and *It's a Dog's Life* (1955).

5   These would include his scores for *The Man with the Golden Arm* (1955), *The Ten Commandments* (1956), *The Magnificent Seven* (1960), *Birdman of Alcatraz* (1962), *To Kill a Mockingbird* (1963), *The Great Escape* (1963), and *Hawaii* (1966).

6   These include *National Lampoon's Animal House* (1978), *Airplane!* (1980), *The Blues Brothers* (1980), *Stripes* (1981), *Trading Places* (1983), *Ghostbusters* (1984), and *¡Three Amigos!* (1986).

7   John Ford's *The Informer* (RKO, 1935) was based on a Liam O'Flaherty novel on the Irish uprisings of 1922.

8   DeMille was not only producer but also director of *The Ten Commandments* (Paramount, 1956).

9   Streamers and punches are visual elements added to a film for the sake of aiding the conductor. A streamer is realized as a diagonal line that seems to move across the projected image; a punch is realized as a single bright flash.

10   The title song in *High Noon* (United Artists, 1952; dir. Fred Zinnemann) is generally known as "Do Not Forsake Me, Oh My Darlin'" but officially bears the title "The Ballad of High Noon." The lyrics are by Ned Washington. Although in the film the song was sung by Tex Ritter, the song's popularization came with the 1952 commercial recording on the Columbia label by Frankie Laine.

11   *The Revolt of Mamie Stover* (Twentieth Century-Fox, 1956; dir. Raoul Walsh) features music by Hugo Friedhofer. The lyrics of the title song are by Paul Francis Webster.

12 *The Man with the Golden Arm* was directed by Otto Preminger and released by United Artists; created by Blake Edwards, the *Peter Gunn* television series ran from 1958 until 1961, first on the NBC network and then on ABC, and included 114 episodes.

13 The song based on that theme, with lyrics by Johnny Mercer, was created in the film's aftermath; during 1945 "Laura" was recorded in at least five different versions, the one by Woody Herman and His Orchestra reaching the No. 1 spot on the Hit Parade.

14 Based on the incomplete *Woyzeck* by the German playwright Georg Buchner, Alban Berg's opera *Wozzeck* was composed between 1914 and 1922 and was given its first performance by the Berlin State Opera in 1925; the American premiere took place in Philadelphia in 1931.

15 Raksin taught film-music composition regularly at the University of Southern California from 1956 until 2003; he taught at the University of California, Los Angeles, from 1970 until 1992, and he occasionally was a visiting lecturer at the University of California, Santa Barbara.

Chapter 13

1 For a full account of production and distribution methods during the studio era, which existed between the time of World War I and approximately 1950, see Thomas Schatz, *The Genius of the System: Hollywood Filmmaking in the Studio Era* (Philadelphia: Temple University Press, 1981).

2 James Wierzbicki, *Film Music: A History* (London and New York: Routledge, 2009), 197.

3 Susan Hayward, *Cinema Studies: The Key Concepts* (London: Routledge, 2000), 64. For an extended definition of the classic-style film, see David Bordwell, Janet Staiger, and Kristin Thompson, *The Classical Hollywood Cinema: Film Style and Production to 1960* (London: Routledge & Keagan Paul, 1985), 3–4.

4 Goldsmith made his Hollywood debut in 1957 with his score for Allen Miner's *Black Patch*. Along with the films cited in this article, his early successes include *Lilies of the Field* (1963), *Seven Days in May* (1964), and *Von Ryan's Express* (1965).

5 Goldsmith's later, and better-known scores, include those for *Planet of the Apes* (1967), *Patton* (1969), *Papillon* (1973), *Chinatown* (1974), *The Omen* (1976), *Star Trek: The Motion Picture* (1979), *Poltergeist* (1982), *Basic Instinct* (1992), *Congo* (1995), *L.A. Confidential* (1997), and *The Haunting* (1999).

6 *Alfie* (1966; dir. Lewis Gilbert) was made in England by Sheldrake Films and released in the United States by Paramount. The score is by jazz musician Sonny Rollins; the title song, which was written after the film's UK release and then affixed to the end titles of the American prints, is by Burt Bacharach.

7 As noted above, the title song for *Alfie* is by Burt Bacharach. The title song as well as the score for *Born Free* (Columbia, 1966; dir. James Hill) are by John Barry. The score for *Dr. Zhivago* (MGM, 1965; dir. David Lean), which includes the melody popularly known as "Lara's Theme," is by Maurice Jarre; after the film's release the melody was fitted with lyrics by Paul Francis Webster and, as "Somewhere, My Love," became an international hit.

8 As mentioned, Rosenman c.1950 studied briefly with Arnold Schoenberg, who famously invented the twelve-tone method in the early 1920s. It should be noted, though, that Rosenman did not study composition—twelve-tone or otherwise—with Schoenberg. Most of what Rosenman knew about serial technique he learned at UC-Berkeley through his sustained work with Roger Sessions and his occasional lessons with visiting professor Luigi Dallapiccola.

9 Rosenman adds this note: "I have been asked many times to extract concert works from film scores I have written. Thus far I have refused, because in the time it would take to refashion the score into a concert piece it would be far simpler to write a new work."

10 The German word "Klangfarben" means, literally, "sound colors."

11 The concert-hall models referenced are the Viennese composer Arnold Schoenberg (1874–1951), Schoenberg's student Anton Webern (1883–1945), and the Polish composer Krzysztof Penderecki (b. 1933).

12   Phillip Lambro (b. 1935) left the film business and returned to writing music for the concert hall shortly after this article appeared. His filmography includes only the documentaries *Father Pat* (1970), *Mineral King* (1971), and *Celebration* (1971), and the low-budget feature films *And Now Miguel* (1966), *Crypt of the Living Dead* (1973), *Git!* (1974), *Murph the Surf* (1975), and *Blood Voyage* (1976). Reflecting on his experiences in Hollywood, in 2010 he self-published an autobiography titled *Close Encounters of the Worst Kind*.

Chapter 14

1   The work cited is Gianni Rondolino's *Cinema e musica* (Torino). See Peter Larsen, trans. John Irons, *Film Music* (London: Reaktion Books, 2007), 14.

2   For detailed information on music in the earliest film exhibitions, see Richard Abel and Rick Altman, eds., *The Sounds of Early Cinema* (Bloomington: Indiana University Press, 2001), and Altman, *Silent Film Sound* (New York: Columbia University Press, 2004).

3   Hugo Riesenfeld, "Music and Motion Pictures," *The Annals of the American Academy of Political and Social Science*, 128, no. 217 (November 1926), 61–62.

4   Ibid., 60.

5   "1920–1929," *Official Website of the American Federation of Musicians*, www.afm.org/about/our-history/1920-1929 (accessed January 31, 2011).

6   "Musical Unemployment," *New York Times*, February 28, 1930, A4.

7   Herman Kenin was a dance band leader who served as AFM president from 1958 to 1970. His Multnomah Orchestra was contemporary with Paul Whiteman and His Orchestra.

8   Hitchcock's *Vertigo* (Paramount, 1958) features a score by Bernard Herrmann; Philip Dunne's *Ten North Frederick* (Twentieth Century-Fox, 1958) features a score by Leigh Harline. The scores for both films were recorded in London.

9   Eliot Daniel was a composer and conductor active in the Hollywood studios from the 1940s to the early 1970s. For Disney, he composed the music to *Make Mine Music, Fun & Fancy Free*, and *Melody Time*. After moving into television, he wrote scores for *Willy* (1954–55), *Those Whiting Girls* (1955), *I Love Lucy* (1951–57). In addition, he served as vocal director for a number of musicals, such as *Belles on Their Toes* (1952), *The Girl Next Door* (1953), and *Gentlemen Prefer Blondes* (1953).

10   Lewis was a piano player based in Oakland, CA. Before founding his own band, he played with Bob Scobey's Frisco Band. During his time working for the AFM, he was also band leader for Tempo, the band that played for all of the union's conventions.

11   At the time, Cecil Read was the principal trumpeter for the Twentieth Century-Fox studio orchestra.

12   Larry Sullivan, the principal trumpeter at Warner Bros., served as treasurer for the MGA. Ted Nash, a saxophonist for Universal, served as the union's recording secretary. Justin Gordon, a flutist at Disney, served as vice-chairman.

13   Michael Melvoin is a jazz pianist who has been working with film studios since 1971. In addition to performing on soundtracks, he has composed for a variety of television series, such as episodes of *Buck Rogers in the 25th Century* (1979), *Fame* (1984), *MacGyver* (1985); and made-for-TV movies, such as *The David Cassidy Story* (2000), and *The Fuzz* (2010).

14   Kim Fellner is a labor activist who has worked for a variety of unions, and who is currently the development director for Working America. At the time of the 1980–81 AFM strike, she was the information director for the Screen Actors Guild. She offered her services to the AFM to help educate the public about the "human side" of the strike.

15   The AFM's Special Payment Fund is a vehicle for paying royalties to those musicians who do recording sessions for either the recording or film industries.

16   Counter died in 2009, after 27 years as president of the AMPTP. During this time he was known for uniting the major film and television companies into a coherent and disciplined bargaining unit for more than 300 labor agreements with the various film and television industry unions.

17   Boddicker is a session musician in Los Angeles who was particularly active in the film industry during the 1980s and early 1990s. In addition, he was closely associated with

Michael Jackson, having performed on "We Are the World," and the albums *Off the Wall*, *Thriller*, *Bad*, and *Dangerous*.

18 The convention took place July 18–20, 2005 at the Riviera Hotel in Las Vegas. Following the 97th AFM Convention, in July 2007, the event switched from a biennial to a triennial schedule.

19 Throughout his career, Post has been associated with action shows and crime dramas. In addition to providing music for the different iterations of *Law & Order*, he has written music for *The Rockford Files* (1974–80), *The A-Team* (1983–87), *Magnum P.I.* (1980–88), *Hill Street Blues* (1981–87), *Doogie Howser, M.D.* (1989–93), *L.A. Law* (1986–94), *Murder One* (1995–97), and *NYPD Blue* (1993–2004).

20 Foliart is a television composer whose credits include episodes of *Laverne & Shirley* (1982–83), *Happy Days* (1981–84), *Roseanne* (1988–94), *Home Improvement* (1991–97), *8 Simple Rules* (2002–05), and *7th Heaven* (1996–2007).

Chapter 15

1 Ted Wick, "Creating the Movie-Music Album," *High Fidelity*, April 1976, 68–71.

2 Richard Lester's *A Hard Day's Night* (1964) was jointly made in England by Maljack Productions, Proscenium Films, and Walter Shenson Films; it was distributed by United Artists. While the film famously features songs by the Beatles, it also features original scoring, and arrangements, by George Martin.

3 David Lean's *Dr. Zhivago* (1975) features a score by Maurice Jarre.

4 The Oscar-winning score for John Sturges's *The Magnificent Seven* (1960) is by Elmer Bernstein.

5 Jules Dassin's *Never on Sunday* (1960) was made by Lopert Pictures and Melinafilm and distributed by United Artists. The Academy Award-winning title song as well as the complete score are by the Greek composer Manos Hatzidakis; in the film the song (as "Ta paidia tou Peiraia") is performed with Hatzidakis's original Greek lyrics; after the film's success, the song was fitted with English lyrics by Billy Towne.

6 Michael Leisen's *Captain Carey, U.S.A.* (Paramount, 1950) has a score by Hugo Friedhofer. The Oscar-winning song "Mona Lisa" was written by Ray Evans and Jay Livingston; the soundtrack version was performed by Nat "King" Cole, and after the film's release Cole's recording was a Number One hit for eight weeks.

7 In the 1970s MGM produced two feature-length films that showcased excepts from its musicals. Directed by Jack Haley Jr., *That's Entertainment!* was released in May 1974; directed by Gene Kelly, *That's Entertainment, Part II* was released in May 1976. Directed by Bud Friedgen and Michael J. Sheridan, a third film—*That's Entertainment! III*—was produced in 1996.

8 Franz Waxman's fanfare for MGM was introduced at the start of his score for *The Philadelphia Story* (1940; dir. George Cukor); Alfred Newman's fanfare for Twentieth Century-Fox was originally composed in 1933 for the Fox Studios, re-done in 1935 when Fox merged with Twentieth Century, and then fitted with a "CinemaScope extension" extension in 1954.

9 Edward Dmytryk's *Raintree County* was released in 1957.

10 The mentioned films are *Laura* (Twentieth Century-Fox, 1944; dir. Otto Preminger), *The Bad and the Beautiful* (MGM, 1952; dir. Vincente Minnelli), and *Forever Amber* (Twentieth Century-Fox, 1947; dir. Otto Preminger).

11 Gershwin's opera *Porgy and Bess* was premiered in New York in 1935.

12 *Farewell My Lovely* (ITC Entertainment, 1975) was directed by Dick Richards.

13 Along with songs by composer Jerome Kern and lyricists Ira Gershwin and E. Y. Harburg, Charles Vidor's *Cover Girl* (Columbia, 1944) features music by Carmen Dragon and Gil Grau; along with songs by Kern and lyricist Johnny Mercer, William A. Seiter's *You Were Never Lovelier* (Columbia, 1942) features original music by Leigh Harline.

14 Former big-band vocalist Nan Wynn (1915–71) appeared in *Million Dollar Baby* (Warner Bros., 1941), *Princess O'Rourke* (Warner Bros., 1943), *Intrigue* (Star Films Inc., 1947) and several other films; she dubbed Rita Hayward's songs not just in *You Were Never Lovelier*

and *Cover Girl* but also in *My Gal Sal* (Twentieth Century-Fox,1942). Soprano Marni Nixon (b. 1930) dubbed the songs of Deborah Kerr in *The King and I* (Twentieth Century-Fox, 1956) and *An Affair to Remember* (Jerry Wald Productions, 1957); over the course of her long Hollywood career Nixon also dubbed for Margaret O'Brien in *The Secret Garden* (MGM, 1949), for Natalie Wood in *West Side Story* (Mirisch Corporation and Seven Arts Productions, 1961), and for Audrey Hepburn in *My Fair Lady* (Warner Bros., 1964).

15 With co-composer Walter Jurmann and lyricist Gus Kahn, Kaper wrote the title song for *San Francisco* (MGM, 1936; dir. Woody Van Dyke). Kaper composed not just the Oscar-winning score for *Lili* (MGM, 1953; dir. Charles Walters) but also (with lyricist Helen Deutsch) the film's featured song, "Hi-Lili, Hi-Lo." For Victor Saville's *Green Dolphin Street* (MGM, 1945), Kaper composed both the score and (with lyricist Ned Washington) the song "On Green Dolphin Street." Along with music from the films just mentioned and from Morton DaCosta's *Auntie Mame* (Warner Bros., 1958), the recording includes Kaper's themes from *Mutiny on the Bounty* (1962), *The Glass Slipper* (1955), *Butterfield 8* (1960), *The Brothers Karamazov* (1958), *The Swan* (1956), and *Lord Jim* (1965).

16 Berkeley's *The Gang's All Here* (Twentieth Century-Fox, 1941) features songs by Leo Robin and Harry Warren as well as original music by Hugo Friedhofer, Alfred Newman, Arthur Lange, Cyril J. Mockridge, and Gene Rose. Along with songs by composer Vincent Youmans and lyricists Gus Kahn and Edward Eliscu, Thornton Freeland's *Flying Down to Rio* (RKO, 1933) includes original music by Max Steiner.

17 Blake Edwards's *The Return of the Pink Panther* was made by ITC Entertainment in 1975. The films with scores by John Williams are *Earthquake* (Universal, 1974; dir. Mark Robson), *The Towering Inferno* (Irwin Allen Productions and Twentieth Century-Fox, 1974; dir. John Guillerman), and *Jaws* (Universal, 1975; dir. Steven Spielberg).

18 Along with underscore by Michel Colombier, Taylor Hackford's *White Nights* (Delphi IV Productions and Columbia, 1985) features songs performed by Chaka Khan, David Pack, Robert Plant, Roberta Flack, John Hiatt, Lou Reed, David Foster, Jerry Burton, Nile Rodgers, Sandy Stewart, Marilyn Martin, and Phil Collins. The song "Separate Lives," by Stephen Bishop, was nominated for an Academy Award.

19 *Streets of Fire* was jointly produced by RKO and Universal in 1984. Along with Bernstein's underscore, *Ghostbusters* (Columbia, 1984) includes songs performed by Alessi, Laura Branigan, the Trammps, the Bus Boys, the Thompson Twins, Air Supply, Mick Smiley, and Ray Parker Jr. Parker's title song was nominated for an Academy Award, but it also triggered a lawsuit, from songwriter Huey Lewis, for plagiarism.

20 Before *White Nights*, for which he sang "Separate Lives," Phil Collins performed songs for *Risky Business* (Geffen Company, 1983: dir. Paul Brickman), *Against All Odds* (Columbia, 1984; dir. Taylor Hackford), and *Electric Dreams* (Virgin, 1984; dir. Steve Barron). In the next few years he performed songs for *Back to the Future* (Universal, 1985; dir. Robert Zemeckis), *No Return, No Exchange* (Urban films, 1986; Jose Wenceslao), *Playing for Keeps* (Miramax, 1986; Bob and Harvey Weinstein), *The Color of Money* (Touchstone, 1986; dir. Martin Scorsese), *You Can't Hurry Love* (Lightning Pictures, 1988; dir. Richard Martini), *Buster* (Movie Group, 1988; dir. David Green), and *Firebirds* (Touchstone, 1990; dir. David Green).

21 Steven Spielberg's *Jaws* (Universal) was released in 1975.

22 Along with underscore by Giorgio Moroder, Adrian Lyne's *Flashdance* (Paramount, 1983) features songs performed by Michael Sembello, Irene Cara, Joan Jett and the Blackhearts, Donna Summer, and Laura Branigan. Herbert Ross's *Footloose* (Paramount, 1984) features songs recorded by Kenny Loggins, Deniece Williams, Bonnie Tyler, Karla Bonoff, Ann Wilson and Mike Reno, Sammy Hagar, Quiet Riot, Moving Pictures, John Cougar Mellencamp, Foreigner, and Shalamar.

23 Cecil B. DeMille's *The Ten Commandments* (Paramount) dates from 1956; Robert Mulligan's *To Kill a Mockingbird* (Universal) dates from 1962.

24 The song, with lyrics by Ned Washington, also goes by the title "The Ballad of High Noon." *High Noon* (Stanley Kramer Productions, 1952) was directed by Fred Zinnemann.

25 The mentioned films are *Citizen Kane* (RKO, 1941; dir. Orson Welles), *Gone with the Wind* (Selznick International and MGM, 1939; dir. Victor Fleming), and *Ben-Hur* (MGM, 1959; dir. William Wyler).

26 The first episode of the *Star Wars* series (Lucasfilm and Twentieth Century-Fox, 1977) was directed by George Lucas.

27 The German synthesizer-based ensemble Tangerine Dream was founded in 1967. At the time the group did the score for *Legend*, its members were Edgar Froese, Christopher Franke, and Paul Haslinger.

28 Featured in Hackford's *An Officer and a Gentleman* (Lomar film Entertainment, 1982), "Up Where We Belong" was written by composers Jack Nitzsche and Buffy Sainte-Marie and lyricist Will Jennings; for the soundtrack it was performed by Joe Cocker and Jennifer Warnes. The title song for *Against All Odds* (Columbia, 1984) was written and performed for the film by Phil Collins.

Chapter 16

1 Based on the same concept that *c.*1930 had allowed filmmakers to record sound on film by photographing filaments that vibrated in response to electrically amplified soundwaves, the ANS synthesizer was developed at the state-run Melodiya studios in the early 1960s by Evgeny Murzin. The instrument takes its name from the initials of Alexander Nikolayevich Scriabin, the Russian composer who with his 1910 *Prometheus: The Poem of Fire* sought to combine music with the projections of colored light.

2 Jackson's *Thriller* was released by Epic Records in November 1982.

3 The acronym SMPTE stands for the Society of Motion Picture and Television Engineers, and it represents a timecode protocol, standardized in 1971, by which each frame of a film or videotape is uniquely identified.

4 The Synclavier, a combination synthesizer and sampler, was developed at Dartmouth College by Jon Appleton and first marketed by New England Digital in 1978.

5 On the market between 1983 and 1986, the Yamaha DX7 was the first commercial digital synthesizer. It was developed by John Chowning at Stanford University.

6 The bracketed insertions throughout the article are the author's.

7 The term "justified," or "quantized," time refers to a computer process by which the attacks of notes in a sequence are adjusted to agree precisely with a specified rhythmic value.

8 Foley effects—sound effects created in a studio and synchronized with filmed action—are named after Jack Foley, a sound recordist who worked for Universal in the early days of the sound film.

9 The bracketed notes are the author's.

10 The bracketed comments are the author's.

11 The franchise to date comprises *Pirates of the Caribbean: The Black Pearl* (2003), *Pirates of the Caribbean: Dead Man's Chest* (2006), and *Pirates of the Caribbean: At World's End* (2007); all three films were produced by Walt Disney Productions and directed by Gore Verbinski.

12 For Gore Verbinski's *The Weather Man* (Paramount, 2005), James S. Levine is credited (with Zimmer) as co-composer.

Chapter 17

1 Jeff Smith, *The Sounds of Commerce: Marketing Popular Film Music* (New York: Columbia University Press, 1998), 209.

2 For a colorful but not necessarily accurate account of how Carl Fischer and other publishers *c.*1917 began to commission license-free film music "by the trainload," see Max Winkler, *A Penny from Heaven* (New York: Appleton-Century Crofts, 1951).

3 Pauline Reay, *Music and Film: Soundtracks and Synergy* (London: Wallflower Press, 2004), 21–22.

4 David T. Friendly, "Seeking the Groove in Movie sound Tracks," *Los Angeles Times*, October 2, 1986, H1.

5　Both *Austin Powers: International Man of Mystery* (Capella International, 1997) and *Austin Powers: The Spy Who Shagged Me* (New Line Cinema, 1999) were directed by Jay Roach and featured music by George S. Clinton. For both films, Chris Douridas is credited as "music consultant"; the credited music supervisor for the 1997 film is John Houlihan, and the credited music supervisors for the 1999 film are Houlihan and Steve Juliani. For Kevin Reynolds's *One Eight Seven* (Icon Entertainment International, 1997; music by David Darling and Michael Stearns), Douridas is credited as music supervisor; for Allison Anders's *Grace of My Heart* (Cappa Productions and Universal, 1996; music by Larry Klein), Douridas is credited (along with Tiffany Anders) as "music consultant."

6　For Bronwen Hughes's *Forces of Nature* (DreamWorks SKG, 1999), the music supervisors were Michelle Kuznitsky and Mary Ramos, and Douridas's name does not appear among the credits. Along with songs performed by such artists as Holly Palmer, the Propellerheads, and R. L. Burnside, the soundtrack includes original music by John Powell.

7　For *Austin Powers: The Spy Who Shagged Me*, Danny Bramson is credited as executive music supervisor.

8　Fritz Lang's *Metropolis* is a silent film dating from 1927; the version with Giorgio Moroder's synthesizer-based soundtrack was released in 1984.

9　The bracketed material is in the original.

10　The song is "The Seeker," the words and music of which are by The Who member Pete Townshend.

11　The Genie Awards are the Canadian equivalent of the United States' Academy Awards. They have been called the Genie Awards only since 1979, but they have been offered since 1949 by the Academy of Canadian Cinema and Television.

12　Jack Rudy has been music supervisor for the 2004 television series *Good Girls Don't . . .*, the 2006 made-for-TV movie *Flirt*, the 2007 film *Waking Dreams*, and the 2009–10 television series *Accidentally on Purpose*.

13　Robert Weston Smith was a radio announcer who developed his outspoken, overtly hip "Wolfman Jack" persona in 1962 when he moved from Newport News, Virginia, to a station in Shreveport, Louisiana. A year later, after he relocated to a high-powered "border blaster" station based in Ciudad Acuña, Mexico, his influential pop music programs were heard all across the United States and even in Canada. In 1971 he worked for station KDAY in Los Angeles, and in 1973 he worked—albeit briefly—for station WNBC in New York. From 1974 until his retirement in 1989 he was based again, as producer of syndicated radio programs, in Los Angeles.

Chapter 18

1　The term "cinema of attraction" owes to film historian Tom Gunning, and it refers to the earliest films (*c*.1895–1902) whose appeal to audiences had to do not at all with narrative content but simply with a moving picture's spectacular novelty. During the period of the "cinema of attraction" music served not to accompany film but simply to enliven the occasions at which films were exhibited. See Tom Gunning, "The Cinema of Attraction: Early Film, Its Spectator and the Avant-Garde," *Wide Angle* 8, nos. 3–4 (1986), 63–70.

2　The first narrative films were produced *c*.1901–03. By 1907 narrative films—usually just one reel in length, but sometimes longer—were the staple of small exhibition spaces that throughout not just the United States but also Europe came to be known as Nickelodeons; the name stems from a theater that opened in Pittsburgh, Pennsylvania, in 1905 and which charged just a nickel—a five-cent coin—for admission. The nickelodeon period extends roughly from 1905 to 1915, when film culture was taken over by multi-reel 'features' exhibited in large "movie palaces."

3　For an explanation of the classical-style film, see Chapter 7, note 2.

4　For information on how the "studio system" worked, see, for example, Douglas Gomery, *The Hollywood Studio System: A History* (London: British Film Institute, 2008), and Thomas Schatz, *The Genius of the System: Hollywood Filmmaking in the Studio Era* (Minneapolis: University of Minnesota Press, 2010).

5   In Noël Coward's 1930 *Private Lives*, the character Amanda observes: "Extraordinary how potent cheap music is."

6   Along with the music of Mozart, Bo Widerberg's (1967) *Elvira Madigan* features an original score by Ulf Björlin.

7   Along with excerpts from the 1862 Verdi opera, Claude Berri's 1986 *Jean de Florette* features original music by Jean-Claude Petit.

8   Along with the diegetic Caruso recordings, Werner Herzog's 1982 *Fitzcarraldo* features original music by the group Popol Vuh.

9   Along with various pieces by Mahler, the soundtrack for Luchino Visconti's 1971 *Morte a Venezia* (*Death in Venice*) includes pre-existing music by Beethoven, Mussorgsky, and Armando Gil.

10   Along with music by Gyorgy Ligeti and Johann Strauss Jr., Stanley Kubrick's 1968 *2001: A Space Odyssey* features music by Richard Strauss and Aram Khatchaturian.

11   Based on a Broadway musical produced by Billy Rose, Otto Preminger's 1946 *Carmen Jones* is an adaption of Bizet's 1875 opera *Carmen*, with the music arranged by Dimitri Tiomkin and Leon Birnbaum and the lyrics re-written by Oscar Hammerstein II. In Sam Wood's 1935 *A Night at the Opera*, a diegetic production of Verdi's 1853 opera *Il Trovatore* provides the situation for the comical climax.

12   The reference is to Milos Forman's *Amadeus* (Saul Zaentz Company, 1984), an adaption for film of Peter Shaffer's same-titled play of 1977.

13   Along with the music from Mozart's 1790 opera, John Schlesinger's 1971 *Sunday, Bloody Sunday* features original music by Ron Geesin.

14   Based in Winnipeg, Manitoba, K-Tel is a television marketing company that since 1966 has thrived by manufacturing and selling, among other things, compilation albums.

15   The original Italian version of Vittorio De Sica's *After the Fox* (*Caccia alla volpe*) (Cinecitta, 1966) featured underscore by Piero Piccioni; Burt Bacharach provided music, including a title song, for the English-language release. Bacharach wrote the underscore, including the title song, for *What's New, Pussycat?* (Famous Artists Productions, 1965; dir. Clive Donner and Richard Talmadge); along with an original score by Bacharach, the song "What's New Pussycat?" was featured in the 1966 James Bond film *Casino Royale* (Columbia; dir. Val Guest and Ken Hughes). The *Painted from Memory* album was released in September 1998 by Mercury Records.

16   Krzysztof Komeda scored such Polanski films as *Gdy spadaja anioly* (*An Old Woman*; 1959), *Nóz w wodzie* (*Knife in the Water*; 1962), *Wenn katelbach kommt* (*Cul-de-sac*; 1966), and *Dance of the Vampires* (1967).

17   Michelangelo Antonioni's *Blow-Up* (Bridge Films) dates from 1966; Federico Fellini's *La Dolce Vita* (Rama Film and Pathé Consortium) dates from 1960.

18   Peer Raben scored such Rainer Werner Fassbinder films as *Der amerikanische Soldat* (1970), *Satansbraten* (1976), *Die Ehe der Maria Braun* (1979), and the fourteen episodes of the television series *Berlin Alexanderplatz* (1980).

19   Bill Conti scored five films in John Avildsen's and Sylvester Stallone's "Rocky" series: *Rocky* (1976), *Rocky II* (1979), *Rocky III* (1982), *Rocky V* (1990), and *Rocky Balboa* (2006); the 1985 *Rocky IV* was scored by Vince DiCola.

20   Along with the underscore by Gavin Friday and Maurice Seezer, Jim Sheridan's *The Boxer* (Universal, 1997) features songs performed by Josie Doherty, the Rolling Stones, and Final Cut.

21   Bernardo Bertolucci's *The Last Emperor* (Recorded Picture Company and Hemdale, 1987) features original music not just by Ryuichi Sakamoto but also by David Byrne and Cong Su. Sakamoto is the sole composer for John Maybury's *Love Is the Devil: Study for a Portrait of Francis Bacon* (British Broadcasting Corporation, 1998).

22   The score for Lisa Cholodenko's *High Art* (391 Productions and Antidote Films, 1998) is credited to Stuart Hill, Nathan Larsen, and Craig Wedren, who together make up the group Shudder To Think.

23   The bracketed word is a conjectural insertion on the part of this volume's editors. As printed in *Billboard*, the sentence reads, cryptically: "Film's to non-traditional composers . . . ."

Chapter 19

1   By the time of Schiff's writing, John Williams had provided the music for four of George Lucas's "Star Wars" films: the original *Star Wars, Episode IV: A New Hope* (1977) and the variously titled sequels, or prequels, from 1980, 1983, and 1999; he would continue with the music for *Star Wars, Episode II: Attack of the Clones* (2002) and *Star Wars, Episode III: The Revenge of the Sith* (2005). Steven Spielberg's *Jaws* (Universal) dates from 1975; *Close Encounters of the Third Kind* (Columbia) dates from 1977.

2   Godfrey Reggio's *Koyaanisqatsi* (IRE Productions) dates from 1982. In addition to scoring *Koyaanisqatsi*, Philip Glass provided the music for Reggio's *Powaqqatsi* (1988), *Anima Mundi* (1992), and *Naqoyqatsi* (2002).

3   Along with excerpts of Stravinsky's *The Rite of Spring*, Walt Disney's 1940 *Fantasia* included animated settings of music by Bach, Beethoven, Schubert, Tchaikovsky, Mussorgsky, Ponchielli, and Dukas.

4   John Farrow's *Commandos Strike at Dawn* (Columbia, 1942) features a score by Louis Gruenberg.

5   Despite Schoenberg's efforts, Sidney Franklin's *The Good Earth* (MGM, 1937) was eventually scored by Herbert Stothart.

6   Selznick was the executive producer of *Duel in the Sun* (Selznick International, 1946); the film's director was King Vidor.

7   The pejorative term "mickey-mousing," used to describe music-action synchronization that was considered excessive, likely originated with producer David O. Selznick. See the comments from Selznick on pp. 104 of this volume.

8   The title music for William Wyler's *The Heiress* (Paramount, 1949) is largely an arrangement of the traditional song "Plaisir d'amour."

9   The title is given incorrectly, in a way that suggests that a Chihara piece called *Clouds* is excerpted from a score for a film called *Out of the Past*. In fact, Paul Chihara's 2001 *Clouds (. . . from out of the past)* is not an example of film music but, rather, an orchestral work commissioned by the American Composers Orchestra. It has nothing to do either with Jacques Tourneur's *Out of the Past* (RKO, 1947) or with Jeffrey Dupre's same-titled but otherwise not related film (Unapix Films) from 1998.

10   The television series *China Beach* aired from 1988 to 1991, and *100 Centre Street* aired for two seasons in 2001 and 2002.

11   THX is a protocol that in effect certifies motion-picture theaters to be capable of reproducing recorded sound according to certain industry specifications. It was introduced in 1983, in conjunction with the second film (*Return of the Jedi*) in George Lucas's *Star Wars* series.

12   John Adams's *The Chairman Dances: Foxtrot for Orchestra* is a thirteen-minute work for orchestra that was composed in 1985; it is similar in style, and to a certain extent in themes, to parts of *Nixon in China*, the opera that Adams was working on in the mid-1980s.

13   John Adams's *Gnarly Buttons* is a work for clarinet and thirteen-piece chamber ensemble—including two musicians who play digital samplers—that was premiered in London in 1996.

14   Ralph Steiner's and Willard Van Dyke's *The City* (American Documentary Films Inc.) was made in 1939 and was exhibited at the New York World's Fair. Lewis Milestone's *The Red Pony* (Lewis Milestone Productions) was made in Hollywood in 1949.

15   Based on themes from the film, John Corigliano's *Concerto for Violin and Orchestra: The Red Violin* was premiered by the Baltimore Symphony Orchestra and violinist Joshua Bell in 2005. Aaron Copland's *Red Pony* Suite was composed simultaneously with Copland's work on the film score and was premiered in 1948, a year before the film's release, by the Houston Symphony Orchestra.

16   Bernard Herrmann's score for *Psycho* (1960) includes music originally written for his 1935 *Sinfonietta for Strings*; the concert suite of music from the *Psycho* score dates from the early 1970s.

17   Along with songs by such groups as Godsmack, Nickelback, Flaw, and Mushroomhead, the soundtrack for Chuck Russell's *The Scorpion King* (Universal, 2002) features underscore by John Debney. Along with songs performed by such artists as Sly and the Family Stone, Herb Albert and the Tijuana Brass, Bob Dylan, and Jethro Tull, Brad Silberberg's *Moonlight Mile* (Epsilon and Touchstone, 2002) features underscore by Mark Isham.

18   Along with songs performed by such artists as Whitney Houston, Kenny G, and Lisa Stansfield, the soundtrack for Mick Jackson's *The Bodyguard* (Kasdan Pictures and Warner Bros., 1992) features underscore by Alan Silvestri. Along with songs performed by such artists as Queen, Ugly Kid Joe, Soundgarden, and the Red Hot Chili Peppers, the soundtrack for Penelope Spheeris's *Wayne's World* (Paramount, 1992) features underscore by J. Peter Robertson.

19   Along with songs performed by such artists as Charlotte Martin, the Freestylers, Jewel, The Calling, Cheryl Crow, and the Charlie Daniels Band, the soundtrack for Andy Tennant's *Sweet Home Alabama* (Original Film and Pigeon Creek Films, 2002) features underscore by George Fenton.

20   Along with songs performed by such artists as Rammstein, Drowning Pool, Moby, and The Chemical Brothers, the soundtrack for Rob Cohen's *xXx* (Original Film and Revolution Studios, 2002) features underscore by Randy Edelman.

21   Mark Motherbaugh is credited as composer for all four of the mentioned films. The films are Wes Anderson's *The Royal Tenenbaums* (American Empirical Pictures and Touchstone, 2001), Igor Kovalyov's and Norton Viergien's *The Rugrats Movie* (Grimsaem Animation Co. and Nickelodeon Movies, 1998), Stig Bergqvist's and Paul Demeyer's *Rugrats in Paris; The Movie—Rugrats II* (Nickelodeon Movies and Paramount, 2000), and Anthony Russo's *Welcome to Collinwood* (Gaylord Films and Pandora Cinema, 2002).

22   Along with a variety of pop/rock songs, Jay Roach's *Austin Powers in Goldmember* (New Line Cinema, 2002) features underscore by George S. Clinton, and Mark Ross's *Lil' Pimp* (Gifted Men Productions and Revolution Studios, 2005) features underscore by Jorge Corante and Frank Fitzpatrick.

23   Joyce Hatto (1928–2006) was a British pianist whose husband, William Barrington-Coupe, in the last decade of her life privately produced a large number of solo and concerto recordings supposedly featuring Hatto. These recordings won high praise from many critics, but after suspicious listeners subjected them to computer analysis it was revealed, in February 2007, that almost all of them were digital manipulations of commercially released work by other pianists.

24   For his contribution to *The Red Violin*, Corigliano won the Academy Award for Best Original Score. His only other film credit is for Hugh Hudson's *Revolution* (1985); in 2009 it was announced that Corigliano was slated to score Martin Campbell's *Edge of Darkness*, but the film when released the next year featured music by Howard Shore.

25   These range from Godfrey Reggio's dialogue-free documentaries *Koyaanisqatsi* (1982) and *Powaqqatsi* (1988) to such more conventional fare as *Mindwalk* (1990), *Candyman* (1992), *Kundun* (1997), *The Hours* (2002), *The Fog of War* (2003), *Notes on a Scandal* (2006), *The Illusionist* (2006), *Cassandra's Dream* (2007), and *Mr. Nice* (2010).

26   Based on material from his score for François Girard's *The Red Violin* (Rhombus Media and New Line International, 1998), John Corigliano's *The Red Violin: Suite for Violin and Orchestra* was premiered by violinist Joshua Bell and the Eos Orchestra in New York in 1999; Corigliano's more extensive *Concerto for Violin and Orchestra: The Red Violin* was premiered by Bell and the Baltimore Symphony Orchestra in 2005.

27   Madras, India's fourth largest city and the capital of the Tamil Nadu state, has recently come to be known as Chennai.

28   For his contributions to *Slumdog Millionaire*, A. R. Rahman won Oscars both for Best Original Score and (with lyricist Gulzar) for Best Song (for "Jai Ho").

29   The parenthetical insertions are in the original. Hugh Hudson's *Chariots of Fire* (Enigma Productions) dates from 1981.

30   Howard Shore provided the music for all three of Peter Jackson's "Lord of the Rings" (New Line Cinema) films: *The Fellowship of the Ring* (2001), *The Two Towers* (2002), and *The Return of the King* (2003).

31   The print version of Martens's article bore the headline "Sterling Scores"; this headline, and the expanded text, comes from the on-line version, available at www.latimes.com/entertainment/news/la-en-composers-20101207,0,4687703.story.

32   Joseph Kosinski's 2010 *Tron* is a remake of a same-titled film directed by Steven Lisberger and released in 1982; the score for the first film is by Wendy (née Walter) Carlos.

33   The section on composer Carter Burwell does not appear in this article's print version.
34   The Coen brothers' 2010 *True Grit* is a remake of a same-titled 1969 film directed by Henry Hathaway; the 1969 film featured a score by Elmer Bernstein.
35   The acronym EMI stands for Electric and Musical Industries. Founded in 1931 with the merger of the Gramophone Company and the Columbia Graphophone Company, the British organization manufactured not only recordings but also electronic equipment with applications in the recording and broadcasting industries.

CONTRIBUTORS

Abby Anderton is a doctoral candidate at the University of Michigan. Her dissertation topic concerns postwar musical culture in Berlin and the American military influence on classical music. She is currently engaged in archival research in Berlin, funded by the Fulbright Commission and the Germanistic Society of America.

Kevin Bartig is an assistant professor of musicology at Michigan State University. His research interests include music of Russia and the Soviet Union, music and politics, film music, and musical diplomacy. He is completing a book on Sergei Prokofiev's work in the Soviet film industry.

Joys H. Y. Cheung holds a Ph.D. in musicology/ethnomusicology from the University of Michigan and now teaches at the Chinese Civilisation Centre at the City University of Hong Kong. Her research interests include Chinese musical modernity, music and communist ritual, and music in Chinese screen productions. Her 2010 publication on the "musical translation" of Huang Zi (1904–38) in *Asian Music* discusses an art song composed for a 1935 film.

Andrew S. Kohler is a doctoral student in musicology and music theory at the University of Michigan. His areas of interest include the works of Beethoven, Mahler, Britten, and Carl Orff, the last of whom is the subject of his dissertation research. Kohler's compositions have been performed at the University of Michigan, and he has worked for organizations that advocate civil and human rights.

Stefano Mengozzi is an associate professor of music at the University of Michigan. His research focuses on music and music theory of the Renaissance period.

Nathan Platte is an assistant professor of musicology at the University of Iowa. His interests in film music, creative agency, and musical adaptations are reflected in articles recently published in *Music and the Moving Image* and *19th-Century Music*. He is co-author of a forthcoming monograph on Franz Waxman's score for the film *Rebecca*.

Colin Roust teaches music history at Roosevelt University's Chicago College of the Performing Arts. His research focuses primarily on French composer Georges Auric and on twentieth-century music in general, examining questions about the relationships of music to politics and of music to the other arts in genres such as film, song, opera, and ballet.

Joan Titus is an assistant professor of musicology at the University of North Carolina, Greensboro, and studies cultural politics/policy in North Africa, the American southwest, and the film music of Russia. Her recent publications include book chapters on Shostakovich's *Odna* and the idea of transnationalism as reflected in the Arizona-based music known as waila. She is currently doing fieldwork on festivals in Morocco and completing a book on narratology, Shostakovich, and film.

James Wierzbicki teaches musicology at the University of Sydney; along with exploring questions of modernity and the postmodern, his research focuses on twentieth-century music in general and film music in particular. His recent books include *Film Music: A History* (Routledge, 2009) and monographs on Elliott Carter and the electronic score for the 1956 film *Forbidden Planet*.

FILMOGRAPHY

127 Hours (USA/UK, 2010)
Dir.: Danny Boyle; Prod. Co.: Cloud Eight Films; Mus.: A. R. Rahman
300 (USA, 2006)
Dir.: Zack Snyder; Prod. Co.: Warner Bros.; Mus.: Tyler Bates
2001: A Space Odyssey (USA, 1968)
Dir.: Stanley Kubrick; Prod. Co.: Warner Bros.; Mus.: Pre-existing music by Gyorgy Ligeti, Johann Strauss Jr., Richard Strauss, Aram Khatchaturian
À Nous la Liberté! (France, 1931)
Dir.: René Clair; Prod. Co.: Sociétés de Films Sonores Tobis; Mus.: Georges Auric; Mus. Dir.: Armand Bernard
The Adventures of Milo and Otis (*Koneko monogatari*) (Japan, 1986, and USA, 1989)
Dir.: Mazonori Hata; Prod. Co.: Fuji Television Network; Mus: Ryûichi Sakamoto for Japanese version, Michael Boddicker for USA version
After the Fox (*Caccia alla volpe*) (Italy, 1966)
Dir.: Vittorio De Sica; Prod. Co.: Cinecitta; Mus.: Piero Piccioni (and Burt Bacharach, for the American release)
Against All Odds (USA, 1984)
Dir.: Taylor Hackford; Prod. Co.: Columbia; Mus.: Michel Colombier, Larry Carlton
L'Age d'Or (*The Age of Gold*) (France, 1930)
Dir.: Luis Buñuel; Prod. Co.: Vicomte Charles de Noailles; Mus.: Luis Buñuel, Georges Van Parys
Alexander Nevsky (*Aleksandr Nevskiy*) (USSR, 1938)
Dir.: Sergei Eisenstein; Prod. Co.: Mosfilm; Mus.: Sergei Prokofiev
Alfie (USA, 1966)
Dir.: Lewis Gilbert; Prod. Co.: Sheldrake Films; Mus.: Sonny Rollins; Title Song: Burt Bacharach
All That Money Can Buy (USA, 1941)
Alternate titles: *The Devil and Daniel Webster* and *Here Is a Man*
Dir.: William Dieterle; Prod. Co.: RKO; Mus.: Bernard Herrmann
Altered States (USA, 1980)
Dir.: Ken Russell; Prod. Co.: Warner Bros.; Mus.: John Corigliano
Amadeus (USA, 1984)
Dir.: Milos Forman; Prod. Co.: Saul Zaentz Company; Mus.: Pre-existing music by Mozart, Antonio Salieri, and others
American Graffiti (USA, 1973)
Dir.: George Lucas; Prod. Co.: Lucasfilm Ltd.; Mus. Coord.: Karin Green
American History X (USA, 1998)
Dir.: Tony Kaye; Prod. Co.: New Line Cinema; Mus.: Anne Dudley
Anatomy of a Murder (USA, 1959)
Dir.: Otto Preminger; Prod. Co.: Carlyle Productions; Mus.: Duke Ellington

Anchorman: The Legend of Ron Burgundy (USA, 2004)
  Dir.: Adam McKay; Prod. Co.: Dreamworks; Mus.: Alex Wurman
The Andromeda Strain (USA, 1971)
  Dir.: Robert Wise; Prod. Co.: Universal; Mus.: Gil Mellé
Anna Karenina (USA, 1935)
  Dir.: Clarence Brown; Prod. Co.: MGM; Mus.: Herbert Stothart
As You Like It (UK, 1936)
  Dir.: Paul Czinner; Prod. Co.: Inter-Allied; Mus.: William Walton
L'Assassinat du Duc de Guise (France, 1908)
  Dir: André Calmettes; Prod. Co.: Pathé's Films d'Art; Mus.: Camille Saint-Saëns
At Long Last Love (USA, 1975)
  Dir.: Peter Bogdanovich; Prod. Co.: Twentieth Century-Fox; Mus. Supervisors: Artie Butler,
  Lionel Newman
At Six in the Evening after the War (*V 6 chasov vechera posle voynï*) (USSR, 1944)
  Dir.: Ivan Pyrev; Prod. Co.: Mosfilm; Mus.: Tikhon Khrennikov
At the Bluest Sea (*U sumogo sinyego morya*) (USSR, 1936)
  Dir.: Boris Barnet; Prod. Co.: Mezhrabpomfilm; Mus.: Sergei Pototsky
Auld Robin Gray (USA, 1910)
  Dir.: Lawrence Trimble; Prod. Co.: Vitagraph
Austin Powers in Goldmember (USA, 2002)
  Dir.: Jay Roach; Prod. Co.: New Line Cinema; Mus.: George S. Clinton and others
The Aviator (USA, 2004)
  Dir.: Martin Scorsese; Prod. Co.: Miramax; Music.: Howard Shore
The Bad and the Beautiful (USA, 1952)
  Dir.: Vincente Minnelli; Prod. Co.: MGM; Mus.: David Raksin
Batman (USA, 1989)
  Dir.: Tim Burton; Prod. Co.: Warner Bros.; Mus.: Danny Elfman and others
Battleship Potemkin (*Bronenosets Potyomkin*) (USSR, 1925)
  Dir.: Sergei Eisenstein; Prod. Co.: Goskino; Mus.: Edmund Meisel (German release), Nikolai
  Kryukov (USSR release)
Beaches (USA, 1988)
  Dir.: Garry Marshall; Prod. Co.: All Girl Productions and Touchstone; Mus.: Georges Delerue
The Bears and I (USA, 1974)
  Dir.: Bernard McEveety; Prod. Co.: Walt Disney Productions; Mus.: Buddy Baker (title song by
  John Denver)
The Bear's Wedding (*Medvezhya svadba*) (USSR, 1926)
  Dir.: Konstantin Eggert; Prod. Co.: Mezhrabpom
La Belle et la Bête (Beauty and the Beast) (France, 1946)
  Dir.: Jean Cocteau; Prod. Co.: DisCina; Mus.: Georges Auric
Ben-Hur: A Tale of the Christ (USA, 1925)
  Dir.: Fred Niblo; Prod. Co.: MGM; Mus.: William Axt and David Mendoza
Ben-Hur (USA, 1959)
  Dir.: William Wyler; Prod. Co.: MGM; Mus.: Miklós Rózsa
The Better 'Ole (USA, 1926)
  Dir.: Charles Reisner; Prod. Co.: Warner Bros.; Mus.: Herman Heller, Maurice Baron, Fred
  Heff, Edward Kilenyi
Beverly Hills Cop (USA, 1984)
  Dir.: Martin Brest; Prod. Co.: Paramount; Mus.: Harold Faltermeyer
The Big Chill (USA, 1983)
  Dir.: Lawrence Kasdan; Prod. Co.: Columbia; Mus. Consultant: Meg Kasdan
The Bigamist (USA, 1953)
  Dir.: Ida Lupino; Prod. Co.: Filmakers Productions; Mus.: Leith Stevens

Bird of Paradise (USA, 1932)
    Dir.: King Vidor; Prod. Co.: RKO; Mus.: Max Steiner
The Birth of a Nation (USA, 1915)
    Dir.: D. W. Griffith; Prod.: David W. Griffith Corp.; Mus.: Joseph Carl Breil and others
Blackboard Jungle (USA, 1955)
    Dir.: Richard Brooks; Prod. Co.: MGM; Mus. Adaptation: Charles Wolcott
Black Rain (*Kuroi ame*) (Japan, 1989)
    Dir.; Shohei Imamura; Prod. Co.: Hayashibara Group; Mus.: Toru Takemitsu
Blade Runner (USA, 1982)
    Dir.: Ridley Scott; Prod. Co.: Warner Bros; Music: Vangelis
Das Boot (West Germany, 1982)
    Dir.: Wolfgang Petersen; Prod. Co.: Columbia; Mus.: Klaus Doldinger
Born Free (USA, 1966)
    Dir.: James Hill; Prod. Co.: Columbia; Mus.: John Barry
Born on the Fourth of July (USA, 1989)
    Dir.: Oliver Stone; Prod. Co.: Ixtlan; Mus.: John Williams and others
The Bourne Identity (USA, 2002)
    Dir.: Doug Liman; Prod. Co.: Universal; Mus.: John Powell
The Bourne Supremacy (USA, 2004)
    Dir.: Paul Greengrass; Prod. Co.: Universal Pictures; Mus.: John Powell
The Breakfast Club (USA, 1985)
    Dir.: John Hughes; Prod. Co.: Universal Pictures; Mus.: Keith Forsey, Gary Chang, and others
Broadway Melody (USA, 1929)
    Dir.: Harry Beaumont; Prod. Co.: MGM; Mus.: Nacio Herb Brown, Arthur Freed, George M. Cohan, and Willard Robison
Bullitt (USA, 1968)
    Dir.: Peter Yates; Prod. Co.: Solar Productions and Warner Bros.; Mus.: Lalo Schifrin
Business and People (*Dela i lyudi*) (USSR, 1932)
    Dir.: Aleksandr Macheret; Prod. Co.: Soyuzkino; Mus.: Nikolai Kryukov
The Cabinet of Dr. Caligari (Germany, 1920)
    Dir.: Robert Wiene; Prod. Co.: UFA; Mus.: Giuseppe Becce
Captain Carey, U.S.A. (USA, 1950)
    Dir.: Mitchell Leisen; Prod. Co.: Paramount; Mus.: Hugo Friedhofer ("Mona Lisa" by Ray Evans and Jay Livingston)
Carmen Jones (USA, 1946)
    Dir.: Otto Preminger; Prod. Co.: Carlyle Productions; Mus. Arr.: Dimitri Tiomkin and Leon Birnbaum
Casablanca (USA, 1942)
    Dir.: Michael Curtiz; Prod. Co.: Warner Bros.; Mus.: Max Steiner
The Charge of the Light Brigade (USA, 1936)
    Dir.: Michael Curtiz; Prod. Co.: Warner Bros.; Mus.: Max Steiner; Mus. Dir.: Leo Forbstein
Chariots of Fire (UK, 1981)
    Dir.: Hugh Hudson; Prod. Co.: Enigma Productions; Mus.: Vangelis
The Chess Player (*Le Joueur d'échecs*) (France, 1927)
    Dir.: Raymond Bernard; Prod. Co.: Société des Films Historique; Mus.: Henri Rabaud
Chinatown (USA, 1974)
    Dir.: Roman Polanski; Prod. Co.: Paramount; Mus.: Jerry Goldsmith
Cinderella Liberty (USA, 1973)
    Dir.: Mark Rydell; Prod. Co.: Sanford; Mus.: John Williams
Citizen Kane (USA, 1941)
    Dir.: Orson Welles; Prod. Co.: RKO; Mus.: Bernard Herrmann

Clairvoyant (UK, 1935)
Dir.: Maurice Elvey; Prod. Co.: Gaumont; Mus.: Arthur Benjamin

Class of '44 (USA, 1973)
Dir.: Paul Bogart; Prod. Co.: Warner Bros.; Mus.: David Shire

Claudine (USA, 1974)
Dir.: John Berry; Prod. Co.: Third World Cinema, Twentieth Century-Fox; Mus.: Curtis Mayfield; Mus. Arr.: Richard Tufo

Cloak and Dagger (USA, 1946)
Dir.: Fritz Lang; Prod. Co.: Warner Bros.; Mus.: Max Steiner

Close Encounters of the Third Kind (USA, 1977)
Dir.: Steven Spielberg; Prod. Co.: Columbia; Mus.: John Williams

Cocktail (USA, 1988)
Dir.: Roger Donaldson; Prod. Co.: Interscope Communications and Touchstone

Contact (UK, 1933)
Dir.: Paul Rotha; Prod. Co.: Imperial Airways; Mus.: Clarence Raybould

The Conversation (USA, 1974)
Dir.: Francis Ford Coppola; Prod. Co.: American Zoetrope; Mus.: David Shire

Cool Hand Luke (USA, 1967)
Dir.: Stuart Rosenberg; Prod. Co.: Jalem Productions and Warner Bros.; Mus.: Lalo Schifrin

Cover Girl (USA, 1944)
Dir.: Charles Vidor; Prod. Co.: Columbia; Mus.: Carmen Dragon, Gil Grau (Songs by Jerome Kern, Ira Gershwin, and E. Y. Harburg)

Crimson Tide (USA, 1995)
Dir.: Tony Scott; Prod. Co.: Hollywood Pictures; Mus.: Hans Zimmer

Crossing Delancey (USA, 1988)
Dir.: Joan Micklin; Prod. Co.: Warner Bros.; Mus.: Paul Chihara

The Crossing Guard (USA, 1995)
Dir.: Sean Penn; Prod. Co.: Miramax Films; Mus.: Jack Nitzsche

Crouching Tiger, Hidden Dragon (Taiwan/Hong Kong/USA/China, 2000)
Dir.: Ang Lee; Prod. Co.: Asia Union and Columbia; Mus.: Tan Dun

The Crowthers of Bankdam (also: *The Master of Bankdam*) (UK, 1947)
Dir.: Walter Forde; Prod. Co.: Holbein Films; Mus.: Arthur Benjamin

The Crow: City of Angels (USA, 1996)
Dir.: Tim Pope; Prod. Co.: Dimension Films; Mus.: Graeme Revell

The Curious Case of Benjamin Button (USA, 2008)
Dir.: David Fincher; Prod. Co.: Warner Bros. and Paramount; Mus.: Alexandre Desplat

The Da Vinci Code (USA, 2006)
Dir.: Ron Howard; Prod. Co.: Columbia; Mus.: Hans Zimmer

David Copperfield (USA, 1935)
Dir.: George Cukor; Prod. Co.: MGM; Mus.: Herbert Stothart

The Day the Earth Stood Still (USA, 1951)
Dir.: Robert Wise; Prod. Co.: Paramount; Mus.: Bernard Herrmann

The Day the Earth Stood Still (USA, 2008)
Dir.: Scott Derrickson; Prod. Co.: Twentieth Century-Fox; Mus.: Tyler Bates

Dementia (USA, 1955)
Dir.: John Parker; Prod. Co.: J. J. Parker Productions; Mus.: George Antheil; Mus. Dir.: Ernest Gold

Destination Moon (USA, 1950)
Dir.: Irving Pichel; Prod. Co.: George Pal Productions; Mus.: Leith Stevens

The Devil's Rejects (USA, 2005)
Dir.: Rob Zombie; Prod. Co.: Lions Gate Films; Mus.: Tyler Bates, Terry Reid, Rob Zombie

Dirty Dancing (USA, 1987)
  Dir.: Emile Ardolino; Prod. Co.: Great American Films Limited; Mus.: John Morris and others
Dirty Harry (USA, 1971)
  Dir.: Don Siegel; Prod. Co.: Malpaso Company and Warner Bros.; Mus.: Lalo Schifrin
Dishonored (USA, 1931)
  Dir.: Josef von Sternberg; Prod. Co.: Paramount; Mus.: Karl Hajos and Herman Hand
La Dixième Symphonie (France, 1918)
  Dir.: Abel Gance; Prod. Co.: Le Films d'Art
Do the Right Thing (USA, 1989)
  Dir.: Spike Lee; Prod. Co.: 40 Acres & A Mule Filmworks; Mus.: Bill Lee and others
Don Juan (USA, 1926)
  Dir.: Alan Crosland; Prod. Co.: Warner Bros.; Mus.: William Axt and David Mendoza
Don Quixote (France, 1933)
  Dir.: Georg Wilhelm Pabst; Prod. Co.: Vandor Film; Mus.: Jacques Ibert
Don't Knock the Rock (USA, 1957)
  Dir. Fred F. Sears; Prod. Co.: Clover Productions, Columbia; Mus.: Ross Di Maggio; Mus. Supervisor: Fred Karger
Double Indemnity (USA, 1944)
  Dir.: Billy Wilder; Prod. Co.: Paramount; Mus.: Miklós Rózsa
The Dowryless Girl (*Bespridannitsa*) (USSR, 1937)
  Dir.: Yakov Protazanov; Prod. Co.: Mezhrabpomfilm; Mus.: David Blok
Dreams That Money Can Buy (USA, 1947)
  Dir.: Hans Richter; Prod. Co.: Films International of America; Mus.: Louis Applebaum, John Cage, Paul Bowles, David Diamond, Darius Milhaud
Dr. Zhivago (USA, 1965)
  Dir.: David Lean; Prod. Co.: MGM; Mus.: Maurice Jarre
Die Dreigroschenoper (*The Three Penny Opera*) (Germany, 1932)
  Dir.: George Wilhelm Pabst; Prod. Co.: Tobias-Klangfilm; Mus.: Kurt Weill; Mus. Dir.: Theo Mackeben
Drive, He Said (USA, 1971)
  Dir.: Jack Nicholson; Prod. Co.: BBS Productions; Mus.: David Shire
Duel in the Sun (USA, 1946)
  Dir.: King Vidor; Prod. Co.: Selznick Releasing Organization; Mus.: Dimitri Tiomkin
Earthquake (USA, 1974)
  Dir.: Mark Robson; Prod. Co.: Universal; Mus.: John Williams
Easy Rider (USA, 1969)
  Dir.: Dennis Hopper; Prod. Co.: Rayburt Productions, Columbia; Mus. Editor: Synchrofilm, Inc. (Songs performed by The Byrds, Smith, The Holy Modal Rounders, Little Eva, The Band, Fraternity of Man, Jefferson Airplane, The Electric Prunes, and Roger McGuinn)
Elevator to the Scaffold (*Ascenseur pour l'échafaud*) (France, 1958)
  Alternate titles: *Elevator to the Gallows*, *Frantic*
  Dir.: Louis Malle; Prod. Co.: Nouvelles Éditions de Films; Mus.: Miles Davis
Elmer Gantry (USA, 1960)
  Dir.: Richard Brooks; Prod. Co.: United Artists; Mus.: André Previn
Elvira Madigan (Sweden, 1967)
  Dir.: Bo Widerberg; Prod. Co.: Europa Film; Mus.: Ulf Björlin and others
L'Empreinte ou La main rouge (France, 1908)
  Dir. Henri Burguet; Prod. Co.: Pathé Frères; Mus.: Fernand Le Borne
End of Days (USA, 1999)
  Dir.: Peter Hyams; Prod. Co.: Beacon Communications; Mus.: John Debney
Enter the Dragon (USA, 1973)
  Dir.: Robert Clouse; Prod. Co.: Concord Productions; Mus.: Lalo Schifrin

Entr'acte (France, 1923)
 Dir.: Francis Picabia and René Clair; Prod. Co.: Les Ballets Suédois; Mus.: Erik Satie
E.T.: The Extraterrestrial (USA, 1982)
 Dir.: Steven Spielberg; Prod. Co.: Universal; Mus.: John Williams
A Face in the Crowd (USA, 1957)
 Dir.: Elia Kazan; Prod. Co.: Newtown Productions; Mus.: Tom Glazer
Fantasia (USA, 1940)
 Prod. Co.: Walt Disney; Mus.: various; Mus. Dir.: Leopold Stokowski
Fantastic Voyage (USA, 1966)
 Dir.: Richard Fleischer; Prod. Co.: Twentieth Century-Fox; Mus.: Leonard Rosenman
Farewell My Lovely (USA, 1975)
 Dir.: Dick Richards; Prod. Co.: ITC Entertainment; Mus.: David Shire
Fido (Canada, 2006)
 Dir.: Andrew Currie; Prod. Co.: Anagram Pictures; Mus.: Don MacDonald
Fighting Caravans (USA, 1931)
 Dir.: Otto Brower, David Burton; Prod. Co.: Paramount; Mus.: Max Bergunker, Emil Bierman,
 A. Cousminer, Karl Hajos, Herman Hand, Emil Hilb, Sigmund Krumgold, John Leipold, Oscar
 Potoker
Fitzcarraldo (Germany, 1982)
 Dir.: Werner Herzog; Prod. Co.: Filmverlag der Autorem; Mus.: Popol Vuh
Flashdance (USA, 1983)
 Dir.: Adrian Lyne; Prod.Co.: Paramount; Mus.: Giorgio Moroder and others
Flight to India (UK, 1933)
 Prod. Co.: Steuart Films; Mus.: Clarence Raybould
The Flim-Flam Man (USA, 1967)
 Dir.: Irvin Kerschner; Prod. Co.: Twentieth Century-Fox; Mus.: Jerry Goldsmith
Flubber (USA, 1997)
 Dir.: Les Mayfield; Prod. Co.: Walt Disney Pictures; Mus.: Danny Elfman
Flying Down to Rio (USA, 1933)
 Dir.: Thornton Freeland; Prod. Co.: RKO; Mus.: Max Steiner (Songs by Vincent Youmans, Gus
 Kahn, Edward Eliscu)
Footloose (USA, 1984)
 Dir.: Herbert Ross; Prod. Co.: Paramount; Mus.: Various performers
Forbidden Planet (USA, 1956)
 Dir.: Fred McLeod Wilcox; Prod. Co.: MGM; Electronic Tonalities: Louis and Bebe Barron
Forever Amber (USA, 1947)
 Dir.: Otto Preminger; Prod. Co.: Twentieth Century-Fox; Mus.: David Raksin
Forever and a Day (USA, 1943)
 Dir.: René Clair, Edmund Goulding, Cedric Hardwicke, Frank Lloyd, Victor Saville, Robert
 Stevenson, and Herbert Wilcox; Prod. Co.: RKO; Mus.: Anthony Collins
The Fortune (USA, 1975)
 Dir.: Mike Nichols; Prod. Co.: Columbia; Mus.: David Shire
The Four Musketeers (USA, 1974)
 Dir.: Richard Lester; Prod. Co.: Film Trust, S.A.; Mus.: Lalo Schifrin
Four Wives (USA, 1940)
 Dir.: Michael Curtiz; Prod. Co.: Warner Bros.; Mus.: Max Steiner
Francesca Da Rimini (USA, 1910)
 Dir.: J. Stuart Blackton; Prod. Co.: Vitagraph
The French Connection (USA, 1971)
 Dir.: William Friedkin; Prod. Co.: D'Antoni Productions; Mus.: Don Ellis
Freud (USA, 1962)
 Dir.: John Huston; Prod. Co.: Universal; Mus.: Jerry Goldsmith

Fury (USA, 1936)
   Dir.: Joseph L. Mankiewicz; Prod. Co.: MGM; Mus.: Franz Waxman
The Gang's All Here (USA, 1941)
   Dir.: Busby Berkeley; Prod. Co.: Twentieth Century-Fox; Mus.: Hugo Friedhofer, Alfred Newman, Arthur Lange, Cyril J. Mockridge, and Gene Rose (Songs by Leo Robin and Harry Warren)
The Garden of Allah (USA, 1936)
   Dir.: Richard Boleslawski; Prod. Co.: Selznick International Pictures; Mus.: Max Steiner
Garden of Youth (*Qingchun de yuandi*) (China, 1955)
   Dir.: Wang Weiyi; Prod. Co.: Shanghai Film Studios; Mus.: Wang Yunjie
Gaslight (USA, 1944)
   Dir.: George Cukor; Prod. Co.: MGM; Mus.: Bronislau Kaper
The Gay Divorcee (USA, 1934)
   Dir.: Mark Sandrich; Prod. Co.: RKO; Mus.: Mack Gordon, Harry Revel, Con Conrad, Herb Magidson, and Cole Porter; Mus. Dir.: Max Steiner
Geheimnisse einer Seele (*Secrets of a Soul*) (Germany, 1926)
   Dir.: Georg Wilhelm Pabst; Prod. Co.: UFA; Mus.: Giuseppe Becce
Genevieve (UK, 1953)
   Dir.: Henry Cornelius; Prod. Co.: Arthur Rank Organization; Mus.: Larry Adler
Ghostbusters (USA, 1984)
   Dir.: Ivan Reitman; Prod. Co.: Columbia; Mus.: Elmer Bernstein and others
Ghostbusters II (USA, 1989)
   Dir.: Ivan Reitman; Prod. Co.: Columbia; Mus.: Randy Edelman and others
Girl No. 217 (*Chelovek No. 217*) (USSR, 1945)
   Dir.: Mikhail Romm; Prod. Co.: Mosfilm and Tashkent Studios; Mus.: Aram Khachaturian
Gladiator (USA, 2000)
   Dir.: Ridley Scott; Prod. Co.: DreamWorks SKG; Mus.: Hans Zimmer
The Godfather (USA, 1972)
   Dir.: Francis Ford Coppola; Prod. Co.: Alfran Productions and Paramount; Mus.: Nino Rota
Godzilla (USA, 1998)
   Dir.: Roland Emmerich; Prod. Co.: Centropolis Films and Sony; Mus.: David Arnold, Michael Lloyd
The Gold Rush (USA, 1925)
   Dir.: Charles Chaplin; Prod. Co.: Charles Chaplin Productions
Gone with the Wind (USA, 1939)
   Dir.: Victor Fleming; Prod. Co.: Selznick International Pictures; Mus.: Max Steiner
The Good Earth (USA, 1937)
   Dir.: Sidney Franklin; Prod. Co.: MGM; Mus.: Herbert Stothart
The Graduate (USA, 1967)
   Dir.: Mike Nichols; Prod. Co.: Embassy Pictures; Mus.: Paul Simon, Art Garfunkel, Dave Grusin
Grand Hotel (USA, 1932)
   Dir.: Edmund Goulding; Prod. Co.: MGM; Mus.: William Axt, Charles Maxwell
The Grapes of Wrath (USA, 1940)
   Dir.: John Ford, Prod. Co.: Twentieth Century-Fox; Mus. Dir.: Alfred Newman
Green Dolphin Street (USA, 1947)
   Dir.: Victor Saville; Prod. Co.: MGM; Mus.: Bronislau Kaper ("On Green Dolphin Street" by Kaper and Ned Washington)
Halloween (USA, 2007)
   Dir.: Rob Zombie; Prod. Co: Dimension Films; Mus.: Tyler Bates
Hangover Square (USA, 1945)
   Dir.: John Brahm; Prod. Co.: Twentieth Century-Fox; Mus.: Bernard Herrmann

A Hard Day's Night (UK, 1964)
   Dir.: Richard Lester; Prod. Co.: Maljack Productions, Proscenium Films, Walter Shenson Films;
   Mus.: George Martin, the Beatles
Heaven and Earth (USA, 1993)
   Dir.: Oliver Stone; Prod. Co.: Alcor Films; Mus.: Kitarô
The Heir to Genghis Khan (*Potomok Chingis-Khana*) (USSR, 1928)
   Dir.: Vsevolod Pudovkin; Prod. Co.: Mezhrabpomfilm; Mus.: Nikolai Kryukov
The Heiress (USA, 1949)
   Dir.: William Wyler; Prod. Co.: Paramount; Mus.: Aaron Copland
Hellboy (USA, 2004)
   Dir.: Guillermo del Toro; Prod. Co.: Revolution Studios; Mus.: Marco Beltrami
Hellzapoppin (USA, 1941)
   Dir.: H. C. Potter; Prod. Co.: Universal; Mus.: Frank Skinner; Mus. Dir.: Charles Previn
Heaven and Earth (USA, 1993)
   Dir.: Oliver Stone; Prod. Co.: Ixtlan; Mus.: Kitaro
Henry V (UK, 1989)
   Dir.: Kenneth Branagh; Prod. Co.: BBC; Mus.: Patrick Doyle
High Noon (USA, 1952)
   Dir.: Fred Zinnemann; Prod. Co.: Stanley Kramer Productions; Mus.: Dimitri Tiomkin
The Hindenburg (USA, 1975)
   Dir.: Robert Wise; Prod. Co.: Filmakers, Universal; Mus.: David Shire
Un homme marche dans la ville (*A Man Walks in the City*) (France, 1950)
   Dir.: Marcello Pagliero; Prod. Co.: Films Sacha Gordine
Hoodlum (USA, 1997)
   Dir.: Bill Duke; Prod. Co.: United Artists; Mus.: Elmer Bernstein
The Hours (USA, 2002)
   Dir.: Stephen Daldry; Prod. Co.: Paramount; Mus.: Philip Glass
Huddle (USA, 1932)
   Dir. Sam Wood; Prod. Co.: MGM
I, Robot (USA, 2004)
   Dir.: Alex Proyas; Prod. Co.: Twentieth Century-Fox; Mus.: Marco Beltrami
An Ideal Husband (UK, 1948)
   Dir.: Alexander Kord; Prod. Co.: London Film Productions; Mus.: Arthur Benjamin
Images (USA, 1972)
   Dir.: Robert Altman; Prod. Co.: Hemdale Film, Columbia; Mus.: John Williams
The Incredibles (USA, 2004)
   Dir.: Brad Bird; Prod. Co.: Disney, Pixar; Mus.: Michael Giacchino
Independence Day (USA, 1996)
   Dir.: Roland Emmerich; Prod. Co.: Centropolis Entertainment; Mus.: David Arnold
An Indian's Gratitude (USA, 1910)
   Dir.: James Young Deer; Prod. Co.: Pathé Frères
Indiana Jones and the Last Crusade (USA, 1988)
   Dir.: Steven Spielberg; Prod. Co.: Lucasfilm and Paramount; Mus.: John Williams
The Informer (USA, 1935)
   Dir.: John Ford; Prod. Co.: RKO; Mus.: Max Steiner
In the Hero's Footsteps (*Po sledam geroya*) (USSR, 1936)
   Dir.: Vladimir Nemolyayev; Prod. Co.: Mezhrabpomfilm; Mus.: Sergei Pototsky
In Like Flint (USA, 1967)
   Dir.: Gordon Douglas; Prod. Co.: Twentieth Century-Fox; Mus.: Jerry Goldsmith
Invasion (*Nashestviye*) (USSR, 1945)
   Dir.: Abram Room; Prod. Co.: Central United Art Film Studio; Mus.: Iurii Biryiukov

Iris (Italy, 1918)
   Dir: Giuseppe de Liguoro; Prod. Co.: Lux-Artis
The Island of Dr. Moreau (USA, 1996)
   Dir.: John Frankenheimer; Prod. Co.: New Line Cinema; Mus.: Gary Chang
Ivan Nikulin, Russian Sailor (*Ivan Nikulin, russkiyi matros*) (USSR, 1944)
   Dir.: Igor Savchenko; Prod. Co.: Mosfilm; Mus.: Sergei Pototsky
Ivan the Terrible, Part I (*Ivan Groznïy*) (USSR, 1944)
   Dir.: Sergei Eisenstein; Prod. Co. Mosfilm; Mus.: Sergei Prokofiev
I Wonder Who's Kissing Her Now (USA, 1947)
   Dir.: Lloyd Bacon; Prod. Co.: Twentieth Century-Fox; Mus.: David Buttolph; Mus. Dir.: Alfred
   Newman
Jaws (USA, 1975)
   Dir.: Steven Spielberg; Prod. Co.: Zanuck/Brown Company; Mus.: John Williams
The Jazz Singer (USA, 1927)
   Dir.: Alan Crosland; Prod. Co.: Warner Bros.; Mus.: Louis Silvers
Jean de Florette (France, 1986)
   Dir.: Calude Berri; Prod. Co.: DD Productions and films A2; Mus.: Jean-Claude Petit and others
Jenny Lind (USA, 1931)
   Dir.: Arthur Robison; Prod. Co.: MGM; Mus.: William Axt
Jonathan Livingston Seagull (USA, 1973)
   Dir.: Hall Bartlett; Prod. Co.: JSL Partnership and Paramount; Mus.: Neil Diamond, Lee
   Holdridge
Jungle Book (USA, 1942)
   Dir.: Zoltan Korda; Prod. Co.: Alexander Korda Films; Mus.: Miklós Rózsa
La Kermesse Héroïque (also *Carnival in Flanders*) (France/Germany, 1935)
   Dir.: Jacques Feyder; Prod. Co.: Film Sonores Tobis; Mus.: Louis Beydts
Kill Bill: Vol. 1 (USA, 2003)
   Dir.: Quentin Tarantino; Prod. Co.: BuenaVista; Music: RZA (a.k.a. Robert Diggs) and others
Kill Bill: Vol. 2 (USA, 2004)
   Dir.: Quentin Tarantino; Prod. Co.: BuenaVista; Music: Robert Rodriguez
King Kong (USA, 1933)
   Dir.: Merian C. Cooper, Ernest B. Schoedsack; Prod. Co.: RKO; Mus.: Max Steiner
The King's Speech (UK/Australia/USA, 2010)
   Dir.: Tom Hooper; Prod. Co.: See Saw Films; Mus.: Alexandre Desplat
Kinsey (USA, 2004)
   Dir.: Bill Condon; Prod. Co.: Fox Searchlight; Mus.: Carter Burwell
Koyaanisqatsi (USA, 1982)
   Dir.: Godfrey Reggio; Prod. Co.: IRE Productions; Mus: Philip Glass
Kundun (USA, 1997)
   Dir.: Martin Scorsese; Prod. Co.: De Finna-Cappa, Dune Films, and Refuge Productions; Mus.:
   Philip Glass
L.A. Confidential (USA, 1997)
   Dir.: Curt Hanson; Prod. Co.: Regency Enterprises; Mus.: Jerry Goldsmith
Lady on a Train (USA, 1945)
   Dir.: Charles David; Prod. Co.: Universal; Mus.: Miklós Rózsa
The Last American Hero (USA, 1973)
   Dir.: Lamont Johnson; Prod. Co.: Rojo Productions and Twentieth Century-Fox; Mus.: Charles
   Fox ("I Got a Name" by Charles Fox and Norman Gimbel)
The Last Emperor (China/Italy/UK/France, 1987)
   Dir.: Bernardo Bertolucci; Prod. Co.: Recorded Picture Company; Mus.: Ryuichi Sakamoto,
   David Byrne, and Cong Su

The Last of Sheila (USA, 1974)
Dir.: Herbert Ross; Prod. Co.: Warner Bros.; Mus.: Billy Goldenberg ("Friends" by Buzzy Lindhardt and Mark Klingman)

The Last Picture Show (USA, 1971)
Dir.: Peter Bogdanovich; Prod. Co.: BBS Productions; Mus.: Hank Williams (songs)

The Last Temptation of Christ (USA, 1988)
Dir.: Martin Scorsese; Prod. Co.: Cineplex-Odon and Universal; Mus.: Peter Gabriel

The Last Time I Committed Suicide (USA, 1997)
Dir.: Stephen Kay; Prod. Co.: Tapestry Films; Mus.: Tyler Bates

Laura (USA, 1944)
Dir.: Otto Preminger; Prod. Co.: Twentieth Century-Fox; Mus.: David Raksin

The Legacy (USA, 1910)
Prod. Co.: Vitagraph

Legend (USA, 1985)
Dir.: Ridley Scott; Prod. Co.: Universal; Mus.: Tangerine Dream

Leonardo da Vinci (Italy, 1952)
Dir.: Luciano Emmer, Enrico Gras; Prod. Co.: Documento Film; Mus.: Roman Vlad

Letty Lynton (USA, 1932)
Dir.: Clarence Brown; Prod. Co.: MGM; Mus.: William Axt

Der letzte Mann (*The Last Man*) (Germany, 1924)
Dir.: Wilhem Murnau; Prod. Co.: UFA; Mus.: Giuseppe Becce and Florian C. Reithner

The Life and Death of King Richard III (France, 1912)
Dir.: André Calmette; Prod. Co.: Le Film d'Art

The Life of Lu Xun (China, 1956)
Dir.: Sun Yu; unreleased

Lili (USA, 1953)
Dir.: Charles Walters; Prod. Co.: MGM; Mus.: Bronislau Kaper ("Hi-Lili, Hi-Lo" by Kaper and Helen Deutsch)

Lion King (USA, 1994)
Dir.: Roger Allers and Rob Minkoff; Prod. Co.: Walt Disney Productions; Mus.: Hans Zimmer, Elton John

Little Fugitive (USA, 1953)
Dir.: Raymond Ashley; Prod. Co.: Little Fugitive Production Co.; Mus.: Eddie Manson

Live and Let Die (USA, 1973)
Dir.: Guy Hamilton; Prod. Co.: Eon Productions; Mus.: George Martin (Title song by Paul McCartney and Linda McCartney)

The Lord of the Rings Trilogy (New Zealand/USA)
The Fellowship of the Ring (2001); *The Two Towers* (2002); *The Return of the King* (2003)
Dir.: Peter Jackson; Prod. Co.: New Line Cinema; Mus.: Howard Shore

The Lost Patrol (USA, 1934)
Dir: John Ford; Prod. Co.: RKO; Mus.: Max Steiner

The Lost Weekend (USA, 1945)
Dir.: Billy Wilder; Prod. Co.: Paramount; Mus.: Miklós Rózsa

The Louisiana Story (USA, 1948)
Dir.: Robert J. Flaherty; Prod. Co.: Standard Oil Company; Mus.: Virgil Thomson

Love and Learn (USA, 1947)
Dir.: Frederick de Cordova; Prod. Co.: Warner Bros.; Mus.: Max Steiner and others

Love Is a Many-Splendored Thing (USA, 1955)
Dir.: Henry King; Prod. Co.: Twentieth Century-Fox; Mus.: Alfred Newman (song by Sammy Fain and Paul Francis Webster)

Love Parade (USA, 1930)
   Dir.: Ernst Lubitsch; Prod. Co.: Paramount; Mus.: John Leipold, W. Franke Harling, Oscar Potoker, Max Terr
Love Story (USA, 1970)
   Dir.: Arthur Hiller; Prod. Co.: Paramount; Mus.: Francis Lai
The Macomber Affair (USA, 1947)
   Dir.: Zoltan Korda; Prod. Co.: Benedict Bogeaus Productions; Mus.: Miklós Rózsa
Mad at the World (USA, 1955)
   Dir.: Harry Essex; Prod. Co.: Filmakers Productions; Mus.: Leith Stevens
The Magnificent Seven (USA, 1960)
   Dir.: John Sturges; Prod. Co.: United Artists; Mus.: Elmer Bernstein
The Man Who Knew Too Much (UK, 1934)
   Dir.: Alfred Hitchcock; Prod. Co.: Gaumont-British; Mus.: Arthur Benjamin
The Man with the Golden Arm (USA, 1955)
   Dir.: Otto Preminger; Prod. Co.: United Artists; Mus.: Elmer Bernstein
Married to the Mob (USA, 1988)
   Dir.: Jonathan Demme; Prod. Co.: Mysterious Arts and Orion Pictures; Mus.: David Byrne
Marnie (USA, 1964)
   Dir.: Alfred Hitchcock; Prod. Co.: Universal; Mus.: Bernard Herrmann
Mayerling (France, 1936)
   Dir.: Anatole Litvak; Prod. Co.: Nero-Film AG; Mus.: Arthur Honegger
McCabe and Mrs. Miller (USA, 1971)
   Dir.: Robert Altman; Prod. Co.: David Foster Productions and Warner Bros.; Mus.: Leonard Cohen
Men in Black (USA, 1997)
   Dir.: Barry Sonnenfeld; Prod. Co.: Amblin Entertainment; Mus.: Danny Elfman
Men in War (USA, 1957)
   Dir.: Anthony Mann; Prod. Co.: Security Pictures; Mus.: Elmer Bernstein
Midnight Express (USA, 1978)
   Dir.: Alan Parker; Prod. Co.: Casablanca Filmworks; Mus.: Giorgio Moroder
Le Million (France, 1931)
   Dir.: René Clair; Prod. Co.: Film Sonores Tobis; Mus.: Armand Bernard, Phillipe Parès, George Van Parys
Million Dollar Baby (USA, 2004)
   Dir.: Clint Eastwood; Prod. Co.: Warner Bros.; Mus.: Clint Eastwood
The Misfits (USA, 1961)
   Dir.: John Huston; Prod. Co.: Seven Arts; Mus.: Alex North
Mishima: A Life in Four Chapters (USA/Japan, 1985)
   Dir.: Paul Schrader; Prod. Co.: Zoetrope Studios and Lucasfilm; Mus.: Philip Glass
The Mission (UK, 1986)
   Dir.: Roland Joffé; Prod. Co.: Goldcrest Films and Warner Bros.; Mus.: Ennio Morricone
Modern Times (USA, 1936)
   Dir.: Charles Chaplin; Prod. Co.: Charles Chaplin Film Corp.; Mus.: Charles Chaplin
The Moderns (USA, 1988)
   Dir.: Alan Rudolph; Prod. Co.: Nelson Entertainment; Mus.: Mark Isham
Monte Carlo (USA, 1930)
   Dir.: Ernst Lubitsch; Prod. Co.: Paramount; Mus.: W. Franke Harling, Karl Hajos, Herman Hand, John Leipold, Sigmund Krumgold
The Month of May (*Mesyats May*); also titled *A Chance Encounter* (*Sluchaynay vstrecha*) (USSR)
   Dir.: Igor Savchenko; Prod. Co.: Mezhrabpomfilm; Mus.: Sergei Pototsky

Moonstruck (USA, 1987)
  Dir.: Norman Jewison; Prod. Co.: MGM; Mus.: Dick Hyman and others
Morte a Venezia (*Death in Venice*) (Italy, 1971)
  Dir.: Luchino Visconti; Prod. Co.: Alfa Cinematografica; Mus.: Pre-existing music by Beethoven, Mussorgsky, and Armando Gil
Moss Rose (USA, 1947)
  Dir.: Gregory Ratoff; Prod. Co.: Twentieth Century-Fox; Mus.: David Buttolph; Mus. Dir.: Alfred Newman
Mousehunt (USA, 1997)
  Dir.: Gore Verbinski; Prod. Co.: DreamWorks SKG; Mus.: Alan Silvestri
Mr. Holland's Opus (USA, 1995)
  Dir.: Stephen Herek; Prod. Co.: Hollywood Pictures; Mus.: Michael Kamen
Der müde Tod (*Destiny*) (Germany, 1921)
  Dir.: Fritz Lang; Prod. Co.: UFA; Mus.: Giuseppe Becce
Mutiny on the Bounty (USA, 1935)
  Dir.: Frank Lloyd; Prod. Co.: MGM; Mus.: Herbert Stothart
My Man Godfrey (USA, 1936)
  Dir.: Gregory La Cava; Prod. Co.: Universal; Mus.: Charles Previn
Navajo (USA, 1953)
  Dir.: Norman Foster; Prod. Co.: Lippert Pictures; Mus.: Leith Stevens
Nell Gwyn (UK, 1934)
  Dir.: Herbert Wilcox; Prod. Co.: Herbert Wilcox Productions; Mus.: Philip Braham
Never on Sunday (*Pot tin Kyriaki*) (Greece, 1960)
  Dir.: Jules Dassin; Prod. Co.: Lopert Pictures and Melina Film; Mus.: Mano Hatzikakis (English lyrics to title song by Billy Towne)
New Babylon (*Novyi Vavilon*) (USSR, 1929)
  Dir.: Grigori Kozintsev, Leonid Trauberg; Prod. Co.: Sovkino; Mus.: Dmitry Shostakovich
New York Stories (USA, 1989)
  Dir.: Martin Scorsese; Woody Allen, Francis Ford Coppola; Prod. Co.: Touchstone
A Night at the Opera (USA, 1935)
  Dir.: Sam Wood; Prod. Co.: MGM; Mus. Dir.: Herbert Stothart
Nora Prentice (USA, 1947)
  Dir.: Vincent Sherman; Prod. Co.: Warner Bros.; Mus.: Franz Waxman
No Sun in Venice (*Sait-on jamais . . .*) (France, 1957)
  Dir.: Roger Vadim; Prod. Co.: Carol Film and Iéna Productions; Mus.: John Lewis
Now, Voyager (USA, 1942)
  Dir.: Irving Rapper; Prod. Co.: Warner Bros.; Mus.: Max Steiner
O Lucky Man! (UK, 1973)
  Dir.: Lindsay Anderson; Prod. Co.: Memorial Enterprises; Mus.: Alan Price
Objective, Burma! (USA, 1945)
  Dir.: Raoul Walsh; Prod. Co.: Warner Bros.; Mus.: Franz Waxman
Odds Against Tomorrow (USA, 1959)
  Dir.: Robert Wise; Prod. Co.: Harbel Productions; Mus.: John Lewis
Odna (*Alone*) (USSR, 1931)
  Dir.: Grigori Kozintsev, Leonid Trauberg; Prod. Co.: Soyuzkino; Mus.: Dmitry Shostakovich
Of Mice and Men (USA, 1939)
  Dir.: Lewis Milestone; Prod. Co.: Hal Roach Productions; Mus.: Aaron Copland
An Officer and a Gentleman (USA, 1982)
  Dir.: Taylor Hackford; Prod. Co.: Lorimar Film Entertainment; Mus.: Jack Nitzsche
Orphée (Orpheus) (France, 1950)
  Dir.: Jean Cocteau; Prod. Co.: André Paulvé; Mus.: Georges Auric

Our Town (USA, 1940)
   Dir.: Sam Wood; Prod. Co.: Sam Loesser Productions; Mus.: Aaron Copland
The Pagan (USA, 1929)
   Dir.: W. S. Van Dyke; Prod. Co.: MGM; Mus.: Arthur Freed, Nacio Herb Brown, and others
Papillon (USA, 1973)
   Dir.: Franklin J. Schaffner; Prod. Co.: Allied Artists and Solar Productions; Mus.: Jerry Goldsmith
Les Parents terribles (*The Terrible Parents*) (France, 1948)
   Dir.: Jean Cocteau; Prod. Co.: Les Films Ariane; Mus.: Georges Auric
Passion (also *Madame DuBarry*) (Germany, 1920)
   Dir.: Ernst Lubitsch; Prod. Co.: Projektions-AG Union
The Passion of the Christ (USA, 2004)
   Dir.: Mel Gibson; Prod. Co.: Icon Productions; Mus.: John Debney
A Patch of Blue (USA, 1965)
   Dir.: Guy Green; Prod. Co.: Filmways Pictures; Mus.: Jerry Goldsmith
Pat Garrett and Billy the Kid (USA, 1973)
   Dir.: Sam Peckinpah; Prod. Co.: MGM; Mus.: Bob Dylan
The Patriot (USA, 2000)
   Dir.: Roland Emmerich; Prod. Co.: Columbia; Mus.: John Williams
Patton (USA, 1970)
   Dir.: Franklin J. Schaffner; Prod. Co.: Twentieth Century-Fox; Mus.: Jerry Goldsmith
Patty Hearst (USA, 1988)
   Dir.: Paul Schrader; Prod. Co.: Atlantic; Mus.: Scott Johnson
Peter Ibbetson (USA, 1935)
   Dir.: Henry Hathaway; Prod. Co.: Paramount; Mus.: Ernst Toch
Petersburg Nights (*Petersburgskaya noch'*) (USSR, 1934)
   Dir.: Grigory Roshal, Ver Stroyeva; Prod. Co.: Moskinokombinat; Mus.: Dmitri Kabalevsky
La p'tite Lilie (France, 1929)
   Dir.: Alberto Cavalcanti; Prod. Co.: Studio Films; Mus.: Darius Milhaud
The Philadelphia Story (USA, 1940)
   Dir.: George Cukor; Prod. Co.: MGM; Mus.: Franz Waxman
Pirates of the Caribbean: The Black Pearl (USA, 2003)
Pirates of the Caribbean: Dead Man's Chest (USA, 2006)
Pirates of the Caribbean: At World's End (USA, 2007)
   Dir. (for all three): Gore Verbinski; Prod. Co.: Walt Disney Pictures; Mus.: Klaus Badelt (*The Black Pearl*), Hans Zimmer (*Dead Man's Chest* and *At World's End*)
The Plow That Broke the Plains (USA, 1936)
   Dir.: Pare Lorentz; Prod. Co.: Resettlement Administration; Mus.: Virgil Thomson
Pocket Money (USA, 1972)
   Dir.: Stuart Rosenberg; Prod. Co.: First Artists; Mus.: Alex North (title song by Carole King)
Pooh's Heffalump Movie (USA, 2005)
   Dir.: Frank Nissen; Prod. Co.: Disney; Mus.: Joel McNeely
Portrait of a Young Man in Three Movements (USA, 1931)
   Dir.: Henwar Rodakiewicz
The Poseidon Adventure (USA, 1972)
   Dir.: Ronald Neame; Prod. Co.: Kent Productions and Twentieth Century-Fox; Mus.: John Williams
Powaqqatsi (USA, 1988)
   Dir.: Godfrey Reggio; Prod. Co.: Golan-Globus Productions; Mus.: Philip Glass
The Pride and the Passion (USA, 1957)
   Dir.: Stanley Kramer; Prod. Co.: Stanley Kramer Productions; Mus.: George Antheil

Private Hell 36 (USA, 1954)
  Dir.: Don Siegel; Prod. Co.: Filmakers Productions; Mus.: Leith Stevens
The Private Life of Henry VIII (UK, 1933)
  Dir.: Alexander Korda; Prod. Co.: London Film Productions; Mus.: Kurt Schröder
Psycho (USA, 1960)
  Dir.: Alfred Hitchcock; Prod. Co.: Shamley Productions; Mus.: Bernard Herrmann
Quo Vadis? (Italy, 1913)
  Dir. Enrico Guazzoni; Prod. Co.: Cinés
Rain Man (USA, 1988)
  Dir.: Barry Levinson; Prod. Co.: United Artists; Mus.: Hans Zimmer
Raintree County (USA, 1957)
  Dir.: Edward Dmytryk; Prod. Co.: MGM; Mus.: John Green
Rango (USA, 1931)
  Dir.: Ernest B. Schoedsack; Prod. Co.: Paramount; Mus.: Karl Hajos, Max Bergunker, Gerard Carbonara, Herman Hand, W. Franke Harling, Sigmund Krumgold, John Leipold, George Steiner
Ray (USA, 2004); alternate title *Unchain My Heart: The Ray Charles Story* (working title)
  Dir.: Taylor Hackford; Prod. Co.: Anvil Films; Mus.: Craig Armstrong and others
Rebecca (USA, 1940)
  Dir.: Alfred Hitchcock; Prod. Co.: Selznick International Pictures; Mus.: Franz Waxman
The Red Violin (Canada, 1998)
  Dir.: Paul Girard; Prod. Co.: Rhombus Media, Mikado Film, and New Line International; Mus.: John Corigliano
The Reivers (USA, 1969)
  Dir.: Mark Rydell; Prod. Co.: National General; Mus.: John Williams
The Return of the Pink Panther (USA, 1975)
  Dir.: Blake Edwards; Prod. Co.: ITC Entertainment; Mus.: Henry Mancini
The Revolt of Mamie Stover (USA, 1956)
  Dir.: Raoul Walsh; Prod. Co.: Twentieth Century-Fox; Mus.: Hugo Friedhofer
Revolution (USA, 1985)
  Dir.: Hugh Hudson; Prod. Co.: Goldcrest Films International and Viking Films; Mus.: John Corigliano
Richard Wagner (Germany, 1913)
  Dir.: Carl Froelich; Prod. Co.: Messter-Film; Mus.: Giuseppe Becce
Rio Rita (USA, 1929)
  Dir.: Luther Reed; Prod. Co.: RKO; Mus.: Joseph McCarthy, Harry Tierney, Max Steiner; Mus. Dir.: Victor Baravalle
Rising Tide (UK, 1933)
  Dir.: Paul Rotha; Mus.: Clarence Raybould
The River (USA, 1938)
  Dir. Pare Lorentz; Prod. Co.: Resettlement Administration; Mus.: Virgil Thomson
Road to Perdition (USA, 2002)
  Dir.: Sam Mendes; Prod. Co.: Dreamworks SKG; Mus.: Thomas Newman
Robin Hood (USA, 1973)
  Dir: Wolfgang Rietherman; Prod. Co.: Walt Disney Productions; Mus.: George Bruns ("Love" by George Bruns and Floyd Huddleston)
Rock around the Clock (USA, 1956)
  Dir.: Fred F. Sears; Prod. Co.: Clover Productions, Columbia; Mus. Supervisor: Fred Karger
The Rogue Song (USA, 1930)
  Dir.: Lionel Barrymore; Prod. Co.: MGM; Mus.: Franz Lehár, William Axt, Herbert Stothart, Dimitri Tiomkin

Romeo and Juliet (USA, 1936)
    Dir.: George Cukor; Prod. Co.: MGM; Mus.: Herbert Stothart
Rose-Marie (USA, 1936)
    Dir.: W. S. Van Dyke; Prod. Co.: MGM; Mus.: Rudolf Friml, Herbert Stothart, Gus Kahn, Harry Akst, Sam Lewis, Joe Young, Shelton Brooks; Mus. Dir.: Herbert Stothart
La Roue (*The Wheel*) (France, 1923)
    Dir.: Abel Gance; Prod. Co.: Films Abel Gance; Mus.: Arthur Honegger
The Royal Tenenbaums (USA, 2001)
    Dir.: Wes Anderson; Prod. Co.: American Empirical Pictures; Mus.: Mark Mothersbaugh
Saint Joan (USA, 1957)
    Dir.: Otto Preminger; Prod. Co.: Wheel Productions; Mus.: Mischa Spoliansky
Salammbô (France, 1925)
    Dir.: Pierre Marodon; Prod. Co.: Gaumont-Franco Film-Aubert
Sand Pebbles (USA, 1966)
    Dir.: Robert Wise; Prod. Co.: Twentieth Century-Fox; Mus.: Jerry Goldsmith
San Francisco (USA, 1936)
    Dir.: W. S. Van Dyke; Prod. Co.: MGM; Mus.: Gus Kahn, Bronislau Kaper, Walter Jurmann, Nacio Herb Brown, and Arthur Freed
Le Sang d'un poète (*The Blood of a Poet*) (France, 1930)
    Dir.: Jean Cocteau; Prod. Co.: Vicomte de Noailles; Mus.: Georges Auric
Saturday Night Fever (USA, 1977)
    Dir.: John Badham; Prod. Co.: Paramount; Mus.: Barry Gibb, Robin Gibb, Maurice Gibb
The Scarlet Pimpernel (UK, 1935)
    Dir.: Harold Young; Prod. Co.: London Film Productions; Mus.: Arthur Benjamin
The Scorpion King (USA, 2002)
    Dir.: Chuck Russell; Prod. Co.: Universal; Mus.: John Debney and others
The Sea Hawk (USA, 1940)
    Dir.: Michael Curtiz; Prod. Co.: Warner Bros.; Mus.: Erich Wolfgang Korngold
Secret Agent (UK, 1936)
    Dir.: Alfred Hitchcock; Prod. Co.: Gaumont-British; Mus. Dir.: Louis Levy
She Done Him Wrong (USA, 1933)
    Dir.: Lowell Sherman; Prod. Co.: Paramount; Mus.: John Leipold, Ralph Rainger
Sing (USA, 1989)
    Dir.: Richard J. Baskin; Prod. Co.: TriStar Pictures; Mus.: Jay Gruska and others
Sisters (USA, 1973)
    Dir.: Brian De Palma; Prod. Co.: American International; Mus.: Bernard Herrmann
The Skin Game (USA, 1971)
    Dir.: Paul Bogart; Prod. Co.: Cherokee Productions; Mus.: David Shire
Slither (Canada, 2006)
    Dir: James Gunn; Prod. Co.: Gold Circle Films; Mus.: Tyler Bates
Slumdog Millionaire (UK, 2008)
    Dir.: Danny Boyle; Prod. Co.: Celador Films; Mus.: A. R. Rahman
The Social Network (USA, 2010)
    Dir.: David Fincher; Prod. Co.: Columbia Pictures; Mus.: Trent Reznor, Atticus Ross
Sodom and Gomorrha (Germany, 1922)
    Dir.: Michael Curtiz; Prod. Co.: Sascha-Film; Mus.: Giuseppe Becce
Some Like It Hot (USA, 1959)
    Dir.: Billy Wilder; Prod. Co.: Ashton Productions; Mus.: Adolph Deutsch
Song Jingshi (*The Rebels*) (China, 1955)
    Dir.: Zheng Junli, Sun Yu; Mus.: Wang Yunjie

The Song of Bernadette (USA, 1943)
Dir.: Henry King; Prod. Co.: Twentieth Century-Fox; Mus.: Alfred Newman
Song of Scheherazade (USA, 1947)
Dir.: Walter Reisch; Prod. Co.: Universal; Mus.: Miklós Rózsa (based on themes by Nikolai Rimsky-Korsakov)
A Song to Remember (USA, 1944)
Dir.: Charles Vidor; Prod. Co.: Columbia; Mus.: Miklós Rózsa (based on themes by Chopin)
The Song that Reached His Heart (USA, 1910)
Dir: J. Searle Dawley; Prod. Co.: Edison
The Sound of Music (USA, 1965)
Dir.: Robert Wise; Prod. Co.: Twentieth Century-Fox; Mus.: Richard Rogers, Oscar Hammerstein II; Mus. Dir.: Irwin Kostal
Spanglish (USA, 2004)
Dir.: James L. Brooks; Prod. Co.: Gracie Films; Mus.: Hans Zimmer
The Spanish Earth (USA, 1937)
Dir.: Joris Ivens; Prod. Co.: Contemporary Historians, Inc.; Mus.: Virgil Thomson, Marc Blitzstein
Spartacus (USA, 1960)
Dir.: Stanley Kubrick; Prod. Co.: Bryna Productions; Mus.: Alex North
Speed (USA, 1994)
Dir.: Jan de Bont; Prod. Co.: Twentieth Century-Fox; Mus.: Mark Mancina
Spellbound (USA, 1945)
Dir.: Alfred Hitchcock; Prod. Co.: Selznick Releasing Organization; Mus.: Miklós Rózsa
Star Wars (USA, 1977)
Dir.: George Lucas; Prod. Co. Lucasfilm and Twentieth Century-Fox; Mus.: John Williams
Steelyard Blues (USA, 1973)
Dir.: Alan Myerson; Prod. Co.: Warner Bros.; Mus: David Shire
Stigmata (USA, 1999)
Dir.: Rupert Wainwright; Prod. Co.: MGM; Mus.: Elia Cmiral, Billy Corgan
The Sting (USA, 1973)
Dir.: George Roy Hill; Prod. Co.: Zanuck/Brown Productions and Universal; Mus.: Scott Joplin; Mus. Arr.: Marvin Hamlisch
The Strangeness of Love (*O strannostyakh lyubvi*) (USSR, 1936)
Dir.: Yakov Protazanov; Prod. Co.: Mezhrabpomfilm; Mus.: David Blok
Street Scene (USA, 1931)
Dir.: King Vidor; Prod. Co.: United Artists; Mus.: Alfred Newman
Street Singer (USA, 1932)
Dir.: Monte Brice; Prod. Co.: Universal
A Streetcar Named Desire (USA, 1951)
Dir.: Elia Kazan; Prod. Co.: Charles K. Feldman Group; Mus.: Alex North
Streets of Fire (USA, 1984)
Dir.: Walter Hill; Prod. Co.: RKO and Universal; Mus.: Ry Cooder
The Student from Prague (*Der Student von Prag*) (Germany, 1913)
Dir.: Stellan Rye and Paul Wegener; Prod. Co.: Deutsche Bioscop GmbH; Mus.: Joseph Weiss
Sunday, Bloody Sunday (USA, 1971)
Dir.: John Schlesinger; Prod. Co.: Vectia; Mus.: Ron Geesin
Sundown (USA, 1941)
Dir.: Henry Hathaway; Prod. Co.: Walter Wanger Productions; Mus.: Miklós Rózsa
Sunset Boulevard (USA, 1950)
Dir.: Billy Wilder; Prod. Co.: Paramount; Mus.: Franz Waxman

La Suprême Epopée (France, 1919)
   Dir.: Henri Desfontaines; Prod. Co.: Service Cinématographique des Armées
Sweet Home Alabama (USA, 2002)
   Dir.: Andy Tennant; Prod. Co.: Original Film and Pigeon Creek Films; Mus.: George Fenton and others
The Sweet Smell of Success (USA, 1957)
   Dir.: Alexander Mackendrick; Prod. Co.: Curtleigh Productions and Hill-Hecht-Lancaster Productions; Mus.: Elmer Bernstein
Symphony of Six Million (USA, 1932)
   Dir.: Gregory La Cava; Prod. Co.: RKO; Mus.: Max Steiner
Syncopation (USA, 1942)
   Dir.; William Dieterle; Prod. Co.: RKO; Mus.: Leith Stevens
Tabu (USA, 1931)
   Dir.: F. W. Murnau; Prod. Co.: Golden Bough; Mus.: Hugo Riesenfeld
The Taking of Pelham One Two Three (USA, 1974)
   Dir.: Joseph Sargent; Prod. Co.: Palladium Productions; Mus.: David Shire
The Ten Commandments (USA, 1956)
   Dir.: Cecil B. DeMille; Prod. Co.: Paramount; Mus.: Elmer Bernstein
Ten North Frederick (USA, 1958)
   Dir.: Philip Dunne; Prod. Co.: Twentieth Century-Fox; Mus.: Leigh Harline
That's Entertainment! (Parts I, II, III) (USA, 1974, 1976, 1996)
   Dir.: Jack Haley Jr. (Part I), Gene Kelly (Part II), Bud Friedgen and Michael J. Sheridan (Part III); Prod. Co.: MGM
Thief of Baghdad (USA, 1924)
   Dir.: Raoul Walsh; Prod. Co.: Douglas Fairbanks Pictures
The Thin Blue Line (USA, 1988)
   Dir.: Errol Morris; Prod. Co.: American Playhouse; Mus.: Philip Glass
The Thing from Another World (USA, 1951)
   Dir.: Christian Nyby; Prod. Co.: RKO; Mus.: Dimitri Tiomkin
Things to Come (UK, 1936)
   Dir.: William Cameron Menzies; Prod. Co.: London Film Productions; Mus.: Arthur Bliss
The Third Man (UK, 1949)
   Dir.: Carol Reed; Prod. Co.: British Lion; Mus.: Anton Karas
This Is the Night (USA, 1932)
   Dir. Frank Tuttle; Prod. Co.: Paramount; Mus.: W. Franke Harling, Ralph Rainger, Rudolph G. Kopp, Arthur Lange, John Leipold
Those Endearing Young Charms (USA, 1945)
   Dir.: Lewis Allen; Prod. Co.: RKO; Mus.: Roy Webb
Time Out of Mind (USA, 1949)
   Dir.: Robert Siodmak; Prod. Co.: Universal; Mus.: Miklós Rózsa
Titanic (USA, 1997)
   Dir.: James Cameron; Prod. Co.: Twentieth Century-Fox; Mus.: James Horner
Tobacco Road (USA, 1941)
   Dir.: John Ford; Prod. Co.: Twentieth Century-Fox; Mus.: David Buttolph
To Kill a Mockingbird (USA, 1962)
   Dir.: Robert Mulligan; Prod. Co.: Universal; Mus.: Elmer Bernstein
Tomorrow Never Dies (USA, 1997)
   Dir.: Roger Spottiswoode; Prod. Co.: Danjaq Productions and MGM; Mus.: David Arnold
A Touch of Class (USA, 1973)
   Dir.: Melvin Frank; Prod. Co.: Brut Productions and Gordon Film Productions; Mus.: John Cameron ("All That Love Went To Waste" by George Barrie and Sammie Cahn)

The Towering Inferno (USA, 1974)
  Dir.: John Guillermin; Prod. Co.: Irwin Allen Productions, Twentieth Century-Fox; Mus.: John Williams
Trouble about a Small White Flag (*Xiao bai qi de feng bo*) (China, 1956)
  Dir.: Heng Gao; Prod. Co.: Shanghai Film Studio; Mus.: Wang Yunjie
Trouble in Mind (USA, 1985)
  Dir.: Alan Rudolph; Prod. Co.: Pfeiffer/Blocker; Mus. Mark Isham
The Trouble with Harry (USA, 1955)
  Dir.: Alfred Hitchcock; Prod. Co.: Paramount; Mus.: Bernard Herrmann
True Grit (USA, 2010)
  Dir.: Ethan Coen, Joel Coen; Prod. Co.: Paramount; Mus.: Carter Burwell
True Lies (USA, 1994)
  Dir.: James Cameron; Prod. Co.: Twentieth Century-Fox; Mus.: Brad Fiedel
Twist (Canada, 2003)
  Dir.: Jacob Tierney; Prod. Co.: Victorious Films; Mus.: Ron Proulx
The Two Mrs. Carrolls (USA, 1947)
  Dir.: Peter Godfrey; Prod. Co.: Warner Bros.; Mus.: Franz Waxman
Two People (USA, 1973)
  Dir.: Robert Wise; Prod. Co.: Filmakers and Universal; Mus.: David Shire
Under Siege (USA, 1992)
  Dir.: Andrew Davis; Prod. Co.: Warner Bros.; Mus.: Gary Chang
Urban Cowboy (USA, 1980)
  Dir.: James Bridges; Prod. Co.: Paramount
The Vagabond Lover (USA, 1929)
  Dir.: Marshall Nielan; Prod. Co.: RKO; Mus.: Harry M. Woods, Phil Baxter, Ruby Cowan, Philip Bartholomae, Phil Boutelje, Clifford Grey, Nat D. Ayer, Gus Kahn, Ernie Erdman, Billy Meyers, Elmer Schoebel, Edward Heyman, Ken Smith, Louis Herscher, Harold Raymond, Nat Simon, Rudy Vallee, and Leon Zimmerman
Vertigo (USA, 1958)
  Dir.: Alfred Hitchcock; Prod. Co.: Paramount; Mus.: Bernard Herrmann
Via delle Cinque Lune (Italy, 1942)
  Dir.: Luigi Chiarini; Prod. Co.: Centro Sperimentale di Cinematografi; Mus.: Achille Longo
The Violinist of Florence (*Der Geiger von Florenz*) (Germany, 1926)
  Dir.: Paul Czinner; Prod. Co.: UFA; Mus.: Giuseppe Becce
Viva Villa! (USA, 1934)
  Dir.: Jack Conway; Prod. Co.: MGM; Mus.: Herbert Stothart
The Volga Boatman (USA, 1926)
  Dir.: Cecil B. DeMille; Prod. Co.: DeMille Pictures; Music: R. H. Bassett (LA premiere), Hugo Riesenfeld (NY premiere)
The War of the Roses (USA, 1989)
  Dir.: Danny DeVito; Prod. Co.: Gracie Films; Mus.: David Newman
The War of the Worlds (USA, 1953)
  Dir.: Byron Haskin; Prod. Co.: Paramount; Mus.: Leith Stevens
Watchmen (USA, 2009)
  Dir.: Zack Snyder; Prod. Co.: Warner Bros.; Mus.: Tyler Bates
The Way We Were (USA, 1973)
  Dir.: Sydney Pollack; Prod. Co.: Columbia; Mus.: Marvin Hamlisch (lyrics to "The Way We Were" by Alan and Marilyn Bergman)
We Are from Kronstadt (*Mï iz Kronshtadta*) (USSR, 1936)
  Dir.: Yefin Dzigan; Prod. Co.: Mosfilm; Mus.: Nikolai Kryukov

The Weather Man (USA, 2005)
  Dir.: Gore Verbinski; Prod. Co.: Paramount; Mus.: Hans Zimmer, James S. Levine
Well Wishes (*Zhufui*); alternate title: *New Year Sacrifice* (China, 1956)
  Dir.: Hu Sang; Prod. Co.: Beijing Film Studio; Mus.: Ruzeng Liu
Wharves and Strays (UK, 1935)
  Dir.: Bernard Browne; Prod. Co.: Alexander Korda; Mus.: Arthur Benjamin
Where the Road Begins (UK, 1933)
  Prod. Co.: Steuart Films; Mus.: Clarence Raybould
White Nights (USA, 1985)
  Dir.: Taylor Hackford; Prod. Co.: Delphi IV Productions and Columbia; Mus.: Michel Colombier
  and others
The Wild One (USA, 1953)
  Dir.: Laslo Benedek; Prod. Co.: Stanley Kramer Productions; Mus.: Leith Stevens
Wilson (USA, 1944)
  Dir.: Henry King; Prod. Co.: Twentieth Century-Fox; Mus.: Alfred Newman
Wings of the Morning (UK, 1937)
  Dir.: Harold D. Schuster; Prod. Co.: New World Pictures Ltd.; Mus.: Arthur Benjamin
Woman in the Dunes (*Sunna no onna*) (Japan, 1964)
  Dir.: Hiroshi Teshigahara; Prod. Co.: Toho Film Company; Mus.: Toru Takemitsu
A Woman of Paris: A Drama of Fate (USA, 1923)
  Dir.: Charles Chaplin; Prod. Co.: Charles Chaplin Production
Works of Calder (USA, 1950)
  Dir.: Herbert Matter; Prod.: Herbert Matter; Mus.: John Cage
A World Apart (UK, 1988)
  Dir.: Chris Menges; Prod. Co.: Atlantic Entertainment Group and British Screen Productions;
  Mus.: Hans Zimmer
xXx (USA, 2002)
  Dir.: Rob Cohen; Prod. Co.: Original Film and Revolution Studios; Mus.: Randy Newman and
  others
You Were Never Lovelier (USA, 1942)
  Dir.: William A. Seiter; Prod. Co.: Columbia; Mus.: Leigh Harline (Songs by Jerome Kern and
  Johnny Mercer)

PERMISSION ACKNOWLEDGMENTS

For use of material in this collection that is not in the public domain, permission granted by the following copyright holders is gratefully acknowledged.

Edwin Evans, "Music and the Cinema," *Music & Letters* 10, no. 1 (January 1929): 65–69. Reproduced by permission of Oxford University Press.

Philip K. Scheurer, "Musical Picture Quietly Undergoes Renaissance," *Los Angeles Times*, February 22, 1931, B9, B20. Reproduced by permission of the *Los Angeles Times*.

Edwin Schallert, "Film Music Experiences Its Sanest Development," *Los Angeles Times*, May 22, 1932: B16. Reproduced by permission of the *Los Angeles Times*.

Clarence Raybould, "Music and the Synchronized Film," *Sight and Sound* 2, no. 7 (Autumn 1933): 80–81. Reproduced by permission of *Sight and Sound*.

Arthur Benjamin, "Film Music," *The Musical Times* 78, no. 1133 (July 1937): 595–97. Reproduced by permission of *The Musical Times*.

Franz Waxman, "History of Motion Picture Music" (1940). Reproduced by permission of The Harry Ransom Center, University of Texas at Austin.

David O. Selznick, "Memoranda" (1937, 1941). Reproduced by permission of The Harry Ransom Center, University of Texas at Austin.

Erich Leinsdorf, "Music and the Screen," *New York Times*, June 17, 1945, X3. Reproduced by permission of the *New York Times*.

Bernard Herrmann, "Music in Films—A Rebuttal," *New York Times*, June 24, 1945, 27. Reproduced by permission of the *New York Times*.

Bosley Crowther, "Heard Melodies," *New York Times*, June 24, 1945, 25. Reproduced by permission of the *New York Times*.

Antony Hopkins, "Music: Congress at Florence," *Sight and Sound* 19, no. 6 (August 1950): 243–44. Reproduced by permission of *Sight and Sound*.

Hans Keller, "Hollywood Orchestrators: The Dragon Shows His Teeth," *Music Review* 12, no. 3 (August 1951): 221–25. Reproduced by permission of The Cosman Keller Art and Music Trust.

Georges Auric, "Voici comment est née et comment se fait aujourd'hui la musique de cinema" ("How Film Music Was Born and How It Is Made Today"), *Arts* (July 17, 1952). Reproduced by permission of Michèle Auric.

John Cage, "A Few Ideas about Music and Film," *Film Music News* 10, no. 3 (January–February 1951): 12–15. Reproduced by permission of the John Cage Trust.

Pierre Schaeffer, "Concrete Music," *UNESCO Courier 3*, 1954: 18–20. Reproduced by permission of UNESCO.

Philip K. Scheurer, "Scorers Skip Classics, Seek New Approach," *Los Angeles Times*, August 29, 1954: D2. Reproduced by permission of the *Los Angeles Times*.

John S. Wilson, "Three Movie Scores Issued on LP Disks," *New York Times*, December 20, 1959: X15. Reproduced by permission of the *New York Times*.

Thomas P. Ronan, "British Rattled by Rock 'n' Roll," *New York Times*, September 12, 1956: 40. Reproduced by permission of the *New York Times*.

Mae Tinee, "'Real Crazy' Mansfield in Raucous Film," *Chicago Tribune*, January 28, 1957: B10; and "Film's Appeal Is Based on Rock 'n' Roll," *Chicago Tribune*, February 7, 1957: C9. Reproduced by permission of the *Chicago Tribune*.

Jane Brockman, "The First Electronic Filmscore—*Forbidden Planet*: A Conversation with Bebe Barron," *The Score* 7, no. 3 (Fall–Winter 1992): 5, 12–13. Reproduced by permission of Jane Brockman.

Martin Bernheimer, "Electronic Strains Reinforce 'Andromeda' Film Score," *Los Angeles Times*, January 17, 1971: Y1, Y42. Reproduced by permission of the *Los Angeles Times*.

Elmer Bernstein, "What Ever Happened to Great Movie Music?" *High Fidelity*, July 1972: 55–58. Reproduced by permission of Hachette Filipacchi Media U.S., Inc, and the Estate of Elmer Bernstein and the Bernstein Family Trust.

David Raksin, "Film Music: Beauty and the Beast?: Raksin Raps State of Art," *Variety* 275, no. 1 (May 1974): 59 (reprinted as "Whatever Became of Movie Music?" in *Film Music Notebook* 1, no. 1 (Autumn 1974): 24–28). Reproduced by permission of *Variety*.

Charles Champlin, "Sound and Fury over Film Music," *Los Angeles Times*, March 12, 1967: C14. Reproduced by permission of the *Los Angeles Times*.

Leonard Rosenman, "Notes from a Sub-Culture," *Perspectives of New Music* 7, no. 1 (Autumn–Winter 1968): 128–133. Reproduced by permission of *Perspectives of New Music*.

Charles Higham, "You May Not Leave the Movie House Singing Their Songs, But . . . ," *New York Times*, May 25, 1975: 119. Reproduced by permission of the *New York Times*.

Howard Kennedy, "Musicians to Picket Two Films in 20 U.S. Cities," *Los Angeles Times*, June 24, 1958: B1–2. Reproduced by permission of the *Los Angeles Times*.

Thomas M. Pryor, "Musicians Guild Wins Coast Vote," *New York Times*, July 12, 1958: 16. Reproduced by permission of the *New York Times*.

"Musicians Guild Wins 14% Hike in Studio Pay," *Los Angeles Times*, August 28, 1958: B3. Reproduced by permission of the *Los Angeles Times*.

Eric Malnic, "Musicians Could Be Left Out When Actors Settle," *Los Angeles Times*, September 19, 1980: A12. Reproduced by permission of the *Los Angeles Times*.

"Tentative Pact Reached in Musician Strike," *Los Angeles Times*, January 15, 1981: A6. Reproduced by permission of the *Los Angeles Times*.

"AFM, Film Producers Reach New Three-Year Pact," *International Musician* 88, no. 12 (May 1990): 1, 8. Reproduced by permission of the *International Musician*.

Florence Nelson, "Keeping Film Scoring on Our Shores," *International Musician* 103, no. 6 (June 2005): 4. Reproduced by permission of the *International Musician*.

Jon Burlingame, "Union Drumbeat's Growing," *Variety* 418, no. 12 (May 3–9, 2010): 65. Reproduced by permission of *Variety*.

Vincent Canby, "Music Is Now Profit to the Ears of Filmmakers," *New York Times*, May 24, 1966: 52. Reproduced by permission of the *New York Times*.

Tom Shales, "The Sound of (Movie) Music: Re-releases of Soundtracks Past," *Washington Post*, July 18, 1976: H1, H6. Reproduced by permission of the *Washington Post*.

Steven Smith, "Movie Music: Is It Becoming Hit or Miss?" *Los Angeles Times*, January 5, 1986: S67. Reproduced by permission of the *Los Angeles Times*.

Jeff Burger, "Synthesizer Upstarts Conquer Hollywood," *Keyboard* (September 13, 1987): 58–61, 64, 69–72, 77. Reproduced by permission of NewBay Media LLC.

Lachlan Westfall, "Computers in the Movies: How Desktop PCs Help Create Hollywood's Amazing Music and Sound Effects," *Music & Computers* 4, no. 4 (May–June 1998): 26–28, 30, 32. Reproduced by permission of NewBay Media LLC.

Michael Prager, "The Unreal Orchestra, Part 1: The Virtual Film Score," *Keyboard* 30, no. 2 (February 2004): 26–28, 30. Reproduced by permission of NewBay Media LLC.

Matt Hurwitz, "Sound for Picture: Hans Zimmer's Scoring Collective—Composer Collaboration at Remote Control Productions," *Mix* 31, no. 9 (September 2007): 49, 53. Reproduced by permission of Penton Media.

Jeff Rona, "Making Soundtracks, Part 1: Those Pesky Songs that Show up in Between Your Cues—Who Puts 'Em There, Anyway?" *Keyboard* 26, no. 3 (March 2000): 118; and "Making Soundtracks, Part 2: More on the Differences between the Score and the Soundtrack," *Keyboard* 26, no. 4 (April 2000): 139. Reproduced by permission of NewBay Media LLC.

Nick Krewen, "Music in Movies and TV: Filling the Bill," *Words & Music* 12, no. 3 (Fall 2005): 12–14. Reproduced by permission of Nick Krewen.

Mike Levine, "Music Business Insider: Q&A: Jack Rudy," *Electronic Musician* 23, no. 2 (February 2007): 80, 82. Reproduced by permission of Penton Media.

Donal Henahan, "Film Music Has Two Masters," *New York Times*, July 19, 1987: H1, H23. Reproduced by permission of the *New York Times*.

David Mermelstein, "In Hollywood, Discord on What Makes Music," *New York Times*, November 2, 1997: AR17, AR30. Reproduced by permission of the *New York Times*.

James Hunter, "Keeping Scores: Good Old-Fashioned Movie Music Is as Healthy as It Ever Was," *The Village Voice*, November 10, 1998: 43, 45. Reproduced by permission of James Hunter.

Catherine Applefeld Olson, "Many Ways to Score," *Billboard* 111:43 (October 23, 1999): 22. Reproduced by permission of Prometheus Global Media.

David Schiff, "Taking Movie Music Seriously, Like It Or Not," *New York Times*, April 22, 2001: AR1, AR36. Reproduced by permission of the *New York Times*.

Dylan Callaghan, "The Soundtrack Game Is Attracting Fresh and Edgy Artists," *Billboard* 114, no. 41 (October 12, 2002): S3–S4, S6. Reproduced by permission of Prometheus Global Media.

Jed Distler, "When Is Film Music Classical?" *Gramophone* 84, no. 1014 (January 2007): 28–29. Reproduced by permission of *Gramophone*.

Kevin Cassidy, "Hollywood Composers Tune In for Rare Gathering," *The Hollywood Reporter*, December 22, 2008: 92. Reproduced by permission of Prometheus Global Media.

Todd Martens, "'127 Hours' and Other Films Take Experimental Turns in Music," *Los Angeles Times*, December 7, 2010: S22. Reproduced by permission of the *Los Angeles Times*.

INDEX